融跃ACCA®
助您备考无忧

✓ 尊享五大会员特权

前导课程
带你快速入门

备考资料
题库笔记干货

干货直播
提分技巧攻略

社群交流
考试指南答疑

考试资讯
考纲政策解读

扫码免费领取

ACCA 知识精要(上)

融跃教育 ACCA 研究院　编著

图书在版编目(CIP)数据

ACCA 知识精要：全 2 册：汉文、英文 / 融跃教育 ACCA 研究院编著. —上海：立信会计出版社，2021.1
ISBN 978-7-5429-6755-8

Ⅰ.①A… Ⅱ.①融… Ⅲ.①会计学—资格考试—自学参考资料—汉、英 Ⅳ.①F23

中国版本图书馆 CIP 数据核字(2021)第 039299 号

策划编辑　　方士华　孙　勇
责任编辑　　方士华

ACCA 知识精要(全 2 册)
ACCA Zhishi Jingyao

出版发行	立信会计出版社			
地　　址	上海市中山西路 2230 号	邮政编码	200235	
电　　话	(021)64411389	传　　真	(021)64411325	
网　　址	www.lixinaph.com	电子邮箱	lixinaph2019@126.com	
网上书店	http://lixin.jd.com		http://lxkjcbs.tmall.com	
经　　销	各地新华书店			
印　　刷	河南美图印刷有限公司			
开　　本	787 毫米×1092 毫米	1/16		
印　　张	51.25			
字　　数	1248 千字			
版　　次	2021 年 1 月第 1 版			
印　　次	2021 年 1 月第 1 次			
书　　号	ISBN 978-7-5429-6755-8/F			
定　　价	218.00 元			

如有印订差错，请与本社联系调换

编委会主要成员

张　昊　　汪晓敏
石　佳　　梅　梅
丛玉翠　　张　璞

　　特许公认会计师公会（The Association of Chartered Certified Accountants，ACCA）是全球最具规模的国际专业会计师组织，为全世界有志投身于财务、会计以及管理领域的人才提供首选的资格认证。ACCA 于 1988 年进入中国，是第一个进入中国的国际专业会计师团体。ACCA 在中国拥有多个代表处，分别位于北京、上海、成都、广州、深圳、香港及澳门等地。ACCA 在中国设有 30 多个考点。在中国，90 余所高校开设了 ACCA 方向班，ACCA 在中国与超过 600 家 ACCA 认证雇主有着密切的合作。

　　ACCA 受到在中国的跨国公司、大型企业和国际"四大"会计师事务所的高度认可。持有 ACCA 专业资格证书的人在就业市场上具有极高的竞争力。全球有超过 8 500 家雇主已经加入 ACCA 认证雇主计划，为 ACCA 学员和会员提供培训及发展机会。ACCA 在全球设有 80 个代表处和办事机构，以其广泛的支持网络为企业提供优质高效的服务。ACCA 在中国拥有超过 500 家雇主企业，它们都优先录用及提升 ACCA 会员及学员。许多企业将 ACCA 作为晋升的依据之一。据统计，ACCA 会员的年薪一般在 10 万～80 万元，高于市场上一般财务人员的收入。

　　融跃教育专注于 ACCA/CFA、FRM 等金融培训，坚守"品质"和"品位"，以"工匠精神"专注于 ACCA 知识体系的"二次挖掘"，通过系统的思考、梳理以及持续的教学实践，不断为全球的华人考生提供优质的备考资源。

　　本知识精要依据考纲和 BPP 教材编写，涵盖了各科目每个章节的重要知识点，能够使考生的学习更加快捷高效。

　　ACCA 的学习过程也许注定是一个人孤军奋战的过程，但融跃教育愿一路陪您一起奋战，做您学海里的灯塔，照亮您学习的道路，陪伴您通过每一科 ACCA。人不是生来就拥有一切，而是要靠从学习中所得到的一切来造就自己，发奋努力的背后必有加倍的赏赐，希望每一个奋斗的 ACCAer 在本书的帮助下最终都能成为 ACCA 持证人！

融跃教育 ACCA 研究院
2021 年 1 月

BT BUSSINESS AND TECHNOLOGY

Part A The business organization, its stakeholders and the external environment ········· 003
- Chapter 1   Business organizations ·· 004
- Chapter 2   Stakeholders in business organization ······························· 008
- Chapter 3   Political and legal factors affecting business ······················ 011
- Chapter 4   The macro-economic environment ····································· 014
- Chapter 5   The micro-economic environment ····································· 022
- Chapter 6   Social-cultural, technological and environmental factors ·········· 029
- Chapter 7   Business analysis models ·· 032

Part B Business organization structure, functions and governance ····················· 036
- Chapter 8   Business organization and its structure ····························· 037
- Chapter 9   Basic organisational structure concepts ····························· 039
- Chapter 10 Types of business organisation structure ·························· 042
- Chapter 11 Function of main departments in business organization ·········· 046
- Chapter 12 Organizational culture ·· 048
- Chapter 13 Committees in business organization ································ 051
- Chapter 14 Corporate governance and social responsibility ···················· 053

Part C Accounting and reporting systems, controls and compliance ················· 059
- Chapter 15 Function of accounting in business ·································· 060
- Chapter 16 Law and regulation governing accounting ··························· 062
- Chapter 17 Financial systems and procedures ···································· 064
- Chapter 18 Information technology and information systems ··················· 067
- Chapter 19 IT systems security and safety ······································· 072
- Chapter 20 Fraud and fraudulent behaviour and their prevention in business ······ 074

Part D Leading and management individuals and teams ... 077

- Chapter 21 Nature of management ... 078
- Chapter 22 Leadership and styles ... 081
- Chapter 23 Recruitment and selection of employees ... 085
- Chapter 24 Equal opportunities and managing diversity ... 090
- Chapter 25 Individual and group behaviour in business organisation ... 092
- Chapter 26 Team formation, development and management ... 094
- Chapter 27 Motivating individuals and groups ... 098
- Chapter 28 Training and development ... 102
- Chapter 29 Review and appraisal of individual performance ... 105

Part E Personal effectiveness and communication in business ... 109

- Chapter 30 Personal effectiveness techniques ... 110
- Chapter 31 Communication in business ... 113
- Chapter 32 Conflicts in business ... 116

Part F Professional ethics in accounting and business ... 118

- Chapter 33 Ethical consideration ... 119

MA MANAGEMENT ACCOUNTING

- Chapter 1 Accounting for management ... 125
- Chapter 2 Sources of data ... 128
- Chapter 3 Presenting information ... 132
- Chapter 4 Type of cost and cost behaviour ... 133
- Chapter 5 Forecasting ... 137
- Chapter 6 Accounting for materials ... 142
- Chapter 7 Accounting for labour ... 148
- Chapter 8 Accounting for overhead ... 151
- Chapter 9 Absorption costing and marginal costing ... 156
- Chapter 10 Process costing ... 159
- Chapter 11 Job, batch and service costing ... 165
- Chapter 12 Alternative costing principles ... 166
- Chapter 13 Budgeting ... 169
- Chapter 14 Standard costing ... 175
- Chapter 15 Variance analysis ... 176
- Chapter 16 Performance measurement ... 179

FA FINANCIAL ACCOUNTING

Chapter 1	Introduction of accounting	185
Chapter 2	The regulatory framework	190
Chapter 3	Conceptual framework	192
Chapter 4	Sources, records and books of prime entry	196
Chapter 5	Ledger accounts and double entry	200
Chapter 6	From trial balance to financial statements	203
Chapter 7	Sales and purchases	205
Chapter 8	Inventory	208
Chapter 9	Tangible assets	212
Chapter 10	Intangible assets	217
Chapter 11	Accruals and prepayments	219
Chapter 12	Provisions and contingencies	221
Chapter 13	Irrecoverable debts and allowance	224
Chapter 14	Control accounts	227
Chapter 15	Bank reconciliation	230
Chapter 16	Correction of errors	232
Chapter 17	Incomplete records	235
Chapter 18	Preparation of financial statements for sole traders	236
Chapter 19	Introduction to company accounting	238
Chapter 20	Preparation of financial statements for companies	243
Chapter 21	Events after the reporting period	246
Chapter 22	Statement of cash flow	248
Chapter 23	Introduction of group	253
Chapter 24	The consolidated statement of financial position	256
Chapter 25	The consolidated statement of profit or loss	261
Chapter 26	Interpretation of financial statements	262

LW CORPORATE AND BUSINESS LAW

Chapter 1	Essential elements of the legal system: court structure	267
Chapter 2	Sources of law	271
Chapter 3	Formation of contract I	277
Chapter 4	Formation of contract II	284
Chapter 5	Content of a contract	291

Chapter 6	Breach of contract and remedies	298
Chapter 7	The tort of law and professional negligence	306
Chapter 8	Contract of employment	313
Chapter 9	Dismissal and redundancy	320
Chapter 10	Agency law	324
Chapter 11	Partnership	328
Chapter 12	Corporations and legal personality	331
Chapter 13	Company formation	336
Chapter 14	Constitution of a company	340
Chapter 15	Share capital	344
Chapter 16	Loan capital	349
Chapter 17	Capital maintenance and dividend law	353
Chapter 18	Company directors	357
Chapter 19	Other company officer	364
Chapter 20	Company meetings and resolutions	367
Chapter 21	Insolvency and administration	370
Chapter 22	Fraudulent and criminal behaviour	378

BUSSINESS AND TECHNOLOGY

Part A

The business organization, its stakeholders and the external environment

Chapter 1

Business organizations

1. Definition and purpose of organization 组织的定义和目的

An organization is a **social arrangement** which pursues **collective goals**, which **controls** its own **performance** and which has a boundary separating it from its environment.

组织的三要素:

1) **collective goals** 共同目标

组织的存在是由人构成的,这群人要朝着共同的方向而努力。比如,公司的目标是盈利。

2) **social arrangement** 社会分工

组织中不同的人在做不同的事情,每个人各司其职,做自己擅长的事情,使组织高效运营。

3) **control performance** 控制业绩表现

组织通过一系列的规章制度来控制成员的业绩表现,以实现组织目标。

考点:通过这三个要素来判断是否为组织

2. Why do organizations exist? /Advantages of organization 组织存在的意义/组织的优点

- Overcome people's individual limitations 克服个人的局限性
- Enable people to specialize in what they do best 实现专业化的分工
- Accumulate and share skills and knowledge 聚集以及分享知识
- Pool resources — whether money or time 汇聚资源:钱或时间
- Save time 节约时间,提高效率
- Enable **synergy**: 1+1＞2, Organizations can achieve more than the individuals could on their own

关键理解:Synergy 协同效应,简单来说,就是1+1＞2,即一群人在组织当中共同的产出会大于他们单独工作的产出之和

3. Types of organizations 组织的分类(四种分类方式)

3.1 Profit-orientated vs. Not-for-profit orientated(根据是否以 profit 为目标分为营利组织和非营利组织)

1) **Profit organization**

The primary goal is to maximize profit and secondary goal is to provide goods or service.

Profit organization 在考试中会出现的别名：Business organization/Profit-seeking organization/commercial organization。营利组织的首要目标是 maximize profit，考试中也会出现其他表达方式，如 maximize shareholder's wealth 最大化股东价值/Increase shareholder's long-term value 提高股东长期价值

2）**Non-profit organization（NFPs or NPOs）**

The primary goal is to provision of goods/service and secondary goal is to minimize cost of primary goal.

非营利组织，即不以盈利为目标的组织。别名：non-for-profit organization/non-trading organization/non-profit seeking organization。

3.2 By ownership/control：Private sector vs. Public sector

按照所有权结构来分，分为：

Private sector 私营部门：私人所有。

Public sector 公共部门：国家或者全体公民所有。

3.2.1 Private sector（commercial business or business organization）

Organizations not owned or run by central or local government, or government agencies. These organizations can be categorized into sole proprietorship（sole trader）, a partnership, or a limited company according to legal status.（私营部门，即不是由政府或政府代理机构运营的组织，根据法律形式可以分为：个体户、合伙制、有限公司）

1）**Sole trader and partnership**

Sole trader is setting up business by individuals alone and partnership is by partners. Their risk is not restricted to their investment in the business and they need to be responsible for all the debts.

个体户：个体户所有者是 individual 个人。

合伙制：由两个或两个以上个人共同拥有的，其所有者是合伙人 partner

他们承担的是什么风险：不以出资额为限（not restricted to their investment in the business），也就是他们承担的是无限责任（unlimited liability）；无限责任相对的是有限责任。

无限责任是指当企业的全部财产不足以清偿到期债务时，投资人应以个人的全部财产用于清偿。

2）**Limited companies（重要考点）**

A limited company has a separate legal personality from its owners（shareholders）. The shareholders can not normally be sued for the debts of the business unless they have given some personal guarantee. Their risk is generally restricted to the amount that they have invested in the company when they buy the shares. This is called limited liability.

有限公司的所有者叫 shareholders 股东，有限责任公司具备独立法人资格，即一个企业一旦成为有限公司之后，在法律上把它视为独立的人：企业拥有自己的资产，承担自己的负债。若资不抵债，破产清算，还款责任是公司的，和股东无关。股东不会被起诉还款，除非他为公司的债务提供了个人担保。所以，对股东来说，他承担的是有限责任，他的风险是有上限的，上限是其在公司全部的投资额。

The ownership and control of a limited company are legally separated even though they may be vested in the same individual or individuals (e.g. the shareholders are also the directors of the company).

有限公司的所有权和控制权(管理权)在法律上是分离的。

Ownership 是我出钱去设立这家企业,我就拥有这个企业了,股东是具有所有权;

Control 管理权,是去管理这家公司的日常经营。董事拥有的是管理权,比如职业经理人。

现实生活中,股东也可以是董事,同时拥有所有权和经营权,但在法律上这两个权力是分离的。

The LLC can be further categorized into 有限公司有两种分类:

a) Private limited company (with 'Ltd' after their name) — these tend to be smaller businesses, often owned by a few shareholders. Shares cannot be offered to the general public.

(私公司/有限责任公司:公司规模较小,股东数量少,不能公开募集资本)

b) Public limited company (with 'plc' after their name) — these can be much larger businesses. Shares can be offered to the general public, meaning that there can be millions of different shareholders. This makes it easier for the company to raise finance, enabling further growth.

(公公司/股东有限公司:公司规模较大,可以公开募集资本,股东数量多)

What is the difference? 公公司和私公司的区别

a) Number of shareholders 股东数量(公公司股东数量多;私公司股东数量少)。

b) Transfer abilities of shares 股份的可转让性。即股票从一个人转移到另一个人的过程是否方便容易:公公司可转让性强,可以在股票交易市场上公开买卖;私公司可转让性差。

c) Directors as shareholders 股东是否是董事。公公司股东往往不是董事,所有权和经营权的分离更加彻底;私公司股东也可能是董事,也就是经营权所有权同时在一拨人身上。越是上市公司,股权越分散,高管往往不是股东,而是股东聘用的一些职业经理人。

d) Source of capital 资金来源。公公司公司股票可以公开发行,资金来源于整个社会,资金来源更广;私公司由于不能面向公众公开集资,资金来源较窄。

3.2.2 Public sector

Organisations owned or run by central or local government or government agencies. Public sector organisations are accountability to the People, the Government, and the Parliament. They are funded by public funds, such as taxpayers' money, charges (e.g. bus tickets, hospital charges) and sometimes borrowing (e.g. Treasury bonds).

由政府拥有或运营的组织叫 public sector 公共部门。公共部门要对人民,对议会,对政府负责。

他的资金来源于公共资金,比如,税收、收费(地铁票、医院收费等)及国债。

3.3 Non-government organization (NGO) 非政府组织

This type of organisation is basically an **independent voluntary association** of people acting together for some common purposes, aimed at promoting social, political, or environmental change **for the good of the public at large.**

非政府组织是独立于政府存在的、自发形成、独立运营的一个组织。它们的成立是为了一些共同的目的，旨在为了广大人民群众的利益而推动社会、政治或者环境改变。

However, NGOs are not generally measured in respect of customer satisfaction or profitability, but rather in terms of **effectiveness and efficiency** in how they manage their resources — in other words, '**value for money**'.

由于 NGO 一般不以营利为目的，也不是商业组织，所以我们去衡量他的 performance 的时候，不看盈利指标或者是客户满意度，而是看 3E，也叫作 value for money，即 effectiveness，efficiency，economy，对应中文为效果、效率和经济。

3.4 Co-operative societies and mutual associations 合作社

Co-operative societies: These are businesses owned by their workers or customers, who share the profits.

A co-operative is an autonomous association of persons united **voluntarily** to meet their common economic (such as, to share the profit), social and cultural needs and aspirations through **a jointly owned and democratically controlled enterprise.**

合作社是由人自发成立的自治的组织，是为了实现共同的目的，这些目的可能是经济、社会、文化等各种目的，即它可以是为了赚钱，也可以不是为了赚钱。它是由其成员**共同拥有，民主管理的**。

Features:

○ Open membership — everybody is welcome 开放的会员制度。

○ Democratic control — one member one vote 民主管理：做决定的时候，是一人一票，投票表决，少数服从多数。

○ Distribution of the surplus in proportion to purchases (customers) 按购买额即股份来分配利润。

Chapter 2

Stakeholders in business organization

1. What is stakeholder? 利益相关者的定义
Stakeholders are those individuals or groups that, potentially, have an interest in what the organization does. 利益相关者是对组织的行为有潜在兴趣的个人或群体。

2. Examples of stakeholder
- Shareholders 股东
- Finance providing parties 债权人（又名：creditor）
- Suppliers and customers (trade creditors) 供应商和客户
- government and Taxation agencies 政府和税务机关
- Financial and investment analysts 投资机构的分析师
- Managers，employees 公司里的经理、员工
- Trade union 工会
- Public at large/Local community 公众和当地社区

3. Types of stakeholders 利益相关者的分类（重要考点）
3.1 Internal, connected and external
根据利益相关者与企业的联系紧密程度划分为内部的、有联系的和外部的。

Stakeholder	Examples
Internal	Employees, management
Connected	Shareholders, customers, suppliers, financiers
External	Government, pressure groups, the public, the community

Notes：
Internal 内部的，即处在企业内部的利益相关者：普通员工、管理者。
Connected 有联系的，处于企业外部但是与企业有交易往来或者契约关系的利益相关者，如股东、客户、供应商、债权人。
External 完全处在企业外部的，和企业没有什么交易往来的，但是又和企业相互影响的利益相关者。例如，政府、压力组织、社区、公众。

Chapter 2　Stakeholders in business organization

3.2　Primary and secondary stakeholders

按照重要性或优先级，分为主要的利益相关者和次要的利益相关者。

a) Primary stakeholders are stakeholders who have a contractual relationship with the organization.

Primary stakeholders = internal + connected stakeholders

Notes：Primary stakeholders 是跟企业有契约关系的、有合同关系的，包括 Internal 和 Connected。

举例：Internal，如员工和经理与企业有劳动合同。

Connected，如债权人：借款合同；股东：股权协议；上下游：买卖合同。

b) Secondary stakeholders do not have such a relationship with the company.

Secondary stakeholders = external stakeholders

Notes：Secondary stakeholders 和企业之间没有合同契约关系，比如，政府、公众、社区、压力组织。

考点：考试的时候，会在题干中列举几个利益相关者，问他们分别是属于哪一类 stakeholder。

4. Conflict of interest among stakeholders and management of stakeholders

Since their interest may be widely different，conflict between stakeholders can be quite common. A relationship in which conflict between stakeholders is vividly characterized is that between managers and shareholders. 利益相关者对组织有不同的诉求，这些诉求各不相同，甚至是互相冲突的。

比如，一个常见的冲突关系是经理和股东之间的冲突（后面章节会讲到经理和股东之间有利益冲突，即代理问题），因此，我们需要对利益相关者进行管理。

Mendelow matrix：(How to manage stakeholders)　重要考点

○ Power：the power they have over the organization

○ Level of interest：the interest they have in a particular decision

Notes：Mendelow 把 stakeholders 放在一个矩阵里面，从两个维度把利益相关者分为四类。

Power：stakeholders 客观拥有的权力，即这个利益相关者对我企业的影响力的高低。

Level of interest：stakeholders 对企业活动的兴趣或利益。

企业通过这些因素来对 stakeholders 分类，从而确定如何管理这些 stakeholders 的诉求。

	LEVEL OF INTEREST	
POWER	Low	High
Low	A Minimal Effort	B Keep Informed
High	C Keep Satisfied	D Key Players

A：Minimal effort：As these stakeholders have lowest influence and least interests，so we may ignore them，least efforts to be input for them.

在 A 区域的 stakeholders，他们称为 Minimal effort，他们没有太大的权力，也没有很高的积极性，所以企业一般不在乎他们。

B：Kept satisfied： must be treated with care. Although often these stakeholders are passive；they are capable of moving to key players.

对于 B 区域的 stakeholder：我们的决策是一定要让他们满意的。因为他们的 power 是高的，但 interest 是低的，客观上他们有很高的 power，但是他们不 care 我们，一旦我们的决策没有使他们满意，他们的 interest 就会变高，就会转移到 D 区域，所以我们要小心对待他们。比如，大的机构投资者、政府。

C：Kept informed： These stakeholders do not have great ability to influence strategy，but their views can be important in influencing more powerful stakeholders，perhaps by lobbying，forming of associations，etc.

在 C 区域的通常没有太大的权力，但是他们的积极性很高，所以企业有什么重要的决定一定要通知他们，保持信息的透明度，否则，他们就会游说那些有更高权力的人去影响我们企业的决策。比如，社会上的一些团体、压力组织。

D：Key players： strategy must be acceptable to them.（major customer）

对于 D 区域的 stakeholder，我们的决策是一定要让他们接受的，因为他们的 power 和 interest 都很高。比如：企业的大客户。

Chapter 3

Political and legal factors affecting business

1. Political factors 政治因素

1.1　How can the political environment affect an organization? 政治环境影响组织的方式

○ A basic legal framework generally exists 基本的法律框架

○ The Government can take a particular stance on an issue of direct relevance to a business or industry 针对企业或者某些行业的直接政策

○ The Government's overall conduct of its economic policy is relevant to the business 政府整体的经济政策，比如，财政政策或货币政策

1.2　Business are able to influence government policies in a number of ways（重要考点）

a) They can employ lobbyists to put their case to individual ministers or civil servants. 雇用说客游说政府官员（部长或公务员）。

b) They can give MPs non-executive directorship, in the hope that the MP will take an interest in all legislation that affects them. （MPs：members of Parliament）让议员担任企业的 NED（非执行董事的职位），以期望议员在立法时考虑企业利益。

c) They can try to influence public opinion. 影响公众舆论，从而影响政府。

2. Legal factors 法律因素

2.1　Employment protection 劳动保护法

Within many countries, the governments have passed legislation which protects employees from unfair treatment. All forms of termination of employment must be treated with great care.

解除雇佣关系的几种形式如下。

1) Retirement 退休

The organizations encourage retirement for a variety of reasons 企业鼓励员工退休的原因：

○ Promotion opportunities for younger workers 给年轻员工提供机会

○ Early retirement is an alternative to redundancy 变相裁员

○ The age structure of an organization may become unbalanced 调整年龄结构

○ The cost of providing pensions rises with age 节约养老金成本

2）Resignation 辞职

When the employee resigns, there should be exit interview and a period of notice.
Period of notice：通知期限，员工离职前，应提前通知公司，一般要提前一个月。

3）Dismissal 解雇

两种违法的解雇方式（考点）：

a) Wrong dismissal — Breach the employment contract.

错误解雇：违背劳动合同，即没有 period of notice，企业没有按合同提前一个月通知员工被解雇。

b) Unfair dismissal — Dismissal without good reasons.

不公平解雇：解雇理由明显不合理，比如因员工的性别、年龄、是否怀孕、婚姻状况而解雇。

4）Redundancy 裁员

In the following cases, an employee is not entitled to the compensation.
三种情况下，企业裁员不需要补偿员工（考点）：

a) The employee unreasonable rejected the offer of an alternative employment by the employer. 该员工主动拒绝了雇主提供的其他工作岗位。

b) The employee is of pensionable age or over, or has less than two years' continuous employment. 该员工超过了退休年龄或者在企业连续工作不满两年。

c) The employee's conduct merits dismissal without notice. 员工的行为违背了规章制度。

2.2 Data protection and security 数据隐私保护法

2.2.1 The Data Protection Act 1998

The Act is an attempt to protect the individual. The term of Act cover data about individuals — not data about corporate bodies.

Note：该法律主体是针对员工个人，保护员工个人隐私未经授权不披露，而不是指保护公司数据。

2.2.2 Definition of terms used in the Act 相关术语

○ **Personal data** is information about a living individual, including expression of opinion about him or her. Data about organizations is not personal data. 隐私信息本身。

○ **Data users** are organizations or individuals who control personal data and the use of personal data. 拥有信息的公司。

○ **Data subject** is an individual who is the subject of personal data. 数据所描述的对象。

举例：BHG 公司知道 A 员工身高 155 cm。
Personal data：A 员工身高 155 cm。
Data user：BHG 公司。
Data subject：A 员工。

2.2.3 The data protection principles 数据保护的原则

a) Personal data shall be accurate and, where necessary, kept up-to date. 信息必须

要准确，必要时候要更新。

b) Personal data must not be kept for longer than is necessary. 个人信息不能被保留超过其必要的时间。例如，当 A 员工不再是 BHG 公司员工时，该信息应及时删除。

c) A data user is responsible for the security and protection of data against unauthorized access, alternation, disclosure or accidental loss. 数据的拥有者有责任保护数据免受未经授权的接触、修改、披露或者丢失。

d) Personal data shall be obtained for one or more specified and lawful purposes and shall not be further processed by the data user in any manner incompatible with those purposes. 信息的使用者获取这个信息，只能是为了特定、合法的目的，不能用于不合理的、随意的目的。

2.3　Health and safety law 工作场合的健康安全法

（在工作场合的健康和安全是谁的责任？Employer & employee）

2.3.1　Employer's responsibilities

a) Employers must carry out ri**sk assessments, generally in writing,** of all work hazards. Assessment should be **continuous.** They must assess the risks to anyone else affected by their work activities. 雇主首先需要进行风险评估，排查工作场所有没有安全隐患，并且要把它写下来，而且这种排查风险必须要持续不断地进行。

b) Information, instruction, training and supervision should encourage safe working practices. Employers must provide training and information to all staff. 告知、指导、培训、监督员工遵守安全条例。

c) The safety policy should be clearly communicated to all staff, and employer should also share hazard and risk information with other employers. 制定相应的安全政策，并且将政策传达给所有员工。

2.3.2　Employee's responsibilities

a) Take reasonable care of themselves and others.

b) Inform the employer of any situation which may be a danger. 发现有危险，要及时地告知雇主。

Chapter 4

The macro-economic environment

1. Define macro-economics 宏观经济学的定义

Macro-economics is the study of the aggregated effect of the decisions of individual economic units (such as households or businesses). It looks at a complete national economy, or the international economy as a whole.

宏观经济研究的是 aggregate effects,即社会所有经济单元聚集在一起会产生总效应。个体经济单元是指一个人、一个家庭或者一个企业(households or business)。

2. Related terms 相关术语

2.1 Aggregate demand and aggregate supply

1) Aggregate demand (AD)

The total demand in the economy for goods and services is called the aggregate demand and it is made up of serval components of the circular flow. These components include consumption, investment, government spending and exports minus imports.

社会总需求:整个社会在一定价格水平下所愿意购买的产品和服务的总量。

社会总需求＝消费需求＋企业购买投资品的需求＋政府采购需求＋外国购买本国产品和服务的净需求,即 $AD = C + I + G + X$。

2) Aggregate supply (AS)

The aggregate supply refers to the ability of the economy to produce goods and services.

社会总供给:一个国家或地区在一定时期内(通常为 1 年)由社会生产活动实际可以提供给市场的可供最终使用的产品和劳务总量。

2.2 Equilibrium national income

1) Inflationary gap

In a situation where resources are already full employed, there may be an inflationary gap since increases in demand will cause price changes, but no variations in real output.

通胀缺口:当充分就业的情况下,社会总需求超过社会总供给的差额。如果社会总需求上升,会引起价格上升,但社会总产出不变。

2) Deflationary gap

In a situation where there is unemployment of resources. Prices are fairly constant and real output changes as aggregate demand varies.

通缩缺口:指实际总需求水平度低于充分就业时的国民收入水平所形成的缺口。在存在通货紧缩缺口的情况下,社会总供给会随着社会总需求的变化而变化,但价格保持不变。

3. The business cycle

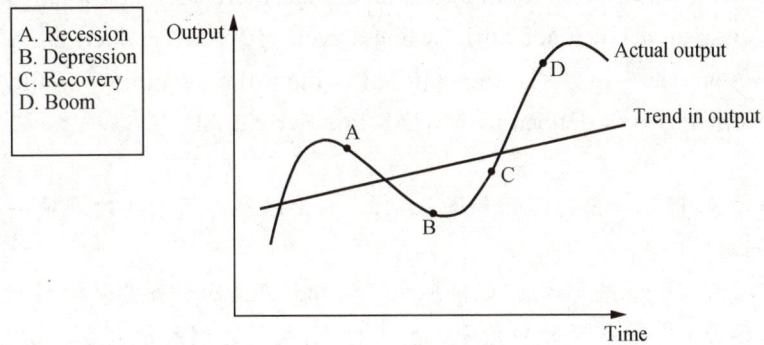

Note: 图中上升的直线叫经济发展趋势,即如果没有出现其他的问题,理论上按照人口的增长、资源的开发等,我们的经济应该呈现稳步的增长。但是事实上并不是这样的,我们经济是有周期的,它是在不断地循环波动上升。

掌握经济循环周期经历的四个阶段:

A：Recession 衰退期

B：Depression 萧条期

C：Recovery 复苏期

D：Boom 繁荣期

4. Government policy related to macro-economic

Macro-economic policy of a country refers to the economic policy that was managed by the Government that affects the economy, and has the following main economic objectives.

政府宏观调控的四个目标:

a) To achieve economic growth. 实现经济增长。

b) To control price inflation. 控制通货膨胀。

c) To achieve full employment. 实现完全/充分就业。

d) To achieve a balance between exports and imports. 实现进出口平衡。

4.1 To achieve economic growth

4.1.1 GDP VS GNP

GDP（gross domestic products）

GNP（gross national products）

Economic growth may be measured by increases in the real gross national product (GNP) per head.

Note： 衡量经济增长的两个指标如下。

GDP 国内生产总值：本国居民在本国的收入＋外国居民在本国的收入（属地原则）。

GNP 国民生产总值：本国居民在本国的收入＋本国居民在外国的收入（属人原则）。

考点：通过 GDP 或 GNP 去判断这个国家经济是增长的，还是下降的，或者增速的高低。

4.1.2 Actual economic growth VS. potential economic growth

Actual economic growth is the annual percentage increase in national output, which typically fluctuates in accordance with business cycle. It is determined by AD and AS.

Potential economic growth is the rate at which the economy would grow if all resources are utilized. It is determined by AS rather than AD.

Note：

实际经济增长：国民产出的实际年增长率，基本上跟经济周期的波动是一样的，它是由 AD 和 AS 共同决定的。

潜在经济增长：指一国（或地区）经济所生产的最大产品和劳务总量的增长率，或者说一国（或地区）在各种资源得到最优和充分配置条件下，所能达到的最大经济增长率。它是由 AS 决定的。

4.2 To control price inflation

4.2.1 Definition

○ **Inflation** is an increase in price levels generally. It means the decline in the purchasing power of money.

○ **Deflation** is a decrease in the general price level of goods and services.

○ **Economic stagnation**, slow or no economic growth.

○ **Stagflation**, a portmanteau of stagnation and inflation, is a term used in economics to describe a situation where an inflation rate is high, the economic growth rate slows down, and unemployment remains steadily high.

考点：掌握四个名词的定义以及会带来哪些经济现象，通过下面这个表格进行总结，考试的时候结合表格灵活应用。

	Price	Cost of living	Investment/Economic growth	Employment rate
Inflation	Increase	Increase	Increase	Increase
Deflation	Decrease	Decrease	Decrease	Decrease
Economic stagflation	—	—	Zero/Decrease	—
Stagflation	Increase	Increase	Decrease	Decrease

4.2.2 Causes of inflation 引起通货膨胀的原因

a) Demand pull factors 需求拉动型（demand＞supply 供不应求，价格上升）

b) Cost push factors 成本推动型（生产成本上升，比如，原材料、人工成本上升，导致物价上升）

c) Import cost factors 进口成本上升（进口成本也是产品成本组成的一部分）

d) Expectations 未来价格的预期（预计未来涨价会导致囤货现象，其实是无形当中把未来的需求提前，供不应求，价格上升）

e) Excessive growth in the money supply 超额货币供应（产出不变，货币供应量变多，导致价格上升）

4.2.3　How to measure inflation

One important measure of the general rate of inflation in the UK used over many years has been the Retail Prices Index（RPI）. The RPI measures the percentage changes month by month in the average level of prices of the commodities and services, including housing costs, purchased by the great majority of households in the UK. CPI excluded housing costs.

Note：衡量通胀率的两个指数：RPI 零售物价指数和 CPI 消费者价格指数。

一般情况下，题干中出现 CPI 和 RPI，是让你通过指数的涨幅来判断这个国家现在处于 inflation 还是 deflation，或者 inflation 的状况是严重还是不严重。

4.2.4　High rates of inflation are harmful to an economy 恶性通胀对经济的危害（考点）

1) **Redistribution of income and wealth**　收入与财富的再分配

Redistribution of wealth might take place from accounts receivable to accounts payable. 财富由债权人流向债务人，从而债务人获利，债权人损失。（考点）

2) **Balance of payments effects** 影响国际收支平衡

If a country has a higher rate of inflation than its major trading partners, its exporters will become relatively expensive and imports relatively cheap. As a result, the balance of trade will suffer, affecting employment in exporting industries. Eventually, the exchange rate will be affected.

如果一个国家和它的主要贸易国相比，它的通胀率更高，那么出口商品会变贵，进口商品变得便宜，后果是：该国的贸易平衡被打破，出口行业的就业率下降，最终影响汇率。

3) **Uncertainty of the value of money and prices** 对货币价值和价格的不确定性

If the rate of of inflation is imperfectly anticipated, no one has certain knowledge of the true rate of inflation. As a result, no one has certain knowledge of value of money or the real meaning of prices. If the rate of inflation becomes excessive, and there is 'hyperinflation', this problem becomes so exaggerated that money becomes worthless, so that people are unwilling to use it and are forced to barter trade.

如果通胀率是不完全预期的，没有人知道真实的通胀率到底是多少，后果就是没有人知道货币的真实价值，也没有人知道 price 的真实含义。如果通货膨胀率进一步升高，变成恶性通胀，那么钱变得不值钱，人们不愿意使用它，就会回到最传统的 barter trade 方式，即以物易物，金融体系崩溃。

4.3　To achieve full employment

4.3.1　The rate of unemployment

$$\frac{\text{Number of unemployed}}{\text{Total workforce}} \times 100\%$$

Note：失业率的计算：

分母 total workforce 总劳动力，包括有能力也有意愿参加工作的人。如未成年人、学生、退休人员、丧失劳动能力的人或者家庭主妇等没有意愿或者没能力参加工作的人，不算劳动力。

分子 number of unemployed 失业人口，包括有能力有意愿去工作，但没有找到工作的人。

4.3.2 Causes of unemployment 六种失业类型

应用性考点，通过一段描述来判断失业的类型。

1) Real wage unemployment

Labor supply > labor demand, often caused by strong labor unions or minimum wages.

真实工资失业：是指劳动力供应量大于劳动力需求所导致的失业，一般是由于工会或者最低工资标准引起的。

2) Temporary frictional wage unemployment

Short-term. It takes time to match employees with employers, and individuals will be unemployed during search period for a new job

摩擦性失业：人们寻找最适于自己的工作的时候，是需要时间去匹配的，会造成短期的暂时性失业。从长期来看，这些人找到了合适的工作，就会从失业人口中流出。

3) Seasonal fluctuation

Short-term. This occurs in certain industries. E.g. tourism and farming.

季节性失业：有些行业有淡季和旺季，在淡季的时候劳动力需求减少，从而引起失业。常见于农业和旅游业。

4) Structural unemployment

Long-term changes occur in the conditions of an industry.

5) Technological unemployment

Long-term changes due to new technologies introduced.

Note：结构性失业和技术性失业都是由于新技术的引进带来的失业。

不同点在于：技术性失业是只是新技术的引进淘汰其中部分低端岗位，但整个行业没有发生结构性的转变，比如旅游业中人工检票的岗位被机器售票所淘汰，但旅游业整体是没有问题的。而结构性失业是新技术的引进造成整个行业发生了长期变化，可能导致整个行业被淘汰。比如，小灵通BB机的整个行业已经被淘汰，行业中的员工自然也失业了。

6) Cyclical or demand-deficient unemployment

Long-term, caused by the business cycle.

周期性失业和和经济周期有关，在经济萧条期的时候失业率往往上升。

4.4 To achieve a balance between exports and imports

4.4.1 The balance of payment

A country's BOP records all financial transactions made between individuals, businesses and its government with foreign consumers and organizations.

国际收支平衡：一段时间内，通常是一年，某个国家付出去的钱和收到的钱是大体相当的。

Chapter 4　The macro-economic environment

我们用下面三个账户来分别记录不同种类的资金流动。

1) Current account 经常性账户：记录国与国之间的经常往来

a) Balance of trade：trade in service or goods. 如果 import ＞ export 叫作贸易逆差（deficit）；反过来，Import＜export，叫作贸易顺差（surplus）。

b) Net factor income from abroad：investment income from dividend and interest on credit and payer to foreign taxes. 国际投资回报，注意这里是回报，不是本金。

c) Net unilateral transfer from abroad：foreign aid，grants，gift and remittances. 国际单边转移：国际捐助、礼物以及侨汇。

2) Capital account 资本账户：记录国与国之间的资本或者大型资产往来

Records the international flow of transfer payment relating to capital items （country's inflows and outflow of payment and transfer of ownership of fixed asset-capital goods such as heavy machine, large input in infrastructure, facilities, premises, etc.）

3) Financial account 金融账户：记录国与国之间的投资活动

a) Foreign direct investment.

b) Portfolio investment（trade in stock）.

c) Other investment（bank deposits）.

d) Movements on government foreign currency reserves.

Note：投资本金流动记录在 financial account；投资回报流动记录在 current account。要了解这三个账户分别记录什么内容。

考试的时候可能会问：题目中的这笔资金的流动应该记录在哪个 account 当中。

4.4.2　Government resolution to rectify a current account deficit

政府有哪些措施去纠正 current account 的逆差？（outflow＞ inflow）

a) A depreciation of the currency/devaluation 本币贬值

贬值有利于出口，不利于进口，增加 inflow，减少 outflow。

b) Direct measures to restrict imports quotas or exchange control regulations

采取直接措施限制进口，如进口配额或者外汇管制，这是降低 outflow。

c) Domestic deflation to reduce aggregate demand in the domestic economy

国内采取紧缩政策，降低经济热度，国民需求下降，对进口的需求也降低，从而降低了 outflow。

Note：政府会采取哪些措施去实现宏观调控的四大目标？

两种政策：一是 fiscal policy 财政政策；二是 monetary policy 货币政策。

在本章我们会学习三种财政政策和四种货币政策。

如果考试问你：下面哪些属于财政或者货币政策？你要能区分出来。

5. Fiscal policy

Fiscal policy is a kind of government policy which focus on **taxation, public borrowing and public spending.** This formal planning of fiscal policy is usually done once a year and is set out in the **Budget**.

Note: 财政政策有三种：税收、国债和公共支出。其中税收和国债属于财政收入，公众支出属于财政支出。无论是收入还是支出的政策，最终都会反映在 national budget 预算当中。

国家每年都会制定财政预算，如果国家预算是财政收入大于支出，就称为财政盈余(budget surplus)；反过来，支出大于收入称为财政赤字(budget deficit)。

5.1 Budget surplus and budget deficit

PSNCR/PSBR：

When the government's expenditure exceeds its income, it must borrow to make up the difference. The amount that government must borrow each year is known as the Public Sector Net Cash Requirement (**PSNCR**) which former name was Public Sector Borrowing Requirement (**PSBR**), we say that the government is running at a **budget deficit**. Running a deficit is known as an '**expansionary** strategy', it is often used when a **deflationary** gap exists.

Note: 当政府支出大于收入的时候，这个国家正在经历的是财政赤字，也叫 PSNCR 净现金需求，曾用名是 PSBR，即公共部门借款需求。

PSNCR = PSBR = Budget deficit，这三种表达方式，都有可能在题干中出现。

如果实行财政赤字，说明政府采取的是扩张性的财政政策，就是通过花钱去刺激经济，往往是存在通缩缺口的时候使用。

When a government's income exceeds its expenditure, and there is a **negative PSNCR** or **PSDR**（public sector debt repayment), we say that the government is running at a **budget surplus**. Running a surplus is known as an '**contractionary strategy**', it is often used when a **inflationary** gap exists.

Note: 如果收入大于支出，这个国家正在经历的是财政盈余，别名 Negative PSNCR 或者 PSDR。

Negative PSNCR = PSDR = Budget surplus

盈余往往是存在 inflationary gap 的时候用，政府要实行紧缩的财政政策去降温。

5.2 Taxes

5.2.1 Types of tax 税的分类

1) Regressive taxes, proportional taxes & progressive taxes

看你的应纳税所得额。也就是随着收入上升，你的税率是上升、下降还是不变来分类的。

- **Regressive tax:** a regressive tax takes a higher proportion of a poor person's salary than of a rich person's (Television licenses and road tax are examples of regressive taxes since they are the same for all people).
- **Proportional tax:** takes the same proportion of income tax from all levels of income.
- **Progressive tax:** takes a higher proportion of income in tax as income rises. (Income tax as a whole is progressive).

2) Direct tax and indirect tax

- **Direct tax** is paid direct by a person to Revenue Authority (e.g. income tax, corporation tax，capital gain tax，inheritance taxes）.

○ **Indirect tax** is controlled by the revenue authority from an intermediary who the attempts to pass on the tax to consumers in the price of goods they sell.

<u>Note</u>：直接税和间接税的分类是看税负的承担人（谁要负责这笔钱）和税负的缴纳人（跑到税务局那边亲自去交）是否为同一人。如果是同一人，叫直接税；不是同一人，是间接税。

常见的直接税：个税、公司税、资本利得税、遗产税。

间接税：税负缴纳人只是 intermediary，最后他会把这个税负转移给消费者，变成价内税。

放在价格里让消费者承担，主要有 sales tax 和 VAT。

5.2.2 Functions of tax

a) To raise revenue for the government. 政府财政收入的来源。

b) To discourage certain activities regarded as undesirable. 用税收调节政府不鼓励的行为。

c) To redistribute income and wealth such as UK inheritance tax. 社会财富的再分配，如遗产税。

d) To protect industries from foreign competition. 保护本国产业不受到外来竞争的冲击，如 tariffs 关税。

5.2.3 Qualities of good tax

a) Flexibility 灵活性，要适应经济的发展

b) Efficiency 税收效率原则

c) Without distorting economic behavior 不能扭曲正常的经济行为

6. Monetary policy

The monetary policy is a kind of government policy which uses money supply, interest rates，exchange rates or credit control to influence aggregate demand.

<u>Note：四种货币政策：</u>

① money supply 增加或降低货币供应量来调节经济。

② Interest rates 利率。

思考：如果国家实行降低存贷款利率的政策会带来什么效果？

对消费者而言，钱存在银行，利息太少，还不如去消费，可以刺激消费。

对企业而言，借钱成本降低，企业会去借钱，扩大生产，可以刺激投资。

用 common sense 就可以判断。

③ Exchange rates 汇率。如果汇率上升，出口相对变贵，进口变得便宜，不利于出口行业的发展，出口行业的失业率上升。

④ Credit controls 信贷控制，分为宽松的和紧缩的信贷政策。宽松的信贷政策，有利于刺激投资和经济增长，增加就业率；紧缩的信贷政策不利于投资和经济增长。

Chapter 5

The micro-economic environment

1. Micro-economics and related concepts

The micro-economic environment refers to the **immediate operational environment** including suppliers, competitors, customers, stakeholders and intermediaries. (More specific and detail than macro). It focuses on how the individual parts of an economy make decisions about how to allocate scarce resources. It attempts to examine how supply and demand decisions made by these individuals affect the selling prices of goods and services within an industry or market.

Note: 微观经济学的定义:

微观经济研究的是个量,即个人、家庭和企业这种单个经济单元的经济行为。它研究的是单个的市场到底是怎么去分配资源、买卖关系和价格问题。

Utility 效用:通过消费带来的满足感。

Utility is the word used to describe the pleasure or satisfaction or benefit derived by a person from the consumption of goods.

Total utility is the total satisfaction that people derive from spending their income and consuming goods.

一种商品会给你带来一个 utility,但是你在一段时间内,会消费很多的商品。

那么,很多的商品给你带来的效用之和就是总效用。用一个公式表示:

$$TU = U_1 + U_2 + U_3 + \cdots U_N$$

Marginal utility is the satisfaction gained from consuming one additional unit of a good or the satisfaction forgone by consuming one unit less. 边际效用:每多消费1单位商品,所增加的效用有多少?

Consumer rationality. Acting rationally means that the consumer attempts to **maximize the total utility** attainable with a **limited income**. 理性的消费者希望在有限的收入下,实现总效用最大化。

2. Demand

Demand for a good or service is the quantity of that good or service that potential purchasers would be willing and able to buy, or attempt to buy, at any possible price.

需求:人们在一定时期内,在各种可能的价格下愿意并且能够购买某个具体商品的数量。

2.1 Demand curve (for a good or service)

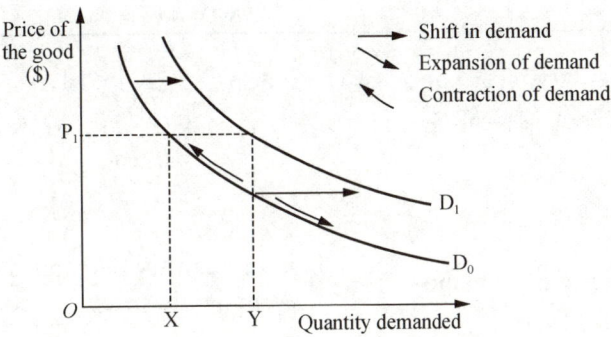

Factors determining demand for a good 需求曲线会受到哪些因素的影响?

a) The price of the good(商品价格越高,需求量越低)

b) Households' income(假设其他条件不变,居民收入上升,需求量上升)

c) The price of other substitute goods

假设 A 商品和 B 商品互为替代品,A 商品价格上升,B 商品需求量上升。

假设 A 商品和 B 商品互为互补品,A 商品价格上升,B 商品需求量下降。

d) Tastes and fashion(假设其他条件不变,流行的东西,需求量上升)

e) Expectations of future price changes(假设其他条件不变,预期未来价格上升,需求量上升)

2.2 Price elasticity of demand (PED) 需求的价格弹性:反映的是需求量的变化受价格变化的影响

计算公式(考点):分母——某商品价格变动的百分比;分子——需求量变化的百分比。

$$\frac{\text{Percentage change in quantity demanded}}{\text{Percentage change in price}}$$

Description	PED	Actual examples
Relatively inelasticity 缺乏弹性	<1	Tea, salt
Unit elasticity 单一价格弹性	=1	—
Relatively elastic 具有弹性	>1	Cameras, air travel

2.3 Income elasticity of demand 需求的收入弹性,反映家庭收入的变化对某件产品需求量变化的影响

计算公式:

$$\text{Income elasticity of demand} = \frac{\text{\% change in quantity demanded}}{\text{\% change in income}}$$

Elasticity	Value	Type of good	Example
Negative 负弹性	＜0	Inferior 劣等品	Inter-city bus travel
Inelastic 缺乏弹性	0～1	Necessity 生活必需品	Basic food stuffs
Elastic 富有弹性	＞1	Luxury 奢侈品	Yachts, sports cars

2.4 Cross elasticity of demand (CED) 需求的交叉弹性 CED

它研究的是：假设 A 商品价格不变，B 商品价格发生变化，对 A 商品需求量有什么影响？

计算公式：

$$\text{Cross elasticity of demand} = \frac{\text{\% change in quantity demanded of good A}}{\text{\% change in price of good B}}$$

Cross-elasticity	Value	Example
Complements 互补品	＜0	Bread and butter
Unrelated products	＝0	Bread and cars
Substitutes 替代品	＞0	White bread and brown bread

考点：三个系数的计算公式和三个系数在不同的数值下，分别代表什么类型的商品？

3. Supply

Supply refers to the quantity of a good that existing suppliers or would-be suppliers would want to produce for the market at a given price.

供给：厂商在一定时期内在一定的价格条件下，生产者愿意并可能为市场提供某种商品或服务数量。

3.1 Short-run supply curve 短期供给曲线

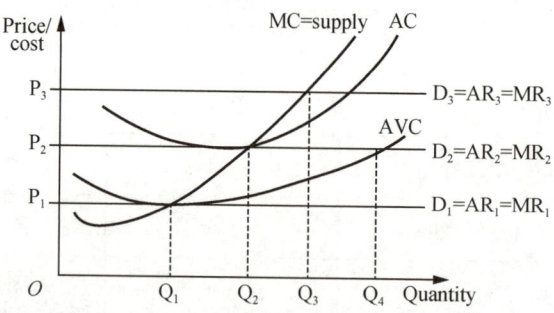

MC：Marginal cost AC：Average cost AVC：average variable cost

We assume price = demand = average revenue = marginal revenue in order to study the supply curve

The supply curve is its marginal cost curve above the variable cost curve (AVC).

MC 在 AVC 以上的部分是 supply curve。

Chapter 5　The micro-economic environment

The firm will supply where MR＝MC in order to maximize profit
当 MR＝MC 的时候，生产者总利润是最大的。

3.2　Factors influencing the supply curve

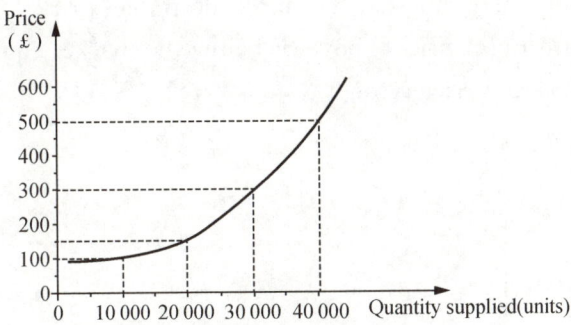

Factors influencing the supply curve：需求曲线会受到哪些因素的影响？

a) Price of goods（商品价格越高，供给量越低）
b) The costs of making the good（其他条件不变，生产成本越高，供给量越低）
c) Price of other goods（substitutes and complements）
假设 A 商品和 B 商品互为替代品，A 商品价格上升，B 商品供给量上升。
假设 A 商品和 B 商品互为互补品，A 商品价格上升，B 商品供给量下降。
d) Expectations of price changes（其他条件不变，预计未来价格上涨，现有供应量下降）
e) Changes in technology（其他条件不变，技术进步，供给量上升）
f) Other factor such as weather（其他因素，如天气）

4. The equilibrium price 均衡价格

The competitive market process results in an equilibrium price, which is the price at which market supply and market demand quantities are in balance. In any market, the equilibrium price will change if market demand or supply conditions change.

均衡价格：在完全竞争市场下，会出现均衡价格，当市场供应和市场需求相等时，所对应的价格就是均衡价格。

The **price mechanism** brings demand and supply into equilibrium, and the equilibrium price for a good is the price at which the volume demanded by consumers and the volume that firms would be willing to supply is the same. This is also known as the **market clearing price**, since at this price there will be neither surplus nor shortage in the market.

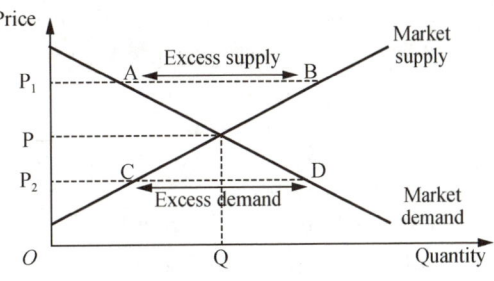

价格机制：在自由市场中，商品价格会围绕着均衡价格上下不断波动，最终停留在均衡价格上。

5. Maximum and minimum prices (Price regulation) 价格管制：最高限价和最低限价

There may be occasions when the equilibrium price established by the market forces of demand and supply may not be the most desirable price. With such cases the government might wish to set prices above or below the market equilibrium price.

5.1 Maximum prices (Price ceiling) 最高限价/价格天花板

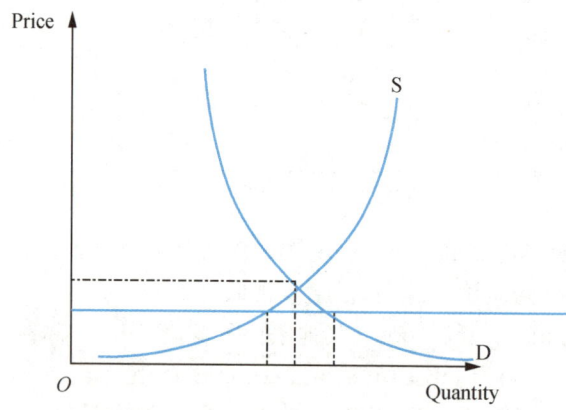

Result：Demand > Supply

Solution：rationing, waiting list and black marketer.

Notes：

① 如果最高限价低于均衡价格,会导致 Demand > supply,供不应求。
   解决方法：配给制；排队；黑市交易。
② 如果最高限价低于均衡价格,对市场无影响,会达到均衡价格。

5.2 Minimum price (Price floor) 最低限价/价格地板

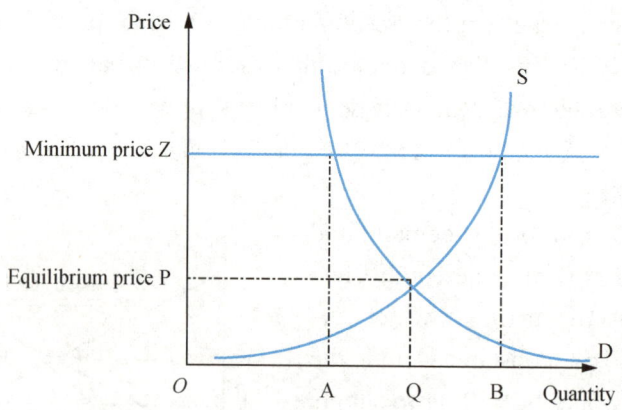

Result：Supply > Demand.

Solution：Production quotas.

Notes：

① 如果政府最低限价高于均衡价格,会导致 supply 大于 demand,生产者会积压存货,卖不出去。

解决方法是：production quotas 生产配额，常见于农产品行业。
② 如果政府最低限价低于均衡价格，no effect，市场的价格机制会趋向于均衡价格。

6. Types of market 四种市场类型（重要考点）

完美市场：完全竞争市场。
不完美市场：寡头市场、垄断市场、垄断竞争市场。

6.1 Perfect competition 完全竞争市场

Perfect market is defined by several conditions, collectively called perfect competition. Among these conditions are：完全竞争市场需要同时满足四个条件：

　　a) Perfect market information 买房和卖方知道同样多的价格信息

　　b) No participant with market power to set prices 没有任何一个参与者有能力制定价格：市场价格是由价格机制的波动决定

　　c) No barriers to entry or exit 没有进入和退出门槛

　　d) Equal access to production technology 市场所有的市场参与者可以平等的获得生产技术

Stock markets and foreign exchange markets are commonly said to be the most similar to the perfect market. The real estate market is an example of a very imperfect market.

现实中，比较接近完美竞争市场的是股票市场和汇率市场。

6.2 Monopoly 垄断市场

　　a) A monopoly describes the situation where a market has only one producer. That is the pure definition, although the term is often used to describe a firm that has a very high share of a market.

定义：垄断即市场上只有一家生产者或者市场上某一家生产者占较大当市场份额

　　b) Monopolies are characterized by a lack of economic competition to produce the good or service and lack of viable substitute goods.

垄断市场的特征是：市场上缺乏经济竞争，并且缺乏替代品。

　　c) A monopoly may come about because the producer has a statutory right to be the only producer, perhaps a 'state owned enterprise'.

垄断市场的出现往往是因为市场上只有某一个生产商获得法定权利去生产商品和服务。比如，国有企业。

　　d) If left uncontrolled, a monopoly can set its own price in the marketplace, which can result in what economists refer to as 'super-normal profits'. For this reason, monopolies are usually subject to control by government or a government agency.

若不加控制，垄断企业可以自己设置价格的话，会导致他们出现"超额利润"。正是因为这个原因，垄断企业往往是由政府控制。

6.3 Oligopoly 寡头市场

An oligopoly arises when a market has a few dominant producers. Each of the few producers has a high level of influence — and a high level of knowledge of their competitor strategies. Oligopolies can result from various form of collusion which reduce competition and lead to higher costs for customers. If an oligopoly has only two firms, it is referred to as a duopoly.

寡头是指市场上有少数几家主要的生产者,每一家生产者都对市场有很大当影响,并且很了解竞争者的战略。寡头企业之间往往会相互勾结串通以减少竞争,制定较高的市场价格。如果市场上只有两家生产者,我们把它叫作"双头垄断"。

Characteristics:

a) Profit maximization conditions 利润最大化
b) Ability to set price 生产者有能力制定价格
c) Barriers to entry are high 进入门槛很高
d) Interdependence 寡头之间相互依赖
e) No-price competition 市场上几乎没有价格竞争

6.4 Monopolistic competition 垄断竞争市场

Monopolistic competition is a type of imperfect competition such that many producers sell products that are differentiated from one another as goods but not perfect substitutes (such as from branding, quality, or location).

垄断竞争市场属于不完全竞争市场中的一种,它是一种介于完全竞争和完全垄断之间的市场组织形式。在垄断竞争市场上,有很多的生产者销售差异化的产品,他们彼此之间不能完全替代(由于品牌、质量、产地等不同)。在这种市场中,既存在着激烈的竞争,又具有垄断的因素。垄断竞争市场是指一种既有垄断又有竞争,既不是完全竞争又不是完全垄断的市场,是处于完全竞争和完全垄断之间的一种市场。

Characteristics:

a) There are many producers and many consumers in the market, and no business has total control over the market price. 市场上有无数的生产者和消费者,没有任何一家企业可以完全控制市场价格。

b) Consumers perceive that there are non-price differences among the competitors' products. 消费者认为竞争者的产品之间没有价格差异。

c) There are a few barriers to entry and exit. 进入和退出市场的门槛较低。

d) Producers have a degree of control over price. 生产者对价格有一定程度的控制权,但没有绝对的控制权。

Chapter 6

Social-cultural, technological and environmental factors

1. Social-cultural factors 社会文化因素

1.1 Demography factors

The study of human population and population trends is known as Demography. 人口统计学：研究人口构成和人口趋势。

有哪些人口统计方面的因素，会对企业经营产生影响？
- Growth and age 人口的增长和年龄构成
- Geography 人口的地理分布
- Ethnicity 种族构成
- Households and family structure 家庭结构
- Social structure 社会结构
- Employment 就业率
- Changes in wealth accumulation and distribution tendency 财富的累积和分配趋势

1.2 Social trends

1.2.1 Social structure

A **social class** refers to a group of people who have the same social, economic or educational status. Organization may be able to link the social position of a given group to its buying patterns.

社会阶层：根据一些分类标准，把具有相同特征的人划分为同一个阶层。例如，根据职业、收入水平或受教育水平进行划分。社会阶层会影响消费者的偏好（preference），划分社会阶层对企业研究市场，进行市场划分有重要的意义。

1.2.2 Values 价值观的改变对企业的影响

a) Health and diet issues — growing market, employee health, new foods, organic foods.

b) Women in work — Overt discrimination, indirect discrimination.

c) Environmentalism — more and more concern for environment.

d) Ethical issues.

现代流行的价值观：健康膳食、环保主义、女性参与工作。

2. Technological factors

The effects of technological change on the organization structure：

1) Downsizing

It is a term used for reducing the number of employees in an organization without necessarily reducing the work or the output.

Downsizing 削减人数：相同工作产量的前提下，组织整体人数的减少。

2) Delayering

It is the process of removing layers of management. This is to change the organisation from one framework with numerous layers into a flatter organization with minimal layers of management.

Delayering 去层：削减管理层级/组织扁平化。它是指组织管理层级的减少，由 tall structure 变为 flat structure 的过程。

3) Outsourcing

It is the contracting out of specified operations or services to an external vendor.

Outsourcing 外包：企业将自己内部的活动交给外部第三方来做。

3. Environmental factors

3.1 The ways in which businesses can limit damage to the environment 企业会有哪些手段减少环境污染？

a) Redesign of products to use fewer raw materials. 重新设计产品包装，节约原材料。

b) Reduction in packaging on products. 减少过度包装。

c) Recycling. 回收利用。

d) Improve energy efficiency. 提高能源利用效率：使用高效能清洁能源。

e) Buying raw materials locally to save transportation emissions. 就近采购原材料。

f) Selecting suppliers carefully, select environmental-friendly suppliers, to reduce pollution, emissions. 选择环保的供应商。

3.2 Sustainability

It means that organisations should use resources in such a way that they do not compromise the needs of future generations. 可持续发展：满足当代人的需求，同时又不损害后代人满足其需求的能力。

3.2.1 Sustainability report

A sustainability report is an organisational report that gives information about economic, environmental social and governance performance such as environmental management, employment, climate change hazardous waste, product formulations, waste management, water use, ethics, and human rights.

The key drivers for the quality of sustainability reports are the guidelines of the Global Reporting Initiative (GRI). The GRI Sustainability Reporting Guidelines enable all organisations worldwide to assess their sustainability performance and disclose the results in a similar way to financial reporting.

可持续发展报告:提供关于经济、环境、社会以及治理方面的信息。

其编制标准是根据国际报告组织(GRI)所提出来的标准来编制。

可持续发展报告除了披露财务数据,更主要的是披露的一些非财务数据(non-financial data)。

3.2.2 Integrated report

Integrated reporting is a process that results in communication by an organisation, most visibly a periodic integrated report, about value creation over time. An integrated report is a concise communication about how an organisations strategy, governance, performance and prospects, in the context of its external environment, lead to the creation of value over the short, medium and long term. An integrated report should be prepared in accordance with the International Integrated Reporting Framework.

Integrated report 综合报告:强调企业的价值增长(value creation),这种价值增长主要是立足现在,着眼未来。它的披露里包括企业拥有哪些资源,资源包括经济、社会、环境等方面的资源,而且包括我们企业在过去、现在以及未来是怎样创造价值的。这份报告既可以综合传统报告的优势,又加上对未来价值的判断,从而给投资者、消费者以及其他利益相关者更多的参考。

Chapter 7

Business analysis models

1. SWOT analysis

SWOT analysis is to assess the **strength, weakness, opportunities and threat** of the organization and **aim to identify the key internal and external factors** to help the organization to achieve success.

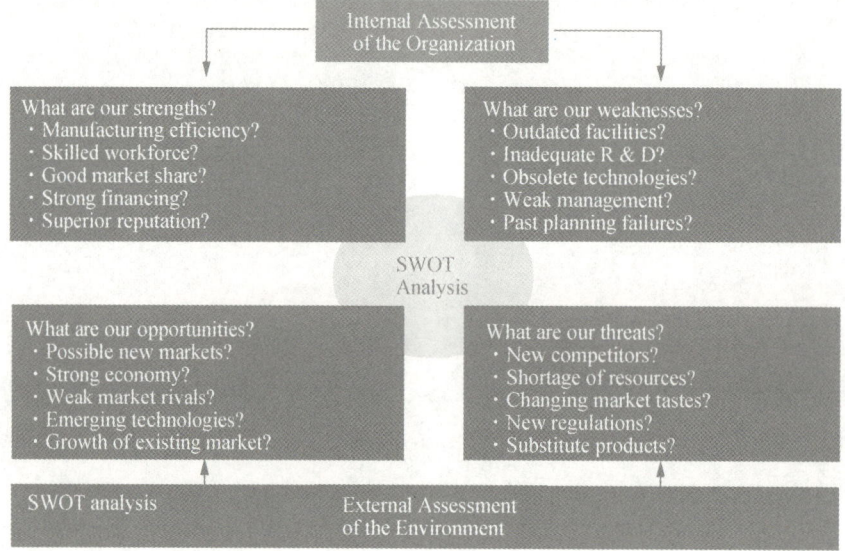

Notes:
① 掌握 SWOT 四个字母分别代表什么含义。
S: Strength 优势。W: Weakness 劣势。O: Opportunity 机会。T: Threat 威胁。
② SWOT 模型既可以帮助分析企业内部的优势和劣势,又可以分析外部的机会和威胁。

2. Porter's five competitive forces model 五力模型(重要考点)

Five forces model provides a simple perspective for **assessing and analyzing the completive strength** and **position** of a corporation or business organization.

The competitive environment is structured by **five forces**:

Chapter 7 Business analysis models

a) Threat of new entrants 新进入者的威胁
b) Substitute products or services 替代品的威胁
c) The bargaining power of customers 下游消费者的议价能力
d) The bargaining power of suppliers 上游供应商的议价能力
e) Competitive rivalry 行业中现有竞争者竞争的激烈程度

2.1 The threat of new entrants (and barrier to entry to keep them out)
如何降低新的进入者的威胁？提高进入门槛。

Main barriers to entry：常见的几类进入门槛

a) Economies of scale 经济规模效应：在一定范围内，随着产量增加，产品单位成本下降。
b) Product differentiation 产品差异化。
c) Good brand name and customer loyalty 品牌效应和消费者忠诚度。
d) Capital requirements 资金门槛。
e) Switching costs 转换成本：客户从购买一个供应商的产品转向购买另一个供应商的产品时所增加的费用。
f) Access to distribution channels 销售渠道。
g) Learning curve advantages 学习曲线优势：随着产量上升，单位产品的生产时间下降。

2.2 Substitute products or services 来自替代品的威胁

A substitute product is a good or service produced by another industry which satisfies the same customer needs. 替代品是来自其他行业的商品同样能满足消费者的需求。

a) The organization would be threatened if the **customers are willing to use substitute products**.
b) The threat of substitute products or services also depend on the **number of them available** in the market.

如何阻止替代品的威胁？提高 Switching cost 转换成本（转换成本，即当我现在已经使用 A 商品，我要换成 B 商品要花费的成本，包括时间、金钱、精力等）

2.3 The bargaining power of customers 下游的议价能力由什么因素决定的

a) How much the customer buys?
消费者购买数量越多，其议价能力越强。

b) How critical the product is to the customer's own business?
本企业产品对客户行业的重要性：越重要，客户的议价能力越弱。

c) Switching cost (the cost of switching supplier).
下游消费者转换成本是高还是低：转换成本越高，消费者议价能力越弱。

d) Whether the products are standard items (hence easily copied) or specialized.
本企业提供的产品是同质化还是差异化的：同质化越强，客户的议价能力越强。

e) The customer's own profitability：a customer who makes low profits will be forced to insist on low prices from suppliers.
下游消费者的利润要求：利润越薄的消费者，议价能力越强。

2.4 The bargaining power of suppliers 上游供应商的议价能力由什么因素决定的

a) Whether there are just one or two dominant suppliers to the industry who are able to charge monopoly prices. 如果企业的上游市场只有一两家主要供应商，那么供应商可以征收一个垄断价格，供应商的议价能力更强。

b) The threat of new entrants or substitute products to the supplier's industry. 供应商行业是否有来自新进入者和替代品的威胁：威胁越大，供应商议价能力下降。

c) Whether the suppliers have other customers outside the industry, and do not rely on the industry for the majority of their sales. 供应商是否有其他行业的客户，如果有的话，供应商议价能力上升。

d) The importance of the supplier's product to the customer's business. 供应商提供的商品对本企业是否重要，越重要，供应商议价能力越强。

e) Whether the supplier has a differentiated product which buyers need to obtain. 供应商的产品是否是差异化的，越差异化，供应商的议价能力越强。

f) Whether switching costs for customers would be high. 对本企业来说，转换成本高不高，转换成本越高，供应商议价能力越强。

2.5 Competitive rivalry

Intensity of existing competition will depend on the following factors：
行业中已有竞争者竞争的激烈程度取决于哪些因素？

a) Number and strength of competitors. 行业中企业数量越多，竞争越激烈。

b) Rate of growth-where the market is expending, competition is low key. 市场增长率：市场增长越快，竞争相对下降。

c) The level of fixed costs. 固定成本越高，竞争激烈程度下降。

d) Buyer switching costs. 消费者转换成本越低，竞争越激烈。

3. Porter's Value chain analysis 价值链分析

The **margin** is the excess the customer is prepared to **pay** over the **cost** to the firm of obtaining resource inputs and providing value activities. It represents the **value created** by the **value activities** themselves and by the **management of the linkages** between them.

Linkages connect the activities of the value chain.

○ **Primary activities** are involved in the **production** of goods and services.

Chapter 7 Business analysis models

○ **Support activities** provide necessary assistance.

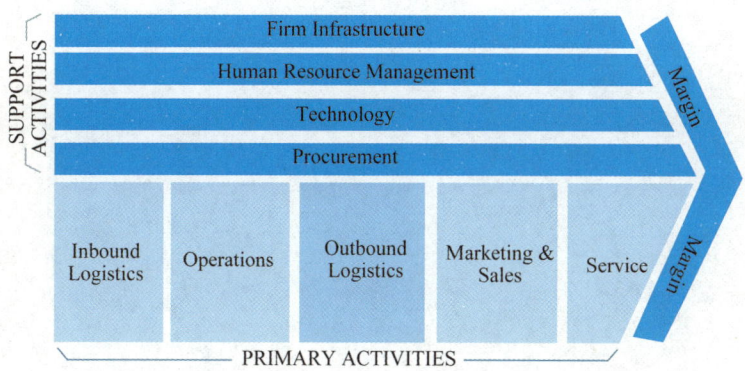

Notes:
① 主要活动：可以直接增加产品价值的活动。
○ Inbound logistics. 进货物流：原材料的储存和运输。
○ Operation. 生产过程：生产、组装、测试。
○ Outbound logistics. 出货物流：产成品的仓储和运输。
○ Marketing and sales. 营销：打广告、促销、定价策略、销售渠道。
○ Service. 售后服务：安装、维修配件。
② 支持性活动：secondary 使 primary activity 做得更好，从而间接地提高产品价值。
○ Firm infrastructure. 企业的基本构造：综合管理、会计核算、融资、战略计划。
○ Human resource management. 人力资源管理：员工招聘、培训、发展。
○ Technology development. 技术发展：产品研发、流程研发。
○ Procurement. 采购。

Part B

Business organization structure, functions and governance

Chapter 8

Business organization and its structure

1. Informal organization and its relationship with formal organization

Formal organization has a **well-defined, fixed structure** of **task-focused** roles and relationships which remains stable regardless of changes of membership.

正式组织中有的角色是明确定义的,结构是固定的,并且以工作为导向。即使团队中的成员发生变化,正式组织中的角色和关系是稳定的。通俗来讲,就是铁打的营盘流水的兵。

However, **within and under each organization,** there is a **complex** informal organization alongside the actual organization structure, known as the informal organization.

正式组织必然伴随非正式组织,有正式组织的地方就有非正式组织。

2. Features of informal organization 非正式组织的特点

a) Informal social network and groups — e.g. cliques, clubs, buddies. 社交关系的非正式:派系、俱乐部、伙伴。

b) Informal communication — e.g. the 'grapevine'. 沟通方式非正式:信息通过小道消息的方式传播。

c) Informal ways of doing things — e.g. shortcuts, lobbying. 行为方式非正式:抄近路、游说。

d) Informal power structures — e.g. a charismatic supervisor can be a more authoritative figure than the departmental manager. 权利结构非正式:大家拥戴的是具有人格魅力的人,而并非具有职权的人。

3. The informal organization can influence the formal organization

Positive: (assume boss has a good relationship with employees)

a) Speed the spread of information 加快信息传播的速度
b) Encourage horizontal and upward communication 提升水平沟通和对上沟通
c) Meet employees' social needs and improve their commitment 满足员工的社会性需求
d) Knowledge sharing 分享知识
e) Co-operation 加强合作

Negative:

a) Social grouping may act against organizational interests 影响正式组织的利益

b) Grapevine effect (inaccurate and carry rumors) 小道消息往往是不准确的，并且会夹带谣言

c) Informal working methods may cut corners in terms of reduction in quality or health and safety hazard 非正式的工作方法（如抄近路）会降低产品质量，增加员工健康和安全风险

4. Manager can minimize problems in following ways

经理有哪些方法减少非正式组织对正式组织的负面影响？

a) Meet employee's needs as far as possible via the formal organization. 尽可能通过正式组织满足员工的需求。

b) Harnessing the dynamics of the informal organization by using informal leaders. 利用非正式组织的领导，来带领员工实现正式组织的目标。

c) Involve managers into the informal structure. 经理加入非正式组织中，甚至成为非正式组织的领导。

Chapter 9

Basic organisational structure concepts

1. Anthony hierarchy
Robert Anthony identified 3 types of management activities:

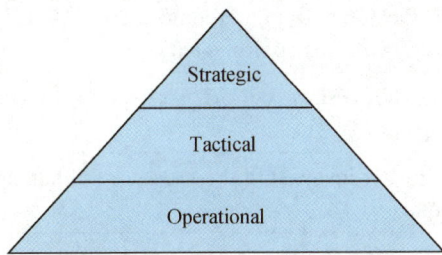

a) **Strategic management** (carried out by **senior** management) is concerned with **direction-setting, policy making and crisis handling**. The time frame of decisions made at strategic management level would typically have implications for **3-5 years**.
战略层：由高管组成，主要职责是制定企业方向和政策，危机处理。
战略层的决策对企业有长期的影响。

b) **Tactical management** (carried out by **middle** management) is concerned with establishing **means** to the corporate ends, **mobilizing resources and innovating** (finding new ways to achieve business goals). Decisions made at this level would have a **medium-term** implications.
战术层：由中层管理者组成，主要职责是制定实现战略的方法，调用资源以及创新。
战术层的决策对企业有中期的影响。

c) **Operational management** (carried out by **supervisors and operatives**) is concerned with **routine activities** to carry out tactical plans. Decisions at this level would deal with **short term** matters.
执行层：由监工/主管等最低一级管理者组成，主要职责是执行日常活动以实现战术层制订的计划。
执行层的决策对企业有短期的影响。

2. Minzberg's five components of the organization
Minzberg believes that all organizations can be analyzed into five basic components

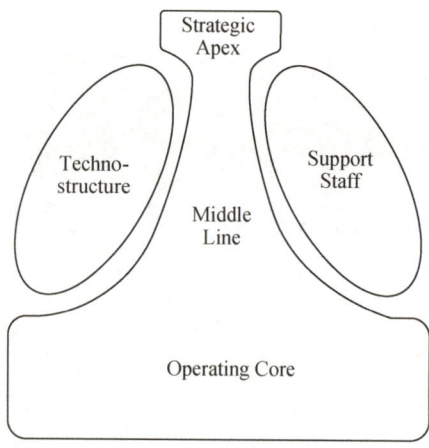

Strategic apex 战略顶点	Ensures the organization follows its mission. Manages the organization's relationship with the environment
Middle line 中间线	Converts the desires of the strategic apex into the work done by the operating core
Operating core 运营核心	People directly involved in the process of obtaining inputs, and converting them into outputs
Technostructure 技术结构	Analyzers determine the best way of doing a job (e.g. Process Engineer) Planners determine outputs (e.g. goods must achieve a specified level of quality, Product Engineer) Personnel analysts standardize skills (e.g. Trainer)
Support staff 支持性员工	Ancillary services such as public relations, legal counsel, the cafeteria Support staff do not plan or standardize production. They function independently of the operating core

考点：
① 了解企业结构的五要素分别包含哪五部分，记住准确的名称。
② 理解五要素分别包括哪些员工。其中最常考的是 technostructure 和 support staff。
如：process engineer, product engineer, trainer 属于 technostructure；public relations, legal counsel 属于 support staff。

3. Basic organizational structure concepts

3.1 Span of control

It refers to the number of subordinates immediately reporting to its superior official.
控制幅度：一个上级直接领导的下级的人数，关键词是 immediate。

3.2 Scalar chain

There is a chain of authority running from top of the organization hierarchy to the bottom. Also called chain of command.
命令链条：命令从最上层传达到最底层要经过多少层级？

3.3 Tall and flat organization

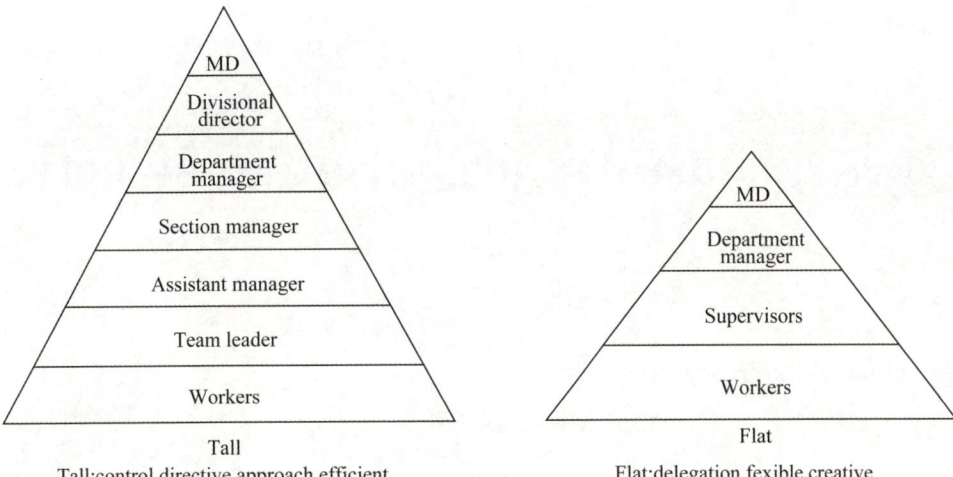

Tall: control directive approach, efficient

Flat: delegation, fexible, creative

3.4 Centralization and decentralization

A centralized organization is one in which authority is concentrated in one place.
定义：集权即做决定的权力仅集中在组织顶层。

3.4.1 Advantages of centralization

a) Decisions are made at one point and hence it easier to execute and coordinate the activities that follows.

b) Senior management can have a wide view of issues at hand and the consequences.

c) It is easier for senior management to maintain a balance between different departments, and makes better decisions in terms of resources allocation.

d) Higher quality of decision due to the senior manager's skills and experience.

e) Since lesser managers will be involved, management cost in terms of time spent could be cheaper.

f) Crisis decisions can be made very quickly.

3.4.2 Advantages of decentralization

a) Overburdening on top managers in terms of workload and stress can be avoided.

b) Improves junior manager's motivation and experience as they are given new opportunities and responsibilities.

c) Greater awareness of localized problems and the relative differences in geographically dispersed organization which should be decentralized on a regional/area basis.

d) Greater speed of decision-making as the decisions process is being decentralized.

e) Facilitate the development of junior managers to gain experience and progressed to more responsible situations or posts.

f) Separate sphere of responsibility can be identified. In other words, controls, accountability, performance measurements can be better implemented.

Chapter 10

Types of business organisation structure

1. Simple/Entrepreneurial structure

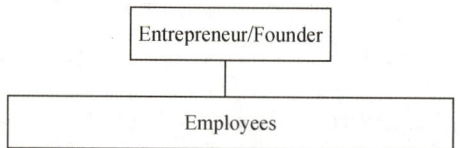

This structure is typical of small businesses in the early stages of their development.

a) This structure is adopted by sole traders who employ others, some small partnerships and some small companies.

b) The center of authority and responsibility normally resting in the founder. Charismatic leaders who exercise direct control over the people making the operation level.

c) It is simple, informal and very fluid, in that it may change on a day-to-day basis. It can handle an environment which is relatively simple but fast moving.

| Advantages:
○ Fast decision making 做决策速度快
○ Good control 有利于控制员工
○ Goal congruence 目标一致性
○ Close bond to workforce 与员工紧密联系
○ More responsive to market 对市场反应快 | Disadvantages:
○ Lack of career structure 缺乏职业结构
○ Dependent on the capabilities of the owner/manager 过于依赖管理者的能力
○ Cannot cope with diversification/growth |

```
                    Board of directors
        ┌───────────────┬───────────────┬───────────────┐
    Marketing        Sales         Production      Accounting
    department    department      department      department
```

2. Functional structure

Advantages:

a) Specialization 专业化分工

b) Expertise is pooled 汇聚专家能力
c) Synergy 协同效应
d) Standardization 标准化
e) Economies of scale 规模效应
f) Avoid duplication 避免重复

Disadvantages：

a) Focus on internal process and input, rather than the customer and outputs. Inward-looking are less able to adapt to changing demand. 只关注内部流程，忽略客户和产出。

b) Poor-coordination, especially if rooted in a tall organization functions. 不利于部门间的合作沟通。

c) Create vertical barrier to information and work flow. 纵向障碍。

3. Divisional structure (geographic, product, customer) 多分部制结构

In divisional structure, each section known as division is more or less **autonomously operated**. The divisions have their own revenue, expenditure, marketing program, capital assets purchasing policies, and hence each with its own profit and loss responsibilities.

特点：高度自治（每个分部独立的核算收入和支出，独立的制定市场战略和采购策略）。

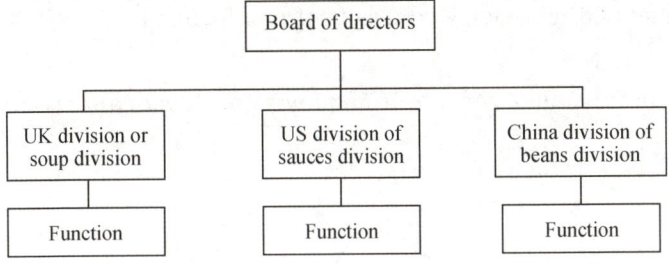

Advantages:	Disadvantages:
○ Focuses the attention of management below 'top level' on business performance ○ Reduces the likelihood of unprofitable products and activities being continued ○ Give more authority to junior managers 给基层经理更多职权 ○ Top management would be much free to concentrate on strategic matters	○ It is not always practical. Sometimes it is impossible to identify completely independent products or markets for which separate divisions can be set up ○ Resource problems. Some divisions get the resources from head office in competition with the others 资源争夺问题 ○ Lack of goal congruence 缺乏目标一致性

4. Matrix 矩阵式结构

The matrix structure evolved in companies that sought to overcome some of the rigidities of the functional organization structure.

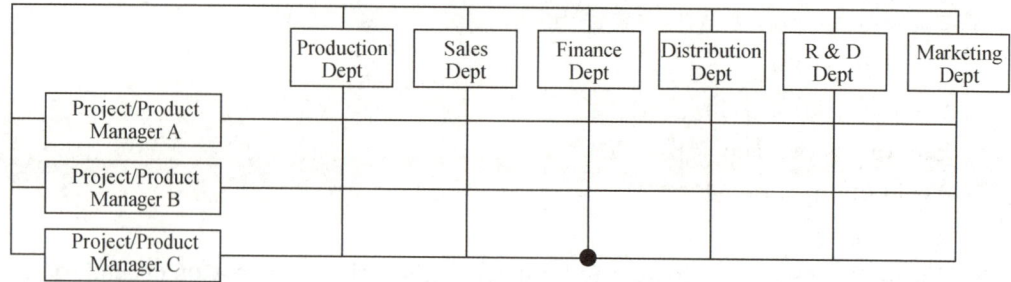

Advantages:	Disadvantages:
○ Greater flexibility of people, workflow and decision-making 灵活性上升 ○ Inter-disciplinary co-operation 加强合作 ○ Motivation and employee development ○ Marketing awareness, more customer or quality focus 对市场反应灵敏 ○ Horizontal workflow: bureaucratic obstacles are removed, and department specialisms become less powerful 加强横向沟通	○ Dual command and conflict 双重指令和冲突 ○ Dual identify suffer from conflicting demands or ambiguous roles 身份模糊 ○ Cost: product management posts are added, meetings have to be held, and so on 管理成本上升 ○ Slower decision making due to added complexity 做决策速度慢

5. Shamrock organization — Handy

Largely driven by pressure to reduce personnel costs, there has been an increase in the use of part-time and temporary contracts of employment.

目的:减少人工成本。

Four leaves: professional core, self-employed professionals, contingent workforce and customers.

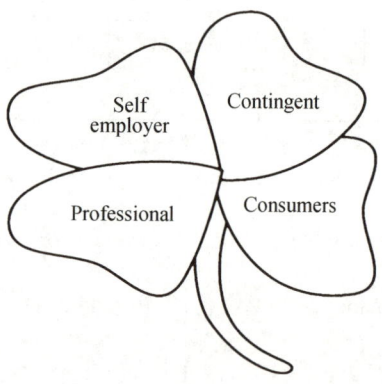

考点:记住四个部分的准确名称。

6. The new organization

1) **Virtual organization** 虚拟组织

Members are geographically dispersed and the organization usually only exists electronically on the Internet, without any physical premises.

Chapter 10 Types of business organisation structure

2) **Hollow organization** 空心化组织

People and activities are split into core and non-core competencies. All non-core processes and activities are outsourced.

3) **Modular organization** 模块化组织

Different elements or components of the product or service the organization produces are outsourced to different suppliers.

4) **Boundaryless organization** 无边界组织

It is an organization that is not defined by, or limited to, the horizontal, vertical, external or geographic boundaries imposed by a predefined structure.

无边界组织：企业经营的过程中，不要把组织局限于水平的、垂直的、外部的或者地理位置的边界。

7. Outsourcing and offshoring

7.1 Outsourcing 外包

It is the contracting out of specified operations or services to an external vendor.

Advantages:

a) Remove uncertainty of cost. 去除成本的不确定性。

b) Long-term contracts encourage planning for the future. 鼓励为未来做长期计划。

c) Bring the benefits of economies of scale. 带来经济的规模效应。

d) A specialist organization is able to retain skills and knowledge. 获得专家的技能和知识。

Disadvantages:

a) Risky in confidential information. 不利于信息保密。

b) If a third party is handing IT/IS services, there is no upon internal management to keep up with new developments or to suggest new ideas.

c) An organization may find itself locked in an unsatisfactory contract. 被捆绑在不满意的合同中。

d) The use of an outside organization does not encourage awareness of the potential costs and benefits of IT/IS within the organization.

7.2 Offshoring involves sending work overseas 离岸

Work sent overseas may still be done within the organization.

7.3 Shared services organizations 服务共享中心

Shared services refer to the provision of a service by one part of an organization or group where that service had previously been found in more than one part of the organization or group. Thus, the funding and resourcing of the service is shared and the providing department effectively becomes an internal service provider. The key is the idea of 'sharing' within an organization or group.

定义：把几个部分相同的工作放在某一个地方来做，由这一个集中的地方给企业其他部分集中地提供服务。

Chapter 11

Function of main departments in business organization

1. Purchasing

1) **Purchasing mix**：采购四要素（数量、质量、价格、运输）
- Quantity
- Quality
- Price
- Delivery

The ideal purchasing mix is one which **holds a proper balance between** each of these elements.

2) **Just-in-time (JIT) purchase strategy**：即时采购战略
- More reliable on suppliers 过于依赖供应商
- Frequent delivery 运输频繁
- Inventory holding costs are minimized 最小化储存成本

2. Service 服务的四个特点

a) **Intangibility** 服务是无形的

b) **Inseparability**：service is created at the same time as it is consumed.
服务产生的过程和消费过程不可分割，是同时发生的过程。

c) **Variability**：it may be hard to attain precise standardization of the service offered.
多样性：服务很难标准化。

d) **Ownership**：service does not normally result in the transfer of property.
服务的所有权不发生转移。

3. Sales and marketing

The marketing function manages an organization's relationship with its customers **Marketing** is the management process which **identifies**, **anticipates** and **satisfies** customer needs.
市场营销即发现、预测以及满足消费者需求的过程。

3.1 Marketing mix for product

1) Product

2) Pricing

Two categories of pricing:

a) **Penetration pricing:** a low price is charged to persuade as many people as possible to buy the product at its early stages. 渗透定价法:先制定低价,再抬高价格。

b) **Skimming:** prices are set to cream off the highest level of profits even though this may restrict the number of people who are able to afford the product. 撇脂定价法:先制定高价,再降低价格。

3) Promotion

Promotion is intended to stimulate the potential customer through four behavioral stages (AIDA).

a) Awareness of the product 提升消费者对产品的意识

b) Interest in the product 引起消费者对产品的兴趣

c) Desire to buy 增加消费者购买的欲望

d) Action of actual purchase 促成实际的购买行为

4) Place

The ideal marketing mix is one which **holds a proper balance between** each of these elements.

3.2 The marketing mix for service: 3P more

- People 以人为卖点
- Process 以流程为卖点
- Physical evidence 以物理证据为卖点

4. Administration and Human Resource

Administration can be defined as the universal process of organizing people and resources efficiently so as to direct activities toward common goals and objectives.

Human resource management: The process of HR is evaluating the HR needs, finding people. Getting best work from employees by providing right incentives and environment.

5. Finance

Role:

a) Financial accounting 财务会计

b) Management accounting 管理会计

c) Treasury 司库(财务管理)

Chapter 12

Organizational culture

1. Definition of the organizational culture

In every organization, there has evolved over time a system of beliefs, values, and norms of behavior, that are shared by members of the organization.

Organization culture has been described as the 'way things are done around here'.

每个组织中,随着时间的推移所形成的一套信念、价值观及行为方式,是组织中每个成员都认可的。

2. Different theory related to corporate cultural

2.1 Schein's three level of culture 文化三层次论

2.1.1 The first level 第一层:表象的,看得见的

The observable, expressed or explicit elements of culture.

Behavior: Norms of personal and interpersonal behavior; customs and rules about behaviors which is acceptable or unacceptable.

Artifacts: Concrete expression such as architecture and interior design, dress codes and symbols.

Attitudes: Patterns of collective behavior such as greeting styles, business formalities, social courtesies and ceremonies.

2.1.2 The second level 第二层:看不见,但可以一定方式表达出来

Beneath these observable phenomena lie **values and beliefs** and the professed culture, which give the behaviors and attitudes their special meaning and significance.

Values and beliefs may be overtly expressed in **slogans** or the **mission statement**.

2.1.3 The third level 第三层:看不见、难以用语言表达出来

Beneath values and beliefs lie assumptions: Foundational ideas (unspoken rules).

2.2 Handy's four cultural stereotypes

2.2.1 The power culture (Zeus) 权力文化

There is only one source or power and influence, which comes normally from the owner or founder of the organization. The power person will strive to **maintain absolute control over the subordinates.**

组织中的影响力来源只有一个,一般是来自组织的所有者或创立者。这个人对下属有绝对的控制权。

2.2.2 The role culture (Apollo) 角色文化

People describe their jobs by its duties and purposes. It is a bureaucratic organization, where the structure determines the authority and responsibility. The culture is based on status, position and hierarchy.

人们的角色是由他们在组织中的职责决定的。这种文化常见于官僚化组织，它是基于组织中每个人的地位、职责和层级。

2.2.3 The task culture (Athena) 任务文化

Task culture has best been seen in **teams** established to achieve **specific task, such as** in **project teams**. People associate themselves with the results they are achieving and nothing is allowed to get in the way of task accomplishment.

This is prevalent in modern western industries where flexibility and sensitivity to the market or environment are vital.

任务文化常见于小组的形式中。在这种文化下，人们注重自己是否达到了任务的目标。这种文化常见于现代西方行业中，这些行业很注重市场的灵活性和对市场的敏感度。

2.2.4 The person culture (Dionysus) 以人为本的文化

The organizational culture existed and presents to satisfy the requirements of the particular individuals involved in the organization.

The culture though rare is to be found in a small, highly participatory organization where individuals undertake all the duties themselves, for example, a barrister in chambers, accounting firm, etc.

这种文化尊重个体差异，注重满足个人需求。常见于小型的高度参与式的组织中，比如会计师事务所、律师事务所等。

2.3 Hofstede's international perspectives on culture 从国际视角看文化

2.3.1 Power distance (PD) 权力距离

The extent to which unequal distribution of power is accepted.

High PD cultures (as in Latin, near Eastern and less developed Asian countries) accept greater centralization, a top-down chain of command and closer supervision. Subordinates have little expectation of influencing decisions.

权力距离远：集权式的管理、从上到下的命令链条、严格的监督、下属不希望影响决策。

Low PD cultures (as in Germanic, Anglo and Nordic countries) expect less centralization and flatter organizational structures. Subordinates expect involvement and participation in decision-making.

权力距离近：分权式的管理、扁平化组织结构、下属希望影响决策。

2.3.2 Uncertainty avoidance (UA)

The extent to which security, order and control are preferred to ambiguity, uncertainty and change.

High UA cultures (as in Latin, near Eastern and Germanic countries and Japan) respect control, certainty and ritual. They value task structure, written rules and regulations, specialists and experts, and standardization.

愿意规避不确定性:尊重控制、确定性和规则。这种文化欣赏结构性的任务、写下来的规章制度、专家和标准化。

Low UA cultures (as in Anglo and Nordic countries) respect flexibility and creativity They have less task structure and written rules, more generalists and greater variability. There is more tolerance of risk, dissent conflict and deviation from norms.

不愿意规避不确定性:不喜欢结构化的任务和写下来的规则,喜欢不确定性和多样性。这种文化能够容忍风险、冲突和偏离常规。

2.3.3　Individual/Collectivism 个人主义/集体主义

The extent to which people prefer to work in individualist or collectivist ways.

High individualism cultures (as in Anglo, more developed Latin and Nordic countries) emphasis **autonomy** and **individual choice and responsibility**. They prize individual initiative. **Task achievement is more important** than relationships. Management is seen in an individual context.

个人主义:强调自治、自主选择和责任。这种文化激励个人的主观能动性,认为完成任务比维护关系更重要。

Low individualism (or collectivist) cultures (as in less developed Latin, near Eastern and less developed Asian countries) emphasis interdependence, social acceptability.

Relationships are more important than task achievement. Management is seen in a team context.

集体主义:强调相互依赖、社会接受度。认为维护关系比完成任务更重要。

2.3.4　Masculinity/Feminine 男性主义/女性主义

The context to which social gender roles are distinct.

High Masculinity cultures (as in Japan and Germanic and Anglo countries) clearly differentiate gender roles. Masculine values of assertiveness, competition and decisiveness and material success are dominant.

男性主义:强调自信、竞争、果断、成功。

Feminine values of modesty, tenderness, focus on relationships and quality of working life are less highly regarded, and confined to women.

女性主义:注重人际关系、生活质量。

Chapter 13

Committees in business organization

1. What is committee

A committee is a group of people to which some matter is committed.

定义：一群具有一定权力的人聚集在一起共同致力于某件事，民主地做出一些决策。

2. Purposes of committees

a) Creating new ideas 集思广益
b) Excellent means of communication 较好的沟通方式
c) Facilitate problem solving 促进解决问题
d) Pooling and combinations of abilities 汇聚知识和能力
e) Coordination 加强协作
f) Representations 代表各方利益
g) Making recommendations 做出好的决策

3. Types of committee

a) **Executive committees** — have the power to govern or administer such as the Board of Directors.

高级管理委员会：由高管组成，行使管理职能。

b) **Management committees** — formed with a number of executives from different levels for decisions not necessarily to be taken by the Board of Directors.

中级管理委员会：由不同层级的管理者组成，行使管理职能。

c) **Standing committee** — are formed for a particular purpose on a permanent basis.

常务委员会：为经常性的事务而设立的、永久存在的委员会。

d) **Ad hoc committee** — formed to complete a particular task on a temporary basis.

临时委员会：为某个目的或任务而暂时组成的委员会。

e) **Joint committee** — formed to coordinate the activities of two or more committees on either permanent or short basis.

总委员会：由两个以上的子委员会组成。

f) **Sub-committee** — appointed to relieve the parent committee of some routine work.

分委员会

4. The committee chair and committee secretary

4.1 Committee chair 委员会主席

a) Have to give immediate ruling on points of dispute or doubt 当出现争议时，给出一些规章制度

b) Be impartial 公平

c) Have the discretion to know when to insist on strict observance and when a certain amount of relaxation 有管理艺术，张弛有度

d) Should be punctual and regular in attendance at meetings 准时经常参加会议

4.2 Committee secretary 委员会秘书

a) Duties before the committee meeting：Fixing the date and time of the meeting, choosing and preparing the location of the meeting, and preparing and issuing various documents.

会前：确定会议时间、地点，准备相关文件。

b) Duties at the meeting：assessing the chair, making notes.

会中：协助主席、做笔记。

c) Duties after the meeting：preparing minutes, acting on and communicating decisions.

会后：整理会议纪要、传达会议精神。

5. Advantages and disadvantages of committees

5.1 Advantages

a) Consolidation of power and authority 结合职权和权力

b) Improves coordination between work groups 加强合作

c) Collective decisions and responsibility 共同决策、共同负责

5.2 Disadvantages

a) May take longer time as large committee will take longer time of decision.

b) Time consuming and expensive. Often meeting takes too much executive times.

c) Too much committee decisions may delay routine matters which can be better decided upon by individual manager.

d) Incorrect or ineffective decisions may be taken by committee members who are not familiar with the issue. At times, it may even leads to failure of reaching decisions.

e) As decisions are made collectively, poor judgement can be hid under the committee.

f) Compromise instead of clear cut decisions can happen due to fact saving.

Chapter 14

Corporate governance and social responsibility

1. Separation of ownership and control

Corporate governance is the system by which organizations are directed and controlled by senior officers. 公司治理即组织中高管控制和管理公司的一套系统。

1.1 Separation of ownership and control

1) **Board of directors**

In simple words, BOD is responsible for managing and controlling the operations of company. Decisions made by consensus (simple majority) though the meeting of BOD.

董事会:负责管理公司的日常经营。董事会中做决策的方式是一人一票,少数服从多数。

2) **Shareholders**

A company's members or equity shareholders are the owners of company Decisions made by voting rights attached to each category of shares, through the general meeting (Annual General Meetings — AGM; Extraordinary General Meetings — EGM).

股东是公司的所有者。股东做决策的方式是根据股份数投票。股东大会分为年度股东大会和临时股东大会。

1.2 Agency theory 代理理论

The situation of 'divorce' of ownership and control could lead to the issues guided by agency problem. 所有权和管理权的分离导致代理问题。

Principals — shareholders 委托人:股东

Agent — BOD 代理人:董事会

Principles would delegate right or authority to agents. 委托人授权给代理人。

Agents should act in the best interest of principles. 代理人应当维护委托人的利益。

1.3 The agency problem

If the agents have moral hazard, that will lead to notorious agency problem. E.g. the directors do not act in the best interest of shareholders instead of satisfying the own self-interest as the result of sacrificing the shareholder interest. This is known as the 'agency problem' where managers have to be motivated to act in the best interests of the company as a whole. 如果代理人有道德瑕疵,会导致代理问题。如:代理人追求自己的利益而牺牲委托人的利益。

2. How to solve agency problem

2.1 Introducing the role of external auditor

The purpose of an audit is to enhance the degree of confidence of intended users in the financial statements. This is achieved by the **expression of an opinion** by the auditor on whether the financial statements are prepared, in all material respects, show **true and fair view.**

审计的目的是增强财报使用者对财报的信心程度。审计就财报是否在所有重大方面真实公允发表意见。

Finally, communicate the result to shareholder through **external audit report** (e.g. **Unqualified Opinion Report** — good report; **Qualified Opinion Report** — bad report, **Adverse Opinion Report** — worst report, and **Disclaimer of Opinion Report** — no opinion).

审计报告有四种类型：无保留意见报告、保留意见报告、否定意见报告、无法发表意见报告。

2.2 Introduction the role of non-executive director (majority)

2.2.1 Definition of NEDs

They are directors who attend to board meetings, and committee meetings when required and do not involve in the day-to-day running of organization. 非执行董事：参与董事会,但是不参与到组织的日常经营中。

2.2.2 Sub-committee

1) **Remuneration committee** 薪酬委员会：制定执行董事的薪酬

Consists of only NEDs in order to determine remuneration policy and package related to executive directors.

2) **Nomination committee** 提名委员会：提名执行董事进入董事会中

Consist of majority of NEDs in order to select suitable candidates to sit in the board and evaluate the individual director performance.

3) **Audit committee** 审计委员会：提名外审

Consist only of NEDs, one of them should posses current development knowledge of accounting and auditing.

Duties:

a) Review of financial statements and systems 审查财报和财报系统
b) Liaison with external auditors 协助外审
c) Review of internal audit 审查内审的工作
d) Review of internal control 审查内控
e) Review of risk management 进行风险管理

3. Internal control system

An internal control is any action taken by management to enhance the likelihood that established objectives and goals will be achieved. 内控即管理层采取的一系列措施来实现公司的目标。

Chapter 14 Corporate governance and social responsibility

The **responsibility** related to design, implementation and monitoring of the internal control system lie with BOD. 设计、运行和监督的内控的责任是董事会的责任。

3.1 Nature and purposes of internal control system

Risk are uncertain events or factors relating to any activities that would make the organization not to achieve its objectives. Risk consists of fraud and error.

The overall objective of internal control system is to avoid, reduce or eliminate risks in order to achieve the corporate objectives. 内控系统的目的是避免、减少、消除风险以实现组织目标。

3.2 Types of internal control system

1) **Related to financial reporting** 和财报相关的内控

Make sure that the financial statements show **true and fair view.**

2) **Related to operation of entity** 和企业经营相关的内控

Make sure that the company's operation achieves '3Es' or 'value for money' (VFM).

3.3 How to establish the internal control system 如何建立内控系统

a) Identifying business risks relevant to financial reporting objectives 识别潜在的风险
b) Estimating the significance of the risks 评估风险的重要性
c) Assessing the likelihood of their occurrence 评估风险发生的可能性
d) Deciding about actions to address those risks 制定应对风险的措施
e) Continuing monitoring the risk 持续的监督风险

3.4 Control environment and control procedure

3.4.1 Control environment 控制环境:环境、氛围、意识

It is the overall context of control, in particular the attitude of directors and managers towards control.

The control environment **sets the tone** of an organization, influencing the control consciousness of its people.

3.4.2 Control procedures 控制程序:具体的控制活动

They are the detailed controls in place.

Types of financial control procedure (SPAMSOAP):

a) Segregation of duties 权责分离
b) Physical control 物理控制
c) Authorization and approval 授权和批准
d) Management 常态化的管理
e) Supervision 监督
f) Organization 通过组织控制
g) Arithmetic and accounting 数字和会计
h) Personnel 控制人员

3.4.3 Three types of control (control consequence)

1) **Prevention** 预防式控制

Prevent all threats cost-effectively from happening in the first place.

2）**Detection** 侦测式控制

Controls that are designed to detect error once they have happened.

3）**Corrective controls** 纠正式控制

Controls that address any problems that have occurred. So where problems are identified，the controls ensure that they are properly rectified.

3.5 Internal checks

Internal checks are the checks on the day-to-day transactions. 内核:检查日常交易的方法。

Arithmetical internal checks include：

- **Pre-list** is a list that is drawn up before any processing takes place 事前清单
- **Post-list** is a list that drawn up during or after processing 事后清单
- **Control totals** is a total of any sort used for control purposes by comparing it with another total that ought to be the same 控制总数

3.6 The limitation on the effectiveness of internal control 内控的缺陷

- Cost-effectiveness 成本效益原则
- Potential for human error or fraud 人为错误和舞弊
- Segregation of duties can be avoided by collusion 通过串通避开权责分离
- Control being by-passed by management 管理凌驾控制之上
- Controls being designed to cope with routine but not non-routine transactions 内控只针对常规风险，无法避免非常规风险

4. Internal auditor

An internal audit is defined as：

a）Internal audit is an independent appraisal activity established within an organization as a service to it. 内审是一个独立的评估活动。

b）It is a control which functions by examining and evaluating the adequacy and effectiveness of other controls. 内审是一种控制:检查和评估内控程序的充分性和有效性。

c）Independent checking，examination and evaluation the internal control system established by executive director. 内审的职责是检查以及评估由董事会建立的内控系统。

Generally，there are five types of internal audit：

a）**Operational audit** concerned with any sphere of company's activities. The objective is the monitoring of management's performance at every level. They are also known as 'management' 'efficiency' or 'value for money' audits. 经营审计:检查公司日常经营的各个方面。

b）**Systems audit** is based on a testing and evaluations of the internal controls within an organization so that those controls may be relied on to ensure that resources could be managed effectively. It includes compliance tests（seeking evidence that the internal controls are being applied as prescribed）and substantive tests. 系统审计:测试和评估组织中的内部控制是否能够被依赖于保证资源能够被有效使用。它包括实质性测试和符合性

Chapter 14 Corporate governance and social responsibility

测试。

c) **Transactions audit/probity audit**: checks account entries to identify errors or omissions which may indicate fraud. A transactions or probity audit aims to detect fraud and uses only substantive tests. If the compliance tests reveal that internal controls are working satisfactorily, then the amount of substantive testing can be reduced. 交易审计：检查会计分录是否有错误和遗漏。只有实质性测试的结果可以作为交易审计的证据。但如果符合性测试显示组织的内控运行是令人满意的，实质性测试的工作量可以减少。

d) **Social audit**: measures the social responsibility or social impacts of the business. 社会审计：针对社会责任的审计。

e) **Management Audit**: management investigation. 针对管理层的检查。

5. Social and environmental responsibilities of business organization

5.1 Proactive strategy

Companies prepare to take full responsibility for its actions. For example, the recalling of defective parts or manufactured products. 主动型战略：主动承担所有的社会责任。

5.2 Reactive strategy

This involves allowing a situation to remain unsolved until the public, government or consumers find out about it. 被动型战略：直到公众、政府或消费者发现时，才会承担社会责任。

5.3 Defense strategy

This involves minimizing or avoid additional obligations arising from a particular problem. 抵御型战略：最小化或逃避社会责任。

5.4 Accommodation strategy

This approach involves taking responsibility when encouraged by interest parties or a failure will result government intervention. 适应型战略：当承担社会责任有直接的好处或者不承担社会责任会导致政府干预时，才承担社会责任。

6. Features of poor corporate

a) Domination of a single person 一个人占有主导地位

b) Lack of involvement of board 缺乏董事会的参与

c) Lack of adequate control function 缺乏足够的控制职能

d) Lack of supervision 缺乏监督

e) Lack of independent scrutiny 缺乏独立审查

f) Lack of contact with shareholders 缺乏和股东的联系

g) Emphasis on short-term profitability 强调短期利益

h) Misleading accounts and information 有误导性的信息（财务报表或数据缺乏真实公允）

7. Principles VS rules

Principles：The codes of governance should be guidelines rather than rules 原则导向

Rules（The Sarbanes-Oxley Act）：The codes of governance should be set in rules 规则导向

8. Public oversight 公共监督

A public oversight board is to be formed for the purpose of monitoring and enforcement of legal and compliance standards.

Part C

Accounting and reporting systems, controls and compliance

Chapter 15

Function of accounting in business

1. What is accounting

Accounting is a way of recording, analysing and summarizing transactions of a business. 会计是记录、分析、汇总企业交易的方式。

2. Financial accounting (financial controller, financial accountant)
财务会计的职责:
○ Routine accounting 日常记录
○ Providing accounting reports 准备财务报告
○ Cashier' duties and cash control 管理现金

In summary, the normal sequence of steps in the accounting functions is:

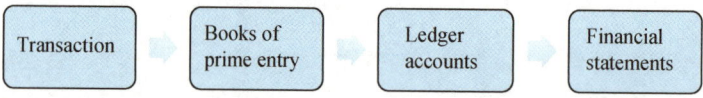

3. Cost and management accounting (cost accountant, management accountant)
管理会计的职责:
○ Budgetary control 预算控制
○ Breakeven analysis 盈亏平衡点分析
○ Key factor analysis 敏感性分析
○ Pricing decisions 定价决策

4. Financial management (Treasurer) 财务管理

Investment appraisal is concerned with long-term investment decisions, such as whether to build a new factory, buy a new machine for the factory, buy a rival company, etc. Typically, money is paid out now, with an expectation of receiving cash inflows over a number of years in the future.

Duties:
○ Financing 融资
○ Working capital management 营运资本管理

○ Risk management 风险管理

5. Taxation

a) Tax avoidance is the legal use of the rules of the tax regime to one's own advantage, in order to reduce the amount of tax payable by means that are within the law. 避税是合理的利用法律最小化税负。

b) Tax evasion is the use of illegal means to reduce one's tax liability, for example by deliberately misrepresenting the true state of your affairs to the tax authorities. 逃税是使用非法手段减少税负。

Chapter 16

Law and regulation governing accounting

1. The regulatory system 有哪些规定或者法律会去约束企业中的会计和审计人员

1) **Company law** 公司法
○ Limited companies are required by law to prepare and publish accounts **annually**. The form and contents of accounts are regulated and accounting standards have to be complied 法律要求有限公司每年要准备财务报表
○ True and fair view 公司法要求财报必须真实公允
○ A company can be **fined** for failing to keep proper accounting records or failing to file financial statements after the year end 如果公司没有保存正确的会计记录或财报,会被罚款

2) **The European union** 欧盟的要求

3) **Accounting standards** 会计准则
○ International Accounting Standards(IAS)
○ International Financial Reports Standards (IFRS)

4) **Generally accepted accounting practice (GAAP)** 美国:一般会计准则
GAAP is a set of rules governing accounting which may derive from: Company law, accounting standards, statutory requirements in other countries, stock exchange requirements.

5) **Ture and fair view** 真实公允

2. Broad consequences of failing to comply with the legal requirements for maintaining and filling accounting records 没有按照法律要求归档和准备财报是董事会的责任
○ Directors are responsible for producing financial statement that give a true and fair view
○ This is delegated within the company to the Finance Director or CFO

3. International accountancy profession 国际会计职业机构
The international accountancy profession through its many regulatory organizations such as the International Accounting Standards Board (IASB) has played the role of both

Chapter 16 Law and regulation governing accounting

self-regulatory and policing body in ensuring a high and acceptable level of professional standards for financial reporting and practices.

The objectives of the IASB: 国际会计准则编制委员会的目标

a) To develop, in the public interest, a single set of high quality, understandable and enforceable global accounting standards. 制定高质量的会计准则。

b) To promote the use and rigorous application of those standards. 推行准则的应用。

c) To bring about convergence of national accounting standards and International Accounting standards (IAS) to high quality solutions. 推动不同国家和地区会计准则的趋同融合。

Chapter 17

Financial systems and procedures

1. **Main systems in financial areas**

1.1 **Sales cycle 销售循环**

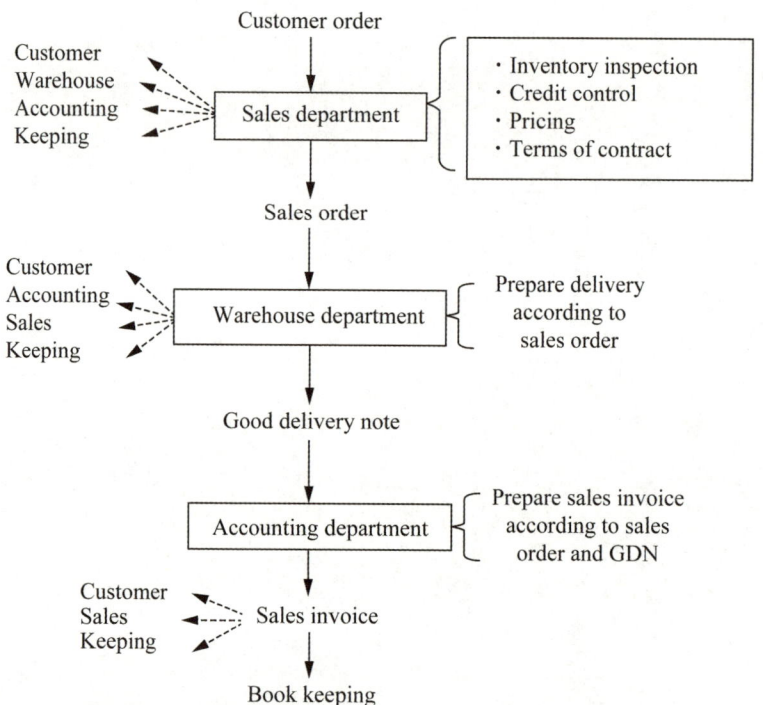

The aims of control over receivables and sales:
  ○ Sale are only made to customer with good credit rating 销售之前做好客户的信用评估
  ○ Accounted correctly 正确的记账
  ○ Identify potential doubtful debt 识别可疑坏账

1.2 **Purchasing cycle 采购循环**

Chapter 17 Financial systems and procedures

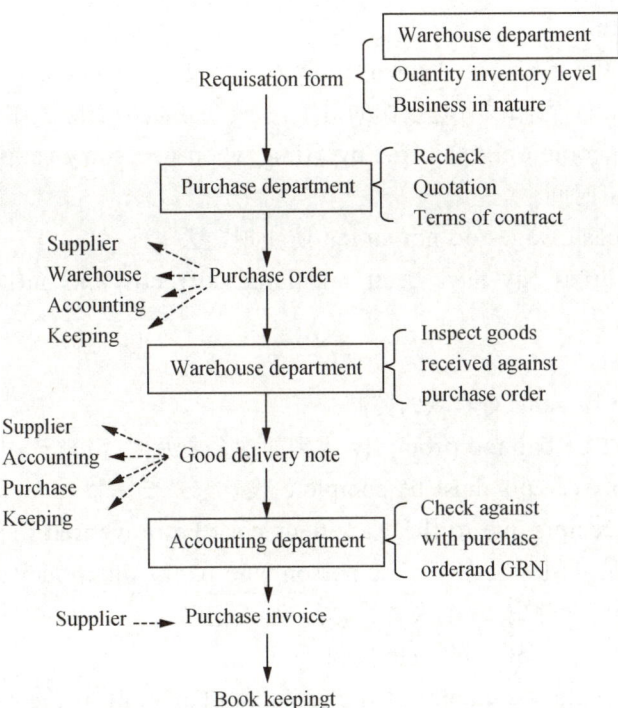

Aims of control over payables and purchase:

○ Proper authorizations 合适的授权

○ Purchase are only made to authorized suppliers at competitive prices 只向经过授权的供应商采购

○ Goods are only accepted if ordered 只接收订单上的货物

○ Accounted correctly 正确地记账

○ Prompt payments to due claims 及时付款

1.3 Payroll system 工资系统

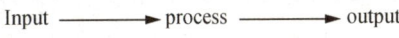

○ Input：hour worked（clock cards or time sheet）and overhead hours（amount of bonus）.

○ Process：payroll calculation.

○ Output：pay slips, payroll analysis, a floppy disk with payment details, etc.

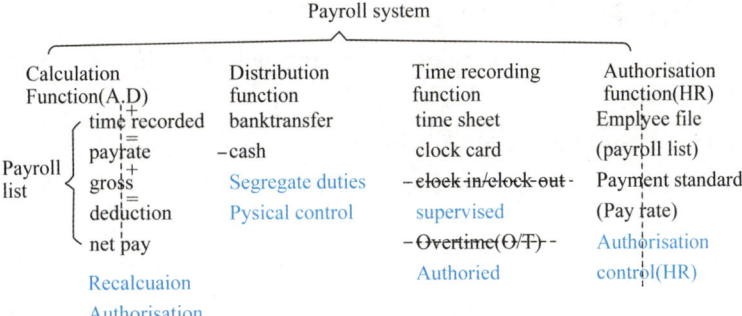

Main control aims：

○ Ensure that there are no 'ghost' employees, people being paid but who do not work for the company 确保没有吃空饷的员工，只支付工资给实际工作的员工

○ Ensure that people only paid for overtime when necessary (approved) 加班工资只支付给被授权的加班时间

○ Ensure that cash wages do not stolen 防止现金丢失

○ Ensure that gross pay have been calculated correctly and authorized 正确的计算工资

1.4 Cash system control

1) Control over receipts 对收款的控制

○ Receipts must be banked promptly 收到的现金要及时存银行

○ The record of receipts must be complete 收款记录要完整

○ The loss of receipts due to theft accident must be prevented 防止偷盗现金的行为

○ Segregation of duties between the person who banks the money and the person who records the money 权责分离：一个人收钱，另一个人记账

2) Control over payments 对付款的控制

○ Obtain documentary evidence of the reason and amount of the payment 获取付款理由和金额的文件证据

○ Each payment must be approved by an authorized person 每一笔付款要经过合适的人授权

○ Restricting the authority to special individuals 限制个别人权力过大

The most important controls designed to detect fraud and error are reconciliations. 检查舞弊和错误最重要的控制方式是对账。

2. Purpose of financial control procedures

a) Financial transactions are property carried out 财务交易可以合理执行

b) The assets are safeguarded 保护企业资产

c) Accurate and timely management information is produced 信息及时准确

3. Signals of poor control procedures

a) Cash or cheques missed 现金或支票丢失

b) Excessive bad or doubtful debts 过多坏账

c) Customers not paying or suppliers not being paid on time 客户未及时付款或企业未及时支付货款

d) Unauthorized purchases 采购未经授权

e) Failure to produce accounts at the specified time 未及时出具财务报表

Chapter 18

Information technology and information systems

1. Information vs. data
○ Data consists of numbers, letters, symbols, raw facts, events and transactions, which have been recorded but not yet processed into a form that is suitable for making decision 数据包含数字、符号、原始事实、事件、交易等形式。但它不能直接用来做决策,需要经过处理

○ In nature, data and information can be regarded as the same thing. But in form, data is the raw materials, information is the processed data to make data more meaningful 信息是处理过的数据,可以帮人们作决策

2. IT vs. IS
○ Information system (IS) refer to the provision and management of information to support the running of the organization (信息系统:提供和管理一些信息来支持整个组织运行)

○ Information technology (IT) describes any equipment concerned with the capture, storage, transmission or presentation of information (信息技术:抓取、存储、转换、呈现信息的技术)

○ The IT is the supporting hardware that provides the infrastructure to run the information systems

3. The attributes of good quality information
a) Accurate 准确性
b) Complete/comparability 完整性
c) Cost-benefit 成本效益
d) User-targeted 以使用者为目标
e) Relevant 相关性
f) Authoritative 授权
g) Timely 及时性
h) Easy to use 方便使用

4. Comparison of different software applications
4.1 Manual systems and computerized systems
Disadvantages of manual system (advantages of computerized system) 手工记账的缺点
a) Lower productivity 产量低
b) Slower processing speed 处理速度慢

c) Risk of error 容易出错

d) Less accessible 不易接触

e) Difficult to alter 不易修改

f) Quality of output 产出质量低

g) Bulky both to handle and store 占用储存空间大

4.2 Database and spreadsheets

4.2.1 Advantages of database system

a) Avoidance of unnecessary duplication 避免重复

b) Data is looked upon as serving the organization as a whole, not just for individual departments 数据是服务于组织的整体,而不仅仅是某一部门

c) Encourage management to analyze data, relationships between data items and data applications 鼓励管理者分析数据

d) Consistency — because data is only held once, the possibility of holding conflicting data on the same subject is reduced 一致性:数据只输入一次,减少了数据冲突的可能性

e) Data on file is independent if the user programs that access the data. This allows greater flexibility in the ways that data can be used 每个使用者接触数据是互相独立的,增加使用数据的灵活性

4.2.2 Disadvantages of database system

a) There are problems of data security and data privacy 数据安全性和隐私性方面的问题

b) Since there is only one set of data, it is essential that the data should be accurate and free from corruption 由于数据只设置一次,可能存在准确性方面的问题

c) Since data is held once, but its use is widespread, the impact of system failure would be greater 系统出现问题,会影响整个组织

d) If an organization develops its own database system, the costs will be high 企业开发自己的数据库,成本高

4.3 Integrated software vs. Separate/stand-alone system 综合性软件 vs.单独软件

4.3.1 Advantages of integrated software

a) Make just one entry in one ledgers which would automatically update the others 只需要输入一次数据,会自动更新其他相关数据

b) Users can specify report, and the software will automatically extract the required data from all the relevant files 软件会自动抓取相关数据和文件,为使用者形成具体的报告

c) Reduce the workload of user, simplify the work procedures and improve work efficiency 减少使用者的工作负担,简化工作程序,提高工作效率

4.3.2 Disadvantages of integrated software

a) More computer memory required 需要更多储存空间

b) Fewer facilities of the program than a set of specialized module 专业性不如单独软件

5. New digital technologies
5.1 Cloud computing as a capability in accountancy and its benefits
5.1.1 Cloud computing

Cloud computing involves the sharing of a pool of physical and/or virtual resources via the internet rather than using locally based systems and networks. 云计算是通过互联网进行物理或虚拟资源共享。

云计算提供四种类型的服务：

a) Cloud hosting services（云储存）offer remote storage and data management solutions.

b) Software as a service（软件即服务）provides access to software applications hosted on a central server (rather than stored on the hard drive of the users' computer).

c) Infrastructure as a service（基础设施即服务）provides a complete architecture service for a customer's systems which are accessed over the Internet.

d) Platform as a service（平台即服务）offers a platform for programmers to develop applications very quickly，without the complexity of building the infrastructure typically associated with developing and launching new apps.

5.1.2 Benefits and Risks

Benefits：
○ More cost effective than in-house 从成本效益原则来看，更加节约成本
○ Greater flexibility as there are lots of service providers to choose from and faster than in-house 更加灵活：可以随时变换服务供应商
○ Accessible anywhere around the world 不受地理位置的限制
○ Available to both large and small organizations 既适合大企业、也适合中小企业
○ Disaster recovery and back-ups 有利于数据恢复和备份

Risks
○ Organization may give up control of its data to an external party being the cloud-based service provider and may have risk suffer from disaster event 不利于企业自己控制数据
○ Data held by the service provider may be stolen，lost or corrupted，or service provider's own staff may interfere with data stored on its servers 数据被第三方保存，可能会被偷、丢失或者发生舞弊行为
○ Regulatory risks 监管风险
○ Failure to keep up payments，lead to a loss of access 未及时付款会导致丧失权限

5.2 Artificial intelligence (AI)
5.2.1 Concepts of AI

Artificial intelligence（AI）is an area of computer science that emphasizes the creation of intelligent machines that work and react like humans by machine learning and deep learning. 人工智能是一种计算机科学，通过机器学习和深度学习的技术让计算机更像人类一样地去工作和反应。

Some of the activities computers with artificial intelligence are designed for include:
- Speech recognition 识别对话
- Learning 学习
- Planning 作计划
- Problem solving 解决问题

5.2.2 Opportunities to apply AI in finance 人工智能在财务领域的应用

- Accountants are now performed by artificial intelligence (AI), allowing professionals to focus on more advisory roles that brings greater value to company and clients 会计人员可以关注在更加增值的工作上，为企业和客户提供价值
- Intelligent accounting- Identify and booking without being programmed, create RPA [Robotic Process Automation（财务流程自动化）process chains where data is captured through chatbots, entered using RPA tools and errors resolved using machine learning]
- Intelligent taxation（智能税务）— complex taxation process by machine learning
- Intelligent auditing（智能审计）— Prevent and detect fraud and error, for example, using forms of AI to address some of the data validation errors encountered in RPA（Robotic Process Automation）processes by applying machine learning to the errors
- Non-financial reporting, more insights on non-financial data and issues

5.3 Big data and data analytics

Big data is extremely large data sets that may be analysed computationally to reveal patterns, trends and associations, especially relating to human behavior and interactions.
- High-volume, high-velocity and varied 数据量大、更新速度快
- Variable and complex 形式多样
- Value-added to business 对企业有价值
- Veracity 可信度高

5.3.1 Application of big data 大数据的应用

- Data mining, identifying trends in data 数据挖掘
- Predictive analytics, involves using data patterns to predict the future behavior 预测性分析
- Text (social) analytics, involves analysing text, typically on social media sites to identify the opinions of participants on those sites 文本分析
- Statistical analytics, can identify trends and changes in behavior 数据分析

5.3.2 Analytics in finance

- More accuracy of data and more effective analytics
- Using external and unstructured data can add a dimension to the level of insight

5.4 Blockchain and distributed ledgers 区块链和分布式账本技术

5.4.1 Blockchain

Blockchain, the technology behind Bitcoin. This creates a ledger of information that is distributed, encrypted and incorruptible. It may be reliably used to store any type of information which may in time include payments, share ownership and even land ownership.

5.4.2 Distributed Ledgers

A distributed or shared ledger is a digital database of records where all participants are looking at a common view — in contrast to a typical situation currently where participants (for example, in different organisations) are looking at different databases that are independently managed and updated.

When a change or update to any participant's record is confirmed, the technology ensures that the view seen by each participant in the network synchronises to reflect the latest update.

5.4.3 Impact on accountancy

○ Without the need for a central authority and share information in a secure and timely fashion 可以及时安全的共享信息

○ Prevent and detect fraud and errors in transactions, as information in ledger is cryptoed 阻止交易中发生错误和舞弊,防止信息被篡改

○ Automated auditing, more efficiency and effective 自动化审计:提高工作效率和效果

○ More practices in financial services, such as a new payment network and cryptocurrency 在金融服务中的应用:确保付款信息的安全性、准确性

Chapter 19

IT systems security and safety

Security is the protection of data from accidental or deliberate threats and the protection of information system from such threats. 信息安全即保护信息系统免于面临故意或者无意的威胁。

1. **Physical threats**

Physical threats to security may be natural or man-made. They include fire, flooding, weather, lightening, terrorist activity and accidental damage. 物理威胁：可能是自然的或人为的，包括火灾、天气灾害、恐怖袭击和故意损坏等情况。

2. **Physical access controls**

a) **Personnel**（人员控制）including receptioists and outside working hours, security guards, can help control human access.

b) **Door locks**（锁门）can be used where frequency of use is low. Locks can be combined with:
  ○ **A keypad system**: requiring a code to be entered 密码控制
  ○ **A card entry system**: requiring a card to be swiped 打卡控制

3. **Building controls into an information system — Integrity controls 完整性控制**

3.1 Input controls 输入控制

Input controls should ensure the accuracy, completeness and validity of input.
  ○ Check digits 位数控制
  ○ Control totals 总数控制
  ○ Hash totals 人员控制
  ○ Range checks 范围控制
  ○ Limit checks 上限/下限控制
  ○ Pre-list 下拉列表

3.2 Processing controls

Processing controls should ensure the accuracy and completeness of processing (e.g. periodic running of test data)

Chapter 19 IT systems security and safety

3.3 Output controls

Output controls should ensure the accuracy, completeness and security of output (e.g. labeling of disks)

4. Back-up controls

A **back-up** and **archive** strategy should include:
- Regular back-up data (at least daily) 日常备份(至少每天一次)
- Archive plans 定期归档
- A disaster recovery plan including off-site storage 建立数据恢复计划

5. Password and logical access systems

A password is a set of characters which may be allocated to a person, a terminal or facility which is required to be keyed into the system before further access is permitted.

An **audit trail** shows who has accessed a system and the operations performed.

Chapter 20

Fraud and fraudulent behaviour and their prevention in business

1. **Prerequisite for fraud 舞弊的前提条件**
   - Dishonesty 不诚信
   - Motivation 动机
   - Opportunity 舞弊的机会

2. **Different types of fraud in the organization**

   For an organization，fraud can fall into one of the following two categories.
   a) Removal of fund/assets 偷钱/物品
   b) Intentional misrepresentation of the financial position of a business 财报的故意错报

   2.1 **Examples of removal of fund/assets 偷钱/物品的例子**
   - Theft of cash 偷钱
   - Theft of inventory 偷存货
   - Payroll fraud 工资造假
   - Teeming and lading 拆东墙、补西墙（常见于销售部）
   - Fictitious customers 虚假客户
   - Collusion with customers 和客户串通
   - Bogus supply of goods or services 虚假供应
   - Paying for goods not received 支付虚假货款
   - Meeting budgets/target performance measures 为达到业绩考核指标造假
   - Manipulate of bank reconciliations or cashbooks 伪造银行余额调节表或现金日记账
   - Misuse of pension fund or other assets 滥用养老金
   - Disposal of assets to employees 贱卖公司资产给员工

   2.2 **Examples of Intentional misrepresentation of the financial position of the business**
   - Over-valuation of inventory 高估存货价值
   - Irrecoverable debt policy may not be enforced 有坏账政策不执行
   - Fictitious sales 伪造虚假销售，虚增销售额
   - Manipulations of years end events 伪造年末事项

Chapter 20 Fraud and fraudulent behaviour and their prevention in business

   ○ Understanding expenses 低估费用
   ○ Manipulation of depreciation figures 伪造折旧金额

3. Implications of fraud for the organization
1) **Immediate financial implications** 短期直接影响
Loss of cash, assets, or profits, loss of working capital, or even loss of reputation
2) **Long term effects on company performance** 长期影响
Working capital shortage, liquidity problems, loss of goodwill, collapse of brand name, or even result in the collapse 营运资本短缺、流动性问题、损失商誉和品牌形象,最终破产

4. Responsibility for detecting & preventing fraud
The responsibility for fraud occurrence and its prevention rest with the board of directors, who deals with the daily operation of the organization and are responsibility of safeguarding the assets of the company. 预防和组织舞弊的责任在于董事会。
However, the managers and staff should be also aware that they share the same responsibility to help in detecting fraud.
   a) **Internal audit staffs** 内审
   b) **External audits** 外审
   c) **Non-executive directors** 非执行董事
   d) **Operational directors, Finance staff and fraud officer** 运营董事、财务部员工、反舞弊员工
   e) **Personnel staffs** 普通员工
Note: It is the responsibility of the directors to take reasonable steps to detect and prevent fraud and error. (考点:会出现在选择题的选项中)

5. Whistleblowing 举报
A whistleblower is a person who tells the public or someone in authority about alleged dishonest or illegal activities (misconduct) occurring in a government department or private company or organization.
Whistleblowing can assist BOD in the discharge of their duty of prevention and the detection of fraud. 举报帮助董事会更好地履行防止和检查舞弊的责任。

6. Money laundering 洗钱
Money laundering is the process by which the proceeds of crime, either money or other property, are converted into assets, which appears to have a legitimate rather than an illegal origin. The aim of the process is to disguise the source of the property in order to allow the holder to enjoy it free from suspicion as to its source. 洗钱是将非法所得经过一系列的投资运作变成看起来的合法所得并自由地享用它。

6.1 Money laundering process 洗钱的三个步骤

1) **Placement** 处置:把钱放出去

The initial disposal of the proceeds of illegal activity into legitimate activity. For example, small amounts are banked with a number of institutions.

2) **Layering layer** 掩藏:洗钱运作的过程

Transfer of money from business to business, or place to place, in order to conceal its initial source.

3) **Integration** 整合:把钱从合法途径收回来

The culmination of the previous procedures through which the money takes on the appearance of coming from a legitimate source.

Three categories of criminal offence in relation to money laundering:

a) Laundering 洗钱罪

b) Failure to report 知情不报

c) Tipping off 通风报信

Part D

Leading and management individuals and teams

Chapter 21

Nature of management

1. Fayol — The five functions of management 管理的五大职能
a) Planning 做计划
b) Organizing 分配任务
c) Commanding 命令员工执行
d) Co-ordinating 协调
e) Controlling 控制绩效

2. Taylor：Scientific Management (establish the most efficient method)泰勒：科学管理理论(常考点)

Taylor thinks that management should be based on 'well-reorganized, clearly defined and fixed, principles, instead of depending on 'more or less' hazy ideas.

Principles of scientific management：科学管理理论的原则

a) Development of a true science of work（establish the most efficient method）. 用科学管理替代原来的人为经验（建立最有效率的科学工作方法）。

b) Scientific selection and progressive development of workers（only the most suitable people should be chosen trained and developed for each job）. 用科学的方法去管理和筛选员工。

c) Application of techniques to plan，measure and control work for maximum productivity（micro-designed jobs）. 最终目的：产量最大化。

d) Constant cooperation between management and workers（pay is the only incentive）. 经理和工人要进行持续不断的密切的合作。

In practice, scientific management techniques included the following key elements.

○ Work study techniques were used to analyze tasks and establish the most efficient methods to use. No variation was permitted in the way work was done, since the aim was to use the one best way. 用最科学的方法去分析工作任务，建立一个最有效率的方式去完成工作，不允许有任何偏差偏离标准。

○ Planning and doing were separated. 作计划的人和做事的人是分开的。

○ Jobs were micro-designed. 工作被无限细分，分解成一个个简单的工作。

○ Workers were paid incentives on the basis of acceptance of the new methods and

output norms
- Pay was assumed to be the only one important motiving force. 用金钱来激励工人。

3. Mayo: human relations 人际关系理论

People are motivated by a variety of psychological needs, including social or 'belonging' needs, rather than working practices or physical conditions (e.g lighting and noise). 人们会受到一系列心理因素的激励，包括社会需求和归属感需求，而不是工作的物理条件。

This approach recognized the role of interpersonal relations in determining workplace behavior and it demonstrated that factors other than pay can motive workers. 这个理论承认了工作场合中人际关系的重要性，并且揭示了工资并不是唯一的激励因素。

Limitations: ignore economic issues (there is no proven link between job satisfaction and motivation)

4. Drucker: the management process   管理流程理论

Management process be grouped into five categories:
a) Setting objectives for the organization 设置组织目标
b) Organizing the work needed to achieve these objectives 分配任务
c) Motivating the employees 激励员工
d) The task of measurement 衡量业绩表现
e) Developing people 发展员工

5. Mintzberg: the manager's role

Types of managerial role:

Role category	Role	Comment
Interpersonal 人际角色	Figurehead 代表	Representing the company 对外代表企业
	Leader 人事管理	Hiring, firing, training, motiving employees and reconciling individual goals with objectives of the organization. 任免、培训、激励、协调
	Liaison 联络	Making contacts outside the vertical chain of demand. Some managers speed up to half of their meeting time with their peers rather than their subordinates 和外部的同僚联系
Information 信息传递	Monitor 监督	Monitor the environment; receiving information from subordinates, superiors and peers 监督外界大环境；从上下级几同僚那里获取各种信息
	Spokesperson 发言人	Providing information on behalf of the unit and organization to interested parties 代表部门、企业向外界感兴趣的利益相关者传播公司的内容
	Disseminator 传播	Disseminating information to subordinates 向下级传递信息

(Continued)

Role category	Role	Comment
Decisional 决策角色	**Entrepreneur** 企业家	Initiates projects to improve the department or to help it react to a changed environment 带领团队的人完成新的项目、开拓新市场、应对变动的环境
	Disturbance handler 解决问题	Respond to unexpected pressure, take decisions when there is the deviations from plan 危机处理、应对突发状况
	Resource allocator 资源分配	Distribute resources to achieve objectives 合理分配资源以实现组织目标
	Negotiator 协商	Negotiate both inside and outside the organization 对内协调不同职能部门；对外协调与客户及供应商的关系

Chapter 22

Leadership and styles

1. Trait or 'qualities' theories 特征学派

Early theories suggested that there are certain personality characteristics common to successful leaders. In other words, **'leaders are born, not made'**. 早期理论认为：成功的领导身上有些共同的特征，即领导是天生的，而不是靠后天培养的。

The qualities of a good leader consist of: judgement, initiative, integrity, foresight, human relation skills, fairness, energy, etc.

The arguments on the theory: 关于早期理论的争论：

a) Certain qualities in the theory have never been substantiated. 理论中的某些领导特征并没有被证实。

b) The qualities listed have been vast, varied and contradictory. 这个理论所列出的领导特质有很多，有些是相互冲突的。

c) The trait theories ignore the complexities of the leadership situation, and not everybody with leadership 'traits' turns out to be a good leader. 特征理论忽略了环境的复杂性，并不是拥有这些好品质的人都能成为一个好的领导。

2. Style theories 风格学派

There are many styles of leadership. In this theory, leadership came from a range of styles from two seemingly extremes：

a) Wholly task-focused, directive leadership behaviors (high control). 任务型风格：注重目标、注重工作内容、高度控制性的。

b) Wholly people-focused, supportive relationship leadership behaviors (high subordinates' discretion). 以人为本型风格：关注人、注重领导和下属之间的关系。

2.1 The Ashridge Management College model（考点）

a) **Tells**（autocratic）— The leader makes decisions and orders have to be obeyed

b) **Sells**（persuasive）— The leader makes decisions but motivate subordinates to accept decisions

c) **Consults**（partial involvement）— Leaders takes the subordinate' views into consideration when making decisions

d) **Joins**（democratic）— The leaders and followers make the decision on the basis of consensus

> Note：这四种风格是从专制到民主的一个过程：

Tells：领导做决策，下属只要服从。

Sells：领导做决策，然后努力地说服员工。

Consults：领导在作决策之前，会和员工讨论，听取下属的意见，但是最终决策权还是属于领导。

Joins：领导和下属一起做决策，一人一票，少数服从多数。

前三种风格都是领导做决策，但是员工参与度不一样；最后一种是员工也参与到做决策的过程中，是最民主的风格。考试的时候要通过题目的描述去判断它是属于哪种风格。

2.2 Blake and Mouton's Managerial Grid（考点）

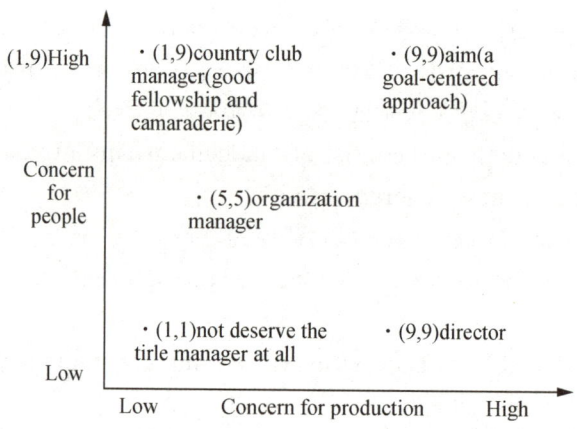

> Note：记住图中5个点的名称以及对应的风格描述。

(1,1) **impoverished**: the manager is lazy, showing little interest in either staff or work. Not deserve a manager at all. 既不关心工作，也不关心人：这种经理很懒，什么也不做，是一个不称职的领导。

(1,9) **country club**: the manager is attentive to staff needs and has developed satisfying relationships. However, there is little attention paid to achieving results. 乡村俱乐部经理：不关心公司的目标和实际事务，只关心人，注重满足下属的需求，营造和谐的氛围。

(9,1) **task management**: almost total concentration on achieving results. People's need are virtually ignored. 任务型领导：只关注实现工作结果，忽视人的需求。

(5,5) **middle of the road or the dampened pendulum**: adequate performance through balancing (or switching between) the necessity to get out work with team morale. 中间路线：对人的关心和对工作的关心维持在中间状态，求的是维持一般的工作效率和士气。

(9,9) **team**: high work accomplished through 'leading' committed people who identify themselves with the organizational aims. 团队/以目标为中心的管理：既特别关心人，也特别关心工作。

2.3 Limitations of style approach 风格理论的局限性

a) The manager's personality may simply not be flexible enough to utilize different

Chapter 22　Leadership and styles

styles effectively. 每个经理的性格不一样，不能切换性格去灵活的适用所有的风格。

b) The demands of the task, technology, organisation, culture and other managers constrain the leader in the range of styles effectively open to him. 有一些环境因素，比如任务的需求、企业文化、技术发展等因素会约束领导风格的具体实施。

c) Consistency is important to subordinates. If a manager adapts his style to changing situations, they may simply perceive him to be fickle/change or may suffer insecurity and stress. 对下属保持风格的一致性很重要。

3. Contingency approaches to leadership

In essence, contingency theory sees effective leadership as being dependent on a number of variable or contingent factors. **There is no one right way to lead that will fit all situations.** 权变思想的核心：这个世界没有一种最好的领导方法，需要根据环境的变化来选择适合的风格。

3.1　F. E Fiedler

Two types of leader：

a) **Psychologically distant managers**（PDMS）maintain distance from their subordinates.

○ They formalize the roles and relationships between themselves and their superiors and subordinates 领导将自己和下属之间的关系正式化

○ They choose to be withdrawn and reserved in their inter-personal relationships within the organization (despite having good inter-personal skills) 领导选择保留自己的人际关系，不参与非正式组织

○ They prefer formal consultation methods rather than seeking the opinions of their staff informally 领导喜欢正式的沟通方式，如开会、邮件等

PDMs judge subordinates on the basis of performance and are primarily task-oriented：Fiedler found that leaders of the most effective work groups tend to be PDMs.

b) **Psychologically close managers**（PCMS）are closer to their subordinates.

○ They do not sick to formalize roles and relationships with superiors and subordinates

○ They are more concerned to maintain good human relationships at work than to ensure that tasks are carried out efficiently

○ They prefer informal contacts to regular formal staff meetings

Note： PCM 和 PDM 的特点完全相反。

Fiedler suggested that the effectiveness of a work group depended on the situation, made up of three key variables：选择 PCM 还是 PDM 的领导风格取决于下面三个变量：

a) The relationship between the leader and the group 领导和团队之间的关系是否亲密

b) The extent to which the task is defined and structured 下属的任务是否是清晰以及结构化的

c) The power of the leader in relation to the group 领导在团队中的权力大小

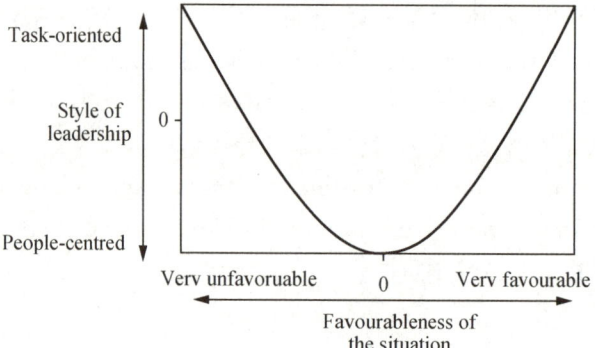

The conclusion:

PDMs performs well when the situation is either very favorable or very unfavorable to the leader.

PCMs perform well when the situation is moderately favorable to the leader.

3.2　John Adair: action-centred leadership/functional leadership 行动中心领导模式

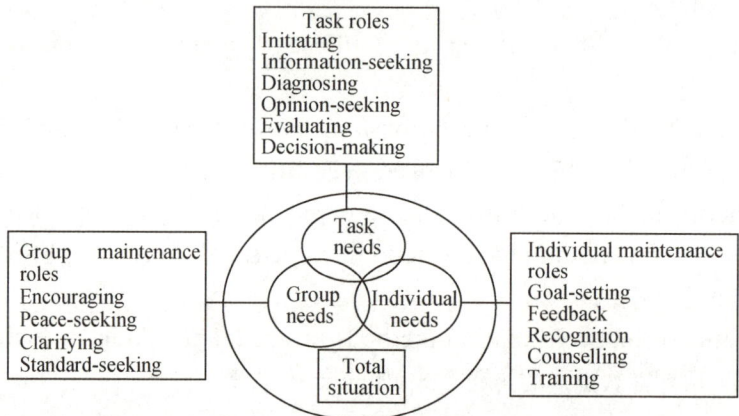

It sees the leadership process in a context made up of **task needs**, the **individual needs** of group members and the **group needs** as a whole. Effective leadership is a process of identifying and acting on the priority of these activities, exercising a relevant cluster of roles to meet the various needs. 环境是由三个相互之间有影响的变量构成的，分别是任务需求、个人需求、团队建设需求。

领导需要在这三个需求之间寻求平衡，根据这三个变量的优先次序来决定哪一个需求更关键，从而去选择合适的领导风格。

3.3　Heifetz: dispersed leadership 离散领导力

The approach recognizes the importance of social relations, the needs for a leader to be accepted and the fact that **no one will be an ideal leader in every circumstance.** 在不同的情况下会有不同的领导，一种领导风格可能适用某一种环境，但不一定适用另外一种环境，因此没有一个领导风格是适用于所有环境的。

A leader's individual qualities are less important than the leadership process, the relationships created and sustained within it.

Chapter 23

Recruitment and selection of employees

1. Define recruitment and selection

Recruitment is the part of the process concerned with **finding applicants**: It is a **positive** action by management, going into the labour market, communicating opportunities and information, generating interest. 招聘就是找到应聘者的过程，它是一个正向的行为。

Selection is the part of the employee resourcing process which involves **choosing** between **applicants** for jobs: It is largely a 'negative' process, eliminating unsuitable applicants.筛选的过程是剔除不合适的人，它是负向的过程。

2. Recruitment process

2.1　Job description 对工作的描述：岗位的职责、岗位目标，以及岗位的具体工作任务

Job description set out the purposes, context, accountabilities and tasks of the job.

Content of a job description:

a) Job title 职位名称

b) Reporting to (immediate boss) 向谁汇报

c) Overall purpose of the job, distinguishing it from other jobs 岗位的总体目标

d) Principal accountabilities or main tasks 岗位具体的工作内容及职责

e) Group the main activities into a number of board areas 具体活动

f) Define each activity as a statement of accountability: what the job holder is expected to achieve

2.2　Person specification 对人员的要求

A person specification is a reworking of the job description in terms of the kind of person needed to perform the job. Possible areas the specification may cover include:

a) Personal skills 个人能力

b) Qualifications 资质证书

c) Innate ability 天资

d) Motivation 动机

e) Personality 性格

2.3　Seven-point plan 招聘七步法：从 7 个角度来审核人员的资质

Rodgers devised a framework for the selection process that includes seven points

point	examples
Physical make-up 外表	Strength, health, appearance
Attainments 成就	Qualifications, career achievements
General intelligence 智力水平	Average, above average
Special aptitudes 天资	Manual dexterity, mental sharpness
Interests 兴趣爱好	Mechanical, people-related
Disposition 性情	Calm, independent
Circumstances 境况	Location, car owner

3. Advertising vacancies

Job advertising is aimed at attracting quality applicants and aiding self-selection.

The object of recruitment advertising is to attract suitable candidates and deter unsuitable candidates. 广告的目的：吸引有质量的应聘者以及让他们进行一定的自我筛选。

3.1 Contents of a job advertisement

a) The organization its main business and location, at least

b) The job: title, main duties and responsibilities and special features

c) Conditions: special factors affecting the job

d) Qualifications and experience required and preferred

e) Rewards: salary, benefits, opportunities for training, career development and so on

f) Application process: how to apply, to whom, and what by date

g) It should encourage a degree of self-selection, so that target population begins to narrow itself down

3.2 Advertising media

a) In-house magazine, notice-boards, e-mail or intranet 内部杂志：适合内招

b) Professional newspapers or magazine 专业报纸杂志：适合招聘专业人员

c) National newspapers 全国报纸

d) Local newspapers 当地报纸

e) Local radio, television and cinema 当地电视、广播、电影院

f) Job centre 职业介绍所：招聘普通技工

g) School and university 学校：招聘应届生

h) The internet 网络招聘

4. The main selection methods

The process of selection begins when the recruiter receives details of candidates interested in the job. A systematic approach includes shortlisting, interviewing, decision-making and follow-up.

Chapter 23　Recruitment and selection of employees

Selection methods 主要的筛选方法
- Interview 面试
- Selection tests 笔试
- Reference checking 推荐信
- Work sampling 样本测试（如：使用）
- Group selection methods 小组筛选

5. Interviews

5.1　Types of interview

5.1.1　Individual interview 一对一面试

Individual，**one-to-one or face-to-face** interviews are the most common selection method

Advantages：

a) Direct face-to-face communication，with opportunities for the interviewer to use **both verbal and non-verbal** cues to assess the candidate. 有机会看应聘者的肢体语言和语言表达。

b) Rapport between the candidate and the interviewer：each has to give attention solely to the other，and there is potentially a relaxed atmosphere，if the interviewer is willing to establish an **informal style**. 有利于形成一种放松的、非正式的氛围。

c) **Flexibility** in the direction and follow-up questions. 提问方式更加灵活。

Disadvantages：

a) The candidate may be able to disguise lack of knowledge in a specialist area of which the interviewer knows little. 面试官缺乏某方面的专业知识而让面试者蒙混过关。

b) The interviewer's perception may be selective or distorted，and this lack of objectivity may go unnoticed and unchecked. 面试官的本身对一些问题的看法缺乏客观性。

c) The greater opportunity for personal rapport with the candidate may cause a weakening of the interviewer's objective judgement. 建议亲密关系不利于面试官的客观判断。

5.1.2　Panel interview (2~3个面试官面试一个人)

A panel may consist of two or three people who together interview a single candidate：most commonly，an HR specialist and the departmental manager. This saves firm time and enables better assessment. 面试官通常包括一个 HR 和一个部门经理,有利于节约时间，更好地评估。

5.1.3　Selection boards 选拔委员会

Large formal panels，or selection boards，may also be convened where there are a number of individuals of groups with an interest in the selection.

Advantages（save time& share information）多对一：节约时间 & 分享信息

a) A number of people see candidates，and share information about them at a single meeting.

b) They can compare their assessments on the spot, without a subsequent effort at liaison and communication.

Disadvantage:

a) Questions tend to be more varies and more random, the candidate may have trouble switching from one topic to another quickly. 问题太过分散会使得面试者难以转换。

b) Dominating member may influence other members. 某一个主导者会影响其他面试官。

c) Not suitable for some candidates who feels stressful. 会让某些面试者感到紧张。

d) Conflicts among members. 面试官之间意见不合。

5.2 Advantages and limitations of interviews

5.2.1 Advantage of interviews

a) Highly interactive, allowing flexible questions and answers. 互动性强,灵活性强。

b) They offer opportunities to use non-verbal communication, which might confirm or undermine spoken answer. 给面试者机会使用非语言化的沟通方式。

c) They offer opportunities to assess a candidate's personal appearance, interpersonal and communication skills. 面试官有机会评估面试者的外表、人际沟通能力等。

d) They offer initial opportunities to evaluate rapport between the candidate and their potential colleagues/bosses. 面试中建立的关系为之后成为同事建立基础。

5.2.2 Limitation of interviews

Limitations include: limited scope; artificial situation; the halo effect; bias; stereotyping; incorrect assessment; logical error; inexperienced interviewers.

Note: Halo effect 光环效应/初次印象:面试官第一眼印象会影响后续的客观判断。

6. Selection testing

Types of selection test 选拔测试

a) Proficiency, attainment or competence test 胜任能力的测试

b) Intelligence tests 智商测试

c) Personality tests 性格测试

d) Aptitude tests 天资测试

e) Medical test 体能测试

7. Group selection methods (assessment centres) 评估中心:多个面试官对多个面试者

Assessment centres are attended by a group of candidates and consists of a series of tests, interviews and group situation. The candidate may feel ease in the test. Two methods are often used.

a) Group role-play exercise 角色扮演

b) Case studies 案例分析

8. Reference 背景调查

a) A reference should contain two types of information
- Straightforward factual information 事实性信息
- Opinions about the applicant's personality and other attributes 观点性信息

b) At least two employer references are desirable, providing necessary factual information, and comparison of personal views 至少要有两个以上的前雇主提供事实性信息的证明

c) Types of reference: written references and telephone references

9. Evaluation of recruitment and selection process

How to appraise the efficiency

a) Performance indicators 绩效指标是否达成

b) Cost-effectiveness data 成本效益原则

c) Monitoring the workforce — observation of staff turnover rates, absenteeism and other workforce trends will reveal the effectiveness of the recruitment or selection of personnel 监控现有员工的表现,如流转率、缺勤率等

d) Attitudes survey — questionnaires and surveys can prove to be very revealing and telling 员工满意度问卷调查

e) Actual individual job performance 个人工作实际表现

Chapter 24

Equal opportunities and managing diversity

1. Equal opportunity 平等机会法案

1.1 Definition

It is an approach to the management of people at work based on **equal access and fair treatment**, irrespective of gender, race, ethnicity, age, disability, sexual orientation or religious belief.

企业在招聘以及员工管理中,应该给与每个人公平待遇,不管他们的性别、种族、年龄、残障、性取向以及宗教信仰。这是一个法案,如果企业没有做到,就是违法。

1.2 Types of discrimination

1) **Direct discrimination 直接歧视**:在一些明显的场合对某些人不公平

One interested group is treated less favourably than another it is unlikely that a prospective employer will practice direct discrimination without being aware of it.

2) **Indirect discrimination 间接歧视**:形式上公平,但是设置门槛让某些人很难达到

Occurs when a policy or practice is fair in form, but discriminatory in operation.

3) **Victimization 处罚反对歧视者**

A person is penalized for giving information or taking action in pursuit of a claim of discrimination.

4) **Harassment 骚扰**:使用威胁、恐吓、攻击言论、侮辱性语言或行为来针对某人

The use of threatening, intimidatory, offensive or abusive language or behaviour.

5) **Positive discrimination 积极歧视**:过度保护弱势群体,从而对大部分人不公平

Actions which give preference to protected people regardless of genuine suitability and qualification for the job.

Note: Training cannot be regarded as positive discrimination.

2. Diversity 人力资源多元化

2.1 Definition

It goes **further** than equal opportunity. 它比公平机会走得更远,要求更高。

It refers to the ways in which people meaningfully differ in the work place include not only race and ethnicity, age and gender, but **personality, preferred working style,**

individual needs and goals and so on.

企业主动招聘各种背景的人：不同的种族、年龄、性别、性格、工作方式等。

2.2 Managing diversity

It implies the need to be **proactive** in managing the needs of a diverse workforce in areas beyond the requirements equal opportunity and discrimination regulations.

a) Tolerance of individual differences

b) Communicating effectively with (and motivating) ethnically diverse work forces

c) Managing workers with increasingly diverse family structure and responsibilities

d) Managing the adjustments to be made by an increasingly aged work force

e) Managing increasingly diverse career aspirations/patterns, flexible working ect

f) Dealing with differences in literacy, numeracy and qualifications in an international work force

g) Managing co-operative working in ethnically diverse teams

Chapter 25

Individual and group behaviour in business organisation

1. **Individual behavior** 个人的行为受到哪些因素的影响?

1.1 **Personality** 性格

Personality is the total pattern of characteristic **ways of thinking, feelings** and **behaviours** that constitutes the individual's distinctive method of relating to the environment.

If an individual's **personality is incompatible** with the work requirements. How can the manager deal with? 作为团队的管理者,如果下属性格跟工作要求不相容时,该如何做?

1) **Restore compatibility** 重塑相容性:给下属重新分配一个适合他性格的工作任务

Reassign an individual to tasks more suited to his personality type.

2) **Achieve a compromise** 达成妥协:鼓励员工对自己的行为做出适当的更改

Individuals should be encouraged to understand the nature of their differences and modify their behaviour if necessary.

3) **Remove the incompatible personality** 把性格不合的人从小组中移除出去

In the last resort, obstinately difficult or disruptive people may simply have to be weeded out of the team.

1.2 **Perception** 知觉/认知

Perception is the processes by which the brain selects and organizes information in order to make sense of it. People behave according to what they perceive, not according to what the reality is.

Different people see things differently. Each individual behaves in a way that reflects their own interpretation of the world. The same thing 'reality' may be perceived differently by different people.

1.3 **Attitudes** 态度

People develop attitudes about things, based on what they think, what they fell and what they want to do about it. Attitudes are formed by perception, experience and personality which in turn are shaped by wider social influence. Attitudes are our general standpoint on things: the positions we have adopted in regard to particular issues, things and people, as we perceive them.

Chapter 25 Individual and group behaviour in business organisation

1.4 Intelligence 智力

Intelligence is a wider and more complex concept than the traditional view of 'IQ'. It includes useful attributes such as:

a) Analytic intelligence 分析能力

b) Spatial intelligence 空间想象能力

c) Practical intelligence 动手能力

d) Intra-personal intelligence: self-awareness, self-expression 自我认知/自我表达

e) Inter-personal intelligence: such as empathy, cooperation ect 人际交往能力

1.5 Role theory 角色理论

It suggests that people behave in any situation **according to other people's expectations** of how they should behave in that situation. 人在某种环境下的行为会根据外界对他的期望是怎么样来表现。

A role set is a group of people who respond to you in a given role.

Role ambiguity may occur if you do not know what role you are operating in at a given time. 角色模糊:不知道你现在应该用什么角色去面对别人。

Role incompatibility (conflict) is where you would perform in two roles at once.

Role signs indicate what role you are in. At a given moment, so that others relate to you in that role without ambiguity or confusion. 角色信号:通过这个信号,别人知道你是什么角色。

Role models are the individuals you aspire to be like.

2. Groups

2.1 Definition

A group is a collection of individuals who perceive themselves as a group. 一群人聚集在一起,认为自己属于某个团体,就是 group。

2.2 Characteristics of groups

a) A sense of identify 身份的认同感

b) Loyalty to the group 对群体的忠诚度

c) Purpose and leadership 共同的目标和领导

Chapter 26

Team formation, development and management

1. Definition of team

Two important features of the 'team':

1) Complementary skills 技能互补

Members of a team usually bring in many skills which could be complementary to each other. At times, due to the larger number of individuals involved in a team, human and skill resources can be plentiful and useful in carry out the common objectives.

2) Mutually accountability 相互负责

For the striving towards a common goal, each member is responsible for the task he is assigned to and accountable to other member as well as to the team as a whole.

2. Types of teams

1) Multi-disciplinary teams 跨部门小组: 团队当中每个人的技能是互补的

Multi-disciplinary teams **bring together individuals with different skills and specialization** so that the collective expertise is pooled together and exchanged.

2) Multi-skilled teams 全能小组: 每个成员都可以完成小组里的任意一项工作

The team brings together a number of individuals who can perform any of the group's tasks. These tasks can then be shared out in a more flexible way between group members according to who is available and best placed to do a given job at the time it is required.

3) Self-managed teams 自我管理小组: 团队成员自主的集体的决定所有重要的事情

This is the most highly-developed form of team working. The **members act autonomously and collectively as a team and collaboratively decide all the major issues** affecting their work. The major characters of self-managed teams are self-control and self-direction.

4) Virtual teams 虚拟小组: 小组成员之间通过网络沟通

The team brings together individuals working in remote locations using Information and Communications Technology (ICT).

3. Theories related to the team

3.1 Belbin's team roles theory 小组角色理论（掌握每个角色的特征）

Role	Description	Team-role contribution	Allowable weakness
Plant 智多星	Creative, imaginative, Unorthodox	Solve difficult problems 解决难题	Ignore details
Resource investigator 交际花	Extrovert, enthusiastic, communicative	Explore opportunities, develop contacts 开拓机遇，寻求资源	Over-optimistic, lose interest once initial enthusiasm has passed
Coordinator (Chairman) 协调者	Mature, confident, a good chair person	Clarify goals, promote decision-making, delegate well 指明方向、促进做决策、分配任务	Manipulative, delegate personal work
Shaper 鞭策着	Challenging, dynamic, strive on pressure	Has the drive and courage to overcome obstacles 帮助团队跨越障碍，情感上鼓励大家	Provoke others, hurt people's feelings
Monitor-evaluator 监控人/评估人	Sober, strategic, discerning	Sees all options, judges accurately 评估各种方案，做出正确的判断	Lacks drive and ability to inspire others, overly critical
Team worker 合作者	Co-operative, mild, perceptive and diplomatic	Listens, builds, averts friction and calm the waters 抚平摩擦、修补团队关系	Indecisive in crunch situations, can be easily influenced
Implementer 执行者	Disciplined, reliable and efficient	Turns ideas into practical actions 将想法转变为实际行动	Somewhat inflexible, slow to respond to new possibilities
Completer/Finisher 完成者	Painstaking, conscientious, anxious	Searches errors and omissions, delivers on time 帮小组发现错误和遗漏，还有掌握时间，督促小组及时完成工作	Inclined to worry unduly
Specialist 专家	Single-minded, self-starting, dedicated	Provides knowledge and skills 提供专业技能	Contributes only on a narrow front, overlooks the 'big picture'

The most important is the mix and balance of the team。

3.2 Tuckman's stages of development 小组发展理论（掌握每个阶段的特征）

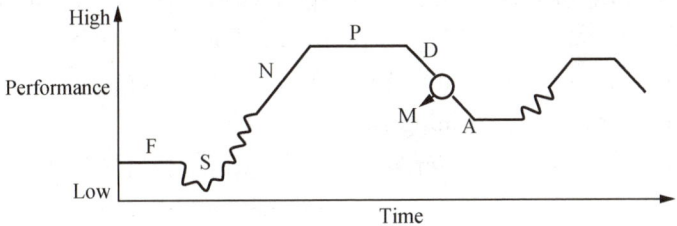

Step1：Forming 形成期

This is the initial stage when things get warmed up. The individuals will be trying to find out about each other, and about the aims and norms of the team. At this stage, the objectives being pursued may as yet not be unclear and **a leader may not yet have emerged.** 团队成员初步了解的阶段,这个阶段领导还未产生。

Step2: Storming 风暴期

This is the growing stage of the team at work when open conflict cannot be avoided. When the team has arrived at some sort of 'settled' disagreement, the team will be entering a fruitful stage as more realistic targets will be set and trust between member increases. 团队成员之间出现一些冲突,一旦某些冲突解决,团队的绩效会增长。这一阶段,绩效是波动上升。

Step3: Norming 规范期

This is a period of settling down when there will be agreements about work sharing, individual requirements and expectations of output. Norm and procedures may evolve consequently. This is the maturing stage. **The team will be able to accept delegated tasks and projects from the leader**. 从这一阶段开始,团队成员有一个统一方向,从领导那里接受分配的任务和项目。这一阶段绩效迅速上升。

Step4: Performing 执行期

The team sets to work to execute its task. The difficulties of growth and development no longer hinder the group's objectives. The team has a **shared vision** and can stand on its own feet with **no interference or participation from the leader**. There is a common focus on achieving goals, and the team **makes most of the decisions consistent with criteria agreed by the leader.** 这一阶段,团队绩效保持在高位持续输出,团队成员可以根据领导留下的标准来做决策。

Later writers add two stages:

Step5: Dorming 怠惰期

Once the team has been performing well for some time, it may get to complacency, and fall back into **self-maintenance** functions, at the expense of the task at work. 任务快完成时,进入维持的阶段,团队绩效略微下降。

Step6: Mourning (Break up)/Adjourning (Disconnection) 解散或完成新的任务

At this stage the group sees itself as having fulfilled its purpose:

○ If it is a temporary group, dissolution may seem logical. This is a stage of confusion, sadness and anxiety as the group breaks up. The group may evaluate of its achievements and experience a gradual withdrawal of group members.

○ If the group is to continue, going on to a new task, there will be a renegotiation of aims and roles: a return to the forming stage.

3.3 Inter-personal skills of communicating in team 人际交往技巧

Category	Behavior	Example
Proposing 提建议	Putting forward suggestions, new concepts or courses of action	Why don't we look at …?

(Continued)

Category	Behavior	Example
Supporting 支持	Supporting another person or his proposal	Yes, I agree
Seeking information 寻求信息	Asking for more facts, opinions or clarification	What do you mean
Giving information 给出信息	Offering facts, opinions or clarification	There is information
Blocking/difficulty stating 设置障碍	Putting obstacles in the way of a proposal, without offering any alternatives	It would bring problems ...
Shutting-out 打断别人	Interrupting or overriding others taking over	Nonsense
Bring-in 鼓励他人发表意见	Involving another member and encouraging contribution	I'd like to hear from
Testing understanding 测试大家是否理解	Checking whether points have been understood	So ..., have I got that right?
Summarizing 总结	Drawing together or summing up previous discussion	Firstly ... secondly ...

4. Evaluating team effectiveness 评估团队的绩效

The criteria for team effectiveness include:

a) **Task performance**: fulfilment of task and organizational goals 任务目标是否完成

b) **Task functioning**: constructive maintenance of team working, managing the demands of team dynamics, roles and processes 团队合作的默契度

c) **Team member satisfaction**: fulfilment of individual development and relationship needs 团队成员个人满意度

5. Limitations of teamwork

Although teams and teamwork are very much favored, there are many drawbacks:

a) Not suitable for all types of tasks 团队形式不适合所有的任务(如:创作型工作适合个人完成)

b) Making people feel better rather than getting better performance 团队形式是为了更好的绩效,而不是人们会觉得在团队工作中感觉好

c) Slower decision making 做决策速度慢

d) Restrict individual personality and flair 限制个人的天资

e) Group think leads to riskier decisions 团体思维有时是错误的

f) Personality clashes 团队成员存在性格冲突

g) Compromise rather than clear-cut decisions 做出的决策是妥协后的

Chapter 27

Motivating individuals and groups

Motivation is a decision-making process through which the individual chooses desired outcomes and sets in motion the behaviour appropriate to acquiring them. 激励是通过一些方式诱发人的主观能动性，让他更愿意做某件事。

1. Content theories of motivation 内容学派，研究有哪些东西可以激励员工

Content theories of motivation suggest that the best way to motivate an employee is to find out what their needs are and offer them rewards that will satisfy those needs.

1.1 Maslow's hierarchy of needs 马斯洛需求层次论（重要考点）

Maslow described five needs and put forward certain propositions about the motivating power of each need.

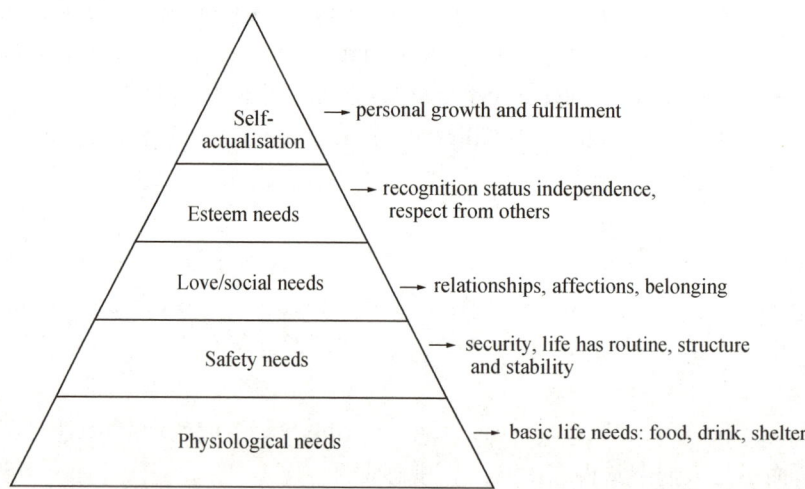

Note：记住五个需求层次的顺序：
第一层，生理需求；第二层，对安全感的需求；第三层，爱和社交需求；第四层，对于尊重的需求；第五层，自我实现需求。

In addition, Maslow described：马斯洛在晚年补充的两个需求：
a) Freedom of enquiry and expression needs 言论自由
b) Knowledge and understanding needs 求知欲

Chapter 27　Motivating individuals and groups

Maslow demonstrates and theories that:

a) Any individual needs can be arranged in a 'hierarchy of relative prepotency' (relative importance/strength). 个人的需求按金字塔中的需求顺序从低到高的排序。

b) Each level of need is dominant until satisfied, then up to next level of needs. 低层次需求不被满足，人不会追求高层次的需求。

c) Once satisfied, the level of need is no longer motivates the individual. 低层次需求一旦被满足，必然追求高层次的需求。

Limitations of Maslow's theory:

a) An individual behavior may be in response to several needs at the same time. 有些人会同时追求好几种需求。

b) The same need may evoke different responses to different individuals. 不同的人对需求重要性的排序不一样。

c) The theory ignores what is known as 'deferred' needs that an individual may prepare to suffer for the promise of future benefits. 递延需求：有些人会为了追求高层次的需求，暂时放弃低层次的需求。

d) The empirical verification is hard to come by and the 'pay' factor influence is ambiguous. 马斯洛的实验方法是经验主义的验证，不具备科学性。对薪酬因素影响的研究比较模糊。

e) The actualization is highly subjective and quite abstract. 个人实现需求毕竟主观抽象，很难定义。

f) Culture values may affect the hierarchy and the individual's responses to these needs. 不同文化背景下对需求重要性排序不一样。

1.2　McClelland's theory of needs

David McClelland identified three types of motivating needs:

a) **The need for power** 对于权力的需求 —— the power to influence and control power

b) **The need for affiliations** 对亲密感的需求 —— the yearning for a sense of membership and belonging of a social group

c) **The need for achievement** 对成就的需求 —— the strong sense of success and the fear of failure

1.3　Herberg's two-factor theory 双因素论（重要考点）

a) The need to avoid unpleasantness is satisfied through **hygiene factors.** Hygiene factors are to do with the environment and conditions of work.

Note: 保健因素是让人从不满意的状态回顾归到正常水平的因素，它常常与工作环境有关

- Company policy and administration 公司的政策和综合管理
- Salary 工资
- The quality of supervision 监督质量
- Interpersonal relations 人际关系
- Working conditions 工作环境

- Job security 工作稳定性

b) The need for personal growth is satisfied by **motivator factors.**

Note：激励因素是让人从正常水平变得满意的因素,可以充分调动人的积极性。

- Status (although this may be a hygiene factor, too) 地位
- Advancement (or opportunities for it) 成就
- Recognition by colleagues and management 他人的认可
- Responsibility 责任
- Challenging work 有挑战性的工作
- A sense of achievement 成就感
- Growth and development in the job 个人成长和发展
- Training program 培训

2. Process theories of motivation 过程学派,研究人应该怎么样被有效地激励

Process theories of motivation help managers to understand the dynamics of employees' decisions about what reward are worth going for.

Vroom's expectancy theory 期望值理论

Human motivation can be calculated by a formula as follows：

$$F = V * E$$

Where：

F = the force or strength of the individual's motivation to behave in a particular way 激励效果

V = valence：the strength of the individual preference for a given outcome or reward 对结果的渴望程度

E = expectancy：the individual's expectation of the results from the behavior 预期,即你现在的行为能多大程度导致结果的实现

In this formula, the motivation force is the product of other two. In other words, the lower the valence or expectancy, the motivation will be lesser. Or, the motivation is directly proportional to the expectancy and desirability of the individual.

Note：激励效果是由 valence 和 expectancy 两个因素同时影响,必须两个值都高,才带来比较强的激励效果。如果一大一小,激励效果就很弱。

3. Management style as a motivator

McGregor：Theory X and Theory Y（考点:掌握 X 型和 Y 型人的特点）

a) **Theory X** suggests that most people dislike work and responsibility and avoid both if possible. They should be threatened or forced to get their work and managers should adopt and authoritarian, repressive style with tight control.（X 人天生不喜欢工作,尽可能逃避责任。管理 X 人要严格的监督、控制）

b) **Theory Y** suggests that physical and mental effort in work is as natural as play or rest. The ordinary person does not inherently dislike work. They are assumed to be

Chapter 27 Motivating individuals and groups

motivated to take responsibility, and exercise self-control and self-direction in order to achieve goals. Managers should adopt a more participative or democratic in their approach.(Y 人天生热爱工作,觉得工作就跟休息玩乐一样是件自然而然的事情。对于 Y 人的管理:只要你给他一定的激励,他自然而然会去承担一定的责任)

4. Reward and incentives
Intrinsic and extrinsic factors 内在激励和外在激励

a) **Extrinsic rewards** are separate from the job itself and depending on the decisions of others.(i.e the workers have no control over these rewards). Pay, benefits, non-cash incentives, working conditions, etc. 外在激励是跟工作本身无关的因素,约等于双因素论中的保健因素。

b) **Intrinsic rewards** are those which arise from performance of the work itself. Intrinsic rewards include the feeling of satisfaction that comes from completing work, the status conveyed by jobs, the feeling of achievement, etc. 内在激励是来自于工作本身的一些因素,指工作给你带来心理上的满足感、成就感,从而激发员工内在的动力,类似于双因素论中的激励因素。

5. Job design as a motivator
1) Job enrichment 工作丰富化

It is planned, deliberate action to build greater responsibility, breadth and challenge of work into a job. It is similar to **empowerment** and represents a '**vertical**' extension of the job into greater levels of responsibilities and challenges. 给员工更多的责任和挑战,让他做更有难度的工作,给予更多的自由决策权。这是对工作的纵向拉伸。

2) Job enlargement 工作扩大化

It is the attempt to widen jobs by increasing the number of operations in which a job holder is involved. It is a '**horizontal**' extension of jobs. 扩大工作的内容,但在难度和决策权上是没有变化的,这是对工作的横向拉伸。

3) Job rotation 轮岗

It is the **planned transfer** of staff from one job to another to increase task variety. It is a '**sequential**' extension of the job to enable the workers gets more training and experience in a greater variety of jobs. 有计划地、系统性地让员工从一个岗位到另一个岗位轮换,使得员工在轮换过程中得到更多的锻炼和经验。

4) Job optimization 工作优化的方法:

○ Skill variety 技能的多样化
○ Task identify 工作任务要明确
○ Task significance 明确任务的重要性
○ Autonomy 给员工一定的自主权
○ Feedback 给员工一些反馈

Chapter 28

Training and development

1. The learning process

1.1 The learning cycle：Kolb 经验学习循环

Kolb's learning cycle is also called as **experiential learning cycle**. It involves doing and puts the learner in an active problem-solving role：a form of self-learning which encourages learners to formulate and commit themselves to their own learning objectives.

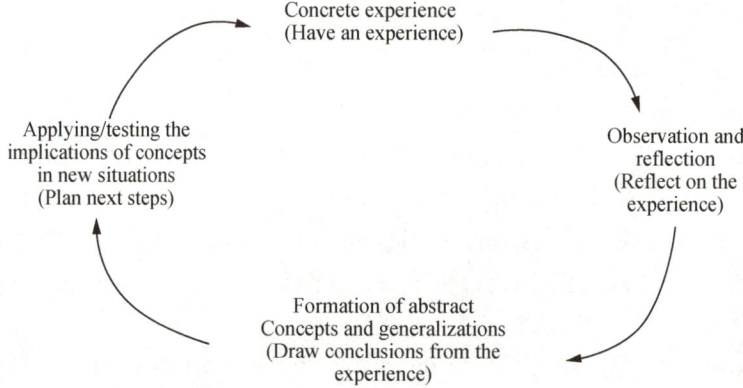

Note：学习圈理论认为学习是一个循环往复的过程,人们的知识在这种不断地学习循环中得以增长。也就是说,学习这件事情是没有终点,不断循环的过程。

1.2 Four learning styles：Honey and Mumford（考点:掌握四种学习风格的特征）

1) **Theorists 思考家**:喜欢基本的概念和原理、理论性的东西
- Programmed and structure
- Designed to allow time for analysis
- Provided by teachers who share their preference for concepts and analysis

2) **Reflectors 观察家**
- Observe phenomena，think about them and choose how to act
- Need to work on their own phase
- Find learning difficult if forced into a hurried programme
- Produce carefully thought-out conclusions after research and reflection
- Tend to be fairly slow，non-participative and cautious

Chapter 28 Training and development

3) **Activists** 行动家：喜欢上手实操
- Deal with practical, active problems and do not have patience with theory
- Require training based on hands-on experience
- Are excited by participation and pressure, such as new projects
- Are flexible and optimistic, but tend to rush at something without due preparation

4) **Pragmatists** 实用主义者：只学在工作中能够用的东西，喜欢直接上手实操
- Only like to study if they can see a direct link to real, practical problems or work-related payoff
- Are good at learning new techniques through on-the-job training
- Aim to implement action plans and/or do the task better
- May discard good ideas which only require some development

1.3 The learning organization

The learning organisation is an organisation that facilitates the acquisition and sharing of knowledge, and the learning of all its members, in order continuously and strategically to transform itself in response to a rapidly changing and uncertain environment. 学习型组织：注重对员工技能的培养，强调不断地获取知识，分享知识。其目的是应对外界快速变化的环境，通过不断的学习就可以保证企业的员工掌握多种技能。

2. Define training, development and education （考点：区分三个概念）

a) **Development** is the growth or realisation of a person's **ability and potential** through the provision of learning and educational experience. 发展指一个人通过学习和教育获得能力和潜力的不断提升。

b) **Training** is the **planned** and **systematic** modification of behavior through learning events, programmes and instructions which enable individuals to achieve the level of knowledge, skills and competence to carry out work effectively. 培训是通过有计划、有系统学习的去修正一个人的行为，来获得知识技能和能力。培训往往是和工作直接相关的。

c) **Education** is acquiring knowledge **gradually** by learning and instruction. 教育是通过学习和指导逐步获取知识的过程。

3. Training methods （考点：区分 on-the job training & off-the job training 及掌握各自优缺点）

3.1 On the job training 在岗培训

On the job training utilizes real work tasks as learning experiences. Methods of on the job training include the following:
a) Demonstration/instruction 示范/指导
b) Job rotation 轮岗
c) Temporary promotion 暂时升职
d) 'Assistant to' positions (or work shadowing) 见习
e) Action learning 参与一个具体的行动

f) Committees 参与委员会

g) Project work 参与项目工作

3.1.1 Advantages

a) Takes account of job context：high relevance and transfer of learning 和工作相关度高

b) Suits 'hands on' learning styles：offers 'learning by doing' 适合喜欢实践性的学习风格

c) No adjustment barriers to application of learning on the job 在工作和学习之间不需要调整

d) Develops working relationships as well as skills 有利于培养同事间的关系

3.1.2 Disadvantages

a) Undesirable aspects of job context also learned 学到不好的工作习惯

b) Doesn't suit 'hand off' learning styles 不适合 theorist 和 reflector 这两种学习风格

c) Trial and error may be threatening 实践中的错误可能会影响工作

d) Distractions and pressures of the workplace may hamper learning focus 工作压力会影响学习的专注度

3.2 Off the job training 脱产培训：单独拿出一段时间参加培训

These are either carried in-house but not at the work place，or externally based on learning relevant to but separate from the job itself.

3.2.1 Advantages

a) Low risk 不会带来工作中的风险

b) Focus on learning 学习的专注度上升

c) Standardisation of training, suits a variety of learning styles 可以学到标准化的培训

d) Confer status 获得学习认证

3.2.2 Disadvantages

a) May not be directly relevant or transferable to the job and job content 和工作的相关度不够高

b) Wastes of working time 浪费工作时间

c) Slower feedback 反馈较慢

d) Tends to be more theoretical：not suit 'hands on' learning styles 不适合喜欢实操性的学习风格

4. Responsibility for training and development

a) The trainee

b) HR department

c) Line manager

d) Training manager

Chapter 29

Review and appraisal of individual performance

1. General purposes of appraisal 评估的目的
a) Reward review 确定奖金
b) Performance review 确定培训需求
c) Potential review 潜力挖掘

2. Performance appraisal process

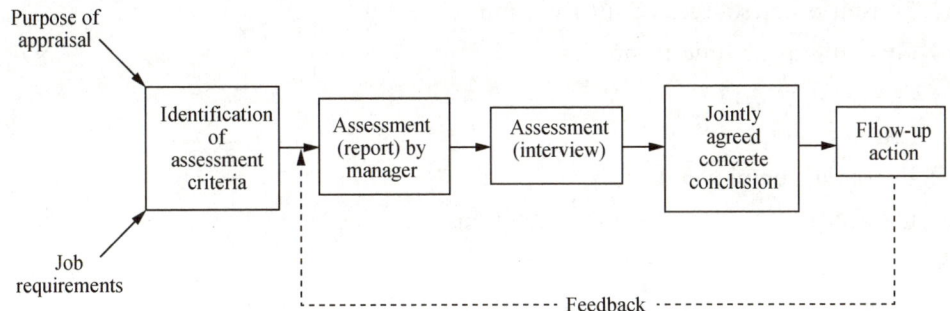

3. The techniques of appraisal 评估技巧

1) Overall assessment

The manager writes in **narrative form** his adjustments about the appraisee. There will be no guaranteed consistency of the criteria and areas of assessment, however, and managers may not be able to convey clear, effective judgements in writing. 综合评估：以叙述性的形式对这个人从总体上评价几句。

2) Guided assessment

Assessors are required to **comment on a number of specified characteristics and performance elements**, with guidelines as to how terms such as 'application', 'integrity' and 'adaptability' are to be interpreted in the work context. This is more precise, but still rather vague. 分类评估：针对一系列具体的特点或要素分门别类进行评估。

3) Grading

Grading adds a comparative frame of reference to the general guidelines, whereby managers are asked to select one of a number of levels or degrees to which the individual in question displays the given characteristic. There are also known as **rating scales.** 打分制：把被评估者划分为一系列的不同的层级。

4) **Behavioral incident methods**

These concentrate on employee behaviour, which is measured against typical behaviour in each job, as defined by common critical incidents of successful and unsuccessful job behaviour reported by managers. 以行为导向的评估方式：将被评估者的行为和一个典型的行为去对比。

5) **Results oriented schemes**

This reviews performance against specific targets and standards of performance agreed in advance by manager and subordinate together. 以结果为导向的方式：上级跟下属之间提前设置好一个专门针对员工个人的目标，每个人的评估标准都不一样。

4. The appraisal interview 面谈的流程

4.1 Prepare 面谈前

a) Planning the place, time and environment

b) Review employee's history

c) Consult other sources of information

d) Give appraisee time to prepare

4.2 Interview 面谈中

a) Listen to employee

b) Encourage employee to talk

c) Identify problems and explore solutions

4.3 Gain commitment 达成共识

a) Arrange and get agreement on plan of action

b) Summaries and ensure understanding

c) Complete the appraisal/improvement/development report

4.4 Follow up 后续行动

a) Take action as agreed

b) Monitor progress

c) Keep employee informed

5. Interview approaches 面谈的风格

a) Tell and sell method 领导对下属评估并告知下属评估结果

b) Tell and listen method 领导先倾听下属的想法，再对下属评估

c) Problem-solving method 以解决问题为目的的评估方式：最民主的方式

6. Other types of appraisal system

6.1 Upward appraisal 下对上的评估

6.1.1 Advantages

a) Subordinates tend to know their superior better than superiors know their subordinates. 下属相对于上级的上级更加了解他们的上司。

b) As all subordinates rate their managers statistically these ratings tend to be more reliable — the more subordinates the better. Instead of the biases of individual managers' ratings, the various ratings of the employee can be converted into a representative view. 一个上级往往有多个下级，越多的下属参与评估，评估的结果就更加可靠准确。

c) More useful to collect information 收集的信息更加有用

6.1.2 Disadvantages

a) Fear of reprisals 下属担心领导报复

b) Some bosses refuse to act 领导拒绝下属的建议

6.2 Self-appraisal 自我评估

6.2.1 Advantage

a) It saves the manager time, as the employee identifies the areas of competence which are relevant to the job and his relative strengths. 节约领导的时间，自己才是最了解自己的人。

b) It offers increased responsibility to the individual, which may improve motivation. 提升员工个人的责任感和动力。

c) This reconciles the goals of the individual and the organization. 将个人的目标与企业的目标相挂钩。

d) In giving the responsibility to an individual, the scheme may offer more flexibility in terms of the timing and relevance of the appraisal. 自我评估的形式和时间更加灵活。

6.2.2 Disadvantages 自我评估缺乏客观性

a) People is often not the best judges of their own performance.

b) People may deliberately over- (or under-) estimate their performance, in order to gain approval or reward- or to conform to group norms.

6.3 360-degree feedback（360度全方位评估：由上级、下级、同事、客户以及你自己都来评估）

360-degree feedback covers appraisal from many sources among which are:

a) The person's immediate manager.

b) People who report to the appraisee, perhaps divided into groups.

c) Peers and co-workers: most people interact with others within an organisation, either as members of a team or as the receivers or providers of services. They can offer useful feedback.

d) Customers: if sales people know what customers thought of them, they might be able to improve their technique.

e）The manager personally：all forms of 360 degree appraisal require people to rate themselves. Those 'who see themselves as others see them will get fewer surprises'.

7. Barriers to effective appraisal（应用型考点）
a）Appraisal as confrontation 把评估当成对抗
b）Appraisal as judgement 把评估作为对一个人的判断
c）Appraisal as 'chit-chat' 把评估作为闲聊
d）Appraisal as bureaucracy 评估过于官僚
e）Appraisal as unfinished business 把评估当成未完成的事项，没有 follow-up action
f）Appraisal as annual report 把评估当作例行公事

Part E

Personal effectiveness and communication in business

Chapter 30

Personal effectiveness techniques

1. Principles of time management（时间管理的原则——六步法）

1.1　Goals 设置目标

To be useful, goals need to be **SMART**

a）Specific 具体的

b）Measurable 可衡量

c）Attainable 可达到

d）Realistic 实际的

e）Time-bounded 有时间范围

1.2　Action plans — written 制定具体的行动计划

1.3　Priorities 根据事情的紧急程度进行排序

Prioritizing tasks involves ordering tasks in order of preference or priority, based on：

a）The relative consequences of timely or untimely performance importance

b）Dependency of other people of tasks urgency

c）Defined deadlines, timescales and commitments

1.4　Focus：one thing at a time 专注：一次只做一件事

1.5　Urgency：do it now！紧急的事情立刻去做

1.6　Organisation 组织和统筹

An **ABCD method** of in-tray management. Resolve to take one of the following approaches

　a. Act on the item immediately

　b. Bin it, if you are sure it is worthless, irrelevant and unnecessary

　c. Create a definite plan for coming back to the item：get it on your schedule. Timetable or to do list

　d. Delegate it to someone else to handle

2. The role of information technology

工作学习中常见的信息技术（了解）：

a）Modems and digital transmission 调制解调器和数字传输

b) Mobile communications 电话

c) Voice messaging systems 语音信箱留言

d) Computer bulletin boards 电子白板

e) Video conferencing 视频会议

f) Electronic data interchange 邮箱

g) Internet and intranet 因特网和内联网

h) Computerized operation, presentation, accounting and management software 电算化软件

The effect of office automation on business:

a) Routine processing

b) The paperless office 无纸化办公

c) Management information

d) Customer service

e) Homeworking or remote working 远程办公

3. The purpose and processes of coaching, mentoring and counselling and their benefits(重要考点:区分三个角色的特征)

3.1 Coaching 教练

Coaching is an approach whereby a trainee is put under the guidance of an experienced person (who may be his superior or co-worker) who shows the trainee how to perform tasks correctly and effectively. Coaching focuses on achieving **specific objective.** 专门针对一些 specific area 进行"手把手"的教授,教练一般由直属上司或者同事担任,往往是和工作相关的指导。

3.2 Mentoring 导师

Mentoring is a **long-term relationship** in which a more experienced person as a teacher, counsellor, role model, supporter and encourager, to foster the individual's personal and career development. 导师是一个长期的关系,一般是由一个更有经验的人担任,作为你的老师、模范、支持者或精神上的引导者鼓励你,培养你个人发展和职业发展。导师提高的指导范围更广,更加宏观。

3.3 Counselling 咨询

It is a **purposeful relationship** in which one person **helps another to help himself.** The aim is to facilitate another person in identifying and working through a problem. 咨询者会倾听你,让你自己知道解决问题的办法。

3.3.1 Benefits of counselling

a) Prevent underperformance 帮企业规避员工业绩水平下降的状况

b) Demonstration of an organization's commitment to and concern of its employees 体现了公司对员工的人文关怀

c) Improvement of employee's confidence, morale royalty and commitment in the organization 增强员工的自信、士气

d) Improvement of employees' job attitude, task responsibility and performance 增加员工的工作热情和动力

3.3.2 Counselling skills

a) Active listening: the listener ensures they are trying to understand 积极地倾听

b) Using different questing styles 使用不同的提问技巧

c) Using body language and interpreting the other person's body language carefully 使用肢体语言

Chapter 31

Communication in business

1. **Purpose of communication 沟通的五大目的**
   a) To inform
   b) To persuade
   c) To request
   d) To confirm
   e) To build a relationship

2. **The communication process 沟通的要素（考点）**

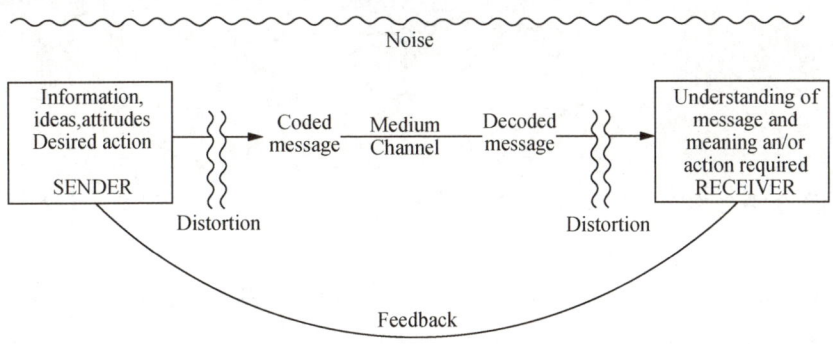

Process	Comment
Encoding of a message 编码	The code or 'language' of a message may be verbal (spoken or written) or it may be non-verbal, in pictures, diagrams, numbers or body language
Medium for the message 媒介	There are a number of channels for communication, such as a conversation, a letter, a notice board or via computer. The choice of medium used in communication depends on a number of factors such as urgency, permanency, complexity, sensitivity and cost
Feedback 反馈	The sender of a message needs feedback on the receiver's reaction. This is partly to test the receiver's understanding of it and partly to gauge the receiver's reaction
Distortion 扭曲	The meaning of a message can be lost at the coding and decoding stages. Usually the problem is one of the language and the medium used; it is very easy to give the wrong impression in a brief e-mail message

(Continued)

Process	Comment
Noise 噪音（物理/技术/ 社会/心理）	Distractions and interference in the environment in which communication is taking place may be physical noise（passing traffic），technical noise（a bad telephone line），social noise（differences in the personalities of the parties）or psychological noise（anger，frustration，tiredness）

3. Direction of communication（应用型考点）

a) Vertical communication — Downward or upward，flows up and down the scalar chain from superior to subordinate and back 纵向沟通（上对下、下对上）

b) Horizontal/lateral communication 横向沟通：不同部门同一级别的沟通

c) Diagonal or cross-functional communication 对角线沟通：不同部门、不同级别的人之间的沟通

4. Communication patterns 沟通的模式（集权/分权沟通）

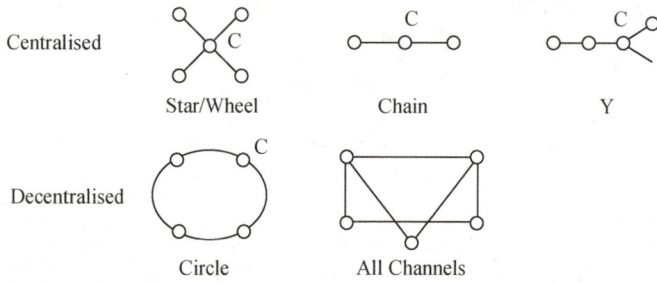

Note：区分哪些属于集权式沟通，哪些属于分权沟通

5. Describe the attributes of effective communication 有效的沟通应当具备什么特征?

a) Clear 清晰的

b) Concise 简明扼要

c) Complete 完整的

d) Correct 准确的

e) Courteous 有礼貌的

6. Barriers to communication

6.1 General faults in the communication process 沟通中常见的问题

a) Distortion or omission of information by sender 发出者发出的信息扭曲或者缺失

b) Misunderstanding due to lack of clarify or technical jargon 使用专业的术语而导致的误解

c) Non-verbal signs contradicting the verbal message，so that its meaning is in doubt 肢体语言和语言化的信息冲突，给对方造成疑惑

d) Overload 信息量过多

e) Noise 干扰（四种类型）

f) People hearing only what they want to hear in a message 人在接收信息的过程中是有选择性

g) Differences in social, racial or educational background, compounded by age and personality differences, creating barriers to understanding and co-operation 人与人之间所处的社会环境、教育背景、种族背景不同而导致沟通的误解

6.2 Categories of communication problems 导致沟通失败的原因

a) **System** — There may be a bad formal communication system 系统问题

b) **Misunderstanding** — There may be misunderstanding about the actual content of a message 误解

c) **Personality** — Inter-personal difficulties may hamper communication 性格不合

7. Describe the main methods and patterns of communication

a) Written (verbal) communications 书面沟通

b) Oral (verbal) communication 口头沟通

c) Non-verbal communications 非语言化的沟通

Generally, non-verbal communications can present as 常见的非语言化沟通方式：

○ Facial expression 面部表情
○ Gestures 手势
○ Movement 动作
○ Positioning 位置
○ Contact 接触
○ Posture 姿势
○ Sounds 声调
○ Silence 沉默

Chapter 32

Conflicts in business

1. Source of conflict 冲突的来源（了解）

a) **Power and resources are limited**（and sometimes scare）in the organisation. Individuals and groups **compete for them**, fearing that the more someone else has, the less there is to go around. 企业中为了争夺有限的资源和权利而产生冲突。

b) Individuals and teams **have their own goals, interests and priorities** — which may be incompatible. 组织中个人及团队的目标、利益、优先次序是不一样的。

c) There may be **differences and incompatibilities of personality** between individuals, resulting in clashes. 性格不合产生的冲突。

d) There may be **differences and incompatibilities of work methods, timescales and working style**, so that individuals or teams frustrate each other with apparent lack of co-ordination（especially if one person's task depends on the others）. 工作方法、工作风格的差异而产生的冲突。

2. Conflict resolution and avoidance

a) Conflict resolution is a wide range of methods of addressing sources of conflict and of finding means of resolving a given conflict or of continuing it in less destructive forms than, say, armed conflict. Processes of conflict resolution generally include **negotiation, mediation, diplomacy and creative peace building.** 解决冲突的方法：谈判、调停、外交手段、有创造力的方式和平地解决问题。

b) Avoidance is not a resolution way, it will be useful as a temporary measure to buy time or as an expedient means of dealing with very minor, non-recurring conflicts, by ignoring it, changing the subject, severing a relationship or leaving a group, etc. 逃避冲突：忽视、转移话题、中断关系、离开团队。

3. Managing your own interpersonal conflicts

3.1 General methods to manage conflicts 管理人际冲突的三个步骤

a) Communicate 沟通

b) Negotiation 协商

c) Separate 把矛盾双方分开

Chapter 32　Conflicts in business

3.2　Managing conflicts in the team or group 在团队或项目中，作为领导，应该怎么样去处理冲突?

Response	Comment
Denial/withdrawal 否认	Sweeping it under the carpet. If the conflict is very trivial, it may indeed blow over without an issue being made of it, but if the causes are not identified, the conflict may grow to unmanageable proportions. 对于琐碎的细小的矛盾视而不见，当作不存在。但是如果忽略了冲突背后的原因，那么矛盾可能会变得不可收拾
Suppression 抑制	Smoothing over to preserve working relationships despite minor conflicts. 抑制矛盾双方的冲突，缓和氛围
Dominance 支配	The application of power or influence to settle the conflict. The disadvantage of this is that it creates all the lingering resentment and hostility of win lose situations 作为领导，用自己的权力判断对错
Compromise 妥协	Bargaining negotiating conciliating. To some extent, this will be inevitable in any organisation made up of different individuals. However, individuals tend to exaggerate their positions to allow for compromise, and compromise itself is seen to weaken the value of the decision, perhaps reducing commitment. 调节安抚双方，鼓励双方达成妥协，各退一步
Integration 整合	Emphasis must be put on the task, individuals must accept the need to modify their views for its sake, and group effort must be seen to be superior to individual effort. 要求矛盾双方关注团队的目标
Encourage co-operative behavior 鼓励合作	Joint problem-solving team, goals set for all teams/departments to follow. 设置团队的整体目标，让成员为共同目标达成合作

3.3　Limits in conflict management

a) Beyond your authority 超出职权范围

b) Beyond ability 超出能力范围

Part F

Professional ethics in accounting and business

Chapter 33

Ethical consideration

1. What is ethics
There are three main sources of rules that regulate behavior of individuals and businesses. These are: 规范个人和企业的三个规则来源:
a) The law 法律(最低要求)
b) Non-legal rules and regulations 规章制度
c) Ethics 道德

2. Approaches to ethics
2.1 Teleology vs. Deontology
1) Teleology

It judges actions by reference to their outcomes or consequences. (Result in the greatest good for the greatest number of people) 结果论:只要这件事情让大多数人满意, 这件事就是对的。

2) Deontology

Behaviour should be governed by absolute moral rules that apply in all circumstances. 义务论:任何一个行为本身,受到一个绝对的道德准则约束。这个道德准则适用于所有的情况。

2.2 Relativism vs absolutism
1) Ethical relativism 相对主义:不同的情况下有不同的道德标准

Relativism is the view that a wide variety of acceptable ethical beliefs and practices exist. The ethics that are most appropriate in a given situation will depend on the conditions at that time.

2) Ethical absolutism 绝对主义:有唯一的道德准则适合所有的情况

Absolutism is the view that there is an unchanging set of ethical principles that will apply in all situations, at all times and in all societies.

3. Corporate ethics
3.1 Fiduciary responsibility 信托责任
Managers do not exist to serve their own purposes or those of their organizations.

They have **a fiduciary responsibility (duty of faithful service)** in this respect and their behavior must always reflect it. 代理人的任何行为都要以委托人的最佳利益为出发点，而不满足自己的利益。

3.2　Ethical problems facing managers（案例分析考察）

a) **Extortion.** Foreign officials have been known to threaten companies with the complete closure of their local operations unless suitable payments are made. 敲诈：企业被迫向政府交保护费。

b) **Bribery.** This refers to payments for services to which a company is not legally entitled. There are some fine distinctions to be drawn：for example，some managers regard political contributions as bribery. 贿赂：企业主动给政府钱去获得本不该属于自己的东西或权力。

c) **Grease money.** Multinational companies are sometimes unable to obtain services to which they are legally entitled because of deliberate stalling by local officials. Cash payments to the right people may then be enough to oil the machinery of bureaucracy. 人情费：企业通过给政府钱去获取一个企业本来就具备的资格。

d) **Gifts.** In some cultures（such as Japan）gifts are regarded as an essential part of civilized negotiation，even in circumstances where to Western eyes they might appear ethically dubious. Managers operating in such a culture may feel at liberty to adopt the local customs. 送礼是否道德取决于各地的文化礼仪。

4.　Ethics in organization

Organizational values that promote ethics：企业推行的价值观

a) Openness 开放
b) Trust 信任
c) Honesty 诚信
d) Respect 尊重
e) Empowerment 赋权
f) Accountability 问责

5.　Professional ethics

1) Integrity 正直即言行一致

A professional accountant should be straightforward and honest in all professional and business relationships. Integrity also implies fair dealing and truthfulness.

2) Objectivity 客观性

A professional accountant should not allow prejudice or bias，conflict of interest or undue influence of others to override professional or business judgements. 专业人员在做出一些专业决策不能受到偏见、利益冲突和他人的不当影响。

3) Professional competence and due care 专业胜任能力和小心谨慎

To maintain professional knowledge and skill at the level required to ensure that a client or employer receives the advantage of competent professional service based on current developments in practice, legislation and techniques. To act diligently in accordance with applicable technical and professional standards in all professional and business relationships. 作为专业人士首先要具备相关的专业能力胜任这份工作；其次在执行工作的过程中，要小心谨慎。

4) **Confidentiality 保密性**

A professional accountant should respect the confidentiality of information acquired as a result of professional and business relationships and **should not disclose any such information to third parties without proper and specific authority unless there is a legal or professional right or duty to disclose**. Confidential information acquired as result of professional and business relationships should **not be used for the personal advantage** of the professional accountant **or third parties**. 在进行专业工作时，对于客户的机密消息，不能在未经允许的情况下，把这些消息披露给第三方，也不能用来自己获利，除非法律要求。

5) **Professional behaviors 职业行为**

A professional accountant should comply with relevant laws and regulations and should avoid any action that discredits the profession. 作为一个专业的会计人员，不仅要符合法律法规的要求，而且任何有损专业形象的事前情不能做。

6. Ethical threats

6.1　Self-interest threats 自我利益威胁

a) Auditors receive excessive gifts or hospitality from a client 审计师从客户那里收取贵重的礼物

b) Auditors receive a large proportion of their fees from one client 审计收入过多依赖某一个大客户

c) Auditors have personal or business relationships with a client 审计师和客户之间有商业往来或个人关系

d) Audit fees are agreed on contingent basis 审计费是浮动的

e) Auditors and clients lend each other money 审计师和客户之间互相借钱

6.2　Self-review threats 自我检查威胁：自己检查自己做的工作会影响独立性

This threat arises when auditors perform work/produce information for the client that they end up reviewing themselves as part of an assurance engagement.

6.3　Familiarity threats 亲密性威胁

Familiarity threats arise when the auditors develop a close relationship with the client and as a result become too sympathetic to their interests or too trusting of their work. 审计师和客户之间有过于亲近的关系，导致审计师可能过于同情客户或者过于信任客户的工作，从而影响独立性。

Examples of familiarities threats are：

a) The auditors audit a company where friends or relatives work

b) The auditor has been auditing the company many years

c) There are people working at the client who recently worked for the audit form

6.4 Advocacy threat 支持性威胁

This may occur when the auditor is asked to promote the client's position or represent them in some way. In this situation the auditor would have to be biased in favor of the client and therefore cannot be objective. 审计师在外行的人看来有推销或代表客户的倾向,会威胁独立性。

Examples of advocacy threats include：

a) Representation an audit client in a legal case or tax enquiry 在法律案件或税务案件中代表客户

b) Auditor to promote their shares for a stock exchange listing 审计师在公开场合推销客户的股票

6.5 Intimidation threats 威胁和胁迫

This threat is caused by a client being in a position to put pressure on an auditor to prevent them acting objectively. This could arise from family and personal relationships. Litigation or close business relationships. As a result，the intimidation threat is very closely related to the self-interest and the advocacy threat to the safeguards are the sam.

MANAGEMENT ACCOUNTING

Chapter 1

Accounting for management

1. Information

Data is the raw material for data processing. Data relates to facts, events and transactions and so forth. 原始数据

Information is data that has been processed in such a way as to be meaningful to the person who receives it. Information is anything that is communicated. 加工处理后的数据

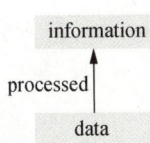

- Processed data
- Meaningful to users 行为有指导意义

Raw material
- such as:
numbers, raw facts, events, transactions

Qualities of good information 好的信息特征
- **A**ccurate: accurate enough for the purpose (not completely accurate)
- **C**omplete: all the necessary information
- **C**larity: be clear to users
- **U**nderstandability: understandable to users, minimum level of jargon
- **R**elevant: relevant to purpose
- **A**ccessible: the best way to communicate with the related person
- **T**imely: be available at the right time
- Cost-**E**ffective: benefit > costs

2. Planning, control and decision making

Management accounts assist in **planning** and **controlling** an organization's activities and help the **decision-making** process.

Planning involves: 计划
a) Establishing **objective** 目标
b) Selecting appropriate **strategies** to achieve those objectives 战略即实现目标的方法

Control involves: 控制
a) **Comparing** the actual performance with planning performance 对比
b) **Reviewing** the corporate plan 反思

c) Corrective action 调整

Decision-taking：决策

Decision making always involves a choice between alternatives. 在不同的选项中做出选择(贯穿整个过程)。

Anthony's view of management activity 安东尼的管理活动理论

Strategic level 战略层

The process of deciding on **objectives of the organisation**, on changes in these objectives, on the **resources** used to attain these objectives, and on the policies that are to govern the **acquisition**, **use and disposition** of these resources. 整个公司的目标，资源的分配。

Characteristic of information-Strategic level
- Used by senior managers
- Long-term (>1 year)
- Focused on organisation as a whole 关注整个公司不同部门
- Financial & non-financial
- Internal & external
- Qualitative & quantitative 质化和量化

Tactical level 战术层

The process by which managers assure that **resources are obtained and used effectively and efficiently** in the accomplishment of the organisation's objectives. 获得的资源有效的使用。

Characteristic of information-Tactical level
- Used by middle management
- Medium term (quarterly, monthly)
- Focused on departments
- It is prepared routinely and regularly

Operational level 经营层

The process of assuring that **specific tasks** are carried out **effectively and efficiently**. 特定的任务工作

Characteristic of information-Operational level
- Used by 'front-line' managers/supervisor

Chapter 1 Accounting for management

- Immediate term
- Task-specific
- Internal
- Quantitative 具体的事项
- It is prepared constantly, or very frequently.

Management control system 管理控制系统

A system which **measures** and **corrects** the performance of activities of subordinates to ensure that the aims of an organization are being met and the plan devised to attain them are **being carried out**. 评估修改及控制

3. Financial accounting and cost and management accounting

Financial accounting systems ensure that the assets and liabilities of a business are **properly accounted for**, and provide information about profits and so on to shareholders and to other interested parties (including external users). 财务会计系统:恰当的记录SOFP;提供给股东和其他感兴趣的人。

Management accounting systems provide information specifically for the use of managers within an organization. 管理会计系统:提供给管理层的。

相同点:
- Both a branch of Accounting
- **Use the same source of data** 使用的是相同的原始信息。

不同点:

	Financial	Management
User	External and Internal	Internal
Legal requirement	✓	✗
Precision	True and Fair	As accurate as possible for users need
Rules	GAAP/IFRS	No rules but some established techniques
Extent	Past data	Past and data about future
Frequency	Annual	As required
Format	Governed by Companies Act	No set format
Measurement	Monetary	Monetary, Non-monetary

Chapter 2

Sources of data

1. Types of data

1.1 Internal data VS. external data 内部数据 VS.外部数据

Internal data: Accounting system, Payroll system, Office automation system

External data: Government source, Banks, Financial newspapers, Trade journals, Internet

Type	Benefits	Limitations
Internal	○ Data can easily be sorted and analyzed ○ Reports can easily be produced when required ○ Data relates to the organization concerned	○ Ignore other factors which may impact the organization
External	○ Wide expanse of external source of information ○ Easily accessible especially using the internet ○ More general information available	○ Data may not be accurate ○ Finding relevant information can be time consuming

1.2 Quantitative data VS. Qualitative data 定量数据 VS.定性数据

Quantitative data is data that can be measured.

Qualitative data is data that have attributes which cannot be measured.

1.3 Primary data VS. Secondary data 一手数据 VS.二手数据

1) Primary data

○ Data collected (in person) specifically for a particular purpose.

○ Noted: the data must serve the original purpose to be primary data, otherwise they are secondary data.

○ Primary data can be collected through survey, experiment, observation.

2) Secondary data

○ Have already been collected elsewhere, for some other purpose, but which can be used or adapted here.

1.4 Discrete data VS. Continuous data 离散数据 VS.连续数据

1) Discrete data

Can only take on a finite or countable number of values within a give range.

2) Continuous data

Can take on any value within a give range.

Measured rather than counted.

1.5 Sample data VS. Population data 样本数据 VS.总体数据

1) Population data

Data arising as a result of investigating the population.

A population is the group of people or objects of interest to the data collector.

2) Sample data

Data arising as a result of investigating a sample.

A sample is a selection from the population.

2. Characteristics of good information

○ **A**ccurate：accurate enough for the purpose（not completely accurate）
○ **C**omplete：all the necessary information
○ **C**larity：be clear to users
○ **U**nderstandability：understandable to users，minimum level of jargon
○ **R**elevant：relevant to purpose
○ **A**ccessible：the best way to communicate with the related person
○ **T**imely：be available at the right time
○ Cost-**E**ffective：benefit > costs

3. Sampling

○ If the whole population is examined，the survey is called a census（人口普查）.
○ Problem of census：Cost & Out of date 成本过高&过时
○ Data are often collected from sample rather than from a population.
○ Best case scenario/perfect sample. 抽样结果是完美的。
○ Sample selected should be **representative/cover all areas** of the population（not biased）. 没有偏见（结果）
○ **A sampling frame is a numbered list of all items in a population.** 样本框架,将研究对象的整个整体全部拿过来编上序号。

3.1 Random sampling 简单随机抽样

○ A simple random sample is selected so that every item in the population has an **equal chance of being selected**.
○ Sampling frame is required 需要样本框架

Adv：

○ If a sample is selected using random sampling，it will be **free from bias**（过程没有偏见）= **truly/completely random** = **each item have equal chance of being selected**.

Disadv：

○ A random sample is **not** necessarily a **perfect sample.**/An **unrepresentative** sample may result.（就结果而言）不一定是具有代表性的。
○ An adequate sampling frame might not exist.

○ The numbering of the population might be **laborious**.（费劲的）

3.2 Stratified random sampling 分层随机抽样

○ Stratified random sampling is where the population is divided into categories from which random samples are taken. 先将整体按照特点分成组，每组分别进行随机抽样。

○ No sampling frame is required 不需要样本框架

Adv：

○ The **structure of the sample** will **reflect that of the population** as the same proportion of individuals is chosen from each stratum.

○ The sample selected will be **representative/unbiased**.

Disadv：

○ The method requires **prior knowledge** of each population item.

○ **Not truly random**. 结果具有代表性，抽样过程是具有偏见的。

3.3 Systematic sampling 系统抽样

○ Systematic sampling：involves selecting **every nth** item after **a random start** 第一个随机抽样，每隔 N 个抽出来一个。

○ Quality check in manufacturing company. 应用于生产制造业的质检。

○ Sampling frame is required.

Adv：

○ It is easy to use & cheap. 简单便宜

Disadv：

○ It is possible that a **biased sample** might be chosen if there is a regular pattern to the population which coincides with the sampling method. 不具有代表性

○ It is not completely random since some items have a zero chance of being selected. 抽样过程有偏见

3.4 Multistage sampling 多级抽样

○ Multistage sampling involves dividing the population into a number of sub-populations and then selecting a small sample of these sub-populations at random. 分成各种下级成员

○ Each sub-population is then **divided further**, and then a small sample is again selected at random. This process is repeated as many times as necessary.

○ No sampling frame is required 不需要样本框架

Adv：

○ Fewer investigators are needed.

○ It is not so costly to obtain a sample. 便宜

Disadv：

○ It is not completely random as only a small number of regions are selected. 不是真正意义上的随机

3.5 Cluster sampling 整群抽样

○ Cluster sampling is a **good alternative** to multistage sampling.

○ Cluster sampling involves selecting **one definable subsection** of the population as the sample, that subsection taken to be representative of the population in question. 最后一步的样本放在一起整体抽样。

3.6 Quota sampling　配额抽样

○ Investigators are told to interview all the people they meet **up to a certain quota**. 首先碰到的确定数量。

○ First come first served. 先到先得

○ No sampling frame is required 不需要样本框架

Adv:

○ It is cheap and administratively easy. 简单

○ A much larger sample can be studied

○ It may be the **only possible approach** in certain situations, such as television audience research. 是有些抽样唯一的方法，电视台随机采访。

Disadv:

○ The sample selected will be unrepresentative. 结果不具有代表性

是否知道每个个体进入到样本中的概率：

Probability sampling method is a sampling method in which there is known chance of each member of the population appearing in the sample.

EG：Random，Stratified random，Systematic，Multistage，Cluster

A non-probability sampling method is a sampling method in which the chance of each member of the population appearing in the sample is not known.

EG：**Quota sampling**

总结：

Sampling frame	Ransom sampling Systematic sampling
Truly random	Random sampling
Representative	Stratified random sampling
Non-probability sampling	Quota sampling

Chapter 3

Presenting information

1. Written reports

The purpose of a report must be **clear**, and certain **general principles** should be followed in planning and giving structure to a report. 清晰表达

Reports are usually intended to initiate **a decision or action**.

Stylistic qualities of reports include objectivity and balance and ease of understanding. 客观 内容包含所有项,不含有太多专业词。

2. Presenting and interpreting information in tables

Since a table is two-dimensional, it can only show **two variables**.

3. Presenting and interpreting information in charts

a) Bar charts 柱状图

○ simple bar chart

○ component bar chart

○ multiple bar chart

○ Percentage component bar chart

b) Pie charts 饼图

c) Scatter diagrams 散点图

d) Line graph 折线图

Chapter 4

Type of cost and cost behaviour

1. Cost classification

Cost accounting 成本会计

Cost accounting is **part of management accounting**. 成本会计是管理会计的组成部分。

Cost accounting information is, in general, **unsuitable for decision making**. 仅依赖于成本会计做决策是不合适的。

Decision-making information should be relevant and incorporate **uncertainty**.

Classified by	Costs are classified as
Element 要素	Material, Labour, Expense
Function 职能	Production, Non-production
Nature 本质	Direct, Indirect
Behavior 习性	Fixed, Variable, Semi-variable, Stepped fixed

1.1 Function

1) Production cost 生产成本

Costs associated with the production of goods and services, from the **supply of raw materials** to the **completion of the product ready for warehousing** as a finished goods item. 发生在生产流程中或者为我们的生产流程提供支持的。

EG: Raw material purchase cost(√); Factory canteen cost(√); Raw material warehouse staff cost(√); Finished goods warehouse staff cost(×)

2) Selling cost 销售成本

Selling costs, sometimes known as **marketing costs**, are the costs of creating demand for products and securing firm orders from customers.

EG: Advertisement cost(√); Trade discount(√) 折扣

3) Distribution cost 配送成本

Distribution costs are the costs of the sequence of operations with the **receipt of finished**.

goods from the production department and making them ready for dispatch and ending with the **reconditioning for reuse of empty containers**.

EG：Finished goods warehouse staff cost（√）；License for lorries（√）；Depreciation of lorries

4）Financing cost 融资成本

Costs incurred to **finance** the business，such as **loan interest**.

5）Administration costs 管理成本

Costs of managing an organisation，that is，planning and controlling its operations，but only insofar as such administration costs are not related to the production, selling, distribution or financing functions.

EG：Remuneration CEO

1.2 Nature

1）Direct cost/prime cost 直接成本

Costs that can be **directly identified** with a specific cost unit or cost center.（Cost per unit 清晰&生产必要的）

EG：Component parts；Wages of quality check staff；Royalties paid to a designer

2）Indirect cost/overhead 间接成本

EG：Supervisor salary；Rent，Rates of a factory

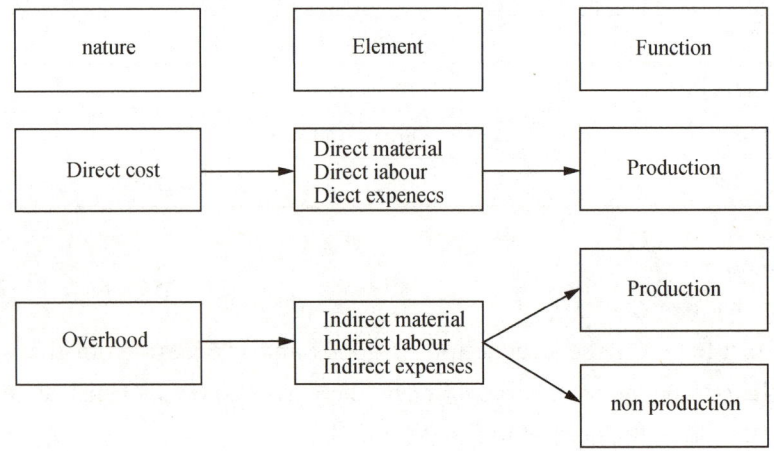

1.3 Managing cost 如何管理成本

1）Cost centers：成本中心

Collecting places for costs before they are further analyzed. Costs are further analyzed into cost units once they have been traced to cost centers（functional department）

2）Cost units：成本单位

A cost unit is a unit of product or service in relation to which costs are ascertained.

3）Cost objects：成本对象

a cost object is any activity for which a separate measurement of cost is desired

Responsibility accounting 责任会计

Responsibility centers 责任中心

Chapter 4　Type of cost and cost behaviour

○ **Cost centers** are collecting places for costs before they are further analyzed. Costs are further analyzed into cost units once they have been traced to cost centers.

○ **Revenue centers** are accountable for **revenues only**. Its managers should normally have control over how revenues are raised.

○ **Profit centers** are accountable for **costs and revenues**.

○ **An investment center** is a profit center with additional responsibilities for **capital investment** and possibly for **financing**, and whose performance is measured by its return on investment or return on capital employed. 在 profit 的基础上又对投资资源进行负责,还有怎么融资的(可能)。

Investment decision：usage of spare money(闲钱的决策)；decisions relating to PPE (做 PPE 相关的决策)

Controllable cost 可控成本

A controllable cost is 'a cost that can be controlled, typically by a cost, profit or investment center manager'. 可以控制的、说了算的成本

Managers should only be held **accountable for costs over which they have some influence**. (Apportioned head office costs)

Cost code 成本代码(用数字管理成本数据,而非文字描述)

Adv of a coding system：

○ A code is usually **briefer** than a description, thereby saving clerical time in a manual system and storage space in a computerized system. 简洁

○ A code is more **precise** than a description. 准确

○ Coding facilitates data processing.

Disadv of a coding system：

○ **Wider issues** are more suited to communication through a 'free text' description rather than the use of codes.

2. Cost behaviour

Classified by the **relationship between costs (total cost) and activity level (volume of output)**.

○ Fixed cost
○ Variable cost
○ Semi-variable cost
○ Stepped fixed cost

1) Fixed cost 固定成本

Cost which is unaffected by changes in the level of activity.

EG：rent of factory, business rates

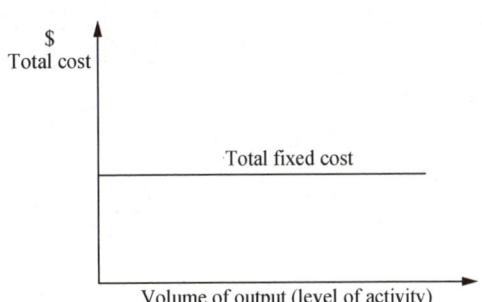

2) Variable cost 变动成本

Cost which tends to vary with the level of activity. Y = kX

EG: direct materials, direct labor

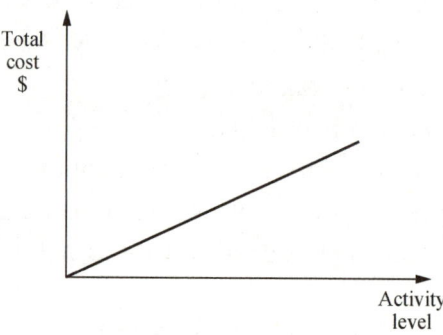

3) Semi-variable cost 半变动成本

Cost which contains both fixed and variable elements. $Y = a + bX$

Semi-variable cost = semi-fixed cost = mixed cost

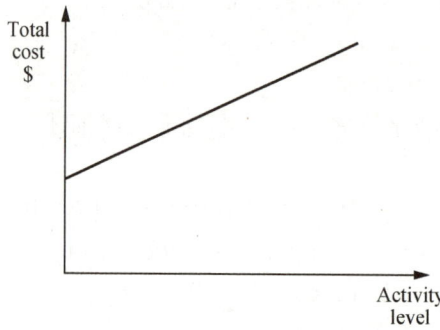

4) Step fixed cost 阶梯式固定成本

Cost which is fixed in nature but only within certain level of activity.

EG: factory rent if new space has to be rented

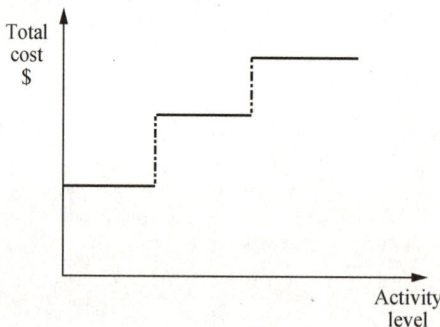

Chapter 5

Forecasting

1. High low method

1) Cost estimation 成本假设

Departmental costs within an organization are assumed to be **mixed costs**, with a fixed and a variable element. Y = a + bX

Departmental costs are assumed to rise in a straight line as the volume of activity increases. In other words, these costs are said to be **linear**. 具有线性关系

2) Cost equation

Y = a + bx

y = total costs   dependent variable 因变量
a = the fixed cost   intercept 截距
b = the variable cost per unit   Slop 斜率
x = the number of units of activity   independent variable 自变量

3) High low method 高低点法

Step 1: select the highest and lowest activity levels, and their associated costs.

Step 2: find the variable cost per unit.

Step 3: find the fixed cost by substitution, using either the high or low activity level. 两点确认，高低点代入是自变量的高低点代入。

➢ High-low method with stepped fixed cost (Fixed cost 会上升，阶梯式，a 发生变化)

➢ High-low method with changes in the variable cost per unit (Variable cost 会下降，比例式，b 发生变化)

2. Linear regression/least square method 线性回归法/最小二乘法

Linear regression analysis (the least squares method) is one technique for estimating a **line of best fit**. Once an equation for a line of best fit has been determined, forecasts can be made. 最佳线

（考试会提供）

Regression analysis

$$y = a + bx$$

$$a = \frac{\sum y}{n} - \frac{b \sum x}{n}$$

$$b = \frac{n\sum xy - \sum x \sum y}{n\sum x^2 - (\sum x)^2}$$

Correlation 相关

Two variables are said to be correlated if a change in the value of one variable is accompanied by a change in the value of another variable.

This is what is meant by correlation.

Positive correlation means that low values of one variable are associated with low values of the other, and high values of one variable are associated with high values of the other. 正相关

Negative correlation means that low values of one variable are associated with high values of the other, and high values of one variable with low values of the other. 负相关

Perfectly correlated 完美相关

An *exact linear relationship* exists between the two variables. 完美的线性关系

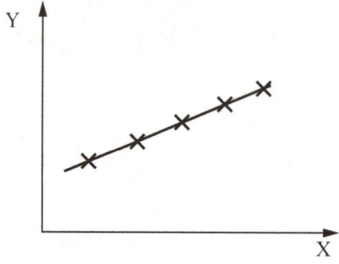

Partly correlated 部分相关

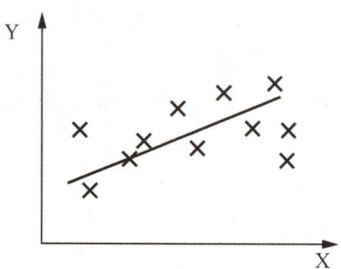

Uncorrelated 不相关

The values of Y these two variables are not correlated with each other.

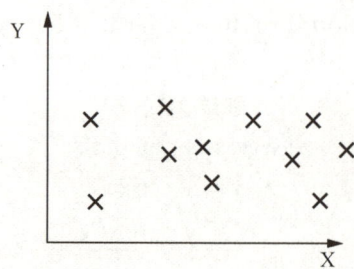

Chapter 5 Forecasting

Correlation coefficient 相关系数（r）

The degree of linear correlation between two variables is measured by the correlation coefficient, r 线性相关的程度

The correlation coefficient, r must always fall between -1 and $+1$. The nearer r is to $+1$ or -1, the stronger the relationship.

r = +1 means that the variables are perfectly positively correlated
r = −1 means that the variables are perfectly negatively correlated
r = 0 means that the variables are uncorrelated

$$r = \frac{n\sum xy - \sum x \sum y}{\sqrt{(n\sum x^2 - (\sum x)^2)(n\sum y^2 - (\sum y)^2)}} [-1, +1]（考试会提供）$$

Coefficient of determination(r^2) 决定系数

The coefficient of determination, r^2, measures the proportion of the total variation in the value of one variable that can be **explained** by variations in the value of the other variable. 一个变量的变化他有多大程度上被另外一个变量所解释。

It also denotes the strength of the linear association between two variables. 线性关系的强弱。

Linear regression 的优缺点

Advantages：

○ It gives a definitive line of best fit, taking account of all of the data. (compare with high-low method) 完美的线，考虑所有点

○ Linear regression makes efficient use of data and good results can be obtained with relatively small data sets.

○ The significance/reliability of the relationship between variables can be statistically tested. 统计学做背书

Disadvantages：

○ It assumes a linear relationship exists between the two variables whereas a non-linear relationship might exist. 不一定有线性关系，假设就不对，两种方法都有这个缺点。

○ Value of Y might depend on several other variables, not just X.

○ When it is used for forecasting, it assumes that what has happened in the past will provide a reliable guide to the future.

○ The amount and reliability of data available is very important. 原始数据可靠程度很重要。

3. Time series analysis 时间序列分析

A time series is a series of figures or values recorded over time. 数字怎么随着时间的变化而变化的。自变量是时间，因变量不固定。

Four components of a time series:

a) Trend: underlying long-term movement over time in the values of the data recorded. 趋势

One method of finding the trend is by the use of moving averages. 抹去波动即平均值,求 trend 使用移动平均值法。

b) Seasonal variations: short-term fluctuations in recorded values. 短期波动/季节性波动

○ **additive model 加法模型**

Seasonal variations are the difference between actual and trend figures. 所有 Seasonal variations 加起来为零。

Y＝Trend＋Seasonal variation

○ **multiplicative model 乘法模型**

In multiplicative model, each actual figure is expressed as a proportion of the trend. 所有 Seasonal variations 的平均值等于1。

Y＝Trend × Seasonal variation

Note that the proportional model is better than the additive model when the trend is increasing or decreasing over time. 如果趋势是上升或者下降的事态,不是一成不变的时候,使用乘法模型比加法模型要好。

c) Cyclical variations: fluctuations which take place over a longer time period. 长期波动/周期波动(经济周期)20年以上

d) Random variations: caused by unforeseen circumstances. 随机波动

4. Index 指数

An index is a measure, over time, of the average changes in the value (price or quantity) of a group of items relative to the situation at some period in the past. 一个数字表示一段时间数据的变化,使用倍数表示。

a) A **price index** measures the change in the money value of a group of items over time. 与钱相关管的指数

b) A **quantity index** (also called a volume index) measures the change in the non-monetary values of a group of items over time.

1) **Single item Index**

$$\text{Price index} = P_n / P_0 \times 100$$

Where P_n is the price for the period under consideration and P_0 is the price for the base period.

$$\text{Quantity index} = Q_n / Q_0 \times 100$$

Where Q_n is the quantity for the period under consideration and Q_0 is the quantity for the Base Period.

○ In the **fixed base method**, a base year is selected (index 100), and all Subsequent changes are measured against this base. P_0 不变

○ In the **chain base method**, changes are calculated with respect to the value of the commodity in the period immediately before. P_0 是前一年

2) **Composite item Index**

Most practical indices cover more than one item and are hence termed composite index numbers.

○ **Weighted aggregate index** 先用数量为权重再算指数。

a) **Laspeyre indices** use weights from the base period and are therefore sometimes called base weighted indices. (which uses quantities/prices from the **base period** as the weights) 拉式指数

b) **Paasche indices** use current time period weights. In other words the weights are changed every time period. (which uses quantities/prices from the **current period** as the weights) 帕式指数

Which to use — Paasche or Laspeyre?

○ A **Paasche index requires quantities to be ascertained each year**. A Laspeyre index only requires them for the base year. Constructing a Paasche index may therefore be costly.

○ The weights for a Laspeyre index become **out of date**, whereas those for the Paasche index are updated each year. 拉式指数过时

√ **Fisher's ideal index**

$$\text{Fisher's ideal index} = \sqrt{\text{Laspeyre} \times \text{Paasche}}$$

Chapter 6

Accounting for materials

1. Inventory

Classifications of inventories:
- Materials (Spare parts/consumables) 原材料
- Work in progress (WIP) 半成品
- Finished goods 产成品

Inventory Control System

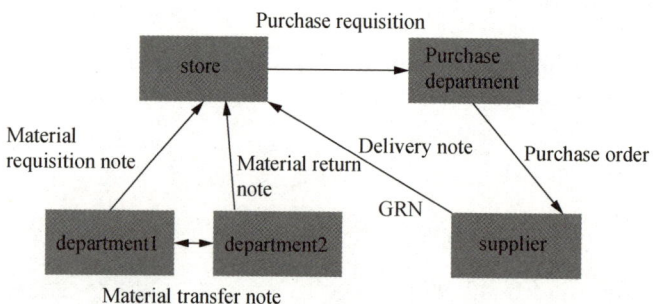

Inventory Control System

Perpetual inventory 永续盘存

Perpetual inventory refers to an **inventory recording system** whereby the records are **updated for each receipt and issue of inventory as it occurs**.

Stocktake 存货盘点

The inventory count (stocktake) involves counting the physical inventory on hand at a certain date, and then checking this against the balance shown in the inventory records.

The inventory count can be carried out on a continuous or periodic basis.

- **Periodic stocktaking** is a process whereby all inventory items are physically counted and valued at a set point in time, usually **at the end of an accounting period**. 一个时间点全部盘点
- **Continuous stocktaking** is counting and valuing selected items at different times on a rotating basis. 循环盘点
- **Discrepancies** (investigate & take appropriate action to ensure that does not happen again.)

2. Inventory control level

2.1 Free inventory

Free inventory represents **what is really available for future use** and is calculated as follows. 未来一段时间可供我们使用的存货

Free inventory level = | Materials in inventory
+ Materials on order from suppliers
− Materials requisitioned, not yet issued | （需要记忆）

2.2 Cost involved with inventory

○ Purchase costs/production cost
○ Holding costs
○ Ordering costs

The overall objective of inventory control is, therefore, to maintain inventory levels so that **the total of the above costs is minimized**.

2.2.1 Holding cost 仓储成本

○ warehouse rental and stores operations
○ interest charges-Holding inventories involves the **tying up of capital** （cash）on which interest must be paid. 占用资金的利息
○ insurance costs 保险
○ risk of obsolescence, deterioration

2.2.2 Ordering cost 采购成本

1) Purchased from external sources 外购
○ Clerical and administrative costs associated with purchasing, accounting for and receiving goods 采购行为导致的费用
○ Transport costs

2) Manufacture inventory for its own use 自产
○ **Production run costs/set-up cost**, for inventory which is manufactured internally rather than purchased from external sources 机器设备的调试

2.3 Economic order quantity (EOQ)-Purchase 经济订货量

The EOQ is the order quantity which **minimizes inventory costs**

Assumption：(背诵)

○ Annual Demand and Price per unit of inventory is constant (i.e no bulk discount)
○ no safe inventory
○ Inventory is replenished instantaneously
○ Inventory is used on a constant speed basis

Conclusion：

Average inventory = order quantity/2 = Q/2

Relevant cost：

Holding cost = $Q/2 \times C_h$

Ordering cost = D/Q×C_o

Economic order quantity (EOQ)

$$EOQ = \sqrt{\frac{2C_0 D}{C_H}}$$ (given to you in the exam)

where C_H = cost of holding one unit of invertory for one time period

C_0 = cost of ordering a consignment from a supplier

D = demand during the time period

2.4 Bulk discounts 批量折扣

Discounts may be available if the order quantity is above a certain size.

Relevant cost: purchase cost, holding cost and ordering cost.

2.5 Economic batch quantity (EBQ)-Production

Manufacturing inventory for its own use.

The EBQ is a modification of the EOQ and is used when **resupply is gradual** instead of **instantaneous.** 企业订购的存货不是一次性到位的情况。

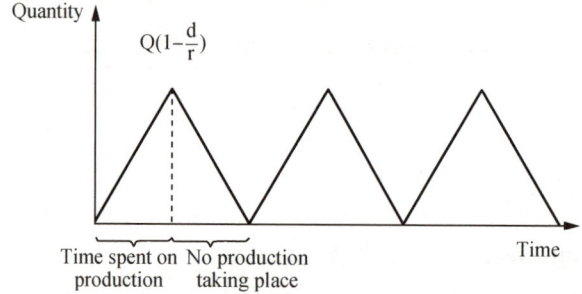

$$EBQ \text{ is } \sqrt{\frac{2C_0 D}{C_H(1-D/R)}}$$ (given in exam)

where R = the production rate per time period (which must exceed the inventory usage)

Q = the amount produced in each batch

D = the usage per time period

C_0 = the set-up cost per batch

C_H = the holding cost per unit of invertory per time period

Average inventory = Q * (1 − D/R)/2

Total holding cost = Q * (1 − D/R)/2 * C_h

Ordering cost = D/Q * C_o

2.6 When to re-order

The reorder level is determined by consideration of the following:

The maximum rate of consumption

The maximum lead time

(Lead time is the time between placing an order with a supplier, and the inventory becoming available for use.)

- **Reorder level = maximum usage × maximum lead time**

Purpose of Reorder level: to avoid stock out risk 避免没有存货的风险

- **Maximum level 警示值(太多)**

This acts as a **warning level** to signal to management that inventories are reaching a potentially wasteful level. 资源浪费

Maximum level = reorder level − (minimum usage × minimum lead time) + reorder quantity

- **Minimum level 警示值(太少)**

This is a warning level to draw management attention to the fact that inventories are approaching a dangerously low level and that stockout is possible.

Minimum level = reorder level − (average usage × average lead time)

- **Safety/Buffer inventories** are the level of units maintained in case there is **unexpected demand**. 安全存货(极限)

- **Total holding cost**

No safety inventory 没有安全存货时

Place order from supplier: total holding cost = $Q/2 * C_h$

Manufacturing inventory for its own use, holding cost = $[Q * (1 - D/R)]/2 * C_h$

With safety inventory 有安全存货时

total holding cost = $(Q/2 + \text{safety inventory}) * C_h$

3. Inventory valuation

SOFP:

For financial accounting purposes, inventories are valued at the lower of cost and net realizable value(NRV). 成本与可变现净值孰低 NRV = revenue-selling cost

P/L:

Cost of sales = opening inventory + purchase/production-closing inventory

- **FIFO(first in, first out) 先进先出法**

FIFO assumes that materials are issued out of inventory in the order in which they were delivered into inventory; issues are priced at the cost of the earliest delivery remaining in inventory.

- **LIFO(last in, first out) 后进先出法**

LIFO assumes that materials are issued out of inventory in the reverse order to which they were delivered: the most recent deliveries are issued before earlier ones, and issues are priced accordingly.

- **AVCO(cumulative weighted average pricing) 累计加权平均法**

A new weighted average price is calculated when a new receipt of material occurs. Each issue is charged at a this average cost.

The balance of inventory remaining would have the same unit valuation.

○ **AVCO（periodic weighted average）期间加权平均法**

The periodic weighted average pricing method calculates an average price at the end of the period, based on the total purchases in that period.

$$\text{Periodic weighted average} = \frac{\text{Cost of opening inventory} + \text{total cost of receipts}}{\text{Units of opening inventory} + \text{total units received}}$$

定性分析：

○ 假设存货单价随着时间而上升

FIFO 跟 AVCO 相比 cost of sales understated　INV overstated

LIFO 跟 AVCO 相比 cost of sales overstated　INV understated

○ 假设存货单价随着时间而下降

FIFO 跟 AVCO 相比 cost of sales overstated　INV understated

LIFO 跟 AVCO 相比 cost of sales understated　INV overstated

优缺点：

	Advantages	Disadvantages
FIFO	Logical, probably represents what is physically happening 符合实际逻辑	Cumber some to operate (need to identify each batch separately)
	Easy to under standard explain	Difficult to make cost comparison and decision making due to price variation of the same materials
	Inventory values at SOFP are close to market value 存货接近市场价值 SOFP 准确	Issue prices can lag behind market value if inflation is high P/L 不准确

	Advantages	Disadvantages
LIFO	Issues are at close to market value P/L 准确	Inventory values at SOFP lag behind market values SOFP 不准确
		Cumber some to operate
		Opposite to what is physically happening normally; Difficult to explain
		Decision making can be difficult due to price variations

	Advantages	Disadvantages
AVCO	Price fluctuations are smoothed out so decision making is easier 容易做决策	Resulting price rarely an actual price 数据不是真实的
	Easier to administer than FIFO and LIFO	Prices lag a little behind market values if there is gradual inflation

4. Accounting for materials costs

Double entry book keeping 复式记账

有借必有贷,借贷必相等。

- Raw materials of $500,000 were purchased on credit from a supplier

  Debit: Material control account $500,000

  Credit: Payables control account $500,000

- Raw materials costing $10,000 were returned to the same supplier due to defects.

  Debit: Payables control account $10,000

  Credit: Material control account $10,000

- The total stores requisitions for direct material for the period were $400,000.

  Debit: Work In Process account $400,000

  Credit: Material control account $400,000

- Total issues for indirect materials during the period were $15,000.

  Debit: Factory overheads account $15,000

  Credit: Material control account $15,000

- $5,000 of unused material was returned to stores from production.

  Debit: Material control account $5,000

  Credit: Work In Process account $5,000

Material control account

1-Payables control account	500,000	2-Payables control account	10,000
5-Work in process account	5,000	3-Work in process account	400,000
		4-Factory overhead account	15,000
		Closing inventory (bal. figure)	80,000
	505,000		505,000

Chapter 7

Accounting for labour

1. Measuring labour activity

1) **Capacity ratio** = Actual hours worked/Hours budgeted

2) **Efficiency ratio** = Expected hours to make actual output/Actual hours taken

3) **Production volume ratio**

= actual output/budgeted output

= Capacity ratio × Efficiency ratio

(These ratios are usually expressed as '%'.)

4) **Labour turnover 员工流动性**

Labour turnover is the rate at which employees leave a company and this rate should be kept as low as possible.

Labour turnover rate = replacements/average number of employees in period

5) **Remuneration methods**

Time work

Piece work

Bonus/Incentive scheme

○ **Time work 计时工资**

Wages = Hours worked × rate of pay per hour

If an employee works for more hours than the basic daily requirement he may be entitled to an **overtime payment**. Hours of overtime are usually paid at a **premium rate**.

Overtime payment rate = basic rate + overtime premium

Idle time 空闲时间

Idle time occurs when employees cannot get on with their work, through **no fault of their own**. 不是员工的原因

Idle time has a cost because employees will still be paid their basic wage or salary for these unproductive hours and so there should be a record of idle time. 一般情况下在正常的时间当中才会发生空闲时间

Idle time ratio = idle hours/total hours

○ **Piece work 计件工资**

Differential piecework schemes offer an incentive to employees to increase their output by paying higher rates for increased levels of production.

Employers should obviously be careful to make it clear whether they intend to pay the increased rate on **all units produced**, or on the **extra output only**.

○ **Bonus/Incentive schemes** 奖励机制（针对小时工资的员工制定）

A **high day-rate system** is a system where employees are paid a **high hourly wage rate in the expectation that they will work more efficiently** than similar employees on a lower hourly rate in a different company. 支付最高小时工资

An **individual bonus scheme** is a remuneration scheme whereby individual employees qualify for a bonus on top of their basic wage，with each person's bonus being calculated separately. 个人奖励机制

A **group bonus scheme** is an incentive plan which is related to the output performance of an entire group of workers，a department，or even the whole factory. 团队奖励机制

2. Accounting for labour costs

The **wages control account** acts as a sort of 'collecting place' for net wage paid and deductions made from gross pay.

The first step is to determine which wage costs are direct and which are indirect. The **direct labour cost** will be debited to the **work in progress account** and the **indirect labour cost** will be debited to the **production overhead account**.

Dr：Work in progress account
　　Cr：Wages control account
Dr：Production overhead account
　　Cr：Wages control account

Direct Workers	
Normal Basic Pay	Direct cost
Over time basic pay element	Direct cost
O/T Premium(溢价)	Indirect cost

Indirect Workers	
Normal Basic Pay	Indirect cost
Overtime basic pay element	Indirect cost
O/T Premium	Indirect cost

OT Worked at the **specific request** of a customer to get the order completed.

		Direct workers	Indirect workers
Specific Order	Basic pay rate	Direct cost	Direct cost
	O/T premium	Direct cost	Direct cost

Worked regularly by a production department in the normal course of operations

		Direct workers	**Indirect workers**
Work regularly	Basic pay rate	Direct cost	Indirect cost
	O/T premium	Direct cost	Indirect cost

Bonuses, NIC, idle time cost	Indirect cost

Chapter 8

Accounting for overhead

1. Absorption costing

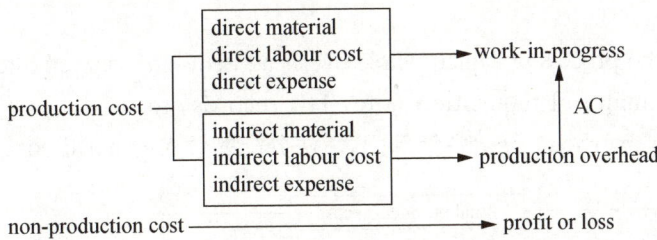

1.1 Pricing decision

The selling price can be expressed as a percentage margin or a percentage mark-up.

A selling price based on a 20% mark-up means that profit is 20% of cost.

A selling price based on a 20% margin means that profit is 20% of selling price.

1) **Mark-up** Cost   100%
               Profit   20%
               Selling price   120%
2) **Margin** Cost   80%
               Profit   20%
               Selling price   100%

The **objective** of absorption costing is to include in the total cost of a product an appropriate share of the organization's total overhead.

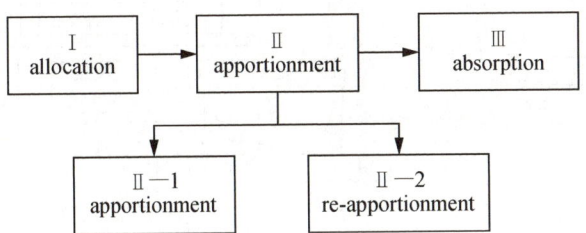

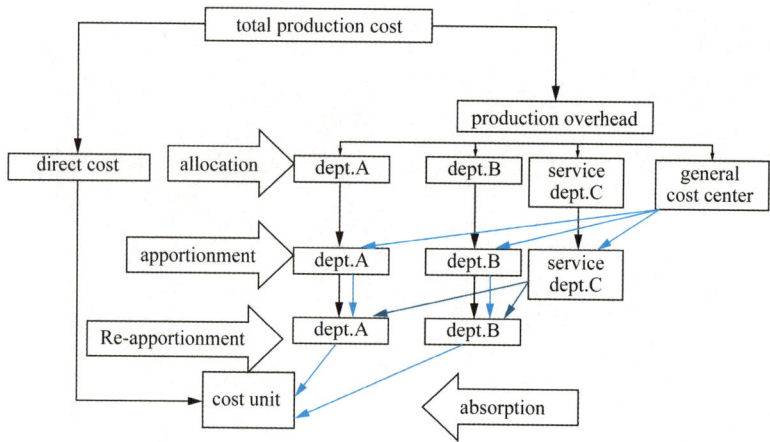

1.2 Three stages of absorption costing

Ⅰ Allocation

Allocation is the process by which whole overhead items are charged direct to a cost center According to material requisition note，HR records etc.

将 production overhead 分给各个部门，无法分配的放入 general cost center。

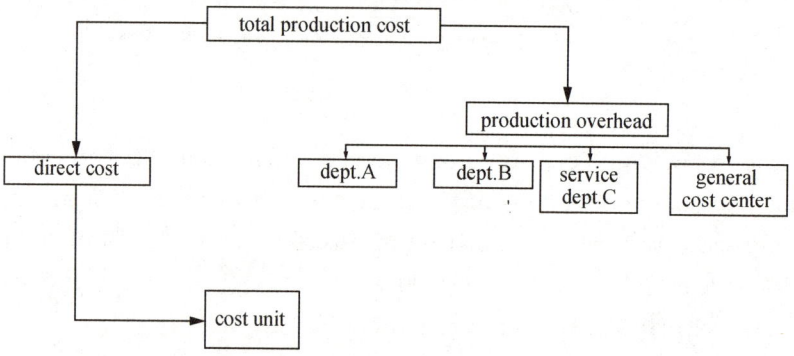

Ⅱ-1 Apportionment

Apportionment is a procedure whereby indirect costs are spread fairly between cost centers. 将 general cost center 通过 OAR 分摊给各个部门。

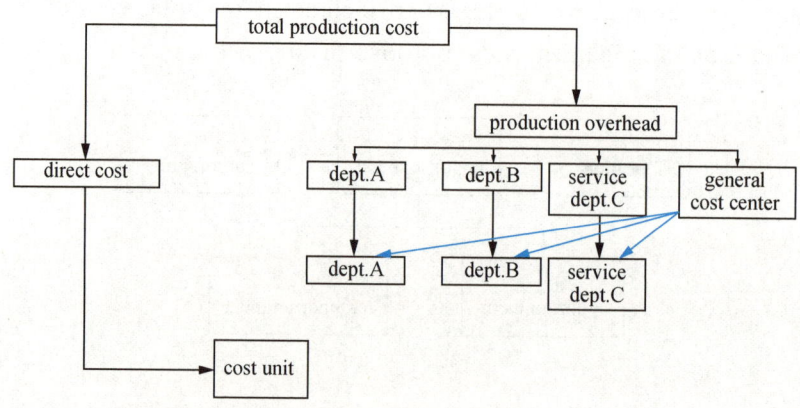

Chapter 8 Accounting for overhead

Overhead costs should be shared out on a fair basis.

Overhead to which the basis applies	Basis
Rent, rates, heating and light, repairs and depreciation of buildings	Floor are a occupied by each cost centre
Depreciation, insurance of equipment	Cost or book value of equipment
canteen, welfare, first aid	Number of employees, or labour hours worked in each cost center

Ⅱ-2 reapportionment

Our aim is to reapportion all the service department costs to the production departments as only production departments produce goods that will ultimately be sold. 将服务部门的成本再分摊给生产部门。

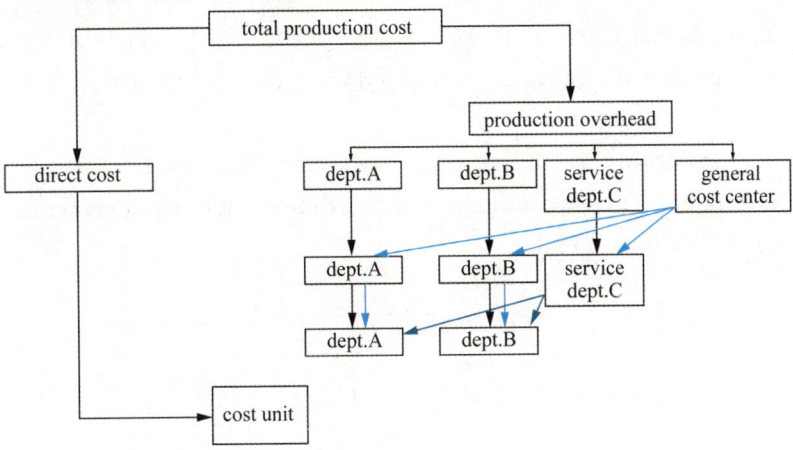

Basis of reapportionment should be fair:

Service cost center	Possible basis of apportionment
Stores	Number or cost value of material requisitions
Maintenance	Hours of maintenance work done for each cost centre
Production planning	Direct labour hours worked in each production cost centre
Canteen	Number of employees

Applying situation:

Two or more service cost centers work for each other — that is, service departments use each other's services.

1) **Direct method**

The direct method of reapportionment involves apportioning the costs of each **service cost center to production cost center only**.

Remember that **all service department costs** must be allocated — that is, both general overheads that were apportioned and those overheads that are specific to the individual departments (allocated overhead). 只让服务部门的成本进入生产部门，不考虑服务部门之间的分摊。

2) **Step-down method**

Step 1

Reapportion **one of the service cost center's overheads** to all the other centres which make use of its services (production and service). 挑出一个服务部门按照实际情况分摊。

Step 2

Reapportion the overheads of the remaining service cost center to the production departments only. The other service cost center is ignored. 其他服务部门只分摊给生产部门，不再考虑服务部门之间的分摊。

3) **Reciprocal method**

a) **Reciprocal method/algebraic method/repeated distribution method**

Where service center costs are reapportioned to both the production departments and service departments that use services. 按照实际情况分摊。手动方法或者方程式方法。

Ⅲ Overhead absorption

Overhead absorption is the process whereby overhead costs allocated and apportioned to production cost centers are added to unit, job or batch costs. 将各个生产部门的成本吸收入产品的单位成本中。

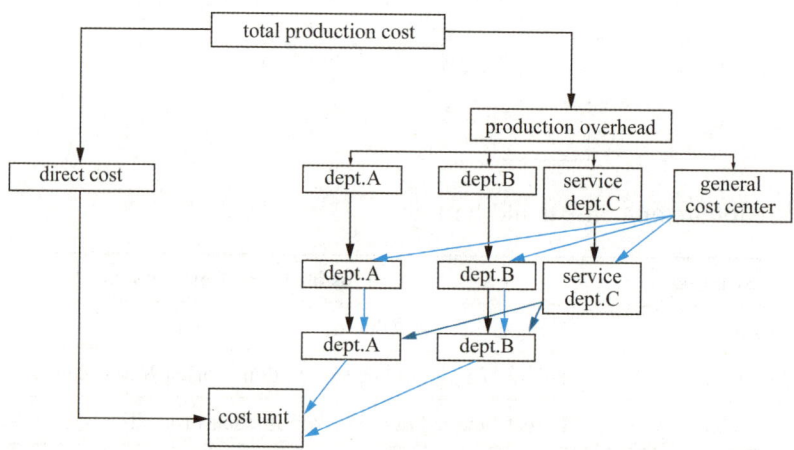

b) **Predetermined OAR = budgeted overhead/budgeted activity level**

◆ **Over and under absorption**

Over and under absorption of overheads occurs because the predetermined overhead absorption rates are based on estimates.

➢ Over absorption means that the overheads charged to the cost of sales are greater then the overheads actually incurred.

Absorbed overhead＞actual overhead 吸收＞实际

➢ Under absorption means that insufficient overheads have been included in the cost of sales.

Absorbed overhead＜actual overhead 吸收＜实际

2. Accounting for overhead

EG：

Mariott's Motorcycles absorbs production overheads at the rate of ＄0.50 per operating hour. Actual data for one month was as follows.

Production overheads　　46,500

Operating hours　　　　　90,000

Absorbed overhead＝90,000×0.5＝45,000

Under absorption：

Production overheads account			
Cash/payable	46,500	Absorbed into WIP	45,000
		Under/over absorption	1,500
	46,500		46,500

Under/over absorption account			
Production overheads	1,500	profit or loss	1,500
	1,500		1,500

Over absorption：(if Production overheads is 50,000)

Production overheads account			
Cash/payable	46,500	Absorbed into WIP	50,000
Under/over absorption	3,500		
	50,000		50,000

Under/over absorption account			
profit or loss	3,500	Production overheads	3,500
	3,500		3,500

Chapter 9

Absorption costing and marginal costing

1. Profit using absorption costing (AC profit)
Method 1:

Sales		X
cost of sales		
opening inventory	X	
(DM+DL+DE+absorbed OH/unit)		
Production	X	
closing inventory	(X)	(X)
less: under absorbed overhead		(X)
add: over absorbed overhead		X
gross profit		X
non-production overhead-fixed		(X)
non-production overhead-variable		(X)
Net profit/(loss)		X/(X)

Method 2:

Sales	X
cost of sales	
(value/unit X units sold)	(X)
less: under absorbed overhead	(X)
add: over absorbed overhead	X
gross profit	X
non-production overhead-fixed	(X)
non-production overhead-variable	(X)
Net profit/(loss)	X/(X)

2. Marginal costing

Marginal cost is the **variable cost** of one unit of product or services.
边际成本法下的计算均为实际数据。

Chapter 9 Absorption costing and marginal costing

The marginal production cost per unit of an item usually consists of the following:
- Direct materials
- Direct labour
- Direct expenses
- Variable production overheads

Marginal costing: Cost of sales 卖掉的产品所对应的边际成本（生产＋非生产）

Opening inventory + Production cost − Closing inventory + Variable selling cost/variable non-production overhead

Contribution is an important measure in marginal costing, and it is calculated as the **difference between sales value and marginal(variable) cost of sales.** 边际贡献

Profit = Contribution − fixed overhead

3. Profit using marginal costing (MC profit)

Method 1:

Sales		X
cost of sales		
opening inventory		X
(DM + DL + DE + variable production OH/unit)		
Production		X
closing inventory	(X)	(X)
variable non-production overhead		(X)
(sales units X variable selling cost/unit)		
Contribution		X
production fixed cost		(X)
non-production fixed cost		(X)
net profit/(loss)		X/(X)

Method 2:

Sales	X
cost of sales	
variable production cost	(X)
(DM + DL + DE + VPOH/unit) X sales units	
variable non-production overhead	(X)
Contribution	X
production fixed cost	(X)
non-production fixed cost	(X)
net profit/(loss)	X/(X)

4. Absorption costing VS Marginal costing

AC profit

sales		x
cost of sales		
opening inventory (DM+DL+DE+absorbed OH/unit)	x	
production	x	
closing inventory	(x)	(x)
less: under absorbed overhead		(x)
add: over absorbed overhead		x
gross profit		x
non-production overhead-fixed		(x)
non-production overhead-variable		(x)
Net profit/(loss)		x/(x)

MC profit

sales		x
cost of sales		
opening inventory (DM+DL+DE+VPOH/unit)	x	
production	x	
closing inventory	(x)	(x)
variable non-production overhead		(x)
contribution		x
production fixed cost		(x)
non-production fixed cost		(x)
net profit/(loss)		x/(x)

5. Reconciling profits

AC profit = MC profit + fixed production overhead/unit (closing inventory-opening inventory)

- If inventory levels have **gone up** (that is, closing inventory > opening inventory or production > sales) then absorption costing profit will be greater than marginal costing profit. 存货水平上升,AC>MC
- If inventory levels have **gone down** (that is, closing inventory < opening inventory or production < sales) then absorption costing profit will be less that marginal costing profit. 存货水平下降,AC<MC
- 关于 **closing inventory valuation**, AC>MC

Chapter 10

Process costing

1. Process costing

Process costing is a costing method used where it is **not possible to identify separate units** of production, or jobs, usually because of the **continuous nature** of the production processes involved. 分布成本法：成本是连在一起的，无法分开，例如水、油、饮料、蛋糕、化学试剂。

1) Feature of process costing 特征

a) The output of one process becomes the input to the next. 一个流程的产出是下一个流程的投入。

b) There is often a loss in process due to spoilage, wastage, evaporation an so on. 有损失

c) There will usually be closing work in progress which must be valued. 在产品出现 WIP

d) Output from production may be a single product, but there may also be a **by-product** or **joint products**. 产出不一定是单个产品，副产品、联产品。

2) **Conversion cost**: direct labour and production O/H 转换成本：直接劳动力加生产费用

3) Losses in process costing

a) Normal/expected loss is the loss expected during a process. It is not given a cost. 正常损失 cost = 0

b) Abnormal loss is the extra loss resulting when actual loss is greater than normal or expected loss, and it is given a cost. 非正常损失 cost = value of finished good

c) Abnormal gain is the gain resulting when actual loss is less than the normal or expected loss, and it is given a 'negative cost'. 非正常收获 negative cost = value of finished good

4) Cost per unit of output = cost incurred/expected output

5) Four key steps: 四步曲

a) Determine output and losses

b) Calculate cost per unit of output, losses and WIP

c) Calculate total cost of output, losses and WIP

d) Complete account

6) Losses with scrap value 损失有残余价值

Scrap is 'Discarded material having some value.'

√ The **scrap value of normal loss** is usually **deducted** from the **cost of materials**. 正常损失的残余价值可以扣减

Cost per unit of output = cost incurred − scrap value of normal loss/expected output

√ The **scrap value of abnormal loss (or abnormal gain)** is usually **set off against its cost**, in an abnormal loss (abnormal gain) account. 非正常损失的残余价值不可以扣减,影响最终的 P/L。

EG:

JJ has a factory which operates two production processes, cutting and pasting. Normal loss in each process is 10%. Scrapped units out of the cutting process sell for $3 per unit whereas scrapped units out of the pasting process sell for $5. Output from the cutting process is transferred to the pasting process; output from the pasting process is finished output ready for sale.

Relevant information about costs for control period 7 is as follows.

	Cutting process		Pasting process	
	Units	$	Units	$
Input materials	18,000	54,000		
Transferred to pasting process	16,000			
Materials from cutting process			16,000	
Added materials			14,000	70,000
Labour and overheads		32,400		135,000
Output to finished goods			28,000	
Required				

Prepare accounts for the cutting process, the pasting process, abnormal loss, abnormal gain and scrap.

◇ **Cutting:**

Step 1

Input	18,000
Normal loss (10%)	(1,800)
Expected output	16,200
Actual output	16,000
Abnormal loss	200

Step 2

Cost per unit of output = cost incurred − scrap value of normal loss/expected output

$= (54,000 + 32,400 − 1,800 * 3)/16,200$

$= 5$

Step 3

	Units		$
Normal loss	1,800	* 3	5,400
Abnormal loss	200	* 5	1,000
Output	16,000	* 5	80,000
			86,400

Step 4

Cutting process account

Material	54,000	Normal loss (scrap value)	1,800	5,400
DL&OH	32,400	Abnormal loss	200	1,000
		Output	16,000	80,000
	86,400			86,400

Abnormal loss account

Cutting process A/C	200	1,000	Scrap value A/C	200	600
			Profit or loss		400
		1,000			1,000

Scrap value account

Cutting process A/C		5,400	Profit or loss		6,000
Abnormal loss		600			
		6,000			6,000

◇ **Pasting:**

Step 1
Input

Material from cutting process	16,000
Added material	14,000
Normal loss (10%)	(3,000)
Expected output	27,000
Actual output	28,000
Abnormal gain	1,000

Step 2

Cost per unit of output = cost incurred − scrap value of normal loss/expected output

$$= (80{,}000 + 70{,}000 + 135{,}000 - 3{,}000 * 5)/27{,}000$$
$$= 10$$

Step 3

	Units		$
Normal loss	3,000	*5	15,000
Abnormal gain	1,000	*10	(10,000)
Output	28,000	*10	280,000
			285,000

Step 4

Pasting process account					
Material			Normal loss		
From cutting process	16,000	80,000	(scrap value)	3,000	15,000
Added material	14,000	70,000	Output	28,000	280,000
DL&OH		135,000			
Abnormal gain	1,000	10,000			
		295,000			295,000

Abnormal gain account				
Scrap value A/C	5,000	Pasting process A/C	1,000	10,000
Profit or loss	5,000			
	10,000			10,000

Scrap value account			
Cutting process A/C	5,400	Profit or loss	16,000
Abnormal loss	600	Abnormal gain	5,000
Pasting process A/C	15,000		
	21,000		21,000

7) Losses with disposal cost 损失需要处理成本

Increase the process costs by the cost of **disposing of the units of normal loss** and use the resulting cost per unit to value good output and abnormal loss/gain.

只有 abnormal loss 对应的 disposal cost 才会影响 cost per unit。

Cost per unit of output = cost incurred ＋ disposal cost of normal loss/expected output

Chapter 10 Process costing

8) **Valuing closing WIP 期末在产品价值（没有 opening WIP）**

Equivalent units are notional whole units which represent incomplete work, and which are used to apportion costs between work in process and completed output. 约当产量

Equivalent units = amounts of WIP × degree of completion

Degree of completion：

✓ **General condition：**
- Direct materials. These are added in full at the start of processing, and so any closing WIP will have 100% of their direct material content.
  Direct materials 开始时全部放入 100%
- Direct labour and production overhead. These are usually assumed to be incurred at an even rate through the production process.
  Direct labour and production overhead 按照百分比

✓ **Special condition：**
- Output from a previous process may be introduced into the subsequent process all at once, so that closing inventory is 100% complete in respect of these materials.
  一类 Direct materials 开始时全部放入 100%
- Further materials may be added gradually during the process, so that closing inventory is only partially complete in respect of these added materials.
  另一类 Direct materials 按照百分比放入
- Labour and overhead may be 'added' at yet another different rate. When production overhead is absorbed on a labour hour basis, however, we should expect the degree of completion on overhead to be the same as the degree of completion on labour.
  Direct labour and production overhead 按照百分比

Step 1

计算 Equivalent units

Step 2

计算 Cost per EU

Step 3

分别计算 FG & Closing WIP 的价值

9) **Valuing opening WIP 期初在产品价值**

✓ **FIFO method**

The FIFO method of valuation deals with production on a first in, first out basis.

The assumption is that the first units completed in any period are the units of opening inventory that were held at the beginning of the period.

先加工 opening WIP 成 FG，看对产出的贡献计算对应价值。

✓ **Weighted average cost method**

An alternative to FIFO is the weighted average cost method of inventory valuation which calculates a weighted average cost of units produced from both opening inventory and units introduced in the current period.

By this method no distinction is made between units of opening inventory and New units introduced to the process during the accounting period. The cost of opening inventory is added to costs incurred during the period, and completed units of opening inventory are each given a value of one full equivalent unit of production. 类似于 Valuing closing WIP 的计算

2. Joint products and by-products

The point at which joint products and by-products become separately identifiable is known as the **split-off point** or **separation point**.

Costs incurred up to this point are called **common costs or joint costs**.

是不是主要销售的产品(主营业务):

√ **Joint products** are two or more products which are output from the same processing operation, but which are indistinguishable from each other up to their point of separation. 联产品

√ A **by-product** is a supplementary or secondary product (arising as the result of process) whose value is small relative to that of the principal product.

By-product 处理方式:

1) The most common method of account for by-products is to deduct the **net realizable value** of the by-product from the cost of the main products.

(By-product sales revenue is **credited to the process account.**)

2) By-product sales revenue is **credited to the sales account**

Common/Joint cost

√ **Physical measurement** 物理特点

√ **Sales value of production** 销售价值

It assumes that all joint products achieve the same profit margin.

Chapter 11

Job, batch and service costing

1. Job costing

A job is a cost unit which consists of a single **order** or **contract**.

Job costing is a costing method applied where work is undertaken to **customers' special requirements** and each order is of comparatively short duration. 适用于非标准化生产产品或服务，根据顾客要求量身定制。

2. Batch costing

A batch is a group of similar articles which maintains its identity during one or more stages of production and is treated as a cost unit.

Batch costing is **similar to job costing** in that each batch of similar articles is separately identifiable. The cost per unit manufactured in a batch is the total batch cost divided by the number of units in the batch. 适用于标准化生产产品，批次生产。

3. Service costing

Service costing is a costing method concerned with establishing the costs, not of items of production, but of **services** rendered. 提供标准化服务。

Service costing VS. product costing

The cost of **direct materials** consumed will be relatively small compared to the labour, direct expenses and overheads cost. 服务行业 direct materials 占比较少

Composite cost unit：复合成本单位

Service	Cost unit
Road, rail and air transport services	Passenger/mile, ton/mile, tonne/kilometre
Hotels	Occupied bed-night
Maintenance	Man-hour

Chapter 12

Alternative costing principles

1. Activity based costing (ABC)

An alternative to the traditional methods of **absorption costing** is activity based costing (ABC). ABC 是 AC 的变形。

ABC involves the identification of the factors (**cost drivers**) which cause the costs of an organization's major activities. Support overheads are charged to products on the basis of their usage of an activity.

识别行为,将导致的成本分到总行为当中,谁发生该行为就分摊成本。

Advantages of ABC:

a) ABC uses cost driver as absorption base and attempts to provide meaningful product costs.

b) ABC recognizes the complexity of manufacturing with its multiple cost drivers.

c) ABC facilitates a good understanding of what drives overhead costs.

Criticisms of ABC

a) Some measure of arbitrary cost apportionment may still be required at the cost pooling stage for items.

b) If an ABC system has many cost pools, the amount of apportionment needed may be greater than ever.

2. Total quality management (TQM) 全面质量管理

Total quality management (TQM) is the process of applying a zero defect philosophy to the management of all resources and relationships within an organization as a means of developing and sustaining a culture of continuous improvement which focuses on meeting customer expectations. 没有任何质量问题的发生

Principles:

a) One of the basic principles of TQM is that the cost of preventing mistakes is less than the cost of correcting them once they occur. The aim should therefore be to get things right first time. 防止错误发生的成本＜修正错误的成本

b) A second basic principle of TQM is dissatisfaction with the status quo: the belief that it is always possible to improve and so the aim should be to '**get it more right next**

Chapter 12 Alternative costing principles

time.'

下次做总比这次做得更好,总有办法做得更好。

c) Good quality saves money; Poor quality costs money. 好的质量会节省成本

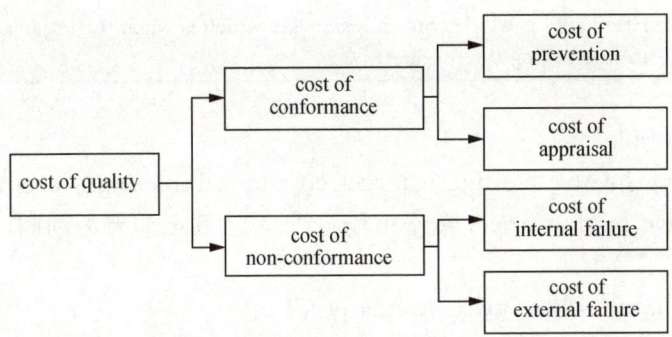

与质量相关的成本可以分成 cost of conformance(以生产完成从生产线下来的时间节点为区分)和 cost of non-conformance,在生产完成从生产线下来时间节点之前发生的成本为 cost of conformance,之后发生的成本为 cost of non-conformance。

Cost of prevention:生产产品之前和生产过程当中,如生产流程优化成本。

Cost of appraisal:生产完后,运下生产线之后发生的成本,如 inspection 质检成本。

产品离开运给消费之前是 cost of internal failure,如 re-inspection 再检查;之后是 cost of external failure,如赔偿费。

3. Life cycle costing

Life cycle costing tracks and accumulates costs and revenues attributable to each product over the entire product life cycle. 考虑产品整个生命周期的全部成本,而非一个会计年度。

A product life cycle can be divided into **four phases**.
- Introduction 引入期
- Growth 增长期
- Maturity 成熟期
- Decline 下降期

Introduction	○ Product is introduced to the market ○ Potential customers will be **unaware** of the product or service, therefore may have to **spend further on advertising**
Growth	Product gains a **bigger market** as demand builds up. Sales Revenues increase and the product **begins to make a profit**
Maturity	○ **Growth** in demand for the product will **slow down** and it will enter a period of relative maturity ○ It will continue to be profitable. The product may be **modified or improved**, as a means of sustaining its demand

Decline	○ The market will have bought enough of the product and it will therefore reach 'saturation point' ○ Demand will start to fall ○ Eventually it will become a **loss-maker** which is when the organization should decide to stop selling the product

4. Target costing

Target costing involves setting a target cost by subtracting a desired profit margin from a competitive market price. 拿来市场定价，减去我们想要的利润，得出我们的目标成本。

Target cost = target selling price − target profit

Cost gap = estimated cost − target cost 识别成本差额，并使其缩小。

Chapter 13

Budgeting

1. Budgetary planning and control systems

A budget is a **quantified plan** of action for a forth coming accounting period.

A budget is a plan of what the organisation is aiming to achieve and what it has set as a target whereas a forecast is an estimate of what is likely to occur in the future.

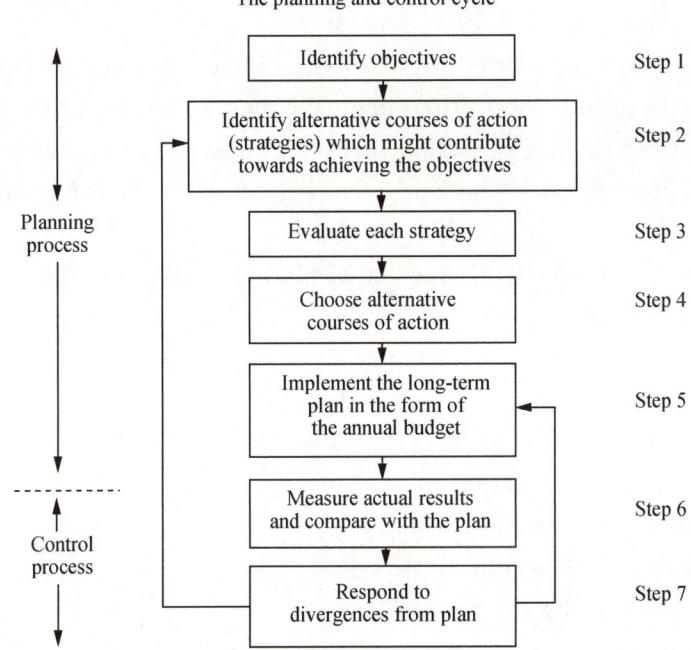

The planning and control cycle

The **objectives** of a budgetary planning and control system are as follows.
- To ensure the achievement of the organization's objectives
- To communicate ideas and plans
- To coordinate activities
- To provide a framework for responsibility accounting
- To establish a system of control
- To motivate employees to improve their performance

2. Fixed flexible and flexed budgets

A fixed budget is a budget which is designed to remain unchanged regardless of the volume of output or sales achieved. 固定预算，不可调整，发生在计划阶段。

A flexible budget is a budget which, by recognizing different cost behavior patterns, is designed to change as volumes of output changes. 弹性预算，做多个预算备用，发生在计划阶段。

A flexed budget is a budget that is prepared at the actual activity level that was achieved in the period. 弹性预算，根据实际情况做出的预算，发生在分析复核阶段。

3. Spreadsheet

A spreadsheet is an electronic piece of paper divided into rows and columns. 电子表单

The intersection of a row and a column is known as a cell. Excel 表格

4. The budgetary process

◆ Budget preparation process 预算流程步骤

Step 1 Communicating details of the budget policy and budget guideline

➢ The long-term plan is the starting point for the preparation of the annual budget.

➢ The budget manual is a collection of instructions governing the responsibilities of persons and the procedures, forms and records relating to the preparation and use of budgetary data.

➢ The budget committee is the co-ordinating body in the preparation and administration of budgets.

Step 2 Determining the factor that restricts output

The principal budget factor (or key budget factor or limiting budget factor) is the factor that limits an organisation's performance for a given period and is often the starting point in budget preparation.

Step 3 Preparation of the sales budget

Step 4 Initial preparation of budgets

✓ Finished goods inventory budget
✓ Production budget
✓ Raw material usage budget
✓ Raw materials inventory budget
✓ Raw materials purchase budget

Step 5 Negotiation of budgets with superiors

Step 6 Co-ordination of budgets

Step 7 Final acceptance of the budget

They are summarised into a Master budget which consisting of a budgeted statement of profit or loss, budgeted statement of financial position and cash budget.

Step 8　Budget review

◆ **Functional budgets 部门预算**

Functional (or departmental) budgets are the budgets for the various functions and departments of an organisation. They therefore include production budgets, marketing budgets, sales budgets, personnel budgets, purchasing budgets and research and development budgets

◆ **Cash budget 现金预算**

Background：purchase/sales on credit

√ Cash in = opening receivables + sales − closing receivables
√ Cash out = opening payables + purchase − closing payables
√ Purchases = cost of sales + closing inventory − opening inventory

5. Making budgets work

1) Top-down budget 自上而下的预算

An imposed/top-down budget is 'A budget allowance which is set without permitting the ultimate budget holder to have the opportunity to participate in the budgeting process'.

高层直接制定预算，不需要下层人员参与，效率高但可能不切实际，下层人员不满。

The times when imposed budgets are effective 适用的公司情况：

a) In newly-formed organisations 新型公司
b) In very small businesses 小公司
c) During periods of economic hardship 公司处于经济困难时期
d) When operational managers lack budgeting skills 下层管理人员缺乏预算能力
e) When the organization's different units require precise coordination 公司各部门需要精确协调合作

➢ **Advantages of top-down budget**

√ Strategic objectives are likely to be incorporated into planned activities.
√ They use senior management's awareness of total resource availability.
√ They decrease the input from inexperienced or uninformed lower- level employees.
√ They decrease the period of time taken to draw up the budgets.

➢ **Disadvantages of top-down budget**

√ Lower-level management initiative may be stifled.
√ Dissatisfaction, defensiveness and low morale amongst employees. It is hard for people to be motivated to achieve targets set by somebody else.
√ The acceptance of organizational goals and objectives could be limited.
√ Managers who are performing operations on a day to day basis are likely to have a better understanding of what is achievable.

2) Bottom-up budget 自下而上的预算/参与型预算

Participative/bottom-up budgeting is 'A budgeting system in which all budget holders are given the opportunity to participate in setting their own budgets'. 下层管理人员参与制定预算,效率低但可能会更加符合实际情况,下层人员满意度高。

> **Advantages of participative budgets**
  - ✓ They are based on information from employees most familiar with the department.
  - ✓ In general they are more realistic.
  - ✓ Morale and motivation is improved.
  - ✓ They increase operational managers' commitment to organizational objectives.
  - ✓ Co-ordination between units is improved.
  - ✓ Individual managers' aspiration levels are more likely to be taken into account.

> **Disadvantages of participative budgets**
  - ✓ They consume more time.
  - ✓ Budgets may be unachievable of managers are not qualified to participate.
  - ✓ They may cause managers to introduce budgetary slack(budget padding)
  - ✓ They can support 'empire building' by subordinates.

6. Capital expenditure budgeting

Capital expenditure results in the acquisition of non-current assets or an improvement in their earning capacity, often represents a significant investment by company. 金额较大

Revenue expenditure is expenditure which is incurred for the purpose of the trade of the business or to maintain the existing earning capacity of non-current assets. 保持公司状态,金额较小。

Compound interest 复利

The amount of interest earned each year gets larger because we earn interest on both the original capital and also on the interest now earned in earlier years. 利滚利 $A(1+r)^n$

Time value of money 时间价值

$$S = P(1+r)^n$$

where
S = future value of the investment after n years
P = the amount invested now
r = the rate of interest
n = the number of years of the investment

Discounting 折现

To build up an investment to $5,000 after four years at 6% interest, we would need to invest now:

$$P = \frac{S}{(1+r)^n} = S \times \frac{1}{(1+r)^n}$$

Interest rate 利息率

A **nominal rate** of interest is an interest rate expressed as a per annum figure although the interest is compounded over a period of less than one year. 名义利率

An **effective annual rate** of interest is the corresponding annual rate when interest is compounded at intervals shorter than a year. 有效年利率

7. Methods of project appraisal 项目评估方法

1) Net present value 净现值

NPV＝PV of all cash inflow－PV of all cash outflows

It is often suggested that the discount rate which a company should use as its **cost of capital** is one that reflects the return expected by its investor in shares and loan notes, the opportunity cost of finance or **required rate of return.**

➤ **Annuity 年金**

Annuities are an annual cash payment or receipt which is the same amount every year for a number of years. 每年收到或支出相同金额，年限固定。

➤ **Perpetuity 永续年金**

A perpetuity is an annuity that lasts forever. The present value of a perpetuity of 'a' per annum, commencing in one year, is **PV＝a/r** where r is the cost of capital as a proportion. 每年收到或支出相同金额，一直持续，没有年限。

2) The payback period 投资回报期

The payback period is the time taken for the initial investment to be recovered in the cash inflows from the project.

The payback method is particularly relevant if there are **liquidity problems.** 避免发生流动性问题

➤ **Advantage of payback period**
- ✓ It is easy to calculate and understand. 简单易计算
- ✓ It is widely used in practice as a first screening method.
- ✓ It identified quick cash generators.

➤ **Disadvantage of payback period**
- ✓ The time value of money is ignored. 忽视时间价值
- ✓ It ignores any cash flow that occur after the project has paid for itself.

3) Discounted payback period 折现的投资回报期

The discounted payback method applies discounting to arrive at a payback period after which the NPV becomes positive.

4) Internal rate of return (IRR) 内含回报率

The internal rate of return technique uses a trial and error method to discover the discount rate which produces the NPV of zero. This discount rate will be the return forecast for the project. 使 NPV＝0 时的折现率

$$IRR = A + \left[\frac{a}{a-b} \times (B-A)\right]$$

Where

A is the discount rate which provides the positive NPV

a is the amount of the positive NPV

B is the discount rate which provides the negative NPV

b is the amount of the negative NPV

❖ 计算可使用相似三角形法

➢ **单个项目要不要做问题：**

想要从项目取得的回报率(r)＜IRR，项目可以做，否则不可以做。

➢ **在众多项目中优先做哪个项目：**

IRR 越大的越优先。

➢ **Advantage of IRR**

It takes into account the time value of money. 考虑时间价值

➢ **Disadvantage of IRR**

✓ Projects with unconventional cash flow can produce negative or multiple IRRs 可能会有多个 IRR

✓ It assumes that funds can be re-invested at a rate equivalent to the IRR. 再投资假设

✓ It may give conflicting recommendations with mutually exclusive projects，because the result is give in relative terms（%），and not in absolute term（$）As with NPV。

➢ **Relevant cash flow 相关现金流**

Relevant cost are future incremental cash flows. 直接由项目投资导致的

✓ **Avoidable costs** are costs which would not be incurred if the activity to which they relate did not exist. 可避免成本

✓ **Differential cost** is the difference in relevant cost between alternatives. 由于不同的选择导致的不同的成本

✓ **Opportunity cost** is the benefit which has been given up，by choosing one option instead of another. 机会成本 由于做 A 而不能做 B 导致的损失 B 的收益

➢ **Non-relevant cash flow 非相关现金流**

✓ A **sunk cost** is a cost which has already been incurred and hence should not be taken account of in decision making. 历史成本

✓ A **committed cost** is a future cash outflow that will be incurred anyway，whatever decision is taken now about alternative opportunities. 做不做都会发生的成本

✓ A **notional (imputed) cost** is a hypothetical accounting cost to reflect the use of a benefit for which no actual cash expense is incurred. 名义成本，并没有实质的现金流的来往，例如折旧。

Chapter 14

Standard costing

1. Standard costing

A **standard cost** is a predetermined estimated unit cost, used for inventory valuation and control. 标准成本,提前预测好的单位成本的预算。

Type of standard	Description
Ideal 完美标准	These are based on **perfect** operating conditions Maximise efficiency and minimise waste **Unfavourable motivational** impact
Attainable 可实现标准	Some allowance is made for wastage and inefficiencies Realistic but **challenging** target of efficiency
Current 现实标准	Based on current working conditions Do not attempt to improve on current levels of efficiency
Basic 平均标准	These are kept unaltered over a long period of time, and may be **out of date**

Standard costing is a control technique which compares standard costs and revenues with actual results to obtain variances which are used to improve performance. 把预算与实际情况相比较,求得差异并分析。

Chapter 15

Variance analysis

1. Basic variance analysis

1) Direct material cost variance

The **direct material total variance** is the difference between what the output actually cost and what it should have cost, in terms of material.

公式：direct material usage variance + direct material price variance = direct material total variance

The **direct material usage variance** is the difference between the standard quantity of materials that should have been used for the number of units actually produced, and the actual quantity of materials used, valued at the standard cost per unit of material. In other words, it is the difference between how much material should have been used and how much material was used, valued at standard cost.

公式：(material that should have been used − material that have been used) × standard cost per kg (基于：actual production units)

The **direct material price variance** is the difference between the standard cost and the actual cost for the actual quantity of material used or purchased. In other words, it is the difference between what the material did cost and what it should have cost.

公式：(actual cost per kg − standard cost per kg) × actual usage per kg

2) Direct labour cost variances

The **direct labour total variance** is the difference between what the output should have cost and what it did cost, in terms of labour.

公式：direct labour rate variance + direct labour efficiency variance = direct labour total variance

The **direct labour rate variance** is similar to the direct material price variance. It is the difference between the standard cost and the actual cost for the actual number of hours paid for. In other words, it is the difference between what the labour did cost and what it should have cost.

公式：(standard rate per hour − actual rate per hour) × actual hours worked or paid

The **direct labour efficiency variance** is similar to the direct material usage variance. It is the difference between the hours that should have been worked for the number of units actually produced, and the actual number of hours worked, valued at the standard rate per hour.

公式:(hours that should have been used - actual hours used) × standard rate per hour(基于:actual production units)

3) Variable production overhead variances

The **variable production overhead total variance** can be subdivided into the variable production overhead expenditure variance and the variable production overhead efficiency variance

公式:variable production OH efficiency variance + variable production OH expenditure variance = variable production overhead total variance

The **variable production OH efficiency variance** is exactly the same in hours as direct labour efficiency variance, but priced at the standard variable production overhead rate per hour.

公式:(actual active hours - standard hours) × standard variable production OH(基于:actual production units)

The **variable production OH expenditure variance** is the difference between the amount of variable production overhead that should have been incurred in the actual hours actively worked, and the actual amount of variable production overhead incurred.

公式:actual active hours × standard variable production OH - actual total variable production OH

It is usually assumed that variable overheads are incurred during active working hours.

假设以 hours 来吸收 POH,假设实际工作状态没有 idle time。

4) Fixed production overhead variances

Fixed overhead total variance is the difference between fixed overhead incurred and fixed overhead absorbed. In other words, it is the under- or over-absorbed fixed overhead.

公式:Fixed overhead expenditure variance + Fixed overhead volume variance = Fixed overhead total variance

Flexed budget - FOH 与 Actual FOH 的差异

Fixed overhead expenditure variance is the difference between the budgeted fixed overhead expenditure and actual fixed overhead expenditure.

Fixed budget - FOH 与 Actual FOH 的差异

Fixed overhead volume variance is the difference between actual and budgeted (planned) volume multiplied by the standard absorption rate per unit.

公式:Fixed overhead volume efficiency variance + Fixed overhead volume capacity variance = Fixed overhead volume variance

Fixed budget - FOH 与 Flexed budget - FOH 的差异

Fixed overhead volume efficiency variance is the difference between the number of hours that actual production should have taken, and the number of hours actually taken (that is, worked) multiplied by the standard absorption rate per hour.

公式:(standard hours - actual hours) × standard OAR(基于:actual production units)

Fixed overhead volume capacity variance is the difference between budgeted (planned) hours of work and the actual hours worked, multiplied by the standard absorption rate per hour.

公式:(actual hours worked - planned hours worked) × standard OAR

2. Further variance analysis

◆ Sales variance

The **selling price variance** is calculated as the difference between what the sales revenue should have been for the actual quantity sold, and what it was.

公式:(standard selling price - actual selling price) × actual quantity sales

The **sales volume variance** is the difference between the actual units sold and the budgeted (planned) quantity, valued at the standard profit/contribution per unit.

公式:(planned sales volume - actual sales volume) × standard selling profit per unit (AC) or standard contribution per unit(MC)

Chapter 16

Performance measurement

1. Performance measurement

Mission statements are formal statements of an organization's mission which describe the organization's basic purpose and what it is trying to achieve. 使命

A hierarchy of SMART goals and objectives cascades downwards from the mission statement, eventually providing the targets for the periodic budget process.

好目标特征:
- **S**pecific
- **M**easurable
- **A**ttainable
- **R**elevant
- **T**ime-bounded

A **critical success factor(CSF)** is 'An element of the organizational activity which is central to its future success. 关键成功因素

An organization can measure how well it is achieving the critical success factors through the use of key performance indicators (KPIs). KPIs 是判断 CSF 有没有实现达成的标准。

1.1 Financial performance measures

Performance measurement aims to establish how well something or somebody is doing in relation to a plan. 好？不好？

1.1.1 Profitability 盈利能力

1) Gross profit margin/Net profit margin

Gross profit margin = gross profit/sales

Net profit margin = net profit/sales

盈利能力,越高越好。

2) Return on investment(ROI)

Return on investment, also called return on capital employed (ROCE), is calculated as (profit/capital employed) × 100% and shows how much profit has been made in relation to the amount of resources invested.

ROCE = Controllable(traceable) profit/Controllable(traceable) investment * 100%

3) Residual income(RI)

RI = Controllable (traceable) profit － imputed interest charge on controllable (traceable) investment

1.1.2　Liquidity 流动性

1) Current ratio

Current ratio = current asset/current liability

2) Quick ratio (acid test ratio)

Quick ratio = (current asset－inventory)/current liability

1.1.3　Efficiency 效率

1) Accounts receivable days (accounts receivable payment periods)

Accounts receivable days = trade receivable/sales × 365

2) Inventory days (inventory turnover period)

Inventory days = inventory/cost of sales × 365

3) Accounts payable days (accounts payable payment period)

Accounts payable days = trade payable/cost of sales × 365

4) Inventory turnover

'**Cost of sales ÷ inventory**' is termed inventory turnover, and is a measure of how vigorously a business is trading.

5) Asset turnover is a measure of how well the assets of a business are being used to generate sales. It is calculated as: (**sales/capital employed**).

$$\text{Profit margin} \times \text{asset turnover} = \text{ROI}$$

$$\frac{\text{Profit}}{\text{Sales}} \times \frac{\text{Sales}}{\text{Capital employed}} = \frac{\text{Profit}}{\text{Capital employed}}$$

Capital structure 资本结构

1) Gearing ratio

Capital gearing is concerned with the amount of debt in a company's long-term capital structure. Gearing ratios provide a long-term measure of liquidity.

$$\text{Gearing ratio} = \frac{\text{Prior charge capital (long-term debt)}}{\text{Prior charge capital} + \text{shareholders' equity}}$$

2) Interest coverage(times)

The interest cover ratio shows whether a company is earning enough profits before interest and tax to pay its interest costs comfortably, or whether its interest costs are high in relation to the size of its profits, so that a fall in profit before interest and tax (PBIT) would then have a significant effect on profits available for ordinary shareholders.

公司取得的利润够交多少次银行利息

$$\text{Interest cover} = \frac{\text{PBIT}}{\text{Interest charges}}$$

1.2 Non-financial performance measures

Balanced scorecard 平衡记分卡

1) Customer satisfaction

Gives rise to targets that matter to customers: cost, quality, delivery, inspection, handling and so on.

2) Process efficiency

Aims to improve internal processes, decision making and resource utilization.

3) Growth

Considers the business's capacity to maintain its competitive position through the acquisition of new skills and the development of new products the organisation must keep learning and developing.

4) Financial success

Covers traditional measures such as growth, profitability and shareholder value but set through talking to the shareholder or shareholders direct

1.3 Non-profit organisation 非营利组织

Performance of not for profit organisation is judged in terms of inputs and outputs, hence the **value for money** criteria of economy, efficiency and effectiveness. ("**3E**")

1) **Effectiveness** is the relationship between an organisation's outputs and its objectives.

结果要实现最终目标。

2) **Efficiency** is the relationship between inputs and outputs.

Input 与 output 的转化效率高，即投入一定量的 input，output 尽量多；或者产出一定量的 output，投入尽量少。

3) **Economy** is attaining the appropriate quantity and quality of inputs at the lowest cost. Input 便宜

2. Applications of performance measurement

Benchmarking 标杆管理

Benchmarking is an attempt to identify best practices and by comparison of operations to achieve **improved performance**.

1) Functional benchmarking

Internal functions are compared with those of the best external practitioners of those function, regardless of the industry they are in. 跟最好的相比

（also known as **operational or generic benchmarking**）

2) Internal benchmarking

A method of comparing one operating unit or function with another within the same industry. 跟同行业同部门相比

3) Competitive benchmarking

Information is gathered about direct competitors, through techniques such as reverse engineering. 跟直接竞争者相比

4) Strategic benchmarking

A type of competitive benchmarking aimed at strategic action and organizational change. 将战略行为跟直接竞争者相比

Cost reduction is a planned and positive approach to reducing expenditure. 成本尽量的小

Cost control is concerned with regulating the costs of operating a business and keeping costs

Value analysis is a planned, scientific approach to cost reduction, which reviews the material composition of a product and the product's design so that modifications and improvements can be made which do not reduce the value of the product to the customer or user. 价值分析,价值重要保留,不重要就去掉。

Value engineering is the application of value analysis techniques to new products, so that new products are designed and developed to a given value at minimum cost.

将 Value analysis 运用在新产品中就是 Value engineering

Four aspects of 'value' should be considered.

○ Cost value is the cost of producing and selling an item.

○ Exchange value is the market value of the product or service.

○ Use value is what the article does, the purposes it fulfills.

○ Esteem value is the prestige the customer attaches to the product

Work study is a means of raising the productivity of an operating unit by the reorganization of work. There are two main parts to work study:

○ **Method study** is the systematic recording and critical examination of existing and proposed ways of doing work in order to develop and apply easier and more effective methods, and reduce costs. 以最好的方式

○ **Work measurement** involves establishing the time for a qualified worker to carry out a specified job a specified level of performance.

FINANCIAL ACCOUNTING

Chapter 1

Introduction of accounting

1. Related definition 相关定义

Financial accounting is mainly a method of reporting the financial performance and financial position of a business. 财务会计是一种记录企业财务状况及财务表现的方法

The principle function is to satisfy the information needs of persons not involved in running the business. 其主要目的是满足非企业经营参与者的信息使用需求

Financial reporting is a way of recording, analyzing and summarizing financial data. 财务报告是一种企业记录、分析及总结财务数据的方式

Financial data is the **name given to the actual transactions** carried out by a business.

2. Financial Reports 财务报告(包含"四表一注")

a) Statement of Financial Position at the end of the period（SOFP）资产负债表
b) Statement of profit or loss and other comprehensive income for the period（SPL & OCI）利润及其他综合收益表
c) Statement of Cash Flows for the period（SOCF）现金流量表
d) Statement of Changes in Equity for the period（SOCIE）所有者权益变动表
e) Notes

3. Elements in financial statements（财务报表要素）

1) **Asset 资产**

An asset is a resource **controlled** by an entity as a result of **past events** and from which future **economic benefits** are expected to **flow to** the entity. 关键理解:"由企业所控制的,过去的交易或事项导致的,经济利益的流入"

资产分为:
a) Non-current assets（fixed assets）(**more than one year**)
b) Current assets（**within the next 12 months**）

* Definition allows **inventory or receivables** to qualify as current assets, even if they may not be realized into cash **within 12 months**. 存货及应收账款划分为"流动资产"

2) **Liabilities 负债**

A liability is a **present obligation** of the entity arising from **past events**, the settlement of which is expected to result in an **outflow from** the entity of resources embodying economic benefits. 关键理解:"过去的交易或事项导致的,经济利益的流出,现时义务"

负债分为:

Current liabilities(due to be settled **within 12 months**)

Non-current liabilities(**all other**)

3) Equity 所有者权益

The **residual interest(剩余权益)** in the assets of the entity after deducting all its liabilities.

引出会计恒等式"ACCOUNTING EQUATION":

Net assets(equity)= Total assets - Total liabilities

Assets = Liabilities + Equities

4) INCOME 收益

Income is increases in **economic benefits** during the accounting period in the form of **inflows** or enhance-ments of assets or decreases of liabilities that result in increase in equity, **other than those relating to contributions from equity participants**. 关键理解:"会导致所有者权益增加并且与所有者投入资本无关的"

5) Revenue 收入

Revenue is the gross inflow of economic benefits(cash,receivables,other assets)arising from the **ordinary operating activities** of an enterprise. 关键理解:"日常经营活动中的"

* Income 的概念范围更广,包含了 Revenue。

6) Expenses 费用

Expenses are decreases in **economic benefits** during the accounting period in the form of **outflows** or depletions of assets or incurrences of liabilities that result in decreases in equity, **other than those relating to distributions to equity participants**. 关键理解:"会导致所有者权益减少并且与向所有者分配利润无关的"

4. The business entity concept 会计主体(假设)

For accounting purposes,all three entities(**sole trader, partnership, limited liability company**)are treated as **separate from their owners.** This is called the business entity concept. 三种形式的组织都会作为独立的会计主体,独立于其投资者。

In law, **sole traders and partnerships are not separate entities** from their owners. However,a **limited liability company is legally a separate entity** from its owners. 在法律上,个体户和合伙企业不具有法人资格,但有限责任公司具有独立法人资格。

1) Sole trader

A sole trader-ship is a business **owned and run by one individual**. The individual's business and personal affairs are, for legal and tax purposes, **identical**.

Advantages:

a) Owner has **complete control** over the business 自己能完全控制企业

Chapter 1　Introduction of accounting

　　b) Owner is **entitled to** profits and the ownership of assets 资产、利益都是自己的

　　c) **Less stringent** reporting obligations compared with other business structures 报告监管要求较少

Disadvantages：

　　a) Owner is personally liable for all debts(**unlimited liability**) 无限责任风险高

　　b) Personal property maybe **vulnerable** for debts and other business liabilities 私人财产容易受到影响

　　c) Large sums of **capital are less likely** to be available to a sole trader，leading to reliance on overdrafts and personal savings 资金来源狭隘

　　d) May lead to **long working hours** without the normal employee recreation leave and other benefits. 想要赚钱就需要更多的工作时间，休息时间少

　　e) Maybe issues of continuity of business in the event of **death or illness of the owner** 老板生病，就很难经营下去

2) Partnership 合伙企业

　　Partnerships occur when **two or more people** decide to **run a business together**.

　　Partnerships are **arrangements** between individuals to carry on business in common with a view to profit. Unless it is a limited liability partnership（LLP），partners will be **fully liable(unlimited)** for debts and liabilities，for example if the partnership is sued. 除非是有限合伙企业，则合伙企业通常都是无限连带责任。

Advantages：

　　a) **Less stringent** reporting obligations 报告要求较少

　　b) **Sharing of risk** and losses between more people 合伙人共担风险

　　c) **No company tax** on the business（profits are distributed to partners and **subject to personal tax**）没有企业所得税，而是计征个人所得税

Disadvantages：

　　a) Partners are **jointly personally liable for all debts（unlimited liability）** unless they have formed an　LLP 同样是无限连带责任

　　b) There are **costs associated** with setting up partnership agreements 建立合伙企业协议成本较高

　　Slower decision making due to the need for consensus between partners 需要合伙人一致决策，导致决策效率低下

　　c) Unless a clause is written into the original agreement，when one partner leaves，the partnership is **automatically dissolved** and another agreement is required between existing partners 若合伙协议没约定，其中有人退出，原合伙协议自动解除。

3) Limited liability company

　　A limited liability company is **legally a separate entity** from its owners.

　　Limited liability status means that the business's debts and the personal debts of the business's owners（shareholders）are **legally separate.**

Advantages:

a) **Less risky** than sole trader or partnership because of limited liability 有限责任风险小

b) Raising **finance easier** e.g. issue of shares 融资更容易

c) **Separate legal entity** from its owner so that company continues to exist **regardless of the identity of its owners** 独立法人主体，就算老板不在了公司也还在！

d) Relatively **easy to transfer shares** to another 股票转让容易，比如上市公司股票可通过交易所转让！

Disadvantage:

a) **Publish** annual financial statements so that anyone can see how good or bad the business is. 年报需要进行公布，比如上市公司

b) Have to **comply with** legal and accounting requirements. 需要严格遵守法律及会计制度

c) Financial statement of large companies has to be **audited** which is time consuming and expensive. 大公司需要审计，审计费贵！

d) **Share issues** are regulated by law. 股票发行被严格地监管

5. Users' and stakeholders' needs 各类财务报表信息使用者的需求一览表

Internal stakeholders	Management 管理的好不好
	Employee 要不要跟着你干
Related stakeholders	Shareholders 给我赚了多少钱
	Creditors (debt holders) 债权人能不能还上钱
	Supplier 能不能换上我的货款
	Customer 售后服务
External stakeholders	Taxation authority 有没有好好缴税
	Government 要不要对你进行补助
	The public 潜在投资人

6. Responsibility for the financial statements

The **objective** of financial statement is **to provide information** about the **financial position**, **performance** and **changes in financial position** of an entity that is useful to a wide range of **users in making economic decisions**.

Directors' responsibility for the preparation of the financial statements:

a) **The preparation** of the financial statements of the company **in accordance with** the applicable financial reporting framework（e.g. IFRS）按照准则要求编制报告！

b) **The internal controls** to enable the preparation of financial statements that are free from material misstatement, whether due to error or fraud. 建立完善的内控体系防止错误或舞弊导致的错报！

  c) The **prevention and detection of fraud**. 不能舞弊！

Chapter 2

The regulatory framework

1. Factors that have shaped financial accounting:（影响财务会计的因素）

a) National/local legislation 法律法规的影响

b) Accounting concepts and individual judgment 会计概念与假设及个人主观判断的影响

c) Accounting standards 会计准则的影响

d) Other international influences 国际上其他事项的影响

e) Generally accepted accounting principles(GAAP) 通用会计准则的影响

2. International accounting standards board(IASB)

a) The **IASB develops**(**issue, produce, promote, formulate**) IFRSs.（IASB 颁布准则！括号里的词都是表示颁布！）The International Accounting Standards Board (IASB) is an **independent, privately funded body** that develops and approves IFRSs.（IASB 是独立民办的组织）

b) The main objectives of the **IFRS Foundation** are **to raise** the standard of financial reporting and eventually **bring about global harmonisation**（协同）of accounting standards.（IFRS Foundation 主要是促进国际协同作用！）

c) **The IASB operates under the oversight of the IFRS Foundation.**（IASB 受 IFRS Foundation 监督）

d) The **IFRS Foundation** is a **not for profit, private sector body** that **oversees** the IASB（IFRS Foundation 是非营利、民办组织）

e) The **objectives** of the IFRS Foundation are to：

○ Develop a single set of high quality, understandable, enforceable and globally accepted IFRSs through its standard-setting body, the IASB（仍然是通过 IASB 颁布准则）

○ Promote the use and rigorous application of those standards（促进准则的应用）

○ Take account of the financial reporting needs of emerging economies and small and mediumsized entities（SMEs）（考虑新兴经济体及中小规模企业的需求）

○ Bring about **convergence** of national accounting standards and IFRSs to **high quality solutions** 促进国家间的会计准则达到一个高水平

f）he **IFRS Advisory Council** is essentially a forum used by the IASB to **consult with the outside world.**（与外界交流）

g）The **IFRS Interpretations Committee provides guidance** on specific practical issues in the interpretation of IFRSs.（提供应用指南）and：

○ To review，on a timely basis，newly identified financial reporting issues not specifically addressed in IFRSs.（复核准则现在存在的问题）

○ To clarify issues where unsatisfactory or conflicting interpretations have developed.（准则的矛盾问题，给出一个官方的回答）

3. International Financial Reporting Standards（IFRSs）

The use and application of IFRSs（如何使用 IFRSs？）

IFRSs have helped to both improve and harmonise financial reporting around the world. The standards are used in the following ways.

a）As national requirements（作为国家要求）

b）As the basis for all or some national requirements（作为国家要求的基础）

c）As an international benchmark for those countries which develop their own requirements（作为标准参考使用）

d）By regulatory authorities for domestic and foreign companies（国家法律法规规定使用）

e）By companies themselves（企业自身愿意使用）

Chapter 3

Conceptual framework

1. The IASB's Conceptual Framework is the basis on which IFRSs are formulated.
(概念框架本身并不是准则,但是准则需要在这个范围内,其作为 IFRSs 形成的基础)

1) Introduction to the conceptual framework

a) The Conceptual Framework for Financial Reporting ('Conceptual Framework') is a set of **principles** which **underpin** the foundations of financial accounting.

b) It is a conceptual framework on which **all IFRSs are based** and hence determines how financial statements are prepared and the information they contain.

2) The going concern concept

The Conceptual Framework sets out one important underlying assumption for financial statements, the **going concern concept**. The financial statements are normally prepared on the assumption that an entity is a **going concern** and will **continue in operation for the foreseeable future**.

If the going concern assumption is **not followed**, that fact must be **disclosed**, together with the following information.

a) The **basis** on which the financial statements have been prepared

b) The **reasons why** the entity is not considered to be a going concern

3) Accrual basis

The effects of transactions and other events are **recognised when they occur** (and not as cash or its equivalent is received or paid) and they are recorded in the accounting records and reported in the financial statements of the **periods to which they relate**.

According to the **accruals assumption**, in computing profit **revenue earned must be matched against the expenditure incurred** in earning it. This is also known as the **matching convention**.

2. The qualitative characteristics of financial information

The Conceptual Framework states that **qualitative characteristics** are the attributes that make the information provided in financial statements **useful to users**.

The **two fundamental** qualitative characteristics are **relevance and faithful representation**.

Enhancing qualitative characteristics are **comparability, verifiability, timeliness and**

understandability.

1) RELEVANCE

Only **relevant information** can be useful. Information should be released on a timely basis to be **relevant to users**.（强调与财务报表使用者相关）

Relevant information is capable of making a difference in the **decisions made by users**. Financial information is capable of making a difference in decisions if it has **predictive value**, **confirmatory value** or **both**.

The relevance of information is affected by its **nature and materiality**.

So，what is **materiality?**

Information is material if omitting it or misstating it could **influence decisions** that **users make** on the basis of financial information about a specific reporting entity.

判断重要性一定要从金额(amount)与性质(nature)两个方面去理解!

2) FAITHFUL REPRESENTATION

To be useful，financial information must **not only represent relevant phenomena** but must **faithfully represent** the phenomena that it purports to represent.（必须实事求是反映经济现象/实质）

To be a faithful representation information must be **complete**，**neutral and free from (material)error**.

a) A **complete** depiction includes all information necessary for a user to understand the phenomenon being depicted，including all necessary descriptions and explanations.

b) A **neutral** depiction is without bias in the selection or presentation of financial information.

c) **Free from(material)error** means there are no errors or omissions.

d) SUBSTANCE OVER FORM

Substance：economic substance（经济实质）and **Form：legal form**（法律形式）

This is not a separate qualitative characteristic under the Conceptual Framework.

The IASB says that to include it would be redundant because it is **implied in faithful representation**. Faithful representation of a transaction is only possible if it is accounted for according to its substance and economic reality.（只有在反映经济实质的情况下,才能做到 **faithful representation**）

3) COMPARABILITY

Information about a reporting entity is more useful if it can be compared with **similar information about other entities(横向比)** and with similar information about the **same entity for another period or date (纵向比)**.

Consistency(一致性)，although related to comparability，is not the same. It refers to the use of the **same methods for the same items**（ie **consistency of accounting treatment**）either from **period to period** within a reporting entity or in a single period **across entities**.

4) VERIFIABILITY

It means that **different** knowledgeable and independent **observers could reach consensus** that a particular depiction is a faithful representation.

5) TIMELINESS

Timeliness means having information available to decision-makers **in time** to be capable of influencing their decisions. Generally, the older information is the less useful it is.

There is a balance between timeliness and the provision of reliable information. (若过度追求及时性可能会导致信息不可靠,相反,若过度追求信息的可靠性,可能会导致信息延迟。)

6) UNDERSTANDABILITY

Understandability. Classifying, characterising and presenting information **clearly and concisely makes it understandable**.

Financial reports are prepared for users who have **a reasonable knowledge** of business and economic activities and who review and analyse the information diligently. (当然得是具有一定专业知识的人才能"understand") Some phenomena are **inherently complex** and cannot be made easy to understand. (但有的信息本来就是带有"固有的复杂性",很难去做到让人清楚"understand")

3. Other accounting concepts

There are **other accounting concepts** which are useful in the preparation of financial statements.

1) CONSISTENCY 一致性

To maintain consistency, the presentation and classification of items in the financial statements should **stay the same from one period to the next**, **except as follows**.

a) There is a **significant change in the nature** of the operations or a review of the financial statements indicates a more appropriate presentation

b) A change in presentation is required by an IFRS.

2) THE BUSINESS ENTITY CONCEPT 会计主体假设

Financial statements always treat the business as a separate entity.

Always to treat a business as a separate entity from its owner(s).

This means the transactions of the owner should **never be mixed with** the business's transactions. This applies **whether** or not the business is recognised **in law as a separate legal entity**.

3) Prudence 谨慎性

Assets and income are not overstated and liabilities or expenses are not understated. (不能高估资产和收益,不能低估负债和费用)

However, the exercise of prudence does not allow, for example, the creation of hidden reserves or excessive provisions, the deliberate understatement of assets or income, or the deliberate overstatement of liabilities or expenses … (但是也不能故意低估资产和收益,故意高估负债和费用)

Chapter 3 Conceptual framework

SUM: 记忆关键词!

Qualitative Characteristics	
1. Relevance	relevant to users/predictive value and confirmatory value/affected by its nature and materiality
2. Faithful representation	economic phenomena/complete: all information necessary/neutral: without bias/Free from error: no errors or omissions
3. Comparability	similar information about other entities/the same entity for another period or date
4. Verifiability	reach consensus
5. Timeliness	the older information is the less useful it is
6. Understandability	clearly and concisely/reasonable knowledge

Accounting Concepts	
1. Materiality	influence decisions that users make/nature and amount
2. Substance over form	economic substance/legal form
3. Going concern	underlying assumption/continue in operation for the foreseeable future/neither the intention nor the need to liquidate or curtail
4. Business entity concept	treat the business as a separate entity/whether or not the business is recognised in law as a separate legal entity
5. Accruals	recognised when they occur/the periods to which they relate/matching convention
6. Prudence	assets and income are not overstated and liabilities or expenses are not understated
7. Consistency	the use of the same methods for the same items/presentation and classification/except

Chapter 4

Sources, records and books of prime entry

1. The role of source documents（原始凭证）

Business transactions are recorded on source documents. Examples include **sales and purchase orders**（订单），**invoices**（发票）**and credit notes.**（退款单）

1) Quotation（卖方给买方的报价单）

A document **sent to a customer** by a company stating the fixed **price** that would **be charged** to produce or deliver goods or services.

2) Purchase order（买方给卖方的采购订单）

A document of the company that details goods or services which the company **wishes to purchase** from another company.

Purchase orders are often **sequentially numbered.**（连续编号）

3) Sales order（卖方给买方的订单）

A document of the company that **details an order placed by a customer for goods or services.** The customer may have sent a purchase order to the company from which the company **will then generate a sales order.**（通常客户会寄送一个采购订单 然后才会有销售订单）

4) Goods received note（GRN,收货单）

A document of the company that lists the goods that a business **has received from a supplier.**

5) Goods despatched note（GDN,发货单）

A document of the company that lists the goods that the company **has sent out to** a customer.

6) Statement（对账单）

A document sent out by **a supplier to a customer listing** the transactions on the customer's account，**including all invoices and credit notes issued and all payments received** from the customer.

7) Credit note（退货退款单,卖方给买方的）

A document sent by a **supplier to a customer** in respect of goods returned or overpayments made by the customer. It is a **'negative' invoice.**

8) Debit note（退货退款单,买方给卖方的,退货申请）

A document sent by **a customer to a supplier** in respect of goods returned or an

Chapter 4 Sources, records and books of prime entry

overpayment made. It is a **formal request** for the supplier to issue a credit note.（先有退货申请 debit note，才有退款单 credit note）

9）Remittance advice（汇款单）

A document **sent to a supplier with a payment**, detailing which invoices are being paid and which credit notes offset.

10）Receipt（收据，收款单）

A document confirming confirmation that **a payment has been received.**

11）Invoices（发票）

An invoice relates to a sales order or a purchase order.

When a business sells goods or services on credit to a customer, it sends out an **invoice.**

The **details** on the invoice should **match** the details on the sales **order.**

The invoice is a request for the customer to pay what they owe.

When a business buys goods or services on credit it receives an invoice from the supplier. The details on the invoice should match the details on the purchase order.

（*一般是依据发票，才能请求买方进行付款。买方：收到发票。卖方：发出发票）

Contents of invoice：

a）**Name** and **address** of the seller and the purchaser

b）**Date** of the sale

c）**Description** of what is being sold

d）**Quantity and unit price** of what has been sold

e）Total amount of the invoice including（usually）details any of **sales tax（增值税）**

SUM：关键词记忆

1. Quotation（卖方给买方的报价单）	sent to a customer/price would be charged
2. Purchase order（买方给卖方的采购订单）	wishes to purchase from another company/sequentially numbered
3. Sales order（卖方给卖方的订单）	placed by a customer for goods and service
4. Goods received notes（GRN）收货单	received from a supplier
5. Goods despatched note（GDN）发货单	goods has sent out to a customer
6. Statement（对账单）	a supplier to a customer/invoices/credit notes/payments received
7. Credit note（退货退款单，卖方给买方的）	sent by a supplier to a customer/'negative' invoice
8. Debit note（退货退款单，买方给卖方的退货申请）	sent by a customer to a supplier/formal request
9. Remittance advice（汇款单）	A document sent to a supplier with a payment/show which invoices have been paid and which are still outstanding
10. Receipt(收据，收款单)	confirmation that a payment has been received.
11. Invoices（发票）	sells/invoice/match on sales order/a request for the customer to pay what they owe/contents

2. Books of prime entry

1) 做账流程

原始数据 → 日记账 → 总账 → 试算平衡表 → 报表

2) Books

a) sales day book → 记录 credit sales 的日记账

b) Purchase day book → 记录 credit purchase 的日记账

c) Sales return day book → 记录 credit sales return 的日记账（站在卖方角度，客户退货"回来"）

d) Purchase return day book → 记录 credit purchase return 的日记账（站在买方角度，"退回"给供应商）

e) Cash book（银行存款日记账）→ The cash book，used to keep a record of **money received and money paid out** by the business.

It deals with money paid into and out of the **business bank account.**

One side（the left）— receipts of cash

The other side（the right）— payments

Bank statements（银行对账单） should be used to **check** that the amount shown as a balance in the cash book agrees with the amount on the bank statement.

正确情况下：Cash book should = bank statement

f) Petty cash imprest system（备用金系统）

Most businesses keep petty cash on the premises，which is topped up from the main bank account. Under the imprest system，the petty cash is kept at an agreed sum，so that each topping up is equal to the amount paid out in the period.

Float(the imprest amount or pre-set limit)（备用金额度）= cash in the petty cash box（备用金盒子里的钱）+ total of expense vouchers since last reimbursement（拿出去花了钱换回来的小票）*任何时间节点上这个"额度，float"都会等于"盒子里剩下的钱"+"买了东西拿回来的小票"

g) journal 其他日记账

Record transactions not recorded in any of the other books of prime entry.（除了上面所列示的日记账当中记录的内容，都记录在此）

其主要用于：Adjustment and correction of errors（调整及纠错）

Remember that one of the books of prime entry is the journal!（一定要记住 journal 就是日记账当中的一种！）

Chapter 4 Sources, records and books of prime entry

SUM: 关键词记忆

BOOKS OF PRIME entry	
1. sales day book（销售日记账）— credit sales（赊销）	date/invoice/customer/total amount invoiced/products
2. purchase day book（采购日记账）— credit purchase（赊购）	date/internal inv no./supplier inv no./supplier/total amount invoiced/products
3. sales return day book（销售退回日记账）— credit sales return（赊销的退回）	credit notes/date/credit note/customer and goods/amount
4. the purchase return day book（采购退回日记账）— credit purchase return（赊购产生的退回）	debit note/date/supplier and goods/amount
5. cash book（银行存款日记账）	bank account/receipts of cash/payments
6. the petty cash — small expenditure 备用金——小额支出	receipts/date/narrative/total/products-IMPREST SYSTEM
7. journal（其他类）日记账	Record transactions not recorded in any of the other books of prime entry

Chapter 5

Ledger accounts and double entry

1. Why do we need ledger accounts?

Ledger accounts **summarise all** the individual transactions listed in the books of prime entry. 会计账户是我们汇总所有日记账的工具。

The records of transactions, assets and liabilities should be kept in the following ways. In chronological order（时间顺序）, and Built up in cumulative totals.（累计金额）

F3 中介绍的为 T-account，即为 T 字账户，如下所示。

	NAME OF ACCOUNT	
DEBIT SIDE $	CREDIT SIDE	$

2. LEDGER ACCOUNT

The principal accounts are contained in a ledger called the general or nominal ledger.（总账）

The need for a personal account（明细账）for each customer.（针对每个客户，会有明细账）

The general ledger is a ledger for all customers and suppliers.（总账金额 = 明细账金额之和）

Examples of accounts in the nominal ledger 总账举例：

a) Plant and machinery at cost（non-current asset）（机器与设备）

b) Motor vehicles at cost（non-current asset）（机动车辆）

c) Plant and machinery, provision for depreciation（contra accounts 备抵账户）（计提的折旧费用）

d) Motor vehicles, provision for depreciation（contra accounts 备抵账户）（计提的折旧费用）

e) Inventories — raw materials（current asset）存货——原材料

f) Inventories — finished goods（current asset）存货——产成品

g) Total trade accounts receivable（current asset） 应收账款总账

3. The Accounting Equation 会计恒等式

ASSETS = CAPITAL（sole trader 和 partnership 中一般叫 capital）or Equity（limited liability company 一般叫 equity）+ LIABILITIES.

"Drawings"（这个概念相对特殊，一般用于 sole trader and partnership 中作为分红的意思，而公司中一般用"dividend 股利"）

引出公式：Closing capital = opening capital + capital introduction + profit − drawing

其实资产负债表中的科目都是这样：

Closing balance = opening balance + movement

期末余额 = 期初余额 + 本期增加 − 本期减少

Double entry bookkeeping 复式记账法

Double entry bookkeeping is based on the idea that each transaction has an equal but opposite effect.

Every accounting event must be entered in ledger accounts both as a debit and as an equal but opposite credit.

"有借必有贷，借贷必相等"

Double entry bookkeeping is the method used to transfer the weekly/monthly totals from the books of prime entry into the nominal ledger.

（*我们的做账方法：从日记账怎么记录到总账？用复式记账法写分录，就是从日记账到总账的过程。）

老师的手写稿：

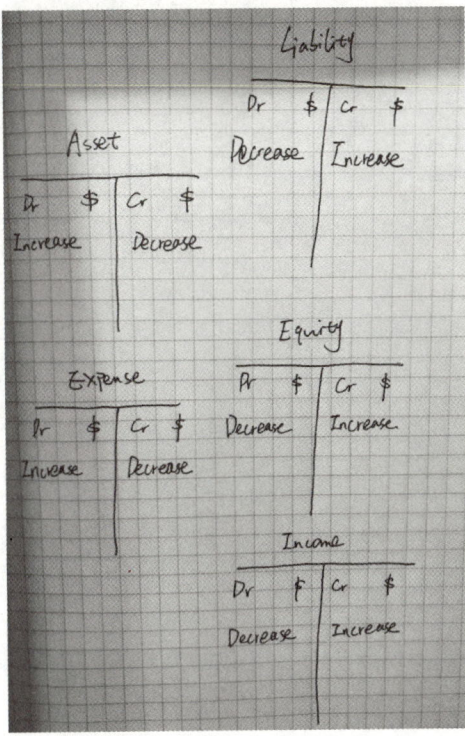

E.g.

以银行存款购进固定资产，分录如下：

DR：PPE cost　　　　　　　　　　　　　　　　　　　　　　　10,000
　　CR：Bank account　　　　　　　　　　　　　　　　　　　 10,000

4. How to balance off and close the Ledger account?

Steps：

a) Total both sides and find the larger total. 将T字账两边所有金额加总求和

b) Put the larger total in both total boxes. 找到金额更大的那一边，然后把这个金额同时写在两边

c) The balance is the difference between the total of Dr side and total of Cr side. 倒挤出差额

d) If the Dr side is larger, there is a Dr balance; if the Cr side is larger, there is a Cr balance. 哪方更大，余额就在哪个方向

举例：

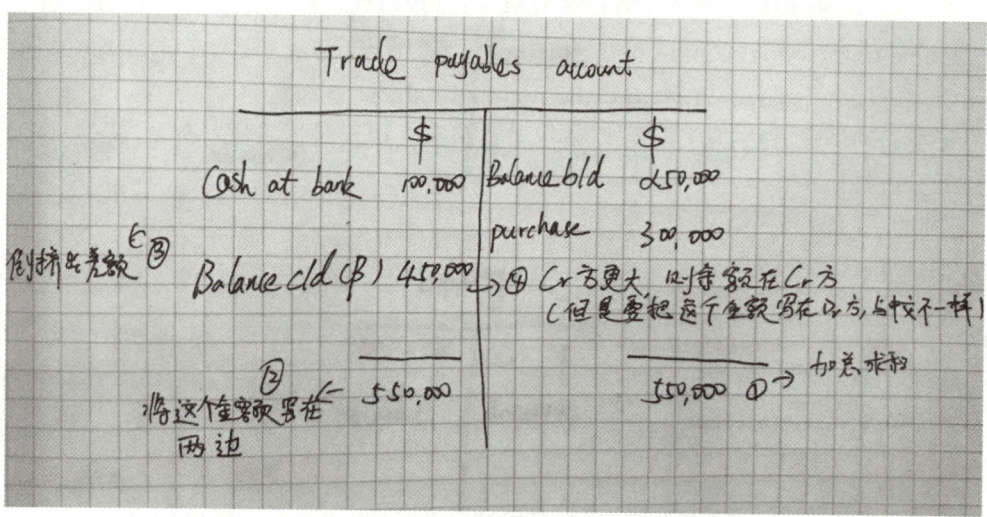

Chapter 6

From trial balance to financial statements

1. The trial balance (TB 试算平衡表)

At suitable intervals, the entries in each ledger account are totalled and a balance is struck. **Balances are usually collected in a trial balance** which is then used as a basis for preparing a statement of profit or loss and a statement of financial position.

A trial balance is **a list of ledger balances** shown in debit and credit columns.

For example:

	DR($)	CR($)
Cash at bank	6,000	
Share capital		7,000
Loan		1,000
Trade accounts receivable	2,000	
	8,000	8,000

A trial balance can be used to test the **accuracy of the double entry** accounting records. The **total debits should equal total credits.** 借贷必相等
试算平衡表如果不平衡,那一定有错;试算平衡表平衡,那也不一定对。

a) The complete omission of a transaction, because neither a debit nor a credit is made 整个交易完全遗漏,但借贷仍然平衡

b) The posting of a debit or credit to the correct side of the ledger, but to a wrong account 比如该记资产的记费用了,但借贷仍然平衡

c) Compensating errors (e.g. an error of $100 is exactly cancelled by another $100 error elsewhere) 两个错误相互抵销,借贷平衡

d) Errors of principle 没有按照准则要求做账,可能不会影响借贷平衡。

2. The statement of profit or loss (利润表)

The first step in the process of preparing the financial statements is to open up another ledger account, called the profit or loss account.

A profit or loss ledger account is opened up to gather all items relating to income and expenses. "profit or loss"这个账户用来结转所有损益类科目，和中文"本年利润"科目道理相同。

The balances on all remaining ledger accounts (including the profit or loss account) can be listed and rearranged to form the statement of financial position. 剩下的所有没结转的账户，包括 profit or loss 这个账户，直接过到资产负债表中，形成资产负债表。

Balances in statement of financial position are carried down in the books of the business.

This means that they become opening balances for the next accounting period and indicate the value of the assets and liabilities at the end of one period and the beginning of the next.

（**Balance at the end of one period＝Balance at the beginning of the next period**）

Balance of profit or loss account will be transferred to equity account. "Profit or loss"账户最终会形成"equity"（＊损益类科目期末无余额）

Chapter 7

Sales and purchases

本章开始进入具体业务的分录学习。

1. Sales return and Purchase return

Cash sales:
DR: Cash
　　CR: Sales revenue

Credit sales:
DR: Trade accounts receivable
　　CR: Sales revenue

Cash purchase:
DR: purchase
　　CR: cash

Credit purchases:
DR: Purchases
　　CR: Trade accounts payable

Purchase return/Return outwards（采购退回/退回去）
DR: Cash/Trade accounts payable
　　CR: Purchase return

Sales return/Return outwards（销售退回/退回来）
DR: Sales return
　　CR: Cash/Trade accounts receivable

2. Discount

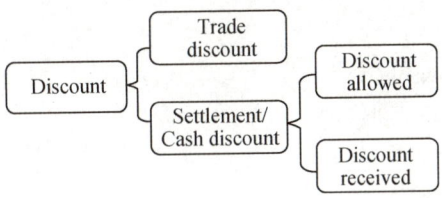

2.1　Trade discount

A trade discount is a reduction in the list price of an article, given by a wholesaler or manufacturer to a retailer. It is often given in return for bulk purchase orders.（promote sales）(为了促进销量提升,鼓励客户多买产品)（商业折扣说白了就是"打折"）

Trade discounts received are deducted from the cost of purchases.

For example, Company A purchases inventory on credit from Supplier B at a gross cost of $1,000, and receives a trade discount of 5% from the supplier. The double entry for the purchase is as follows:

Dr: Inventory   950
    Cr: Trade payables   950

（大家可以看到商业折扣直接扣减掉，实质上就是没做账的。）

2.2 Cash discount

A cash (or settlement) discount is a reduction in the amount payable in return for payment in cash, or within an agreed period.（鼓励客户早点还钱）

For example, a supplier charges $1,000 for goods, and offers a trade discount of 10%, at the same time offers a discount of 5% if the goods are paid within 10 days.

看下站在客户和供应商角度分别怎么做账。

1) 客户角度

当交易发生时：

DR: Purchase[1,000*(1-10%)]（交易发生时直接扣除商业折扣）   900
    CR: Trade payable   900

当实际在十天内付款时：

DR: Trade payable   900
    CR: Cash [900*(1-5%)]   855
    CR: Discounts received（作为 other income 计入利润表）   45

2) 供应商角度（分为预期客户会取得现金折扣与预期客户不会取得现金折扣两种情况）

a) Expect customer to take up the discount

销售发生时：

DR: TR [900*(1-5%)]   855
    CR: Sales   855

结算时客户实际取得了现金折扣（符合预期），customer takes up the discount：

DR: cash   855
    CR: trade receivable   855

结算时客户没有取得现金折扣（不符合预期），customer dose not take up the discount：

DR: Cash   900
    CR: Trade receivable   855
    CR: Sales（补记 45 的收入）   45

b) Expect customer not to take up the discount

销售发生时：

DR: TR   900
    CR: Sales   900

结算时客户确实没有取得现金折扣：

DR: Cash   900
    CR: Trade accounts receivable   900

Chapter 7　Sales and purchases

结算时客户取得了现金折扣：

DR：Cash　　　　　　　　　　　　　　　　　　　　　　　　　855
DR：Sales（扣除 45 的收入）　　　　　　　　　　　　　　　45
　　　CR：Trade accounts receivable　　　　　　　　　　　　900

3. Sales tax（增值税）

a) **Registered businesses** charge output sales tax on sales and suffer input sales tax on purchases.

Sales → collect VAT on behalf of tax authority → liable to tax authority → Output tax.

Purchase → paid VAT to supplier → has a right to reclaim the amount from tax authority → Input tax.

Output sales tax = Sales price (**exclusive of sales tax**) * Tax rate

Input sales tax = Purchase price (**exclusive of sales tax**) * Tax rate

Example：

A company sells goods for list price of $600 (**exclusive of sales tax**) in cash and the sales tax rate is 20%.

DR：Cash（600+600×20%）　　　　　　　　　　　　　　720
　　　CR：Output sales tax（600×20%）　　　　　　　　　120
　　　CR：Sales　　　　　　　　　　　　　　　　　　　　600

A company purchase goods for list price of $600 (**inclusive of sales tax**) in cash and the sales tax rate is 20%.

DR：Purchase [600/(1+20%)]（先做价税分离还原成不含税价）　500
　　　CR：Input sales tax [600/(1+20%)×20%]（再算税额）　　100
　　　CR：Cash　　　　　　　　　　　　　　　　　　　　　　600

(* In the statement of financial position，Cash/Trade receivable/Trade payable is inclusive of sales tax.

In the statement of profit or loss，Sales/Purchase is exclusive of sales tax)

b) Irrecoverable sales tax must be regarded as part of the cost of the items purchase. (不可抵扣的税一定要记得作为成本！)

○ A trader is not registered for sales tax

○ Inputs are not related to taxable business activities

Chapter 8

Inventory

1. Introduction

Statement of financial position → Closing inventory

Statement of profit or loss → Cost of sales

2. Definition

Inventories are assets:

Held for sale in the ordinary course of business（在正常经营过程中**持有待售**的）

In the process of production for such sale（**work in progress** 在产品）

In the form of **materials**（原材料）

3. Cost of inventory

The cost of inventory should **comprise all** the followings:

a) Costs of purchase 采购过程中发生的成本

b) Costs of conversion 生产转换过程中的成本

c) Other costs incurred in bringing the inventory to their present location and condition 其他使存货达到预定可销售状态所必需的成本

Purchase cost:

Purchase price（买价）

Non-recovered duty and tax（irrecoverable）（不可抵扣的税费）

Transport, handling, carriage inwards（往里面运的运费）and others

Less any trade discount and rebates（扣除任何形式的商业折扣）

Conversion costs:

Cost directly related to unit production e.g. direct material, direct labour（直接材料 直接人工）

Fixed and variable production overhead that incurred in converting materials into finished goods, allocated on systematic basis（制造费用，比如折旧费）

＊**Fixed production overhead:** Indirect costs of production that remains relatively constant **regardless of the volume of production.**（与产量无关的费用,固定费用）

E.g. Cost of factory management and administration (Salary of factory manager 车间管理人员的工资)

Allocated to inventories **based on normal capacity** (标准水平) of the production facility

* **Variable production overhead:** Indirect costs of production, that **vary directly with the volume of production** (随着产量会改变的,变动费用)

E.g. Indirect material and labour

Allocation of variable overhead is based on the **actual (实际水平) use** of production facility.

Excluded cost: (着重记忆:不应包含进存货成本的有哪些?)

a) Abnormal wastage (however, normal wastage is included as cost of inventory)(非正常损耗不计入成本,正常损耗计入成本)

b) Selling costs (marketing, carriage outwards)

c) Storage cost (except costs which are necessary in the production process before a further production stage 除非是为了进入下一个生产环节所必须得仓储成本才能计入成本,否则仓储成本都不计入存货成本)

d) Administrative overheads unrelated to production

e) Foreign exchange difference

f) Interest costs on Cr purchase of inventory

4. Counting inventory

1) Continuing counting (continuous/perpetual) 永续盘存制

A business holds **considerable** quantities of **varied** inventory

A card, or a **computerised record**, is kept for every item of inventory, showing receipts and issues from the stores, and a running total. (时时刻刻都在计算存货"收发存"数量)

2) Physical count/Periodic count 实地盘存制/定期盘存制

A business holds **easily counted** and **relatively small amounts** of inventory quantities of inventories on hand at the reporting date can be determined by physically counting them in an inventory count at that date. (在期末实地去盘点我们的存货有多少)

做账区别如下:

	Continous count	Periodic count
Purchase of inventory $8	Dr: Inventory $8 Cr: Cash $8	Dr: Purchase $8 Cr: Case $8
Sales of inventory $12	Dr: Cash $12 Cr: Sales $12	Dr: Cash $12 Cr: Sales $12
Cost of goods sold	Dr: Cost of sales $8 Cr: Inventory $8	

3) Physical count 实地盘存制下的存货怎么做账?

a) Opening inventory ＄8（假设期初库存有8美元的存货）

DR：Cost of sales	＄8
CR：Opening inventory	＄8

b) Purchase ＄10（假设本期购进10美元的存货）

DR：Cost of sales	＄10
CR：Purchase	＄10

c) Closing inventory ＄2（期末，实际去仓库盘点发现我们有2美元的存货）

DR：closing inventory	＄2
CR：cost of sales	＄2

Cost of sales $= 8 + 10 - 2 =$ ＄16

为什么是这样？

逻辑是在实地盘存制下，我们先假设期初（＄8）及本期增加的（＄10）存货在当期都卖出去了，到了期末的时候去仓库实地盘点，得到还有＄2的存货，倒挤出实际卖出去的存货只有＄16。

得到公式，实地盘存制下：

Cost of sales＝Opening inventory＋Purchase－Closing inventory

5. Valuing inventory－price

5.1 Items not ordinarily interchangeable

Cost of inventories should be assigned by **specific identification** of their **individual costs**. 针对不可互换、不可互相替代的产品，应当单独确认每个存货的成本。

5.2 Interchangeable items 针对同质、可相互替换的存货

1) First in，first out（FIFO）先进先出法

Components are used in the order in which they are received from suppliers

2) Last in，first out（LIFO）后进先出法（了解即可，准则不允许使用）

Components used formed part of the most recent delivery，and inventories are the oldest receipts. And LIFO is not permitted by IAS2 Inventory.

3) Weighted average cost（AVCO）加权平均法

As purchase prices change with each new consignment，the average price of components held is **constantly changed.** Each component is valued at the average price of all components held at that moment.

a) Moving(continuous)weighted average cost 移动加权平均法

Cost of inventory = cost of inventory currently in the store + cost of new items received − cost of issued/No. Of inventory currently in the store + No. Of new items received − No. Of inventory issued

b) Periodic weighted average 期末一次加权平均

Cost of inventory = cost of opening inventory + cost of all purchase in the period/No. Of opening inventory + No. Of all purchase in the period

3) Impairment of inventory

Inventory should be valued at the lower of cost and net realisable value. (IAS2) (背下这句话!)

Net realisable value is the estimated selling price in the ordinary course of business less the estimated costs of completion and the estimated costs necessary to make the sale.

文字变公式:NRV = Selling price − Cost of completion − Cost necessary to make the sale

If cost of inventory is larger than net realisable value, then impairment loss occurs.

Dr: Impairment loss (SPL)   XXX
    Cr: Inventory (SOFP)   XXX

SUM:

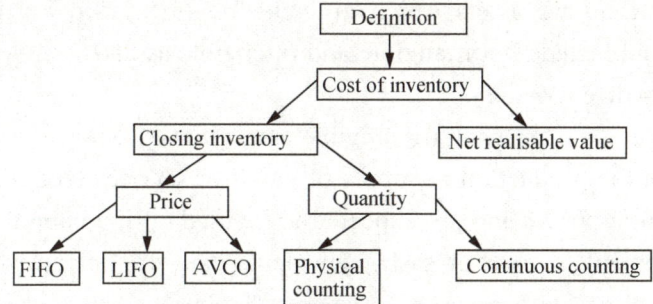

Chapter 9

Tangible assets

1. Definition

Non-current assets are assets which are **intended to be used by** the business on a continuing basis and include both tangible and intangible assets.

Tangible non-current assets:

Property, plant and equipment are tangible assets that:

held for use in the production or supply of goods or services, for rental to others, or for administrative purposes; and are expected to be used during **more than one period**.

Cost is the amount of cash or cash equivalents paid or the fair value of the other consideration given to acquire an asset **at the time of its acquisition or construction.** (在取得时或建造时的成本,即为历史成本**"historical cost"**)

Fair value is the price that would be received to sell an asset or paid to transfer a liability in an **orderly transaction**(有序公平的市场) between market participants **at the measurement date.** (各位在F3的学习中FV通常=MV)

Carrying amount (net book value) is the amount at which an asset is recognised **after deducting any accumulated depreciation and impairment losses**.

Carrying amount = Cost（历史成本）— Accumulated depreciation（累计折旧）— Accumulated impairment（累计减值）

2. Recognition

Recognised when the following two criteria met:

It is **probable (>50%)** that the **future economic benefit** associated with the asset will **flow to** the entities(经济利益很可能流入)

The cost of the asset to the entity can be **measured reliably**(成本能够可靠的计量)

Dr: Non-current asset — cost   XX

    Cr: Cash/Payable   XX

3. Initial measurement

The property, plant and equipment are initially **measured at cost**. (以历史成本初始计量)

The component of cost will include following:(成本包含哪些?)

Chapter 9 Tangible assets

1) Purchase Price 购买价款

a) Including import duties,（包含进口关税）excluding any trade discount and sales tax（不含商业折扣及可抵扣的进项税）

b) Initial estimate of costs of dismantling and removing the item and restoring the site on which it is located（弃置费用，F3中考的较少）

2) Directly attributable costs of bring the asset to working condition for intended use（使资产达到预定可使用状态的直接相关成本）

a) Site preparation 场地整理费

b) Initial delivery and handling 初始装卸费

c) Professional fees（比如请建筑师、工程师的费用）

d) **Costs of testing** whether the asset is working properly, **after deducting** the net proceeds from **selling samples** produced when testing equipment（测试成本，注意一定要扣除卖掉"样品"的收入）

e) Staff costs arising directly from the construction or acquisition of the asset（为了建造或取得资产的直接人工成本）

3) Costs may not be capitalized（不能被资本化的费用）

a) **Staff training** costs（员工培训费用）

b) **Maintenance contracts** purchased with the assets（正常维修费用）

c) **Initial operating losses** before asset reaches planned performances（资产达到预定生产状态前产生的亏损）

d) **Administration** and other general overhead costs（管理费用）

e) **Start-up** and similar pre-production costs（开办期间及生产前的成本）

4. Subsequent expenditure

1) Capital expenditure 资本化支出 → 进 SOFP

Improvements to existing non-current assets.:（关键是判断是否有"improvements"）

Modification **to extend its useful life,** including **increased capacity** 使用年限延长，生产力提升

Upgrade to improve the quality of output 提高产品产出质量

Adoption of a new production process leading to **large reductions in operating cost**. 经营成本减少

2) Revenue expenditure 费用化支出 → 进 SPL

For trading（**selling expense**）销售费用（为了卖固定资产出去）

To maintain the existing earning capacity of non-current（只是维持现状，没"improvements"）

3) Capital income 资本性收益（简单了解）

Proceeds(cash received) from the **sale of non-trading assets**（出售非交易性资产）

4) Revenue income 收益性收益（简单了解）

The sale of trading assets(held for sell), such as goods held in inventory 销售商品

The provision of services 提供服务

Interest and dividends received from investments held by the business 投资性收益

5. Depreciation

1) Depreciable assets

Depreciable assets are expected to be used during **more than one accounting period**, have a **limited useful life**; and are held by an enterprise **for use** in the production or supply of goods and service, for rental to others, or for administrative purpose.

Depreciable amount = Historical cost − estimated residual value

Depreciation is the **allocation of the depreciable amount** of an asset over its **estimated useful life**.

Dr: Depreciation expense (SPL)
    Cr: Accumulated Depreciation (SOFP)

2) Depreciation method

a) Straight-line method 直线法

Annual depreciation charge = (Cost − residual value)/expected useful life

b) Reducing balance method 余额递减法（最后两年需通过倒挤平均摊销。）

Depreciation amount = (Depreciation rate% × Carrying amount 账面价值)

3) Change in method of depreciation

If there is a **significant change in the pattern** that the assets generating benefits, then the depreciation method should be changed to best reflect the new pattern. The remaining carrying amount is depreciated under the new method, ie. **only current and future periods are affected**; the **change is not retrospective**(折旧方法的变更属于会计估计的变更,采用"未来适用法",不进行追溯调整）

6. Revaluation(重估)(F3 中考重估增值,不考重估减值)

IAS 16 requires that when an item of property, plant and equipment is revalued, **the whole class** of assets to which it belongs **should be revalued**. 分录如下：

Dr: PPE — Cost（revalued amount-cost）
Dr: Accumulated Depreciation
    Cr: Revaluation surplus（Revalued amount − carry amount）

为什么分录是这样？带着大家看下逻辑：(视为将该资产卖出再买回来,只是不涉及现金的交付。)

1) 卖出资产,冲掉其成本(假设为 10)及累计折旧(假设为 6)(则 carrying amount 为 4)：
DR: Accumulated depreciation   6
    CR: Cost(old)   10

2) 买进资产,增加资产成本(假设新成本即 Revalued amount 为 12)
DR: Cost(Revalued amount)   12
    CR: Revaluation surplus(差额作为 RS)(12−4)   8

3) 将上述分录合并就得到图中分录：

DR：PPE-cost（12－10）　　　　　　　　　　　　2
DR：Accumulated depreciation　　　　　　　　　6
　　CR：Revaluation surplus（12－4）　　　　　　　　　　　8

7. Excessive depreciation

IAS 16 allows entities **to transfer an amount equal to the excess depreciation** from the **revaluation surplus to retained earnings** in the equity section of the statement of financial position, **if they wish to do so.**

（针对重估增值后多提的折旧怎么处理？**将多提的折旧从未实现损益 revaluation surplus 转到已实现损益 retained earnings 中！**）分录如下：

Excess depreciation = depreciation after revaluation − depreciation before revaluation

DR：Revaluation surplus　　　　　　　　　　　　XXX
　　CR：Retained earnings　　　　　　　　　　　　　　XXX

8. Disposal of fixed assets（PPE）steps（纯处置）

a) Remove the cost of the non-current asset disposed（第一步，去掉固定资产成本）
Dr：Disposal account　　　　　　　　　　　　　XX
　　Cr：Non-current asset cost account　　　　　　　　XX

（*固定资产处置账户"disposal account"只是一个过渡科目，不属于资产、负债或是权益等要素）

b) Remove accumulated depreciation of the fixed asset disposed（第二步，去掉固定资产累计折旧）
Dr：Accumulated depreciation　　　　　　　　　XX
　　Cr：Disposal account　　　　　　　　　　　　　　XX

c) Cash received（记录收到的钱）
Dr：Cash　　　　　　　　　　　　　　　　　　XX
　　Cr：Disposal account　　　　　　　　　　　　　　XX

d) 看结果
Profit on disposal = Proceeds − carrying amount
Loss on disposal = Carrying amount − proceeds

9. Disposal of fixed assets-part exchange（"以旧换新"固定资产）

a) New asset：记录新资产成本
Dr：NCA（cost of new asset）　　　　　　　　　XXX
　　Cr：Disposal account　　　　　　　　　　　　　　XXX

b) Old asset：去掉旧资产账面价值
Dr：Disposal account　　　　　　　　XXX（carrying amount）
　　Cr：NCA　　　　　　　　　　　　　　　　　　　XXX

c) Cash paid：支付出去的钱

Dr：Disposal account XXX
　　Cr：Cash XXX

d) Balance of the disposal account is profit or loss on disposal.

Chapter 10

Intangible assets

1. Definition (IAS 38)

Intangible assets are non-current assets **with no physical substance**. 无实物形态
An intangible asset is an **identifiable non-monetary** asset **without physical substance**.
(可辨认的:F3 中的学习理解为"单独区分,可以单独买卖")
(非货币性:指其在将来为企业带来的经济利益是不固定的或不可确定的)
回顾 Asset 关键定义:
Controlled by the entity as a result of **events in the past**
Something from which the entity expects future **economic benefits to flow**
a) Externally acquired:Software 软件 and Patents 专利权
b) Internally generated:Brands and Customer list

2. Recognition

The recognition of an item as an intangible asset:(同时满足下列两项)
※ **the definition** of an intangible asset
※ the **recognition criteria** (if,and only if)
It is **probable** that the expected **future economic benefits** that are attributable to the asset will **flow to** the entity; and The **cost** of the asset can be **measured reliably**

3. Research and development cost

Research is original and planned **investigation** undertaken with the prospect of gaining new scientific or technical **knowledge and understanding**.(理解为只是获得了一些简单的认知或了解)

Research(研究阶段) costs should be recognised as an expense when they incurred. (研究阶段的支出一定要费用化)

Development(开发阶段) is the **application of research findings** or other knowledge to a plan or design for the production of new or substantially improved materials,devices,products,processes,systems or services **prior to the commencement of commercial production** or use.

Development expenditure *must be recognised as an intangible asset if, and only if, all of the criteria in IAS 38 have been met*. (开发阶段资本化的条件,必须同时满足下列各项,且若全部满足,必须资本化:"pirate"原则)

P: how the assets will generate *Probable* future economic benefits (可能性)

I: its *Intention* to complete the intangible asset and use or sell it (管理层意愿)

R: whether adequate technical, financial and other *Resources* to complete the development (是否有足够的资源来支持开发)

A: its *Ability* to use or sell the intangible asset (开发完了有没有能力卖出去或者自己使用)

T: the *Technical feasibility* of completing the intangible asset (技术上的可行性)

E: its ability to measure reliably the *Expenditure* attributable to the intangible asset (成本能否可靠计量)

4. Amortization

1) Intangible assets with finite useful life (使用寿命有限的无形资产)

An intangible asset with a *finite useful life* should *be amortised over its used life*.

The amortisation will *begin* when the asset is *available for use*.

The amortisation should be *reviewed annually*.

Dr: Amortised expense (SPL)

　　Cr: Accumulated amortisation (SOFP)

2) Intangible assets with indefinite life (使用寿命不确定的无形资产)

An intangible asset with indefinite life should not be amortised. (记住这句话)

The asset should be assessed for impairment in accordance with IAS 36. (每年进行减值测试,记住这句话)

Chapter 11

Accruals and prepayments

1. Introduction

The **matching concepts（权责发生制/配比原则）** state that **income and expenses incurred in the period should be accounted for in that period**, regardless of when invoices are raised or received.

The fundamental rule is that income and expenditure are recognised as they are earned or incurred, **not as money is received or paid**.

Income			
Accrued	Prepaid	Accrued	Prepaid
Liability	Asset	Asset	Liability
已发生，未支付的费用 → 负债	已支付，未发生的费用 → 资产	已发生，未收到的收入 → 资产	已收到，未发生的收入 → 负债

2. Accrued Expenditure

a) **Accruals** are **expenses due and unpaid** that **have not been recorded** in the books for accounting period concerned. Accruals will appear in the **SOFP as current liabilities.**

　　Dr：Expense
　　　　Cr：Accruals（liability）

b) Accrual vs. trade payable

Accruals generally represent liabilities to pay for goods or services received in a period, **that have not yet been invoiced** for by the suppliers.（通常没开票的就是accruals）**Trade accounts payables** are liabilities to pay for goods or services received in a period **that have been invoiced** for by the suppliers（已经开票的就是 **trade accounts payables**）

c) Prepaid expenditure

Prepayments are expenses paid **in excess of** the accounting period concerned. They are treated as **unexpired values** to be placed in the **SOFP as a current asset**.

　　Dr：Prepayment（SOFP）
　　　　Cr：Expense（P/L）

d) Accrued income

Arises where income **has been earned** in the accounting period but **has not yet been received**. E.g interest

Dr: Accrued income (SOFP)
    Cr: Income (P/L)

e) Prepaid income

Also referred to as **"deferred income"**, arising where income **has been received** in the accounting period but which **related to the next accounting period**. (liability)

Dr: Income (P/L)
    Cr: Prepaid income (SOFP)

Chapter 12

Provisions and contingencies

1. Provision

1) Definition

A provision **is a liability of uncertain timing or amount**.（记住这句话,首先要满足负债的定义＋不确定性）

回顾负债定义:A liability is a **present obligation** of an entity **to transfer economic benefits** as a result of **past transactions or events**.

2) Recognition

A provision should be recognized **as a liability in the financial statements** when **meeting all** following three conditions:

a) An entity has a **present obligation**（legal or constructive）（法律或推定的义务）as a result of a **past event**.

b) It is **probable**（more than 50%）that a **transfer of economic benefits** will be required to settle the obligation.

c) A **reliable estimate** can be made of the obligation

When first set up provision, the **full amount of provision** should be **charged to profit or loss**:

Dr: Expenses (SPL)
　　Cr: Provisions (SOFP)

3) Measurement

The amount recognized as provision should be the best estimate of the expenditure required to settle the obligation at the end of reporting period.

a) If the provision relates to just **one item**, the **best estimate** will be the **most likely outcome**.（针对一次性的事项,选可能性最大的那个金额来计量!）比如最常考的就是"**Legal case**"

b) If the provision involves **a lot of items**,（e.g. warranty provision 质保服务,each sold product has a warranty attached to it）, then the provision is calculated by **expected value approach**.（若是多次事项,则要用期望值法进行计量!）比如最常考的就是"**warranty provision**"

2. Contingent liability

1) Definition

IAS 37 defines a **contingent liability** as:

A **possible (5%＜possible＜50%) obligation** that arise from **past events** and whose existence will be confirmed only by the **occurrence or non-occurrence of uncertain future events not wholly within the entity's control**.

A contingent liability **must not be recognized as a liability** in the financial statements because:（或有负债不能确认为负债,而应当披露!）

It is **not probable** that a transfer of economic benefits will be required to settle the obligation, or The **amount of the obligation cannot be measured** with sufficient reliability Instead **it should be disclosed** in the notes to the accounts, unless the possibility of an outflow of economic benefits is remote（小于5%）（若可能性小于5%,remote,则披露都不用）

2) Disclosure

A **brief description** of nature of the contingent liability

An estimate of its **financial effect**

An **indication of uncertainty** that exist

The **possibility** of any reimbursement

3. Contingent asset

1) Definition

IAS 37 defines a **contingent asset** as:

A **possible asset** that arises from past events and whose existence will be confirmed by the **occurrence of one or more uncertain future events not wholly within the enterprise's control**.

2) Recognition

A **contingent asset must not be recognized** as an asset in the financial statements.（或有资产不能确认为资产!）

If the flow of economic benefit associated with the contingent asset becomes **virtually certain (＞95%)**, it should **then be recognized as an asset** in the statement of financial position as it is no longer a contingent asset.（只有基本确定,**virtually certain,＞95%,才能确认**）

3) Disclosure

It **should be disclosed** in the notes to the accounts, **if it is probable (＞50%)** that the **economic benefits** associated with the asset will flow to the entity.（只有当可能性＞50%才披露）The required disclosure:

A **brief description** of contingent asset

An estimate of its likely **financial effect**

SUM

Chapter 12 Provisions and contingencies

	Provision	Contingent liability	Contingent asset
Probable	Recognise	Recognise	Disclose
Possible	Disclose	Disclose	Do nothing
Remote	Do nothing	Do nothing	Do nothing

Chapter 13

Irrecoverable debts and allowance

1. Relationship

Trade receivables → 确定收不回来了 → Bad debts 坏账

Trade receivables → 可能收不回来了 → Doubtful debts 疑账（疑账又分为 specific allowance 针对特定客户的；general allowance 针对其他客户的）

2. Bad debts/irrecoverable debts

An **irrecoverable (or 'bad') debt** is a **debt which is definitely not expected to be paid**. （比如客户破产了"Bankrupt"）

When a credit sale is made to a customer：

Dr：Trade accounts receivables

    Cr：Sales

Write off if the customer can't pay：

Dr：Irrecoverable debts expense (P/L)

    Cr：Trade accounts receivables (SOFP)

An irrecoverable debt which has been written off might **occasionally be unexpected 意外的 paid**(若坏账产生了，客户又还钱了怎么处理？)

第一步：Reverse bad debts written off

Dr：Trade receivables

    Cr：Irrecoverable debt expense

第二步：Record cash received

Dr：Cash

    Cr：Trade receivables

合并两个分录即为：

Dr：Cash

    Cr：Irrecoverable debt expense

3. Allowance for receivables

1) Types of allowances

There may be some debts which the business thinks **might not be paid**, these are

Chapter 13　Irrecoverable debts and allowance

known as **doubtful debts**.

Specific allowance

The doubtful debt may be a particular invoice or perhaps the whole balance outstanding from a **particular customer**. (能具体到某一个交易或某一个客户的疑账)

General allowance

Created to provide against the remaining trade receivable balance，**after** writing off **bad debts and** after accounting for **specific doubtful debts**.

General allowance＝X% * (Trade receivables-bad debts-specific allowance)

2) Accounting for allowance

a) When an allowance is first made：

Dr：Irrecoverable debts expense (P/L)

　　Cr：Allowance for receivables (SOFP)

b) Subsequently adjustment in allowance：

If a higher allowance is required：

Dr：Irrecoverable debts expense (P/L)

　　Cr：Allowance for receivables (SOFP)

If a lower allowance is needed now：（reversal）

Dr：Allowance for receivables (SOFP)

　　Cr：Irrecoverable debts expense (P/L)

Trade receivables in SOFP：

Net of allowance＝(Trade receivables-closing allowance)(资产负债表中列式的应收账款是扣除掉坏账准备之后的！实际上坏账准备就是应收账款的一个备抵科目"Contra account")

3) From allowance to bad debts（疑账真的变成坏账了怎么办?）

From allowance to bad debts：

a) Reverse：

Dr：Allowance for receivables

　　Cr：Irrecoverable debts expense

b) Record bad debts：

Dr：Irrecoverable debts expense

　　Cr：Trade receivables

Dr：Allowance for receivables
Cr：Trade receivables

4. **Credit control**

1) The **costs** of offering **credit facilities** to customers includes：(信贷措施的成本可能有哪些?)

a) **Interest** costs of an overdraft，if customers do not pay promptly

b) Costs of trying **to obtain payment** 比如催账费用

c) **Court costs** 比如打官司的费用

d) Cost businesses control receivables by setting up credit limit and credit period（事

先建立信贷额度及信贷期间的审核成本,比如调查客户征信)

2) Aged receivables analysis(应收账款账龄分析) is an important tool in credit control. (记住这句话!下面的文字了解即可)

An aged receivables analysis is a report of all receivables analysed **by customer and by age of the receivable**, e.g. balances outstanding for 30 days, 60 days and 90 + days or more.

If a balance has been outstanding for a **long period of time**, it may indicate that a customer is unable to pay. Most credit controllers will have a system of chasing up payment for long outstanding invoices.

Chapter 14

Control accounts

1. General ledger & personal ledger

General ledger → (for all customer/suppliers) → total of books of prime entry

Personal ledger → (for specific customer/suppliers) → each transaction in books of prime entry

General ledger is also called Nominal ledger or Control account. (总账)

Subsidiary ledger is also called personal ledger. (明细账)

Cash books and day books are totalled periodically and the totals posted to the control accounts. At suitable intervals, the balances on the personal accounts are extracted and totalled.

These balance totals should agree to the balance on the control account.

2. Purpose of control account

Provide a check on the accuracy of entries made in the personal accounts and control accounts. (检查准确性)

Assist in the location of errors. (检查错在哪儿了)

Provides an internal check-separation of duty check (职责分离，做明细账的人和做总账的人不是一个人，企业内控的一种体现)

Balance extracted more simply and quickly (平时就加总求余额，加总更快)

3. Dishonored cheques

When cheque is received: (收到 cheque 就认为是收到了 cash)

Dr: Cash
    Cr: Trade receivables

Dishonored by the bank: (银行拒付，重新变为应收账款)

Dr: Trade receivables
    Cr: Cash

4. Overpayment (客户多付钱的处理)

When sales is made:

Dr：Trade receivables	$ 100
Cr：Sales	$ 100

When overpayment is made by customer：

Dr：Cash	$ 150
Cr：Trade receivables	$ 150

Cash paid to clear credit balances/Cash refunds to customers：

Refunds to customer：

Dr：Trade receivables	$ 50
Cr：Cash	$ 50

5. Contra

For example，C buys hardware from you and you buy software from C. In the receivables ledger，C owes you $130. However，you owe C $250. You may reach an agreement to offset the balances receivable and payable. This is known as a 'contra'. The double entry is as follows.

Dr：Payables control account	$ 130
Cr：Receivables control account	$ 130

6. Overpayment（"我们"多付钱的处理）

When purchase is made：

Dr：Purchase	$ 100
Cr：Trade payables	$ 100

When overpayment is made：

Dr：Trade payables	$ 150
Cr：Cash	$ 150

Cash refunds received from suppliers

Dr：Cash	$ 50
Cr：Trade payables	$ 50

7. Supplier statements reconciliation（供应商与客户的对账单）

A supplier will frequently send a statement showing **invoices issued**，**credit notes**，**payments received** and **discounts given**.

Any **discrepancies** between this statement and the supplier's personal ledger should be **identified and any errors corrected**.

1) Payment in transit 在途资金

A payment will go in the payables ledger when the cheque is issued. There will be delay（postal，processing）before this payment is entered in the records of the supplier. （比如，我们开出支票，直接记录 cash 减少 TP 减少，而供应商还未去银行请求付款，则其 TR 尚未减少，cash 尚未增加）

2）Goods in transit（在途物资）

Timing difference（比如，supplier 已发货我们还未收货）

3）Omitted invoices and credit notes（直接漏掉了交易，没做账）

4）Invoices or credit notes may appear in the ledger of one business but not in that of the other due to error or omission.（一方遗漏未做账，一方正常做账）

5）Error（记账过程中的错误，比如金额记错了）

Chapter 15

Bank reconciliation

1. Introduction

A **bank statement**（银行对账单）is **sent by a bank** to its customers itemising the **balance** on the account at the **beginning** of the period, **receipts into** the account and payments from the account during the period, and the **balance** at the **end** of the period.

In theory, the entries appearing on a **business's bank statement should be exactly the same as those in the business cash book**（企业银行存款日记账）.

The balance shown by the bank statement should be the same as the cash book balance on the same date.（银行对账单与企业银行存款日记账的余额应当一致。）

	Deposit	Overdraft
Cash book	Debit balance	Credit balance
Bank statement	Credit balance	Debit balance

For example, If a business has $800 cash in the bank, it will have a debit balance in its own cash book, but the bank statement, if it reconciles exactly with the cash book, will state that there is a credit balance of $800.（银行的记账方向与企业的记账方向是相反的,比如我们的存款800是资产,但对于银行来说我们的存款800就是负债。）

2. Errors made by bank statement（银行对账单会出现的"错误"）

1) Un-presented cheques/Outstanding cheque（未承兑支票）

Cheques drawn (ie paid) by the business and credited in the cash book, which **have not yet been presented to the bank**, or 'cleared', and so do not yet appear on the bank statement.（企业已付,银行未付）

2) Deposits in transit/Outstanding deposit/Bank lodgement（Add）在途存款

Cheques received by the business, paid into the bank and debited in the cash book, but which **have not yet been cleared and entered in the account by the bank**, and so do not yet appear on the bank statement.（企业已收,银行未收）

如何调整?

Balance per bank statement

X

Chapter 15　Bank reconciliation

Add outstanding lodgements	**X**
Less unpresented cheques	**X**
Correct bank balance after adjustment	**X**

3. Errors made by cash book（企业银行存款日记账会出现的"错误"）

a) Dishonored cheques　空头支票

Cheques included in our deposit **may not be paid by the drawer's（出票人）** bank due to some irregularities or lack of sufficient funds to cover the cheque. Our bank then notifies us of the dishonored cheque.

　Dr：Receivables
　　　Cr：Bank

b) Direct debit or standing orders（银行自动扣款，企业不知道）

Payments made into the bank account or from the bank account by way of standing order or direct debit，which **have not yet been entered in the cash book.**

c) Credit transfers（Add）（直接转账进来，企业不知道）

Cash is directly transferred into bank account

d) Bank charges（银行自动扣手续费，企业不知道）

e) Bank interest（银行自动给我们结算利息收入，企业不知道）

以下 T 字账户代表企业银行存款日记账应当怎么调整，借方表示调增，贷方表示调减。

Cash book			
Opening balance	X		
Bank interest	X	Bank charges	X
Credit transfer	X	Direct debit	X
		Dishonored cheque	X
Closing balance/Correct cash book balance	X		

在银行对账单与企业银行存款日记账调整完后，二者金额应当相等！！！

Chapter 16

Correction of errors

1. Types of error

Types of error	Description	Example	Trial balance
Errors of transposition 记账错位	Two digits（数字）in a figure are accidentally recorded the wrong way round.	A sale is recorded in the sales account as ＄643, but it has been incorrectly recorded in the total receivables account as ＄634	Dr ≠ Cr
Errors of omission 记账遗漏	Failing to record a transaction at all 借贷双方都没记账	An invoice from a supplier for ＄520 is omitted from the books entirely	Dr = Cr
	Making a debit or credit entry, but not the corresponding double entry 借贷只记录了一方	An invoice from a supplier for ＄520 is credited in payable but no other entries made	Dr ≠ Cr
Errors of principle 原则性错误（根本没有按照会计准则的要求来记）	Accounting entry breaks the 'rules' of an accounting principle or concept.	Treat certain revenue expenditure incorrectly as capital expenditure.	Dr = Cr
Errors of commission	Putting a debit entry or a credit entry in the wrong account 记错会计科目	Telephone expenses of ＄520 are debited to the electricity expenses account	Dr = Cr
	Errors of casting (adding up). 日记账加总错误 对总账没有影响 试算平衡表仍然平衡（因为试算平衡表是根据总账编的）	The total daily credit sales in the sales day book should be ＄425, but are incorrectly added up as ＄825	Dr = Cr
	Making two debit or credit entry 同时记录了两遍同一方向	Recording a sales invoice of ＄300 Dr：Trade receivables ＄500 Dr：Sales ＄500	Dr ≠ Cr

Chapter 16 Correction of errors

(Continued)

Types of error	Description	Example	Trial balance
Compensating errors 互补性错误 两个没关系的错误相互抵消了	Errors which are, coincidentally, equal and opposite to one another	Sales is credited incorrectly by $500, While bank deposit is debited incorrectly by $500	Dr = Cr
Error of original entry （科目正确，金额错了）	An incorrect figure is entered in the records and then posted to the correct account	Cash $2,000 for plant repairs is entered as $200; plant repairs account is debited with $200	Dr = Cr

错误本身是什么并不重要，关键要知道是否会影响借贷平衡以及如何纠错！

2. Correction of errors

Once an error has been detected, it needs to be put right.

TB 表平衡的情况 → DR＝CR → 直接通过分录进行调整

TB 表不平衡的情况→ Dr≠CR → 要通过 suspense account（临时性纠错的账户）来调整

1) 纠错步骤（借贷平衡时）

a) 先把错误的分录反写过来（reverse incorrect entry）

b) 写正确的分录（correct entry）

c) 将 1、2 的分录进行合并（合并）

For example：

Repairs worth $520 were incorrectly debited to the non-current asset (machinery) account instead of the repairs account.

用分录体现为：

DR：NCA   520
　　CR：Cash   520

纠错：

a) 先把错误的分录反写过来（reverse incorrect entry）

DR：Cash   520
　　CR：NCA   520

b) 写正确的分录（correct entry）

DR：repair expense   520
　　CR：cash   520

c) 将 1、2 的分录进行合并（合并）就得到调整分录（adjusting entry）

DR：repair expense   520
　　CR：NCA   520

2) 纠错步骤：（借贷不平衡时）

a) 用临时账户（suspense account）补足金额

b) 反写（a) 的分录

c) 写出正确分录

d) 合并(b)(c)分录，写出调整分录

For example：

$800 paid for plant maintenance has been correctly entered in the cash book and credited to the plant asset account.

a) 用临时账户（suspense account）补足金额

DR：Suspense account（此时贷方多了1 600，借方为0，故用临时账户补足金额）

	1,600
CR：Plant	800
CR：Cash	800

b) 反写(a) 的分录

DR：Plant	800
DR：Cash	800
CR：Suspense account	1,600

c) 写出正确的分录

DR：Maintenance expense	800
CR：Cash	800

d) 合并上述(b)(c)分录，写出调整分录：

DR：Plant	800
DR：Maintenance expense	800
CR：Suspense account	1,600

Chapter 17

Incomplete records

1. Mark up and margin

Gross profit margin = gross profit/sales * 100%

Mark up on cost = gross profit/cost of sales * 100%

Mark up on sales = gross profit/sales * 100%

	Gross profit margin = 20%	Mark up on cost = 20%	Mark up on sales = 20%
Sales	100%	120%	100%
Profit	20%	20%	20%
Cost of sales	80%	100%	80%

2. Accounting for inventory loss

Since the loss is not a trading loss, the cost of goods lost is not included in the cost of sales.

If the goods were not insured, the business must bear the loss:

Dr: Expenses (e.g. administrative expenses)

    Cr: Cost of sales

If the goods were insured, the business will not suffer a loss, because the insurance will pay back the cost of lost goods.

Dr: Insurance claim account (receivable account)

    Cr: Cost of sales

When the claim is paid, the account is then closed by:

Dr: Cash

    Cr: Insurance claim account

Chapter 18

Preparation of financial statements for sole traders

1. 回顾做账流程

编制报表步骤：
a）先编制利润表再编制资产负债表
b）对 TB 表分类，看哪些属于 SOFP，哪些属于 SPL
c）写出格式（根据 TB 表及 notes）
d）填数字（注意看 notes 需要怎么调整数字）

2. F3 层次中利润表格式

XX

Statement of profit or loss for the year ended XX.XX.XXXX

	$
Sales	X
Cost of sales	X
Gross profit	X
Other income	X
Depreciation Expense	X
Other expense	X
Finance cost	X
…	X
Profit before tax	X
Tax expense	X
Profit after tax	X

3. F3 层次中资产负债表格式

XX

Statement of financial position as at XX.XX.XXXX

	$
Assets	
Non-current assets	
Property	X
Equipment	X
...	X
Current assets	
Inventory	X
Trade accounts receivable	X
Cash in hand	X
Bank	X
Prepayment	X
...	
Total assets	X
Equities and liabilities	
Capital (Sole trader and Partnership)	X
Total equities	X
Non-current liabilities	
Long term Loan	X
...	X
Current liabilities	
Accruals	X
Trade accounts payable	X
Total liabilities	X
Total equities and liabilities	X

Chapter 19

Introduction to company accounting

1. Equity
Equity is the **residual interest** in the assets of the entity after deducting all its liabilities.

1) **Ordinary shares（普通股）**
Ordinary shares are shares which are **not preferred with** regard **to dividend payments**.（普通股：没有优先获得股利分配的权利）

Ordinary shareholders are thus the **effective owners** of a company(**voting rights**)（但是有投票权可以参与决策）

2) **Preference shares（优先股）**
Preference shares are shares which confer **certain preferential rights** on their holder.
Priority right to return their capital over ordinary shareholders in **liquidation.**（破产清算时有一定的优先偿还权，还钱先还了债权人，再还优先股，再普通股）

Priority right to pay preference **dividends**（同时优先支付优先股股利）

3) Classification of preference shares
按是否可累积进行分类：

a) Cumulative preference shares 可累积优先股

If the dividend is not paid in a given year，it is **still owed to** the shareholders in the following year，and must be paid ahead of any ordinary dividend.（指在某个营业年度内，如果公司所获得的盈利不足以分派固定的股利时，日后优先股的股东对往年未付给的股利，有权要求如数补给。）

b) Non-cumulative preference shares 不可累积优先股

If the dividend is not paid in a given year，then in the following year，**only that year's** dividend need to be paid before an ordinary dividend.（指在某年度内，如公司由于某种原因不能如数支付优先股股息时，其所欠部分，即使以后年度内有盈余，也不能要求公司给予补发的优先股。）

按是否可以赎回进行分类：

a) Irredeemable preference shares 不可赎回优先股

Preference shares which are not redeemable.（投资本金不可赎回）

b) Redeemable preference shares（NCL）可赎回优先股

Preference shares repayable by the company at a specific future date（投资本金可

赎回）

4) **Share capital**

a) **Authorised（or legal）capital**: the **maximum amount** of share capital a company is empowered to issue

b) **Issued capital**: the par amount of share capital that **has been issued** to shareholders

c) **Called-up capital**（催缴股本）: when shares are issued or allotted, a company does not always expect to be paid the full amount for the shares at once.

d) **Paid-up capital**（实缴股本）: the amount of called-up capital that **has been paid**

For example, if a company issues 400,000 ordinary shares of $1 each, calls up 75 cents per share, and receives payments of $290,000, we would have:

	$
Allotted or issued capital	400,000
Called-up capital	300,000
Paid-up capital	290,000
Capital not yet paid-up	10,000

5) **Value of shares**

Face value/Par value（票面价值）

in units of 25 cents, 50 cents, $1 or whatever seems appropriate

Market value 市场价值

the price at which someone is prepared **to purchase shares** in the company from an **existing shareholder.**

Share capital = number of shares * **par value**

6) **Share premium**

Share premium is the amount of cash received for issue of shares in excess of their par value.

Share premium is a **capital reserve, which cannot be paid out in dividends.**

Share premium **can be used** to finance the issue of **bonus shares.**

For example, A Co issues 5,000 50c shares for $6,000. What are the entries for share capital and share premium in the statement of financial position?

Dr: Cash	6,000
Cr: Share capital	2,500
Cr: Share premium	3,500

7) **Bonus issue (CAPITALIZATION ISSUE)**（红利股/送股）

Extra shares may be issued to **existing** shareholders **without** them having to **pay anything.**

The new shares are issued to the existing shareholders **in proportion** to their current shareholdings, e.g. 1 for every 50 shares held.

　　Dr: Reserves(冲减顺序: share premium → retained earnings → revaluation surplus)
　　　Cr: Ordinary share capital

Advantages	Disadvantages
Increases capital without diluting 不稀释 current shareholders' holdings	Does not raise any cash
Capitalises reserves, so they cannot be paid as dividend 不能作为股利分配	Could jeopardise 危机 payment of future dividends if profits fall

8) Rights issue

Existing shareholders are given the right (not an obligation) to buy shares in the company at a discounted price.

A rights issue differs from a bonus issue in that cash actually flows from the shareholders to the company.

　　DR: Cash
　　　CR: Share capital
　　　CR: Share premium

Advantages	Disadvantages
Raises cash for the company	Dilutes shareholders' holdings if they do not take up rights issue
Keeps reserves available for future dividends	

9) Reserves

Statutory reserves: required to set up by law, not available for distribution of dividends — capital reserve.

Non-statutory reserves: distributable as dividends if the company so wishes — revenue reserve

10) Revaluation surplus

The result of an upward revaluation of a non-current asset is a revaluation surplus.

It is another capital reserve, non-distributable.

When the relevant asset is sold, the revaluation surplus can be transferred to retained earning within equity.

　　Dr: Revaluation surplus
　　　Cr: Retained earning

11) Retained earnings (未分配利润)

Retained earnings are accumulated earnings of a company since its inception less dividends, This is the account from which dividends are paid.

12) Dividends

Dividends are appropriation of profit after tax to shareholders.

Chapter 19 Introduction to company accounting

Some companies may pay dividends in **3 stages** within one financial year.

a) Proposed — Disclose 董事会提议-披露

Proposed dividends are not adjusted for, they are simply disclosed by notes.

b) Declared — Recognise 宣告发放-确认

Dr: Retained earnings
   Cr: Dividend payable

c) Paid — Recognise 支付-确认

Dr: Dividend payable
   Cr: Cash

Dividends are not shown in statement of profit or loss, while they are shown in the statement of changes in equity (SOCIE) and statement of financial position (SOFP).

Dividend = no of shares * dividend per share

2. Statement of changes in equity(考试不常考,稍微记下格式)

	Share Capital	Share Premium	Revaluation surplus	Retained Earning	Total
Opening balance	X	X	X	X	X
Prior year adjustment					
Rights issue	X	X			X
Bonus issue	X	(X)	(X)		X
Revaluation of assets			X		X
Net profit for the year				X	X
Dividends	—	—	—	(X)	(X)
Closing balance	X	X	X	X	X

3. loan note

A **debenture**（公司债券）is a **long-term** debt instrument（债务工具）issued by a company in exchange for cash. The company promises to pay a **principal** amount at a specific date as well as **interest** on that principal amount at a specific rate per period.（还本付息）Upon issuance（发行）the debenture（公司债券）becomes **a long-term liability** in the statement of financial position, since repayment date can be 2, 5 or even for 10 years from date of issue.

Dr: Cash
   Cr: Non-current liability

Interest is always paid based on the **nominal value, regardless its market value.**

Dr: Finance cost (SPL)
   Cr: Cash/Interest payable (SOFP)

4. Income tax

The difference between the **estimated tax** on profits for one year and the **actual tax charge** finally agreed for the year is made **as an adjustment to taxation expense in the following year,** resulting in the disclosure of either an **underprovision or an overprovision** of tax.

Income tax：**All companies** pay corporate taxation on the profits they earn.

Statement of financial position	Statement of profit or loss
Tax payable to the Government is generally shown as a current liability, as it is usually due within 12 months of the year end	Deducted from profit for the year
Tax payable＝current tax payable（Estimated amount）	Tax expense＝Tax charge for the year（本年度预计金额）＋under provision(以前年度少付金额)－以前年度 over provision(以前年度多付金额) 这个公式需要记住
For various reasons, the tax on profits in the statement of profit or loss and the tax payable in the statement of financial position are not normally the same amount	

Tax payable(liability)

		Balance b/d	X
Tax paid	X	Tax expense	X
Balance c/d	X		
	X		X

Chapter 20

Preparation of financial statements for companies

1. Financial statements

IAS 1 lists the required contents of a company's **financial statements**. It also gives guidance on how items should be presented in the financial statements.

A complete set of financial statements includes the following.

Statement of financial position (SOFP)

Statement of profit or loss and other comprehensive income (SPL&OCI)

Statement of changes in equity (SOCIE)

Statement of cash flows (SOCF)

Notes, including a summary of significant accounting policies and other explanatory information

Statement of profit or loss and other comprehensive income of ABC Company for the year ended XX.XX.XXXX

	$
Sales revenue	X
Cost of sales	(X)
Gross profit	X
Other income	X
Distribution cost	(X)
Administration cost	(X)
Other operation expenses	(X)
Profit from operating	X
Finance cost	(X)
Profit before tax	X
Tax	(X)
Profit for the year	X

(Continued)

	$
Other comprehensive income:	
Gains on property revaluation	X
Total comprehensive income	<u>X</u>

Statement of financial position of ABC Company as at XX.XX.XXXX

Assets	$	$
Non-current assets		
Property, plant and equipment	X	
Intangible assets	X	
Goodwill	X	
Investments	X	
		<u>X</u>
Current assets		
Inventory	X	
Trade receivable	X	
Other current assets	X	
Cash and cash equivalents	X	
		<u>X</u>
Total assets		<u>X</u>
Equities and liabilities		
Equity		
Share capital	X	
Retained earnings	X	
Other components of equity	X	
		<u>X</u>
Non-current liabilities		
Long-term loan	X	
Long-term provisions	X	
		<u>X</u>
Current liabilities		
Trade and other payable	X	
Short term borrowing (Bank overdraft)	X	
Current portion of long-term borrowings	X	
Short-term provisions	X	

Chapter 20　Preparation of financial statements for companies

(Continued)

Assets	$	$
Current tax payable	X	
		X
Total equity and liabilities		X̲

Statement of changes in equity of ABC Company for the year ended 31 December 20X8

	Share capital $	Share premium $	Revaluation surplus $	Retained earnings $	Total $
Balance at 1.1.XXXX	X	X	X	X	X
Changes in accounting policy				(X)	(X)
Restated balance	X̲	X̲	X̲	X̲	X̲
Changes in equity for XXXX					
Dividends				(X)	(X)
Total comprehensive income for the year			X	X	X
Issue of share capital	X	X			X
Balance at 31.12.XXXX	X̲	X̲	X̲	X̲	X̲

2. IFRS 15 Revenue from contracts with customer

Revenue is recognized and measured using a five step model

Step 1　Identify the contract with the customer（识别与客户订立的合同）

Step 2　Identify the separate performance obligations（识别单项履约义务）

Step 3　Determine the transaction price（确定交易价格）

Step 4　Allocate the transaction price to the performance obligations（将对价分摊至各单项履约义务）

Step 5　Recognise revenue when a performance obligation is satisfied（确认收入）

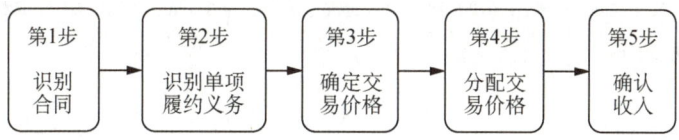

编制报表步骤总结

第一步　先对 TB 表分类，看哪些属于 SOFP，哪些属于 SPL，哪些属 SOCIE

第二步　写出格式（根据 TB 表及 notes）

第三步　填数字（看 notes 需要怎么调整数字）

第四步　先编制利润表再编制资产负债表

Chapter 21

Events after the reporting period

1. Definition

Events after the reporting period are those events, **both favorable and unfavorable** 有利与不利的, that occur **between the reporting date** and the date on which the financial statements are **authorized for issue**.（Reporting date — authorizing date）.

2. Adjusting events

Events that provide further evidence of conditions that **existed at the reporting date should be adjusted** for in the financial statements. Example as following：

a）Evidence of a **permanent diminution（永久减值）** in **property** value prior to the year end

b）Sale of inventory after the end of the reporting period for **less than its carrying value** at the year end（存货减值）

c）**Insolvency 破产** of a customer with a balance owing at the year end（比如应收账款收不回来了）

d）Amounts received or paid in respect of **legal or insurance claims** which were in negotiation at the year end（期末已经存在的诉讼，而非期后存在的诉讼事项，考试重点）

e）Discovery of **fraud or errors** showing the financial statements are incorrect

f）**Determination** after the year end of the sale or purchase **price** of assets sold or purchased before the year end

g）Evidence of a **permanent diminution（永久减值）** in the value of a **long-term investment** prior to the year end

3. Non-adjusting events

Events which do not affect the situation at the reporting date should not be adjusted for，but should **be disclosed** in the financial statements.

a）Acquisition of，or disposal of，a subsidiary **after the year end**（期后收购、处置子公司）

b）Announcement of a plan to discontinue an operation（期后宣告终止部分经营）

c）Announcement or commencing implementation of a major restructuring（期后宣

告重大重组）

　　d）Major purchases and disposals of assets（期后重大资产的购买和处置）

　　e）Destruction of a production plant by fire after the end of the reporting period

　　f）Share transactions after the end of the reporting period（期后发行股票）

　　g）Litigation（诉讼）commenced after the end of the reporting period（期后才开始的法律诉讼，考试重点，注意与前面调整事项的区分）

　　h）Dividends（股利）**proposed or declared after the end of the reporting period are not recognized as a liability in the accounts at the reporting date, but are disclosed in the notes to the accounts.**（稍微记下这句话）

　　调整事项中：减值及法律诉讼常考

　　非调整事项中：期后的诉讼、火灾等常考

4. Disclosure requirements

If disclosure of events occurring after the reporting period is required by this standard, the following information should be provided:

The nature of the event（性质是什么）

An estimate of the financial effect or a statement that such an estimate cannot be made（披露可能的财务影响或无法估计的原因）

Chapter 22

Statement of cash flow

1. The need for statement of cash flow

a) Cash flow statement concentrates on the sources and uses of cash and are a useful indicator of a company's liquidity and solvency.（反映一个公司的流动性及偿付能力的重要指标）

b) Shareholders might believe that if a company makes a profit after tax，then this is the amount which it could afford to pay as a dividend.

c) Survival of a business entity depends not so much on profits as on its ability to pay its debts when they fall due.（债务到期，有钱还，企业才能活下去）

d) Cash is less likely to be manipulated than profit（相比利润，现金相对来说不容易被操纵）

2. Definition

IAS 7 (Revised) Cash Flow Statements defines the followings：

Cash comprises **cash on hand and deposits** payable on demand；

Cash equivalents are **short-term（3个月内可变现）**, highly liquid investments that are convertible to **known amounts of cash** and which are subject to **insignificant risk** of changes in value.

An investment maturity date should **normally be three months** from its acquisition date.

The **bank overdrafts** are repayable on demand and will be included in cash and cash equivalents.（**bank overdrafts** 记着作为现金及现金等价物的减项）

Cash flows are inflows and outflows of cash and cash equivalents.

3. Presentation of statement of cash flow

IAS 7 requires statements of cash flows to report cash flows during the period classified by **operating, investing and financing activities.**

1) Operating activity (CFO) 经营活动产生的现金流量

Operating activities are the **principle revenue** producing activities of enterprise and other activities **that are not investing or financing activities.**

Most of operating cash flows will be those items which determine the net profit or loss of the entity. Examples of cash flow from operating activities：

a）Cash receipts from the sale of goods and the rendering of services 销售商品及提供劳务收到的现金

b）Cash receipts from royalties，fees，commissions and other revenue

c）Cash payments to suppliers for goods and services 采购商品及接受劳务支付的现金

d）Cash payments to and on behalf of employees（eg.工资）

2）Investing activities(CFI)投资活动产生的现金流量

Investing activities are the acquisition and disposal of long-term assets and other investments not included in cash equivalents.

Examples of cash flows arising from investing activities：

a）Cash payments to acquire non-current assets 购买 NCA

b）Cash receipts from sales of non-current assets 处置 NCA

c）Cash payments to acquire other investment（shares or debentures of other enterprises）购买其他公司股票或债券

d）Cash receipts from sales of other investment 处置投资

e）Cash advances（预付款）and loans made to other parties 对其他企业进行贷款

f）Cash receipts from the repayment of advances and loans made to other parties 其他企业偿还贷款

3）Financing activities(CFF)筹资活动产生的现金流量

Financing activities are activities that result in changes in the composition of the equity capital and borrowings of the enterprise.（改变企业债务和股权比例的）

Examples of cash flows which might arise under these headings：

a）Cash proceeds from issuing shares 发行股票获得的现金

b）Cash payments to owners to redeem the enterprises' shares 赎回股票支付的现金

c）Cash proceeds from borrowings 借款

d）Cash repayments of debt 偿还负债

IAS 7（Revised）allows **two methods** of reporting cash flows from operating activities：

The **DIRECT method** whereby major classes of gross cash receipts and gross cash payments are disclosed

The **INDIRECT method**. whereby net profit or loss is adjusted for the effects of：

√ transactions of a non-cash nature 非现金交易(非收现收入/非付现成本)

√ any deferrals or Accruals of past or future operating cash receipts or payments，and

√ items of income or expense associated with investing or financing cash flows

IAS 7（Revised）**encourages** enterprises to report cash flows from operation activities doing the **direct method**. It is believed that the direct method will provide more useful information about an entity's cash flows，**but it may not be practical or cost effective** in many circumstances.

When the indirect method is adopted, the net cash flow from operating activities is determined by adjusting net profit or loss for the effects of:（间接法是通过调整"PBT"税前利润来反映现金流）

Changes during the period in inventories and operating receivables and payables 存货/应收/应付 Non-cash items such as depreciation 折旧调整

All other items for which the cash effects are investing or financing cash flows 投资/筹资相关的调整

4. Interest and dividends

Cash flows from interest and dividends received and paid should each be disclosed separately.（利息及股利需要单独披露）Each should be classified in a **consistent manner** from period to period.

Interest paid should be classified as an operating cash flow（正常经营活动中的利息）or a financing cash flow.（为了融资支付的利息）（支付的利息，题干中未明确说明就放在经营活动中）

Interest received and dividends received should be classified as operating cash flows or, **more usually, as investing cash flows.**（收到的利息/股利通常作为投资活动的现金流量）

Dividends paid by the enterprise should be classified as an operating cash flow, so that users can assess the enterprises' ability to pay dividends out of operating cash flows, or **more usually, as a financing cash flow**, showing the cost of obtaining financial resources.（支付的股利通常作为筹资活动的现金流量）

5. Format

Statement of Cash Flow for the year ended XXXX

Cash flow from operating activities

Cash receipts from customers	x
Cash paid to suppliers and employees	(x)
Cash generated from operations	x
— Interested paid	(x)
— income tax paid	(x)
Net cash flow from operation activity	x

Other parts is same as indirect format

a) **Direct method format**

b) **Indirect method format**

Statement of cash flows of ABC Company for the year ended XX.XX.XXXX

Chapter 22　Statement of cash flow

	$
Cash flows from operation activities	
Profit before taxation	X
Adjustment for:	
Depreciation/amortization charged	X
Loss/profit on disposal on non-current assets	X/(X)
Finance costs	X
Investment income	(X)
Net cash flow before working capital changes	X
Working capital changes:	
(increase)/(decrease)in inventory	(X)/X
(increase)/(decrease)in trade receivable	(X)/X
Increase/(decrease)in trade payable	X/(X)
Cash generated from operations	X
-interest paid	(X)
-income tax paid	(X)
Net cash flows from operation activity	X
Cash flows from investing activities:	
Purchase of property, plant and equipment	(X)
Proceeds from sale of equipment	X
Interest received/investment income received	X
Dividends received	X
Net cash flows from investing activities	X
Cash flows from financing activities:	
Proceeds from issuance of share capital	X
Proceeds from long-term borrowing	X
Loan repayment	(X)
Dividends paid	(X)
Net cash flows from financing activities	X
Net increase/decrease in cash and cash equivalents	X/(X)
Cash and cash equivalents at the beginning of period	X
Cash and cash equivalents at the end of period	X

Preparing a statement of cash flows is **very straightforward**. You should therefore **simply learn the format and apply the steps noted** in the example below. **Although you won't**

have to prepare a full statement of cash flows in your exam, the examiner has highlighted the importance of practicing full questions so that you fully understand the underlying principles.

（通常来说，考试是不会考到现金流量表的，但是还是要掌握。）

6. 编表步骤

a）记住间接法格式，考试若考到编报表的时候直接先上格式

b）T字账的working一定要会写（一般tax、PPE、retained earnings是必写working）

c）各类调整的方向一定不要搞错（究竟是调增现金流还是调减现金流）

d）期末现金及现金等价物若有overdraft一定要减去

Chapter 23

Introduction of group

1. Trade investment(通常持股比例在小于 20%)

A trade investment is a **simple investment** in the shares of another entity **that is not an associate or a subsidiary**.

A trade investment is a simple investment in the shares of another entity, that is **held for the accretion of wealth** 财富增值(为了增值买卖或是长期获利), and is **not an associate or a subsidiary.**

  Dr：Investment（在报表上通常列式在非流动资产部分） XX
    Cr：Cash XX

2. Associate

Associate：An entity over which the investor **has significant influence**. 重大影响(IAS 28)

The existence of significant influence is usually evidenced in the **following ways**：

a) Representation on the board of directors（董事会）(or equivalent) of the investee（董事会当中有代表

b) **Participation** in the policy making process（可参与决策）

c) Material transactions between investor and investee（有重大交易，比如为主要供应商）

d) Interchange of management personnel（内部高管的互换）

e) Provision of essential technical information（提供核心技术信息）

Note：

If an investor **holds 20% or more of the voting power（投票权）of the entity**, it can be presumed that the investor has **significant influence** over the entity, unless it can be clearly shown that this is not the case.（通常来说持股比例超过20%就代表有重大影响）

1) Equity method in consolidated financial statements — IAS28

a) P acquire A 40% shares in cash for 1,000

  Dr：Investment in associate 1,000
    Cr：Cash 1,000

b) After acquisition, A makes a profit of $500

Dr：Investment in associate　　　　　　　　　　　200（500*40%）
　　　　Cr：Share of profit of associate　　　　　　　200（500*40%）
c) At the same time，A make a dividend $ 200
　　Dr：Cash　　　　　　　　　　　　　　　　　　80（200*40%）
　　　　Cr：Investment in associate　　　　　　　　　80（200*40%）

The F3/FFA syllabus requires you to **understand the principle** of equity accounting，**but** you will **not be expected to perform calculations** using equity accounting techniques in your exam.（理解即可，F3中不会考到你复杂的计算）

2) COST METHOD IN SINGLE FINANCIAL STATEMENTS

a) P acquire A 40% shares in cash for 1,000
　　Dr：Investment in associate　　　　　　　　　　1,000
　　　　Cr：Cash　　　　　　　　　　　　　　　　　　　1,000
b) After acquisition，A makes a profit of $ 500—Do nothing
c) P received dividend from A 200
　　Dr：Cash　　　　　　　　　　　　　　　　　　　200
　　　　Cr：Investment income　　　　　　　　　　　　　200

3. Group

The parent has **power over more than 50% of the voting rights** by virtue of agreement with other investors.

The parent has power to **govern（监管控制）** the financial and operating policies of the entity by statute or under an agreement（控制财务经营决策）

The parent has the power to **appoint or remove a majority** of members of the board of directors（or equivalent governing body）（任命或罢免董事会大多数成员）

The parent has power to cast **a majority of votes** at meetings of the **board of directors**（董事会当中大多数的投票权）

Control can usually be assumed to exist when the parent owns **more than half（ie over 50%）of the voting power** of an entity unless it can be clearly shown that such ownership does not constitute control（these situations will be very rare）.（通常来说持有拥有投票权的股权超过50%即形成控制）

1) Definition

Subsidiary 子公司

An entity that is controlled by another entity（known as the parent）.

Parent 母公司

An entity that has one or more subsidiaries.

Group 集团

A parent and all its subsidiaries.

Control

The power to govern the financial and operating policies of an entity so as to obtain benefits from its activities.

Consolidation means presenting the results, assets and liabilities of a group of companies **as if they were one company.**

2) Basic principle for consolidation

IFRS 10 requires a parent to present consolidated financial statements 母公司编制合并报表（also referred to as group accounts）in which the accounts of the parent and subsidiary (or subsidiaries) **are combined and presented as a single entity.**

This presentation means that the **substance, rather than the legal form**, of the relationship between parent and subsidiaries will be presented.

Consolidated financial statements **ignore the legal boundaries** of the separate legal entities.

They are important because the users of the parent's financial statements need to know about the financial position, results of operations and changes in financial position of the **group as a whole.**

IFRS 10 requires that, when a parent issues consolidated financial statements, it should **consolidate all subsidiaries, both foreign and domestic**

Basis principle of consolidation is:

Adding together 加总求和

Cancellation of like items internal to the group 抵销内部交易

Consolidate as if you owned everything then show the extent to which you do not own everything（先假设你拥有100%，再体现你不拥有的东西"少数股东权益"）

Chapter 24

The consolidated statement of financial position

1. Introduction

1）日期

DOA：date of acquisition（收购日，形成控制那一天）

DOC：date of consolidation（合并日，母公司会计期末）

2）P → 100% 控股的情况

Investment in subsidiary：对子公司的投资（即为我们花了多少钱买子公司）

= Fair value of net assets of S + Goodwill

= Net assets + Fair value adjustment + Goodwill

= Total assets − Total liabilities + Fair value adjustment + Goodwill

即为：**Goodwill 商誉 = investment in subsidiary − FV of net assets**（考试更常用的公式是这个）

3）P → 50%～100%（非 100%）控股的情况

Investment in subsidiary：对子公司的投资（即为我们花了多少钱买子公司）

= Fair value of net assets of S + Goodwill − **Non-controlling interest（NCI）**

= **Net assets + Fair value adjustment + Goodwill − NCI**

= **Total assets − Total liabilities + Fair value adjustment + Goodwill − NCI**

即为：**Goodwill 商誉 = investment in subsidiary + NCI − FV of net assets of S**（考试更常用的公式是这个）

2. Consolidation principle

Basic consolidation consists of two procedures

Cancelling out items which appear as an asset in one company and a liability in another（内部交易，比如应收应付的抵销）

Then **adding together all the uncancelled assets and liabilities** on a line by line basis.（逐行相加剩下的所有资产负债）

The asset 'investment in subsidiaries' in the parent company accounts always cancels with the share capital of the subsidiary companies. The only share capital in the consolidated accounts is that of the parent company.

Chapter 24 The consolidated statement of financial position

（这段话在 F3 层次中先简单理解，到了后期 F7 和 SBR 会逐渐形成更深入的理解；这儿简单理解为：花了"investment in subsidiaries"账户里所列示的钱把子公司的 equity 从子公司股东那儿买过来了，买过来的形式是相关的资产和负债一起打包买过来，所以如果再加一遍 equity 就会重复，所以 equity 应当抵销。）

3. Goodwill arising on consolidation

Goodwill is **the difference between consideration paid and the fair value of net assets of subsidiary at acquisition**.

Fair value adjustment：

The **land and buildings**（考试中通常这两项都是公允价值会高于账面价值）of the subsidiary may be worth more than their carrying amount at acquisition. If this is the case, it must be taken into account in the consolidated financial statements.

Goodwill calculation：

Consideration transferred	X
Non-controlling interest	X
Less fair value of identifiable net assets of subsidiary company at acquisition date:	
Share capital	X
Share premium	X
Retained earnings at acquisition	X
Fair value adjustments at acquisition	X
	(X)
Goodwill	X

The **consideration paid** by the parent for the shares in the subsidiary can take **different forms**. (收购所支付的对价有不同的形式)

The calculation of goodwill **must be based on the fair value** of the consideration transferred.

a) Cash

b) Shares of parent company — fair value of shares is their **market price** on the date of acquisition (number of shares issued * share price of P)

4. Non-controlling interest(NCI)（少数股东权益）

The **non-controlling interest (NCI)** shows the extent to which net assets controlled by the group are **owned by other parties**.

IFRS 10 defines non-controlling interest as the equity in a subsidiary not attributable, directly or indirectly, to a parent.

NCI is **shown in the equity section** of the consolidated statement of financial position and is included in the consolidated financial statements at its fair value plus the NCI's share of post-acquisition retained earnings and other reserves.

Fair value of NCI at date of acquisition (DOA)	X
Plus: NCI's share of S's post-acquisition retained earnings	X
NCI at reporting date/date of consolidation (DOC)	X

5. Intra-group sales

There may be intra-group trading (内部交易) within the group.

For example, Subsidiary Co may sell goods on credit to Parent Co.

Parent Co would then be a receivable in the accounts of Subsidiary Co, while Subsidiary Co would be a payable in the accounts of Parent Co.

详细讲解逻辑如下，会比教材更复杂，但是希望大家掌握原理。

In the buying company's accounts, inventory will be valued at acquisition cost which now includes the profit element earned by the selling company.

The problem is that from the group's point of view this profit has not yet been realised because no sale has been made outside the group and therefore closing inventories are overstated by the profit element.

直接看例子：

P公司系S公司的母公司。P公司本期个别利润表的营业收入中有2 000万元，系向S公司销售商品实现的收入，其商品成本为1 400万元，销售毛利率为30%。S公司本期从P公司购入的商品本期均未实现销售，期末存货中包含有2 000万元从P公司购进的商品，该存货中包含的未实现内部销售损益为600万元。编制合并报表内部交易的抵销分录：

借：营业收入　　　　　　　　　　　　　　　　2 000
　　贷：营业成本　　　　　　　　　　　　　　　　1 400
　　　　存货　　　　　　　　　　　　　　　　　　 600

DR: Sales　　　　　　　　　　　　　　　　　　2,000
　　CR: Cost of sales　　　　　　　　　　　　　1,400
　　CR: Inventory　　　　　　　　　　　　　　　 600

分录归纳整理：

借：期初未分配利润（年初存货中包含的未实现内部销售利润）（注：F3中一般不考这个金额，记住下面的分录就行）

借：营业收入（本期内部商品销售产生的收入）
　　贷：营业成本
　　　　存货（期末存货中未实现内部销售利润）

上述抵销分录的原理为：本期发生的未实现内部销售收入与本期发生存货中未实现内部销售利润之差即为本期发生的未实现内部销售成本。抵销分录中的"期初未分配利润"和"存货"两项之差即为本期发生的存货中未实现内部销售利润。

变为F3中的分录即为：

1) P-S 母公司卖给子公司的情况

Chapter 24 The consolidated statement of financial position

　　a) 资产负债表中（SOFP）：

DR：Retained earnings（Unrealized profit）

　　CR：Inventory（Unrealized profit）

　　b) 利润表中（SOP/L）：

DR：Sales（Intra-group sales）

　　CR：Cost of sale（Intra-group sales — URP）

　　将上述分录合并：

DR：Retained earnings b/f（URP b/f）（F7 中一般此项为 0，即为期初无未实现内部销售利润）

DR：Sales（Intra-group sales）

　　CR：Cost of sales（Intra-group sales — URP）

　　CR：Inventory（Unrealized profit）

　　2) S to P（子公司卖给母公司）

　　子公司卖给母公司存货就会产生一个问题，即"少数股东是否承担未实现内部交易损益？"

　　合并财务报表准则第三十六条：母公司向子公司出售资产所发生的未实现内部交易损益，应当全额抵销"归属于母公司所有者的净利润"。子公司向母公司出售资产所发生的未实现内部交易损益，应当按照母公司对该子公司的分配比例在"归属于母公司所有者的净利润"和"少数股东损益"之间分配抵销。

　　则分录变为：

　　a) 资产负债表中（SOFP）

DR：Group retained earnings（Unrealized profit * P% shareholding）

DR：Retained earnings of NCI（Unrealized profit * NCI% shareholding）

　　CR：Inventory（Unrealized profit）

　　b) 利润表中（SOP/L）

DR：sales（intra-group sales）

　　CR：cost of sale（intra-group sales — URP）

　　合并则为：

DR：Retained earnings b/f of Parent（URP b/f * P% shareholding）（F3 中一般此项为 0，即为期初无未实现内部销售利润）

DR：Retained earnings b/f of NCI（URP b/f * NCI% shareholding）（F3 中一般此项为 0，即为期初无未实现内部销售利润）

DR：Sales（Intra-group sales）

　　CR：Cost of sales（Intra-group sales — URP）

　　CR：Inventory（Unrealized profit）

　　看例子：

　　S 公司系 P 公司子公司，P 公司拥有 S 公司 80% 的股份。2×19 年 3 月 1 日，S 公司向 P 公司出售一批存货，成本为 80 万元，未计提存货跌价准备，售价为 100 万元，至 2×19 年 12 月 31 日，P 公司将上述存货对外出售 70%。编制合并报表内部交易的抵销分录：

计算未实现损益(URP) = (100 − 80) * (1 − 70%) = 6(万元)
抵销分录：
a) 资产负债表中：

DR：Retained earnings (6万元 * 80%)　　　　　　　48,000
DR：NCI(6万元 * 20%)　　　　　　　　　　　　　　12,000
　　CR：Inventory　　　　　　　　　　　　　　　　　　60,000

b) 利润表中：

DR：Sales (1,000,000)　　　　　　　　　　　　　1,000,000
　　CR：Cost of sales (1,000,000 − 60,000)　　　　940,000

6. Retained earnings

Group's retained earnings	$
P's retained earnings（per question）	X
Group's share of post R. E.（X * S%）	X
Less unrealised profit	(X)
Group's returned earnings @DOC	X

7. Sum

Consolidated statement of financial position of P group as at XX.XX.XXXX

Non-current assets	Equity and liabilities
Investment = 0	Share capital（only P）
Goodwill（working）	Share premium（only P）
Tangible NCA（P + S + FV_adj）	Retained earning（working）
	NCI（working）
Current assets	Total equity
Inventory = P + S − PUP	
TR = P + S − Intra	Current liabilities
Bank and cash（P + S）	TP = P + S − Intra
	Tax（P + S）
Total assets	Total equity and liabilities

Chapter 25

The consolidated statement of profit or loss

1. Consolidated principle

If a subsidiary is acquired during the year, **only the post-acquisition** element of the statement of profit or loss balances is included on consolidation.

Consolidated sales＝P's sales＋S's sales－intra－sales price

Consolidated cost of sales＝P's cost of sales＋S's cost of sales－(sales－urp)

Unrealised profit＝(Intra－sales price－Cost of sales) * percentage unsold

(内部交易的抵销处理见上一章)

Statement of profit or loss of P Group for the year ended XX.XX.XXXX

	$
Sales revenue (P + S * n/12 − intra sales price)	X
Cost of sales (P + S * n/12 − intra sales price + unrealised profit)	(X)
Gross profit(P + S * n/12 − unrealised profit)	X
Distribution cost(P + S * n/12)	(X)
Administration costs(P + S * n/12)	(X)
Profit before tax	X
Tax(P + S * n/12)	(X)
Profit for the year	X
Profit attributable to:	
Owners of parent (profit for the year — NCI)	X
Non-controlling interest(NCI% * S's post-acquisition profit)	X

Chapter 26

Interpretation of financial statements

1. Ratio classification

Ratios provide information through comparison, which can be analyzed from four aspects: Profitability and return(衡量盈利能力)

Liquidity, cash and other working capital(衡量短期偿债能力)

Debt and gearing(Long term solvency)(衡量长期破产迹象)

2. Profitability and return

1) Gross profit margin = Gross profit/sales * 100% 毛利率

This ratio is of fundamental importance in the analysis.(每一块钱销售收入能带来多少毛利润)

2) Operating profit margin = PBIT(Profit before interest and tax)/Sales * 100%

A high profit margin means a high profit per \$1 of sales, but if this also means that sales prices are high, there is a strong possibility that sales turnover will be depressed, and so asset turnover lower.(每一块钱销售收入能带来多少息税前利润)

3) *Asset turnover* = ("Sales revenue" × 100%)/(*Capital employed*)(资产周转率,每一块钱的资本能为企业带来多少收入)

Capital employed = equity + long term liability 占用的资本(占用资金的"长期"来源)
$$= \text{Total assets} - \text{Current liability}$$

Reflect the pure business profitability, without considering the cost of capital employed.

Can be interpreted by comparing it with previous period or competitor or market borrowing rates

A high asset turnover means that the company is generating a lot of sales, but to do this it might have to keep its prices down and so accept a low profit margin per \$1 of sales.

4) Return on Capital Employed = (PBIT×100%)/(Capital employed)

ROCE = Operating profit margin × Asset turnover

ROE = (Profit after tax and preference dividend)/(Equity shareholder 'funds')

ROCE measures the overall efficiency of a company in employing the resources available to it.

Chapter 26　Interpretation of financial statements

3. Liquidity

A simple measure of how much of the total current assets is financed by current liability.（衡量多少短期负债支撑着多少短期资产）

1) Current ratio = (Current asset)/(current liability)

If, for example the result is 2∶1, this means only a limited portion of assets are funded by the current liabilities. Acceptable current ratio is 1.5

2) Quick ratio (or acid test ratio 酸性测试比率) = (Current asset − inventoryinventory)/(Current liability)

Inventory are not very liquid asset

Acceptable 0.8, but ideally be at least 1

3) Working capital

Working capital analysis can help us to interpret the liquidity ratio more in depth. Through the analysis we can assess the management's efficiency in controlling the main elements of working capital: inventory, receivable and payable.

a) Receivables days = (trade receivables balance * 365)/(credit sales)

Estimated average receivable collection period（应收账款平均回收周期,多少天能收回应收账款）

Increased receivable days may indicate poor credit control. However, some companies must allow generous credit terms to win customers.

b) Payable days = (trade payable balance * 365)/(credit purchase)

Estimated average period to settle the payment to suppliers

Increased payable days may indicate deteriorated liquidity.（暗示资金流动性出现了问题）

c) Inventory turnover = (inventory balance × 365)/(cost of sales)

Indicate the average number of days that inventory **is held for** in a business（存货持有的天数）

Increased inventory days may indicate inefficiency of inventory management.

d) Operating cycle = inventory days + receivable days − payable days（企业一个经营循环需要多少天）

4. Debt and gearing (long-term solvency)

Debt ratios are concerned with how much the company owes in relation to its size, whether its **debt burden** seems heavy or light.

1) Gearing ratio = [(long-term debts) × 100%]/(capital employed)

Shows a company's long term capital structure

No absolute limit, over 50% is said to be highly geared.

If gearing is too high, company may find it difficult to borrow in future.（比如获得新借款难、借款成本更高）

2) Leverage = (Shareholder's equity)/(capital employed)

3) Debt ratio＝(Total debts×100％)/(Total assets) 资产负债率

Reflect the debt burden of a company

The safe limit varies amount companies, depending on the nature of business

General bench marking: 50％

4) Interest coverage＝(Profit before interest and tax)/(Interest charge) 利息保障倍数

Shows whether a company earns enough profit to pay interest.

A fall on PBIT would have significant influence on profits available for ordinary shareholder.

3 times is considered to be acceptable limits.

5. Problems of ratio analysis

1) Information problems

a) Base information is out of date, so timeliness of information leads to a problem of interpretation.

b) Historical information is not appropriate to make decision

c) Summarized information can not provide details

d) Analysis identifies symptoms not causes and thus of limited use (只看到了问题,但不知道原因所在)

2) Comparison problems: trend analysis

a) Effects of price changes make comparisons difficult unless adjustments are made

b) Impacts of changes in technology on the price of assets, the likely return and the future markets

c) Impacts of a changing environment on the results reflected in the accounting information

d) Potential effects of changes in accounting policies on the reported results

e) Problems associated with establishing a normal base year to compare other years with

CORPORATE AND BUSINESS LAW

Chapter 1

Essential elements of the legal system: court structure

1. What is law?

Law is a formal mechanism of social control.

It provides a **structure** for dealing with and resolving disputes that may arise, as well as providing some **deterrent** to those wishing to disrupt **social order**.

2. Types of law

The English legal system distinguishes several different types of law.

Common law & Equity	Statute law
Private law & Public law	Criminal law & Civil law

2.1 Common law and equity

Common law: a system of **rigid rules** laid down by royal courts.

Remedies under common law are **monetary** (**damages**).

Equity: resolve disputes where damages are not a suitable remedy and to introduce **fairness** into the legal system.

2.2 Statute law

Parliament is responsible for **statute law**.

Statute law is usually made in areas so **complicated** or **unique** that suitable common law alternatives are unlikely, or would take an unacceptable length of time, to develop

2.3 Private law and public law

Private law: law which deals with **relationships** and **interactions** between businesses, and **private individuals**, **groups** or **organisations**.

Public law: mainly concerned with **government** and the **operation** and **functions** of **public organisations** such as councils doctrine of judicial precedent and local authorities.

The doctrine of judicial precedent

该原则要求法院将遵循先前确定的判决先例,具体而言,同样的案件将获得同样的处理。这样一来,英国法的规则不会因为时间的经过而灭失效力。这样一来,英国法的规则不会因为时间的经过而灭失效力。

2.4 Criminal law and civil law

Criminal law is a part of **public** law and deals with behaviour that the **state** considers unwelcome and wishes to prevent. Criminal law also decides how those guilty of committing unlawful behaviour should be **punished**.

Civil law is a form of **private law** used by individuals to assert their rights against other individuals, the aim being to **provide compensatory remedies,** not punish them.

The **distinction** between criminal and civil liability is central to the English legal system and to the way the court system is structured.

Distinction between criminal and civil cases

Feature	Civil	Criminal
Who brings action?	Claimant	Prosecution by state(CPS)
Standard of Proof	Balance of probabilities	Beyond reasonable doubt
Decisions	Liable/not liable (Judge)	Guilty/not guilty (Jury)
Aims	Compensation	Punishment
Remedies	Damages	Prison/Fines
Law	Private law	Public law

3. The system of courts

3.1 court structure

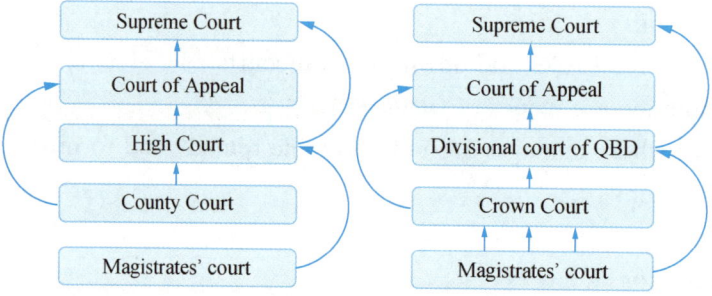

3.2 Operation of Civil procedures

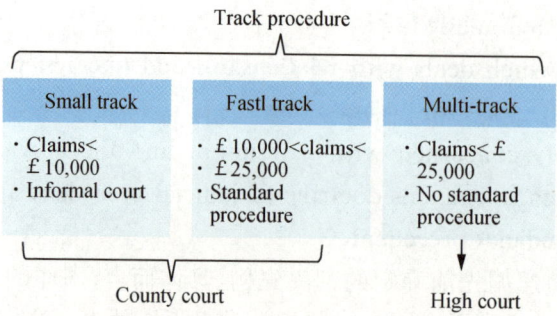

Chapter 1 Essential elements of the legal system: court structure

Magistrates court

In civil cases the magistrate may hear family proceedings in addition to having powers of recovery in relation to council tax and domestic bills.

County court (have civil jurisdiction only)

Broadly speaking the County court will hear cases of small claims and fast track basis.

High court

a) The Queen Bench Division — hears cases relating to contract and tort, its judges are specialists in commercial law.

b) The Chancery Division — hears cases relating to: Trusts and mortgages; Revenue matters; Bankruptcy; Disputed wills and administration of estates of deceased persons; Partnership and company matters.

c) The Family Division — hears all cases related to Matrimonial; Family property; Proceedings relating to children (wardship, guardianship, adoption, legitimacy); Appeals from Magistrates' Courts on family matters; Appeals from County Courts on family matters.

Court of appeal

The Court of Appeal will hear appeals from the three divisions of the High Court, the county court and the Employment Appeal Tribunal. The appeals rocedure takes the form of a rehearing of the case, using a transcript of the case and the udge's notes. Witnesses are not re-examined and new evidence is not usually ermitted.

Supreme court

Justices of the Supreme Court hear appeals from the Court of Appeal, and occasionally leap frog appeals from the High Court.

European Court of Human Rights (ECHR)

The European Court of Human Rights is the supreme court of those European states who have signed up to the European Convention of Human Rights. Any individual who alleges that their human rights have been violated can bring an action against those responsible.

European Court of Justice (ECJ)

Sited in Luxembourg the function of the ECJ is to ensure that 'in the interpretation and application of this Treaty, the law is observed'. It is the ultimate authority on EC law. The court hears disputes between nations and institutions of the EU.

The Privy Council

The Judicial Committee of the Privy Council is the final Court of Appeal for certain Commonwealth countries. Their decisions are also important to cases heard in the UK as they have persuasive influence over hearings concerning points of law applicable under the UK's jurisdiction.

4. Criminal Courts

The operation of criminal procedures

There are three main categories of criminal offences as follows:

➢ Summary offences — minor crimes those subject to maximum punishments of six months imprisonment and/or £5,000 fine, only triable summarily in Magistrates' Courts.

➢ Indictable offences — more serious offences subject to maximum punishments in excess of six months imprisonment and/or £5,000 fine, that can only be heard in a Crown Court.

➢ Triable either way — offence such as theft, drug and some involving violence against the person which are triable by either the Magistrates or Crown court, is one where the accused has the choice of which court will hear the case.

1) Magistrates

This court is empowered to try summary offences without a jury and committal proceedings for indictable offences.

2) Crown court

Hears all indictable cases, and can confirm, reverse, or vary any part of the judgement of the Magistrates Court.

3) High court

The Divisional Court of the Queen's Bench Division of the High Court will hear case stated appeals only from the magistrates.

4) Court of appeal

The Criminal Division of the Court of Appeal will hear appeals against convictions and sentences imposed by the Crown Court.

5) Supreme Court

The Justices will hear appeals from either the prosecution or the defence from either the Court of Appeal or the High Court.

Chapter 2

Sources of law

1. What is meant by case law?
- The first legal source of law
- Judge-made law: consisting of decisions made in the courts
- A court's decision is expected to be consistent with previous decisions
- Once a legal principle is decided by an appropriate court it is a judicial precedent

Where equitable rules conflict with common law rules, equitable rules prevail.

1.1 What is meant by precedent?

A precedent is a previous court decision which another court is bound to follow by deciding a subsequent case in the same way.

The nature of precedent itself operates through the interpretation of judges' decisions, requiring each decision to be separated into:

- **Ratio Decidendi** (the **reason for the decision**) — this is the **binding** element of the judgment.
- **Obiter Dicta** (**statements made by the way**) — not binding, merely of **persuasive** authority and can be taken into consideration in later cases.

1.2 Court hierarchy

Only decisions of the **higher courts in important cases** can **create** precedent.
- Supreme Court — binds **all** lower courts, but not itself.
- Court of Appeal — binds **all** lower courts, and itself.
- High court — binds **all** lower courts, and usually itself.
- **Magistrates/County/Crown courts cannot create precedent.**

Established precedents will not be binding in the following circumstances:
a) **Overruling**: Court higher in the legal hierarchy overruled precedent
b) **Reversing**: A procedure whereby a court higher in the hierarchy reverses the

decision of a lower court in the same case

c) **Distinguishing**: A precedent is avoided by demonstrating that the material facts of two cases are not the same

1.3 Appraisal of precedent

Advantages	Disadvantages
Consistent	Inconsistent
Efficient	Limit judges' discretion
Flexible	Bulk
Practical	Unfair precedent

2. Legislation

The second major source of law is legislation (known as statute law), and may take form of **Acts of Parliament** or **Delegated legislation** under the Acts.

Parliament is deemed to be the supreme law maker in the UK and consists of 3 bodies, the House of Commons, the House of Lords, and the Monarch.

2.1 Parliamentary sovereignty

Parliament may:
- Repeal earlier statutes
- Overrule or modify case law developed in the courts
- Make new law on subjects which have not been regulated by law before

2.2 Parliamentary procedure

Before a piece of primary UK legislation is passed, two initial stages must be negotiated:

a) Green paper — public consultation document

b) White paper — firm proposal for legislation

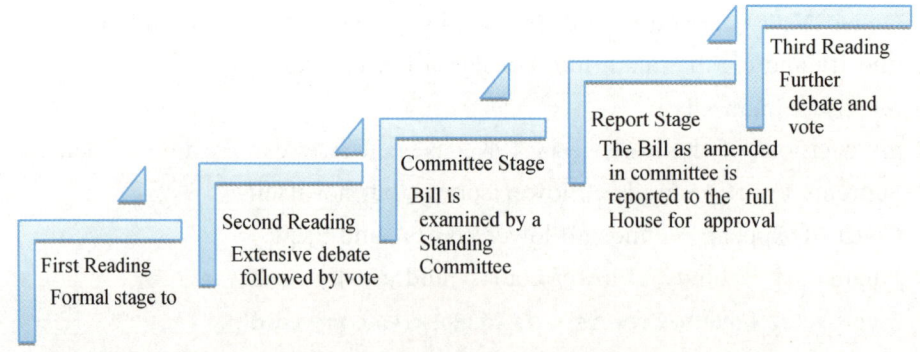

2.3 Categories of legislation

Public Acts: legislation that affects the general public

Private Acts: legislation that affects specific individuals and groups

Enabling legislation: empowers a specific individual or body to produce the detail required by a parent Act

2.4 Appraisal of statute law

Pros	Cons
Responsive To public opinion	Bulky
In theory Deal with any problem	Lacks time to consider sufficient detail
Carefully Constructed	Parliamentary time
New problem can be dealt with	Cannot anticipate every individual case

2.5 Delegated legislation

To save time in Parliament, Acts usually contain a section by which power is given to a minister, or public body such as a local authority, to make subordinate or delegated legislation.

2.6 Delegated legislation appears in various forms

○ **Orders in Council** — created by a non-party political body of parliamentarians known as the Privy Council

○ **Statutory Instrument**s (SI's) — created by Government Ministers

○ **Byelaws** — enacted by Local Government

○ **Professional regulations** — such as those of the ACCA regulating its members

○ **Rules of Court** — may be made by the judiciary to control court procedure.

2.7 Appraisal of delegated legislation

Pros	Cons
Timesaving	Accountability
Expertise	Bulk
Flexibility	Confuse

2.8 Control of delegated legislation

1) Parliament

○ Most new pieces of delegated legislation must be laid before parliament for 40 days, automatically becoming law at this point

○ The joint select committee reviews all SI's

○ Parliament may revoke an enabling act

2) Court

The court may declare any piece of delegated legislation ultra vires (beyond capacity) and void

3. Statutory interpretation

Legislation must be interpreted correctly before judges can apply it fairly.

Although Parliament creates primary legislation in the UK, it is the **courts** that interpret the legislation/status law, thereby giving it legal effect.

3.1 Situations which lead to a need for interpretation

- Ambiguity
- Uncertainty
- Unforeseeable developments
- Broad term

3.2 Statutory interpretation

There are a number of different sources of assistance for a judge in their task of statutory interpretation.

- Rules
- Presumptions
- Other aids (intrinsic or extrinsic)

3.3 Rules of Interpretation

1) Literal rule

Words in the Act should be given their **ordinary dictionary meaning** rather than what the judges thinks they mean.

2) Golden rule

Where the application of the literal rule results in a **manifest absurdity or inconsistency with the rest of the statute,** literal rule may be disregarded, Golden rule applies.

- **Mischief rule**

A judge considers what mischief the act was intended to prevent. A statute is designed to remedy a weakness in the law, the correct interpretation is the one which achieves it. See *Corkery v Carpenter* 1950.

3) The purposive approach

What is the legislation trying to achieve?

4) The contextual rule

That a word should be **construed in its context**: it is permissible to look at the statute as a whole to discover the meaning of a word in it.

3.4 General rules of interpretation

- The ejusdem generis rule — when a general list of words follows a specific example, the list will be interpreted in the light of the specific example.
- Expressio unius est exclusio alterius — To express one thing is by implication to exclude anything else.
- Noscitur a sociis — It is presumed that words draw meaning from the other words around them. If a statute mentioned 'children's books, children's toys and clothes', it would be reasonable to assume that 'clothes' meant children's clothes.

> In pari materia — If the statute forms part of a series which deals with similar subject matter, the court may look to the interpretation of previous statutes on the assumption that Parliament intended the same thing.

3.5 Presumptions of interpretation

In order to avoid uncertainty, the courts may rely on presumptions, rules, and use guidance found within and outside of the Act. As follows:

- **Does not alter the common law.**
- There is **no retrospective effect.**
- An individual will **not be denied liberty.**
- **The Crown is not bound.**
- A statute generally has effect **only in the UK**.
- International laws will not be broken.
- Strict liability will not be imposed.
- A statute does **not repeal other statutes.**

3.6 Other aids of interpretation

3.6.1 Intrinsic Aids

- The title — long or short (consider the Dangerous Dogs Act 1991)
- The preamble
- Interpretation sections to Acts
- Side notes

3.6.2 Extrinsic Aids

a) Reports of the Law Commission, Royal Commissions, the Law Reform Committee and other official committees.

b) Hansard

4. Identify the concept and impact of human rights law

4.1 Concept of human right law

- It protects the civil rights and freedoms of individuals
- **Only binding on public authorities.**
- **European Court of Human Rights** — The **final appeal court** for human rights issues for persons living in the UK

4.2 The impact of the Act

4.2.1 Impact on new legislation

HRA requires the person responsible for a Bill to make a statement of compatibility with the Convention before the Bill's **second reading**. Where a Bill is incompatible with the Convention, a statement to that effect can be made should the government wish to continue with the Bill anyway.

4.2.2 Impact on statutory interpretation

Existing legislation must be interpreted in a way which is compatible with

Convention Rights. However, if a court feels that legislation is incompatible with the Convention and that it cannot interpret it in such a way to make it compatible, it may make a **declaration of incompatibility,** or courts can **strike out secondary legislation** that is contrary to the act.

4.2.3 Impact on the common law

Should any decision from an established decided case be in conflict with the HRA 98 be **set aside.** As such the lower courts are now able to disregard the rulings of even the House of Lords in such instances.

5. Case Summaries

1) Whiteley v Chappell

A statute aimed at preventing election malpractice made it an offence to impersonate any person entitled to vote at an election. The accused was acquitted because he impersonated a dead person, who was clearly not entitled to vote

2) Re Sigsworth

A son murdered his mother. Applying the literal rule to the Administration of Justice Act 1925, it would mean that the son would inherit his murdered mother's estate. The court applied the golden rule, stating that a murderer should not benefit from their crime and therefore the law would not be interpreted literally in this case

3) Corkery v Carpenter

The court held that a bicycle was a carriage for the purpose of the Licensing Act 1872, where a defendant was charged with cycling whilst intoxicated. The purpose of the Act was to prevent people who are in a state of intoxication from operating any form of transport on public roads

4) DPP v Bull

The defendant (a man) charged with prostitution under the Street Offences Act 1959. However, the Magistrate upheld his defence that the Act in question applied only to females and therefore the mischief could not be committed by a male.

Chapter 3

Formation of contract I

1. Analyse the nature of a contract

1.1 Definition of contract

A contract may be defined as an **agreement** which **legally binds the parties.**

In order to form a **valid contract**, the five essential features must be present:

- Offer ⎫
- Acceptance ⎬ Agreement
- Consideration ⎭
- Intention to create legal relations
- Capacity and legality

1.2 Form of a contract

Contracts do not usually have to be in writing except in the following circumstances.

a) Some contracts must be by **deed**.

A contract by deed must be in **writing** and it must be **signed**. Delivery must take place. Delivery is conduct indicating that the person executing the deed intends to be bound by it.

These contracts **must** be by deed.

- **Leases** for three years or more
- A **conveyance** or transfer of a legal estate in land (including a mortgage)
- A promise **not** supported by **consideration** (such as a covenant, for example a promise to pay a regular sum to a charity)

b) Some contracts must be in **writing**.

The following contracts must be in writing and signed by at least one of the parties.

- A transfer of shares in a limited company
- The sale or disposition of an interest in land
- Bills of exchange and cheques
- Consumer credit contracts

In the case of consumer credit transactions, the effect of failure to make the agreement in the prescribed form is to make the agreement unenforceable against the debtor unless the creditor obtains a court order.

c) Some contracts must be **evidenced in writing**.

Certain contracts may be made orally, but are not enforceable in a court of law unless there is written evidence of their terms. The most important contract of this type is the contract of guarantee.

2. Factors affecting the modern contract

The law seeks to protect the idea of 'freedom of contract', although contractual terms may be regulated by **statute**, particularly where the parties are **of unequal bargaining strength**.

The **standard form contract** is a document prepared by many **large organisations** setting out the terms on which they contract with their **customers**.

3. Offer

3.1 Definition of offer

An offer can be defined as '**definite promise** to be **bound on specific terms**' in any forms. The person making the offer is known as the **offeror**, and person in receipt of an offer is known as the **offeree**.

- By definition then offers cannot be vague or imprecise.
- In any form such as express or implied statement;
- Offer can be and not have to be made to a particular person.

Supply of information: A statement which sets out possible terms of a contract is not an offer unless this is clearly indicated.

3.2 Invitation to treat

An **indication** that a person is prepared to receive offers with a view to entering into a binding contract.

This is merely something that acts as an inducement to encourage another person to make an offer.

Types of ITT:

- Auction sales

However, where an auction is stated to be 'without reserve' the auctioneer is offering goods for sale and the bid is the acceptance.

- Most ads.
- Exhibition of goods for sale
- An invitation for tenders.
- A share prospectus
- Circulation of a price list

Case study: *Carlill v Carbolic Smoke Ball Co*

a) The wording was too precise to be deemed an ITT
b) 'Money on the table' signalled intention

c) The advert was addressed to the word at large, not Mrs Carlill, hence world wide offers are possible

4. Termination of an offer

1) **Express rejection** — saying no

2) **Counter offer** — Acceptance must be unqualified agreement to the terms of the offer.
   - A counter-offer is a final rejection of the original offer
   - Request for information is not a counter-offer

3) **Lapse of time**

Expressed specified time.

No express time limit set ⟶ a reasonable time.

4) **Revocation**

a) The offeror may **revoke** their offer at **any time before acceptance**.

b) Revocation may be an **express statement** or may be an **act** of the offeror.

c) The offeror's revocation does not take effect until the revocation is **communicated** to the offeree.

d) **Revocation of offer may be communicated by any third party** who is a sufficiently reliable informant. *Dickinson v Dodds 1876*

e) **Posting a letter of revocation** is not a sufficient act of revocation. *Byrne v Van Tienhoven 1880*

5) **Conditions** — An offer may be conditional. If the condition is not satisfied, the offer is not capable of acceptance. *Financings Ltd v Stimson 1962*

6) **Death**

a) The **death of the offeree** terminates the offer.

b) The **offeror's death terminates the offer**. However, if the offer is accepted **in ignorance of the offeror's death, and the offer is not of a personal nature**, there will be a **binding contract**.

5. Acceptance

5.1 The definition of acceptance

'A positive act by a person to whom an offer has been made which, if unconditional, brings a binding contract into effect.'

5.2 Consequence of acceptance

The contract **comes into effect** once the offeree has accepted the terms presented to them. This is the point of **no return**.

After acceptance, the offeror **cannot withdraw** their offer and both parties will be **bound** by the terms that they have agreed.

5.3 Key points of acceptance

○ Acceptance may be **by express words, by action or inferred from conduct**.
Brogden v Metropolitan Railway Co

○ Acceptance must be **unqualified agreement** to the terms of the offer.

A purported acceptance which introduces any new terms is a counter-offer, which has the effect of terminating the original offer.

○ Acceptance is generally not effective until **communicated** to the offeror.
Silence of the offeree is not an acceptance. Felthouse v Bindley

○ Acceptance 'subject to contract': Acceptance 'subject to contract' means that the offeree is agreeable to the terms of the offer but proposes that the parties should negotiate a formal contract.

○ Neither party is bound until the formal contract is signed.

○ **Letters of intent**: an indication by one party to another that they **may** place a contract with them.

○ **Cross-offers**: If two offers, identical in terms, cross in the post, there is **no contract**.

5.4 Exceptions to communication

5.4.1 Unilateral offer

A unilateral offer is one where one party promises something in return for some **action** on the part of another party.

In relation to unilateral offers, revocation is not permissible once the offeree has started performing the task requested.

Reward cases are examples of such unilateral promises.

5.4.2 Postal rules

When the postal rules apply acceptance is completed as soon as the letter has been posted. **Adams v Lindsell**

The postal rule states that, where the use of the post is **within the contemplation of both the parties**, the acceptance is complete and effective as soon as a letter is posted, even though it may be delayed or even lost altogether in the post.

If the offer stipulates a particular mode of communication, the postal rule may not apply.

6. Collateral contracts

A collateral contract is a contract where consideration is provided by the making of another contract.

There is a contract despite the absence of direct communication between them. For example, if there are two separate contracts, one between A and B and one between A and C, on terms which involve some concerted action between B and C, there may be a contract between B and C.

7. Case Summaries

1) Carlill v Carbolic Smoke Ball Co 1893

The facts: The manufacturers of a patent medicine published an advertisement by which they undertook to pay '£100 reward .... to any person who contracts ....

influenzaafter having used the smoke ball three times daily for two weeks'. The advertisement added that £1,000 had been deposited at a bank 'showing our sincerity in this matter'. The claimant read the advertisement, purchased the smoke ball and used it as directed. She contracted influenza and claimed her £100 reward. In their defence the manufacturers argued against this.

a) The offer was so vague that it could not form the basis of a contract, as no time limit was specified.

b) It was not an offer which could be accepted since it was offered to the whole world.

Decision: The court disagreed.

a) The smoke ball must protect the user during the period of use — the offer was not vague.

b) Such an offer was possible, as it could be compared to reward cases.

2) Harvey v Facey 1893

The facts: The claimant telegraphed to the defendant 'Will you sell us Bumper Hall Pen? Telegraph lowest cash price'. The defendant telegraphed in reply 'Lowest price for Bumper Hall Pen, £900'. The claimant telegraphed to accept what he regarded as an offer; the defendant made no further reply.

Decision: The defendant's telegram was merely a statement of his minimum price if a sale were to be agreed. It was not an offer which the claimant could accept.

3) Byrne v Van Tienhoven 1880

The facts: The defendants were in Cardiff; the claimants in New York. The sequence of events was as follows.

○ October Letter posted in Cardiff, offering to sell 1,000 boxes of tin plates. 8 October Letter of revocation of offer posted in Cardiff.

○ October Letter of offer received in New York and telegram of acceptance sent. 15 October Letter confirming acceptance posted in New York.

○ October Letter of revocation received in New York. The offeree had meanwhile resold the contract goods.

Decision: The letter of revocation could not take effect until received (20 October); it could not revoke the contract made by the telegram acceptance of the offer on 11 October.

4) Dickinson v Dodds 1876

The facts: The defendant, on 10 June, wrote to the claimant to offer property for sale at £800, adding 'this offer to be left open until Friday 12 June, 9.00 am.' On

11 June the defendant sold the property to another buyer, A. B, who had been an intermediary between Dickinson and Dodds, informed Dickinson that the

defendant had sold to someone else. On Friday 12 June, before 9.00 am, the claimant handed to the defendant a formal letter of acceptance.

Decision: The defendant was free to revoke his offer and had done so by sale to a third party; the claimant could not accept the offer after he had learnt from a reliable informant of the revocation of the offer to him.

5) Financings Ltd v Stimson 1962

The facts: The defendant wished to purchase a car, and on 16 March signed a hire-purchase form. The form, issued by the claimants, stated that the agreement would be binding only upon signature by them.

On 20 March the defendant, not satisfied with the car, returned it. On 24 March the car was stolen from the premises of the dealer, and was recovered badly damaged. On 25 March the claimants signed the form. They sued the defendant for breach of contract.

Decision: The defendant was not bound to take the car. His signing of the agreement was actually an offer to contract with the claimant. There was an implied condition in this offer that the car would be in a reasonable condition.

6) Brogden v Metropolitan Railway Co 1877

The facts: For many years the claimant supplied coal to the defendant. He suggested that they should enter into a written agreement and the defendant's agent sent a draft to him for consideration. The parties applied to their dealings the terms of the draft agreement, but they never signed a final version. The claimant later denied that there was any agreement between him and the defendant.

Decision: The conduct of the parties was only explicable on the assumption that they both agreed to the terms of the draft.

7) Felthouse v Bindley 1862

The facts: The claimant wrote to his nephew offering to buy the nephew's horse, adding 'If I hear no more about him, I consider the horse mine'. The nephew intended to accept his uncle's offer but did not reply.

He instructed the defendant, an auctioneer, not to sell the horse. Owing to a misunderstanding the horse was sold to someone else. The uncle sued the auctioneer.

Decision: The action failed. The claimant had no title to the horse.

8) Adams v Lindsell 1818

The facts: The defendants made an offer by letter to the claimant on 2 September 1817 requiring an answer 'in course of post'. It reached the claimants on 5 September; they immediately posted a letter of acceptance, which reached the defendants on 9 September. The defendants could have expected a reply by 7 September, and they assumed that the absence of a reply within the expected period indicated non acceptance and sold the goods to another buyer on 8 September. *Decision*: The acceptance was made 'in course of post' (no time limit was imposed) and was effective when posted on 5 September.

9) Shanklin Pier Ltd v Detel Products Ltd 1951

The facts: The defendants gave assurances to the claimants that their paint would be satisfactory and durable if used to repaint the claimant's pier. The claimants in their contract with X for the repainting of the pier specified that X should use this paint. The paint proved very unsatisfactory. The claimants sued the defendants for breach of undertaking. The defendants argued that there was no contract between the claimants and themselves.

Decision: The contract between the claimants and X requiring the use of the defendant's paint was the consideration for a contract between the claimants and the defendant.

10) Entores Ltd v Miles Far East Corporation

E Ltd, in London, send offer to MFE, in Amsterdam, by teleprinter. Acceptance sent by MFE in Amsterdam by teleprinter to E Ltd in London.

MFE later in breach and question arose as to where contract was made and where litigation should begin.

Held that contract was made where acceptance actually communicated to E Ltd, therefore in London.

Chapter 4

Formation of contract II

1. **Consideration**

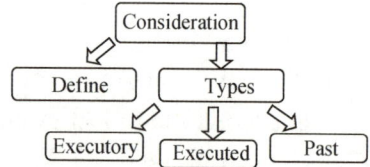

1.1 **What is consideration?**

'A valuable consideration in the sense of the law may consist either in some right, interest, profit or benefit accruing to one party, or some forbearance, detriment, loss or responsibility given, suffered or undertaken by the other.'

Consideration can be in the form of money, goods, services, or the promise of any of these.

1.2 **Types of consideration**

a) **Executory** — the **promise** to perform an action. Executory consideration is a **promise given for a promise**. Hence contracts can be formed by an exchange of promises, known as an executory contract.

b) **Executed** — an **act** given in return for a promise, the promise only becoming enforceable upon execution of the act.

c) **Past** — Anything which has already been **done before a promise** is **not valid** per *Re McArdie*.

If there is an existing contract and one party makes a further promise, no contract will arise. Even if the promise is directly related to the previous bargain, it has been made upon past consideration. See *Roscorla v Thomas* 1842.

In three instances past consideration for a promise is sufficient to make the promise

1.3 **Binding**

a) **Bill of exchange**

b) After six (or in some cases 12) years the right to sue for recovery of a debt becomes **statute barred**. If, after that period, the debtor makes written acknowledgment of the creditor's claim, the claim is again enforceable at law.

c) When a request is made for a service this request may imply a promise to pay for it. If, after the service has been rendered, the person who made the request promises a specific reward, this is treated as fixing the amount to be paid per *Lampleigh v Braithwaite*.

2. Rules of consideration

a) Performance must be legal. The courts will not enforce an illegal agreement.

b) Performance must be **possible.**

c) Consideration must '**be sufficient but need not be adequate**'.

2.1 Adequacy

It is presumed that each party is capable of serving their **own interests**, and the courts will not seek to weigh up the comparative value of the promises or acts exchanged.

See *Thomas v Thomas* 1842 *and Chappell v Nestle*.

2.2 Sufficiency

Consideration is sufficient if it has some **identifiable value**.

The law only requires an element of bargain, **not** necessarily that it should be **a good bargain**.

Given that consideration needs to be sufficient, the courts have defined this term in two contexts:

2.3 Promises to pay extra, and Promises to accept less

2.3.1 Promises to pay extra

➢ Performance of **existing legal obligations** is **not** a sufficient consideration.

➢ Performance of **existing contractual obligations** is **not** sufficient to support a promise of additional reward. For example, where an employer promises to pay an employee extra money this promise will not be enforceable where the employee merely carries out their existing contractual duties — *Stilk v Myrick*.

2.3.2 Exceptions to rule in Stilk v Myrick

a) Should the employee perform **over and above** their existing contractual obligations then the promise will be enforceable. *Hartley v Ponsonby*.

b) Should both parties derive a mutual benefit, then such a promise is enforceable. *Williams v Roffey Bros* 1990

c) If A promises B a reward if B will perform their **existing contract with C**, there is consideration for A's promise since they obtain a benefit to which they previously had no right, and B assumes new obligations.

2.3.3 Promises to accept less

a) Where one party promises to waive a debt i.e. **part-payment** in settlement of a full debt, then this promise to write-off the money is **unenforceable**, per *Foakes v Beer Foakes*.

b) **Exceptions**:

Common law exceptions:
- Pay the debt early
- Pay by goods instead of cash
- Pay at a different location
- Payment is made by a third party

Equitable Doctrine:

- Promissory estoppel: The creditor can b**e estopped from breaking their promise to waive a debt** *per Central London Property Trust v High Trees*: The creditor makes a promise to waive a debt; The debtor relies upon that promise to their detriment; The creditor is aware of the reliance made by the debtor.

3. Intention to create legal relations

An agreement will only become a legally binding contract if the parties intend this to be so. Where there is no express statement as to whether or not legal relations are intended, the courts apply one of two rebuttable presumptions to a case:

a) **Social, domestic and family** arrangements are **not** usually intended to be binding.

b) **Commercial** agreements are usually intended by the parties involved to be legally binding.

3.1 Domestic arrangements

○ **Spouses living together** — no intention presumed Balfour v Balfour, except transfer property.

○ **Spouses separating** — intention resumed, the case of Merritt v Merritt proved that the presumption of no intention between spouses could be rebutted

○ Other friendly agreements — no intention presumed, unless 'Mutuality of Intention' can be proved per Simpkins v Pays

3.2 Commercial arrangements

There is a very strong presumption of intent in such agreements per *Edwards v Skyways*.

However even this can be rebutted for example in transactions deemed to be **binding in honour only** J*ones v Vernons Pools*. If legal relations are not intended, **burden of proof** is **on the party seeking to escape liability.**

3.3 Other arrangements-no intention

1) Statutory provisions

Procedural agreements between employers and trade unions for the settlement of disputes are not intended to give rise to legal relations in spite of their elaborate content under the Trade Union and Labour Relations (Consolidation) Act 1992.

2) Letters of comfort

Holding companies have given 'letters of comfort' to creditors of subsidiaries which purport to give some comfort as to the ability of the subsidary.

4. Capacity

Certain persons do not have the ability to enter into a contract, they include:

Minors, persons defined in law as being under the age of 18. Contracts entered into by

a) minors can be classified in three ways.
- Valid, where the contract is for necessaries such as clothing
- Voidable, such as a minor inheriting an interest in leases
- Void, the most common classification

b) Persons who either **lack mental capacity or are intoxicated**

5. Privity of contract

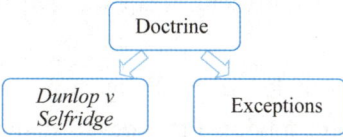

As a general rule, **only a person who is a party** to a contract has **enforceable** rights or obligations under it per *Dunlop v selfridge*.

Exceptions:

a) The third party can sue in another capacity. See *Beswick v Beswick*.
b) Where a collateral contract exists per *Shanklin Pier Ltd v Detel Products Ltd 1951*
c) Where a contract has been validly assigned
d) Foreseeable loss to the third party
e) Statutory exceptions (insurance)
f) Agency
g) Implied trusts
h) The Contracts (rights of Third Parties) Act 1999 whereby the third party has rights provided that: they are expressly identified in the contract; the contract confers a benefit on them

6. Case Summaries

1) Re McArdle

Decorating was done in the family home by a daughter in law and on the subsequent death of the mother-in-law the remainder of the family promised to pay the cost of the decorating to the daughter in law when the estate was settled. This promise was not enforceable as the consideration to 'buy' the promise was provided in the past.

2) Roscorla v Thomas 1842

The facts: The claimant agreed to buy a horse from the defendant at a given price.

When negotiations were over and the contract was formed, the defendant told the claimant that the horse was 'sound and free from vice'. The horse turned out to be vicious and the claimant brought an action on the warranty.

Decision: The express promise was made after the sale was over and was unsupported by fresh consideration.

3) Lampleigh v Braithwaite

B killed a man and later asked L to obtain a Royal pardon. L obtained the pardon at personal expense. B then promised to pay. B then failed to pay and L sued.

It was held that B's request implied a promise to pay and therefore this later actual promise merely fixed the amount.

4) Thomas v Thomas

The executors of a man's will promised to let his widow live in his house, in return for a rent of £1 per year. It was held that £1 was sufficient consideration to validate the contract, although it did not represent adequate rent in economic terms.

5) Chappell v Nestle

Chocolate bar wrappers provided in exchange for a record offered by Nestle were part of the consideration despite having little or no commercial value. It was not cash alone which entitled you to the record.

6) Stilk v Myrick

Two deserters on a sea voyage led to a promise from the captain to the crew to divide the deserters' wages between them if they sailed the ship home. It was held that the promise to pay extra was unenforceable as their contract already obliged them to meet normal emergencies and no additional consideration was provided.

7) Hartley v Ponsonby

More money was promised to sailors if they sailed the ship home when the level of deserters rendered the ship unseaworthy. This promise was enforceable as the sailors provided additional consideration by going beyond their obligation.

8) Williams v Roffey Bros and Nicholls (Contractors) Ltd

Roffey Bros. were main contractors in the refurbishment of a block of flats. In the contract between Roffey Bros. and the employer there was a penalty clause which provided that Roffey Bros would have to pay damages if the work was not completed on time. Roffey Bros. had sub-contracted the carpentry work to Williams and became concerned that Williams would not be able to finish on time. Roffey Bros. therefore offered Williams an extra £10,300 to finish the work on time. They later refused to pay the money when Williams completed on time.

It was held where that there was no evidence of fraud or economic duress and there was a benefit to both parties, a promise backed up by consideration may be enforceable. Hence Roffey Bros. were ordered to pay the £10,300.

Chapter 4 Formation of contract II

9) Foakes v Beer

Foakes owed Beer a sum of about £2,000, awarded in damages from an earlier case. The parties agreed that if Foakes paid £500 at once and the rest of the sum by instalments, then Beer would not take legal action. Foakes eventually paid the debt, but not the interest, which would have accrued since the date the award was made. Beer sued Foakes for the interest. In defence, Foakes claimed that the new agreement (payment of the sum in instalments) cancelled the original obligation, and the Beer had thereby waived her right to the interest. Beer claimed that the agreement was void since Foakes offered no consideration. The Court sided with Beer, allowing Pinnel's case to stand.

10) Pinnel's Case

Pinnel sued the Cole for the sum of £8 10s. The defence was based on the fact that Cole had, at Pinnel's request, tendered £5-2s-6d before the debt was due, which Pinnel had accepted in full satisfaction for the debt.

'Payment of a lesser sum on the day in satisfaction of a greater, cannot be any satisfaction for the whole, because it appears to the Judges that by no possibility, a lesser sum can be a satisfaction to the plaintiff for a greater sum; but the gift of a horse, hawk, or robe, etc. in satisfaction is good ... [as] more beneficial to the plaintiff than the money.'

The case was decided on a technicality. Had Cole secured the agreement of Pinnel the part-payment would have been sufficient.

11) Central London Property Trust v High Trees House

During war, CLPT made a promise not to increase the rent they charged HT. HT, as a result, reduced the rent they charged their tenants. After the war CLPT claimed the back rent from HT. It was held that even though HT had given no

consideration to CLPT for the promise, CLPT were ESTOPPED from going back on the promise. They had entered into the promise freely with the intention that HT relied on it and HT had done so.

12) Dunlop v Selfridge

D imposed a resale price on customers. D then sold tyres to a dealer. Dealer sold tyres on to Selfridge with same price restriction. S sold tyres at below price. D sued S. It was held that D could not recover damages under a contract to which it was not privy.

13) Beswick v Beswick

A coal merchant sold his business to his nephew for a consultancy fee during his lifetime, and an annual annuity of £5 per week, payable to his widow. When the merchant died his widow sued for non-payment of the annuity, and it was held that in her position as a beneficiary of the death estate she was able to gain an order for specific performance, despite not being privy to the original contract.

14) Balfour v Balfour

An informal agreement between husband and wife (who had not broken up) was held not to be legally binding.

15) Merritt v Merritt

A husband and wife separated. The husband agreed to pay the wife £40 per month out of which she agreed to keep up the mortgage payments. The husband signed a note to this effect and in addition agreed to transfer the house to his wife once the mortgage had been paid. On the discharge of the mortgage the husband refused to effect a transfer.

The court held that all the circumstances of the case gave rise to an inference of legal intention and hence the agreement was legally binding.

16) Simpkins v Pays

Agreement to share competition winnings can be enforceable if there is 'mutuality in the arrangements between the parties'.

17) Edwards v Skyways

In commercial arrangements there is a presumption of intention to create legal relations which will have to be discharged by the person seeking to avoid liability.

18) Jones v Vernons Pools

The claimant submitted a correctly forecast pools coupon. The defendant had lost the coupon, but was able to rely on a clause in the coupon stating that 'the transaction was binding in honour only'.

Chapter 5

Content of a contract

1. Terms v Representations: four distinguishing tests

Some promises made during contract formation will not form part of the contract itself, but will merely act to **induce** the other party into the contract. Such pre-contractual statements are known as **representations**.

If something said in negotiations proves to be untrue, the party misled can claim for breach of contract if the statement became a **term** of the contract.

Four distinguishing tests:

○ If a statement is of **such importance** that the promisee would not have entered into the contract without it, it shall be deemed a term.

○ Where is a **time gap** between the statement and contract formation, the statement is more likely to be interpreted as a representation.

○ If an **oral** statement is **omitted from a later written contract**, its exclusion will suggest that it was a representation.

○ Should a party to the formation be **an expert, or possess special skills or knowledge**, statements made by them will be terms. *Dick Bentley Productions v Arnold Smith Motors 1965, Oscar Chess v Williams 1957*

2. Sources of Terms

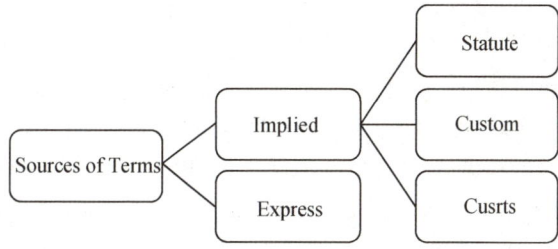

2.1 Express term
Terms clearly included in the contract are **express terms**.

2.2 Implied term
A term deemed to form part of a contract even though not expressly mentioned.

1) Terms implied by statute Sale of Goods Act 1979

Where there is a contract for the sale of goods by description, there is an implied term that the goods will correspond with the description.

Implied terms may **override express** terms in certain circumstances, such as where they are implied **by STATUTE**.

2) Terms implied by custom

The parties may enter into a contract subject to **customs** of their trade.

3) Hutto*n v Warren*

Any **express** term **overrides** a term which might be **implied** by **custom**.

4) Terms implied by the courts

Terms may be implied if the court concludes that the parties **intended those terms** to apply to the contract. *The Moorock 1889*

Where a term is implied as a **'necessary incident'** it has **precedent value** and such terms will be implied into future contracts of the same type.

Liverpool City Council v Lrwin 1997

3. Types of term

1) Condition

A condition is a **vital term**, going to the root of the contract, breach of which entitles the injured party to decide to treat the contract as **discharged** and to **claim damages**. *Poussard v Spiers 1876*

2) Warranty

A warranty is a term **subsidiary** to the main purpose of the contract, breach of which **only** entitles the injured party to **claim damages**. Failure to observe it **does not cause the whole agreement to collapse**. *Bettini v Gye 1876*

3) Innominate terms

It **may not be possible** to determine whether a term is a condition or a warranty. Such terms are classified by the **courts** as **innominate terms**. *Hong Kong Fir Shipping Co Ltd v Kawasaki Kisa Kaisha Ltd 1962*

4. Exclusion clauses

An **exclusion clause** can be described as 'a clause in a contract which purports to exclude liability altogether or to restrict it by limiting damages or by imposing other onerous conditions. They are sometimes referred to as **exemption clauses**.'

The courts are deeply suspicious of such clauses and as such anyone wishing to enforce one would need to pass 3 tests:

a) The clause needs to be correctly **incorporated** into the contract **before the contract is formed**.

b) The clause needs to be properly **constructed**, in such a way that it is worded clearly to exclude the breach.

c) The clause is deemed reasonable per statute.

4.1 Incorporation

a) **By signature** — once a document has been signed, parties are bound by its terms, irrespective of whether or not they have read them — *L'Estrange v Graucob*

b) **By notice** — any exclusion clause must be **an integral part of the contract**, and be given **at** the time that the contract is made. This extends to:

- **Notice boards** *Olley v Marlborough Court*
- **Tickets & Receipts** *Chapelton v Barry UDC*
- Each party must be **aware of the contract's terms before or at the time of entering into the agreement** if they are to be **binding**.
- **Onerous Terms** *Interfoto Pic Library Ltd v Stiletto Visual Programmes Ltd*
- **Unusual and onerous** should **be highlighted**.

c) **By custom** — A history of **consistent dealings** between the parties is sufficient to incorporate terms into a contract. *J Spurling Ltd v Bradshaw 1956*

4.2 Construction/Interpretation

The wording of the clause needs to **be clear and precise**. Any party attempting to rely on **an ambiguous** clause will be **defeated** per the **Contra proferentem rule**— *Hollier v Rambler Motors*.

Contra proferentem rule: In deciding what an exclusion clause means, the courts interpret any ambiguity **against** the person who relies on the exclusion.

Main purpose' rule: Any attempt to construct a clause designed to **defeat the fundamental purpose of a contract will fail** per *Photo Productions v Securicor Transport*.

4.3 Reasonable

The final test of an exclusion clause is whether or not a clause is reasonable per the **Unfair Contract Terms Act 1977** (UCTA 77), and **the Consumer Rights Act** (CRA) **2015**.

4.3.1 The Unfair Contract Terms Act 1977 (UCTA 77)

The Unfair Contract Terms Act 1977 aims **to protect parties** when they enter contracts by stating that some exclusion clauses are **void**, and considering whether others are reasonable.

a) In general, the Act only applies to **business to business contracts.**

b) UCTA 1977 does not apply to contracts of **insurance** or contracts relating to the transfer of an interest in land.

c) Automatically void:

a clause which purports to exclude or limit liability for death or personal injury resulting from negligence.

In a contract for the sale or hire purchase of goods, a clause that purports to exclude the condition that the seller has a right to sell the goods.

d) If a clause is not automatically void, it is subject to a statutory test of reasonableness.

4.3.2 The Consumer Rights Act (CRA) 2015.

The Consumer Rights Act 2015 provides protection for consumers in contracts with businesses. Thus, it provides statutory control in respect of consumer contracts and consumer notice, including business-to-consumer contracts.

a) An **unfair term** is any term which causes a significant imbalance in the parties' rights and obligations under the contract to the detriment of the consumer.

b) **Businesses acting as consumer:** where a business engages in an activity which is merely incidental to the business.

5. Case Summaries

1) Dick Bentley Productions v Arnold Smith Motors 1965

The facts: The defendants sold the claimants a car which they stated to have done only 20,000 miles since a replacement engine and gear-box had been fitted. In fact the car had covered 100,000 miles since then and was unsatisfactory.

Decision: The defendants' statement was a term of the contract and the claimants were entitled to damages.

2) Oscar Chess v Williams 1957

The facts: The defendant, when selling his car to the claimant car dealers, stated (as the registration book showed) that his car was a 1948 model and the dealers valued it at £280 in the transaction. In fact it was a 1939 model, worth only £175, and the registration book had been altered by a previous owner.

Decision: The statement was a mere representation. The seller was not an expert and the buyer had better means of discovering the truth.

3) Hutton v Warren 1836

The facts: The defendant landlord gave the claimant, a tenant farmer, notice to quit the farm. He insisted that the tenant should continue to farm the land during the period of notice. The tenant asked for 'a fair allowance' for seeds and labour from which he received no benefit because he was to leave the farm.

Decision: By custom he was bound to farm the land until the end of the tenancy; but he was also entitled to a fair allowance for seeds and labour incurred.

4) The Moorcock 1889

The facts: The owners of a wharf agreed that a ship should be moored alongside to unload its cargo. It was well known that at low water the ship would ground on the mud at the bottom. At ebb tide the ship settled on a ridge concealed beneath the mud and suffered damage.

Decision: It was an implied term, though not expressed, that the ground alongside the wharf was safe at low tide since both parties knew that the ship must rest on it.

5) Poussard v Spiers 1876

The facts: Mme Poussard agreed to sing in an opera throughout a series of performances. Owing to illness she was unable to appear on the opening night and the next few days. The producer engaged a substitute who insisted that she should be engaged for the whole run. When Mme Poussard recovered, the producer declined to accept her services for the remaining performances.

Decision: Failure to sing on the opening night was a breach of condition which entitled the producer to treat the contract for the remaining performances as discharged.

6) Bettini v Gye 1876

The facts: An opera singer was engaged for a series of performances under a contract by which he had to be in London for rehearsals six days before the opening performance. Owing to illness he did not arrive until the third day before the opening. The defendant refused to accept his services, treating the contract as discharged.

Decision: The rehearsal clause was subsidiary to the main purpose of the contract.

7) Hong Kong Fir Shipping Co Ltd v Kawasaki Kisa Kaisha Ltd 1962

The facts: The defendants chartered a ship from the claimants for a period of 24 months. A term in the contract stated that the claimants would provide a ship which was 'in every way fitted for ordinary cargo service'. Because of the engine's age and the crew's lack of competence the ship's first voyage, from Liverpool to Osaka, was delayed for five months and further repairs were required at the end of it. The defendants purported to terminate the contract, so the claimants sued for breach; the defendants claimed that the claimants were in breach of a contractual condition.

Decision: The term was innominate and could not automatically be construed as either a condition or a warranty. The obligation of 'seaworthiness' embodied in many charter party agreements was too complex to be fitted into one of the two categories. The ship was still available for 17 out of 24 months. The consequences of the breach were not so serious that the defendants could be justified in terminating the contract as a result.

8) L'Estrange v Graucob 1934

The facts: The defendant sold to the claimant, a shopkeeper, a slot machine under conditions which excluded the claimant's normal rights under the Sale of Goods Act 1893. The claimant signed the document described as a 'Sales Agreement' and including clauses in 'legible, but regrettably small print'.

Decision: The conditions were binding on the claimant since she had signed them. It was not material that the defendant had given her no information of their terms nor called her attention to them.

9) Olley v Marlborough Court 1949

The facts: A husband and wife arrived at a hotel and paid for a room in advance. On reaching their bedroom they saw a notice on the wall by which the hotel disclaimed liability for loss of valuables unless handed to the management for safe keeping. The wife locked the room and handed the key in at the reception desk. A thief obtained the key and stole the wife's furs from the bedroom.

Decision: The hotel could not rely on the notice disclaiming liability since the contract had been made previously and the disclaimer was too late.

10) J Spurling Ltd v Bradshaw 1956

The facts: Having dealt with a company of warehousemen for many years, the defendant gave it eight barrels of orange juice for storage. A document he received a few days later acknowledged receipt and contained a clause excluding liability for damage caused by negligence. When he collected the barrels they were empty and he refused to pay.

Decision: It was a valid clause as it had also been present in the course of previous dealings, even though he had never read it.

11) Photo Productions v Securicor Transport 1980

The facts: The defendants agreed to guard the claimants' factory under a contract by which the defendant were excluded from liability for damage caused by any of their employees. One of the guards deliberately started a small fire which destroyed the factory and contents. It was contended that Securicor had entirely failed to perform their contract and so they could not rely on any exclusion clause in the contract.

Decision: There is no principle that total failure to perform a contract deprives the party at fault of any exclusion from liability provided by the contract. In this case the exclusion clause was drawn widely enough to cover the damage which had happened. As the fire occurred before the UCTA was in force, the Act could not apply here. But if it had done it would have been necessary to consider whether the exclusion clause was reasonable.

12) Chapelton v Barry UDC 1940

The facts: There was a pile of deckchairs and a notice stating 'Hire of chairs 2d per session of three hours' The claimant took two chairs, paid for them and received two tickets which were headed 'receipt' which he put in his pocket. One of the chairs collapsed and he was injured. The defendant council relied on a notice on the back of the tickets by which it disclaimed liability for injury.

Decision: The notice advertising chairs for hire gave no warning of limiting conditions and it was not reasonable to communicate them on a receipt. The disclaimer of liability was not binding on the claimant.

13) Interfoto Pic Library Ltd v Stiletto Visual Programmes Ltd 1988

The facts: 47 photographic transparencies were delivered to the defendant together with a delivery note with conditions on the back. Included in small type was a clause stating that for every day late each transparency was held a 'holding fee' of £5 plusVAT would be charged. They were returned 14 days late. The claimants sued for the full amount.

Decision: The term was onerous and had not been sufficiently brought to the attention of the defendant. The court reduced the fee to one-tenth of the contractual figure to reflect more fairly the loss caused to the claimants by the delay.

Chapter 6

Breach of contract and remedies

1. Discharge of contract

a) **Agreement**: Where both parties agree to end the agreement and it is supported by consideration.

b) **Performance**: The most common method of discharge. The contractual obligations are exactly or substantially met (all contract terms are performed).

c) **Breach of contract**: Where one party fails to meet its contractual obligations without lawful excuse.

d) **By frustration**: Where performance of an obligation is impossible due to specific circumstances occurring after formation of the contract:

1.1 Lawful excuse

- Performance is impossible, for some unforeseeable event.
- They have tendered performance but this has been rejected.
- The other party has made it impossible for them to perform.
- The contract has been discharged through frustration.
- The parties have by agreement permitted non-performance.
- Change of law
- Impossibility of performance of obligations due to destruction of subject matter. *Taylor V Caldwell 1863*.
  - Contract for providing personal services
  - Fundamental and radical change or circumstances

1.2 By insolvency, death, lunacy

2. Breach of contract

Types of breach

1) Repudiatory breach

A repudiatory breach occurs where a party indicates, either by words or by conduct, that they do not intend to honour their contractual obligations or commits a breach of condition or commits a breach which has very serious consequences for the injured party. It usually occurs when the performance is due.

Repudiatory breach usually occurs in the following circumstances:
- Refusal to perform (renunciation): no intention to perform
- Failure to perform an entire obligation: Precondition
- Incapacitation
- Breach of condition
- Breach of an innominate term

2) What should the injured party do?

a) Entitles the injured party to **end the contract and claim damages**. They must notify the other of their decision.

b) They can elect to **affirm** the contract. The contract remains fully in force.

3) Anticipatory breach

One party declares **in advance** that they will not perform their sides of the bargain when the time for performance arrives.

This type of breach gives the innocent party the **option** to:

a) Sue immediately on notice of breach

b) Perform their contractual obligations and sue afterwards. Their claim for damages will then depend on what they have actually lost — *White and Carter (Councils) v McGregor 1961*

4) Distinguish between the two types of breach

Types of breach	Repudiatory breach	Anticipatory breach
Time	Usually at the time of performance	Before the due date for performance

5) Termination for repudiatory breach

The innocent party must notify the other of their decisions.

a) They are not bound by their future or continuing contractual obligations, and cannot be sued on them.

b) They need not accept nor pay for further performance.

c) They can also refuse to pay for partial or defective performance already received, unless the contract is severable.

d) They can reclaim money paid to a defaulter if they can and do reject defective performance.

e) They are not discharged from the contractual obligations which were due at the time of termination.

3. Damages

Damages are a common law **remedy**, and they are intended to be compensatory not punitive. Remoteness of damage and measure of damages are the two tests applied to a claim for damages.

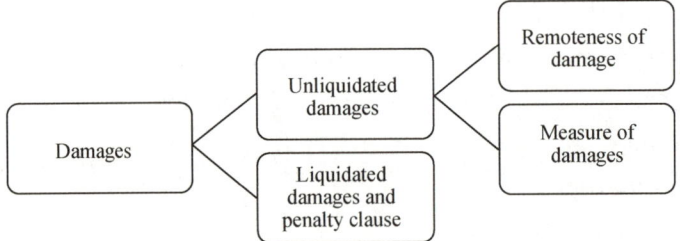

3.1 Assessment of unliquidated damages

Where the contract does not make any provision for damages, the court will determine the damages payable. These are known as unliquidated damages.

- Remoteness of damage (i.e. what losses can be claimed for?)
- Measure of damages (i.e. how much are those losses worth?)

3.2 Remoteness of damage

However not every breach of contract will give rise to a successful claim for damages, as the conditions of 'Remoteness of Damages' must first be satisfied.

- Loss must arise either naturally from the breach. See *Hadley v Baxendale* 1854.
- Be reasonably foreseeable in the eyes of both parties at the time the contract was formed. See *Victoria Laundry v Newman Industries 1949*.
- A loss outside the natural course of events will only be compensated if the exceptional circumstances are within the defendant's knowledge when they made the contract. See *Victoria Laundry v Newman Industries 1949*.

3.3 Measure of damages

The measure of damages is that which will compensate for the loss incurred. It is not intended that the injured party should profit from a claim. Damages may be awarded for financial and non-financial loss.

- Expectation interest: Put the claimant in the position where contract was performed — Doctrine of Restitution.
- Reliance interest: Put the claimant in the position where they had not relied on the contract. *Anglia Television v Reed 1972*

3.3.1 Market price rule

The general principle is to compensate for actual financial loss.

Market price rule: A seller fails to sell the goods, the buyer can go into the market and purchase equivalent goods instead.

The seller (buyer) would have to compensate the buyer (seller) for any additional cost the buyer (seller) incurred over the contract cost. *Thompson Ltd v Robinson (Gunmakers) Ltd 1955*

3.3.2 Non-financial loss

In some cases, damages have been recovered for mental distress where that is the main result of the breach. Contrast with the following cases: *Jarvis v Swan Tours* 1973;

Alexander v Rolls Royce Motor Cars Ltd 1995

3.3.3 Cost of cure

Cost of restitution is too high. *Ruxley Electronics and Construction Ltd v Forsyth 1995*.

3.3.4 Mitigation of loss

The injured party must take all reasonable steps to mitigate their losses.

The injured party is not required to take **discreditable** or **risky measures** to reduce their loss since these are not 'reasonable'. *Payzu v Saunders 1919*

3.4 Liquidated damages and penalty clauses

3.4.1 Liquidated damages

Liquidated damages can be defined as 'a fixed or ascertainable sum agreed by the parties at the time of contracting, payable in the event of a breach, for example, an amount payable per day for failure to complete a building. If they are a genuine attempt to pre-estimate the likely loss the court will enforce payment.'

See *Azimut-Benetti Spa v Darrell Marcus Healey 2010*.

3.4.2 Penalty clause

A **penalty clause** can be defined as 'a clause in a contract providing for a specified sum of money to be payable in the event of a subsequent breach. If its purpose is merely to deter a potential difficulty, it will be held void and the court will proceed to assess unliquidated damages. *Bridge v Campbell Discount Co.* 1962

○ The stipulated sum is extravagant in comparison with the maximum loss that could be incurred.

○ The same sum is payable in respect of one or more breaches, both trifling and serious.

○ The sum stipulated is larger than the amount which would actually be payable if the contract were performed.

3.4.3 Contrast

Liquidated damages	Penalty clause
Equivalent to Actual loss	Larger than actual loss Same amount for any breach
Genuine	Threaten
Enforceable	Not enforceable

3.5 Other common law remedies

3.5.1 Action for the price

A simple action for the price to recover the agreed sum should be brought if breach of contract is failure to pay the price. But property must have passed from seller to buyer, and the agreed sum is due at the time of an anticipatory breach.

3.5.2 Quantum meruit

The phrase quantum meruit literally means 'how much it is worth'. It is a measure of the value of contractual work which has been performed. The aim of such an award is to restore the claimant to the position they would have been in if the contract had never been made, and is therefore known as a restitutory award.

See *De Barnardy v Harding 1853*.

Quantum meruit is likely to be sought where one party has already performed part of their obligations and the other party then repudiates the contract.

4. Equitable remedies

It is an equitable remedy awarded at the discretion of the court when damages would not be an adequate remedy.

4.1 Specific performance

Specific performance can be defined as 'an order of the court directing a person to perform an obligation. Its principal use is in contracts for the sale of land but may also be used to compel a sale of shares or debentures, though this will not be awarded in the following circumstances:
- where the courts cannot supervise enforcement
- where a contract is for personal service or contract of employment
- where minors are involved
- building contracts

4.2 Injunction

An injunction is a discretionary court order and an equitable remedy, requiring the defendant to observe a negative restriction of a contract (not to do sth.). *Warner Bros Pictures Inc v Nelson 1937*.

4.3 Rescission

Rescinding a contract means that it is cancelled or rejected and the parties are restored to their pre-contract condition. Four conditions must be met:
- It must be possible for each party to be returned to the pre-contract condition (restitutio in integrum).
- An innocent third party who has acquired rights in the subject matter of the contract will prevent the original transaction being rescinded.
- The right to rescission must be exercised within a reasonable time of it arising.
- Where a person affirms a contract expressly or by conduct it may not then be rescinded.

5. Case Summaries

1) White & Carter (Councils) v McGregor 1961

The facts: The claimants supplied litter bins to local councils, and were paid not by the councils but by traders who hired advertising space on the bins. The defendant contracted with them for advertising of his business. He then wrote to cancel the contract but the claimants elected to advertise as agreed, even though they had at the time of cancellation taken no steps to perform the contract. They performed the contract and claimed the agreed payment.

Decision: The contract continued in force and they were entitled to recover the agreed price for their services. Repudiation does not, of itself, bring the contract to an end. It gives the innocent party the choice of affirmation or rejection.

2) Hadley v Baxendale 1854

The facts: The claimant owned a mill at Gloucester, the main crank shaft of which had broken. They made a contract with the defendant for the transport of the broken shaft to Greenwich to serve as a pattern for making a new shaft. Owing to neglect by the defendant, delivery was delayed and the mill was out of action for a longer period. The defendant did not know that the mill would be idle during this interval. He was merely aware that he had to transport a broken millshaft. The claimnats claimed for loss of profits of the mill during the period of delay.

Decision: Although the failure of the carrier to perform the contract promptly was the direct cause of the stoppage of the mill for an unnecessarily long time, the claim must fail since the defendant did not know that the mill would be idle until the new shaft was delivered. Moreover, it was not a natural consequence of delay in transport of a broken shaft that the mill would be out of action. The miller might have a spare.

The defendant is liable only if they knew of the special circumstances from which the abnormal consequence of breach could arise.

3) Thompson Ltd v Robinson (Gunmakers) Ltd 1955

The facts: The defendants contracted to buy a Vanguard car from the claimants. They refused to take delivery and the claimants sued for loss of profit on the transaction. There was at the time a considerable excess of supply of such cars over demand for them and the claimants were unable to sell the car.

Decision: The market price rule, which the defendants argued should be applied, was inappropriate in the current market as demand for such cars was so low as to effectively mean that no market for them existed. The seller had lost a sale and was entitled to the profit.

4) Anglia Television v Reed 1972

The facts: The claimants engaged an actor to appear in a film they were making for television. He pulled out at the last moment and the project was abandoned. The claimants claimed the preparatory expenditure, such as hiring other actors and researching suitable locations.

Decision: Damages were awarded as claimed. It is impossible to tell whether an unmade film will be a success or a failure and, had the claimants claimed for loss of profits, they would not have succeeded.

5) Jarvis v Swan Tours 1973

The facts: The claimant entered into a contract for holiday accommodation at a winter sports centre. What was provided was much inferior to the description given in the defendant's brochure. Damages on the basis of financial loss only were assessed at £32.

Decision: The damages should be increased to £125 to compensate for disappointment and distress because the principle purpose of the contract was the giving of pleasure.

6) Ruxley Electronics and Construction Ltd v Forsyth 1995

The facts: A householder discovered that the swimming pool he had ordered to be built was shallower than specified. He sued the builder for damages, including the cost of demolition of the pool and construction of a new one. Despite its shortcomings, the pool as built was perfectly serviceable and safe to dive into.

Decision: The expenditure involved in rectifying the breach was out of all proportion of the benefit of such rectification. The claimant was awarded a small sum to cover loss of amenity.

7) Payzu v Saunders 1919

The facts: The parties had entered into a contract for the supply of goods to be delivered and paid for by instalments. The claimants failed to pay the first instalment when due, one month after delivery. The defendants declined to make further deliveries unless the claimants paid cash in advance with their orders. The claimants refused to accept delivery on those terms. The price of the goods rose, and they sued for breach of contract.

Decision: The seller had no right to repudiate the original contract. But the claimants should have mitigated their loss by accepting the seller's offer of delivery against cash payment. Damages were limited to the amount of their assumed loss if they had paid in advance, which was interest over the period of prepayment.

8) Dunlop v New Garage

A contract for the sale of tyres imposed a minimum resale price. The contract included a fixed payment in the event of breach, at £5 per tyre. NG sold at less than the minimum resale price and, when D sought to recover the fixed sum, argued it was a penalty. It was held that this amount was a genuine attempt at pre-estimate of loss and would be upheld.

9) Warner Bros v Nelson 1937

The facts: Nelson was Bette Davis. N agreed not to work for any other studio — only for WB. However, N commenced work for a British film producer in the UK. Therefore, WB sued for an injunction

Decision: Court imposed an injunction on N stopping her working for the British producer.

10) De Barnardy v Harding 1853

The facts: The claimant agreed to advertise and sell tickets for the defendant, who was erecting stands for spectators to view the funeral of the Duke of Wellington. The defendant cancelled the arrangement without justification.

Decision: The claimant might recover the value of services rendered

11) Azimut-Benetti Spa v Darrell Marcus Healey 2010

The facts: The defendants entered into a ship building contract with the claimants. A liquidated damages clause stated that in the event the contract is terminated by the defendants, the claimants could receive a sum equal to 20% of the contract price (£7.1 million).

Decision: The court held that the clause represented a commercially justified balance between the parties' interests and the claimants could receive the £7.1 million when the defendants failed to pay the first instalment due.

12) Victoria Laundry (Windsor) v Newman Industries 1949

The facts: The defendants contracted to sell a large boiler to the claimants 'for immediate use' in their business of launderers and dyers. Owing to an accident in dismantling the boiler at its previous site, delivery was delayed. The defendants were aware of the nature of the claimant's business and had been informed that the claimants were most anxious to put the boiler into use in the shortest possible space of time. The claimants claimed damages for normal loss of profits for the period of delay and for loss of abnormal profits from losing 'highly lucrative' dyeing contracts to be undertaken if the boiler had been delivered on time.

Decision: Damages for loss of normal profits were recoverable since in the circumstances failure to deliver major industrial equipment ordered for immediate use would be excepted to prevent operation of the plant. The claim for loss of special profits failed because the defendants had no knowledge of the dyeing contracts.

13) Alexander v Rolls Royce Motor Cars Ltd 1995

The facts: The claimant sued for breach of contract to repair his Rolls Royce motor car and claimed damages for distress and inconvenience or loss of enjoyment of the car.

Decision: Breach of contract to repair a car did not give rise to any liability for damages for distress, inconvenience or loss of enjoyment.

14) Bridge v Campbell Discount Co 1962

The facts: A clause in a hire purchase contract required the debtor to pay, on termination, both arrears of payments due before termination, and an amount which, together with payments made and due before termination, amounted to two-thirds of the HP price, and additionally to return the goods.

Decision: This was a penalty clause and void since, in almost all circumstances, the creditor would receive on termination more than 100% of the value of the goods.

Chapter 7

The tort of law and professional negligence

1. Explain the meaning of tort

A tort is a **civil wrong** and the person wronged sues in a civil court for compensation.

In tort, no previous transaction or contractual relationship need exist. Tort is not a breach of contract and not a crime.

2. The tort of passing off

Passing-off is the use of a name, mark or description by one business that **misleads a consumer** to believe that their business is that of another. In such cases one party is accused of misrepresenting themselves to the public in a calculated manner designed to allow them to benefit from parties' goodwill. These actions are most commonly associated with trademarks and company names.

Where it can be proved in passing-off cases that there is a chance of 'genuine public confusion' all lost trading profits can be awarded to the injured party in addition to an injunction over the use of names.

3. Tort of negligence including the duty of care and its breach

3.1 Tort of negligence

Definition:

Which is used to describe **carelessly** carrying out an act and **breaking a legal duty of care** owed to another causing them **loss or damage.**

Negligence is the most important modern tort. To succeed in an action for negligence the **claimant must prove** that:
- The **defendant had a duty of care** to avoid causing injury, damage or loss
- There was a **breach of that duty by the defendant**
- In consequence the **claimant suffered injury, damage or loss**

3.2 Duty of care

A person is not automatically liable for the wrongful acts they commit. The first step in establishing liability is to prove that the defendant owed a duty of care to the injured party. A person's duty of care in tort was initially defined in *Donoghue v Stevenson* via the **neighbour principle**: 'you owe a duty of care to anybody who it may be reasonably foreseen will be affected by your negligent acts or omissions'.

In this way it was established that a **manufacturer owed a duty of care to the ultimate consumer of a product**.

A three stage test for establishing a duty of care:
- Was the harm **reasonably foreseeable**?
- Was there a **relationship of proximity** between the parties?
- Considering the circumstances, is it **fair, just and reasonable** to impose a duty of
- care?

3.3 Breach of duty of care

3.3.1 basic rule

Once it has been successfully proved a duty of care exists the **claimant** next has to prove that this duty has been breached. In order to do this, it must be proved that the defendant '**failed to act reasonably**' per *Blyth v Birmingham*. The standard of care owed by an individual defined in Blyth can be adjusted by the following:

- **Probability of injury**: takes greater precautions when the risk of injury is high
- **Seriousness of the risk**: the more serious the risk, the more the reasonable man would do to mitigate this. *Egg-shell skull*
- **Practicality and cost**: the foreseeable risk must be balanced against the cost and practicability of eliminating the danger. *Latimer v AEC Ltd*
- **Common practice**: where an individual can prove their actions were in line with common practice or custom it is likely that they would have met their duty of care. This is unless the common practice itself is found to be negligent.
- **Social benefit**: where an action is of some benefit to society, defendants may be protected from liability even if their actions create risk. For example, a fire engine that speeds to a major disaster provides a social benefit that may outweigh the greater risk to the public.
- **Professions and skill:** Persons who hold themselves out to possess a particular skill should be judged on what a reasonable person possessing the same skill would do in the situation rather than that of a reasonable man.

3.3.2 Res Ipsa Loquitur

Ordinarily the burden of proof in tort lies with the claimant. However, where the facts speak for themselves the burden may be reversed '**Res Ipsa Loquitur**'— **facts speak** for themselves. The burden of proof is reversed and the **defendant** must prove that they were not negligent.

4. Explain the meaning of causality and remoteness of damage

4.1 Causality

Finally, the claimant must demonstrate that they suffered injury or loss as a result of the breach.

4.1.1 Damage or loss

In order for a claimant to succeed in a negligence claim, he must not only show that the defendant owed him a duty of care and breached that duty of care, but he must additionally prove that the damage or loss he suffered was as a result of the defendant's breach. There are two factors necessary for this element. Firstly the defendant must have caused the claimant's loss or damage (But for test). Secondly, the loss or damage suffered by the claimant must be of a type that was reasonably foreseeable, i.e. the damage must not be too remote (Remoteness of damage).

4.1.2 The 'But for' test

The claimant must prove that if it was not 'but for' the other's actions they would not have suffered damage.

Therefore, claimants are unable to claim for any harm that would have happened to them anyway irrespective of the defendant's actions.

Where there are multiple possible causes, the court must establish that the negligent act was the one that caused the injury. If this is not possible then causality is not established. See *Barnett v Chelsea*.

Novus actus interveniens

There are three types of intervening act that will break the chain of causation. The situation of an intervening act usually applies in circumstances where the negligence of the defendant has triggered a sequence of events leading to the harm suffered by the claimant. The intervening event may be the act of the claimant himself, or a third party over which the defendant had no control. The court has to decide whether the new act is sufficiently serious to be the cause of the damage rather than the original act. A defendant who injures a claimant who has already been injured will be liable only in so far as his act increases or exacerbates the pre-existing injury.

Act of the claimant	Act of a third party	Natural events
Act is unreasonable. McKew v Holland	Where a third party intervenes in the course of events the defendant will normally only be liable for damage until the intervention. Knightly v Johns	Natural event is unforeseeable. Carslogie Steamship Co Ltd

4.2 Remoteness of damage

Eventual outcome is reasonably foreseeable — *The Wagon Mound*.

The 'thin skull principle'(sometimes it is called the 'eggshell skull principle') may overrule the law of remoteness. The principle states that 'you must take your victim as you find them'. If a victim has a particular susceptibility or weakness and suffers a greater injury than a normal person, the defendant will be liable to the full extent of the claimant's injuries.

5. Defences to negligence

The defendant has the following defences available where liability for tort has been established by the claimant:

1) Vicarious liability

An employee can **avoid liability** for negligence if they were acting on their **employer's business** at the time of the incident.

2) 'Volenti non fit injuria'

Voluntary acceptance of the **risk of injury**. For this defence to be successful the defendant must **prove** that the claimant was **fully informed** of the **risks** and that they **consented to them**. An **awareness** of the risk **is not sufficient to establish consent**.

3) Contributory negligence

A court may **reduce** the amount of damages paid to the claimant if the defendant establishes that they contributed to their own **injury or loss**.

Reductions for contributory negligence are **typically** in the range of **10% to 75%**, but it is possible to reduce the claim by **100%**.

Additional information

The Limitation Act 1980 states that claims in tort should be brought to court within six years from the date of negligence. For personal injury claims this has been reduced to three years.

6. Explain and analyse the duty of care of accountants and auditors

6.1 Special relationship

The claimant must prove they were in a '**special relationship**' with the defendant to establish a duty of care, i.e.:

a) A client requested a professional opinion from their accountant/auditor.

b) The accountant/auditor gave an opinion acting in a professional capacity.

c) The client relied upon the opinion, when it was deemed reasonable to do so.

d) The client suffered an economic loss as a result of reliance upon the opinion.

6.2 Accountants and auditors

However, it is still necessary to establish that you were **owed a duty of care** at the time the negligent misstatement occurred. When performing audit services the duty of care was defined in *Caparo v Dickman*:

The Caparo decision

The duty of care when accounts are prepared extends only to the members of a company. This does not extend to members as individuals, or to potential purchasers of shares in a company.

The accountants owe a higher standard of care to the **target company** because the report will be used in a **take-over** bid.

○ The auditors of a subsidiary company owe a duty of the care to both **the parent and subsidiary companies**.

6.3 Limitation of auditors' liability

Per the Companies Act 2006 (CA 2006) it is now possible for an auditor to limit their liability for 'negligence, default, breach of duty or breach of trust occurring in the course of the audit of accounts' to a stated amount.

Limited liability is not, however, a right and in order to secure such indemnity the members of the company must approve such agreements by resolution before the date that such an agreement becomes effective.

In the event that an auditor comes to rely on such a clause they may then be required to prove the liability amount is 'fair and reasonable'. In determining such amounts the courts will have regard for:

a) The auditor's responsibilities

b) The nature and purpose of the auditor's contractual obligations to the company

c) The professional standards expected of him

The liability limitation agreement must be approved on an annual basis; with the company able to withdraw from the agreement via an ordinary resolution at any point before such an agreement become enforceable.

7. Case Summaries

1) Latimer v AEC Ltd

The claimant had suffered injury when he slipped on a floor that had become contaminated with oil during a recent flood. The House of Lords held that the duty imposed at common law and under statute was not an absolute one — the claimant had to show that a reasonable employer would be likely to have acted differently from the defendant. In this case, the only way in which the claimant's injury could have been prevented was to close the plant; there was no evidence that a 'reasonable employer' would have taken such a drastic step, so the claim failed.

2) Barnett v Chelsea

The widow of a night watchman who died of arsenic poisoning claimed in negligence after he had attended the defendant's hospital, but was negligently sent home without adequate treatment. The court was satisfied that even if the defendants had performed their duty of care and admitted the deceased to their hospital, he would still have died of arsenic poisoning five hours after being admitted, and that he therefore suffered no loss as a consequence of the breach of duty complained of.

3) The Wagon Mound

The defendants negligently allowed a spillage of oil from their vessel, which reached the claimant's wharf. The claimants sought advice on whether the oil was flammable and, being told (incorrectly) that it was not, continued welding work they had undertaken. The oil caught fire and did substantial damage. The claimants were able to recover in negligence the cost of repairing the damage caused by the oil spillage, but not of the damage caused by the fire as it was deemed unforeseeable due to the unusual chain of events that caused the oil spill to catch fire.

4) McKew v Holland

As a result of their negligence, the defendant caused an injury to the claimant's leg which significantly weakened it. When later attempting to descend a steep staircase without a handrail or assistance, the claimant broke the ankle in the same leg as a result of jumping to avoid falling headfirst when his weakened leg gave way. Lord Reid said that once a person is injured and that injury produces a loss of mobility, they must act reasonably and carefully.

5) Knightly v Johns

The first defendant caused a road traffic accident. Subsequently, a police inspector negligently handled traffic control following the accident. This negligence led to the claimant, a police officer, being killed (he had been ordered to travel down a tunnel against the flow of oncoming traffic). The first defendant successfully argued that the negligent handling by the police inspector broke the chain of causation between his negligence and the death of the officer.

6) Carslogie Steamship Co Ltd v Royal Norwegian Government 1952

The facts: A ship owned by the claimants was damaged as a result of the defendant's negligence and required repair. During the trip to the repair site the ship was caught in severe weather conditions that resulted in additional damage being caused and therefore a longer repair time was required. The claimants claimed loss of charter revenue for the period the ship was out of action for repairs caused by the original incident.

Decision: The House of Lords held that the defendants were liable for loss of profit suffered as result of the defendants' wrongful act only. Whilst undergoing repairs, the ship ceased to be a profit-earning machine as the weather damage had rendered her unseaworthy. The weather conditions created an intervening act and the claimants had sustained no loss of profit due to the ship being out of action as it would have been unavailable for hire anyway due to the weather damage.

7) Caparo v Dickman

The defendant auditor provided a statutory audit of a company, which was relied on by investors in deciding to purchase shares in the company. However, the auditors report failed to make clear that the company was making a loss. When the investors realised they had made a loss, they sued the auditors in negligence.

The statements of Lord Bridge in *Caparo* are now generally taken to represent the law, where attribution of a Duty Of Care is concerned. If a case has a fact situation in which a duty of care has been attributed in the past, then a duty of care can be attributed without further analysis. If the facts represent a novel situation, then one should ask first of all whether the loss was foreseeable (this is essentially the 'neighbour principle' of Donoghue v Stevenson).

If the loss was foreseeable, one should consider whether there was a sufficient relationship of proximity between the parties. If there was, ask whether it is 'fair, just, and reasonable' to impose liability.

In *Caparo* the loss was foreseeable, and it could be argued that there was sufficient proximity between the parties. However, the claimants failed on the third part of the test. It was held that the auditors were carrying out a duty to the company directors and, while they could have forseen that their report would be seen by the investors, it was not reasonable for investors to rely on it.

8) Donoghue v Stevenson

Donoghue ordered an ice cream float from a Paisley cafe. The proprietor brought the icecream in a tumbler and poured some 'D. Stevenson' ginger beer over it. Mrs D. took a drink and found the decomposed remains of a snail in the ginger beer.

Suffering from severe gastro-enteritis, she issued a writ against David Stevenson, claiming £500 in damages. The case reached the House of Lords where the historic decision that the manufacturer of the ginger beer owed a duty of care to any consumers that used its products.

9) Blyth v Birmingham

Birmingham Waterworks Co. (D) had installed water mains and fire plugs on the street where Blyth (P) lived. After 25 years without problems, an unusually cold frost caused one of the plugs opposite P's house to freeze over. The damaged plug leaked a large quantity of water into P's home. P sued D for damages based on negligence. P was awarded damages for negligence by the jury and D appealed, asserting that the severity of the frost of 1855 was unforeseeable. A reasonable person cannot be held liable for an unforeseeable event. Negligence is an objective standard and has nothing to do with a party's subjective state of mind.

Chapter 8

Contract of employment

1. What is an employee?
- **Employed**-works under a contract of service.
- **Self-employed (independent contractor)**-works under a contract to provide services.
- **An employee** is an individual who has entered into, or works under a contract of employment.

1.1 The tests used to determine employment

1.1.1 The control test
The court will consider whether the employer has control over the way in which the employee performs their duties.

However, this test is unappropriated for skilled workers. See *Mersey Docks & Harbour Board v Coggins & Griffiths (Liverpool)*.

1.1.2 The integration test
Because the control test was not sufficient to deal with all situations, the integration test was formulated. This looks at how much the work is fully integrated into the core activities of the employing organization. Is the work done as an integral part of the business? See case *Cassidy v Ministry of Health*

1.1.3 The multiple (economic reality) test
Courts also consider whether the employee was working on their own account and require numerous factors to be taken into account. See *Ready Mixed Concrete (South East) v Ministry of Pensions & National Insurance*.

1) Relevant factors (employee or self-employed?)
- Provision of tools
- Wearing of uniforms
- Selection, appointment and dismissal
- Holiday/sick pay entitlements
- Method of remuneration
- Use of substitute labor
- Working for a number of different people is not necessarily a sign of self-employment. A number of assignments may be construed as 'a series of employments'.

2) Practical implementation

The case below marks an important shift away from courts accepting as fact the **contents of an employment** contract towards looking at the **actual working arrangement** when deciding on an employee's employment status.

It also means that the **relative bargaining power** between the parties should be considered. *Autoclenz v Belcher*.

1.2 Agency workers

Two key cases have considered length of service of agency workers and control that the client of the agency has over the worker.

a) **Length of service (integration test)**

b) **Control over the worker (employee)**

2. Why does it matter?

The distinction between employed and self-employed is important as to whether **certain rights** are available to an individual and how they are treated for **tax** purposes.

Significance of the distinction

	Employed	Self-employed
Social Security	Employers must pay secondary class 1 national insurance contributions on behalf of employees Employees make primary class 1 national insurance contributions	Independent contractors pay class 2 and 4 contributions
Taxation	Deductions must be made for income tax by an employer	Directly responsible to HM Revenue and customs for tax due
Employment Protection	Minimum periods of notice Remedies for unfair dismissal	Employment protection is not available for contractors
Tortious acts	Employers liable	Independent contractor liable
Implied terms	Rights and duties implied by statute for employers and employees	Implied rights and duties do not apply
VAT	Employees do not have to register for or charge VAT	May have to register for, and charge VAT
Bankruptcy	Employee has preferential rights as a creditor	Contractors are treated as non-preferential creditors
Health and safety	Significant common law and legislation governing employers' duties to employees	Common law provisions and the legislation relating to employees also relates to independent contractors

3. Employment contract: basic issues

An employment contract is a contract of service which may be **express** (either **oral** or **written**) or implied. This means that employment contracts can be simple, straightforward agreements.

3.1 Requirement for written particulars (Express terms)

Within two months of the beginning of the employment the employer must give to an employee a **written statement of prescribed particulars** of their employment.

The statement should identify the following:
- The names of **employer** and **employee**
- The **date** on which employment began
- **Continuous period** of employment
- **Pay** — scale or rate and intervals at which paid
- **Hours** of work (including any specified 'normal working hours')
- Any **holiday** and **holiday pay** entitlement (for a person working five days per week, the holiday entitlement is 5.6 weeks or 28 days)
- The **title** of the job which the employee is employed to do (or a brief job description)
- **Sick leave** and **sick pay** entitlement
- **Pensions** and pension **schemes**
- Length of **notice** of termination to be given on either side

A '**principal statement**', which must include the **first seven items above**, must be provided, but other particulars may be given by way of separate documents.

3.2 Implied terms

Implied terms usually arise out of **custom** and **practice** within a profession or industry. Four requirements should be met before such terms can be read into a contract.
- The terms must be **reasonable, certain** and **notorious**
- They must represent the **wishes** of both parties
- **Proof** of the custom or practice must be provided by the party seeking to rely on the term
- A **distinction** must be made between implying terms that make **minor**, and terms that make **fundamental** changes to the contract.

4. Common law duties

There is an overriding duty of mutual trust and confidence between the employer and the employee.

There is no duty to provide a reference when employees leaveservice. Employers may be liable under negligence for not taking reasonable care over accuracy and fairness if they do provide one.

4.1 Employee's duties

The employee has a fundamental duty of faithful service to their employer. All other duties are features of this general duty. *Hivac Ltd v Park Royal Scientific Instruments Ltd*.

The implied duties of the employee include the following:

○ **Reasonable** competence to do their job.

○ Obedience to the employer's instructions unless they require them to do an unlawful act or to expose themselves to personal danger (not inherent in their work) or are instructions outside the employee's contract.

○ Duty to **account** for all money and property received during the course of their employment except what is customary to be received or is trivial.

○ **Reasonable care and skill**

○ **Personal service** — the contract of employment is a personal one and so the employee may not delegate their duties without the employer's express or implied consent.

4.2 Employer's duties

There is an overriding **duty of mutual trust and confidence** between the employer and the employee.

The employer usually also has **the four main duties** at common law.

○ To **pay remuneration** to employees.

○ To **indemnify the employee** against expenses and losses incurred in the course of employment.

○ To take care of the employees' health and safety at work. This is also provided for in statute.

○ To **provide work** (if there is **no work** available and the employer continues to pay its employees).

4.3 The importance of implied duties

○ **Breach of a legal duty**, if it is important enough, may entitle the injured party to treat the contract as **discharged and to claim damages**

○ In an employee's claim for compensation for unfair dismissal, the employee may argue that it was a case of **constructive dismissal** by the employer

5. Statutory duties

An **employer** has **statutory duties** in the following areas:

○ Pay and equality
○ Time off work
○ Maternity rights and the 'work-life balance'
○ Health and safety
○ Working time

5.1 Pay and equality

There are two key pieces of legislation in relation to pay. These are the **Equality Act 2010** and the **National Minimum Wage Act 1998**.

○ National Minimum Wage Act 1998 -A national minimum hourly wage.

- Pay statement — provide an itemised pay statement.
- Equality — The Equality Act 2010 seeks to ensure equal treatment in employment to outlaw direct discrimination, harassment, victimisation and disability-related discrimination at work.

5.2 Time off work

- Trade union officials are entitled to time off on full pay at the employer's expense to enable them to carry out trade union duties.
- A member of a recognised independent trade union may have time off work (without statutory right to pay) for trade union activities, for example, attending a branch meeting.
- An employee who has been given notice of dismissal for redundancy may have time off to look for work or to arrange training for other work.
- Employers also have a duty to allow an employee to have reasonable time off to carry out certain public duties. There is no statutory provision entitling an employee to time off for jury service, but prevention of a person from attending as a juror is contempt of court.

5.3 Maternity rights and the 'work-life balance'

A woman who is pregnant is given substantial rights under statute, including:
- The right to time off work for ante-natal care
- The right to ordinary maternity leave
- The right to additional maternity leave
- The right to maternity pay
- The right to return to work after maternity leave
- If dismissed, a claim for unfair dismissal

Family-friendly employment policies and the 'work/life balance'

1) Ante-natal care

An employee has a right not to be unreasonably refused time off for ante-natal care during working hours.

2) Maternity leave and pay

Every woman who is an employee is entitled to statutory maternity leave of up to 52 weeks.

Statutory maternity pay is paid for 39 weeks during statutory maternity leave.

3) Paternity leave and pay

A qualified man is entitled to take either one week or two consecutive weeks paid paternity leave.

4) Adoption leave and pay (Adoptive parents)

There is a right to statutory adoption leave(SAL) and statutory adoption pay (SAP).

5) Flexible working

Employees have the right to apply for a change in terms and conditions of employment in respect of hours, time and place of work and not to be unreasonably refused.

6) Parental leave

Any employee with a year's continuous service who has parental responsibility is entitled to **unpaid** parental leave of **18 weeks** to care for each child up to the child's **18th** birthday.

5.4 Health and safety

The Health and Safety at Work Act 1974

a) Provide and maintain **plant** and **systems of work** which are safe and without risk

b) Make **arrangements** to ensure safe use, handling, storage and transport of articles/substances

c) Provide adequate **information, instruction, training** and **supervision**

d) Maintain safe **places** of work and ensure that there is adequate access in and out

e) Provide a safe and healthy working **environment**

The contract of employment contains an **implied right not to be subjected to detriment** by the employer on grounds of health and safety:

a) Carry out activities designated

b) Perform duties as a representative of workers on issues of health and safety

c) Take part in consultation with the employer under the Health and Safety (Consultation with Employees) Regulations 1996

d) Leave their place of work or refused to work in circumstances which they reasonably believed to be serious or imminent and they could not reasonably be expected to avert

e) Take appropriate steps to protect themselves or others from circumstances of danger which they believed to be serious and imminent

5.5 Working time

The Working Time Regulations 1998 provide broadly that a worker's **average working time in a 17-week period**, (including overtime) shall **not exceed 48 hours for each seven days period**, unless the worker has agreed in writing that this limit shall not apply.

6. Continuous employment

Many rights given to employees under **the Employment Rights Act 1996** are only available if an employee has a specified period of **continuous employment.**

The basic rule is that a year is twelve calendar months.

7. Case Summaries

1) Walker v Crystal Palace FC

As a professional football player Walker claimed to be self-employed. However it was ruled that he was employed under a contract of service as he was subject to the control of his master in the form of training, discipline and method of pay.

2) Cassidy v Ministry of Health

In determining for the purposes of vicarious liability whether or not surgeons were employed or self-employed Lord Denning decreed:

'In my opinion authorities who run a hospital, be they local authorities, government boards, or any other corporation, are in law under the self-same duty as the humblest doctor; whenever they accept a patient for treatment, they must use reasonable care and skill to cure him of his ailment. The hospital authorities cannot, of course, do it by themselves; they have no ears to listen through the stethoscope, and no hands to hold the surgeon's knife. They must do it by the staff which they employ; and if their staff are negligent in giving the treatment, they are just as liable for that negligence as is anyone else who employs others to do his duties for him...' Having stated therefore that the surgeon was an employee of the hospital it was the hospital that was held vicariously liable for his negligent acts.

3) RMC v Ministry of Pensions

Following a query over national insurance contributions the question arose as to whether RMC's drivers were employed or independent contractors. Court looked at a multiple of factors to decide: drivers were buying their own lorries on HP from RMC; they were responsible for maintenance; were paid on deliveries made; no provision for holidays or fixed hours of work; substitute drivers were allowed; drivers wore company overalls. Considering all these factors court held that drivers were not employees.

Chapter 9

Dismissal and redundancy

1. Termination by notice

A contract of employment may be terminated by notice.
a) Notice not be less than the statutory minimum
b) May be given without specific reason
c) Only be given in specific circumstances

Minimum period of notice

	Service period(x)	Notice time
Employee notice	≥1 month	≥1 week
Employer notice	1 month≤x<2 yrs	≥1 week
	2 yrs+<x<12 yrs	1 week notice for each year
	≥12 yrs	≥12 week

2. Types of dismissal

a) **Summary dismissal** is where the employer dismisses the employee **without notice**. They may do this if the **employee** has committed a serious **breach of contract**.

b) **Constructive dismissal** is where the **employer** commits a **breach of contract**, thereby causing the employee to resign.

c) **Wrongful dismissal**: without the correct notice period and justification

d) **Unfair/Fair dismissal**: statutory concept

3. Summary dismissal

Summary dismissal: Employer dismisses the employee without notice.

○ They may do this if the employee has committed a serious breach of contract, if so, the employer incurs no liability.

○ Where no serious breach of contract by employee, the employer has summarily dismissed an employee without notice, there may be a claim for damages at common law for wrongful dismissal.

4. Constructive dismissal

Constructive dismissal occurs where the employer, although willing to continue the employment, repudiates some essential term of the contract, for example by the imposition of a complete change in the employee's duties, and the employee resigns.

The employer is liable for breach of contract.

To establish constructive dismissal, an employee must show the following issues:

a) His employer has committed a serious breach of contract.

b) He left because of the breach.

5. Wrongful dismissal

A claim for wrongful dismissal is a common law action for breach of contract. The claim is available to both employees and independent contractors.

Occurs where the employer terminates the contract:

a) without giving proper notice

b) without justification

5.1 Justification of dismissal

a) Wilful disobedience of a lawful order

b) Misconduct: disclosure of confidential information

c) Dishonesty

d) Incompetence or neglect

e) Gross negligence

f) Immorality

g) Drunkenness

5.2 Remedies for wrongful dismissal

a) Damages for wrongful dismissal based on the loss of earnings that would have been earned if proper notice had been given.

b) Wronged party is expected to mitigate their loss such as seeking other employment.

Apply to:

a) Employment tribunal: it's available for the employee to claim within three months to resolve employment disputes.

b) County court/High court: it's available for everyone believes he has been wrongful dismissed to sue within six years.

6. Unfair dismissal

Unfair dismissal is a statutory claim made by 'qualified' employees who have been 'unfair dismissed' that seeks to widen the scope of protection and increase the range of remedies.

Any employee with at least two years' continuous service has the right 'not to be unfairly dismissed.

6.1 Scope

Certain categories of employee are **excluded** from the statutory unfair dismissal code:

a) Persons employed to work **outside Great Britain**

b) Employees dismissed while taking **unofficial strike** or other industrial action

c) Other categories, including members of the police or army

6.2 Remedies

a) Reinstatement: Same job

b) Re-engagement: Same status

c) Compensation:
- Basic award
- Compensatory award
- Additional award

○ **Basic award**

Age	Entitlement (week's pay)
18—21	1/2
22—40	1
41+	3/2

The basic award is limited to a maximum 20 years, up to a statutory maximum per week.

The basic award for unfair dismissal is also suitable for the remedies of constructive dismissal and redundancy.

○ **Compensatory award**

It is for any additional loss of earnings, expenses and benefits, on common law principles of damages for breach of contract. This is limited to a statutory maximum.

○ **Additional award**

a) The employer ignores an order for re-employment or re-engagement.

b) The dismissal is unfair because of race, sex or disability discrimination.

c) A punitive additional award is made of between 26–52 weeks (subject to a statutory weekly maximum).

Reduce the amount:

a) If the employee contributed in some way to their own dismissal

b) If they have unreasonably refused an offer of reinstatement

c) If it is just and equitable to reduce the basic award by reason of some matter which occurred before dismissal

6.3 Justification

6.3.1 Automatically unfair reasons for dismissal

a) Pregnancy or other maternity-related grounds

b) A spent conviction

c) Trade union membership or activities

d) Taking steps to avert danger to health and safety at work

e) Transfer of an undertaking unless reasonable reasons

f) Making a protected disclosure order

g) Seeking to enforce rights relating to the national minimum wage

h) Exercising rights under Working Time Regulations 1998

6.3.2 Automatically fair reasons for dismissal

a) Taking part in unofficial industrial action

b) Being a threat to national security (to be certified by the government)

6.3.3 Potentially fair reasons for dismissal

To justify dismissal as fair dismissal, employers must show:

a) Incapability or not qualifications

b) Misconduct of the employee

c) Legal prohibition

d) **Redundancy** unless: unreasonable selection procedure or trade union membership

e) The employee was married to one of their competitors.

f) The employee refused to accept a reorganisation.

7. Redundancy

7.1 What is redundancy?

a) The employer has **ceased**, or intends to cease, to carry on the business

b) The **requirements** of that business for employees to carry on the work done by the employee have ceased or diminished

7.2 Exceptions to the right to redundancy payment

a) Not employee

b) Not been continuously employed for two years

c) Be dismissed for misconduct

d) An offer to renew the contract is unreasonably refused

e) Claim is made out of time (after six months)

f) Employee leaves before redundant

Misconduct of the employee

An employee who is dismissed for misconduct is **not entitled** to redundancy pay even though they may become redundant.

However, an employee can be dismissed for misconduct but still claim redundancy pay in the event of a **strike**. Strike action after the redundancy notice is served

However, if they are **on strike when the notice is served** they will **not be eligible** for the payment.

Chapter 10

Agency law

1. Role of the agent

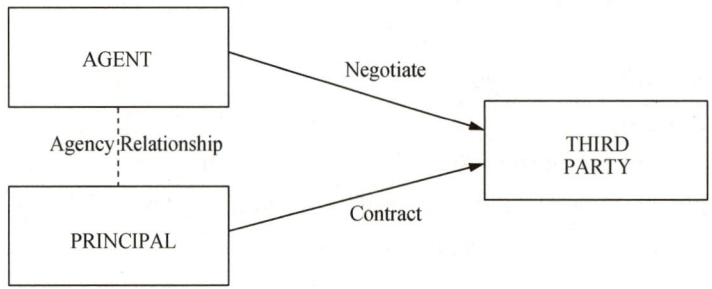

Type of agent:

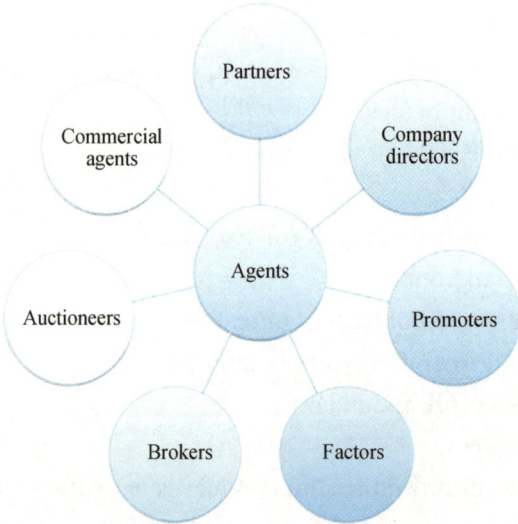

2. The formation of the agency relationship

2.1 Express agreement

Agent is **expressly appointed** by the principal. This may be orally, or in writing.

An agent expressly appointed by the principal has actual authority of the principal to act on their behalf.

2.2 Implied agreement

Two people may be implied by their **relationship** or by their **conduct**.

2.3 Ratification

An agency relationship may be created **retrospectively**, by the 'principal' **ratifying** the act of the 'agent'.

The conditions for ratification are:

a) The principal must have existed at the time of the contract made by the agent;

b) The principal must have had legal capacity at the time the contract was made

c) The ratification must take place within reasonable time

d) They ratify the contract in its entirety

e) They communicate their ratification to the third party sufficiently clearly

2.4 Agent by estoppel

Principal holds out to third parties that a person is their agent, even if the principal and the 'agent' do not agree to form such a relationship. *Freeman & lockyer v buckhurst park properties (mangal) ltd 1964*

2.5 Agent by necessity

In Emergency situation, a person to take action in respect of someone else's goods.

3. Authority of the agent

A contract made by the agent is binding on the principal and the other party only if the agent was acting **within the limits of their authority from their principal**.

3.1 Types of authority

3.1.1 Express authority

Authority explicitly given by the principal to the agent to perform particular tasks.

The extent of the agent's express authority will depend on the **construction of the words used on their appointment**.

If the agent contracts outside the scope of their express (actual) authority, they may be liable to the principal and the third party for breach of warrant of authority.

3.1.2 Implied authority

No express authority, authority may be **implied** from the **nature** of the agent's activities or from what is **usual or customary** in the circumstances.

For example, the Managing Director and Company Secretary are assumed to have the power to bind the company in all commercial and administrative contracts respectively.

3.1.3 Apparent/ostensible authority

Ostensible authority arises in **two** distinct ways.

a) **A person** makes a **representation** to third parties that a particular person has the authority to act as their agent without actually appointing them as their agent.

b) it may arise where a principal has **previously represented** to a third party that an agent has authority to act on their behalf. *Reeman & lockyer v buckhurst park properties (mangal) ltd* **1964**

Ostensible authority must be a representation of fact, **not law**, and must be made to the third party. This distinguishes ostensible authority from actual authority, where the **third party need know nothing of the agent's authority**.

Express and implied authority are sometimes referred to together as actual authority. This distinguishes them from ostensible or apparent authority.

3.2 Revocation of authority

Where a principal has **represented** to a third party that an agent has authority to act, and has subsequently revoked the agent's authority, this may **be insufficient to escape liability**. The principal should inform third parties who have previously dealt with the agent of the change in circumstances.

3.3 Termination of agency

Agency is terminated by **agreement** or by operation of **law** (death, insanity, insolvency).

a) Principal or agent dies

b) Principal or agent becomes insane

c) Principal becomes bankrupt, or the agent becomes bankrupt and this interferes with their position as agent.

4. Agent's rights and obligations

4.1 Agent's rights

The rights of any agent are:

a) To claim remuneration for services performed

b) To be indemnified by the Principal for expenses incurred

c) To exercise lien over property owned by the Principal

4.2 Agent's duties

To perform their duties in line with the instructions of the principal

a) To exercise due care and skill

b) To act in person

c) To be accountable for all transactions

d) To avoid a conflict of interests

e) Not to make a secret profit

f) Not to accept bribes

4.3 General rule of agent's liability

An agent contracting for their principal within their actual and/or apparent authority generally has **no liability** on the contract and is **not entitled to enforce it**.

4.4　Agent will be personally liable

1) Where the agent acts for a disclosed principal

○ Agents intended to **undertake personal liability**.

○ Where it is **usual business practice or trade custom** for an agent to be liable and entitled.

○ The agent **is acting on their own behalf** even though they support to act for a principal.

○ **Breach of warranty of authority**: he warranted or promised that he had authority which he did not possess.

2) Where the agent acts for an undisclosed principal

When the third party discovers the existence of principal, he can **elect** to treat principal of agent as bound by the transaction.

5. Case Summaries

1) Watteau v Fenwick 1893

The facts: The owner of a hotel (F) employed the previous owner (H) to manage it. F forbade H to buy cigars on credit but H did buy cigars from W. W sued F for payment but F argued that he was not bound by the contract, since H had no actual authority to make it, and that W believed that H still owned the hotel.

Decision: It was within the usual authority of a manager of a hotel to buy cigars on credit and F was bound by the contract (although W did not even know that H was the agent of F) since his restriction of usual authority had not been communicated.

2) Freeman and Lockyer v Buckhurst Park Properties

The facts: K and H carried on business as property developers through a company which they owned in equal shares. Each appointed another director, making four in all. H lived abroad and the business of the company was left entirely under the control of K. As a director K had no actual or apparent authority to enter into contracts as agent of the company, but he did make contracts as if he were a managing director without authority to do so. The other directors were aware of these activities but had not authorised them.

The claimants sued the company for work done on K's instructions.

Decision: Although there had been no actual delegation to K, the company had by its acquiescence led the claimants to believe that K was an authorised agent and the claimants had relied on it. The company was bound by the contract.

Partnership

1. Partnerships

Partnership is the relation which subsists between **persons carrying on a business in common** with a view of **profit.**

a) **'Person'** includes a corporation such as a registered company as well as an **individual** living person.

b) A business can consist of **a single transaction** (joint ventures).

2. Unlimited liability partnership

A partnership is formed when **two or more** people agree to **run a business** together Detailed partnership agreements.

A **written** partnership agreement is **not legally required**

2.1 Forming an unlimited liability partnership

Partnership Act 1980

a) to share equally in the capital and profits of the business

b) to be indemnified by the firm for any liabilities

c) to take part in the management of the business

d) to have access to the firm's books

e) to prevent admission of a new partner or a change in partnership nature

2.2 Terminating an unlimited liability partnership

a) Passing of time

b) The **death or bankruptcy** of a partner

c) **Subsequent illegality**

d) **Notice** given by a partner if it is a partnership of indefinite duration

e) **Order of the court** granted to a partner

f) **Agreement** between the partners

Assets are realised and the proceeds applied in this order

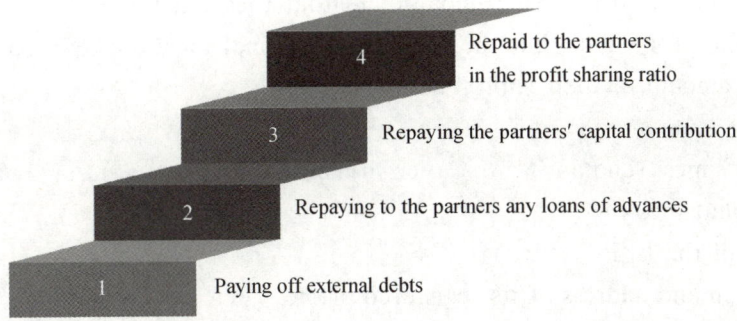

2.3 Authority of partners in an unlimited liability partnership

A partner is the agent of the partnership and their co-partners.

Other than when the partner has **actual authority**, the authority often **depends on the perception of the third party**. If the third party genuinely believes that the partner has authority, the partner is likely to bind the firm.

2.4 Liability of partners in an unlimited liability partnership

Partners are also **jointly liable** for **crimes** and **torts** committed by one of their number in the course of business.

Partners are **jointly liable for all partnership debts** that result from contracts that the partners have made which bind the firm.

a) A new partner admitted to an existing firm is liable for debts incurred only after they become a partner.

b) A partner who retires is still liable for any outstanding debts incurred while they were a partner, unless the creditor has agreed to release them from liability. They are also liable for debts of the firm incurred after their retirement if the creditor knew them to be a partner (before retirement) and has not had **notice** of their retirement.

Partnerships can grant a mortgage or **fixed charge** over property, but cannot grant **floating** changes.

3. Limited partnership

At least one partner (the general partner) must have full, **unlimited liability.** The other partners have limited liability for the debts of the partnership beyond the extent of the capital they have contributed.

a) The partnership must be registered with the Registrar of Companies as a limited partnership.

b) Limited partners may not participate in the management of the business. If they do, they forfeit their limited liability.

c) A limited partner has no power to bind the firm to contracts who is not an agent of the firm.

4. Limited liability partnerships (LLP)

LLPs are similar to limited companies in that they **have separate legal identity** and unlimited liability for debts, but the **liability of the individual partners** (or members) is limited to the amount of their capital contribution.

4.1 Formation

Subscribers must send an **incorporation document** and a **statement of compliance** to the registrar of companies.

- ✓ Name of the LLP
- ✓ Location and address of its registered office
- ✓ Name and address of all members
- ✓ Which of the members are to be designated members (must have two)

4.2 Internal regulation

The **rights and duties** of the partners will usually be set out in a partnership agreement. In the **absence** of a partnership agreement, the rights and duties are set out in regulations under the **act.** LLPs must **have two designated members**, who take responsibility for the publicity requirements of the LLP.

Duties of the two designated members:

a) filing certain notices

b) signing and filling accounts

c) appointing auditors

4.3 External relationships

Every member is an agent of the LLP.

a) The LLP will not be bound by the acts of the member where: They have no authority and the third party is aware of that fact.

b) They have ceased to be a member, and the third party is aware of that fact.

4.4 Dissolution

An LLP does **not dissolve** when a member **leaves.**

An **LLP must be formally wound up.** This is achieved under provisions **similar to company winding up** provisions.

Chapter 12

Corporations and legal personality

1. Sole trader

A sole trader owns and runs business — owns the assets and is liable for all the debts.

Advantages	Disadvantages
No formal procedures	Personal wealth might be lost
Independence Self-accountability	Plough back profits for expansion
Personal supervision	High dependence on the individual
All profits accrue to the sole trader	Death of the proprietor

2. Companies

A company has a **legal personality** separate from its owners (known as members).

2.1 Legal personality

a) An individual human being is a **natural person**.

b) The law also recognises **artificial persons in the form of companies** and limited partnerships.

c) A corporation is a **legal entity separate from the natural persons** connected with it, for example as **members or directors**.

2.2 Limited liability of members

Limited liability is a protection offered to members of certain types of company. In the event of business **failure**, the members will only be asked to contribute **identifiable amounts to the assets of the business**.

a) Protection for members against creditors

b) Protection from business failure

c) Members asked to contribute identifiable amount

— companies limited by shares

— companies limited by guarantee

d) Liability of the company for tort and crime

Identifiable amount

Type of company	Amount owed by member at winding up
Company limited by shares	Any outstanding amount from when they originally purchased their shares from the company
If the member's shares are fully paid, they do not have to contribute anything in the event of a winding up	
Company limited by guarantee	The amount they guaranteed to pay in the event of a winding up

3. Veil of incorporation

Meaning	Company is separate legal entity (Separate from its shareholders) *Salomon v Salomon & Co, Lee v Lee's Air Farming Ltd 1960*
Consequences	○ **Company is liable for its own debts.** Members are liable up to the amount they have contributed in share capital if the company is Insolvent ○ Company has perpetual succession, irrespective of fate of shareholders ○ Separation of management from ownership

'veil of incorporation' as seen below:

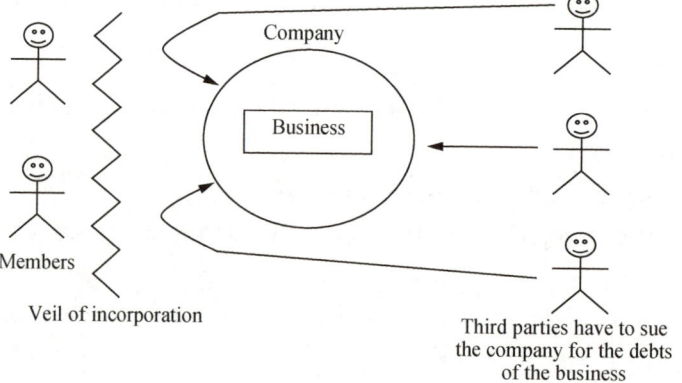

4. Lifting the veil

It is sometimes necessary by law to look at who the owners of a company are. This is referred to as 'lifting the veil'.

Result: members or directors become personally liable for the company's debts. There are three situations in which the veil can be lifted:

a) Lifting the veil by statute to enforce the law

b) Evasion of obligation

c) Group situation

4.1 Lifting the veil by statute to enforce the law

a) Liability for trading without trading certificate

Chapter 12　Corporations and legal personality

b) Fraudulent and wrong trading

c) Disqualified directors

d) Abuse of company names

4.2　Evasion of obligations

4.2.1　Evasion of legal obligations

The veil will be lifted only where "special circumstances exist indicating that it is **a mere facade concealing the true facts**".

Sham companies — *Gilfor Motor Cor Ltd v Horne 1933*

4.2.2　Public interest

Nationality — in times of war it is illegal to trade with the enemy.

Daimler v Continental Tyre & Rubber Co 1916

4.2.3　Evasion of liabilities

The veil of may also be lifted where directors ignore the separate legal personality of two companies and transfer assets from one to the other.

4.2.4　Evasion of taxation

Unit Construction Co Ltd v Bullock 1960

4.2.5　Quasi-partnership

Ebrahimi v Westbourne Galleries

4.3　Group company

There are a number of cases where the courts have lifted the veil between a **holding company** and its various **subsidiaries**.

The subsidiary is acting as **agent** for the holding company.

The group is to be treated as a **single economic entity** because of statutory provision. The **corporate structure** is being used as a **facade** (or sham) to conceal the truth.

Adams v Cape Industries 1990

5. Types of companies

5.1　Classification

Public Company & Private Company

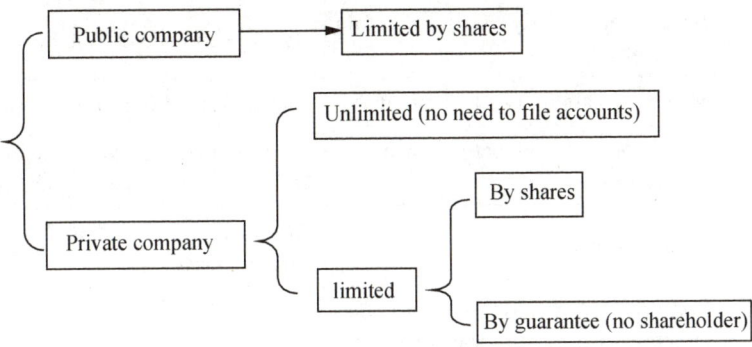

5.2 Public companies vs Private limited companies

	Public companies	Private (limited) companies
Definition	Registered as a public company	Any company that was not a public company
Name	Ends with plc or public limited company	Ends with Ltd or limited
Capital	Not less than the authorised minimum (currently £ **50,000**)	No minimum requirement
Director	Minimum two	Minimum one
Audit	Accounts must be audited	Audit not required if turnover below **£ 10.2 m**
AGM	Must be held each year	Need not hold an AGM

5.3 Small companies' regime

The definition of a small company for the purposes of accounting and auditing are almost identical.

In accounting terms, a company is small if it meets two of the three criteria: Balance sheet total ≤ £ 5.1 m

Turnover ≤ £ 10.2 m

50 employees or fewer on average.

For audit purpose, a company is classed as small if it qualifies on the above criteria, but must meet both of conditions ① & ②

5.4 Unlimited liability companies

An unlimited liability company is a company in which members do not have limited liability. In the event of business failure, the liquidator can require members to contribute as much as may be required to **pay the company's debts in full**.

An unlimited company can only be a private company, by definition, a public company is always limited.

5.5 Companies vs. Partnerships

Factor	Company	Traditional partnership
Entity	Is a legal entity separate from its members	Has no existence outside of its members
Liability	Members' liability can be limited	Partners' liability is usually unlimited
Size	May have any number of members (at least **one**)	Some partnerships are limited to 20 members (professional partnership excluded)
Succession	Perpetual succession	Partnerships are dissolved when any of the partners leaves it
Management	Company must have at least one director (two for a public company)	All partners can participate in management

6. Case Summaries

1) Salomon v Salomon and Co.

S transferred his business as a sole trader into a company legally incorporated with the correct number of shareholders. Sale of assets to the company meant S was owed money by S and Co, which was secured by a debenture. On subsequent liquidation this took priority over unsecured trade creditors who argued it was invalid as the creditor — S — and the debtor — S and Co — were technically one and the same. It was held that this was incorrect.

The company, being validly constituted, was a separate legal entity to S and the debt was upheld.

2) Gilford Motor Co v Horne

H was a car salesman, and left G. His contract stated that he wasn't allowed to sell to G's customers for a period after leaving. H set up a company which then approached his former customers; H argued that firstly his company was approaching the customers, not him; and secondly, if there was wrongdoing, his company was liable and not him. The courts held that the company was sham, and granted an injunction against his company as well as him.

3) Daimler Co Ltd v Continental Tyre and Rubber Co (GB) Ltd

C sued D for debts owing. C was a UK company; however, all shareholders but one was German. D argued that they should not pay the debt to German individuals to prevent money going towards Germany's war effort. The court held that C was German.

4) Ebrahimi v Westborne Galleries

E and friend N set up a gallery in Holland Park. Initially it was a partnership and then N suggested setting up a Ltd Co. to attain limited liability. Shares were allocated on a 50/50 basis with equal management rights.

N then introduced his son to the company, effectively reducing E's shares to 49%. N and his son passed an ordinary resolution sacking E as a director and then paid bonuses to the directors and declared nil dividend. E applied to court for just and equitable winding up. It was held that the company was in legal effect a partnership based on a relationship of mutual trust and confidence which had clearly broken down. The court wound the company up.

5) Adams v Cape Industries

Cape, an English company, was head of a group including wholly owned subsidiaries.

In the United States claimants had been awarded damages for asbestosis against a marketing company NAAC, a subsidiary of Cape.

The Court of Appeal held that the judgement could not be enforced against Cape, as the subsidiary was to be treated as a 'separate legal entity with all the rights and liabilities which would normally attach to separate legal entities...'

Chapter 13

Company formation

1. Definition of a promoter

A person who 'undertakes to form a company and who takes the necessary steps to accomplish that purpose', excluding people just acting in a professional capacity, such as accountant or solicitor.

Duties of a promoter

a) Promoters have a general duty to **exercise reasonable skill and care.**

b) **Some or all the shares** of the company when formed **are to be allotted to other people.**

c) Fiduciary duty:

Promoters must not put themselves in a position where their own **interests conflict** with those of the company and make a 'secret profit'

d) But, a promoter may make a **profit** as a result of their position, if a promoter discloses any interest in transaction to the company and it is allowed.

2. Pre-incorporation expenses and contracts

2.1 Pre-incorporation expenses

a) Pre-incorporation expenses- the cost associated with formation made before the company is formed.

b) A promoter has no automatic right to recover 'pre-incorporation expenses' from company.

c) However, they can arrange directors agree that company shall pay the bills or refund to them their expenditure.

2.2 pre-incorporation contracts

A pre-incorporation contract is where a person enters into a contract before a company has been registered.

A company, prior to its incorporation, does not have contractual capacity and after its formation it **cannot ratify** or formally adopt a pre-incorporation contract.

The promoter is therefore **personally liable** under any such contract.

2.2.1 The promoter can protect his position by

There are various other ways for promoters to avoid liability for a pre-incorporation contract.

a) The contract remains as a draft (so not binding) until the company is formed.

b) Entering into an agreement of novation.

c) Buying an 'off-the shelf' company

2.2.2 Off-the-shelf companies

An "off-the-shelf" company is one that has already been formed.

2.2.3 Advantages

a) Documents will not need to be filed with the registrar by the purchaser such as memorandum and articles, application for registration

b) No risk of potential liability arising from pre-incorporation contracts

2.2.4 Disadvantages

a) The off-the-shelf company is likely to have model articles. The directors may wish to amend these.

b) The directors may want to change the name of the company

3. Registration Procedures

A company is formed and registered under CA06 when it is issued with a certificate of incorporation by the Registrar, after submission to the Registrar of a number of documents and a fee.

3.1 Application for registration

- The company's proposed name
- The location of its registered office (England or Scotland)
- Liability of members is to be limited by shares or guarantee
- Whether the company is to be private or public
- A statement of the intended address of the registered office

3.2 Documents to Registrar

Documents to be delivered	Description
Memorandum of association	A prescribed form signed by the subscribers
Articles of association	Only required if the company does not adopt model articles
Statement of proposed officers	Proposed director(s) and Company secretary
Statement of compliance	Companies Act
Statement of capital and initial Shareholdings	
Registration fee	

3.3 Certificate of incorporation

a) Name of the company

b) Limited private or public

c) Registered office

d) Date of incorporation

e) Registered number

f) Signed by the registrar

3.4 Trading certificate — public companies only

a) A private company can trade as soon has it has obtained a certificate of incorporation from the Registrar of Companies. No trading certificate is required.

b) A public company cannot commence trading until the registrar has issued a trading certificate.

However, if a public company does business or borrows before obtaining trading certificate, the transaction is valid, and company and any officer in default have committed an offence punishable by a fine.

3.5 Re-registration procedures

A private company with share capital may be able to re-register as a public company if the share capital requirement is met. A public company may re-register as a private one.

a) For a private company to re-register as a public company it must fulfil the share capital requirement of a public company: Its allotted share capital must be **at least £50,000** of which **a quarter** must be paid up, plus the whole of any premium

b) If the **share capital** of a public company **falls below £50,000**, it must re-register as a private company.

4. Roles of The Registrar of Companies

Roles are performed by the registrar of companies:

a) Issuing each company's certificate of incorporation

b) Registering companies that will be sold 'off-the-shelf'

c) Filing copies of each company's ordinary and special resolutions

5. Describe the statutory books, records and returns that companies must keep or make

A company must keep registers of certain aspects of its constitution, including the registers of **members, charges and directors.**

The register must include a service address for each director. A register of debentureholders should be kept but there is no statutory compulsion to do so.

5.1 Accounting records

Companies must keep sufficient accounting records to explain the company's transactions and its financial position. (SOFP, I/S)

	Certain specific records
1	Daily entries of sums paid and received
2	A record of assets and liabilities
3	Statements of stocks at the end of each financial year
4	Statements of stocktaking to back up the records in 3
5	Statements of goods bought and sold

a) Must be kept at company's registered office for **3 years** for a private company, **6 years** for a public company.

b) Failure to keep records is an **offence** by the officers in default

5.2 Annual financial statements

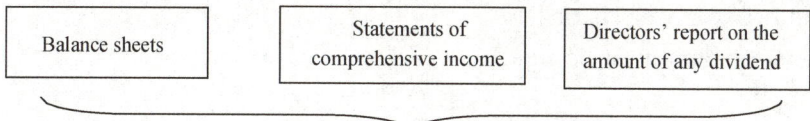

Must be approved and signed on behalf of the board of directors and a copy filed with Registrar.

5.3 Annual return

The annual return must be filed with the Registrar annually within 28 days of the return date. The return must be signed by a director or a secretary.

Chapter 14

Constitution of a company

1. Memorandum of association

The memorandum is a **simple document** which states that the **subscribers wish to form a company** and **become members** of it.

The memorandum must be signed by each **subscriber**.

2. A company's constitution

According to the Companies Act 2006, the constitution of a company consists of:

a) **Articles of Association**: how the company is to be managed and administered

b) **Resolutions and agreements**

2.1 Articles of association

a) Directors' powers and responsibilities

b) Decision making by directors

c) Appointment of directors

d) Organisation and conduct of general meetings

e) Issue and transference of shares

f) Payment of dividends

g) Exercise of members' rights

2.1.1 Legal effect of AOA

a) The articles are enforceable by the members against the company.

b) The articles also operate as a contract between individual members in their capacity as members.

However, the company's constitution does not bind the company to third parties.

2.1.2 Model articles

a) Companies are free to use **any** of the model articles that they wish.

b) If **no articles** are registered then the company will be **automatically incorporated** with the **default model articles** which are relevant to the type of company being formed.

c) Model articles can be **amended** by the members.

2.2 Alteration of the articles

a) The articles may be altered by **a special resolution.**

Chapter 14 Constitution of a company

b) **Bona fide in the interest of the company as a whole.**

c) A private company may pass a **written resolution** with a **75% majority.**

d) The alteration will be valid and binding on **all** members of the company.

e) **Copies** of the amended articles must be sent to **the Registrar**, within **15** days of the amendment, taking effect.

2.3 Restrictions on alteration

a) Confliction with the Companies Act

b) Court's order

c) Not be compelled to subscribe for additional shares

d) Correct rights variation procedure

e) Contract contained in the articles

f) Not acting **bona fide** in what they deem to be the interests of the company as a whole. The case law on the **bona fide test** is an effort to hold the balance between two principles:

○ The **majority** are **entitled** to **alter articles** even though a minority considers that the alteration is prejudicial to its interests.

○ A minority is entitled to protection against an alteration which is intended to **benefit** the **majority** rather than the company and which is **unjustified discrimination** against the minority.

3. Company objects and capacity

A **company's objects** are its aims and purposes. If a company enters into a contract which is outside its objects, that contract is said to be **ultra vires**. However the rights of third parties to the contract are protected.

3.1 Alteration of the objects

As a company's objects are located in its articles, it may alter its objects by **special resolution** for any reason.

3.2 Contractual capacity and ultra vires

Ultra vires is where a company exceeds its objects and acts outside its capacity.

The third party is not required to **enquire** whether or not there are any restrictions placed on the power of directors. They are free to assume the directors have any power they profess to have.

4. Company name and registered office

A company's name is its **identity**. There are a number of rules which restrict the choice of name that a company may adopt.

4.1 Statutory rules on the choice of company name

No company may use a name which is:

a) The **same** as an existing company on the Registrar's index of company names

b) A **criminal offence**, **offensive** or '**sensitive**' (as defined by the Secretary of State)

c) Suggest a connection with the government or local authority (unless approved)

d) The name must end with the word(s):

- Public limited company (plc) if it is a public company

- Limited (or Ltd) if it is a private limited company, unless permitted to omit 'limited' from its name

- The Welsh equivalents of either (i) or (ii) may be used by a Welsh company

4.2 Change of name

A company may decide to change its name by:

a) Passing a special resolution

b) By any other means provided for in the articles (in other words the company can specify its own procedure for changing its name).

4.3 Passing-off action

A company can be prevented by an injunction issued by the court in a passing-off action from using its registered name, if in doing so it causes its goods to be confused with those of the claimant.

If, however, the two companies' businesses are different, confusion is unlikely to occur, and hence the courts will refuse to grant an injunction.

5. Case Summaries

1) Hickman v Kent or Romney Marsh Sheep Breeders Association

The articles provided that disputes between members and the association be resolved by arbitration. Hickman brought an action against the company in the courts. It was held that the association were entitled to have the action stayed as the articles constituted a contract between Hickman and the association in respect of their rights as members.

2) Pender v Lushington

AoA stated maximum votes to be attached to shareholdings. P transferred shares to nominee companies in order to increase his votes. Chairman of company at a general meeting disallowed these votes. It was held that this was improper. P could enforce this provision against the company.

3) Rayfield v Hands

The directors of a company were forced to abide by the AoA, which required them to purchase the shares of any members who wished to transfer their shares. As a professional football player Walker claimed to be self-employed. However it was ruled that he was employed under a contract of service as he was subject to the control of his master in the form of training, discipline and method of pay.

4) Eley v Positive Life Co

E, a solicitor, drafted the original articles and included a provision that the company must always employ him as its solicitor. E became a member of the company some months after its incorporation. He later sued the company for breach of contract in not employing him as a solicitor. It was held that E could not rely on the article since it was a contract between the company and its members and he was not asserting any claim as a member.

5) Greenhalgh v Arderne Cinemas

An alteration of the AoA to remove pre-emption rights, whilst depriving G of his individual shareholder rights, was held to be for the benefit of the company as a whole.

6) Ewing v Buttercup Margarine Co Ltd 1917

The facts: The claimant had since 1904 run a chain of 150 shops in Scotland and the north of England through which he sold margarine and tea. He traded as 'The Buttercup Dairy Co'. The defendant was a registered company formed in 1916 with the name above. It sold margarine as a wholesaler in the London area. The defendant contended that there was unlikely to be confusion between the goods sold by the two concerns

Decision: If, however, the two companies' **businesses are different**, confusion is unlikely to occur, and hence the courts will refuse to grant an injunction.

Chapter 15

Share capital

1. Share capital

A share is a form of personal property, carrying rights and obligations. It is by its nature transferable.

A member who holds one or more shares is a shareholder. **Public and private companies must have a minimum of one member. There is no maximum number**.

The strict definition of a **share** consists of three **elements**, encompassing:

a) **Interest in the company** — the member is entitled to a share of the profits generated by the assets owned by the company

b) **Limited liability** — the liability of the member is limited to the amount they have agreed to pay for their shares

c) **Mutual covenants** — as defined in the previous chapter on the AoA, members are bound together — *Rayfield v Hands*

Name	Definition
Issued/allotted	The nominal value of shares currently in issue
Called up	The amount which the company **required shareholders** to pay now or in the future on the shares issued
Paid up	The amount which shareholders have **actually paid** on the shares issued and called up

When a **public company** issues shares partly paid, the following payment rules apply:

a) at least **25%** of the nominal value must be received **100% of any share premium** must be received

b) Where a shareholder **did not** pay the full nominal value of their share on issue, the debt transfers to the **new shareholder** if the share is sold.

2. Types of share

A company can issue shares of differing types, each having differing values and rights attaching to them. There are five categories you should be aware of:

○ Ordinary shares

- Preference shares
- Redeemable shares
- Treasury shares
- Deferred shares

2.1 Ordinary shares (equity)

All shares are equity shares with the same rights.

Equity share capital is a company's issued share capital less capital which carries preferential rights.

2.2 Preference shares

Preference shares are shares carrying one or more rights such as a fixed rate of **dividend** or preferential **claim** to any company profits available for distribution.

a) The right is merely to receive a dividend at the specified rate. It is **not** a right to compel the company to pay the dividend.

b) The right to receive a preference dividend is deemed to be **cumulative**.

Feature	Ordinary	Preference
Dividends	Variable	Fixed — usually cumulative
Voting rights	Yes	Restricted
General meetings	Attend and vote	Restricted
Liquidation	Rank last Entitled to capital and share of surplus	Rank above ordinary shares Entitled to repayment of capital only

2.3 Redeemable shares

Shares that the company may repurchase at a future specific date. A company must have some irredeemable shares in issue at all time.

2.4 Treasury shares

Treasury shares are created when a **limited company** legitimately **purchases its own shares** out of cash or distributable profit.

- No dividend
- No voting rights exercisable.
- May be reissued for cash without the usual issuing formalities

2.5 Deferred shares

A rare form of capital that **postpones** the rights of a holder to **receive a dividend** until the ordinary shareholders have received a fixed return

3. Class right

Class rights are rights which are attached to particular types of shares by the company's constitution.

- Dividends

○ Return of capital

○ Voting

○ The right to appoint or remove a director

Indeed a company may even have many different classes of the same types of shares such as Ordinary A, Ordinary B, Ordinary C shares etc. Each of these may well have different rights attaching to them, such as the power to vote, or preference over dividends, and these are known collectively as **class rights**.

Alteration of class rights is a contentious area and it is often the role of courts to distinguish between:

a) **Variation of class rights** — such as removing/reducing the rights of a class of shares to vote or receive dividends

b) **Not a variation of class right** — for example sub-dividing 50p shares with one vote each, into five 10p shares, with one vote each, does not constitute the variation of the rights of other classes of shares in the same company.

3.1 Variation of class rights

3.1.1 Special situations:

a) If the class rights are set by the articles and they provide a variation procedure, that procedure must be followed for any variation even if it is less onerous than the statutory procedure.

b) If class rights are defined otherwise than by the articles and there is no variation procedure, the **standard procedure** for variation of class rights requires that a **special resolution** shall be passed by a **three quarters majority** cast either at a **separate meeting** of the class, or by **written consent**.

The rules on notice, voting, polls, circulation of resolutions and quorum relating to general meetings relate also to class meetings when voting on alteration of class rights.

3.1.2 Minority appeals to the court for unfair prejudice

Whenever class rights are varied under a procedure contained in the constitution, a minority of holders of shares of the class may apply to the court to have the variation cancelled. The **objectors** together must:

a) Hold **not less than 15%** of the issued shares of the class in question

b) Not themselves have consented to or voted in favour of the variation

c) Apply to the court within **21 days** of the consent being given by the class

The court can either approve the variation as made or cancel it as 'unfairly prejudicial'. It cannot, however, modify the terms of the variation. To establish that a variation is 'unfairly prejudicial' to the class, the minority must show that the majority was seeking some advantage to themselves as members of a different class instead of considering the interests of the class in which they were then voting.

3.2 Not a variation of class rights

a) To issue shares of the same class to allottees who are not already members of the class.

b) To subdivide shares of another class with the incidental effect of increasing the voting strength of that other class.

c) To return capital to the holders of preference shares.

d) To create and issue a new class of preference shares with priority over an existing class of ordinary shares.

4. Explain allotment of shares, and distinguish between rights issue and bonus issue of shares

4.1 Allotment of shares

Allotment of shares is the issue and allocation to a person of a certain number of shares under a contract of allotment. Once the shares are allotted and the holder is entered in the register of members, the holder becomes a member of the company. The member is issued with a share certificate.

Private company with a single class of shares: in these companies directors need not seek authority to allot new shares unless directed by their AoA.

Public companies and private companies with multiple classes of shares: in order to allot new shares the directors require authority, which is derived from passing an ordinary resolution. Once passed the ordinary resolution is effective for up to five years

Allotments are subject to the following rules:

- where shares are issued wholly for cash pre-emption rights are granted;
- any company may exclude pre-emption rights by special resolution and with court approval
- directors must issue shares for a 'proper purposes

4.2 Public company allotment of shares

There are various methods of selling shares to the public.

- **Public offer:** where members of the public subscribe for shares **directly** to the company.
- **Offer for sale:** an offer to members of the public to apply for shares based on information in a prospectus.
- **Placing:** a method of raising share capital where shares are offered in a small number of large 'blocks', to persons or institutions who have previously agreed to purchase the shares at a predetermined price.

4.3 Payment of shares

The rules governing the methods of payment for shares in both private and public companies are:

a) Private companies may accept payment for shares in the form of:

- money
- goods

○ services

b) Public companies may only issue shares in exchange for: money — subject to the rules in 1.2.1 goods — these must be independently valued six months before allotment, and received within five years of allotment

4.4 Rights issues

A rights issue is a right given to a shareholder to **subscribe for further shares** in the company, usually **pro-rata** to their existing holding in the company's shares.

Pre-emption rights: are the rights of existing ordinary shareholders to be offered new shares issued by the company *pro rata* to their existing holding of that class of shares. Where shares are issued **wholly for cash**, pre-emption rights are granted.

4.5 A bonus issue

A bonus issue is the capitalisation of the reserves of a company by the issue of additional shares to existing shareholders, in proportion to their holdings. Such shares are normally fully paid-up with **no cash** called for from the shareholders.

5. Examine the effect of issuing shares at either a discount, or at a premium

a) **Shares may not be issued at a discount** (below their nominal value). Where this happens the shareholder is liable to the company for the unpaid amount plus interest.

b) Where shares are issued at a premium i.e. in excess of nominal value, whether for cash or otherwise, an **amount equal to the premium must be transferred to a share premium account**.

c) It is common for a company to issue its share **at a premium to the nominal value**. There are however a number of restrictions as to the use of the resulting share premium reserve, being:

○ The issue of fully paid bonus shares
○ Pay issue expenses and commissions in respect of a new share issue
○ Writing off the discount on the issue of debentures
○ Allowing the repurchase of debentures at a premium

Chapter 16

Loan capital

1. Define companies' borrowing powers

All companies registered under the Companies Act 2006 have an implied power to borrow for purposes incidental to their trade or business.

If a company is quoted on the Stock Exchange, a maximum limit on the borrowing arranged by directors should be set.

A contract to repay borrowed money may in principle be unenforceable if either:
- Ultra vires (or restricted) purpose
- Directors exceed their borrowing powers or have no powers to borrow

However

a) In both cases the lender will probably be able to enforce the contract.

b) If the contract is within the capacity of the company but beyond the delegated powers of the directors the company may ratify the loan contract.

2. Explain the meaning of loan capital and debenture

2.1 Loan capital

Loan capital comprises all the longer term borrowing of a company.

a) Borrowing must be repaid.

b) Share capital on the other hand is only returned to shareholders when the company is wound up.

2.2 Debentures

Debentures are a form of loan capital. A debenture is a document stating the terms on which a company has borrowed money. There are three main types.

a) A single debenture: issued to a single provider, this document sets out the terms of the loan

b) Debentures issued in series and usually registered: transferable securities; different lenders may provide different amounts on different dates. Although each transaction is a separate loan, the lenders should rank equally (*pari passu*)

c) Debenture stock: subscribed to by a large number of lenders. Only this form requires a debenture trust deed, although the others may often incorporate one:

○ Only a public company may use this method to offer its debentures to the public

○ The debenture stock can be transferable and non-transferable

○ The trustee is usually a bank, insurance company.

○ The nominal amount of the debenture stock is defined, the date or period of repayment and the rate of interest are specified.

○ If the debenture stock is secured, the deed creates a charge or charges over the assets of the company.

○ The trustee is authorised to enforce the security in case of default.

○ A company is not required to keep a register of debentureholders unless debentures are issued as a series or as debenture stock.

2.3 Rights of debentureholders

2.3.1 Debentureholder VS Shareholder (in common)

a) Both own transferable company securities which are usually long-term investments in the company.

b) The issue procedure is much the same. An offer of either shares or debentures to the public is a prospectus as defined by the Act.

c) The procedure for transfer of registered shares and debentures is the same.

2.3.2 Debentureholder VS Shareholder (difference)

Differences	Shareholder	Debentureholder
Status	Member	Creditor
Voting	May vote	May not vote
Returns	Dividends	Interest
Issued	No discount	Discounted/par
Redemption	Restrictions	No restrictions
Security	None	Fixed/Floating
Liquidation	Rank last	Rank first

3. Explain the concept of a company charge and distinguish between fixed and floating charges

A charge is an encumbrance upon real or personal property granting the holder certain rights over that property. They are often used as security for a debt owed to the charge holder.

Charges may be either fixed, which attach to the relevant asset on creation, or floating, which attach on 'crystallisation'. For this reason it is not possible to identify the assets to which a floating charge relates (until crystallisation).

3.1 Fixed charges

Fixed charges have the following properties:

a) They attach to *specific assets* upon creation

b) The charged asset may *not be disposed* of by the company

c) Default on the loan by the company enables the charge holder to *sell* the asset and recover monies owed

d) Upon liquidation fixed charge holders *rank first*

3.2 Floating charges

Floating charges have the following properties:

a) They do not attach to specific assets upon creation, merely 'hovering' over classes of assets

b) Upon a '*crystallising event*' the charge attaches itself to the remaining assets within the charged class. Such events may include:
- company is unable to pay its debts
- a receiver is appointed
- company ceases business
- company goes into liquidation

c) The company is *free to deal* in charged assets up to the point of crystallisation

d) Upon liquidation the floating charge holders' *rank behind fixed charge holders, the liquidator, and other secured creditors*

3.3 Identification of charges as fixed or floating

The label attached by parties in this way is not a conclusive statement of the charge's legal nature.

The general rule is that a charge over assets will not be registered as fixed if it envisages that the company will still be able to *deal with the charged assets* without reference to the chargee. *R in Right of British Columbia v Federal Business Development Bank*

3.4 Comparison of fixed and floating charges

Advantage of floating charge: current assets which may be easier to realise. If for example a company becomes insolvent it may be easier to sell its inventory than its empty factory.

3.5 Priority of charges

Priority of charges
Fixed charges rank according to the *order of their creation*. If two successive fixed charges over the same factory are created on 1 January and 1 February the earlier takes priority over the later one
A *floating charge created before a fixed charge* will only take priority if, when the latter was created, the *fixed chargee* had *notice* of a clause in the floating charge that prevents a later prior charge
A *fixed charge created before* a *floating one* has *priority*
Two floating charges take priority according to the *time of creation*

Negative pledge clauses

A floating chargeholder may seek to protect themselves against losing their priority by including in the terms of their floating charge a prohibition against the company creating a fixed charge over the same property.

3.6 Sale of charged assets

If a company sells a charged asset to a third party the following rules apply.

a) A chargee with a fixed charge still has recourse to the property in the hands of the third party — the charge is automatically transferred with the property.

b) Property only remains charged by a floating charge if the third party had notice of it when they acquired the property.

4. Describe the need for registering company charges

Charges must be registered with the Registrar within 21 days of their creation — not registration; else they become void, rendering the debt unsecured.

Charges that are delivered late will only be registered to the extent that they do not prejudice the rights of other charge holders.

5. Debentureholders' rights

5.1 Rights of unsecured debentureholders

Any debentureholder is a creditor of the company with the normal remedies of an unsecured creditor. They could:

a) Sue the company for debt and seize its property if their judgment for debt is unsatisfied

b) Present a petition to the court for the compulsory liquidation of the company

c) Apply to the court for an administration order, that is, a temporary reprieve to try and rescue a company

5.2 Rights of secured debentureholders

a) Take possession of the asset

b) Sell debentures

c) Apply to the court for its transfer to their ownership by foreclosure order

d) Appoint a receiver of it, provided an administration order is not in effect

Capital maintenance and dividend law

1. Capital maintenance

Capital maintenance is a fundamental principle of company law, that limited companies **should not be allowed to make payments out of capital to the detriment of company creditors.**

Company Y Balance Sheet at 31/12/200X

Net Assets	1,000
Share capital	100
Share premium	150
Revaluation reserve	200
Capital redemption reserve	100
Retained earnings	450
Shareholders' funds	1,000

Share capital, Share premium, Revaluation reserve, Capital redemption reserve } Creditors' buffer

2. Why reduce capital?

A company may wish to reduce its capital for one or more of the following reasons:

a) Suffering a loss in the value of its assets

b) Wishing to extinguish the interests of some members entirely

c) A part of a complicated arrangement of capital, for instance, replacing share capital with loan capital.

Reduction of share capital

There are **three basic methods of reducing share capital** specified in the Companies Act.

a) **Removing** liability for unpaid calls on issued share capital

b) **Paying back** excess capital to shareholders, on fully paid shares

c) **Cancelling** paid up share capital that has been lost

Private companies	Public companies
A limited company is permitted **without restriction to cancel unissued** shares as that change does not alter its financial position	

(Continued)

Without court approval	With court approval
(a) A special resolution is passed (b) A statement of solvency declared by the directors. It is an criminal offence for directors to deliver to the registrar a solvency statement without having reasonable grounds (c) Copies of resolution, solvency statement and a statement of capital must be filed with Registrar within 15 days	(a) Not been restricted by the company's articles (b) Special resolution (c) Confirmation of the reduction from the court (creditor, member, public) (d) File document to registrar. If share capital falls below £50,000, it must be re-registered as a private company

3. Acquisition of own shares

1) A market purchase

2) Off-market purchase

a) Public companies are forbidden from repurchasing shares out of capital (creditors' buffer)

b) Rules for private companies are relaxed, allowing for purchases out of capital, known as Permissible Capital Payments (PCPs). The rules for PCPs are extremely rigorous, and any payment by a private company out of capital will be unlawful unless:

- Directors produce a statutory declaration of solvency
- The declaration is audited
- Company passes a special resolution within one week of the declaration
- Within one week of resolution the company advertises the PCP on Gazette

4. Distributing dividends

A dividend is an amount payable to shareholders from profits or other distributable reserves. Various rules have been created to ensure that dividends are only paid out of

4.1 Available profits

4.2 Rules related to the power to declare a dividend

The company in general meeting and ordinary resolution
No dividend exceeds the amount recommended by director
Declared payable on the paid up amount of share capital

Paid otherwise than in cash (scrip dividend)
Paid by cheque or warrant
Listed companies generally pay two dividends a year; an interim dividend based on interim profit figures, and a final dividend based on the annual accounts and approved at the AGM
A dividend becomes a debt when it is declared and due for payment

4.3 Distributable profit

Private companies	Public companies
Accumulated realised profits	Accumulated realised profits
Less	Less
Accumulated realised losses	Accumulated realised losses
	less
	Accumulated unrealised losses

4.3.1 Alternative for public companies

A public company may only make a distribution if its **net assets** are, at the time, not less than the **aggregate of its called-up share capital** and **undistributable reserves.**

4.3.2 Undistributable reserves are defined as:

a) Share premium account

b) Capital redemption reserve

c) Any surplus of accumulated unrealised profits over accumulated unrealised losses

d) Any reserve which the company is prohibited from distributing by statute, its constitution or law.

4.3.3 Key points

○ In essence therefore, a **private company** may only pay out its **retained earnings** as a dividend;

○ A **public company** must further deduct any losses it has made, but has yet to realise, such as **negative revaluation reserves**.

○ **Depreciation** must be treated as a **realised loss**, and debited against profit, in determining the amount of distributable profit remaining

4.4 Relevant accounts

Whether a company has profits from which to pay a dividend is determined by reference to its '**relevant accounts**', which are generally **the last annual accounts** to be prepared.

4.5 Infringement of dividend rules

Director is **liable**, if:

○ The directors: declare a dividend which they know **is paid out of capital**.

○ The directors: **without preparing any accounts**, declare or recommend a dividend which proves to be paid out of capital.

○ The directors: make some **mistake** of law or interpretation of the constitution which leads them to recommend or declare an **unlawful dividend**.

The position of **members** is as follows.

○ An injunction

- Members voting in general meeting
- Company can recover from members an unlawful dividend
- Directors can claim indemnity from members who knew of the irregularity
- Members knowingly receiving an unlawful dividend may not bring an action against the directors

Chapter 18

Company directors

1. The role of directors and the different types of directors

1.1 The role of directors

A director is a person who is responsible for the overall direction of the company's affairs.

The directors' function is to take part in making decisions by attending meetings of the board of directors

1.2 Types of directors

a) **De jure directors**: Most directors are **expressly appointed** by a company.

b) **A de facto director**: **Anyone** who is **held out by a company** as a director, **performs the functions** of a director and is **treated by the board** as a director although they have **never been validly appointed**.

c) **Shadow directors**: A person might seek to **avoid the legal responsibilities of being a director** by avoiding appointment as such but using their power, say as a major shareholder, to manipulate the acknowledged board of directors.

d) **Alternate directors**: A director may, if the articles permit, appoint an alternate director to attend and vote for them at board meetings which they are unable to attend.

e) **Executive director** — An executive director is someone employed to be a member of the company's board, involving themselves in the management of the business.

f) **Non-executive director** — A non-executive director does not have a function to perform in a company's management but is involved in its governance.

g) **Managing director** (MD) (The Chief Executive Officer)- a company may optionally appoint one or more managing directors who have the implied actual authority to **enter into any commercial contracts** on behalf of the company and carry out overall **day-to-day management functions**.

h) **The board of directors** — The board of directors is the elected representative of the shareholders acting collectively in the management of a company's affairs.

i) **The Chair** — a company's Chair (or Chairman) is responsible for leading the board and ensuring its effectiveness. This is a very distinct role from that of the CEO/MD, who is responsible for leading the company's operations.

Number of directors — Every company must have at least **one** director and for **a public company** the minimum is **two**. At least one director must be a **natural person**, not a body corporate. A **company** may be a director.

2. Discuss the ways in which directors are appointed, can lose their office or be subject to a disqualification order

2.1 Appointment of directors

2.1.1 Appointment of first directors

The application for registration delivered to the Registrar to form a company **includes particulars of the first directors**, with their consents. On the formation of the company those persons become the first directors.

2.1.2 Appointment of subsequent directors

It can be either to **replace** existing directors or as **additional** directors.

Appointment of further directors is carried out **as the articles provide**. Most company articles allow for the appointment of directors:

a) By **ordinary resolution** of the shareholders

b) By a **decision** of the directors.

2.1.3 Publicity

In addition to giving notice of the first directors, every company must within **14 days** give **notice** to the Registrar of any change among its directors. This includes any changes to the register of directors' residential addresses.

2.1.4 Age limit

The minimum age limit for a director is **16** and, unless the articles provide otherwise, there is no upper limit.

2.2 Directors can vacate office in the following ways

a) **Removal** — by **ordinary resolution with special notice** (28 days)

b) **Resignation** — which must be in writing

c) **Retirement** — not standing for re-election at the end of their term (At the first AGM of the PLC all directors shall retire)

d) **Termination per the articles** — failure to comply with any given requirement of the company's articles i.e. not participating in majority decisions

e) **Disqualification** — under Company Directors Disqualification Act 1986 (CDDA 86)

The court **may** make a disqualification order:

○ Person is convicted of an **indictable offence** in connection with the promotion, formation, management or liquidation of a company or with the receivership or management of a company's property.

○ It appears that a person has been **persistently in default** in relation to provisions of company legislation.

○ It appears that a person has been guilty of fraudulent trading

○ The Secretary of State acting on a report made by the inspectors or from information or documents obtained under the Companies Act, applies to the court for an order believing it to be expedient in the public interest.

○ A director was involved in certain competition violations.

○ A director of an insolvent company has participated in wrongful trading. The court must make a disqualification order:

○ A person has been a director of a company which has at any time become insolvent.

○ Their conduct as a director of that company makes them unfit to be concerned in the management of a company.

The CDDA 86 allows the court to disqualify anyone from being not only a director, but also a liquidator, administrator, receiver, or manager of a company.

Disqualification orders last for periods ranging 2-15 years.

3. Distinguish between the powers of the board of directors, the managing director and the individual directors to bind the company

3.1 Directors' powers

Directors' powers (as a whole) are derived from the articles of the company, and the laws of agency act. The board of directors may exercise 'all the powers of the company', though this power is given to the board, not individual directors.

3.2 Individual directors only have the power (the board gives them):

a) Express actual authority — per their service contract, the articles, or delegated by the board

b) Implied actual authority — from the position held, such as the MD

c) Apparent authority — by virtue of holding out, an agent appears to have to a third party, make contracts attached to their management position.

4. Explain the duties that directors owe to their companies

4.1 Directors' general duties

The CA 2006 has codified directors' duties into a set of seven general duties

4.1.1 Duty to act within powers

Directors have a duty to act in accordance with the company's constitution, and to exercise his powers for the purposes conferred.

What constitutes proper purpose is defined by the circumstances under consideration with a good example being the allotment of new shares. In these instances directors must exercise their powers for a proper purpose per:

√ Not to facilitate a takeover — Howard Smith v Ampol Petroleum

√ Not to prevent a prospective takeover — Hogg v Cramphorn

√ Though such breaches may be retrospectively ratified — Bamford v Bamford

4.1.2 Promote the success of the company (enlightened shareholder value)

A director has a duty to act in a way he considers, in good faith, would be most likely 'to promote the success of the company for the benefit of its members as a whole'.

Unfortunately the CA 2006 does not define what 'promote the success' means and although it is felt to relate to improving the long-term returns to shareholders it is only in time via case law that a true definition will emerge.

In exercising this duty directors must have regard to the following factors:

a) The likely consequences of any decision in the long term,

b) The interests of the company's employees,

c) The need to foster the company's business relationships with suppliers, customers and others,

d) The impact of the company's operations on the community and the environment,

e) The desirability of the company maintaining a reputation for high standards of business conduct, and

f) The need to act fairly as between members of the company

4.1.3 Independent judgment

Directors should not delegate their powers of decision-making or be **swayed by the influence of others**. Directors may delegate their functions to others, but they must continue to make independent decisions.

This duty is not infringed by acting in accordance with any agreement by the company that restricts the exercise of discretion by directors, or by acting in a way authorised by the company's constitution.

4.1.4 Reasonable skill, care and diligence

A director has a duty to his company to exercise reasonable skill, care and diligence and this is judged by two 'tests':

1) An objective test

Did the director act in a manner reasonably **expected** of a person performing the same role? a competent person

2) A subjective test

Did the director act **in accordance with** the skill, knowledge and experience that they **actually have**? degree of skill, *Dorchester Finance v Stebbing*

4.1.5 Avoid conflicts of interest

Directors had traditionally faced a very strong fiduciary duty not to benefit personally from any commercial opportunities that came their way as a result of their directorship. In such cases the directors would have required permission of shareholders before proceeding:

IDC v Cooley — director acts dishonestly

Regal (Hastings) Ltd v Gulliver — failure to gain permission of the company Peso Silver Mines Ltd v Cropper — company declined the opportunity

The impact of the CA 2006 on private companies is that independent directors may now authorise such transactions unless the AofA prohibits such authorisation.

For public companies such authorisation by independent directors must be expressly permitted by the AofA.

4.1.6 Duty not to accept benefits from third parties

Directors are forbidden from accepting benefits from third parties, including bribes. Where a director accepts a benefit that may also create or potentially create a conflict of interest.

4.1.7 Duty to declare interest in proposed transaction or arrangement

At any point a director becomes aware that they have any interest in a contract with the company this must be disclosed to the full board at the next board meeting.

4.2 Directors' statutory duties

Substantial Property Transactions Directors or any person connected to them may not acquire a non-cash asset from the company without approval of the members	✓ Asset's value < £5,000, or less than 10% of the company's asset value. 无需批准 ✓ All sales of assets with a value exceeding £100,000 must be approved. 需要批准
Service contracts The company must keep available for inspection copies of all directors' service contracts both during their service and for at least one year after they have expired	Directors' service contracts lasting more than two years must be approved by the members. Non-contractual payments to directors for loss of office must be approved by the members.
Loans and quasi loans Any loans given to directors, or guarantees provided as security for loans provided to directors, must be approved by members	Loan > £10,000 in value. 需要批准 Expands section 197 to prevent unapproved credit transactions by the company for the benefit of a director of over £15,000 in value (PLCs only). Directors must seek approval of the embers where the company loans them over £50,000 to meet expenditure required in the course of business.

4.3 Consequences of a breach of duty

Should any breach of duty (general or specific) occur the directors may be liable in the following ways:

a) Fined — failure to comply can be a criminal offence

b) Removed from office — for breach of their service contract

c) Indemnify the company — for any losses suffered as a result of breach of duty

4.4 Directors' personal liability

As a general rule a director has **no personal liability for the debts** of the company. But there are certain exceptions.

a) Personal liability may arise by lifting the veil of incorporation.

b) A limited company may by its **articles** or by **special resolution** provide that its directors shall have unlimited liability for its debts.

c) A director may be liable to the **company's creditors** in certain circumstances.

5. Case Summaries

1) Howard Smith v Ampol Petroleum

Directors issued new shares to person seeking to launch a takeover bid to help it succeed. Even though the directors honestly thought that the takeover was in the best interests of the company it was held to be unconstitutional to issue shares for this purpose.

2) Hogg v Cramphorn

An honest belief that directors should seek to maintain their office for the good of the company did not prevent the motive for issuing additional shares to prevent a takeover from being an improper motive.

3) Bamford v Bamford

The improper issue of 500,000 shares by the directors to defend a takeover bid could be ratified by the shareholders and therefore no challenge could be made to the directors' actions.

4) Dorchester Finance Co v Stebbing

Money lending company had 3 directors S and Parsons and Hamilton. S worked full time, P and H paid little attention to the company and came to the premises rarely. H and P were in the habit of signing blank cheques at S's request. No board meetings were held and S used the cheques to make illegal loans. All these were held liable to make good the company's losses on grounds (amongst others) that H and P were experienced in accountancy and signing blank cheques was negligent.

5) IDC v Cooley

C was MD of IDC who provided consultancy to Gas Boards. A Gas Board declined to give a contract to IDC but C realised he could obtain it personally. C resigned from IDC faking ill health and then obtained the contract himself. It was held that C was accountable to IDC for the profit.

6) Regal (Hastings) Ltd v Gulliver

Opportunity arose for the company to acquire two more cinemas through a subsidiary. Company could not proceed alone because it had insufficient funds. The directors subscribed for new shares in the subsidiary and the shares in the two companies were sold on at a profit. The new controlling shareholder sued the directors to recover the profit. It was held that, whilst the directors had no ulterior motive, they were still liable to account for the profit made.

7) Peso Silver Mines v Cropper

A Canadian company voting through its Board of Directors rejected an opportunity to take a prospecting claim. A syndicate comprising some of the directors took the claim themselves. It was held that they were not liable to account for any profit to the company, which had rejected the opportunity bona fide.

8) anorama Development v Fidelis Furnishing

Fidelis' company secretary, Mr Bayne, hired cars from Panorama Development's business, Belgravia Executive Car Rental. Bayne used the Fidelis' paper and represented that he wished to hire a number of Rolls-Royce's and Jaguars for the business while his managing director was away. He was lying and he used them himself. Bayne was prosecuted and imprisoned, but Belgravia had outstanding £570 for the hired cars. Fidelis claimed that it was not bound to the hire contracts, because Bayne never had the authority to enter them. HELD that Fidelis was nevertheless bound on the contract to Panorama. Mr Bayne, as company secretary had ostensible, or apparent, authority to enter such agreements.

Chapter 19

Other company officer

1. Company secretary

Every **public company** must have **a company secretary**, who is one of the officers of a company and may be a director. **Private companies** are **not** required to have a secretary.

1.1 Appointment of a company secretary

Public companies must still appoint a company secretary, who must be qualified by virtue of being any of the following:

a) Qualified accountant: the ACCA, CIMA, ICAEW

b) A solicitor, barrister or advocate

c) Employment as a plc's secretary for **three out of the five years** preceding appointment

d) Employment in a position or membership of a professional body that, in the opinion of the directors, appears to qualify that person to act as company secretary

e) A **sole director** of a private company cannot also be the company secretary, but a company can have **two** or more joint secretaries.

1.2 Duties of a company secretary

The specific **duties** of each company secretary are **determined by the directors** of the company.

a) Establishing and maintaining the company's statutory registers

b) Filing accurate returns with the Registrar on time

c) Organising and minuting company and board meetings

d) Ensuring that accounting records meet statutory requirements

e) **Ensuring** that **annual accounts** are **prepared** and **filed** in accordance with statutory requirements

f) **Monitoring statutory requirements** of the company

g) **Signing company documents** as may be required by law

Under UK Corporate Governance Guidelines, the company secretary should:

a) **Ensure good information flows** within the board and its committees

b) **Facilitate induction of board members** and assist with professional development

c) **Advise** the **chairman** and the **board** on all **governance issues**

As agents to exercise apparent or ostensible authority: enter the company into contracts connected with the administrative side of the company act.

2. Auditors

Every company (except a dormant private company and certain small companies) must appoint auditors for each financial year.

2.1 Appointment

a) By members

b) By directors

c) By Secretary of State

2.2 Ineligibility as auditor

a) An officer or employee of the company being audited

b) A partner or employee of accounting firm if it is ineligible

c) A partner of a partnership

d) Ineligible by virtue of the above for appointment as auditor of any parent or subsidiary undertaking where there exists a connection of any description as may be specified in regulations laid down by Secretary of State

2.3 Reappointing an auditor of a private company

Auditors of private companies are deemed automatically reappointed unless one of the following circumstances apply:

a) The auditor was appointed by the directors

b) The articles require formal reappointment

c) Members holding 5% of the voting rights serve notice that the auditor should not be reappointed

d) A resolution (written or otherwise) has been passed that prevents reappointment

e) The directors have resolved that auditors should not be appointed

2.4 Exemption from audit

a) A company is exempt from the annual audit requirement in a financial year if it meets the criteria for being a small company (two from, turnover being less than £10.2 million, balance sheet total not more than £5.1 million and having 50 or fewer employees).

b) The exemptions do not apply to public companies, banking or insurance companies or those subject to a statute-based regulatory regime.

c) The company is a non-commercial, non-profit making public sector body which is subject to audit by a public-sector auditor.

d) Members holding 10% or more of the capital of any company can veto the exemption.

e) Dormant companies

2.5 Duties of an auditor

The statutory duty of auditors is to report to the members whether the accounts give a **true and fair view** and have been properly prepared in accordance with the **Companies Act**.

a) To **make a report** to the company's members as to whether or not the accounts have been properly prepared, and whether the directors' report is consistent with the accounts.

b) To **give an opinion** on the truth and fairness of the accounts.

c) **To make the necessary investigations in order to be able to deliver their opinions.**

d) To report on the **consistency** of any summary financial statements circularised by the board.

2.6 Power/right of an auditor

a) The right to access at all times, the company's books and accounts

b) To compel the officers to provide such information and explanations as they consider necessary

c) To receive copies of all proposed resolutions

d) To attend general meetings

e) To resign at any time

2.7 Auditors leave office

a) Resignation

b) Removal from office by an **ordinary resolution with special notice** passed before the end of their term

c) Failing to offer themselves for reelection (**decline reappointment**)

d) Not being re-elected at the general meeting at which their term expires.

However, auditors leave office they must either:

a) State there are no circumstances which should be brought to members' and creditors' attention;

b) Or list those circumstances.

Auditors who are resigning can also:

a) Circulate a statement about their resignation to members;

b) Requisition a general meeting;

c) Speak at a general meeting

Chapter 20

Company meetings and resolutions

1. **Distinguish between types of meetings**

   Annual General Meeting (AGM) — called by the company's **directors**.

   Private company — no longer required to hold an AGM

   Public company — must be held within 6 months of the year-end, at least **21 days' notice** should be given

   General Meeting (GM) — called as, and when required, and may be called by the **directors, or, members owning 5% of the share capital.**

   Class Meeting (CM) — called at least 14 days' notice and held for the benefit of members of a particular class of shares, i.e. a variation of class rights.

   AGM vs GM

Feature	AGM-plc	GM-all Co's
Notice	21	14
Frequency	Annual	As required
Called by	Directors	Directors or Members
Business	Routine	Exceptional-insolvency
Short notice period	100%	95%-public or 90% private

2. **Resolutions**

2.1 **Ordinary VS special resolutions**

Feature	Ordinary	Special
Notice	14 days	14 days
Votes	>50%	≥75%
Text	Not necessary	Set out in full
File with registrar?	Very few (only for changes to directors and auditors)	Yes, all
Uses	○ Allot shares ○ Approve dividends ○ Appoint/remove Directors	○ Liquidations ○ Change articles ○ Change company name

2.2 Written resolutions

A **private company** can pass any decision needed by a **written resolution, except for removing a director or auditor** before their term of office has expired.

As we saw earlier, **a private company is not required to hold an AGM**. Therefore the Act provides a mechanism for directors and members to conduct business solely by written resolution.

A **written resolution** is one that is signed by the members. **Members holding 5%** (or lower if authorised by the articles) of the **voting rights** may request a written.

3. Procedure for calling such meetings

3.1 Calling a meeting

The meeting must generally be **called by the board of directors** or other competent person or authority.

a) Sufficient notice must be given (21-AGM, 14-GM)

b) Notices should contain details of time, location, and sufficient detail to allow members, or their proxies, to decide whether or not they need attend

c) An agenda should be circulated

d) The company's auditor should be invited

3.2 Members require the directors to call a meeting

a) They hold at least **5% of the voting rights**

b) They provide a statement of the general business to be conducted and the text of any proposed resolution (delivered at least **six weeks** in advance of an AGM or other general meeting)

c) Special notice is a notice of **28 days** which must be given to a company if the member intended to **remove or appoint an auditor or director**

d) The directors must call a meeting within 21 days of receiving the request, with the meeting held within 28 days of the directors calling the i.e. the meeting itself must be held within 7 weeks of the members' request.

3.3 Proceedings at meetings

A meeting can only reach binding decisions if:

a) It has been properly convened by notice.

b) A quorum is present.

c) A chairman presides.

d) The business is properly transacted and resolutions are put to the vote.

The Chair (chairman)	The meeting should usually be chaired by the chairman of the board of directors. They do not necessarily have a casting vote unless the articles give them one
Quorum	May be two or more

(Continued)

Proxies	✓ Speak at the meeting ✓ Vote on a poll and on a show of hands ✓ Demand a poll at a meeting
Voting on a show of hands	One member, one vote
Voting on a poll	One share, one vote
Minutes of company meetings	must be kept of all general, directors' and management meetings

Chapter 21

Insolvency and administration

1. What is liquidation?

Liquidation means that the company must be dissolved and its affairs 'wound up', or brought to a formal end.

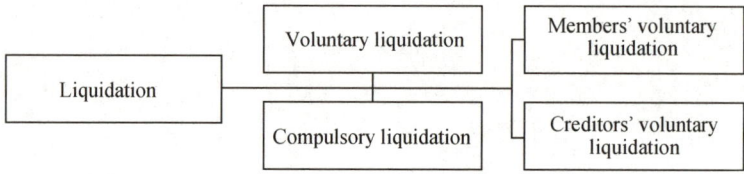

1.1 Role of the liquidator

a) A **qualified** and **authorised** insolvency practitioner

b) **Report** to the secretary of state

1.2 Common features of liquidations

a) The assets are realized, debts are paid out of the proceeds, and any surplus amounts are **returned to members**.

b) **No share dealings** or **changes in members** are allowed

c) All company documents and the website must **state the company is in liquidation**

d) **The directors' power to manage ceases**

2. Voluntary liquidation

2.1 Members' voluntary liquidation

A members' voluntary winding up, where the **company is solvent** and the **members** merely decide to 'kill it off'

The procedure:

a) The winding up **commences on the passing of the special resolution**

b) The directors must make a **declaration of solvency** delivered to the registrar within 15 days

c) Liquidator is appointed by the members.

d) The liquidator convenes a meeting within **3 months** from the commencement of the winding up to report on his transactions.

Chapter 21 Insolvency and administration

e) A final meeting is called up on completion of the liquidation, with the laying of the liquidators final accounts

f) The liquidator informs the registrar of the final meeting and submit a copy of report

g) The registrar registered the report and company is dissolved 3 month later.

Key points

In order to be a members' winding up, the directors must make a declaration of solvency. It is a **criminal offence** to make a declaration of solvency without reasonable grounds.

a) Declaration is made **by all the directors**

b) Declaration includes a statement of the company's **assets and liabilities**

c) **Timing** of the declaration: The declaration must be delivered to the Registrar within **15 days after the meeting.**

2.2 Creditors' voluntary liquidation

A creditors' voluntary winding up, where the company is insolvent and the members resolve to wind up in consultation with creditors

The procedure:

To commence a creditors' voluntary winding up the directors convene a general meeting of members to pass a **special resolution** (private companies may pass a written resolution with a 75% majority).

a) When there is **no declaration of solvency** there is a creditors' voluntary winding up. A meeting of creditors will be called within 14 days of the resolution to liquidate, with at least 7 days' notice given, and advertised in the **Gazette**.

b) **Both creditors' and members' meeting are called**. Both members and creditors have the right to appoint a liquidator but the **creditor prevail**. The members and creditors may appoint up to 5 representatives to serve on a **liquidation committee**.

c) The liquidator convenes a meeting 3 months from the commencement of the **winding up to report** on his transactions.

d) The liquidator represents his report to the final meeting of the members and creditors.

e) The liquidator informs the registrar of the final meeting and submit a copy of report.

f) The registrar registered the report and company is dissolved 3 months later.

2.3 Members' voluntary liquidation VS Creditors' voluntary liquidation

Function	Winding up	
	Members' voluntary	Creditors' voluntary
(1) Appointment of liquidator	By members	Creditors prevail
(2) Approval for liquidator's actions	General meeting of members	Liquidation committee

(Continued)

Function	Winding up	
	Members' voluntary	Creditors' voluntary
(3) Liquidation committee	None	Up to five representatives of creditors
(4) Company position	solvent	insolvent

3. Compulsory liquidation

There are **seven** grounds of compulsory liquidation per s122 IA1986.

a) The company is unable to pay its debts; section 123 (IA) provides that, if a company with a debt exceeding **£750** fails to pay it within **three weeks** of receiving a written demand, then it is deemed unable to pay its debts.

b) The court is of the opinion that it is **just and equitable** that the company should be wound up.

c) The company has passed a **special resolution that it be wound up by the court.**

d) It is a public company which has not **within a year** since its registration obtained a trading certificate with the share capital requirements.

e) It is an 'old public company' which has failed to **re-register.**

f) It has not commenced business **within a year** from its incorporation or has suspended its business for a whole year.

g) A **moratorium for a voluntary arrangement** for the company has passed and no voluntary arrangement is in place.

3.1 Petitioners

The following people may petition to court for a compulsory liquidation

- The company itself
- The official receiver, who is a civil servant in the insolvency service and is an officer of the court
- Contributory. This is any person who is liable to contribute to the assets of the company when the company is wound up
- Creditor who is owed at least **£750**
- Members (just and equitable ground)

3.2 The just and equitable ground

A member who is **dissatisfied** with the directors or controlling shareholders over the management of the company may petition the court for the company to be wound up on the **just and equitable ground.**

a) The **substratum of the company has gone.** *Re German Date Coffee Co*

b) The company was formed for an **illegal or fraudulent purpose** or there is a complete **deadlock** in the management of its affairs. *Re Yenidje Tobacco Co Ltd*

c) The understandings between members or directors which were the basis of the

Chapter 21 Insolvency and administration

association have been **unfairly** breached by lawful action. *Ebrahimi v Westbourne Galleries Ltd*

3.3 Proceedings for compulsory liquidation

a) Liquidation is deemed to have commenced from **the date the petition**

b) The **Official Receiver** is appointed by the courts

c) Within 12 weeks, the official receiver will summon meetings of creditors and contributories in order to appoint a licensed insolvency practitioner to make over the job of liquidator and form a liquidation committee

d) A final meeting of creditors and members is called by liquidator at which the liquidator presents his accounts

e) The liquidator informs the registrar of the final meeting and submit a copy of report

f) The registrar registered the report and company is dissolved 3 months later.

3.4 Effects of an order for compulsory liquidation

a) **The official receiver becomes liquidator**

b) **Commence at the time** when the petition was **first presented**

c) **Disposition** and **transfer is void** unless the court orders otherwise

d) **Legal proceedings** in progress against the company are halted

e) **Employees** of the company are **automatically dismissed**

f) **Any floating charge crystallises**

3.5 Order of payments on liquidation

Contributories are members of a company. At winding up, members may have to make payments to the company in respect of any **unpaid share capital** or guarantees.

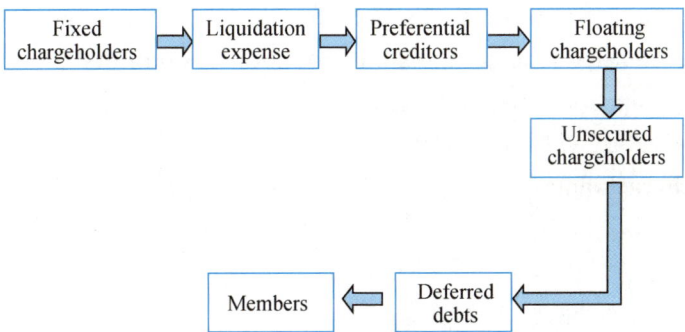

Key points:

✓ **Preferential creditor:**
 ○ wages of salaries due
 ○ all accrued holiday pay

✓ All preferential creditor rank equally

✓ **Unsecured creditors**-rank equally (pari passu)

✓ Any surplus to **members**
✓ **Deferred debts**: declared but unpaid dividend

4. Differences between compulsory and voluntary liquidation

	Members' Voluntary Liquidation	Creditors' Voluntary Liquidation	Compulsory Liquidation
Control	Member	Creditor	Court
Timing	Special Resolution		Petition Date
Liquidator	Liquidator		Official Receiver
Legal Proceedings	Valid		Court may prevent creditor obtaining unfair advantage
Management and staff	Employees are not automatically dismissed		Employees are automatically dismissed

5. Saving a company: administration

The process aims to save the company from liquidation by taking the company out of the hands of the directors, and placing it in the hands of an administrator.

In essence the company is granted breathing space in which to trade its way out of difficulty. The administration may last up to **12** months, and when the administrator feels their business is complete they will resign.

5.1 What is administration?

Its purpose is to **insulate** the company **from its creditors to seek**:

a) To **save itself** as a going concern

b) To achieve a **better result for creditors** than an immediate winding up would secure

c) To **realise property** so as to make a distribution to creditors.

5.2 Who can appoint an administrator?

5.2.1 Appointment without court order

○ Floating chargeholders

○ Directors

○ Company

1) Floating chargeholders

Floating chargeholder may only appoint an administrator if:

○ They have given **two days written notice** to the holder of any prior floating charge where that person has the right to appoint an administrator.

○ Their floating charge is enforceable.

2) Company and directors

A company or its directors may appoint an administrator if the company:

○ Has not done so in the last 12 months or been subject to **a moratorium**

- **Unable to pay its debts**
- **No petition** for **winding up** nor any administration order
- Is **not** in **liquidation**
- **No administrator** or receiver is already in office

5.2.2 Appointment with a court order

Four parties may **apply to the court** for an administration order:
- **The company** [that is, a majority of the members by (ordinary) resolution]
- **The directors** of the company
- One or more **creditors** of the company
- The **Justice and Chief Executive** of the Magistrates Court following non-payment of a fine imposed on the company.

5.3 The effects of appointing an administrator

- A moratorium over the company's debts commences (that is, no creditor can enforce their debt during the administration period without the court's permission)
- Winding up petitions are dismissed/refused
- Assets cannot be reclaimed by secured charge holders
- Assets held under hire purchase agreements cannot be re-possessed
- Any **administrative receiver** in place must **vacate office**.

5.4 Duties of the administrator

The administrator has fiduciary duties to the company as its agent, plus some legal duties:

a) Send notice to creditor, company, and registrar

b) Require certain relevant people to provide a **statement of affairs** of the company. The **statement of affairs** is in a prescribed form, and contains:
- Details of the **company's property**
- The company's **debts** and **liabilities**
- The **names** and **addresses** of the **company's creditors**
- Details of any **security** held by any **creditor**

c) Every business document of the company bears the identity of the administrator

d) Set out proposal **within 8 weeks**

Having considered all information the administrator must within **eight weeks** (subject to possible extension):
- Set out their proposals for achieving the aim of the administration; or
- Set out why it is not reasonable and practicable that the company be rescued.

e) Administrator must manage the affairs of the company

5.5 Administrator's powers

a) Remove or appoint a director

b) Call a meeting of members or creditors

Creditors' meeting

The administrator must **call a meeting of creditors within ten weeks** of their appointment to approve the proposals. The creditors may either accept or reject them.

c) Apply to court for directions regarding the carrying out of their functions

d) Make payments to secured or preferential creditors

e) **With the permission of the court, make payments to unsecured creditors**

5.6 End of administration

The **administration period ends** when:

a) The administration has been **successful**

b) The administrator or a creditor **applies to the court** to end the appointment

c) Twelve months have **elapsed**

d) An **improper motive** of the applicant for applying for the administration is discovered

5.7 Advantages of administration

Advantages of administration	
To the company	Not necessarily cease to exist A temporary breathing space from creditors Prevents creditor applying for compulsory liquidation Provides for past transactions to be challenged
To the members	Continue to have shares If success, share value being enhanced and income being restored
To the creditors	Obtain a return in relation to their past debts Unsecured creditors benefit from asset realisations Apply to the court for an administration order Floating chargeholders may appoint an administrator Have a continued business relationship with the company

6. Case Summaries

1) Yenidje Tobacco Co Ltd

Two persons with separate businesses decided to amalgamate. For this purpose a company was formed with each person a director and equal shareholder. The company made considerable profits but the two members became bitterly hostile and were unable to communicate with each other. The articles did not provide for a casting vote. A provision referring disputes to arbitration proved impractical as there were continuous disputes. The court allowed a winding up on the ground that it was just and equitable to do so.

2) Re Westbourne Galleries

E and friend N set up a gallery in Holland Park. Initially it was a partnership and then N suggested setting up a Ltd Co. to attain limited liability. Shares were allocated on a 50/50 basis with equal management rights.

N then introduced his son to the company, effectively reducing E's shares to 49%. N and his son passed an ordinary resolution sacking E as a director and then paid bonuses to the directors and declared nil dividend. E applied to court for just and equitable winding up. It was held that the company was in legal effect a partnership based on a relationship of mutual trust and confidence which had clearly broken down. The court wound the company up.

3) **Re German Date Coffee Co Ltd**

A company which was incorporated for the purpose of acquiring a German patent for the manufacture of coffee from dates. The company failed to acquire the patent and, when the company tried to obtain a similar Swedish patent, a minority shareholder petitioned successfully for winding up on the ground that the company had been formed for a particular purpose which was not capable of being attained.

Chapter 22

Fraudulent and criminal behaviour

1. Insider dealing

Insider dealing has been defined as a **criminal offence** by The Criminal Justice Act 1993 (CJA 93). In essence it is using unpublished information to **buy/sell securities** in order to make a gain or avoid making a loss.

In order to understand the offence fully the following terms must be defined:

a) **Insider** — anyone who is in receipt of 'inside information', including: Directors, employees, or shareholders.

Anyone else who has access to inside information via their office or profession
Anyone who gains information from any of the above

b) **Inside Information** — information that is price sensitive, being:

Related to specific securities

Is specific or precise

Has not been made public.

Is likely to **have a significant effect on the price** of the securities

c) **Dealing** — the defendant either:

Was an insider who dealt **using** inside information in price-affected securities
Encouraged others to deal

Disclosed the inside information to anyone else

Defences

a) Market makers acting in good faith

b) The defendant did not expect the dealing to result in profit, or the avoidance of a loss

c) The defendant reasonably believed the information was publicly available

d) The defendant would have dealt anyway, even if they did not have the information

As insider dealing is deemed a **criminal offence per the CJA 93**, it is up to the prosecution to prove the defendant is 'guilty beyond reasonable doubt'. Given the range of defences available it is in fact very difficult to successfully secure a conviction.

For those found guilty the maximum sentence is **7** years in prison, and an unlimited fine.

2. Market abuse

Remember that insider dealing is a criminal offence, market abuse is a civil matter. Market abuse relates to behaviour which amounts to abuse of a person's position regarding the stock market.

Market abuse is often connected with activities such as recklessly making a statement or forecast that is misleading, false or deceptive, or engaging in a misleading course of conduct for the purpose of inducing another person to exercise or refrain from exercising rights in relation to investments.

Examples: misuse of information, manipulating devices, market distortion and dissemination of information

3. Money laundering

Money laundering is the process by which the proceeds of crime, which have illegitimate origins, are converted into assets that appear to be legitimate.

3.1 Money laundering process

a) Placement — the disposal of the proceeds of crime into an apparently legitimate business property or activity

b) Layering — the transfer of money from place to place, in order to conceal its criminal origins

c) Integration — the culmination of placement and layering, giving the money the appearance of being from a legitimate source

3.2 Three categories of offence

a) Laundering — being the offences of concealing, disguising, converting, transferring, or removing criminal property from the UK

b) Failure to report — it is an offence for someone who knows or suspects that another person is engaged in money laundering not to report that fact to the appropriate authority (National crime agency). This offence only relates to individuals working in a regulated industry, i.e. accountants

c) Tipping off — it is an offence to make a disclosure likely to prejudice a money laundering offence already being undertaken, or which may be undertaken

3.3 Penalties

a) Laundering — a maximum 14 year prison sentence is possible, and/or a fine. Additionally, the police may seize the illegitimate assets

b) Failure to report — punishable by a maximum 5 years sentence, and/or a fine

c) Tipping off — punishable by a maximum 5 years sentence, and/or a fine

4. Bribery

Bribery is a serious offence which often relates to the offering and receiving of gifts or hospitality.

Bribery offences are regulated by the **Bribery Act 2010** which came into force on the 1st July 2011. The Act created 4 classes of offence:

a) Bribing another person

b) Receiving a bribe from another

c) Bribing a foreign public official (FPO)

d) Corporate failure to prevent bribery, where a company or partnership fails to put in place '**adequate procedures**' to prevent offences being committed by an employee, agent or subsidiary

'Adequate procedures' are not defined by the Act, but the Secretary of State's non-prescriptive published guidance on adequate procedures is based around six principles:

- Proportionate procedures
- Top-level commitment
- Risk assessment
- Due diligence
- Communication
- Monitoring and review

The Act makes it clear that bribery can be committed by both state and privately employed persons and that the scope extends to offences committed **outside of the UK**.

Specific defences are available to members of the armed forces and the secret services when engaged on active duty.

The maximum penalty under the Act is 10 years' imprisonment and/or unlimited fine.

5. Criminal activity relating to companies

Deferred prosecution agreement (DPA) mean that the **organization admits wrongdoing** but stops short of pleading guilty to the offence. In return, a judge awards a fine against the business but **no criminal prosecution takes place**.

5.1 Criminal offences in relation to winding up

a) Declaration of solvency: it is a **criminal offence** punishable by fine or imprisonment for a director to make a **declaration of solvency without** having **reasonable grounds** for it.

b) Fraudulent trading

5.2 Fraudulent trading and wrongful trading

5.2.1 Fraudulent trading

This **criminal offence** occurs under the **Companies Act 2006** where a company has traded with **intent** to defraud creditors or for any fraudulent purpose. Offenders are liable to imprisonment for up to ten years or a fine.

a) There is also a **civil offence** under **Insolvency Act 1986**

b) If the liquidator considers that there has been fraudulent trading they should apply to the court for an order that those responsible are liable to **make good to the company** all or some specified part of the company's debts.

Chapter 22 Fraudulent and criminal behaviour

c) **Intent** must be proved in order to win a case of fraudulent trading.

5.2.2 Wrongful trading (civil remedy)

a) Wrongful trading is a civil offence that is brought by a company's **liquidator**.

b) **No intent to defraud** is required because the directors commit the offence if they allow the company to trade whilst in the knowledge that there is no reasonable prospect of the company avoiding going into liquidation.

5.2.3 Potential criminal activity in the operation, management and liquidation of companies

1) Acting as a director whilst disqualified

A person who **acts as a director whilst disqualified** personally liable for the company's debts.

2) Phoenix companies

Phoenix companies are created by directors of insolvent companies as a method of continuing their business

3) Defrauding creditors

Make a gift of, or transfer company property

6. Case Summary

1) R v Grantham

The jury were directed that they could find dishonesty and intent to defraud if they thought that Mr. Grantham obtained credit when he knew there was no good reason for thinking that his company would be able to repay the debt when it became due. Therefore, intent to defraud was established on proof of intention to dishonestly prejudice creditors in being repaid.

2) Re Produce Marketing

The directors of the loss making and insolvent company, Produce Marketing, claimed that they only became aware of the inevitable liquidation of the company when its annual accounts were delivered 6 months late by its auditors in January 1987. The directors continued to trade after this point, arguing they needed to sell the perishable goods they had in cold store.

The court held that they should have concluded in July 1986 there was no reasonable prospect of avoiding liquidation, and though they did not have the accounts till January 1987 they had an intimate knowledge of the business and must have known turnover was well down on previous years. It did not matter that they may not have actually known about the accounts; they ought to have known the results for the financial year 1985-6. The two had not taken steps they should have under s 214(3). After February 1987, trading was not limited to realise the fruit in cold store. Overall, s 214 was compensatory, not penal, and the right amount to contribute was the amount caused to be depleted by the directors' conduct.

融跃ACCA® 助您备考无忧

 尊享五大会员特权

前导课程
带你快速入门

备考资料
题库笔记干货

干货直播
提分技巧攻略

社群交流
考试指南答疑

考试资讯
考纲政策解读

扫码免费领取

ACCA 知识精要（下）

融跃教育 ACCA 研究院　编著

PM PERFORMANCE MANAGEMENT

Chapter 1	Activity based costing	385
Chapter 2	Target costing	387
Chapter 3	Life cycle costing	389
Chapter 4	Throughput accounting	391
Chapter 5	Environmental management accounting	393
Chapter 6	Cost volume profit analysis	395
Chapter 7	Limiting factor analysis	397
Chapter 8	Pricing	399
Chapter 9	Short term decisions	403
Chapter 10	Risk and uncertainty	406
Chapter 11	Budgeting	409
Chapter 12	Quantitative analysis in budgeting	415
Chapter 13	Standard costing and variance analysis	418
Chapter 14	Advanced variance analysis	420
Chapter 15	Financial performance measurement	429
Chapter 16	Divisional performance measurement	434
Chapter 17	Transfer price	437
Chapter 18	Performance for the not-for-profit sector	439
Chapter 19	External considerations and behavioral aspects	441
Chapter 20	Big data & Security and confidential information	442

TX TAXATION

Chapter 1	The UK tax system	447
Chapter 2	Income tax outline	448
Chapter 3	Trading income	454

Chapter 4　　Basis of assessment ……………………………………………… 458
Chapter 5　　Capital allowance ………………………………………………… 460
Chapter 6　　Property income ………………………………………………… 462
Chapter 7 & 15　Loss relief for individual and corporation ………………… 464
Chapter 8　　Partnerships ……………………………………………………… 467
Chapter 9　　Benefit …………………………………………………………… 469
Chapter 10　 Employment income …………………………………………… 475
Chapter 11　 National insurance contribution（NICs）……………………… 477
Chapter 12 & 17　Self-assessment for individual & corporations ………… 480
Chapter 13 &14　Corporation tax …………………………………………… 486
Chapter 16　 Group relief ……………………………………………………… 489
Chapter 18 & 19　CGT for individual and corporation …………………… 492
Chapter 20　 VAT ……………………………………………………………… 501
Chapter 21　 IHT ……………………………………………………………… 511

FR　FINANCIAL REPORTING

Chapter 1　　The conceptual framework ……………………………………… 519
Chapter 2　　The regulatory framework ……………………………………… 523
IAS 16　Property，plant and equipment ……………………………………… 525
IAS 40　Investment property ………………………………………………… 530
IAS 23　Borrowing costs ……………………………………………………… 534
IAS 38　Intangible assets ……………………………………………………… 538
IAS 36　Impairment of assets ………………………………………………… 541
IAS 20　Government grants …………………………………………………… 543
IFRS 15　Revenue from contracts with customers ………………………… 546
IAS 32　Financial instruments：presentation ………………………………… 552
IFRS 16　Leases ………………………………………………………………… 557
IAS 37　Provisions，contingent liabilities and contingent assets ………… 563
IAS 10　Events after reporting period ……………………………………… 567
IAS 2　Inventory ……………………………………………………………… 569
IAS 41　Agriculture …………………………………………………………… 573
IAS 12　Income tax …………………………………………………………… 575
Group introduction …………………………………………………………… 580
专题介绍　合并报表中的特殊事项处理 ……………………………………… 585
IAS 21　Foreign currency transactions ……………………………………… 598
IAS 8　Accounting policies，changes in accounting estimates and errors ……… 600

IFRS 5	Non-current assets held for sale and discontinued operations	602
IAS 33	Earings per share	605
IAS 22	Statement of cash flow	612

AA AUDIT AND ASSURANCE

Format of the exam ········ 621
Part 1   Introduction ········ 622
Part 2   Audit risk ········ 625
Part 3   Internal control ········ 630
Part 4   Test of control and substantive procedures ········ 633
Part 5   Cycle and substantive procedures ········ 635
Part 6   Subsequent event ········ 647
Part 7   Going concern ········ 651
Part 8   Written representations ········ 653
Part 9   Reporting ········ 654
Part 10 Professional ethics ········ 660
Part 11 Corporate governance ········ 667
Part 12 Other matters ········ 675

FM FINANCIAL MANAGEMENT

Part A Financial management function ········ 683
    Chapter 1 Financial management and financial objectives ········ 684

Part B Financial management environment ········ 688
    Chapter 2 The economic environment for business ········ 689
    Chapter 3 Financial markets and institutions ········ 692

Part C Working capital management ········ 696
    Chapter 4 Working capital ········ 697
    Chapter 5 Managing working capital ········ 702
    Chapter 6 Working capital finance ········ 708

Part D Investment appraisal ········ 715
    Chapter 7 Investment decision ········ 716

Chapter 8   Investment appraisal using DCF methods ……………………………… 720
Chapter 9   Allowing for inflation and taxation ……………………………………… 722
Chapter 10   Project appraisal and risk ………………………………………………… 724
Chapter 11   Specific investment decisions …………………………………………… 728

Part E   Business finance …………………………………………………………………… 734
Chapter 12   Sources of finance ………………………………………………………… 735
Chapter 13   Dividend policy …………………………………………………………… 747
Chapter 14   Gearing and capital structure …………………………………………… 751
Chapter 15   The cost of capital ………………………………………………………… 758
Chapter 16   Capital structure …………………………………………………………… 765

Part F   Business valuations ………………………………………………………………… 772
Chapter 17   Business valuations ………………………………………………………… 773
Chapter 18   Market efficiency …………………………………………………………… 781

Part G   Risk management …………………………………………………………………… 786
Chapter 19   Foreign currency risk ……………………………………………………… 787
Chapter 20   Interest rate risk …………………………………………………………… 797

PERFORMANCE MANAGEMENT

Chapter 1

Activity based costing

Learning objectives
✓ Identify appropriate cost drivers under ABC
✓ Calculate costs per drivers under ABC
✓ Compare ABC and traditional methods of overhead absorption

1. Introduction 基本原理

基本原理：(为什么会有 ABC?)
Production cost：Direct Material — 直接吸收计入各个产品成本
　　　　　　　　Direct Labour — 直接吸收计入各个产品成本
　　　　　　　　Direct Expense — 直接吸收计入各个产品成本
　　　　　　　　Variable Production overhead — 不用吸收，会告知每个产品对应的成本
　　　　　　　　Fixed Production overhead — 需要计算吸收

Fixed Production overhead：使用 OAR（Overhead Absorption Rate）= Fixed Production overhead/labour hours or machine hours or units(计算基础 cost driver)

但一个公司单一地使用一种计算基础就会导致最终吸收的成本不准确。为了成本更准确，就产生了 ABC 方法。ABC 会识别 activities，根据每个 activities 确定对应的 cost driver，再进行后续计算。

Activity Based Costing（ABC）attempts to absorb overheads in a more accurate（and therefore more useful）way. Absorption costing 的升级版。

2. The steps to be followed are as follows 步骤

Step 1　Identify the major activities that give rise to overheads（e.g. machining dispatching of order）.

识别引起相关费用的主要活动，例如订单发送。

Step 2　Determine what causes the cost of each activity-the cost driver(e.g. machine hours，number of despatch orders).

确定每项活动产生成本的原因——成本动因，例如机器工时、发货订单数量。

Step 3　Calculate the total cost for each activity-the cost pool（e.g. total machining costs，total costs of despatch department）.

计算每项活动的总成本——成本池,例如加工总成本、调度部总成本。

Step 4 Calculate an absorption rate for each cost driver.
计算每个成本动因的吸收率(OAR)。

Step 5 Calculate the total overhead cost for each product manufactured.
计算每个产品的总间接成本。

Step 6 Calculate the overhead cost per unit for each product(cost card).
计算每个产品的单位间接成本。

3. Advantages and disadvantages of ABC 优缺点

Advantages:

➢ ABC uses cost driver as absorption base and attempts to provide meaningful product costs.

➢ Management can control overhead costs by managing cost drivers.

➢ It facilitates a good understanding of what drives (causes) overhead costs. Managers can improve the processes using that information and achieve greater efficiency and hence more profits.

Disadvantages:

➢ Time consuming/expensive.

➢ Some measure of arbitrary cost apportionment may still be required at the cost pooling stage for items.

➢ ABC will be of limited benefit if the overheads are volume related.

➢ ABC will be of limited benefit if fixed costs account for a small proportion.

Chapter 2

Target costing

> **Learning objectives**
> ✓ Derive a target cost in manufacturing and service industries
> ✓ Explain the difficulties of using target costing in service industries
> ✓ Suggest how a target cost gap might be closed

1. Concept of target costing

Target costing involves setting a target cost by subtracting a desired profit margin from a target selling price. At the design stage, it is easier and cheaper to make changes that reduce costs.

2. Steps of implementing target costing 步骤

Step 1 Set a selling price at which the organization will be able to achieve a desired market share.

Step 2 Estimate the required profit based on return on sales or return on investment.

Step 3 Calculate the target cost = Target selling price − Target profit.

Step 4 Compile an estimated cost for the product based on the anticipated design specification and current cost levels.

Step 5 Calculate cost gap = Estimated cost − Target cost.

Step 6 Make efforts to close the gap.

3. Closing a target cost gap 缩小目标成本差距的方法

➢ Training staff in more efficient techniques
➢ Acquiring new, more efficient technology
➢ Cutting out non value added components/activities
➢ Using different materials
➢ Using cheaper staff

4. Target costing in service industries 服务行业中的目标成本法

Target costing is difficult to use in service industries due to the characteristics and information requirements of service businesses.

Characteristics of service

- Intangibility: can't be touched
- Simultaneity: created and consumed at the same time
- Heterogeneity: hard to keep standard, rely on people
- Perishability: can't be stored
- No transfer of ownership: service do not result in the transfer of property

Information about services tends to be more qualitative and may not be easy to obtain.

Chapter 3

Life cycle costing

Learning objectives
✓ Identify the costs involved at different stages of the life cycle
✓ Derive a life cycle cost or profit in manufacturing and service industries
✓ Identify the benefits of life cycle costing

1. Product life cycle 产品生命周期

The 'classical' life cycle of a product has five phases or stages:
- Development 研发期
- Introduction 引入期
- Growth 成长期
- Maturity 成熟期
- Decline 衰退期

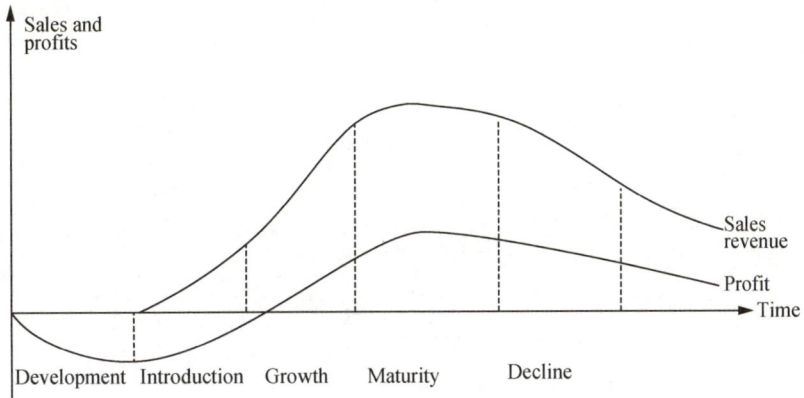

2. Life cycle costing 生命周期成本法

Life cycle costing tracks and accumulates costs and revenues attributable to each product over the entire product life cycle.

Benefits of life cycle costing 优点
- More sensible assessment of profitability by taking into actual costs (e.g. R&D in

initial stage) over product life cycle
- Enable better decision making
- Promote long term thinking and forward planing than short term profitability consideration
- The life cycle concept helps managers to realize early actions to break-even

3. Maximising return over the product life cycle 在产品生命周期内实现回报最大化的方法
- **Design costs out of products 在设计阶段就控制成本**
- **Minimise the time to market 缩短进入市场的时间**

'Time to market' is the time from the conception of the product to its introduction to the market. It is vital for an organization to launch its new product as soon as possible in order to outperform its competitors in terms of greater revenue and longer product life.
- **Minimise break-even time (BET) 缩短到达盈亏平衡点的时间**

A short BET is very important in keeping an organization liquid The sooner the product is launched the quicker the research and development costs will be repaid, providing the organization with funds to develop further products.
- **Maximise the length of the life span. 拉长生命周期的总长度,指拉长成熟阶段时间**

Chapter 4

Throughput accounting

Learning objectives

✓ Identify limiting factors in a scarce resource situation and select an appropriate technique
✓ Determine the optimal production plan where an organization is restricted by a single limiting factor
✓ Discuss and apply the theory of constraints
✓ Calculate and interpret a throughput accounting ratio (TPAR)
✓ Suggest how a TPAR could be improved
✓ Apply throughput accounting to a multi-product decision making problem

1. Throughput accounting 产量会计

Throughput = sales revenue − direct material costs

Throughput accounting (TA) is an approach to production management which aims to maximise sales revenue less materials cost, while also reducing inventory and operational expenses.

Inventory has no value because it does not create throughput until it is used to sell products.

Operational expenses, also known as factory expenses, are all the other costs of operations. They include what in traditional costing would be both direct labour costs and overhead costs.

In throughput accounting, all operational expenses or factory expenses are **assumed** to be 'fixed' costs.

2. Theory of constraints (TOC) 限制因素理论

The concept of throughput accounting has been developed from the theory of constraints (TOC) as an alternative system of cost and management accounting in a **JIT (Just in time) production environment**.

Bottleneck resource or binding constraint is an activity which has a lower **capacity (efficiency)** than preceding or subsequent activities, thereby limiting throughput.

There will be **idle resources** in non-bottleneck areas, but this does not matter. The focus should be on maximising throughput, given the limitation of the bottleneck.

Output through the binding constraint should never be delayed or held up otherwise sales will be lost. To avoid this happening a small **buffer inventory** should be built up immediately **prior** to the bottleneck constraint. 安全存货可以有，并且应该在该流程前。

Five-step approach to summaries the key stages of TOC.

Step 1 Identify the constraint (bottleneck resource).

Step 2 Decide how to exploit the constraint in order to maximise throughput.

Step 3 Subordinate and synchronic everything else to the decisions made in step 2.

Step 4 Elevate the performance of the constraint.

Step 5 If the constraint has shifted during any of the above steps, go back to step 1. Do not allow inertia to cause a new constraint.

3. Performance measures in throughput accounting

In a throughput accounting environment, production priority is given to the products best able to generate throughput.

Performance measures in throughput accounting are based around the concept that the aim is to maximise throughput. This is achieved by maximising the throughput per unit of bottleneck resource.

The throughput accounting ratio (TA ratio) is the ratio of the throughput per unit of bottleneck resource to the factory cost per unit of bottleneck resource. This ratio should be as high as possible, and certainly more than **1.0**.

$$\text{Throughput accounting ratio} = \frac{\text{Throughput per unit of bottleneck resource}}{\text{Factory cost per unit of bottleneck resource}}$$

Improving TPAR：如何提升 TPAR？

➢ Increase the selling price for the product.

➢ Reducing the material cost per unit.

➢ Reduce expenditure on operating costs/factory costs.

➢ Improve efficiency

➢ Improve capacity

Chapter 5

Environmental management accounting

Learning objectives
✓ Discuss the issues business face in the management of environmental costs
✓ Describe the different methods a business may use to account for its environmental costs

1. Managing environmental costs

Environmental costs are important to businesses for a number of **reasons**.
为什么要考虑与环境相关的成本？为什么与环境相关的成本如此重要？
➢ Identifying environmental cost associated with individual products and services can assist with pricing decisions
➢ It ensures compliance with regulatory standards and therefore avoids potential taxes and fines
➢ There is potential for cost savings

Defining environmental costs 定义

There are many varied definitions of environmental costs. The US Environmental Protection Agency makes a distinction between four types of cost.

a) **Conventional costs**, such as raw materials and energy costs, have an impact on the environment. 常规成本

b) **Potentially hidden costs** are relevant costs that are captured within accounting systems but may be 'hidden' within 'general overheads'. 潜藏成本

c) **Contingent costs** are costs that will be incurred at a future date as a result of discharging waste into the environment, such as clean-up costs. 或有成本

d) **Image and relationship costs** are costs incurred to preserve the reputation of the business; for example, the costs of preparing environmental reports to ensure compliance with regulatory standards. 形象及公关成本

2. Accounting for environmental costs

The United Nations Division for Sustainable Development (UNDSD, 2003) identified management accounting techniques which are useful for the identification and allocation of environmental costs. They are **input/output analysis, flow cost accounting,** environmental activity based accounting and life cycle costing.

a) Input/Output analysis 投入产出分析

Input/output analysis operates on the principle that what comes in must go out. Process flow charts can help to trace inputs and outputs, particularly waste.

Input/output analysis measures the input to a production process or system, and the output from the system. Any difference between the amount input and the amount input is 'residual', which is called 'waste'.

- Input and output quantities are measured first, and these can then be given a cost.

b) Flow cost accounting (also known as Material Flow Cost Accounting or MFCA)

Under this technique, material flows through an organization are divided into three categories, and the cost of each category is measured separately.

> **Material**
> **System**: this is the in-house handling that is required (including labour) and its cost
> **Delivery and disposal**: this is the cost of transport and the cost of disposal of waste

Output costs are allocated between **positive products** (good finished output) and **negative product costs** (cost of waste and emissions).

An important focus of management attention with flow cost accounting should be to reduce the proportion of negative products in total output and increasing the proportion of positive products.

c) Environmental life cycle costing

Under this method of environmental cost accounting, environmental costs for a product are considered from the design stage of the product right up to the end of life costs, such as decommissioning and removal.

d) Environmental Activity Based Costing

Environmental activity-based costing combined elements of environmental costing with an activity-based costing system.

Suitable environmental activities should be identified and an activity cost centre created for it. It should be possible to trace environment-driven costs to these cost centres.

Environment costs that have been allocated and apportioned to environmental activity cost centres can then be absorbed into product costs on a suitable basis.

Chapter 6

Cost volume profit analysis

> **Learning objectives**
> √ Explain the nature of CVP analysis
> √ Calculate and interpret the break-even point and margin of safety
> √ Calculate the contribution to sales ratio, in single and multi-product situations, and demonstrate an understanding of its use
> √ Calculate target profit or revenue in single and multi-product situations, and demonstrate an understanding of its use
> √ Prepare break even charts and profit volume charts and interpret the information contained within each, including multi-product situations
> √ Discuss the limitations of CVP analysis for planning and decision making

1. Cost volume profit (CVP)/breakeven analysis 定义

Cost volume profit (CVP)/breakeven analysis is the study of the interrelationships between costs, volume and profit at various levels of activity. 本量利分析/盈亏平衡点分析

Assumptions: 假设

○ Fixed costs per period are same in total, and unit variable costs are a constant amount at all levels of output and sales.
○ Sales prices are constant at all levels of activity. **Selling price 保持不变**
○ Production volume = sales volume. **Inventory level 不变**

2. Cost volume profit (CVP)/breakeven analysis 公式

➢ Contribution = sales revenue − variable cost
➢ Profit = contribution − fixed cost
➢ Breakeven point in unit = FC/contribution per unit
➢ Breakeven point in sales revenue = FC/C/S ratio
➢ C/S ratio = contribution/sales revenue
➢ Margin of safety in unit = budgeted sales units − breakeven sales units
➢ Margin of safety in sales revenue = budgeted sales revenue − breakeven

sales revenue

➢ Margin of safety in % = (budgeted sales units − breakeven sales units)/budgeted sales units

➢ Sale volume to achieve a target profit = target profit + FC/contribution per unit

Chapter 7

Limiting factor analysis

Learning objectives

✓ Formulate and solve multiple scarce resource problem both graphically and using simultaneous equations as appropriate

✓ Explain and calculate shadow prices (dual prices) and discuss their implications on decision-making and performance management

✓ Calculate slack and explain the implications of the existence of slack for decision-making and performance management

1. limiting factor 限制性因素

A limiting factor is any factor that is in scarce supply and that stops the organisation from expanding its activities.

Further, so that there is a maximum level of activity at which the organisation can operate.

- Labour
- Materials
- Machine capacity

计算方法:

➢ **One limiting factor:** contribution/Limiting factor

➢ **Two potentially limiting factors:** 先找出真正的 limiting factor, 再同 one limiting factor 方法。

➢ **Two or more limiting factors:** linear programming 线性回归

2. Shadow price

The **shadow price or dual price** of a limiting factor is the increase in value which would be created by having one additional unit of the limiting factor at its original cost.

3. Slack and surplus

Slack occurs when maximum availability of a resource is not used; slack is the amount of the unused resource or other constraint, where the constraint is a 'less than or equal to' constraint.

Surplus occurs when more than a minimum requirement is used: surplus is the excess over the minimum amount of constraint, where the constraint is a 'more than or equal to' constraint.

Chapter 8

Pricing

Learning objectives

✓ Explain the factors that influence the pricing of a product or service
✓ Explain the price elasticity of demand
✓ Derive and manipulate a straight line demand equation. Derive an equation for the total cost function (including volume based discounts)
✓ Calculate the optimum selling price and quantity for an organisation, equating marginal cost and marginal revenue
✓ Evaluate a decision to increase production and sales levels, considering incremental costs, incremental revenues and other factors
✓ Determine prices and output levels for profit maximisation using the demand based approach to pricing (both tabular and algebraic methods)
✓ Explain different price strategies, including:
  ○ All forms of cost-plus
  ○ Skimming
  ○ Penetration
  ○ Complementary product
  ○ Product-line
  ○ Volume discounting
  ○ Discrimination
  ○ Relevant cost
✓ Calculate a price from a given strategy using cost

1. Factor influencing selling price 影响销售价格的因素

There are a variety of factors which may influence the selling price of a product.
○ Price sensitivity
○ Sensitivity to price levels will vary among purchasers.
○ Price perception
○ Price perception is the way customers react to prices.
○ Quality

- Intermediaries
- Competitors
- Suppliers
- Inflation
- Newness
- Incomes
- Product range
- Ethics

2. Cost plus pricing

Full cost-plus pricing is a method of deciding the sales price by adding a percentage mark-up for profit to the full cost of the product.

Cost + profit = selling price
(以成本为基础,加上一定的利润得到的最终售价)

Advantages:

- It is a quick, simple and cheap method of pricing which can be delegated to junior managers.
- When there is no market price for the product, deciding a price by adding a profit margin to cost is a logical approach, which seeks to ensure that the organisation makes a profit.

Disadvantages:

- There may be a need to adjust prices to market and demand conditions.
- Budgeted output volume needs to be established.
- A suitable basis for overhead absorption must be selected.

3. Optimal selling price-tabular approach

Profits are maximised where **marginal cost (MC) = marginal revenue (MR)**.

The optimal selling price can be determined by deriving equations for MC and MR. Alternatively, the optimum selling price can be determined using **tabulation**.

Steps: MC = MR 的步骤

- Establish the demand function (find the values for 'a' and 'b').
- Obtain a value for MR from the demand curve. $MR = a - 2bQ$
- Establish MC (the marginal cost). This will simply be the variable cost per unit.
- To maximise profit, equate MC and MR to find Q.
- Substitute Q into the demand function and solve to find P (the optimum price).

4. Price elasticity of demand 需求的价格弹性

The **price elasticity of demand (PED)** is a measure of the extent of change in demand for a good in response to a change in its price.

$$PED = \frac{\Delta D\%}{\Delta P\%}$$

Demand is referred to as **inelastic** if the absolute value is less than **1** and elastic if the absolute value is
greater than 1.
- **Inelastic: PED < 1**
- **Elastic: PED > 1**
- **Perfectly inelastic: PED = 0**
- **Perfectly elastic: PED = ∞**

意义：
- In circumstances of inelastic demand，prices should be increased because revenues will increase and total costs will reduce (because quantities sold will reduce). 非弹性，可以提升价格。
- In circumstances of elastic demand，increases in prices will bring decreases in revenue and decreases in price will bring increases in revenue. Management therefore have to decide whether the increase/decrease in costs will be less than/greater than the increases/decreases in revenue. 弹性，不能轻易动价格。

5. Optimal pricing-equations 最优定价等式

Economic theory argues that the higher the price of a good，the lower will be the quantity demanded.

Demand equation **P = a − bQ**. 假设 price 升高，demand 下降。

When demand is linear the equation for the demand curve is：

$$P = a - bQ$$

where P = the price

Q = the quantity demanded

a = the price at which demand would be nil

$$b = \frac{\text{change in price}}{\text{change in quantity}}$$

The constant a is calculated as follows.

$$a = \$(\text{current price}) + \left(\frac{\text{Current quantity at current price}}{\text{Change in quantity when price is changed by } \$b} \times \$b\right)$$

Here are some variables which determine the degree of demand for a good in the market as a whole.
- **Price of other goods 市场上其他商品的价格**
  - Substitutes 替代品
  - Complements 互补品
- **Income 消费者收入**
- **Tastes or fashion 口味和时尚**

- **Expectations** 预期
- **Product life cycle** 生命周期
- **Marketing** 市场宣传

6. Pricing strategies

- **Market skimming** 市场撇脂定价（Maximise short-term profitability 尽快收回利润）
- **Market penetration pricing** 市场渗透定价（As soon as it is launched on the market 抢占市场）
- **Product line pricing**

Pricing jointly

- **Price discrimination** 价格歧视

Sell same product to different markets at different prices

- **Volume discounting**

Discounts for large quantities

Chapter 9

Short term decisions

> **Learning objectives**
> ✓ Explain the concept of relevant costing
> ✓ Identify and calculate relevant costs for a specific decision situations from given data
> ✓ Explain and apply the concept of opportunity costs
> ✓ Explain the issues surrounding make vs. buy and outsourcing decisions
> ✓ Calculate and compare "make" costs with "buy-in" costs
> ✓ Compare in-house costs and outsource costs of completing tasks and consider other issues surrounding this decision
> ✓ Apply relevant costing principles in situations involving shut down, one off contracts and the further processing of joint products

1. Relevant costs 相关成本

Relevant costs are future cash flows arising as a direct consequence of a decision.
- Relevant costs are future costs. 未来成本
- Relevant costs are cash flows. 有现金流的流入流出
- Relevant costs are incremental costs, arising as a direct consequence of the decision. 成本增量

Non-relevant costs：非相关成本
- Sunk cost 沉默（历史）成本
- Committed cost 已承诺成本
- Notional（imputed） 名义（推算）成本

Relevant costs：相关成本
- Differential cost 差异成本
- Avoidable costs 避免成本
- Opportunity cost 机会成本

2. Make or buy decisions 买或卖决策

In a make or buy decision, the choice is between **making items in-house** or **purchasing**

them from an external supplier.

➢ With no limiting factors

The relevant costs are the differential costs between the two options.

➢ With limiting factor

The decision is about which items to make internally and which to purchase externally.

The optimal decision, based on financial considerations alone, is to arrange internal production and external purchasing in a way that minimize total costs.

3. Outsourcing 外包决策

Use of external suppliers for finished products, components or services. Also known as contract manufacturing or sub-contracting, e.g. office building cleaning.

Advantages：优点

○ specialist contractors can offer superior **quality** and **efficiency**.

○ The provider should have **economies of scale** which will lead to cost reductions

○ Contracting out manufacturing frees capital that can then be invested in core activities, such as market research, product definition, product planning, marketing and sales.

○ Contractors have the capacity and flexibility to start production very quickly to meet sudden variations in demand

○ There is not enough work to keep internal staff fully occupied, so it is cheaper to outsource the work.

○ Management time is freed up to focus on core competencies

Disadvantages：缺点

○ It leads to a **reduction of control**, particularly in relation to quality. Firms try to mitigate this by having clear service level agreements in place and devoting resources to relationship management

○ Firms may be tied in to long-term contracts and find it hard to change suppliers even if their supplier is unsatisfactory

○ Outsourcing can mean a firm loses competencies and becomes dependent on suppliers, giving them increased bargaining power even when the contract ends

○ If the function is the of strategic importance the outsourcing can not be accept. 部门很重要，也不可外包。

4. Further processing decisions 进一步加工处理决策

A further processing decision often involves **joint products** from a common manufacturing process. The decision is whether to sell the products at the split-off point, as soon as they emerge from the common process, or whether they should be processed further before selling them.

A joint product should be processed further past the split-off point if the additional sales revenue exceeds the relevant post-separation (further processing) costs. 再次深加工后会产生对应的增量成本及增量收入，那么如果增量收入大于增量成本，则可以选择深加工；如果增量收入小于增量成本，则不选择深加工。

5. Shutdown decisions 关闭决策

A shutdown decision is whether to close down an operation or stop making and selling a particular product or service. 自己不做，也不交给其他人做。

现在关闭？几年后关闭？现在有个新的特殊订单是否接受？

Qualitative factors influence 影响因素

○ What impact will a shutdown decision have on the morale of **employees** who remain?

○ What signal will the decision give to **competitors**? How will they react?

○ How will **customers** react? Will they lose confidence in the company's products?

○ How will **suppliers** be affected? If one supplier suffers disproportionately there may be a loss of goodwill and damage to future relations.

Chapter 10

Risk and uncertainty

Learning objectives

✓ Suggest research techniques to reduce uncertainty e. g. focus groups, market research

✓ Explain the use of simulation, expected values and sensitivity

✓ Apply expected values and sensitivity to decision making problems

✓ Explain and apply the concept of opportunity costs

✓ Apply the techniques of maximax, maximin, and minimax regret to decision making problems including the production of profit tables

✓ Draw a decision tree and use it to solve a multi-stage decision problem

✓ Calculate the value of perfect information

1. Risk and uncertainty 风险和不确定性

Risk VS Uncertainty

是否知道概率 probability

Risk preference 风险偏好

➤ 风险喜好者:

A risk seeker is a decision-maker who is interested in the best outcomes, no matter how small the chance that they may occur.

➤ 风险中立者:

A decision-maker is **risk neutral** if they are prepared to make a decision that balances risk and return. They are concerned with the most likely or 'average' outcome.

➤ 风险厌恶者:

A **risk-averse** decision-maker acts on the assumptions that the worst outcome might occur and will make a decision that limits or minimises the risk.

2. Allowing for uncertainty

One approach to dealing with uncertainty is to **obtain more information**, in order to reduce the amount of uncertainty about what will happen. **Reliable information reduces uncertainty**.可靠的信息会降低不确定性。可通过 market research 市场调研和 focus groups

专项研究组来获取有效可靠的信息。

Types of data collected 信息类型

➤ 一手信息

Primary data is data that is obtained for a specific purpose and collected at first hand, typically from a sample of respondents. Market research and focus groups are sources of primary data. 从必须是自己去获取的，不能是购买的。

➤ 二手信息

Secondary data is data that has been collected by someone else, and not for the specific purpose for which it is now being used. Secondary research is also known as desk research, because it can be carried out in an office by researching files or archives. Government statistics, published by the Government's statistics department or bureau, are widely used by business organizations as a source of secondary data.

3. Sensitivity analysis 敏感性分析

Sensitivity analysis is a term used to describe any technique whereby decision options are tested for their vulnerability to changes in any 'variable', such as expected sales volume, sales price per unit, material costs and labour costs. 能影响决策的变量（key factor）变化多少能引起决策的改变。一次只能有一个变量发生变化。百分比（%）越小说明越敏感，即稍微改变一点就可能会导致改变决策。

It can help to concentrate management attention on the most important factors.

意义：公司找出最敏感的因素，就会时刻地关注该因素，避免因所作决策导致利润变为0或者亏损。

4. Simulation models 仿真模型

Simulation models can be used to deal with decision problems when there are a large number of uncertain variables in the situation. 一次改变多个变量所呈现的最终结果。使用计算机。

5. Other decision rule

Various approaches can be used to deal with risk and uncertainty.

➤ Expected value 平均值
➤ Maximin 最小值最大化法
➤ Maximax 最大值最大化法
➤ Minimax regret 最大后悔值最大化法
➤ Decision tree 决策树

6. Value of perfect information 完美信息的价值

Perfect information is guaranteed to predict the future with 100% accuracy. Imperfect information is better than no information at all but could be wrong in its prediction of the future.

The value of perfect information is the difference between the EV of profit with perfect information and the EV of profit without perfect information.

Chapter 11

Budgeting

Learning objectives

✓ Explain how budgetary systems fit within the performance hierarchy

✓ Select and explain appropriate budgetary systems for an organization, including top down, bottom up, rolling, zero base, activity base, incremental and feed forward control

✓ Describe the information used in budget systems and the sources of the information needed

✓ Explain and apply the concept of opportunity costs

✓ Indicate the usefulness and problems with different budget types (including fixed, flexible, zero based, activity- based, incremental, rolling, top down, bottom up, master, functional)

✓ Prepare flexed budgets, rolling budgets and activity based budgets

✓ Explain the beyond budgeting model, including the benefits and problems that may be faced if it is adopted in an organization

✓ Discuss the issues surrounding setting the difficulty level for a budget

✓ Explain the benefits and difficulties of the participation of employees in the negotiation of targets

✓ Explain the difficulties of changing a budgetary system or type of budget used

✓ Explain how budget systems can deal with uncertainty in the environment

1. Objectives of budgeting systems

A budget is a **quantified plan** of action for a forthcoming accounting period.

➢ Corporate plans or strategic plans

➢ Tactical plans

➢ Operational plans

2. The planning and control cycle

The planning and control cycle has **seven steps**.

Step 1: Identify objectives 确定目标

Step 2: Identify potential strategies 找出实现目标的方法

Step 3: Evaluate strategies 评估

Step 4: Choose alternative courses of action 选择

Step 5: Implement the long-term plan 实施

Step 6: Measure actual results and compare with the plan 实际VS计划

Step 7: Respond to divergences from the plan 反馈给做计划的

Objectives of a budgetary planning and control system are as follows 为什么做计划？

- Ensure the achievement of the organization's objectives
- Compel planning
- Communicate ideas and plans
- Co-ordinate activities
- Provide a framework for responsibility accounting
- Establish a system of control
- Motivate employees to improve their performance

Feedback 反馈

a) **Negative feedback** indicates that results or activities must be brought back on course, as they are deviating from the plan. 负面反馈

b) **Positive feedback** results in control action continuing the current course. You would normally assume that positive feedback means that results are going according to plan and that no corrective action is necessary. 正面反馈

c) **Feedforward control** is control based on **forecast** results: in other words, if the forecast is bad, control action is taken well in advance of actual results. 预测一下有什么结果跟计划对比。

Types of feedback 接到反馈后的反应

a) **Single loop feedback** is control, like a thermostat, which regulates the output of a system. For example, if sales targets are not reached, control action will be taken to ensure that targets will be reached soon. The plan or target itself is not changed, even though the resources needed to achieve it might have to be reviewed. 不改变计划,改变行为。

b) **Double loop feedback** is of a different order. It is information used to change the plan itself. For example, if sales targets are not reached, the company may need to change the plan. 改变计划,行为也将会改变。

3. Top-down budgeting

Top-down budgeting 自上而下的预算

An imposed/top-down budget is 'A budget allowance which is set without permitting the ultimate budget holder to have the opportunity to participate in the budgeting process'. 上级决定,下级执行。

Appropriateness 适用条件

- In newly-formed organisations 刚成立公司

➤ In very small businesses 小公司
➤ During periods of economic hardship 公司或大环境经济形势不好
➤ When operational managers lack budgeting skills 下层管理人员的能力缺乏

Advantages 优点

○ Strategic plans are likely to be incorporated into planned activities.
○ They enhance the coordination between the plans and objectives of divisions.
○ They use senior management's awareness of total resource availability.
○ They decrease the input from inexperienced or uninformed lower- level employees.
○ They decrease the period of time taken to draw up the budgets.

Disadvantages 缺点

○ Dissatisfaction, defensiveness and low morale almost employees. It is hard for people to be motivated to achieve targets set by somebody else.
○ The acceptance of organizational goals and objectives could be limited.
○ The feeling of the budget as a punitive device could arise.
○ Managers who are performing operations on a day to day basis are likely to have a better understanding of what is achievable.
○ Unachievable budgets could result if consideration is not given to local operating and political environments. This applies particularly to overseas divisions.

4. Bottom-up budget 自下而上的预算

Participative/bottom-up budgeting is 'A budgeting system in which all budget holders are given the opportunity to participate in setting their own budgets'. 上下参与

Advantages 优点

○ Morale and motivation is improved.
○ They increase operational managers' commitment to organizational objectives.
○ They are based on information from employees most familiar with the department.
○ In general they are more realistic.
○ Co-ordination between units is improved.
○ Senior managers' overview is mixed with operational level details.
○ Individual managers' aspiration levels are more likely to be taken into account.

Disadvantages 缺点

○ They consume more time.
○ They may cause managers to introduce budgetary slack.

5. Incremental budgeting 增量预算

Incremental budgeting takes the previous year results and then adjusts them by an amount to cover inflation and any other known changes.

Advantages 优点

○ Considered to be the quickest and easiest method of budgeting

○ Suitable for organisations that operate in a stable environment

○ Suitable for organisations whose operations are not subject to improvement

Disadvantages 缺点

○ Builds in previous problems and inefficiencies

○ Uneconomical activities may be continued.

6. Zero based budgeting 零基预算

The principle behind zero based budgeting（ZBB）is that the budget for each cost centre should be made from 'scratch' or zero. Every item of expenditure must be justified in its entirety in order to be included in the next year's budget.

Three-step approach

Step 1：Define items or activities for which costs should be budgeted，and spending decisions should be planned：these are 'decision packages'.

Step 2：Evaluate and rank the packages in order of priority：eliminate packages whose costs exceed their value.

Define decision packages 决策包

Decision packages are activities or items in the budget about which a decision should be made.

○ Mutually exclusive packages 互斥包

These are alternative methods of getting the same job done. The best option among the packages must be selected by comparing costs and benefits and the other packages are then discarded. If there are two mutually exclusive decision packages，the preferred package is selected and the other rejected for budgeting purposes. 同一件事情，不同的解决办法是互斥的。

○ Incremental packages 增量包

These divide an aspect of operations into different levels of activity. The **'base' package** will contain the minimum amount of work that must be done to carry out the activity and the cost of this minimum level. The other incremental packages identify additional **(incremental)** work that could be done，at what cost and for what benefits. 基础包+增量包

Step 3：Allocate resources to the decision packages according to their ranking. Where resources such as money are in short supply，they are allocated to the most valuable activities.

Advantages 优点

○ It is possible to identify and remove inefficient or obsolete operations.

○ It forces employees to avoid wasteful expenditure.

○ It can increase motivation of staff by promoting a culture of efficiency.

○ ZBB documentation provides an in-depth appraisal of an organisation's operations.

○ In summary，ZBB should result in a more efficient allocation of resources.

Disadvantages 缺点

○ Short-term benefits might be emphasised to the detriment of long-term benefits.

○ The organisation's information systems may not be capable of providing suitable information.

○ It may call for management skills both in constructing decision packages and in the ranking process which the organisation does not possess.

7. Activity based budgeting (ABB)

At its simplest, activity based budgeting (ABB) is merely the use of activity based costing methods as a basis for preparing budgets.

Advantages 优点

○ It focuses on the drivers of costs, the budget is more likely to be accurate.

○ It provides useful information by relating the cost of an activity to the level of service provided.

○ the costs can be controlled by control the drivers.

Disadvantages 缺点

○ Time consuming and lots of effort to be given.

○ It may be difficult to identify all the activities.

○ In the short term overhead costs may not be controllable.

8. Rolling budget 滚动预算

A rolling budget is a budget which is **continuously updated** by adding a further accounting period (a month or quarter) to the end of the budget when the corresponding period in the current budget has ended. As a result, a number of rolling budgets are prepared each year and each rolling budget covers the next 12-month period.

Rolling budgets may be used when the pace of change in the **business environment is fast and continual**. They represent an attempt to prepare plans which are **more realistic** by shortening the period between preparing budgets.适用于所处行业环境变化很快且持续不断的公司。

操作步骤：

➢ **Instead of preparing a periodic budget annually for the full budget period, new budgets are prepared every 3 months.** 不同于一年做一次预算，滚动预算要求隔一段时间就要做预算，如3个月。

➢ Each of these budgets would cover the next 12 months so that the current budget is extended by an extra period as the current period ends: hence the name rolling budgets. 时间跨度都是12个月。

➢ **The first 3 months of the budget period would be planned in great detail, and the remaining nine months in lesser detail, because of the greater uncertainty about the longer-term future.** 前3个月的预算做得越详细越好，剩下的9个月就不用做得太详细。

➢ Four rolling budgets would be prepared every 3 month basis, requiring, inevitably, greater administrative effort. 需要时间及精力。

Advantages 优点
○ They reduce the element of uncertainty in budgeting because they concentrate detailed planning and control on the near-term future, where the degree of uncertainty is much smaller.

○ They force managers to reassess the budget regularly, and to produce budgets which are up to date in the light of current events and expectations.

○ Planning and control will be based on a recent plan which is likely to be far more realistic than a fixed annual budget made many months ago.

○ Realistic budgets are likely to have a better motivational influence on managers.

Disadvantages 缺点
○ They involve more time, effort and money in budget preparation.

○ The rolling budget may demotivated managers, as it may concentrates on adjusting budget instead of increasing controls.

9. Beyond Budgeting 超出预算

Beyond Budgeting is a budgeting model which proposes that traditional budgeting should be abandoned.

Adaptive management processes should be used rather than fixed annual budgets. 没有预算。

Advantages 优点
○ Motivation. Managers and employees are often motivated by the corporate values, rather than specific targets set in an annual budget.

○ Faster response to threats and opportunities.

Disadvantages 缺点
○ Resistance to change. Managers who consistently meet their annual budget targets may resist the adoption of beyond budgeting as it threatens their position and bonuses.

○ Resource constraints. In addition, some public sector organisations may struggle to implement a beyond budgeting process due to the constraints on their resources.

10. Difficulties of changing a budgetary system

➢ Resistance by employees

Familiar with current system

Already build in slack

➢ Loss of control

Senior management may take time to adapt to the new system

➢ Training

Could be time-consuming and expensive

➢ Cost of implementation

➢ Lack of accounting information, e.g. when implementing ZBB

Chapter 12

Quantitative analysis in budgeting

Learning objectives

✓ Analyse fixed and variable cost elements from total cost data using high/low method.

✓ Estimate the learning rate and learning effect

✓ Apply the learning curve to a budgetary problem, including calculations on steady states

✓ Discuss the reservations with the learning curve

✓ Apply expected values and explain the problems and benefits

✓ Explain the benefits and dangers inherent in using spreadsheets in budgeting

1. Analyzing fixed and variable costs: high-low method 高低点法

The high-low method is a quantitative technique for analyzing total costs into their fixed cost and variable cost elements. 根据高低点法找出成本的函数表达，$Y = a + bX$，得出公式后将对应的产量代入得出总成本，做好预测，从而做好预算。

Advantages 优点

➢ simple and easy

Disadvantages 缺点

➢ The method ignores all cost information apart from costs at the highest and lowest volumes of activity and these may not be representative of costs at all levels of activity.

➢ Inaccurate cost estimates may be produced as a result of the assumption of a constant relationship between costs and volume of activity.

➢ Estimates are based on historical information and conditions may have changed.

2. Learning curves 学习曲线

Theory:

As cumulative output doubles, the cumulative average time per unit fills to a given percentage of the previous average time per unit.

Conditions 适用条件

➢ There is a significant manual element in the task being considered

- The task must be repetitive
- Production must be at an early stage so that there is room for improvement
- There must be consistency in the workforce
- There must not be extensive breaks in production, or workforce will 'forget' the skill
- Workforce is motivated.

Cessation of learning effect 停止学习的原因
- Machine efficiency restricts any further improvement
- Workforce reach their physical limits
- There might be a 'go-slow' agreement among the workforce

Learning curve effect in management accounting 学习曲线在管理会计中的应用
- Calculate marginal (incremental) cost for extra units
- Help determine selling price for a contract
- Prepare realistic production budgets and schedules
- Prepare realistic standard costs for cost control purposes

3. Expected values in budgeting 平均价值法

Probabilistic budgeting assigns probabilities to different conditions (most likely, best possible, worst possible) to derive an expected value (EV) of budgeted profit.

Advantages 优点
- helping management to assess the risk

Disadvantages 缺点
- Preparing probabilistic budgets is more time consuming than preparing a single fixed budget
- A probabilistic budget represents a weighted average of expectations, and may not reflect an outcome that is actually expected to happen.
- Probabilistic budgets have little practical value for the purpose of planning or control, so the cost of preparing the budgets may exceed the benefits obtained.

4. Using spreadsheet in budgeting 电子表单

Spreadsheet packages can be used to build business models to assist the forecasting and planning process. They are particularly useful for 'what-if?' analysis. **Excel 表格**

Advantages 优点
- Simple format of rows, columns and worksheets
- Easier to master compared with database software
- Readily accessible, one can create the model, input data, generate the report all by himself

Disadvantages 缺点
- Minor error can affect the validity of the whole model and it is difficult to trace

➢ Very easy to corrupt a model with unintended operation
➢ Possible to become over-dependent on them
➢ Qualitative factors cannot be incorporated into spreadsheets
➢ No audit trail, it can be difficult to track different version of budget

Chapter 13

Standard costing and variance analysis

Learning objectives
√ Explain the use of standard costs
√ Outline the methods used to derive standard costs and discuss the different types of cost possible
√ Explain and illustrate the importance of flexing budgets in performance management
√ Explain and apply the principle of controllability in the performance management system

1. The use of standard costs 标准成本

Standard cost: estimated unit cost built up of standards for each cost element. 标准成本指的是单个成本，预算指多个产品。

Standard costing has three main uses.
➢ To value inventories. 管理会计才可以使用。
It is an alternative to FIFO and average cost as a method of inventory valuation.
➢ To budget production costs. 单个成本确定就可确定整个预算。
When a standard per unit of product has been established, budgeting production costs becomes a fairly straightforward process.
➢ To act as a control device. 管理工具，有利于问责。
This is done by establishing standards (expected costs) and comparing actual costs with the expected costs. Variances between actual and standard cost indicate aspects of operations which may be out of control.

2. Deriving standards 标准类型
Types of standard
➢ **Ideal standard 完美标准**
  ○ Assuming perfect conditions apply, e. g. 100% efficiency from workers and machines
  ○ Could form the basis for long-term aims, but not useful for variance analysis

Chapter 13 Standard costing and variance analysis

because unattainable

➤ **Basic standard** 多年前的基础标准
  ○ Long run underlying average standard
  ○ Only useful in very sable situations where here are unlikely to be fluctuations in price, interest rate, etc.

➤ **Attainable standard** 可达到标准
  ○ Challenging but realistic
  ○ Work hard to achieve
  ○ Used as target

➤ **Current standard** 目前标准
  ○ Reflect current conditions
  ○ Useful in period of high inflation
  ○ Can be used for performance appraisal

3. **The principle of controllability**

Responsibility accounting 责任会计

A system of accounting that separates revenues and costs into areas of personal responsibility in order to monitor and assess the performance of each part of an organization.

Controllability principle 可控原则

Controllable costs are items of expenditure which can be directly influenced by a given manager within a given time span.

The controllability principle is that managers of responsibility centre should only be held accountable for costs over which they have some influence.

Chapter 14

Advanced variance analysis

Learning objectives

✓ Calculate, identify the cause of, and explain material mix and yield variances

✓ Explain the wider issues involved in changing material mix e.g. cost, quality and performance measurement issues

✓ Identify and explain the relationship of the material usage variance with the material mix and yield variances

✓ Suggest and justify alternative methods of controlling production processes

✓ Calculate, identify the cause of, and explain sales mix and quantity variances

✓ Identify and explain the relationship of the sales volume variances with the sales mix and quantity variances

✓ Calculate a revised budget

✓ Identify and explain those factors that could and could not be allowed to revise an original budget

✓ Calculate, identify the cause of and explain planning and operational variances for:
  ○ sales, including market size and market share
  ○ Materials
  ○ labour including the effect of the learning curve

✓ Explain and discuss the manipulation issues involved in revising budgets

✓ Analyse and evaluate past performance using the results of variance analysis

✓ Use variance analysis to assess how future performance of an organization or business can be improved

✓ Identify the factors which influence behaviour

✓ Discuss the effect that variances have on staff motivation and action

✓ Describe the dysfunctional nature of some variances in the modern environment of JIT and TQM

✓ Discuss the behavioral problems resulting from using standard costs in rapidly changing environments

Chapter 14　Advanced variance analysis

1. Basic variances 公式

○ A **fixed budget** is a budget which is designed to remain unchanged regardless of the volume of output or sales achieved. (Planning stages)

○ A **flexible budget** is a budget which, by recognizing different cost behavior patterns, is designed to change as volumes of output changes. (Planning stages)

○ A **flexed budget** is a budget that is prepared at the actual activity level that was achieved in the period. **Actual stages**（现实情况已发生的反推出 flexed budget）

➢ **Direct material cost variance**

The **direct material total variance** is the difference between what the output actually cost and what it should have cost, in terms of material.

公式：direct material usage variance ＋ direct material price variance ＝ direct material total variance

The **direct material usage variance** is the difference between the standard quantity of materials that should have been used for the number of units actually produced, and the actual quantity of materials used, valued at the standard cost per unit of material. In other words, it is the difference between how much material should have been used and how much material was used, valued at standard cost.

公式：(material that should have been used － material that have been used) × standard cost per kg (基于：actual production units)

The **direct material price variance** is the difference between the standard cost and the actual cost for the actual quantity of material used or purchased. In other words, it is the difference between what the material did cost and what it should have cost.

公式：(actual cost per kg － standard cost per kg) × actual usage per kg

➢ **Direct labour cost variances**

The **direct labour total variance** is the difference between what the output should have cost and what it did cost, in terms of labour.

公式：direct labour rate variance + direct labour efficiency variance = direct labour total variance

The **direct labour rate variance** is similar to the direct material price variance. It is the difference between the standard cost and the actual cost for the actual number of hours paid for. In other words, it is the difference between what the labour did cost and what it should have cost.

公式：(standard rate per hour － actual rate per hour) × actual hours worked or paid

The **direct labour efficiency variance** is similar to the direct material usage variance. It is the difference between the hours that should have been worked for the number of units actually produced, and the actual number of hours worked, valued at the standard rate per hour.

公式：(hours that should have been used － actual hours used) × standard rate per hour (基于：actual production units)

➢ **Variable production overhead variances**

The **variable production overhead total variance** can be subdivided into the variable production overhead expenditure variance and the variable production overhead efficiency variance

公式：variable production OH efficiency variance＋variable production OH expenditure variance＝variable production overhead total variance

The **variable production OH efficiency variance** is exactly the same in hours as direct labour efficiency variance, but priced at the standard variable production overhead rate per hour.

公式：(actual active hours - standard hours) × standard variable production OH(基于：actual production units)

The **variable production OH expenditure variance** is the difference between the amount of variable production overhead that should have been incurred in the actual hours actively worked, and the actual amount of variable production overhead incurred.

公式：actual active hours × standard variable production OH - actual total variable production OH

It is usually assumed that variable overheads are incurred during active working hours.
假设以 hours 来吸收 POH，假设实际工作状态没有 idle time。

➢ Fixed production overhead variances

Fixed overhead total variance is the difference between fixed overhead incurred and fixed overhead absorbed. In other words, it is the under- or over-absorbed fixed overhead.

公式：Fixed overhead expenditure variance ＋ Fixed overhead volume variance ＝ Fixed overhead total variance

Flexed budget — FOH 与 Actual FOH 的差异

Fixed overhead expenditure variance is the difference between the budgeted fixed overhead expenditure and actual fixed overhead expenditure.

Fixed budget — FOH 与 Actual FOH 的差异

Fixed overhead volume variance is the difference between actual and budgeted (planned) volume multiplied by the standard absorption rate per unit.

公式：Fixed overhead volume efficiency variance ＋ Fixed overhead volume capacity variance＝Fixed overhead volume variance

Fixed budget — FOH 与 Flexed budget — FOH 的差异

Fixed overhead volume efficiency variance is the difference between the number of hours that actual production should have taken, and the number of hours actually taken (that is, worked) multiplied by the standard absorption rate per hour.

公式：(standard hours - actual hours) × standard OAR(基于：actual production units)

Fixed overhead volume capacity variance is the difference between budgeted (planned) hours of work and the actual hours worked, multiplied by the standard absorption rate per hour.

公式：(actual hours worked - planned hours worked) × standard OAR

Chapter 14　Advanced variance analysis

➢ Sales variance

The **selling price variance** is calculated as the difference between what the sales revenue should have been for the actual quantity sold, and what it was.

公式：(standard selling price - actual selling price) × actual quantity sales

The **sales volume variance** is the difference between the actual units sold and the budgeted (planned) quantity, valued at the standard profit/contribution per unit.

公式：(planned sales volume - actual sales volume) × standard selling profit per unit (AC) or standard contribution per unit(MC)

2. Material usage variance & Materials mix & yield variances

The materials usage variance can be subdivided into a materials mix variance and a materials yield variance when more than one material is used in the product. 多种 material 混合比例不同,产出仍是同一产品。例如：奶茶。

○ Materials are interchangeable

The mix variance is calculated as follows.

○ Take the total actual quantity of materials used.

○ Divide this total quantity of materials into the standard mix or standard proportions of the different materials used in the mix.

○ For each item of materials, the difference between the actual quantity used and the quantity in the standard mix is a mix variance.

○ Convert the mix variance for each item of material into a money value by applying the standard price per unit for the material.

○ The total of the mix variance for each of the materials in the mix is the total materials mix variance.

The yield variance is calculated as follows.

○ For the actual number of units of product manufactured, calculate the total quantity of materials that should have been used (a single total for all the materials in the mix).

○ Compare this standard quantity of materials that should have been used with the actual total quantity of materials that was used.

○ The difference is the yield variance in material quantities.

○ Convert this into a monetary value by applying the weighted average cost per unit of material.

Standard usage in standard mix VS actual usage in standard mix → materials yield variance

actual usage in standard mix VS actual usage in actual mix → materials mix variance

EG：

A company manufactures a chemical, Dynamite, using two compounds Flash and Bang.

The standard materials usage and cost of one unit of Dynamite are as follows.

		$
Flash	5 kg at $2 per kg	10
Bang	10 kg at $3 per kg	30
		40

In a particular period, 80 units of Dynamite were produced from 600 kg of Flash and 750 kg of Bang.

Required

Calculate the materials usage, mix and yield variances.

Materials mix variance：

	Actual usage in standard mix	Actual usage in actual mix	variance	standard cost per kg	variance in $
F	450	600	150(A)	2	300(A)
B	900	750	150(F)	3	450(F)
	1,350	1,350			150(F)

OR

materials usage variance = materials yield variance + materials mix variance
= 150(F) + 400(A)
= 250(A)

Meanings：

➢ materials mix variance(A)：比例中单价高的 material 用的多。

➢ materials mix variance(F)：比例中单价低的 material 用的多。

➢ materials yield variance(A)：预计使用量与实际使用量不同，使用效率问题。使用效率比较低。

➢ materials yield variance(F)：使用效率比较高。

materials yield variance：

	Standard usage in standard mix	actual usage in standard mix	variance	variance in $ X standard cost per kg	
F	400	450	50(A)	X2	100(A)
B	800	900	100(A)	X3	300(A)
	1,200	1,350			400(A)

materials usage variance：

	Standard usage in standard mix	actual usage in actual mix	variance	variance in $ X standard cost per kg	
F	400	600	200(A)	X2	400(A)
B	800	750	50(F)	X3	150(F)
	1,200	1,350			250(A)

3. Sales volume variance & Sales mix variance & Sales quantity variance

The sales volume variance can be analyzed further into a sales mix variance and a sales quantity variance.

The sales mix variance is calculated in a similar way to the materials mix variance.
- Take the total actual quantity of units sold, for all the products combined.
- Divide this total quantity of sales units into the budgeted standard mix or budgeted proportions of the different products in the mix.
- For each product, the difference between the actual quantity sold and the sales quantity in the budgeted standard mix is a mix variance.
- Convert the mix variance for each product into a monetary value by applying the standard profit per unit (or standard contribution per unit, where standard marginal costing is used).
- The total of the mix variance for each of the products in the sales mix is the total sales mix variance.

The sales quantity variance is calculated in a similar way to the materials yield variance, as follows.
- Calculate the weighted average standard profit per unit (or weighted average standard contribution per unit). This is calculated from the budget, as the budgeted total profit divided by the budgeted total units of sale.
- Calculate the difference between the actual total sales units and the budgeted total sales units. This difference is the sales quantity variance in units.
- Convert this variance in sales units into a monetary value by applying the weighted average standard profit (or standard contribution) per unit of sale.

Standard sales quantity in standard mix VS actual sales quantity in standard mix → sales quantity variance

actual sales quantity in standard mix VS actual sales quantity in actual mix → sales mix variance

× standard selling profit per unit(AC)

× or standard contribution per unit(MC)

EG:

Just Desserts Limited makes and sells two products, Chocolate Crunch and Strawberry Sundae. The budgeted sales and profit are as follows.

	Sales Units	Revenue $	Costs $	Profit $	Profit per unit $
Chocolate Crunch (CC)	400	8,000	6,000	2,000	5
Strawberry Sundae (SS)	300	12,000	11,100	900	3
				2,900	

Actual sales were 280 units of Chocolate Crunch and 630 units of Strawberry Sundae. The company management is able to control the relative sales of each product through the allocation of sales effort, advertising and sales promotion expenses.

Required

Calculate the sales volume variance, the sales mix variance and the sales quantity variance.

Materials mix variance:

	Actual usage in standard mix	Actual usage in actual mix	variance	standard cost per kg	variance in $
F	450	600	150(A)	2	300(A)
B	900	750	150(F)	3	450(F)
	1,350	1,350			150(F)

OR

sales volume variance = sales mix variance + sales quantity variance
= 480(A) + 870(F)
= 390(F)

Meanings:

➢ sales mix variance(A):卖的比例是不喜欢的情况,多卖的产品不赚钱,利润能力弱。

➢ sales mix variance(F):卖的比例是喜欢的情况,多卖的产品赚钱,利润能力强。

➢ sales volume variance(A):在比例相同下,实际卖出的总量比预计的低,销售人员业绩不好。

➢ sales volume variance(F):在比例相同下,实际卖出的总量比预计的高,销售人员业绩好。

sales quantity variance:

	Standard sales quantity in standard mix	actual sales quantity in standard mix	variane		variance in $ X standard profit per unit
F	400	520	120(F)	X5	600(F)
B	300	390	90(F)	X3	270(F)
	700	910			870(F)

sales volume variance:

	Standard sales quantity in standard mix	actual sales quantity in standard mix	variane		variance in $ X standard profit per unit
F	400	280	120(A)	X5	600(F)
B	300	630	330(F)	X3	990(F)
	700	910			390(F)

4. Planning variances & Operational variances

A planning and operational approach to variance analysis divides the total variance into those variances which have arisen because of inaccurate planning or faulty standards (**planning variances**) and those variances which have been caused by adverse or favourable operational performance, compared with a standard which has been revised in hindsight (**operational variances**).

- Planning and operational variances for sales
- Planning and operational variances for materials
- Planning and operational variances for labour

Planning variances are calculated by comparing the original budget/standard cost with the revised budget/standard cost.

Operational variances are calculated in the same way as 'normal' basic variances, except that they are based on a comparison between actual results and the revised budget/standard cost.

为什么会有 planning variances 与 operational variances？
出现差异想找出差异是计划层面还是操作层面导致的，要进行后期分析。

5. Planing and operational variances for sales: market size and market share variances

- A **sales volume planning variance**, or **market size variance**, which is caused by the difference between the sales volume in the original budget and the sales volume in the revised budget
- A **sales volume operational variance**, or **market share variance**, which is caused by the difference between actual sales volume and the sales volume in the revised budget

➤ **Standard sales volume VS revised sales volume → sales volume planning variance**
➤ **Revised sales volume VS actual sales volume → sales volume operational variance**
  × **selling profit per unit(AC)**
  × **or contribution per unit(MC)**
➤ **Actual sales units × standard selling price VS Actual sales units × revised selling price → sales price planning variance**
➤ **Actual sales units × revised selling price VS Actual sales units × actual selling price → sales price operational variance**
  × **selling profit per unit(AC)**
  × **or contribution per unit(MC)**

6. Planning and operational variances for materials

➤ **Actual usage × standard price per kg VS actual usage × revised price per kg → material usage planning variance**
➤ **Actual usage × revised price per kg VS actual usage × actual price per kg → material usage operational variance**
➤ **Standard usage units × standard selling price per kg VS revised usage units × standard selling price per kg → material price planning variance**
➤ **Revised usage units × standard selling price per kg VS actual usage units × standard selling price per kg → material price operational variance**

7. Planning and operational variances for labour

- Actual hours paid × standard rate VS actual hours paid × revised rate → labour rate planning variance
- actual hours paid × revised rate VS actual hours paid × actual rate → labour rate operational variance
- Standard hours × standard rate VS revised hours × standard rate → labour rate planning variance
- revised hours × standard rate VS actual hours × standard rate → labour rate operational variance

8. Advantages & Limitations of a system of planning and operational variances

Advantages of a system of planning and operational variances：

- The analysis highlights those variances which are controllable (operational variances) and those which are non-controllable (planning variances). 谁的错误谁负责
- The planning and standard-setting processes should improve; standards should be more accurate, relevant and appropriate. 提升 planning 的能力
- Operational variances will provide a more realistic and 'fair' reflection of actual performance.

Limitations of planning and operational variances, which must be overcome if they are to be applied in practice

- It is difficult to decide in hindsight what the realistic standard should have been. 难以界定计划所需时间。
- It may become too easy to justify all the variances as being due to bad planning, so no operational variances will be highlighted.
- Even though the intention is to provide more meaningful information, managers may be resistant to the very idea of variances and refuse to see the virtues of the approach. Careful presentation and explanation will be required until managers are used to the concepts.

Chapter 15

Financial performance measurement

> **Learning objectives**

✓ Describe, calculate and interpret financial performance indicators (FPIs) for profitability, liquidity and risk in both manufacturing and service businesses. Suggest methods to improve these measures

✓ Analyse past performance and suggest ways for improvement

1. Basic concepts of management

Management activity

- Strategic level 考虑公司整体,资源分配。
- Tactical level 中期,怎样使用资源更有效。
- Operational level 每周、每日具体工作。

Strategic management accounting 战略层管理会计

Strategic management accounting is a form of management accounting in which emphasis is placed on information about factors which are external to the organisation, as well as non-financial and internally generated information. 管理会计下的一种

Information system

Types of information systems:

- **Transaction processing systems (TPS)**

collect, store, modify and retrieve the transactions of an organisation

  ○ **Batch transaction processing (BTP)** 隔段更新
  ○ **Real time transaction processing (RTTP)** 同步更新

Characteristics: 标准化

  ○ Controlled processing.
  ○ Inflexibility.
  ○ Rapid response.
  ○ Reliability.

- **Management information systems (MIS)**

MIS extract, process and summarise data from the TPS and provide periodic (weekly, monthly, quarterly) reports to managers.

Characteristics：
- Designed to report on existing operations
- Support structured decisions *analytical* capability 信息分析
- An *internal* focus 内部信息
- Relatively inflexible

➢ **Executive information systems（EIS）**

- Executive information systems draw data from the MIS and allow communication with *external* sources of information. 外部信息
- An EIS summarises and tracks *strategically critical information* from the MIS and includes data from external sources，e.g. competitors，legislation and databases. 汇报给战略层使用

➢ **Executive resource planning systems（ERP）**

Executive resource planning systems（ERP systems）are modular software packages designed to integrate the key processes in an organisation so that a single system can serve the information needs of all functional areas. 资源管理

Open and closed system 开放型和封闭型系统

A closed system is isolated and shut off from the environment. Information is not received from or provided to the environment. 保密

An open system is connected to and interacts with the environment and is influenced by it.

Advantages of an open system：
- It adapts to the changing environment and there is scope for absorbing new pieces of information into the system.
- It highlights the interdependencies of different operations and processes within a business and the environment in which it operates.
- It helps business leaders and managers to focus on the external factors that shape behaviour and patterns within the organisation.

Internal information 内部信息

Internal sources of information include the financial accounting records and other systems closely tied to the accounting system.

Cost of internal information
- Direct data capture 获取成本
- Processing 分析成本
- Inefficient use of information 浪费成本

External information 外部信息

Cost of external information
- Direct search costs 直接搜索成本 e.g. 付费等
- Indirect access costs 间接进入时间
- Management costs 处理成本

- Infrastructure costs 基础设施成本
- Time theft 浪费时间成本

2. Financial performance indicators

Performance measurement aims to establish how well something or somebody is doing in relation to a plan. 好？不好？

Financial performance indicators include three main categories
- Profitability
- Liquidity
- Gearing

Profitability

a) Gross profit margin/Net profit margin

Gross profit margin = gross profit/sales

Net profit margin = net profit/sales

盈利能力，越高越好。

b) Asset turnover

Asset turnover = sales/capital employed

c) Return on capital employed (ROCE)

Return on capital employed (ROCE) = operating profit or PBIT/capital employed

Capital employed = equity + long-term liability
            = asset(NCA + CA) − current liability
            = working capital(CA − CL) + non-current asset

ROCE = operating profit margin × asset turnover

Tip：ROCE 很高，一定代表经营特别好吗？

Answer：也可能是由于 capital employed 的减少导致 ROCE 的升高。这样就会损害未来的盈利能力，从长远利益来看对公司来说并不好。

投资方面的盈利能力，每投入＄1，赚取多少利润。

Liquidity and cash flow

a) Current ratio

Current ratio = current asset/current liability

b) Quick ratio (acid test ratio)

Quick ratio = (current asset − inventory)/current liability

c) Accounts receivable days (accounts receivable payment periods)

Accounts receivable days = trade receivable/sales × 365

d) Inventory days (inventory turnover period)

Inventory days = inventory/cost of sales × 365

e) Accounts payable days (accounts payable payment period)

Accounts payable days = trade payable/cost of sales × 365

Gearing ratio

a) Gearing ratio

Gearing ratio = long-term liability/capital employed

Capital employed = equity + long-term liability

b) Interest coverage(times)

Interest coverage(times) = operating profit or PBIT/interest

3. Non-financial performance indicators

Balanced scorecard 平衡记分卡

The balanced scorecard approach to performance measurement focuses on four different perspectives of performance, and uses both financial and non-financial indicators to set performance targets and monitor performance.

- Customer
- Internal
- Innovation and learning
- Financial

Building Block model 积木模型

Dimensions of performance
Profit
Competitiveness
Quality
Resource utilisation
Flexibility
Innovation

Standards
Ownership
Achievability
Equity

Rewards
Clarity
Motivation
Controllability

Three aspects to setting standards of performance 制定标准三方面

- Individuals need to feel that they 'own' the standards and targets for which they will be made responsible.
- Individuals also need to feel that the targets or standards are realistic and achievable.
- The standards and targets should be seen as 'fair' and equitable for all the managers in the organisation.

Three aspects to consider in a reward system 制定奖励三方面

- The system of setting targets and rewarding individuals for achieving the targets should be clear. Clarity will improve the motivation to achieve the targets.

○ Achievement of performance targets should be suitably rewarded.

○ Individuals should be made responsible only for aspects of performance that they are in a position

Chapter 16

Divisional performance measurement

Learning objectives

√ Explain the meaning of, and calculate, Return on Investment (ROI) and Residual Income (RI), and discuss their shortcomings

√ Compare divisional performance and recognize the problems of doing so

1. Divisionalisation

Divisionalisation 分部门管理

This is a term for the division of an organisation into divisions. Each divisional manager has authority to make decisions and is therefore responsible for the performance of the division. 每个部门经理有权作出决定，因此对部门的业绩负责。

Decentralisation 分散化

In general, a division structure will lead to decentralisation of the decision-making process and divisional managers may have the freedom to set selling prices, choose suppliers, make product mix and output decisions, and so on. Decentralisation is, however, a matter of degree, depending on how much freedom divisional managers are given. 分权是一个程度问题，取决于部门经理有多大的自由度。

Advantages of divisionalisation 部门化管理的优点

➢ Divisionalisation can improve the quality of decisions made because divisional managers (those taking the decisions) know local conditions and are able to make more informed judgement.

➢ Decisions should be taken more quickly because information does not have to pass along the chain of command to and from top management.

➢ The authority to act to improve performance should motivate divisional managers.

➢ Divisional organisation frees top management from detailed involvement in day-to-day operations and allows them to devote more time to strategic planning.

➢ Divisions provide valuable training grounds for future members of top management by giving them experience of managerial skills in a less complex environment than that faced by top management.

Chapter 16　Divisional performance measurement

Disadvantages of divisionalisation

➢ Decisions might be taken by a divisional manager in the best interests of their own part of the business, but against the best interest of other divisions and possibly against the interests of the organisation as a whole.

➢ It is claimed that the costs of activities that are common to all divisions, such as running the accounting.

➢ Department, may be greater for a divisionalised structure than for a centralized structure.

➢ Top management, by delegating decision-making to divisional managers, may lose control since they are not aware of what is going on in the organisation as a whole.

Responsibility accounting 责任会计

Responsibility accounting is the term used to describe decentralisation of authority, with the performance of the decentralised units measured in terms of accounting results. 问责制有利于追责。

Types of responsibility centre (division)

➢ Cost centre: manager has authority over cost but not revenue 成本中心

Cost centers are collecting places for costs before they are further analyzed. Costs are further analyzed into cost units once they have been traced to cost centers. 成本中心是在进一步分析成本之前收集成本的地方。一旦成本被追踪到成本中心，成本就被进一步分析成单位成本。

➢ Revenue centre: authority over revenue only 收入中心

Revenue centers are accountable for revenues only. Its managers should normally have control over how revenues are raised. 收入中心只对收入负责。它的管理者通常应该控制如何增加收入。

➢ Profit centre: authority over cost and revenue, but not new capital investment 利润中心

Profit centers are accountable for costs and revenues. 利润中心负责成本和收入。

➢ Investment centre: authority over cost, revenue and new capital investment 投资中心

An investment center is a profit center with additional responsibilities for capital investment and possibly for financing, and whose performance is measured by its return on investment or return on capital employed. 投资中心对资本投资和融资负有责任，其业绩以其投资回报率或使用的资本回报率来衡量。

什么是投资决策？

Investment decision: usage of spare money; decision relating to PPE

对处置管理闲置资金的使用和做与 PPE 相关的决策

2. Return on investment (ROI) 投资回报率

Return on investment (ROI) shows how much profit has been made in relation to the amount of capital invested. 该项投资赚多少。

ROI = Profit before interest and tax（PBIT）/Capital employed

ROCE　VS　RI

ROCE 考虑的是整个公司 as a whole

RI 考虑的是一个部门

ROCE ＜ New subject ROI ＜ department average ROI

若一个新项目是以上这种形式，说明这个新项目不符合该部门的投资标准，但是对于整个公司而言，是可以投资的；但是如果投资会拉低部门的投资回报率，决策权在部门手里，部门不会投就失去了这个可以增加整个公司利益的新项目，这个就是使用 ROI 评价部门业绩对于公司而言的坏处，从而出现 RI。

Return 回报

Profit after depreciation 扣减折旧后的利润

Controllable costs only 用来控制成本

Investment 投资

Non-current assets plus working capital NCA + CA + CL

Net book value of asset i.g after depreciation　账面净值

3. Residual income(RI) 剩余收益

An alternative way of measuring the performance of an investment centre，instead of using ROI，is residual income（RI）. Residual income is a measure of the center's profits after deducting a notional or imputed interest cost.

RI = Profit - interest cost

衡量投资中心绩效的方法是 RI。

The center's profit is after deducting depreciation on capital equipment. 扣减折旧后

The imputed cost of capital might be the organization's cost of borrowing or its weighted average cost of capital. 借款成本或其加权平均资本成本。

Chapter 17

Transfer price

Learning objectives

√ Explain and illustrate the basis for setting a transfer price using variable cost, full cost and the principles behind allowing for intermediate markets

√ Explain how transfer prices can distort the performance assessment of divisions and decisions made.

1. Transfer price 转让价格

Transfer price is the price at which goods or services are transferred from one department to another, or from one member of a group to another. 转移价格是货物或服务从一个部门转移到另一个部门的价格，或从一个组的一个成员转移到另一个成员。

It is a way to make each division profit accountable. 是一种使每个部门的利润都有人负责的方法。

Limits within which transfer prices:

○ The minimum. The sum of the supplying division's marginal cost and opportunity cost of the item transferred.

Minimum price 从卖方角度考虑:

a) 如果有 space capacity, minimum price = marginal cost

b) 如果是 Full capacity, minimum price = market price − cost saved

○ The maximum. The lowest market price at which the receiving division could purchase the goods or services externally, less any internal cost savings in packaging and delivery.

Maximum price 从买方角度考虑:

a) maximum price = market price

b) maximum price = sales price − processing cost

Problems with transfer pricing 转让定价的问题

➢ Maintaining the right level of divisional autonomy

Decisions might be taken by a profit centre manager in the best interests of the in own part of the business, but against the best interests of other profit centers and possibly the organisation as a whole.

➢ **Ensuring divisional performance is measured fairly**

Transfer prices affect behaviour and decisions by profit centre managers.

➢ **Ensuring corporate profits are maximized**

When there are disagreements about how much work should be transferred between divisions, and how many sales the division should make to the external market, there is presumably a profit-maximising level of output and sales for the organisation as a whole.

Chapter 18

Performance for the not-for-profit sector

> **Learning objectives**
>
> ✓ Comment on the problems of having non-quantifiable objectives in performance management
> ✓ Comment on the problems of having multiple objectives in this sector
> ✓ Explain how performance could be measured in this sector
> ✓ Outline Value for Money (VFM) as a public sector objective

1. Not for profit organizations 非营利组织

Not for profit organizations are those whose prime goal cannot be assessed by economic means. In pursuit of that goal it may undertake profit-making activities. 非营利组织是其主要目标不能通过经济手段来评估的组织。为了实现目标可以从事营利活动。例如慈善机构和国家机构，警察和卫生局。

➢ A major problem with many not for profit organizations, particularly government bodies, is that it is extremely difficult to define their objectives at all. 目标不好确定。

➢ They tend to have multiple objectives, so that even if they could all be clearly identified it is impossible to say which is the overriding objective. 有同样重要的多个目标

➢ It is difficult to judge whether non-quantifiable objectives have been met. 难以量化目标是否实现。

2. Problems with performance measurement of not for profit

a) Multiple objectives
b) The difficulty of measuring outputs
c) Lack of profit measure
d) Financial constraints
e) Political, social and legal considerations

3. Methods of performance measurement

A few methods can be applied to measure performance.
➢ Inputs

> Judgement
> Comparisons

4. Value for money(3E)

Performance of not for profit organisation is judged in terms of inputs and outputs, hence the **value for money** criteria of economy, efficiency and effectiveness.

> **Effectiveness** is the relationship between an organisation's outputs and its objectives. 结果要实现最终目标。

> **Efficiency** is the relationship between inputs and outputs.

Input 与 output 的转化效率高,即投入一定量的 input,output 尽量多;或者产出一定量的 output,投入尽量少。

> **Economy** is attaining the appropriate quantity and quality of inputs at the lowest cost. Input 便宜

Chapter 19

External considerations and behavioral aspects

Learning objectives
✓ Explain the need to allow for external considerations in performance management, including stakeholders, market conditions and allowance for competitors
✓ Suggest ways in which external considerations could be allowed for in performance management
✓ Interpret performance in the light of external considerations
✓ Identify and explain the behaviour aspects of performance management

1. External considerations 外部因素
Stakeholders 利益相关者
Stakeholders are groups of people or individuals who have a legitimate interest in the activities of an organisation. 客户、员工、股东、供应商、借贷人等。

Three broad types of stakeholder
- Internal stakeholders 内部利益相关者(员工、管理层)
- Connected stakeholders 关联利益相关者(股东、客户、供应商、融资者)
- External stakeholders 外部利益相关者(社区、政府)

2. Behaviour aspects of performance management 行为举止方面
The controllability principle 可控性原理
The controllability principle is that managers of responsibility centers should only be held accountable for costs and/or revenues over which they have some influence. 责任中心的管理者只应对他们有影响的成本收入负责。

Chapter 20

Big data & Security and confidential information

Learning objectives

√ Discuss the procedures that may be necessary to ensure security of highly confidential information that is not for external consumption

1. Big data

Benefits of big data analytic

Performance improvements

➢ **Better understanding of customer behaviour**

➢ **Targeted marketing messages**

Big data could facilitate targeted promotions and advertising. 大数据可以促进有针对性的促销和广告。

➢ **Decision-making**

➢ **New products and services**

More generally, big data could also provide new business opportunities in their own right.

➢ **Performance measurement**

Big data can provide more detailed and up-to-date information for performance measurement.

For example, performance reports can be produced in real-time allowing management to react quickly to variances.

Big data and the finance professional

Five traits of a data-enabled finance professional:

➢ Understands the fundamental drivers and metrics of the business
了解业务的基本驱动因素和指标

➢ Has a clear sense of what customers care about and how to track this
对客户所关心的事情有清晰的认识,以及如何追踪它

➢ Embraces new, unconventional sources of data
新的、非传统的数据来源

- Comfortable with uncertainty
  习惯不确定性
- Looks for new visual ways to present data with impact
  寻找新的可视化方式来呈现具有影响力的数据

Risks and challenges of big data

- Critics have argued that although data sets may be big, they are not necessarily representative of the entire data population as a whole
- Quality of data

Data has to be relevant and reliable.

Veracity 真实

In order to be valuable, data also needs to be reliable. (volume, velocity, variety and veracity). 大量的,速度,多样性和准确性

Using big data requires organisations to maintain strong governance on data quality.

- Cost

It is expensive to establish the hardware and analytical software needed, and to comply with data protection regulations which vary from country to country.

- Skills

The scale and complexity of data sets may require a data scientist's level of analytical skills for data mining, deriving algorithms and predictive analytic

- Loss and theft of data

Companies could face legal action if data is stolen.

2. Security and confidential information 安全与保密信息

A number of procedures can be used to ensure the security of highly confidential information that is not for external consumption. 使用一些程序来确保非供外部使用的高度机密信息的安全性。

- **Passwords** — to only allow authorized users to access the system. 密码仅允许授权用户访问系统
- **Physical access control** is concerned with the prevention of unauthorized persons gaining access to the hardware. 物理访问控制涉及防止未经授权的人员访问硬件,例如门锁等。
- **Logical access control** is concerned with preventing those who already have access to a terminal or a computer from gaining access to data or software. 逻辑访问控制是指防止已经访问终端或计算机的人访问数据或软件。

A logical access system performs three operations when access is requested. 当请求访问时,逻辑访问系统会执行的三个操作:
  - Identification of the user 用户标识
  - Authentication of user identity 用户身份验证
  - Check on user authority 检查用户权限

- Database controls 数据库控制
- Firewalls 防火墙
- Encryption 加密
- Authentication 认证
- Dial back security 回拨安全
- System logs 系统日志
- Personal data 个人资料
- Personnel security planning 人员安全规划
- Anti-virus and anti-spyware software 防病毒、防间谍软件

TAXATION

Chapter 1

The UK tax system

1. The overall function and purpose of tax
— Economic factors:
Used to encourage and discourage certain types of activity.
— Social factors:
Redistribution of income and wealth.
— Environmental factors:
To deal with environmental concerns like global warming.

2. Tax avoidance and tax evasion
Tax evasion：逃税漏税
○ Misleading HMRC by suppressing information or deliberately providing false information.
○ Illegal.
Tax avoidance：合理避税
○ Using the legislation to reduce your tax burden.
○ Legal.

3. Ethical and professional approach
If accountant learns of material error or omission in a client's tax return or of a failure to file a required tax return, Accountant has following responsibilities:
(1) Advise and recommend client disclosure to HMRC 给客户提建议
(2) If client refuse, inform the client in writing of ceased acting for that client 如果客户拒绝，就停止服务该客户
(3) Notify HMRC but not required to disclose detailed reasons 通知税务局你停止为他服务
(4) Report to the money laundering reporting officer 报告给反洗钱组织

Chapter 2

Income tax outline

		NSI	SI	Dividend	Total
Trading income	C3, 5, 4, 8	x			
Less: trading loss b/f or terminal loss	C7	(x)			
Employment income	C9, 10	x			
○ salary/bonus/commission		x			
○ benefits: voucher		x			
living accomodation benefit: normal + additional − actual paid					
living accomodation expense benefit: job related(10%)/not job related					
motor car benefit &car fuel benefit					
beneficial loan: lower of, exempt (loan< 10,000)					
private use of employee asset: use of asset/acquisition an asset					
other benefit					
exempt benefit					
(include approved mileage allowance)多报销部分					
less: OPS by employee		(x)			
less: charitable donation under payroll		(x)			
less: subscription fees		(x)			
less: approved mileage deduction		(x)			
pension income		x			

Chapter 2 Income tax outline

(Continued)

		NSI	SI	Dividend	Total
Property business income	C6	x			
○ rent		x			
○ premium		x			
less: allowable expenditure finance cost		(x)			
less: property income finance cost(25%)		(x)			
furnished room		X			
Furnished holiday letting profit (5 conditions)	C6	x			
Interest income	C2		x		
○ Bank and building society interest			x		
○ National Savings & Investments interest including interest from Direct Saver Accounts, Investment Accounts, Income Bonds			x		
○ Interest on government securities or Treasury Stock (these are also called 'gilts').			x		
○ Interest from company loan stock which is listed on a recognized stock exchange			x		
Exempt saving income	C2		0		
○ Interest from Saving Certificates issued by National Savings and Investment Bank			0		
○ Interest from Individual Savings Accounts (ISA) Limit = 20,000			0		
Other exempt income					
○ Prizes received from premium bonds			0		
○ Statutory redundancy money					
○ Scholarships					
○ Interest on damages for personal injuries					
○ Local authority grant					
○ Child benefit (adjusted net income not exceed £50,000)			0		
Dividend	C2			<u>x</u>	
Total income		x	x	x	x

(Continued)

		NSI	SI	Dividend	Total
less: qualifying interest paid (5类)	C2	(x)1st	(x)2nd	(x)3rd	(x)
(a) Loan to buy plant or machinery for partnership use					
(b) Loan to buy plant or machinery for employment use.					
(c) Loan to buy interest in employee-controlled company.					
(d) Loan to invest in a partnership					
(e) Loan to invest in a co-operative					
Less: trading loss (current year) or (loss in the first 4 years of trade)	C7	(x)1st	(x)2nd	(x)3rd	(x)
Net income		x	x	x	x
less: Personal allowance (Be reduced if ANI>100,000)	C2	(12,500)1st	2nd	3rd	−12,500
Taxable income		x	x	x	x
Income tax liability:					
NSI:		∗20%	∗40%	∗45%	x
SI (basic: 1,000, higher: 500)	∗0%(5,000)	∗20%	∗40%	∗45%	x
Dividend (all: 2,000)		∗7.5%	∗32.5%	∗38.1%	x
Total income tax liability					x
Less: tax deducted at source − PAYE	C10				(x)
Less: Marriage allowance	C2				−250
Less: Property income finance cost(75%) B∗20%	C6				(x)
Add: Child benefit income tax charge (adjusted net income over £50,000)	C2				x
Add: Annual allowance charge excess AA ∗ tax rate	C11				x
Income tax payable/repayable (via self-assessment system)	C12				x/(x)

Chapter 2　Income tax outline

1. The UK resident

判断英国公民需要分三步：

Step 1：判断自动非公民测试是否满足

The following people will automatically be treated as non-resident in the UK：

a) A person who is in the UK for less than 16 days during a tax year.

b) A person who is in the UK for less than 46 days during a tax year, and who has not been resident during the three previous tax years.

c) A person who works full-time overseas, subject to them not being in the UK for more than 90 days during a tax year.

Step 2：判断自动是公民测试是否满足

If not meeting any of the automatic overseas tests, the following people will automatically be treated as resident in the UK：

a) A person who is in the UK for 183 days or more during a tax year.

b) A person whose only home is in the UK.

c) A person who carries out full time work in the UK.

Step 3：根据在英国居住天数和以下 5 个条件判断是否满足

5 UK ties

a) Spouse/civil partner or child(under 18) in the UK

b) House in UK which is used during tax year

c) In UK for more than 90 days in either of 2 previous tax years

d) More time in UK than in any other country in tax year

e) Doing substantive work in UK

Days in UK	Previously resident	Not previously resident
Less than 16	Automatically not resident	Automatically not resident
16—45	Resident if 4 UK ties (or more)	Automatically not resident
46—90	Resident if 3 UK ties (or more)	Resident if 4 UK ties
91—120	Resident if 2 UK ties (or more)	Resident if 3 UK ties (or more)
121—182	Resident if 1 UK ties (or more)	Resident if 2 UK ties (or more)
183 more than	Automatically resident	Automatically resident

2. Fiscal year (Tax year)

— The year of assessment 2020/21 is 6 April 2020 ~ 5 April 2021

3. Layout of income tax computation

4. Personal allowance

The personal allowance for the tax year 2020/21 is £12,500

Step 1：计算 ANI

Adjusted net income = total net income - Gross personal pension contributions - Gross gift aid donations（GAD）

Step 2：除二减

If ANI > £100,000, PA = 12,500 - (ANI - 100,000) × 1/2

Step 3：

If ANI ≥ £125,000 (12,500 * 2 + 100,000), PA = 0

5. Tax rate

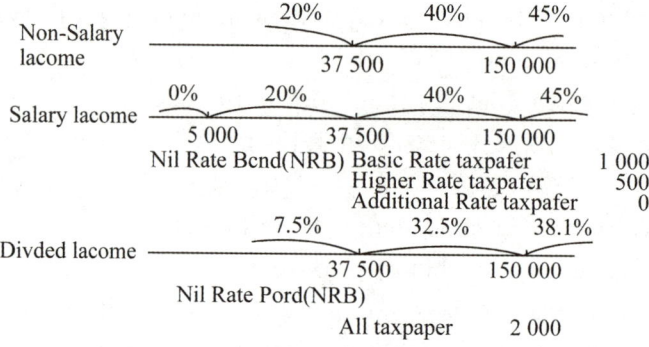

Kinds of taxpayer（depend on **total taxable income**）
- Basic rate taxpayer：Taxable income ≤ 37,500
- Higher rate taxpayer：37,500 < Taxable income ≤ 150,000
- Additional rate taxpayer：Taxable income > 150,000

6. Gift aid donation(GAD) & Personal pension contribution(PPC)

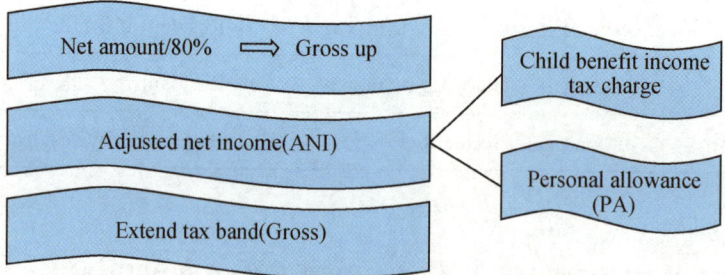

7. Child benefit income tax charge

※ ANI < 50,000

Income tax charge = 0

※ $50{,}000 < \text{ANI} < 60{,}000$

Income tax charge = child benefit received * 1% * (ANI − 50,000)/100

※ ANI > £60,000,

Income tax charge = child benefit received.

Chapter 3

Trading income

1. The badges of trade

1）The subject matter of the transaction
   Are the goods of a type normally used for trading?
2）The frequency of similar transactions
   Frequent transaction indicate trading
3）The length of ownership
   Short period of ownership is more likely to indicate trading
4）Supplementary work, improvements and marketing
   Work is done to make the item more marketable indicate trading
5）A profit motive
   Intention to profit indicating trading
6）The circumstances responsible for realization
   Force sales to raise cash indicates not trading

2. Pro forma for tax adjusted trading profit

5 steps：
Starting point：net profit/operating profit（Income Statement）
a）Add back depreciation
b）Notes adjustment　＋／－
c）Review other items in question
d）Deducted capital allowance（Chapter 5）
e）Deducted non-trading income（e.g. interest income, property income）

3. Adjustment of items

※ Only expenditure incurred **wholly and exclusively** for the purpose of the trade is allowable. 只有百分百用于 trading 目的的费用税法才允许抵扣

※ The following expenditure is non-deductible 以下费用税法都不允许抵扣

○ Is too remote from the purpose of trading — Remoteness test 不是用于 trading 的费用

Chapter 3 Trading income

○ Has more than one purpose and one of them is not trading — Duality test 这项费用有双重目的(不止用于 trading)

Items	Deductible	Non-deductible
Short lease	Renewing charge	Initial granting charge
Appropriations		○ Sole trader's salary and income tax, national insurance ○ Drawing by sole trader (Add back profit or revenue by cost in the book or not) ○ Excessive salary to family member
Car leasing	CO_2 emission rate $\leqslant$ 110 g/km: Fully deductible	CO_2 emission rate $>$ 110 g/km: 15% of leasing costate disallowed.
Pre-trading expenditure	Expense incurred within 7 years of the start of trade (e.g. pretrading advertising expenditure)	
Non-current asset	Capital allowance	Deprecations & amortization
Repairs	The cost of initial repair to remedy normal wear and tear of recently acquired assets is allowable revenue expenditure	The cost of initial repairs to improve an asset recently acquired to make it fit to earn profits is disallowable capital expenditure
Restoration	The cost of restoration of an asset by replacing a subsidiary part of the asset is revenue expenditure, (e.g. expenditure on a new factory chimney replacement was allowable since the chimney was a subsidiary part of the factory)	
Bad debts	○ Only impairment losses where the liability was incurred wholly and exclusively for the purposes of the trade are deductible for taxation purposes. ○ If an impairment loss which has been deducted for tax purposes is later recovered, the recovery is taxable, so no adjustment is required to the amount of the recovery shown in the statement of profit or loss	Loans to employees written off are not deductible
Trade or professional subscriptions	wholly and exclusively for the purpose of trade	

4. Cash basis for small business

Items	Deductible	Non-deductible
Charitable donation	○ Wholly and exclusively for **trading purposes** (E.g. Promoting business name) ○ **Local not national** ○ Made to an educational, religious, cultural or benevolent organization	○ Donations to **political parties** ○ Donations to **national parties** ○ Gift aid donation
Patents	○ Registering fee ○ Copy right ○ Patent royalty	
Fines and penalties	**Parking fine** incurred on business (perform his duty) by employee (not sole trader)	

Format of calculation

Trading profit (or loss) under the cash basis is therefore calculated as follows

Receipts (including sale of plant & machinery) 现金收款(包含变卖 p&m 的金额)	xx
Expense payments (including the purchase of P&M) 现金付款费用(包含购买 p&m 的金额)	(xx)
Trading profit (or loss)	xx

Condition to use cash basis 什么时候可以用 cash basis

○ The cash basis can only be used by

a) unincorporated businesses (sole trader and partnership)非有限责任公司

b) the revenue is 150,000 or less 年收入额小于等于 150,000

○ However a business must cease to use the cash basis if:

Revenue exceeds 300,000 a year.

当年收入超过 300,000 时候就不可以用 cash basis

Taxable cash receipts

○ Cash receipts include all amounts received relating to the business, including amounts received from the sale of plant and machinery (except motor cars).

○ Receipts from the sale of motor cars and capital assets which are not classed as plant and machinery (e.g. land) are not taxable receipts. 变卖非 p&m 以外的资产不能算进 cash receipt (尤其是小汽车)

Deductible business expenses paid

○ Under the cash basis, business expenses are deductible when they are paid.

○ It also includes capital expenditure on plant and machinery (except motor cars).

○ Other capital expenses are not business expenses e.g. purchase of land, motor cars, and legal fees on such purchases

Chapter 3 Trading income

Fixed rate mileage expenses

○ Motor expenses can use the approved mileage allowances to calculate the deduction for business mileage. The rate is 45p per mile for the first 10,000 miles, with a rate of 25p per mile thereafter.

Business mileage	
0—10,000 miles	45p
10,000 miles above	25p

The actual running and capital costs of owning a motor car are ignored.

汽车实际产生的运行成本和资本成本可以忽略不计，取而代之的是按照 fixed rate 计算出来的汽车费用

Losses

Where the use of the cash basis results in a trading loss, the only relief available is to carry the loss forward against future trading profits. There is no relief against total income. 用这种方式算出来的 trading loss 不能递减 total income，只能往以后年度去抵扣未来的 trading income

Chapter 4

Basis of assessment

1. Current year basis (CYB)

The basis period for the tax year is the taxable trading profits for the 12 month period of account ending in that tax year.

a) 税法上规定 Tax year 2020/21 is 6 April 2020 to 5 April 2021（△）

b) 会计期间可能是 1 月 1 日～12 月 31 日（"｜"：accounting date），与 tax year 不匹配，运用 CYB 方法把会计期间和税务年度相匹配，匹配后的 period 叫作 basis period

c) 一个 basis period 通常是 12 个月，并且只能包含一个 5/6 April（△）

d) CYB method

Calculate the taxable trading profit assessable in 2020/21

从 2020 年 4 月 6 日到 2021 年 4 月 5 日之间找"｜"往前数 12 个月，这段 period 就是 2020/21 所匹配后的 basis period.

（公司开始营业的第一年和停止营业那年处理方法例外）

2. Opening basis year rules

BP 1：从⚹到第一个▲，这段时间就是 BP 1

BP 2：从第一个▲后的第一个"｜"往前数 12 个月

There are 3 conditions：

○ A：if 第一个▲后的第一个"｜"往前数的期间≥12 months，那么 BP 2 是从"｜"往前数 12 个月，这段时间就是 BP 2

○ B：if 第一个▲后的第一个"｜"往前数的期间≤12 months，那么 BP 2 就是从⚹往后数 12 个月，这段时间就是 BP 2

○ C：if 第一个▲后面没有看到"｜"就先看到了第二个▲，那么 BP 2 就是第一个▲到第二个▲的这段时间

BP 3：从第二个▲后面找"｜"往前数 12 个月，这 12 个月就是 BP 3

BP 4：从第三个▲后面找"｜"往前数 12 个月，这 12 个月就是 BP 4

Overlap profits 只有在公司停止营业的最后一年才可以抵扣 taxable profits

3. Closing basis year rules

a) If a trade starts and ceases in the same tax year, the basis period for that year is the whole lifespan of the trade. 如果开业日和停业日在同一段两个小▲期间，那么全部期间就是 BP.

b) If the final year is the second year, the basis period runs from 6 April at the start of the second year to the date of cessation. 如果停业日在第二个税务年度，那么第二年就是小▲到停业日.

c) If the final year is the third year or a later year

如果停业日在第三个或第 n 个税务年度，那么

Step 1：从关门日往前数 12 个月，这 12 个月中间包含一个▲

Step 2：被▲分隔开的两段区间分别是①和②

Step 3：减去 overlap profit 即③

Closing year trading income = ① + ② − ③

4. Choice of accounting date — first time

1) An accounting date of just after 5 April (30 April)

a) Will ensure the maximum interval between earning profits and having to pay the related tax liability.

经营期间和计税期间之间有最大的间隔期。

b) Will result in increased overlap profits upon the commencement of trading. But there may be a long delay before relief is obtained.

Overlap profit 最多。

2) An accounting date of just before 5 April (31 March)

a) Will give the shortest interval between earning profits and having to pay the related tax liability.

经营期间和计税期间之间有最短的间隔期。

b) However, there will be no overlap profits.

3) It is usually beneficial to ensure that profits for the first period of trading are kept to a minimum where they are assessed more than once under the commencement rules.

5. Loss in the early years of trade

A loss in an overlap period can only be relieved once. If basis periods overlap, a loss in the overlap period is treated as a loss for the earlier tax year only

Loss 是没有 overlap 的，如果重合，loss 只能算进前一年。

Chapter 5

Capital allowance

Capital allowance 做题步骤：（对应表格）

Step 1：读题

1) Length of period of account 老板自己定的会计期间 AIA/WDA/small pool balance allowance * n/12（n≤＞12 months）

2) 判断题目中提到的资产是否可以申请 CA

Fire regulation capital expenditure Specified for CA {Alterations to buildings needed for the installation of plant. Acquiring computer software.

Not be plant for CA：Land & buildings（walls，floors，ceilings，doors，gates，windows）and structures

3) 把 additional asset 分类标注特征

a) General pool（main pool）18%WDA，AIA2

i) All machinery, fixtures and fittings and equipment

ii) Vans, forklift trucks, Lorries

iii) Cars with CO_2 emissions between 51 g/km — 110 g/km

b) Special rate pool　6%WDA，AIA1

i) Long-life asset

ii) Integral features of a building or structure（可展开）

iii) Cars with CO_2 emission ＞110 g/km

c) Short life asset　18%WDA，AIA3

P&M（except of motor cars and plant used partly for non-trade）＜8 yrs

d) Private used asset（by sole trader）

e) Low emission car　　100%FYA

CO_2≤50 g/km

Step 2：Additions

AIA 最多申请 1,000,000，注意 AIA 顺序，AIA * n/12

AIA、FYA 是否有 private use%

AIA、FYA 在 final year 不用计算

Step 3：Disposal

The disposal value is the lower of sale proceeds and original cost.

Chapter 5　Capital allowance

BC（WDV — Disposal value ＜ 0）　减少 CA,随时产生,随时计算
BA（WDV — Disposal value ＞ 0）　增加 CAGP 和 SRP 只有最后一年才能计算 BA

Step 4：考虑 WDV 期末余额

在计算 WDA 之前,如果 GP 和 SRP 的余额≤1,000,那么直接 claim Small pool balance allowance（别忘了 * n/12）

Step 5：计算 WDA

在计算 WDA 之前,如果 GP 和 SRP 的余额＞1,000,计算 WDA
注意：WDA * n/12,是否有 private use%，在 final year 不用计算

Step 6：计算 SBA

可减免的价格为支付价格－土地价值
注意：SBA * n/12,减免量为@3%（不同于 WDA 的@18%和@6%）

（注：SBA 的关键点）

SBA (structure and buildings allowance)：
- 在33年零4个月内
- @3%
- 办公室、工厂、仓库，包括墙壁、隧道、桥梁等，都符合SBA的资格；
- 住宅不符合SBA的资格；
- 土地价值不符合SBA的资格，因此可使用SBA的金额是：支付价格－土地价值；
- 建筑物必须投入使用后才能有SBA
- 需要根据月份进行调整

Step 7：复查

WDA 和 AIA 是否都乘以 n/12 和所有 private 的资产的 AIA、WDA、FYA、BA、BC、small pool allowance 都乘以 business use%。

注意计算格式

公司所得税中计算 capital allowance 要和个人的两点区别：
a）Not have private used asset pool
b）AIA/WDA * n/12　（n≤12 months）

	GP	SRP	SLA	PUA（Business use %）	Allowance
TWDV b/f					
Additions for A/A	x				
Less：A/A	(1,000,000)				A/A
Transfer to each pool	x	x	x		
Additions for FYA	x1				
Less：FYA (100%)	(x1)				FYA
	0				
Disposal					
BA/BC					BA/(BC)
Less：Small pool allowance					Small pool
Less：WDA 18%/6%					WDA
TWDV c/f					

Chapter 6

Property income

1. 计算步骤

income	Rental	x	一般用 cash basis,除非特别说明。公司要用 accrual basis
	Premium	x	收到 premium 用 Property income = P * (51 − D)/50 支付 premium 用 Deduct from trading profit = P * (51 − D)/50/D
Less:	Revenue expenses (accrual basis)	(x)	○ Insurance ○ Agent's fees ○ Advertising ○ Council tax paid by landlord ○ Water rates paid by landlord ○ Repairs and Redecorations（Revenue Expenditure） ○ Specific bad debts (e.g. tenants leave without payment) ★○ Interest expenses（finance cost）on a loan for acquiring the letting property（25%） (in company this expense is disallowable)
	Replacement furniture relief	(x) A	actual cost of replacement — proceeds from selling old assets（improvement is not available）

	Rent a room income	B	property income = 0
			○ Rent < 7,500
			  Rent − Expense = Property loss
			○ Rent > 7,500 property income = Rent − higher of 7,500
			  Actual rent expense

	Property income profit/(loss)	C	

A loss on a property letting business is carried forward to set against the first available future property income.

Property loss 只能抵扣未来的 property income,不能抵扣其他收入。

2. Furnished holiday letting profit(NSI)

1) Conditions

The property must satisfy the following conditions, and then could be treated as furnished Holiday lettings：同时满足

a) Must be furnished and the accommodation must in UK

b) Must on a commercial basis

c) Available for letting for at least 210 days during the year; and

d) Actually let for at least 105 days during the year

e) Not let to the same person for 31 days in any 155 days period

2) Furnished holiday letting loss

A furnished holiday letting loss could only be carried forward against future profits from furnished holiday lettings.

3) Benefit of furnished holiday lettings (like trading income)

a) Capital allowances are available on furniture instead of replacement furniture relief. 因为作为 trading 这项行为，购买的家具属于 business asset 所以可以申请 capital allowance

b) On the disposal it will qualify as a business asset and capital gains tax roll-over relief, entrepreneur's relief and holdover relief may be available. 作为 trading 这项行为，这些 business asset 可以申请 relief

c) The profit from a furnished holiday letting qualifies as relevant earnings for pension tax relief purposes

Relevant earning：Trading profit + Employment income + FHL

3. 公司所得税计算中的两个区别

1) Property business loss

a) First set off against **non-property income and gains of the company for the current period; and any excess is,**

b) Carried forward for set off against **future income (of all descriptions)**

property loss 可以抵扣全部类型收入

2) Interest paid on a loan to buy or improve property

Not a property business expense

贷款利息不能抵扣 property income

Chapter 7 & 15

Loss relief for individual and corporation

Trading loss for Individuals	Trading loss for Corporations
Step 1:	Step 1:
Against General Income 有四种选择： $\begin{cases} \text{Against General Income for current year} \\ \text{Against General Income for previous one year} \\ \text{Against General Income for previous one and current year} \\ \text{Against General Income for current and previous one year} \end{cases}$ Cap on income tax relief（cap 是用来限制 trading loss 抵减 general income 的） Cap is higher of: $\begin{cases} 50,000 \\ \text{Adjusted total income（total income — PPC gross）} * 25\% \end{cases}$ CAPITAL ALLOWANCE 可以考虑不完全计算 ○ The trader may adjust the size of the loss relief claim by not claiming all the capital allowances he is entitled to. ○ This may be a useful tax planning point to preserve the personal allowance or where the effective rate of relief for capital allowances in future periods will be greater than the rate of tax relief for the loss relief. 如果预计明年的收入高导致税率高或者考虑节省 PA，可以考虑 ○ A reduced claim will increase the balance carried forward to the next year's capital allowances computation. 会导致以后年度的 CA 增多，从而抵扣更多的 trading income	Set the loss against total profits（before gift aid donations）in the following order: （1）Loss making accounting period （2）Preceding 12 months（可以选择，也可以不选择）
Step 2:	Step 2:
Excess Trading loss relieved against capital gains: 多余的 trading loss 可以抵扣 capital gain 1) Extention to trade loss relief against general income 必须先抵扣完 general income 才能抵 CG 2) The capital gains is Net capital gains（after deducted capital loss for the same year or for previous years.）But before Annual Exemption. 一定要抵 net CG，但是在 AE 计算之前	Total Profit 中已经包含 Capital Gains 所以不需要此步骤

Chapter 7 & 15 Loss relief for individual and corporation

(Continued)

Trading loss for Individuals	Trading loss for Corporations
Step 3:	Step 3:
Excess carried forward against the first available future trading profit. 再多余的 trading loss 只能往以后年度去抵扣未来的 trading income	Excess carried forward against the total profits, can consider not waste QCD of future year.多余的 trading loss 可以往以后年度去抵扣未来的 total profit.
Loss in the first four years of a trade for Individuals:	
1) Only loss occurs in the first four years of trade 只有公司经营前四年的亏损可以申请这个 relief 2) Set off against the general income in the preceding 3 years, taking the earliest year first. 抵扣以前三个年度的 general income,最早的一年先抵	
Terminal trade loss relief for Individuals:	**Terminal trade loss relief for Corporations:**
1. A loss on cessation (last 12 months of trading) is called terminal loss: Terminal loss 方法: Step 1: 从停业那天往前数 12 个月 Step 2: 在这 12 个月里面找到△,分成①和②两部分 Step 3: Terminal loss = ① + ② − unrelieved overlap profit From 6 April to the date of cessation ② X The actual trade losses for the period from 12 months before cessation until the end of the penultimate tax year ① X Unrelieved overlap profits $\underline{X}$ X	1. Trading loss during the final 12 months of trading: 经营期间最后 12 个月的亏损
(1) Relief is given in the tax year of cessation	(1) Set against current period profits, then 先抵自己当期的 total profit
(2) And the 3 preceding years, taking the latest year first. And relieved against trade profits only.抵扣以前三个年度的 trade profits,最晚的一年先抵.	(2) Set against total profits of the three years preceding the loss making period, later years first. 抵扣以前三个年度的 total profit ,最晚的一年先抵.
Capital Loss for Individuals:	**Capital Loss for Corporations:**
(1) Losses are set off against gains of the same year and any excess carried forward. Capital loss 先抵减自己当年的 CG,如果还有剩余往以后年度去抵扣未来的 CG	(1) Capital losses can only be set off against current and future capital gains(同个人)

	(Continued)
Capital Loss for Individuals:	**Capital Loss for Corporations:**
(2) Brought forward losses are only set off to reduce net gains down to the amount of the annual exemption. 以前年度带过来的 capital loss 不能让我今年的 AE 浪费	(2) Capital losses may not be set against income. Capital loss 只能抵扣 capital gain，不能抵扣其他收入
Property Loss for Individuals:	**Property Loss for Corporations:**
(1) Against property Income for current year	(1) First set off against non-property income and gains of the company for the current period;
(2) Excess carried forward to set against the first available future property income.	(2) Excess carried forward for set off against future income (of all descriptions)

The choice between loss reliefs

○ The rate of income tax or capital gains tax

○ The timing of the relief obtained，with a claim against total income/capital gains of the current year or preceding year resulting in earlier relief than a claim against future trading profits.

○ The extent to which personal allowances and the capital gains annual exemption may be wasted.

Chapter 8

Partnerships

1. **Assessment of partnerships to tax** 如何匹配每个合伙人的税务利润

Each partner is taxed individually on his share of the partnership, despite the partnership being a single trading entity. 每个股东都要根据自己的股份对应的比例去算利润从而交税

To determine partner's assessable profits：如何计算合伙人企业的利润

○ Firstly, calculate the tax adjusted trading profit for the partnership 先用 Chapter 3 和 Chapter 5 的知识把纳税调整后的利润算出来

○ Secondly, allocate the tax adjusted trading profits to the individual partners. 按照他们的股份比例去计算每个人的纳税调整后的利润

○ Finally, apply the basis of assessment rules to determine a partner's assessable profits in a tax year. 运用 Chapter 4 的画数轴方式匹配出来每个人对应税务年度的利润

2. **Profit allocation** 如何进行利润分配

○ Partner's salary and interest on capital are not deductible expenses in the adjustment of taxable profits as they are merely an allocation of profits. Partners' salaries and interest on capital are allocated first. 先用会计期间的公司利润减掉股东的工资和成本利息

○ The balance after allocating salaries and interests on capital will be allocated in the profit sharing ratio. 剩下的利润按照投资比例分配

○ When there is a change in the profit sharing ratio, the profit or loss will need to be time apportioned prior to allocation. 按照每个人的小旗子和小牌子画数轴匹配出各自的税务年度的利润

3. **Reasons for changes：合伙人企业变动的原因**

The membership of a partnership may change as the result of the admission, death or retirement of a partner. 合伙人企业变化的原因就三个：加入、去世、退休

Deal with changes 如果股权变动，怎么处置

○ Allocate profit and loss first, and 先用上面的利润分配前两步计算出来各自的利润

○ Then apply commencement rules to joiners and cessation rules to leavers. 然后运用

各自的匹配原则(比如是开业原则或者停业原则)去计算各自的利润
  ○ Each partner has his or her own overlap profit, available for overlap relief.每个人有每个人的 overlap profit

Chapter 9

Benefit

General rule:

Taxable Benefit = cost to the employer of providing the benefit − payment by employee

(Time apportioned)

应税福利 = 老板为了提供福利支付的钱 − 员工为了享受福利支付的钱

1. Vouchers

taxable benefit = cost to the employer of providing the voucher. 不管代金券票面价值是多少，应税福利只算老板实际支付的成本

specifically exempt
$\begin{cases} \text{meal vouchers up to 15p/day 午餐券每天 15p 免税} \\ \text{wholly, exclusively and necessarily in the performance of employment} \\ \text{完全用于工作目的的 vouchers 是免税的} \end{cases}$

2. Living accommodation benefit 住房福利

1) Normal benefit

Higher of $\begin{cases} \text{Rent actually paid} \\ \text{Annual value} \end{cases}$

2) Additional benefit on expensive accommodation

If the cost of the accommodation > £75,000

Additional benefit = (cost of providing the accommodation − £75,000) × 2.5% × n/12

Note of "Cost":

❖ Cost = original cost (or M.V.) + Capital improvement prior to the start of current tax year 在 2019 年 4 月 6 日之前发生的资本性支出

❖ Capital expenditure:

usable: Initial installation, legal fee at acquisition

nature: Subsequent improvement: e.g. extension, construction of a new wall to split one room into two

❖ Purchase to provision > 6 years, use MV when first provided to the employee 房龄大于 6 年，用第一次给员工使用时候的市场价值

✧ Purchase to provision ≤ 6 years, use original cost 房龄小于6年，用房子的原始成本

3. Living expenses of accommodation

a) If it is **not job related**，如果住房和工作无关，老板支付的所有的住房费用就是职工应税福利

The full cost of living expenses paid by employer for employee is taxable benefit.

Runing cost：

○ Heating, lighting or cleaning the premises

○ Repairing, maintaining or decorating the premises

住房费用福利

房子的费用应该是谁住由谁承担，如果老板支付就算做员工福利，如果员工支付就不用了处理了。

b) If it is **job related** 如果住房和工作相关，那么住房费用的应税福利不能超过净收入的 10%

Taxable benefit is lower of $\begin{cases} \text{Actual running cost} \\ \text{Net earning} * 10\% \end{cases}$

Employment income（salary + benefits）   X

Less：occupational pension schemes   (X)

Less：allowable expenses (excluding these related expenses). (X)

Net earnings   <u>X</u>

4. Motor car benefits 汽车福利

Motor car benefits = A × a% × n/12 − Contribution for **use**（员工为了**使用汽车**支付给老板的钱）

公式里的 n 代表在 2020.4.6—2021.4.5 之间员工私人使用了多少个月

£

List price（before any discount）

X

Accessories cost

X

Capital contribution for purchase（max £5,000）   (X)   员工在**购买**时候支付给老板的钱

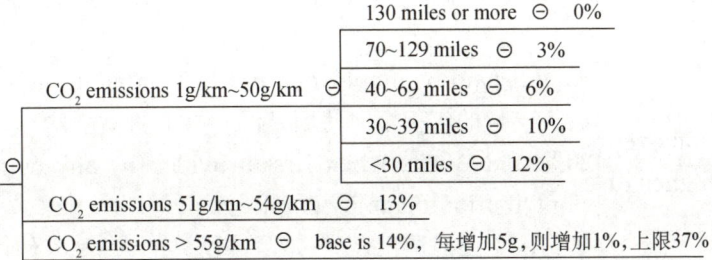

Van

○ If a van is made available for an employee's private use, taxable benefit on the van is £3,490 for a year.

○ If the fuel is also provided for the van, taxable benefit on the fuel is £666 for a year.

○ Time apportion is needed if not used for a whole year.

○ It is not taxable if employees only use the van for ordinary journey (from work to home)

Pool cars

Pool cars are exempt. A car is a pool car if all the following conditions are satisfied:

a) **It is used by more than one employee and is not ordinarily** used by any one of them to the exclusion of the others.

b) Any private use is merely incidental to business use.

c) It is not normally kept overnight at or near the residence of an employee

5. Company car fuel benefit 汽车燃油福利

Car fuel benefit = $24,500 \times a\% \times n/12$

Unlike most benefits, a reimbursement of private use does not reduce the benefit.

There will be a taxable benefit unless the employee reimburses full cost of private fuel.

如果员工没有把私人用途的全部油费补偿给老板，那么就要按照公式计算应税福利，如果只给一部分的话是不能抵扣应税福利的

6. Beneficial loan 贷款应税福利

Lower of $\begin{cases} \text{Average method: } (b/f + c/f)/2 \times 2.5\% \times n/12 - \text{interest paid} \\ \text{Accurate method: actual payable} \times 2.5\% - \text{interest paid} \end{cases}$

The interest benefit is not taxable if the total of all non-qualifying loans to the employee did not exceed £10,000 at any time in the tax year.

如果员工私人用途的借款没有超过£10,000，那么不用算贷款的应税福利

7. Private use of employer's assets 把老板的资产用于私人用途的福利

1) Use of assets

Benefit = higher of $\begin{cases} \text{Rental paid by employer} \times n/12 - \text{Contribution made by employee} \\ \text{老板支付的年租金} * \text{使用月份} - \text{员工的补偿款} \\ 20\% \text{ of MV the when first provided by any employee} \times n/12 - \text{Contribution made by employee} \\ \text{第一次给任意员工(不一定是该题目的人)私人使用时候的市场价值} \times 20\% \times \text{使用月份} - \text{员工的补偿款} \end{cases}$

Exception：first mobile phone，bicycles provided for journeys to work

2) Acquisition an asset

a）New：X = cost 送给员工的资产是老板新买的，那么购买成本就是应税福利

b）Acquisition the asset which previously be used by the employee 送给员工的资产是员工以前使用的，那么应税福利就是两者取高

Benefit = Higher of $\begin{cases} \text{Market value of acquisition} - \text{price paid by employee 老板购买时候的市场价值—员工补偿金} \\ \text{MV when first provided} - \text{amounts already taxed (ignore contribution by the employee)} (MV \times 20\%) - \text{price paid by employee 员工第一次使用的市场价值} - \text{已经计税的金额(市场价值} \times 20\%) - \text{员工补偿金} \end{cases}$

8. Other benefits

Exception：second-hand car & van

a）**Scholarships** given to members of an employee's family — taxable benefit is the cost to employer unless the scholarships fund is not more than 25% of total employment payment.

支付给员工家庭成员的奖学金：如果老板支付的奖学金金额没有超过员工全年收入的25%，那么免税；如果超过了，那么应税福利就是老板支付的钱

b）**Workplace childcare** is an exempt benefit.

c）Other benefits = **cost to the employer** of the benefits （VC）如果员工占用公司经营的产品，那么员工福利就是老板支付的变动成本

9. Exempt benefits

a）**Entertainment provided to employees** by genuine third parties （e. g. seats at sporting/cultural events），even if it is provided by giving the employee a voucher 给员工提供的娱乐活动是免税的

b）**Gifts of goods** from third parties，if the total cost （including VAT）of all gifts by the same donor to the same employee in the tax year is £250 or less. If the £250 limit is exceeded，the full amount is taxable

由第三方送给员工礼物，每个员工从同一个donor那获得的礼物每年不能超过£250，

如果一旦超过全额计税

c) **Non-cash awards for long service** if the period of service was at least 20 years, no similar award was made to the employee in the past 10 years and the cost is not more than £50 per year of service.

如果员工工龄超过 20 年, 发放给员工的奖励金额是 £50 乘以工作年限, 如果超过了, 超过的部分交税

d) The first £8,000 of **removal expenses** is exempt. 给员工的搬家费用 £8 000 是免税的, 如果超过 £8 000, 超过的部分交税

e) **Workplace childcare**

f) **Sporting or recreational facilities available to employees** generally and not to the general public

g) **Assets or services used in performing the duties of employment** provided any private use of the item concerned is insignificant. This exempts, for example, the benefit arising on the private use of employer-provided tools. 只针对员工开放的娱乐和运动设施是免税的

h) **Welfare counselling** and similar minor benefits if the benefit concerned is available to employees 给员工提供的福利咨询之类的福利是免税的

i) **Bicycles or cycling safety equipment** provided to enable employees to get to and from work or to travel between one workplace and another; 上班过程中提供的自行车和安全装备是免税的, 不包括从家去公司

j) Workplace parking 办公地点的停车费

k) Up to £15,480 a year paid to an employee who is on a **full-time course** lasting at least a year, with average full-time attendance of at least 20 weeks a year. If the £15,480 limit is exceeded, the whole amount is taxable 员工参加全日制培训的课程(一年至少 20 周)学费不超过 £15 480 是免税的, 一旦超过全额计税

l) **Work related training and related costs**; this includes the costs of training material and assets either made during training or incorporated into something so made 培训相关的成本免税

m) **Air miles or car fuel coupons** obtained as a result of business expenditure but used for private purposes

n) The cost of **work buses and minibuses** or subsidies to public bus services 班车费用或公共交通补助免税

o) **Transport/overnight costs** where public transport is disrupted by industrial action, late night taxis and travel costs incurred where car sharing arrangements unavoidably breakdown

p) The private use of **one mobile phone**, which can be a smartphone. Top up vouchers for exempt mobile phones are also tax free. 提供的第一个手机和月租费是免税的

q) Employer provided **uniforms** which employees must wear as part of their duties 工作制服是免税

r) The **cost of staff parties** which are open to staff generally provided that the cost per head per year (including VAT) is £150 or less; the £150 limit may be split between several parties 员工派对每人每年不超过£150是免税

s) **Private medical insurance premiums** paid to cover treatment when the employee is outside the UK in the performance of duties. eye tests and glasses for employees using Visual Display Units (VDUs)

t) **Cheap loans** that do not exceed £10,000 in the tax year (see above) 员工贷款额小于£10 000 免税

u) **Employer contributions towards additional household costs** incurred by an employee who works wholly or partly at home. Employers can pay up to £4 per week (or £18 per month to monthly paid employees). 需要在家办公的员工,每周£4或者每月£18的是免税

v) **Incidental overnight expense:** Overseas daily allowance up to £10 per night (£5 per night in the UK). If it exceeds, whole amount is taxable. 出差过夜补助,出国每晚£10,国内每晚£5

w) **Recommended medical treatment** costing up to £500 per employee per tax year paid for by an employer. The treatment must be recommended in writing by a health professional (e.g. doctor)

x) **Trivial benefits:** An exemption has been introduced for trivial benefits which do not cost more than £50 per employee provided these benefits are not cash or cash equivalent (e.g. A box of chocolate given to employee for xmas) 给员工的小礼物,低于£50是免税的

y) **Pensions advice** up to £500 per employee per tax year under certain schemes open to the employer's employees generally. If the payments exceed £500 in a tax year, the first £500 is exempt.

Chapter 10

Employment income

1. Proforma

个人薪酬收入组成部分

Salary	X
Bonus	X
Commission/tips	X
Add: Benefits in kind	X
Less: Allowable deductions	(X)
Employment income	**X**

2. Basis of assessment

1) General employee

入账时点判断,判断出来的时间如果在 2020.4.6 到 2021.4.5 之间才计入 2020/21 的 employment income

General earnings consisting of money are treated as received on the earlier of:

a) The time when payment is made 实际发工资的日期

b) The time when a person becomes entitled to payment 承诺发工资的日期

2) Director

Earliest of

a) The time when payment is made

b) The time when a person becomes entitled to payment

c) The date when the amount is credited in company account 董事薪酬计入公司账的日期

Bonus remuneration

Dr: employee remuneration
　　Cr: director account

d) Where earning are determined 确定董事薪酬的日期

○ Before the end of period: the end of period 如果确定日期在期末之前,那么期末日期作为确定日期

○ After the end of period: the date the earning are determined 如果确定日期在期末

之后，那么确定日期就是确定日期

　　e.g. 1. 1. 2017—31. 12. 2017 is accounting period

　　○ 25/12/2017 determined：取 31/12/2017

　　○ 1/2/2018 determined：取 1/2/2018

3) General earnings not in the form of money（ie benefits）are taxable when they are received by the employee. 职工福利的入账时点就是员工收到福利的那天

4) Pensions are taxed on the amount accruing in the tax year，whether or not it has actually been received in that year. 退休金是权责发生制，只看 2020. 4. 6 到 2021. 4. 5 一共收到多少退休金

3. Allowable deductions

a) Contributions to approved occupational pension scheme. OPS 在职人员保险

b) Employees make tax deductible donations to charity under the payroll deduction scheme. 从工资中直接抵扣的慈善捐赠

c) Subscriptions to professional bodies if relating to the duties of the employment. 和雇佣相关的职业会费

d) Travel expenditure 特定交通费可以抵扣

Home → Client　✓

Company → Client ✓

Client → Client　✓

Company's department 1→Company's department 2（the same company）✓

Home → temporary work place（≤24 months）✓

e) Wholly，exclusively and necessarily for performing the duties of the employment 只有完全用于雇佣目的的费用才可以抵扣，比如普通制服就不可以抵扣

4. Statutory approved mileage allowances

私车公用

○ Employee who uses their own car for business purposes will normally be paid mileage allowance by their employer. 私车公用税法上要求老板报销的金额按照以下计算

○ 0—10,000 miles，45p per mile

　　Up 10,000 miles，25p per mile

○ If the reimbursement is more than HMRC approved amount，taxable benefits are arisen. 如果老板实际补偿的金额大于税法规定，那么多出来的部分算应税福利

○ If business mileage is not reimbursed by employer（or the reimbursement is less than approved mileage allowances），employee can use the approved mileage allowance as a basis for an expense claim. 如果老板实际补偿的金额小于税法规定，那么差值可以抵扣员工收入

Chapter 11

National insurance contribution (NICs)

Self-employed	Employed (employee)
Class 2 NIC ○ **Class 2** are paid at a **flat weekly rate of £3.05/week** and the actual amount of class 2 NIC is based on the number of weeks of self-employment during a tax year ○ Exempted if annual taxable profits are less than the small profit threshold which is £6,475. 如果个体户的一年应税利润没有超过£6,475,可以免掉 Class 2 NIC ○ Class 2 NIC is payable under the self-assessment system and will be due on 31 January following the tax year. 缴纳 Class 2 NIC 的日期是 2021.1.31 (2019/20: 31.1.2021)	**Employee (Primary)** **Class 1** cash earnings (Gross) 现金的收入包含私车公用老板多给报销的部分,不包含 benefits Earnings (excluding benefits). Earnings also include payments for use of the employee's own car on business over the approved amount of 45p per mile. £1 — £9,500 per year　　　　Nil £9,501 — £50,000 per year　　12% £50,001 and above per year　　2%
Self-assessment	**Employer (Secondary)**
Based on tax adjusted trading profits after deducting trading loss. 基于调整后的营业利润(第三章学习)去计算 Class 4 NIC £1 — £9,500 per year　　　　Nil £9,501 — £50,000 per year　　9% £50,001 and above per year　　2% Class 4 NICs are paid at the same time as income tax under self-assessment ※ Class 4 NIC are based on the level of the individual profits. (BPP Q71) 和月份无关	**Class 1** £1 — £8,788 per year　　　　Nil £8,789 and above per year　　13.8% Employment allowance　　　£3,000 每个老板每年都有£3 000 的免征额,除非这个公司就老板一个人 **Class 1A** 13.8% on employee's taxable benefits (Taxable benefit * 13.8%) ○ Class 1A NIC is deductible expenses under employer's trading profit. 当作公司的运营费用抵扣公司的 trading profit ○ Due date: 19 July (by cheque) or 22 July (electronic payment) of the following tax year (2019/20: 21.7.22)

(Continued)

Occupational pension scheme(ops)→→Employee	Personal pension scheme→→anyone
只有员工才能上的职业养老保险	每个人都可以买的商业个人养老保险 如果题目中看到 Personal pension 字眼就从以下四个计算去考虑
1. Employer's contributions: deductible under **trading profit** 2. Employee's contributions: deductible under **employment income**	1. Gross up 100/80 2. Adjusted net income: Child benefit income tax charge & PA (Net income — PPS-GAD) 3. Extend tax band (Gross) 4. AA amount
Tax relief for contributions made by individual **Step 1**: Tax relief base is lower of M: gross pension made(PPC or OPC) (G) 获得减免额的基数A: Higher of 3,600 Relevant earning 英国政府为了避免个人不参与社会活动,仅靠投资收益给自己缴高额养老保险,并且还想获得国家20%的减免,所以做了这个决定,G 不能超过 relevant earning **Step 2**: Tax relief = G * 20% Actual paid = M - tax relief **Step 3**: Higher rate taxpayer: PPS extend tax band by G **Step 4**: Annual allowance charge calculation AA 用来限制每个人当年最多可以缴多少保险不交税,如果 PPS + OPS 的总额超过当年可用的 AA,那么多出来的部分算作 NSI,要按照 NSI 税率交税(annual allowance charge) ↓ (Gross PPS + OPS - Available Annual Allowance) non-saving income The non-saving income is taxed after taxable total income and charged at 20%, 40% or 45%	Relevant earning = taxable trading profit + employment income + furnished holiday letting profit (exclude property income) AA = 40,000 - (Adjusted income - 240,000)/2 ≥ 10,000 Adjusted income = Net income + employee OPS + employer OPS/PPS 1. carry forward any unused allowance for up to 3 years. 没用完的 AA 可以往以后年度带 3 年 2. The individual was a member of a registered pension scheme for that tax year 会员身份 3. AA for current year is used first, then AA from earlier years first 先用自己当年的 AA

Chapter 11 National insurance contribution (NICs)

(Continued)

Choice of business medium
An individual can choose between trading as a sole trader or trading through a company.

Sole trader	Company
○ Pay income tax on trading profit	○ Sole trader becomes director and shareholder of the company.
○ Pay Class 4 NIC on trading profit	○ Income is paid in form of director salary and dividends.
○ Pay Class 2 NIC	○ Company pays corporation tax on its taxable total profits.
	○ Director's salary and employer's class 1 secondary NIC is deductible in calculation of company's taxable profit.
	○ The remaining profit is paid to director in form of dividend.
	○ Director pays income tax and class 1 primary NIC on its salary.
	○ Director pays income tax on dividend income. There is no national insurance contribution on dividend income

Chapter 12 & 17

Self-assessment for individual & corporations

1. Self-assessment: Individual

1.1 Notification of liability to income tax and cgt 个税的纳税申报通知

Individuals who are chargeable to income tax or CGT for any tax year and who have not received a notice to file a return are required to give notice of chargeability to HMRC within six months from the end of the year.

当个人需要缴纳个人所得税或者资本利得税的那一年，如果没有收到税务局的纳税申报通知单，他要在这一年年末后的 6 个月内向税务局主动发通知

Behaviour	Maximum penalty	Minimum penalty with unprompted disclosure		Minimum penalty with prompted disclosure	
Deliberate and concealed	100%	30%		50%	
Deliberate but not concealed	70%	20%		35%	
		≥12 m	<12 m	≥12 m	<12 m
Careless	30%	10%	0	20%	10%

情节严重情况分为：粗心、故意不隐瞒、故意并隐瞒，补救方式又分为主动披露和非主动披露，如果有合理原因的粗心错误可以不用罚款

1.2 Time limits for submission of tax returns 提交纳税申报单

Non-electronic return Later of：

a) 31 October 2021

b) 3 months from the date of issue of return 税务局发出通知后的 3 个月

Electronic return Later of：

a) 31 January 2022

b) 3 months from the date of issue of return

Chapter 12 & 17 Self-assessment for individual & corporations

Penalties for late submission

Late Date	Penalties		
X≤3 months	£100		
3 months<X≤6 months	£100 + £10/day (max 90 days)		
6 months<X≤12 months	£100 + 900 + 5% of tax due (min £300)		
X>12 months	Not deliberate	100 + 900 + 5% of tax due (min 300) + 5% of tax due (min 300)	
	Deliberate but not concealment	100 + 900 + 5% of tax due (min 300) + 70% of tax due (min 300)	
	Deliberate with concealment	100 + 900 + 5% of tax due (min 300) + 100% of tax due (min 300)	

1.3 Keep records

Records must be retained until the later of:

➢ 5 years after the 31 January following the tax year where the taxpayer is in business (as a sole trader or partner or letting property). Note that this applies to all of the records, not only the business records, or

如果是个体经营户或者合伙人企业,这些记录保存5年

➢ 1 year after the 31 January following the tax year otherwise 公司职员的个税记录可以保存到这个税务年度后的1月31日再往后推1年

The maximum penalty for each failure to keep records is £3,000 per tax year.

1.4 Amendment of tax return & claim overpaid tax 修改纳税申报单和申请退回多支付的税款

a) Taxpayer can amend the return within 12 months of 31 January following the end of the tax year. 纳税人修改申报单的期限应该是22.1.31之后的12个月内

b) If an error is discovered at a later date then the taxpayer can make a claim for overpayment relief to recover any tax overpaid. The claim must be made within 4 years of the end of the tax year concerned. 如果纳税人发现以前的税多交了,可以从税务年末往前推4年把多交的税申请退回来

Penalties for incorrect returns

Type of error	Maximum	Minimum	
		Prompted	Unprompted
Careless	30% of PLR (potential lost revenue)	15% of PLR	0% of PLR
Deliberate not concealed	70% of PLR	35% of PLR	20% of PLR
Deliberate and concealed	100% of PLR	50% of PLR	30% of PLR

1.5 Payment of income tax and cgt

Date	Type	Base
31 January in the tax year	First payment on account	(Income tax + class 4 NIC)/2 for the previous year
31 July after the tax year	Second payment on account	(Income tax + class 4 NIC)/2 for the previous year
31 January after the tax year	Balancing payment	[Total income tax + Class 4 NIC − tax deducted at source (PAYE) payments on account] + CGT

1.6 Penalties for late payment 纳税晚了需要罚款

A penalty is chargeable where tax is paid after the penalty date. The penalty date is 30 days after the due date for the tax. Therefore no penalty arises if the tax is paid within 30 days of the due date. 如果交税日期是在罚款日之后缴纳的那么就要罚款了。罚款日是交税日后的第30天。

The penalty chargeable is:

Late Date	Surcharge
1 month < X < 6 months	5% of unpaid tax
6 ≤ X < 12 months	10% of unpaid tax
X ≥ 12 months	15% of unpaid tax

1.7 Interest on underpaid and overpaid tax 少交、晚交的滞纳利息和多交、早交的利息收入

Interest on underpaid tax is 3.25%. Interest on overpaid tax is 0.5%.

1.8 Compliance check enquiries 税务局的检查问卷

○ HMRC has the right (not need to give reason) to enquire into the completeness or accuracy of any return. 税务局有权力询问纳税申报单的完整性和准确性

○ Reason: Such an enquiry may be made on a complete random basis or a suspicion of under payment of tax due to tax payer's failure to comply with tax legislation. 有时候是随机的，有时候是怀疑有目的的

○ HMRC has a limited period within which to commence enquiries into a tax return. 税务局要在有限的期间内进行询问调查

The officer must give written notice of his intention by:

a) The first anniversary of the actual filing date, if the return was delivered on or before the due filing date, or 如果纳税申报单按时或者提前缴纳，那么应该是提交之后的1年以内进行询问

b) The quarter day following the first anniversary of the actual filing date, if the return is filed after the due filing date. The quarter days are 31 January, 30 April, 31 July and 31 October. 如果纳税申报单没有按时申报缴纳，那么应该是在提交之后的1年的季度日(1.31 4.31 7.31 10.31)

2. Self-assessment: Corporation

2.1 Notification of liability to corporation tax 企业税的纳税申报通知

A company that does not receive a notice to file tax return, must notify HMRC within 12 months of the end of the accounting period if it is chargeable to tax.

当公司需要缴纳公司所得税的那一年,如果没有收到税务局发的纳税申报通知单,公司需要在计税期间结束后的12个月内向税务局主动发通知

Behaviour	Maximum penalty	Minimum penalty with unprompted disclosure		Minimum penalty with prompted disclosure	
Deliberate and concealed	100%	30%		50%	
Deliberate but not concealed	70%	20%		35%	
		≥12 m	<12 m	≥12 m	<12 m
Careless	30%	10%	0	20%	10%

情节严重情况分为:粗心、故意不隐瞒、故意并隐瞒,补救方式又分为主动披露和非主动披露,如果有合理原因的粗心错误可以不用罚款

Notification of first accounting period 关于第一个计税期间开始的通知

➢ A company must notify HMRC of the beginning of its first accounting period (i.e. usually when it starts to trade) and the beginning of any subsequent period that does not immediately follow the end of the previous accounting period. The notice must be in the prescribed form and submitted within three months of the relevant date. 公司要给税务局发通知说他们的第一个计税期间,这个通知应该在开始之后的3个月内发出。

➢ Failure to notify, and provide information about, the first accounting period can mean penalty of £300 plus £60 per day the information is outstanding, and a penalty of up to £3,000 for fraudulently or negligently giving incorrect information. 如果没有按照要求通知,那么先罚£300,再加上每天£60直到通知税务局,如果是故意或者欺骗性质的罚款不能超过£3 000。

2.2 Time limits for submission of tax returns 提交纳税申报单

A return is due on or before the filing date. This is normally the later of:

a) 12 months after the end of the period to which the return relates;

计税期间结束后的12个月。

b) 3 months from the date on which the notice requiring the return was made.

发出纳税申报通知单的之后的3个月。

Penalties for late submission

Late Date	Penalties	Preceding two accounting periods was late
Failure to submit on time	£100	£500
>3 months but ≤6 months	£200	£1,000
>6 months but ≤12 months	£200 + 10% of the tax unpaid	£1,000 + 10% of the tax unpaid
>12 months	£200 + 20% of the tax unpaid	£1,000 + 20% of the tax unpaid

2.3 Keep records

Companies must keep records until the latest of:

a) 6 years from the end of the accounting period;

b) The date any enquiries are completed;

c) The date after which enquiries may not be commenced.

Failure to keep records can lead to a penalty of up to £3,000 for each accounting period affected.

2.4 Amendment of tax return & claim overpaid tax

a) Company can amend the return within 12 months of filling date. 公司修改日期应该是提交纳税申报单后的12个月内

b) If a company believes that it has paid excessive tax, for example as a result of an error in its tax return, a claim may be made within 4 years from the end of the accounting period. 如果公司发现以前的税交多了,可以从计税期间末往前推4年把多交的申请退回来

Penalties for incorrect returns:

Type of error	Maximum	Minimum	
		Prompted	Unprompted
Careless	30% of PLR (potential lost revenue)	15% of PLR	0% of PLR
Deliberate not concealed	70% of PLR	35% of PLR	20% of PLR
Deliberate and concealed	100% of PLR	50% of PLR	30% of PLR

2.5 Payment of corporation tax

1) Small and medium companies

Corporation tax is due for payment by nine months after the end of the accounting period 中小公司应该在计税期间解释后的第9个月缴纳企业所得税

2) Large companies

Large companies have to make quarterly installment payments of their corporation tax liability. 大公司要分期季度缴纳所得税

a) On the 14th of the 7, 10, 13, 16 months following the start of the accounting period. 在计税期间开始后的第7、10、13、16个月的14号缴纳企业所得税

b) If an accounting period is less than twelve months long, subsequent installments are due at three monthly intervals but with the final payment being due in the fourth month of the next accounting period. 如果计税期间不是 12 个月，那么就是每隔 3 个月交一次，最后一次交税是下个计税期间开始的第 4 个月的 14 号

c) Basis of payment is estimated corporate taxation for the current period. If tax is under estimated, it will incur interest charges. 季度缴纳金额按照当年预测金额，如果低估了，要交滞纳利息。

The amount of each installment is computed by: 3×(corporate tax/n)

n = No. of months in the period

What is a large company? 什么是大公司定义

a) Paying the full rate of corporation tax at the current year and the previous year: Augmented profit (profit for the year) excess £1,500,000. 要连续两年利润都超过 £1,500,000

b) This limit is reduced where a company has associates. 门槛 £1,500,000 会受到计税期间长度和联属公司数量的影响而减少

c) Installments will not be due if the tax liability is less than £10,000. 如果预计当年的企业所得税小于 £10,000，那么可以不用季度分期付款

d) A company is not required to pay installments in the first year that it is 'large', unless its profits exceed £10 million (reduced proportionately if there are associated companies) 新成立的公司如果第一年利润超过了 £10 million，那么也直接认定为大公司

2.6 Interest on underpaid and overpaid tax

Interest on underpaid tax is 2.75%. Interest on overpaid tax is 0.5%.

2.7 Compliance check enquiries

○ HMRC has the right (not need to give reason) to enquire into the completeness or accuracy of any return.

○ Reason: Such an enquiry may be made on a complete random basis or a suspicion of under payment of tax due to tax payer's failure to comply with tax legislation.

○ HMRC has a limited period within which to commence enquiries into a tax return. The officer must give written notice of his intention by:

a) The first anniversary of the actual filing date, if the return was delivered on or before the due filing date, or

b) The quarter day following the first anniversary of the actual filing date, if the return is filed after the due filing date. The quarter days are 31 January, 30 April, 31 July and 31 October.

Chapter 13 & 14

Corporation tax

1. The UK resident 判断企业是否是英国的先看注册地,再看集中管理控制权是否在英国	
Place of incorporation 公司注册地	Corporation tax treatment
UK	Treated as resident in the UK for corporation tax purposes
Overseas	Only treated as resident in the UK if its central management and control is exercised in the UK

2. Accounting period		
Financial year (FY)	Period of account (POA)	Chargeable accounting period (CAP)
1st April — 31st March	会计期间经营长度	计税期间
仅用于政府规定税率,对于计算不太影响	>or <or = 12 months	<or = 12 months

3. Layout of a corporation tax computation 和 Chapter 2 对比去记忆		
Adjusted Trading profit（accrual）	X	Chapter 3, Chapter 5
Property business income（accrual）	X	Chapter 6
Interest income（accrual）指和 trading 无关的利息收入（见下表）	X	
Miscellaneous income（accrual）	X	
Chargeable gains（after against capital loss current year and b/f）(receipts) 抵减完当年和以前年度资本亏损的净资本利得额	X	Chapter 18, Chapter 19
1. Less: property business loss 房租亏损(当年/以前)	(X)	个人：property loss 只能递减 property income
2. Less: trading loss relief against total profit 营业亏损(当年/以前)	(X)	
3. Less: qualifying charitable donation (GAD) (payment) 慈善机构捐赠	(X)	个人：GAD 不可以递减 total profit
4. Less: group relief 集团减免	(X)	

Chapter 13 & 14 Corporation tax

(Continued)

3. Layout of a corporation tax computation 和 Chapter 2 对比去记忆		
Taxable total profit	X	用来 * tax rate 计算企业所得税
Add： Franked Investment Income（FII）	X	收到的控股小于 50% 公司分的 dividend income 写在此处，如果是控股大于 50% 的公司分的 dividend income 就不能写在此处
Augmented profit	X	用来判断 tax payment 方式，不参与计算税

4. Company VS Individual/Partnership 公司和个人的抵扣费用对比		
Items	Company	Individual or partnership
Private expenses	There is no adjustment to profits needed for private expenses met by the company 公司没有私人用途这个概念	Add back private used expense by sole trader
Salary paid	There is no adjustment to salary paid to director by company 付给公司里的董事薪酬也是税法允许抵扣的	Add back sole trader's salary and excessive salary paid to family member
Trading loan interest	Allowable deducted from trading income	Allowable deducted from total income
Dividend paid	Be not allowable as a trading expense in the calculation of its trading income 发放给股东的股利不能抵扣公司的利润	No dividend paid
Dividend received	Dividend received from non-group companies（<50%）：determined tax payment 如果收到控股比例小于 50% 的公司的 dividend，仅仅用来决定税率	Dividend income
	Dividend received from non-group companies（>=50%）：not be chargeable for tax 如果收到控股比例大于等于 50% 的公司股份，不需要交税	
Capital allowance	Not have private used asset pool 没有私人用途这个概念	Private used asset pool
	AIA/WDA * n/12（n<=12 months）	AIA/WDA * n/12（n<=>12 months）
Property business loss 房租亏损	（1）First set off against non-property income and gains of the company for the current period；and any excess is，先抵扣非房租收入， （2）Carried forward for set off against future income（of all descriptions）如果还有亏损再抵扣未来其他收入	（1）First set off against property income for the current period；and any excess is，先抵扣当年的房租收入 （2）Carried forward for set off against future property income 如果还有亏损再抵扣未来房租收入

(Continued)

Interest paid on a loan to buy or improve property 为了买房或者improve 房子产生的借款利息	Not a property business expense	Be a property business expense
Interest income/expense（non-trading）和 trading 无关的利息收入和支出	Interest charged on underpaid tax and interest received on overpaid tax is assessable under non-trading loan relationship. 比如公司没有按时交税的滞纳利息和提前交税的利息收入，这些都是和 trading 无关的，自己单独罗列一列收入	
GAD（gift aid donation）	Deducted when computing Taxable total profits.	Extend tax band or ANI influence

5. Tax rate

Rate of tax — Financial Year 2019	19%	
— Financial year 2018	19%	
— Financial year 2017	19%	
Profit threshold —用来衡量大小公司的门槛	£1,500,000	当 augmented profit 大于 threshold 的时候，需要季度分期交税
Corporation tax 企业所得税计算公式	Taxable total profit * tax rate	
Profit threshold is reduced in 2 circumstances：	£1,500,000 * N/12	N = Chargeable accounting period 计税期间的长度
门槛会被两种情况影响	£1,500,000 * 1/n+1	n = No. of related 51% group companies 集团拥有联属公司的数量

Chapter 16

Group relief

1. Definition of 75% group 满足条件
   a) One company is a 75% subsidiary of other, or
   b) Both companies are 75% subsidiary of a third company
   c) Each level at least 75% 直接控股要至少75%
   d) Effective holding at least 75% 间接控股要至少75%
   e) Group can be created through companies resident anywhere in the world, but companies actually claiming/surrendering group relief must be resident in UK. 如果想互相抵扣亏损,必须母子公司都是英国的。
   f) Group relief is not restricted according to the percentage of shareholding. 集团的税务减免不受控股比例的影响,只要控股满足75%以上就可以全额互相减免。

2. Current period group relief
   ○ The surrender company is the **loss making** company. 产生亏损的公司
   ○ The claimant company is the company to which the loss is surrendered. 接受亏损的公司(盈利的公司)
   The losses that can be group relieved are:
   — Trading losses 营业亏损
   — Excess property business losses 当年没有抵扣完的房租亏损
   — Excess qualifying charitable donation 当年没有抵扣完的慈善机构捐赠
   ○ Trading loss can be group relieved **any amount** and there is **no requirement** of the surrendering company to relieve the trade loss against its own profits first. 当期的营业亏损递减顺序不受限制,不用先用自己当年的收入去递减,然后剩下的给集团其他公司用。
   ○ Qualifying charitable donations and property income losses can only be group relieved to the extent that they exceed total profits before taking account of any losses of the current period or brought forward or back from other accounting periods. 但是当期慈善机构的捐赠和房租亏损必须要先递减自己当期的利润,如果还有剩余再给当期集团其他公司用。
   ○ Excess qualifying charitable donations should be surrendered **before** excess property business losses. 当期没有抵扣完的慈善机构捐赠一定要先抵,然后再抵当期没有抵扣完的

房租亏损。

　　○ A claimant company is assumed to use its own current year losses. 接受亏损的公司假设已经抵扣完了自己当期的所有亏损。

3. Carry forward group relief

1) Transfer of carried forward loss

A company which has a loss carried forward (the surrendering company) may transfer all or part of this loss to another member of the 75% group (the claimant company).

2) The claimant company

The claimant company must use its own losses to the fullest extent possible in working out the available taxable total profits against which it may claim carry forward group relief.

先用自己的全部 loss,如果还有剩余可以用 carry forward group relief。

3) The surrendering company

The surrendering company may surrender carried forward trading losses and/or property business income losses to other group companies under carry forward group relief.

trading loss 和 property loss 都可以给集团内公司使用。

4. Correspond accounting period 交叉区间（画图很重要）

　　○ If the accounting periods of the two companies do not match, the profits and losses must be time apportioned.

　　○ If a company joins or leaves a group, group relief is only available for the corresponding accounting period (i.e. When both companies have been a member of the same group) 只有两个公司重合的区域才可以互相抵扣亏损。

5. Factors consider when making a choice

a) How quickly relief will be obtained: Group relief is quicker than carry forward loss relief　时效性。越快越好,今年大于明年。

b) The extent to which relief for qualifying charitable donations might be lost:

—— Group relief is deducted after qualifying charitable donations in the claimant company, so QCD is not lost.　不浪费捐赠抵扣,当年一定要能抵多少都抵,因为 QCD 是不可以往以后年度带的

—— By contrast, if the loss-making company claims loss relief against its own current year total profit QCD in that company may be wasted.

6. Chargeable gain group

1) Definition of chargeable gain group

a) At each level, at least direct holding of 75%, this only applies to ordinary share capital. 直接控股原始股超过 75%

　　b) Effective holding more than 50%. 间接控股 50%

　　c) Holding company is must.

2) Transfer of assets within the group

○ When a group company transfers an asset to another group company, there is a transfer of no gain/no loss basis. 集团企业之间互相转移资产，no gain no loss。

○ Two companies can elect that an actual sale of the asset outside the group made by one company is deemed to be made by another company. 只有当资产被处置到集团外的时候才交税，a 公司处置的资产可以视同 b 公司处置的资产。

○ The election has to be made within 2 years of the accounting period in which the asset is sold outside the group. 集团公司要在处置以后的两年内向税务局申请。

Note: only current year capital loss can be transferred, not brought forward losses.

注意：只有当年处置资产产生的亏损可以视同是集团其他公司的，以前年度的亏损不能给其他公司用。

3) Advantage of transfer of assets within the group 集团内部转移的好处

○ Plan to maximize the use of its capital loss as early as possible by matching chargeable gains with capital losses. 最大限度地使用 capital loss。

○ Without having to make actual transfer of an asset, there will be savings in legal and administrative costs. 不是真正意义上的实际转移，所以节省了很多行政法律费用。

4) Roller relief

a) Members of a 75% group are treated as one for the purposes of rollover relief and all trades carried out on by the members of the group are treated as a single trade.

b) It means that a gain on a disposal by one group member can be rolled over against a qualifying reinvestment made by another group company.

如果 a 公司处置了一个资产，b 公司作为同集团的联属公司，在 a 处置前的 1 年或者之后 3 年购买了一个 business asset，那么他们视同是一个公司，所以也可以联合申请 RR。

Chapter 18 & 19

CGT for individual and corporation

Individual		Company	
Not part of income tax		Part of taxable total profit	
Sales proceeds	X	Sales proceeds	X
Less：acquisition cost	(X)	Less：acquisition cost	(X)
Less：allowable expenditure	(X)	Less：allowable expenditure	(X)
		Less：indexation allowance	(X)
Less：relief（business relief，PPR，letting relief）	(X)	Less：relief（business relief）	(X)
Less：chargeable loss in current year	(X)	Less：chargeable loss in current year	(X)
Less：unrelieved trading loss against CG（as much as possible）	(X)		
Less：chargeable loss b/f（restricted to keep AE）	(X)	Less：chargeable loss b/f	(X)
Chargeable gain	X		
Less：AE	−12,300		
Taxable gain	X	Chargeable gain (Taxable gain)	X
CGT @10% OR 20% on taxable gain			

个人和公司在计算 CGT 时候最本质的区别：

a）个人的资本利得税单独计算，公司需要合并在企业所得税中计算

b）个人在计算资本利得税的时候有 annual exemption 的减免，公司没有

c）个人在计算资本利得税的时候没有 indexation allowance，公司需要计算

d）个人在处置房子时候有很多 relief 可以用，比如（PPR，letting relief，ER，IR），公司只有 business relief

e）处置股票的顺序不一样

Chapter 18 & 19　CGT for individual and corporation

1. Disposal 处置

1.1　The date of disposal 处置日期在哪个计税期间，就在哪个期间算资本利得税

a) Normal：the date when the contract for sale is made 签合同的日期

b) Conditional contract：the date when all conditions are satisfied 条件合同完成的日期

c) The date legal title passes, or physical possession is obtained, or the date payment is made, is irrelevant. 和货物是否实际转移，和是否货款没有关系

1.2　Sale proceeds 处置价格

It is the proceeds of sale of the asset, but a disposal is deemed to take place at market value：以下三种情况要用处置资产时候的市场价值作为处置价格

a) Where the disposal is not a bargain at arm's length 不是公平公允的

b) Where the disposal is by way of a gift 赠与形式

c) Where the disposal is made for a consideration which cannot be valued 不能有明确对价的处置

1.3　Acquisition cost 资产成本

a) Purchase price if bought 如果处置的资产是买的，那么购买价格就是成本

b) Market value of asset if gifted 如果处置的资产是别人赠与的，那么当时赠与的市场价值就是成本

c) Probate value if acquired on death 如果处置的资产是遗产继承的，那么经过遗嘱认证的价格就是成本

1.4　Allowable expenditure 允许抵扣的费用

a) Incidental cost on acquisition/disposal of the asset：valuation fees, estate agency fees, advertising costs, legal costs 资产购买和处置的时候发生的一些费用

b) Establish, preserve or defend the company's title to the asset 为了获得这项资产所产生的资本性支出

c) Enhancement expenditure：capital costs of additions and improvements to the asset reflected in the value of the asset at the date of disposal, such as extensions, planning permission and architects fees for extensions. 一些资本性支出费用可以直接反映出资产的价值变化

It exclude any expenditure deducted from trading profit. 从 trading profit 中抵扣的费用就不能在此抵扣了

AE（annual exemption）for 2020/21 is ￡12,000

Payment of CGT：2020/21→→31.01.22 交税日期

○ The rate is linked to level of a person's taxable income. 资本利得税率受 taxable income 的影响。

○ Taxable gains are taxed after taxable income. 资本利得额要累加在 taxable income 之后。

○ The basic rate band is extended by Personal Pension Contribution and Gift Aid Donation.

○ Where a person has residential property gain and other gains, then annual exemption and capital loss should initially be deducted from the residential property gains. AE 和 capital loss 要先抵扣住房处置的资本利得。

Rate of tax	Normal rate	Residential property
Fall within basic rate band	10%	18%
Exceeds basic rate band	20%	28%

2. The following are exempt assets. 免税资产
- Motor vehicles suitable for private use
- National Savings and Investments certificates and premium bonds
- Gilt-edged securities（treasury stock）
- Qualifying corporate bonds（QCBs）
- Certain chattels
- Investments held in new individual savings accounts（NISAs）

3. Transfers between spouses/civil partners 夫妻之间转移资产，视同没有转移，no gain no loss

a）Disposals between spouses or members of a civil partnership are made on a no gain no loss basis.

b）Spouses and civil partners are taxed as separate individual. Each has his own annual exemption，and losses of one spouse or civil partner cannot be set against gains of the other spouse or civil partner. Annual exemption 不能在夫妻之间转移，各用各的

c）Tax planning　在做税收筹划的时候，为了家庭利益最大化，要考虑以下三点
Maximize the use of：
a）Each individual's AE 不要浪费各自的 AE
b）each individual's basic rate band 考虑每个人的税率档，尽量把资本利得额放在低收入人群中去计算
c）Capital loss is used for which one 每个人把自己 capital loss 用完，不要浪费

4. Part disposals
Part cost：

Total cost　※　Market value of disposal part（处置部分的市场价值）
　　　　　　　　Market value of disposal part + Market value of remaining part（处置部分的市场价值 + 剩下部分的市场价值）

5. The damage, loss or destruction of an asset
1）Destruction or loss of an asset　资产被破坏，收到保险公司的赔偿

a）If an asset is destroyed any compensation or insurance monies received will normally be brought into an ordinary CGT disposal computation as proceeds. 如果资产破坏，公司收到保险赔偿金，视同部分处置

b) If all the proceeds are applied for the replacement of the asset within 12 months, any gain can be deducted from the cost of the replacement asset. 如果公司用所有赔偿金在12个月内购置了替换资产，那么我们不能视同部分处置，资本利得额可以抵扣新资产的成本（处理方法类似 roller relief）

Insurance compensation	x
less：Original cost	(x)
Gain	x1
Replacement asset cost	x
less：gain	(x1)
Base cost	x

2）Damage to an asset

a) If an asset is damaged then the receipt of any compensation or insurance monies received will normally be treated as a part disposal.

如果资产破坏，公司收到保险赔偿金，视同部分处置，处置价值就是当时收到的赔偿金

Insurance compensation	x
less：Original cost	(x)
Gain	x

b) If all the proceeds are applied in restoring the asset the taxpayer can elect to disregard the part disposal. The proceeds will instead be deducted from the cost of the asset.

如果公司用赔偿金维修了这个资产，那么可以不视同部分处置，再重新评估该资产的时候，赔偿金可以抵扣原成本

Original cost	x
Less：insurance compensation	(x)
Add：restoration cost	x
Base cost	x

6. Chattles 动产

Useful life ＜50 years (Wasting assets)	Movable (Chattel)	Solution
YES	YES	Wasting chattel—no gain, no loss
NO	YES	Non-wasting chattels—6,000 rules
YES	NO	Wasting assets—depreciate over time
NO	NO	Normal capital gain

1）Wasting chattles

例外：if P&M is sold for a loss, no capital loss is computed. (Balance charge is computed) If P&M is sold for a gain, follow non-wasting chattel rule. 如果机器设备在处

置中产生了 gain, 那么计算 CGT 遵循 non-wasting chattles(6,000 rules)

2) Non-wasting chattels

	Cost ≤ 6,000	Cost > £6,000
Sales ≤ 6,000	Exempt 免税	6,000-cost
Sales > 6,000	CG is lower of 5/3 × (gross proceeds − £6,000) 正常计算	正常计算

3) Wasting assets

○ A wasting asset is one which has an estimated remaining useful life of 50 years or less and whose original value will depreciate over time. (copyrights and registered designs)按照直线折旧法去计算成本

The cost is written down on a straight line basis, and it is this depreciated cost which is deducted in the computation.

7. Principal private residence relief (PPR)

1) The actual occupation periods

2) The last 9 months of ownership

3) Deemed occupation→→前后都有实际居住

a) 任意原因最多 3 年

b) 出国出差所有期间

c) 在英国境内出差最多 4 年

Principal private residence relief (PPR)

Step 1: Total period of ownership

Step 2: Period of occupation = A + B + C (a + b + c)

Step 3: PPR = Total gain × $\dfrac{\text{Period of occupation}}{\text{Total period of ownership}}$

Step 4: letting relief is lowest of:

a) PPR

b) Gain * period of letting/period of ownership

c) £40,000 (Maximum)

Step 5: Chargeable gain = Gain − PPR − letting relief

8. Entrepreneurs' relief 企业家减免

8.1 Conditions for entrepreneurs' relief

a) Assets qualifying 有资格的资产(不包含投资)

A disposal of a business or part of a business by a sole trader or partnership. And relief is only available in respect of gains on business asset. This will exclude chargeable gains arising from investments.

b) The individual has at least a 5% shareholding in the company 个人至少控股 5%

Chapter 18 & 19   CGT for individual and corporation

c) The individual is an officer or employee of the company 个人在公司工作

d) Provided the company is a trading company or holding company of trading group. 公司是一个正在经营的公司

e) The above three qualifying conditions must be met prior to the date of disposal is 2 years. 以上条件都要在处置资产之前满足两年

8.2 Operation of ER

a) CGT = Taxable gain * 10%

b) 判断税率的时候，要先累计 taxable income，然后是可以申请 ER 的 CG，最后是不可以申请 ER 的 CG

c) The annual exemption and any capital losses should be initially deducted in the following order：AE 的递减顺序

— Gain on residential property（18% or 28%）

— Gain not qualifying for ER（10% or 20%）

— Gain qualifying for ER（10%）

d) Entrepreneurs' relief covers the first £10 m of qualifying gains that a person makes during their lifetime.

e) The relief must be claimed within 12 months of the 31 January following the end of the tax year in which the disposal is made. For a 2019/20 disposal，the taxpayer must claim by 31 January 2022.

9. Rollover relief 投资者减免

9.1 Conditions

a) Qualifying assets

○ Land and buildings that are both occupied and used for trading purposes

○ Fixed P & M

○ Goodwill（company goodwill is not a qualifying asset）

b) 前一后三，在处置旧资产之前的 1 年或者处置后的 3 年，购买了替换资产

c) The old asset sold and the new asset bought are both used only in the trade.

9.2 Operation of RR

Step 1: Old asset capital gain

Old asset sale	1,200
Less：Old asset cost	−200
Old asset gain	1,000
Less：roller relief (balance)	100
Chargeable gain	0
(old asset sales− new asset cost)	(1,200−1,800)

Step 2: Base cost

New asset cost	1,800
Less: roller relief	−100
Base cost	800

Step 3: New asset capital gain

New asset sales	3,500
Less: base cost	−800
Chargeable gain	2,700

9.3 Depreciating asset

— Where the replacement asset is a depreciating asset, the gain is not rolled over by reducing the cost of the replacement asset. Rather it is deferred until it crystallizes on the earliest of:

a) Disposal of the replacement asset

b) Ceases to be used for trading purposes

c) 10 years after the asset was acquired (maximum)

10. Gift relief (holdover relief)

10.1 Conditions for gift relief:

Assets qualifying

○ Business assets. (The asset needs only be a qualifying business asset in the hands of the donor)

○ Unquoted shares in a trading company 非上市股票

○ Quoted shares in a personal trading company ($>5\%$)

If an individual gives away a qualifying asset, the transferor and transferee can jointly claim within 4 years of the end of the tax year of the transfer. 捐赠者和受赠方要在4年内向税务局申请 GR

10.2 Operations of GR

Step 1: Donee's Chargeable gain

MV	200
Less: cost	−30
Gain	170
Less: Gift relief(balance)	−150
Chargeable gain (actual received- cost)	50 − 30 = 20

Chapter 18 & 19 CGT for individual and corporation

Step 2: Donee's Base cost

MV	200
Less: Gift relief	−150
Base cost	50

Step 3: Donee's capital gain

Sales proceed	195
Less: base cost	−50
Chargeable gain	145

10.3 Shares GR

Where the gift is shares in personal trading company, and the company has chargeable non-business assets, the relief is restricted to:

Gift relief = Gain * the market value of the chargeable business assets (CBA)

the market value of the chargeable assets (CA)

CA(chargeable assets): CBA: freehold/lease hold + goodwill,

CNBA: shares, securities and other asset held for investment

Exempted asset: motor cars, stocks, debtors, cash

11. Investor's relief

a) Relief has now been extended to gains on disposal of qualifying shares by external investors (other employee and officer of the company) of unquoted trading company.

b) In order to qualify for relief, a share must: 满足条件

○ Newly issued shares acquired by subscription 新认购的股票

○ be in an unlisted trading company 非上市的营业公司

○ have been issued by the company on or after 17 March 2016 and have been held for a period of at least three years from the date of the issue of the shares until the date of disposal. 在16.3.17当年或者之后发行的股票，并且从股票发行到股票处置期间至少大于3年

○ Individual must not be an employee or officer of the company. 处置方不能是公司的员工或者董事

c) The investors' relief has its own separate £10 m lifetime limit, with qualifying gain being taxed at 10%. 直接税率10%

d) An individual must claim investors' relief by the first anniversary of 31 Jan following the end of the tax year of disposal.

For a 2020/21 disposal, the taxpayer must claim by 31 Jan 2023. 个人申请这个relief 要在处置股票的这个税务年度后的1月31日再往后推一年，比如是是在2020/21处置的，

那么申请应再改为 2022.1.31

12. Shares and securities

All shares and securities disposed by an individual are subject to capital gain tax except for the followings：处置以下股票免税
- The government list security（gilt-edged securities and gilts）
- Qualifying corporate bonds（company loan notes）
- Shares held in ISA

Valuing quoted shares

If shares are not disposed at market value，then the market value need to be calculated. 如果处置股票的时候不是用的市场价值，那么我们要用平均法估算出市场价值作为处置价值
- Quoted shares are valued at mid-price based on the day's quoted price.
- For example，if shares are quoted at £5.10 — £5.18，then the value per share to be used is £5.14（£5.10+£5.18)/2）.

The matching rules for individual：

a) Shares purchased on the same day as the disposal

b) Shares purchased within the following 30 days（FIFO）

c) Shares in the share pool

Matching rules for company：

a) Shares acquired on the same day as the sale

b) Shares acquired during the 9 days before the sale（FIFO）

c) Shares in the share pool

Indexation allowance = Cost × Indexation factor

The indexation allowance has been frozen at December 2017.

Cost：acquisition cost，incidental costs，enhancement cost

2017 年 12 月份以后购买的资产都不计算 IA

Operative events
股票数量和价值同时发生变化

Not operative events

Acquisition
Disposal
Right issue
Bonus issue
Reorganization
Takeover

Chapter 20

VAT

1. Classification of supplies

Supplies outside the scope of VAT

Exempt supplies: not register with HMRC and cannot recover input VAT

Taxable supplies   Zero rated: 0 output VAT = 0 (register with HMRC, recover input VAT)   Reduced rated: 5%
                      Standard rated: 20%

The following are items on the exempt supplies：免征增值税的项目

a) Financial services

b) Insurance

c) Public postal services provided by the Royal Mail under its duty to provide a universal postal service (e.g. first and second class letters)

d) Betting and gaming

e) Certain education and vocational training

f) Health services

g) Sale of freeholds of buildings (other than commercial buildings less than 3 years old) and leaseholds of land and buildings.

The following are items on the zero-rated list：零税率的项目

a) Human and animal food

b) Sewerage services and water

c) Printed matter used for reading (e.g. books, newspapers)

d) Construction work on new homes or the sale of the freehold of new homes by builders

e) Transport of goods and passengers

f) Drugs and medicines on prescription or provided in private hospital

g) Clothing and footwear for young children and certain protective clothing, e.g. motor cyclists' crash helmets

2. Registration

2.1 Compulsory registration 强制注册

1) Historical test 历史测试

a) 站在月末看之前 12 个月的 cumulative taxable supplies (excluding VAT and capital asset) exceeds £85,000. (e.g. exceed limit on 31 March)

b) Notify HMRC within 30 days of the end of the month in which the £85,000 limit is exceeded. (by 30 Apr.) 发现超过 limit 那天往后推 30 天以内通知税务局

c) HMRC will then register the person with effect from the end of the month following the month in which the £85,000 was exceeded,(by 1 May.) 税务局正式注册是在下个月月初

d) A trader need not register if his taxable supplies for the next 12 months are expected to be less than the deregistration limit currently £83,000. 尽管之前 12 个月的累计收入已经超过 £85,000,但是如果预测未来 12 个月收入没有超过 £83,000,可以暂时先不注册

2) Future test 未来测试

a) 站在今天看未来 30 天的 taxable supplies (excluding VAT) exceed £85,000. (e.g. Expected limit exceed on 1 Mar)

b) Notify HMRC within 30 days notified by the end of the 30 day period. (by 30 Mar)

c) Registration will be with effect from the beginning of that period. (by 1 Mar)

2.2 Voluntary registration 自愿注册

A business may decide to voluntarily register for VAT where taxable supplies are below the £85,000 registration limit. 如果累计收入没有超过 85,000 也可以注册

Advantages:

a) The business makes zero-rated supplies. Output VAT will not be due but input VAT will be recoverable. 如果从事的零税率业务,注册后销项税不用交,还能获得进项税抵扣

b) The business makes supplies to VAT registered customers. Input VAT will be reclaimed. 如果客户是增值税纳税人,那么进项税可以抵扣

c) Imposes discipline on the business to keep accurate records. 强制企业保存正确的入账记录

d) Lends credibility to a business 增强企业的可信任度

Disadvantage

a) When customers are members of the general public, since such customers cannot recover the output VAT charged. If selling prices cannot be increased, the output VAT will become an additional cost for the business. 当你的客户是普通大众的时候,他们所交的增值税没有办法抵扣。如果销售价格不增长,那么销项税就成为企业额外的负担了。

b) Adds to administrative costs. 增加行政成本

A decision whether or not to register voluntarily may depend upon

a) Whether or not output VAT can be passed on to customers 销项税能不能转给下家

b) The status of the outputs and the image of the business the trader wishes to project 企业的形象目的

c) The administrative burden of registration 注册后的行政成本

2.3 Group VAT registration

2.3.1 Conditions:

a) Common control (such as a parent company and its subsidiary companies) and each of them is resident in the UK. 有共同控制关系的公司(50%)才可以申请集团注册。

b) Single company registered for VAT on its own. 集团所有公司视同一个独立的增值税个体。

c) Representative company is then responsible for completing and submitting a single VAT Return and paying VAT on behalf of the group. 代表公司有责任对纳税申报单的完整性和提交负责，然后代替集团支付增值税。

d) However, all the companies in the VAT group remain jointly and severally liable for any VAT liabilities. 集团内所有的公司有联合责任。

2.3.2 Advantages of group VAT registration

a) There is no need to account for VAT on goods and services supplied between group members. 集团公司之间互相买卖东西不用计算增值税。

b) It is only necessary to complete one VAT return for the whole group, so there should be a saving in administrative costs. 集团就填写一张纳税申报单，降低了行政成本。

3) Disadvantages of group VAT registration

Cash and annual accounting schemes, will apply to the VAT group as a whole rather than on an individual company basis. 集团不能享受一些中小型企业的特殊优惠政策。

2.4 Pre-registration input tax 注册之前的进项税可以在注册的时候抵扣回来

VAT incurred before registration can be treated as input tax and recovered from HMRC subject to certain conditions.

2.4.1 Pre-registration goods, the following conditions must be satisfied.

购入货物满足以下两个条件。

a) The goods must have been acquired for business purposes and not sold or consumed prior to registration. 产品适用于公司用途并且再注册的时候还没有消费掉。

b) The goods were acquired in the 4 years prior to VAT registration. 注册之前4年内购入的产品。

2.4.2 Pre-registration services, the following conditions must be satisfied.

购入服务满足以下两个条件。

a) The services must have been supplied for business purposes. 这个服务是用于公司目的。

b) The services were supplied in the 6 months prior to VAT registration. 注册之前6个月内购物的服务。

3. Deregistration

3.1 Voluntary deregistration 自愿注销

a) Taxable supplies (net of VAT and excluding supplies of capital assets) in the following one year period will＜￡83,000（from 1 April 2019）。预测应税收入在未来一年不超过 83,000。

b）HMRC will cancel a person's registration from the date the request is made or from an agreed later date. 税务局会取消你的 VAT 身份从你申请那天或是两者协商更晚的一天。

3.2 Compulsory deregistration 强制注销

a）A trader who no longer makes taxable supplies may be compulsorily deregistered. 公司不再进行增值税项目的时候要强制注销

b）HMRC must be notified within 30 days，and deregistered from the date of cessation，or from an agreed later date. 税务局要在 30 天以内被通知，注销从停止经营那天或者协商的更晚的一天。

3.3 The consequences of deregistration

VAT charge is made on a deemed supply of trading stock and capital assets on which input VAT has been recovered. Output tax is then paid on the deemed supply. If the amount of output VAT is ￡1,000 or less，it does not have to be paid. 如果仓库里的货物已经在购买的时候都已经抵扣进项税了，那么在公司注销增值税身份后，要视同仓库里的所有产品都已经视同销售了，如果小于 1 000，可以不用管。

3.4 Transfer of a going concern

The transfer of a business as a going concern is outside the scope of VAT.

4. Accounting for and administering VAT

4.1 VAT periods

a）The VAT period is the period covered by a VAT return. It is usually three calendar months. 每个季度缴纳增值税。

b）The return shows the total input and output tax for the tax period and must be submitted（along with any VAT due）within1 month of the end of the period. 在每个季度结束后的 1 个月内报税交税。

4.2 Online filing

File VAT returns online and pay any VAT is by electronically. The deadlines for doing this are extended by seven days. （2020.1.1—2020.3.31：2020.5.7）如果是电子申报时一个月＋7 天。

4.3 Refunds of VAT

Where it is discovered that VAT has been overpaid in the past，the time limit for claiming a refunds is 4 years to the beginning of current VAT period. 如果发现以前的增值税交多了，那么可以从这个季度初往前推 4 年内将多交的增值税要回来。

4.4 The tax point 纳税时点，看在哪个季度就在哪个季度计算增值税

The VAT rules that determine the tax point in respect of a supply of goods，and a supply of services.

a）The basic tax point is the date on which goods are removed or made available to the customer or the date on which services are completed. 基本纳税时点是货物转移的日期或者客户可用的日期或者服务完成的日期。

b) Payment received before the basic tax point：actual tax point is the date of payment. 如果客户付款的日期早于基本纳税时点，那么实际纳税时点就是付款日期。

c) Invoice issued before the basic tax point：actual tax point is the date of invoice. 如果开具发票的日期早于基本纳税时点，那么实际纳税时点就是开发票日期。

d) Invoice issued within 14 days after basic tax point：actual tax point is the date of invoice. 如果开发票日期是在基本纳税时点后的 14 天以内，那么实际纳税时点就是开发票日期。

5. Calculation of VAT

VAT Computation

Output VAT

1 Sales（discounts taken into account）	x
4 Sales of Motor cars	x
5 Fuel costs（partially private-use）	x

Input VAT

2 Purchase and expense	x
2 Material for own use or gift	(x)
3 Entertaining for overseas customers	x
3 Entertaining for employees	x
4 Purchase Motor car	x
5 Motor expenses	x
6 Impaired debts（over 6 months）	(x)
VAT payable/repayable	x

1) **Sales discount**

Output VAT is charged on the actual amount received if a discount is offered for prompt payment.

2) **Purchase and expenses** 只有公司用途的费用才能抵扣进项税

○ goods and services are for business purpose. A VAT invoice is needed to support the claim.

○ Input VAT cannot be claimed in respect of goods or services that are not used for business purposes.

3) **Entertaining** 只有招待员工和海外客户的娱乐费用才能抵扣进项税

Input VAT cannot be recovered in respect of business entertainment.

VAT incurred on staff entertaining and entertaining overseas customers is recoverable.

4) **Motor car**

○ If a car is used wholly for business purposes，the input tax is recoverable，then output VAT must account for if the car is subsequently sold. 只有100%用于公司目的的汽车才能申请进项税返还,在日后变卖的时候计入销项税

- VAT on partly privately used car
  — The purchase of the car:no input VAT
  — The sale of the car:no output VAT
  — Leased car,50% of input VAT is recoverable 如果是租赁的车有私人用途,那么租车费用的50%可以申请进项税返还
- If a car is used for business purposes then any VAT charged on repair and maintenance costs can be treated as input tax. 公司用途的汽车,其修理费和维护费都可以申请进项税返还

(5) Car fuel

- Fuel for business use by employees:input VAT is fully recovered
- Fuel for private use by employees:

Step 1:Reclaim all input VAT

If employee has not paid private fuel to employer:output VAT based on scale charge

Step 2:

If employee has pay private fuel to employer:output VAT based on reimbursed amount

6) Impaired debts

Relief for impairment losses is only available if the debt is over 6 months old. As measured from the time that payment was due to the ending date of VAT period.

从该季度末往前推6个月,6个月以前的坏账可以申请进项税返还

6. VAT invoices and records

6.1 VAT Invoices

A taxable person must supply a VAT invoice within 30 days of supply, and must keep a copy. 要在销售后的30天以内开具增值税发票,并且要保存附件,增值税发票上面包含的内容如下图所示。

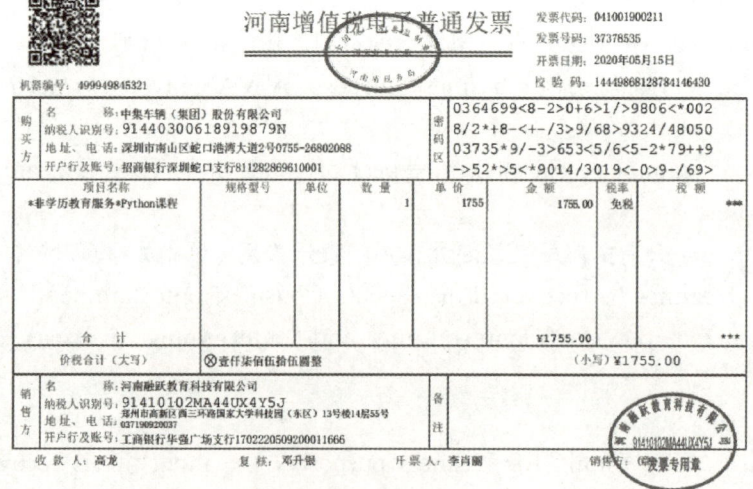

6.2 VAT Records

Every VAT registered trader must keep records for six years 增值税纳税人至少保存发票6年

7. Penalties

7.1 Penalties for late 晚了就罚款

A default occurs when a trader either submits his VAT return late, or submits the return on time but pays the VAT late. 增值税申报晚了或者交税晚了,两者只要有一个发生,就算过错。

The notice specifies a surcharge period running from the date of the notice to the anniversary of the end of the period for which the trader is in default. 第一次犯错不罚款,只是从你犯错那天往后一年是你的监督期,如果在这一年监督期内,你又犯错了,就按照犯错次数按比例罚款

Default involving late payment of VAT in the surcharge period surcharge as a percentage of the VAT outstanding at the due date

First	2%,小于400免掉
Second	5%,小于400免掉
Third	10%,要大于等于30
Fourth or more	15%,要大于等于30

7.2 Penalties for errors

a) Errors on a VAT return not exceeding the greater of:
- £10,000 (net under-declaration minus over-declaration)
- 1% × net VAT turnover for return period (maximum £50,000)

b) If errors on a VAT return not exceeding it, the errors may be corrected on the next return. 如果错误没有超过以上取高者,那么这个错误可以在下次纳税申报时候修改过来

c) If error is large, then penalty will apply (disclosure will reduce the penalty) 如果错误超过了,那么就要有罚款

	Unprompted	Promoted	No disclosure
Disclosure disclosure Careless	0%	15%	30%
Deliberate not concealed	20%	35%	70%
Deliberate and Concealed	30%	50%	100%

7.3 Interest on unpaid VAT (default interest)

少交或交晚了罚 3.25%

多交或早交了奖 0.5%

8. Special schemes

8.1 The cash accounting scheme 现金计税法

The cash accounting scheme allows a business to account for VAT on the basis of cash paid and received, rather than on invoices received and issued. 只以现金收入和现金

支出计算增值税。

1) Required 条件

a) A business can apply to use the cash accounting scheme if its expected taxable supplies (excluding VAT and supplies of capital items) for the next 12 months does not exceed £1,350,000. 预计未来12个月应税收入没有超过£1,350,000。

b) The business must be up to date with her VAT returns and VAT payments. 纳税申报单和税款都要按时申报和缴纳。

c) Businesses already in the scheme may continue to use it until the value of taxable supplies in the previous 12 months exceeds £1,600,000. 公司可以一直用现金计税法去计算增值税直到累计收入超过£1,600,000。

2) Benefits

a) Output VAT does not have to be accounted for until payment is received. 直到收款才计入销项税。

b) Automatic bad debt relief since no output VAT is payable if payment is not received. 坏账自动过滤。

However, input VAT cannot be recovered until the business has actually paid the supplier for purchases. 进项税也只能等到实际付款的日子才能申请进项税返还。

3) Disadvantage

Not suitable for the business with a lot of cash sales or zero-rated supplies which would suffer a delay in the recovery of input VAT. 不适合都是现金销售的公司或者销售的货物都是零税率的。

8.2 The annual accounting scheme

1) Operations

○ The annual accounting scheme allows a business to submit one VAT return a year; This is use within two months of the end of the year. 一年报一次税，在这一年结束后的第二个月月末。

○ Normally 9 payments on account of the VAT liability for at end of months 4 to 12 of the year. Each payment represents 10% of the VAT liability for the previous year. 一般要在这一年开始后的第4个月到第12个月交9次预付款，每次付款金额是去年增值税的10%，最后一次交税是在这一年结束后的第2个月月末，多退少补。

2) Required

a) its expected taxable supplies (excluding VAT and supplies of capital items) for the next 12 months does not exceed £1,350,000.

b) Businesses already in the scheme may continue to use it until the value of taxable supplies in the previous 12 months exceeds £1,600,000.

c) The business must be up to date with VAT payment. 公司按时交税就可以。

3) Benefits

a) The resulting reduced administration should mean that default surcharges are avoided in respect of the late submission of VAT returns. 减少了犯错的次数，以前一年交

Chapter 20 VAT

4次,4次都要严格监管,现在虽然是交10次,但是前9次都是预交,交少了交晚了都不罚款。

b) One additional month to complete the annual return and make the balancing payment. 还额外多了一个月去计算这一年的增值税。

c) The payments on account are normally based on the previous year's VAT liability. This will improve both budgeting, and possibly, where a business is expanding. 前面的9次预交有助于企业做预算。

4) Disadvantage

○ Timing of payments has less correlation with the turnover by the business. 其实预交的税费和当年的销售额相关性有点差。

8.3 Flat rate scheme

1) Operations

A flat rate * VAT inclusive turnover (includes exempt supply, taxable supplies and supplies of capital assets). And there is no deduction for input VAT. 只算销项税(特殊方式)不递减进项税。

The business will issue tax invoices using the normal rules e.g. standard rate, zero rate. It does not have to keep records of the input VAT on individual purchases. 公司一旦用这种方式计税,就不用了保存进项发票了。

2) Required

a) A business can apply to use the flat rate scheme if its expected taxable supplies (excluding VAT) for the next 12 months does not exceed £150,000. 企业预计未来12个月内的应税销售额没有超过£150,000。

b) In addition, the expected total income (inclusive of VAT and including exempt supplies) for the next 12 months must not exceed £230,000. 如果未来没有超过£230,000就还可以继续用这个scheme。

3) Benefits

a) Reduction in the burden of administration of preparing the VAT return as no records of input VAT need be kept. 降低成本(因为计算简单了)。

b) Frequently less VAT payable to HMRC than under the normal rules. 比常规方法计算税要少一点。

c) Especially for those whose customers are not VAT registered, there will be no need to issue VAT invoices. 特别适合客户是普通大众的,这样也可以不用开具增值税发票了。

9. Overseas aspects

Outside EU   Export：Zero-rated

Import：
↓
HMRC hold goods at point of entry into UK
↓
Input VAT paid on value of goods imported
↓
Input VAT deductible on nest VAT return

Dispatch within EU:

If UK supplier has VAT No. of EU recipient: Zero-rated

If UK supplier has no VAT No. of EU recipient: Charge UK local VAT rate

Acquisition within EU:

UK trader accounts for output VAT at point of acquisition
↓
Treated as input VAT (provided tax invoice issued by supplier)
↓
VAT neutral

Chapter 21

IHT

1. Definition

1) A person who is domiciled in the UK is liable to IHT in respect of their worldwide assets. All of a person's estate is generally chargeable to IHT. 在英国定居的人要针对全球的资产交遗产税。

2) Transfer and gift

3) Donor and donee

4) Transfer of value（diminution in value）在 donor 手里损失的价格（参考讲义例题）

5) PET（Potentially Exempt Transfer）：

○ PET is a lifetime transfer made by an individual to another individual. 去世前的转移,个人给个人。

○ A potentially exempt transfer（PET）is exempt from IHT when made and will remain exempt if the donor survives for at least seven years from making the gift. PET 在捐赠的时候不交税,如果捐赠 7 年后去世,那么去世的时候也不交税。

○ If the donor dies within seven years of making the PET, the transfer will become chargeable to IHT. 如果在捐赠 7 年内去世,要交 IHT。

○ However, the value of a PET is fixed at the time that the gift is made. PET 在捐赠时候的价值就是日后计算遗产税的价值。

6) CLT（Chargeable Lifetime Transfer）

○ CLT is a lifetime transfer by an individual（e.g. a gift to trustees）which is not an exempt transfer. 生前捐赠,不是捐赠给个人。

○ A chargeable lifetime transfer（CLT）is immediately chargeable to IHT when made. 捐赠的时候就要交税（预交）。

○ An additional tax liability may then arise if the donor dies within seven years of making the gift. 捐赠的 7 年内去世,确定应该交税总金额。

○ Just as for a PET, the value of a CLT is fixed at the time that the gift is made. CLT 在捐赠时候的价值就是日后计算遗产税的价值。

7) Nil rate bands：Seven-year accumulation（2019/20：325,000）

IHT is a cumulative tax. This means that you need to look back seven years from the date of a chargeable transfer to see whether some or all of the nil rate band has been used up by gross chargeable transfers in that seven year accumulation period. 七年内的累计减免额。

8) AE（Annual Exemption）

○ The first £3,000 of value transferred in a tax year is exempt from IHT.

○ Any unused portion of the annual exemption is carried forward for one year only. 当年没有用完可以带到下一年，只能带1年。

○ The annual exemption is used only after all other exemptions. AE 是最后的抵减项。

○ If several gifts are made in a year, the £3,000 exemption is applied to earlier gifts before later gifts. 如果这一年有很多捐赠，AE 要按照时间顺序抵扣。

○ AE of current year is used first. AE 要先用自己当年的，再用上一年的。

9) Other exemptions before AE

a) Transfers to spouses 夫妻之间转移 100% 免税

b) Small gifts exemption 250 磅以下的小礼物赠与免税，一旦超过，全额征税

Outright gifts to individuals totaling £250 or less per donee in any one tax year are exempt. If gifts total more than £250 the whole amount is chargeable.

c) Gifts in consideration of marriage 婚礼礼金赠与

○ £5,000 if from a parent of a party to the marriage/civil partnership 父母一方是 £5,000 免税

○ £2,500 if from a remoter ancestor (grandparent) or from one of the parties to the marriage/civil 爷爷奶奶一方是 £2,500 免税

○ £1,000 if the gift is made by anyone else 其他人是 £1,000 免税

If gifts exceed the limit, only the excess amount is chargeable 如果赠与的前超过以上限额，超过的部分才交税

2. Tax rate

PET	Gift：0
	If the donor dies within 7 years：**40%**
CLT	Gift：Trust/Donee paid： **20%**
	Donor paid：**25%**，如果题目中没有说谁支付，默认 donor 付
	If the donor dies within 7 years：**40%** — paid IHT in lifetime transfer (if have any)

3. Taper relief

Years before death 捐赠资产距离去世的时间	Percentage reduction %
Over 3 but less than 4 years	20
Over 4 but less than 5 years	40
Over 5 but less than 6 years	60
Over 6 but less than 7 years	80

4. Computation format（画图很重要）

a) 标注去世日期和往前推 7 年的日期
b) 标注生前捐赠的日期, 金额和税率
c) 标注 NRB of gift & NRB of death（£325,000）对应金额
d) 标注每一笔捐赠的 taper relief 金额

口诀：

Step 1：Lifetime transfer

1

Gross	IHT	Net
（donor 总损失）	（donor 净损失）	transfer of value

1. If IHT is paid by donee/trust：Gross = Net
2. If IHT is paid by donor：Gross = IHT + Net

```
        AE              当 N                    看 7
        Transfer to spouses
        Small gift exemption           看这笔 CLT 之前 7 年内
        Gift on consideration of marriage   有没有要交税的 CLT 被
        AE（current year and last year）    捐赠当年 NRB 所 cover
```

Step 2：Additional liability arising on death

算去世前 7 年内的 CLT/PET 在去世时候需要再交多少税（小旗子到小牌子之间的捐赠）

　　　　　　　　　　　　　　2　　　　　　　五　　　　　　看 7

Gross	IHT	Taper relief	IHT paid	IHT payable
CLT (step 1)	working	%	Step 1	x
PET	working	%	0	x

NRB on death ＋ transfer of NRB between spouses

看这笔 CLT/PET 之前 7 年内有没有要交税的 CLT/PET 被去世那年的 NRB 所 cover

Step 3：Death estate 算去世时候遗产需要交多少税

　　　　　　　　3　　　　　　　一　　　　　　　　死 N　　　看 7

Death estate	X
Less：Allowable deduction	(X)
Less：Spouses exemption	(X)
Gross chargeable estate	X
Less： NRB available on death	(X)
Less： additional residence NRB	(X)
Taxable amount	X

NRB on death ＋ transfer of NRB between spouses

看这笔去世之前 7 年内有没有要交税的 CLT/PET 被去世那年的 NRB 所 cover

5. Tax liability on death estate

A person's estate includes the value of everything which they own at the date of death such as:

a) Property, shares, motor vehicles, cash, investments

b) Proceeds from life assurance policies even though these proceeds will not be received until after the date of death. The actual market value of a life assurance policy at the date of death is irrelevant. 只关注保险合同上的金额，不考虑市场价值。

The following deductions are permitted:

a) Funeral expenses 葬礼

b) Debts due for valuable consideration (Gambling debts cannot be deducted) (i.e. illegal debt or oral promise not deducted) 有明确的对价的债务才可以，口头的不行

c) Mortgages on property. This does not include endowment mortgages. Repayment mortgages and interest-only mortgages are deductible 房屋抵押

d) Outstanding tax (income tax and capital gain tax) 欠税

Additional NRB：

Additional NRB has been introduced for main residence inherited on death by direct descendants (children &grandchildren). 如果是把住房捐赠给自己的直系亲属，只包含父母或者祖父母，可以额外有￡150,000 的 NRB

— For tax year 2020/21 the residence nil rate band is 175,000.

— Residence nil rate bands is also transferable between spouse (or registered civil partner) 夫妻之间可以互相转移

6. Payment of IHT

Type	Date	Who paid
Life time transfers	Later of a) 30 April following the end of the tax year in which the gift is made b) 6 months from the end of the month in which the gift is made	a) Donors b) Trust c) Donees
Additional liabilities arising on death	6 months after the end of the month in which the donor died	donee
Death estates	Earlier of a) 6 months after the end of the month in which the donor died b) The personal representatives deliver their account of the estate assets to HMRC	Personal representative

7. Advantages of lifetime transfers 去世之前转移的好处

Lifetime transfers are the easiest way for a person to reduce their potential IHT liability.

a) A PET is completely exempt after seven years. 如果在捐赠 7 年后去世，PET 可完全免税，因为捐赠时候不交税，去世后也不交税。

b) A CLT will not incur any additional IHT liability after seven years. 如果在捐赠 7 年后去世，CLT 只在捐赠的时候交税，去世后不用再交税了。

c) Even if the donor does not survive for seven years, taper relief will reduce the amount of IHT payable after three years. 即使不是捐赠 7 年后去世的，生前捐赠还可以有 taper relief。

d) The value of PETs and CLTs is fixed at the time they are made, so it can be beneficial to make gifts of assets that are expected to increase in value such as property or shares. 对于一些未来会升值的资产（比如房子和股票）在生前捐赠的时候就已经锁定当时捐赠时候的价格作为遗产税的计算基础。

8. Transfer of a spouse's unused nil rate band

○ If one spouse or civil partner does not use up the whole nil rate band on death, the excess may be transferred to the surviving spouse/civil partner. 如果夫妻中一方去世没有用完 NRB，可以转移存活的一方。

○ The amount that can be claimed is based on the proportion of the NRB not used when the first spouse died. 转移的是比例不是具体金额，先计算转移比例，然后用存活的一方在去世时候的 NRB 基数×转移比例。

○ Changes in nil rate band between deaths of spouses/civil partners

For example, if the nil rate band at B's death was £300,000 and B had an unused nil rate band of £90,000, the unused proportion in percentage terms is therefore 90,000/300,000 × 100 = 30%. If A dies when the nil rate band has increased to £325,000, B's unused nil rate band is £325,000 × 30% = £97,500 and this amount is transferred to increase the nil rate band maximum available on A's death.

9. Basic inheritance tax planning

○ Use exemptions 尽量用所有的减免额
○ Make gifts early in life 越早捐赠越好
○ Make use of the nil rate band 尽量多用 NRB
○ Skip a generation 隔辈转移资产

FINANCIAL REPORTING

Chapter 1

The conceptual framework

1. The objective of general purpose financial reporting

The objective of general purpose financial reporting is **to provide information** about the reporting entity that is useful **to existing and potential** investors, lenders and other creditors **in making decisions** about providing resources to the entity. 目的一定是帮助信息使用者进行决策！

2. Accruals basis＝matching

The effects of transactions and other events are **recognized when they occur**（and not as cash or its equivalent is received or paid）and they are **recorded in** the accounting records and reported in the financial statements of **the periods to which they relate**. 权责发生制＋配比原则（收入与成本费用的配比）

3. The qualitative characteristics of financial information

Fundamental characteristics：

1）Relevance

Relevant information is capable of making a difference in the decisions made by users.

It will be regarded as being relevant if it has either **predictive value and/or confirmatory value** to a user.

The relevance of information is affected by its **nature and its materiality.**（重要性的判断一定要从金额和性质两个方面去进行分析）

2）Faithful representation

Financial information must **faithfully represent the phenomena** that it purports to represent.

a）**Complete：** includes **all information necessary** for a user to understand the phenomenon

b）**Neutral：without bias** in the selection or presentation of financial information.

c）**Free from error：** there are **no errors or omissions** in the process of producing financial statements. It does not mean that no inaccuracies can arise, particularly where estimates have to be made.（并不是一定没有误差,尤其是存在会计估计的地方误差的确可能会出现。）

Substance over form 实质重于形式（并不是一个单独的信息质量特征,信息质量特征有且仅有6个。）

This is not a separate qualitative characteristic under the Conceptual Framework，it is implied in faithful representation.Faithful representation of a transaction is only possible if it is accounted for according to its substance and economic reality.（只有反映了经济实质才能做到"faithful representation"）

Enhancing characteristics

3) Comparability 可比性

Compare and contrast［different entities in the same industry(横向比)；One entity in different years(纵向比)］

Consistency 一致性 of methodology, approach or presentation helps to achieve comparability of financial information from period to period within a reporting entity or in a single period across entities.

4) Verifiability 可验证性

Different，knowledgeable and independent observers could reach consensus，although not necessarily complete agreement.

5) Timeliness 及时性

Timeliness means having information available to decision-makers in time to be capable of influencing their decisions. Generally，the older information is the less useful it is.

6) Understandability 可理解性

Classifying，characterizing and presenting information clearly and concisely makes it understandable.

Financial reports are prepared for users who have a reasonable knowledge of business and economic activities and who review and analyse the information diligently.（但是也得是有专业知识水平的人才能够理解）

4. The cost constraint（成本效益问题)on useful financial reporting

When information is provided，its benefits must exceed the costs of obtaining and presenting it.（做什么事都要权衡下成本效益,效益必须要大于成本才去做。)This is a subjective area and there are other difficulties：others, not the intended users，may gain a benefit；also the cost may be paid by someone other than the users. It is therefore difficult to apply a cost-benefit analysis，but preparers and users should be aware of the constraint.（但实际上很难去进行成本效益分析)

5. The elements of financial statements

Elements	Recognized in	Definition	Key point
Asset	Statement of financial position	A resource controlled by an entity as a result of past events and from which future economic benefits are expected to flow to the entity	(1) Future economic benefit (The potential to contribute, directly or indirectly.)（不一定是经济利益的直接流入，也可能是减少经济利益的流出。） (2) Control, not reliant on Physical form nor Legal rights（控制，一定是根据实质来进行判断，而不是依据表面形式或者法律形式上的所有权来进行判断。）
Liability	Statement of financial position	A present obligation of the entity arising from past events, the settlement of which is expected to result in an outflow from the entity of resources embodying economic benefits	(1) Obligation: A duty or responsibility to act or perform in a certain way. Obligations may be legally enforceable or constructive obligation.（可以是法定的义务或推定的义务） (2) Provision: A present obligation which satisfies the rest of the definition of a liability, even if the amount of the obligation has to be estimated.（with uncertain timing or amount）
Equity	Statement of financial position	The residual interest in the assets of the entity after deducting all its liabilities	The amount shown for equity depends on the measurement of assets and liabilities. It has nothing to do with the market value of the entity's shares.（所有者权益为资产—负债的净额，与公司股价无关！）
Income	Statement of profit or loss	Increases in economic benefits during the accounting period in the form of inflows or enhancements of assets or decreases of liabilities that result in increases in equity, other than those relating to contributions from equity participants	Gains（利得）: Increases in economic benefits. As such they are no different in nature from revenue（本质上跟收入没什么区别，但是利得通常指的是一些资产利得，比如 gain on revaluation）
Expenses	Statement of profit or loss	Decreases in economic benefits during the accounting period in the form of outflows or depletions of assets or incurrences of liabilities that result in decreases in equity, other than those relating to distributions to equity participants	Losses（损失）: Decreases in economic benefits. As such they are no different in nature from other expenses.（本质上跟费用没什么区别，但是损失通常指的是一些资产损失，比如 loss on disposal）

Recognition of the elements of financial statements：同时满足下列条件，上述要素才能在报表中进行确认：
(1) meets the definition of an element（满足相关要素的定义）
(2) It is probable that any future economic benefit associated with the item will flow to or from the entity（经济利益很可能会流入或流出）
(3) The item has a cost or value that can be measured with reliability（成本或价值能够可靠计量）

(Continued)

Measurement of the elements of financial statements(财务报表要素的计量标准)：
(1) **Historical cost 历史成本 (This is the most commonly adopted measurement basis 这是最常用的计量标准)**
Assets are recorded at the amount of cash or cash equivalents paid or the fair value of the consideration given to acquire them **at the time of their acquisition**.
Liabilities are recorded at the amount of proceeds **received in exchange for the obligation**（当时借的钱是多少就是多少）, or in some circumstances（for example，income taxes），at the amounts of cash or cash equivalents **expected to be paid**（但也有可能是计算预计的数字，比如递延所得税负债）to satisfy the liability in the normal course of business.
(2) **Current cost 现行成本(≠重置成本)**
Assets are carried at the amount of cash or cash equivalents that would have to be paid **if the same or an equivalent asset was acquired currently**
Liabilities are carried at the **undiscounted amount**（注意是不折现的金额）of cash or cash equivalents that would be required to settle the obligation **currently**
(3) **Realizable (settlement) value**
The amount of cash or cash equivalents that **could currently be obtained by selling an asset in an orderly disposal**.（其实就是**可变现净值**的概念）
＝selling price-estimated to complete-cost necessary to make the sale
The **undiscounted amounts**（也是不折现的金额）of cash or cash equivalents expected to be paid to satisfy the liabilities in the normal course of business.
(4) **Present value 现值**
A **current estimate of the present discounted value of the future net cash flows** in the normal course of business

Chapter 2

The regulatory framework

1. Principles-based versus rules-based systems

a) A principles-based system works within a set of laid down **principles**.（原则导向性）

The Conceptual Framework **provides the background of principles** within which standards can be developed. This system is intended to ensure that standards are not produced which are in conflict with each other and also that any departure from a standard can be judged on the basis of whether or not it is in keeping with the principles set out in the Conceptual Framework.（说白了就是在原则的范围内做自己的就好了。）

b) In the absence of a reporting framework，a more **rules-based** approach has to be adopted.

This leads to a large mass of regulation **designed to cover every eventuality**，as in the US.（有非常详细并且力争完善的具体规则，严格按照每条规则去做。）

2. Advantages and disadvantages of IFRs

ADVANTAGES	DISADVANTAGES
A business can present its financial statements on the same basis as its foreign competitors, making comparison easier	The cost of implementing IFRS（运用成本较高）
Cross-border listing（跨国上市）will be facilitated, making it easier to raise capital abroad	The lower level of detail in IFRS（都是一些原则性的概念，详细度并不高）
Companies with foreign subsidiaries will have a common, company-wide accounting language	The principles-based standards in IFRS requires the application of judgement and give more defence（需要的主观判断较多）
Foreign companies which are targets for takeovers or mergers can be more easily appraised	

3. Setting of international financial reporting standards

Step 1：During the early stages of a project，the IASB may establish an Advisory Committee to give advice on issues arising in the project. Consultation with the Advisory

Committee and the IFRS Advisory Council occurs throughout the project.（首先 IASB 和咨询委员会先沟通）

Step 2：IASB may develop and publish Discussion Papers for public comment.（公布在网站上，集合意见，形成讨论意见稿）

Step 3：Following the receipt and review of comments, the IASB would develop and publish an Exposure Draft for public comment.（Normally 90 days）（在讨论意见稿的基础上形成征求意见稿）

Step 4：Following the receipt and review of comments, the IASB would issue a final International Financial Reporting Standard（复核修改，再进行发布）

IAS 16

Property, plant and equipment

1. Definitions

Property, plant and equipment are tangible assets that:

a) are **held for use** in the production or supply of goods or services, for rental to others, or for administrative purposes

b) are expected to be used during **more than one period**

2. Recognition

The recognition of property, plant and equipment depends on two criteria:

a) It is probable(可能性大于 50%)that **future economic benefits** associated with the asset will **flow to** the entity

b) The **cost** of the asset to the entity can be **measured reliably**

3. Measurement

Once an item of property, plant and equipment qualifies for recognition as an asset, it will **initially be measured at cost**(初始计量是历史成本计量). Cost includes **all costs necessary to bring the asset to working condition for its intended use**.(初始计量的成本是为使资产达到预定可使用状态的所有必要的支出)

1) Components of costs(成本所包含的内容)

➤ **Purchase price**, **less any trade discount or rebate**(扣除 trade discount 后的净额,cash discount 别扣)

➤ **Import duties and non-refundable purchase taxes**(进口关税和不可抵扣的增值税进项税额)

➤ **Directly attributable costs** of bringing the asset to working condition for its intended use(比如 Site preparation cost 场地整理费)

➤ Initial delivery and handling costs(运输装卸费)

➤ Installation costs(安装费)

➤ Testing (testing costs whether the asset is functioning property 为了测试这个资产是不是可以用的必要的测试费)

➤ Professional fees

➢ **Borrowing costs in accordance with IAS 23 Borrowing Costs.**（满足资本化条件的借款费用）

➢ **Present value** of future clean-up costs if the entity has an obligation to incur such costs（**dismantling and removing**）（需要折现计入的环境恢复成本）

2）Excluding cost（成本不包含的内容）

➢ Administration and other general overhead costs（企业的管理费用）

➢ Abnormal costs（self-constructed asset）（管理不善导致的非正常损耗）

➢ Start-up and similar pre-production costs（开办费用）

➢ Initial operating losses before the asset reaches planned performance（达到管理层认为应有业绩前所发生的亏损，此时这个资产已经可以使用了，所以需要费用化而不是资本化）

All of these will be recognised as an expense rather than an asset.

4. Subsequent expenditure

1）Capital expenditure 资本化支出

Subsequent expenditure on property, plant and equipment should only be **capitalized if it improves** the asset beyond its originally assessed standard of performance.（必须是 improve 的话才是资本化，比如增加产量、提高效率、降低成本、延长使用年限等等。）

2）Revenue expenditure 费用化支出

All other expenditure incurred to **maintain the economic benefits** originally expected should be expensed in SPL.（只是维持资产原状的话，就是费用化，比如 repair，只是维修维持原状）

3）Exchanges of assets（非货币性资产交换）

IAS 16 specifies that exchange of items of property, plant and equipment, regardless of whether the assets are similar, **are measured at fair value**.（非货币性资产交换，通常按照公允价值计量，没有公允价值，才用账面价值）

4）Complex assets — separate components 大型、复杂的资产的单独组成部分

These are assets which are **made up of separate components. Each component is separately depreciated over their useful life**.（这种情况一定要注意每一个组成部分要单独计提折旧，比如飞机的各个组成部分）

5）Major inspection or overhaul costs（大修费用）

Satisfying the IAS 16 rules for separate components, such costs should be **capitalized separately** as a non-current asset and depreciated over their useful lives

5. Depreciation

1）Definition

Depreciation is the **systematic allocation** of the **depreciable amount（cost — residual value）** of an asset **over its useful life**.

It is in essence a cost allocation process in compliance with the **accruals/matching** principle. （收入成本费用配比原则的体现）Each accounting period must bear a charge for depreciation to reflect the usage of the asset and benefit it helps to generate.

Depreciable amount is the **cost of an asset less its residual value**.

All assets with a **finite useful life must be depreciated**. **Land** has no finite life, therefore **excluded from depreciation**. （土地别提折旧！）

Depreciation **must be charged from the date the asset is available for use**. This may be earlier than the date it is actually brought into use（资产一定要在达到预定可使用状态时就开始计提折旧，并不一定是实际投入使用。比如在实际投入使用前，资产已经达到预定可使用状态，但是需要对员工进行培训才能使用，那折旧应当从资产达到预定可使用状态时就开始计提。）

Depreciation is continued even if the asset is idle. （即使是资产闲置期间资产也要折旧）

2) Depreciation methods

a) Straight line：Annual depreciation = (Cost − Residual value)/useful life

b) Reducing balance：Annual depreciation = Carry amount * depreciation rate

3) Changes in useful life or method

The useful lives of assets or depreciation method should be **reviewed at least at each financial year-end** and, if there has been a significant **change in the expected pattern of economic benefits** from those assets, the **method should be changed** to suit this changed pattern.

When a material change becomes necessary, the depreciation charge for the **current and future periods should be adjusted**. （未来适用法，不进行追溯调整。）

Change of useful life or method is a **change in accounting estimate** not a change in accounting policy. （折旧政策的改变是会计估计的变更而不是会计政策的变更。）

6. Cost model and revaluation model

a) Cost model：Carry the asset at its cost less depreciation and any accumulated impairment loss.

Initial recognition	Initial measured at cost
Subsequent measurement	Cost — accumulated depreciation — accumulated impairment losses
Depreciation	Based on historical costs DR：Depreciation 　　CR：Accumulated depreciation
Disposal	Profit or loss on disposal = proceeds − carrying amount of the assets

b) Revaluation model：Carry the asset at a revalued amount, being its fair value at the date of the revaluation less any subsequent accumulated depreciation and subsequent accumulated impairment losses.

The revised IAS 16 makes clear that the revaluation model is available **only if the fair** value of the item can be measured reliably.

Initial recognition	Initial measured at cost
Subsequent measurement	Revalued amount — subsequently accumulated depreciation — subsequently accumulated impairment losses
Depreciation	Based on revalued amount DR: Depreciation 　　CR: Accumulated depreciation Excessive depreciation may be transferred from RS to RE: DR: Revaluation surplus 　　CR: Retained earnings
Disposal	Profit or loss on disposal = proceeds — carrying amount of the assets Remaining balance may be transferred from RS to RE（处置了,未实现损益就变成已实现的损益） DR: Revaluation surplus 　　CR: Retained earnings

7. Revaluations

The revaluation model is **available only if the fair value of the item can be measured reliably**.

In the case of plant and equipment, fair value can also be taken as **market value**. Where a market value is not available, however, depreciated replacement cost should be used.（通常按照市场价值来计量,市场价值没有的话,就按折旧后的重置成本来计量。）

When an item of property, plant and equipment is revalued, the **entire class** of assets to which the item belongs must be revalued.（重估了一个资产,那该类型的所有资产都必须重估。）

Revaluation gains are credited to other comprehensive income and equity (revaluation reserve), the increase shall be recognised in profit and loss to the extent that it reveres a revaluation decrease previously recognised in profit and loss.

Revaluation losses should be recognised as an expense to profit and loss.

However the decrease shall be recognised in other comprehensive income to the extent of any credit balance existing in the revaluation surplus.

8. Derecognition

An entity is required to **derecognise the carrying amount** of an item of property, plant or equipment that it disposes of on the date the criteria for the sale in **IFRS 15 Revenue**

from contracts with customers would be met. This also applies to parts of an asset. 当满足收入准则后,(不是继续使用,而是通过处置来实现其经济利益时)就应终止确认该固定资产。

```
         OCI ↘
              ↘
    ↙_____ lost
   ↗        ↖
  P/L       P/L
```

9. Disclosure

a) Measurement bases for determining the gross carrying amount

b) Depreciation methods used

c) Useful lives or depreciation rates used

d) Gross carrying amount and accumulated depreciation

e) Reconciliation of the carrying amount at the beginning and end of the period showing: additions, disposals, acquisitions through business combinations, increases/decreases during the period from revaluations and from impairment losses, impairment losses recognized in profit or loss, impairment losses reversed in profit or loss, depreciation, net exchange differences, and any other movements

IAS 40

Investment property

1. Definitions

Investment property is property (land or a building — or part of a building — or both) held (by the owner or by the lessee as a right-of-use asset) to earn rentals or for capital appreciation or both, rather than for:

a) Use in the production or supply of goods or services or for administrative purposes, or

b) Sale in the ordinary course of business.

投资性房地产,是指为**赚取租金**或**资本增值**,或**两者兼有**而持有的房地产。

下列各项不属于投资性房地产:

1) 自用房地产

即为生产商品、提供劳务或者经营管理而持有的房地产。

2) 作为存货的房地产

作为存货的房地产是指房地产开发企业在正常经营过程中销售的或为销售而正在开发的商品房和土地。这部分房地产属于房地产开发企业的存货,不属于投资性房地产。

如果某项房地产,部分用于赚取租金或资本增值、部分用于生产商品、提供劳务或经营管理,能够单独计量和出售的、用于赚取租金或资本增值的部分,应当确认为投资性房地产。

2. Recognition

Investment property should be recognised as an asset when two conditions are met:

a) It is probable that the future economic benefits that are associated with the investment property will flow to the entity.

b) The cost of the investment property can be measured reliably.

将某个项目确认为投资性房地产,首先应当符合投资性房地产的概念,其次要同时满足投资性房地产的两个确认条件:

a) 与该投资性房地产相关的经济利益很可能流入企业;

b) 该投资性房地产的成本能够可靠地计量。

3. Measurement

3.1 Initial measurement

An investment property should be measured initially at its cost, including transaction costs.

投资性房地产应当按照成本进行初始计量。

3.2 Subsequent measurement

IAS 40 requires an entity to choose between two models.

a) The fair value model 公允价值模型

b) The cost model 成本模型

Whatever policy it chooses should be applied to all of its investment property.

After initial recognition, an entity that chooses the fair value model should measure all of its investment property at fair value, except in the extremely rare cases where this cannot be measured reliably. In such cases it should apply the IAS 16 cost model. (IAS 与企业会计准则稍有差异)

企业通常应当采用成本模式对投资性房地产进行后续计量,满足特定条件时也可以采用公允价值模式对投资性房地产进行后续计量。但是,同一企业只能采用一种模式对所有投资性房地产进行后续计量,不得同时采用两种计量模式。(IAS 与企业会计准则稍有差异)

3.2.1 Fair value model

采用公允价值模式进行后续计量的投资性房地产

Fair value is the price that would be received to sell an asset or paid to transfer a liability in an orderly transaction between market participants at the measurement date. (FV 定义,稍作了解)

企业只有存在确凿证据表明投资性房地产的公允价值能够持续可靠取得的,才可以采用公允价值模式对投资性房地产进行后续计量。

a) A gain or loss arising from a change in the fair value of an investment property should be recognised in net profit or loss for the period in which it arises 公允价值变动计入当期损益

b) The fair value of investment property should reflect market conditions at the end of the reporting period(每个资产负债表日都要反映其相应的 FV)

c) The residual value must be assumed to be zero(残值为 0)

d) No depreciation is charged on the asset.

企业采用公允价值模式进行后续计量的,不对投资性房地产计提折旧或摊销,也不计提减值准备。

3.2.2 Cost model

In those rare cases where the entity cannot determine the fair value of an investment property reliably, the cost model in IAS 16 must be applied until the investment property is disposed of.(当公允价值无法可靠取得的时候,用 cost model)

The cost model is the cost model in IAS 16. (和 PPE 的处理一样)

√ Investment property should be measured at depreciated cost, less any accumulated impairment losses.

√ Residual value must assumed to be zero.

✓ An entity that chooses the cost model should disclose the fair value of its investment property.

3.2.3 Changing models 计量模式的变更

Once the entity has chosen the fair value or cost model，it should apply it to all its investment property.

It should not change from one model to the other unless the change will result in a more appropriate presentation. IAS 40 states that it is highly unlikely that a change from the fair value model to the cost model will result in a more appropriate presentation.

企业对投资性房地产的计量模式一经确定，不得随意变更。以成本模式转为公允价值模式的，应当作为会计政策变更处理，将计量模式变更时公允价值与账面价值的差额，调整期初留存收益。

已采用公允价值模式计量的投资性房地产，不得从公允价值模式转为成本模式。

3.3 投资性房地产的转换

Transfers to or from investment property should only be made when there is a change in use. For example，owner occupation commences so the investment property will be treated under IAS 16 as an owner-occupied property.

3.3.1 Investment property (FV) to PPE or Inventory

When there is a transfer from investment property carried at fair value to owner-occupied property or inventories，the property's cost for subsequent accounting under IAS 16 or IAS 2 should be its fair value at the date of change of use.

3.3.2 PPE or Inventory to Investment property (FV)

Conversely，an owner-occupied property may become an investment property and need to be carried at fair value. An entity should apply IAS16 up to the date of changes of use. It should treat any difference at that date between the carrying amount of the property under IAS 16 and its fair value as a revaluation under IAS16.

分录：

1) Transfer from IAS 40 Investment Property under Fair model to IAS 16 PPE

- Dr PPE（Fair value @ transfer date）
- Cr Investment Property（carry amount）
- Cr Profit or loss β 贷方差额

- Dr PPE（Fair value @ transfer date）
- Dr Profit or loss β 借方差额
- Cr Investment Property（carry amount）

2) Transfer from IAS 16 PPE to IAS 40 Investment Property under fair value model

- Dr Investment Property（Fair value @ transfer date）
- Cr PPE（carry amount）
- Cr Revaluation Surplus β 贷方差额

- Dr Investment property
- Dr P/L β 借方差额

- Cr NCA

3) Transfer from IAS 16 PPE to IAS 40 Investment Property under cost model
- Dr Investment Property（carry amount）——对应,简单。
- Cr PPE（carry amount）——对应,简单。

4) Transfer from IAS 40 Investment Property under cost model to IAS 16 PPE
- Dr PPE（carry amount）——对应,简单。
- Cr Investment Property（carry amount）——对应,简单。

4. Disposal

a) Derecognise (eliminate from the statement of financial position) an investment property on disposal or when it is permanently withdrawn from use and no future economic benefits are expected from its disposal.

当投资性房地产被处置,或者永久退出使用且预计不能从其处置中取得经济利益时,应当终止确认该项投资性房地产。

b) Any gain or loss on disposal is the difference between the net disposal proceeds and the carrying amount of the asset. It should generally be recognised as income or expense in profit or loss.

企业出售、转让、报废投资性房地产或者发生投资性房地产毁损时,应当将处置收入扣除其账面价值和相关税费后的金额计入当期损益

IAS 23

Borrowing costs

1. Definitions

Borrowing costs: Interest and other costs incurred by an entity in connection with the borrowing of funds.

The standard lists what may be included in borrowing costs.

Interest on bank overdrafts and short-term and long-term borrowings

Amortisation of discounts or premiums relating to borrowings

Amortisation of ancillary costs incurred in connection with the arrangement of borrowings

Finance charges in respect of finance leases recognised in accordance with IFRS16

Exchange differences arising from foreign currency borrowings to the extent that they are regarded as an adjustment to interest costs

借款费用是企业因借入资金所付出的代价,它包括借款利息费用(包括借款折价或者溢价的摊销和相关辅助费用的摊销)以及因外币借款而发生的汇兑差额等。

借款费用应予资本化的借款范围既包括专门借款,也包括一般借款。

企业发生的借款费用,可直接归属于符合资本化条件的资产的购建或者生产的,应当予以资本化,计入符合资本化条件的资产成本。其他借款费用,应当在发生时根据其发生额确认为财务费用,计入当期损益。

Qualifying asset: An asset that necessarily takes a substantial period of time to get ready for its intended use or sale

Examples of qualifying assets:

○ Depending on the circumstances, any of the following may be qualifying assets.
○ Inventories
○ Manufacturing plants
○ Power generation facilities
○ Intangible assets
○ Investment properties

Financial assets and inventories that are manufactured, or otherwise produced over a short period of time are not qualifying assets. Assets that are ready for their intended use or sale when purchased are not qualifying assets.

符合资本化条件的资产,是指需要经过相当长时间(一年或一年以上)的购建或者生产活动才能达到预定可使用或可销售状态的固定资产、投资性房地产和存货等资产。

企业发生的借款费用,可直接归属于符合资本化条件的资产的购建或者生产的,应当予以资本化,计入符合资本化条件的资产成本。其他借款费用,应当在发生时根据其发生额确认为财务费用,计入当期损益。

2. Capitalisation

Under the revised treatment, all eligible borrowing costs must be capitalised.

Only borrowing costs that are directly attributable to the acquisition, construction or production of a qualifying asset can be capitalised as part of the cost of that asset.

企业发生的借款费用,可直接归属于符合资本化条件的资产的购建或者生产的,应当予以资本化。

2.1 Borrowing costs eligible for capitalisation

Those borrowing costs directly attributable to the acquisition, construction or production of a qualifying asset must be identified.

These are the borrowing costs that would have been avoided had the expenditure on the qualifying asset not been made.

2.2 Borrowing costs related to specific asset

Once the relevant borrowings are identified, which relate to a specific asset, then the amount of borrowing costs available for capitalisation will be the actual borrowing costs incurred on those borrowings during the period, less any investment income on the temporary investment of those borrowings.

It would not be unusual for some or all of the funds to be invested before they are actually used on the qualifying asset.

为购建或者生产符合资本化条件的资产而借入专门借款的,应当以专门借款当期实际发生的利息费用,减去将尚未动用的借款资金存入银行取得的利息收入或进行暂时性投资取得的投资收益后的金额确定。

对专门借款而言,资本化期间的借款费用全部资本化,费用化期间的借款费用全部费用化。

2.3 Borrowings obtained generally

In a situation where borrowings are obtained generally, but are applied in part to obtaining a qualifying asset, then the amount of borrowing costs eligible for capitalisation is found by applying the 'capitalisation rate' to the expenditure on the asset.

The capitalisation rate is the weighted average of the borrowing costs applicable to the entity's borrowings that are outstanding during the period, excluding borrowings made specifically to obtain a qualifying asset. However, there is a cap on the amount of borrowing costs calculated in this way: it must not exceed actual borrowing costs incurred.

Sometimes one overall weighted average can be calculated for a group or entity, but in some situations it may be more appropriate to use a weighted average for borrowing costs for individual parts of the group or entity.

为购建或者生产符合资本化条件的资产而占用了一般借款的,企业应当根据累计资产支出超过专门借款部分的资产支出加权平均数乘以所占用一般借款的资本化率,计算确定一般借款应予资本化的利息金额。资本化率应当根据一般借款加权平均利率计算确定。

相关计算公式如下:

一般借款利息费用资本化金额 = 累计资产支出超过专门借款部分的资产支出加权平均数 × 所占用一般借款的资本化率

资产支出加权平均数 = $\sum$(每笔资产支出金额 × 该笔资产支出在当期所占用的天数/当期天数)

3. Commencement of capitalization

Three events or transactions must be taking place for capitalisation of borrowing costs to be started.

a) Expenditure on the asset is being incurred

b) Borrowing costs are being incurred

c) Activities are in progress that are necessary to prepare the asset for its intended use or sale

Expenditure must result in the payment of cash, transfer of other assets or assumption of interest-bearing liabilities. Deductions from expenditure will be made for any progress payments or grants received in connection with the asset.

Activities necessary to prepare the asset for its intended sale or use extend further than physical construction work. e.g. obtaining permits. They do not include holding an asset when no production or development that changes the asset's condition is taking place, e.g. where land is held without any associated development activity

借款费用开始资本化的时点:

(1) 资产支出已经发生(包括支付现金、转移非现金资产和承担带息债务形式发生的支出,赊购形式发生的支出不属于资产支出)

(2) 借款费用已经发生(已经发生了专门借款费用或者占用了一般借款的借款费用)

(3) 为使资产达到预定可使用或者可销售状态所必要的购建或者生产活动已经开始(是指符合资本化条件的资产的实体建造或者生产工作已经开始)

4. Suspension of capitalisatoin

If active development is interrupted for any extended periods, capitalisation of borrowing costs should be suspended for those periods.

Suspension of capitalisation of borrowing costs is not necessary for temporary delays or for periods when substantial technical or administrative work is taking place.

符合资本化条件的资产在购建或者生产过程中发生**非正常中断**、且中断时间**连续超过3个月**的,应当暂停借款费用的资本化。在中断期间所发生的借款费用,应当计入当期损益,直至购建或者生产活动重新开始。

但是,如果中断是使所购建或者生产的符合资本化条件的资产达到预定可使用或者可销售状态必要的程序,所发生的借款费用应继续资本化。

项目	概念	示例
正常中断	为使资产达到预定可使用状态或可销售状态所必要的程序、可预见的不可抗力因素导致的中断	正常测试、调试停工 严寒地区冬季无法施工而停工
非正常中断	企业管理上导致的或其他不可预见的原因等导致的中断	与施工方的质量纠纷 工程物资未得到及时供应 资金周转困难 发生安全事故 发生劳动纠纷

5. Cessation of capitalisation

Once substantially all the activities necessary to prepare the qualifying asset for its intended use or sale are complete, then capitalisation of borrowing costs should cease.

After the cessation of capitalisation, borrowing costs should be debted to profit or loss

When physical construction of the asset is completed, although minor modifications may still be outstanding → Cessation of capitalisation

The asset may be completed in parts or stages, where each part can be used while construction is still taking place on the other parts. Capitalisation of borrowing costs should cease for each part as it is completed

购建或者生产符合资本化条件的资产达到预定可使用或者可销售状态时,借款费用应当停止资本化。

停止资本化的判断:
(1) 实体建造已经完成;
(2) 基本符合设计要求;
(3) 后续支出金额很少;
(4) 试生产出合格产品;
(5) 分别建造、分别完工的资产,如果完工部分能够独立使用或销售,完工部分借款费用应当停止资本化;
(6) 分别建造、分别完工的资产,必须等到整体完工后才可使用或者可对外销售的,应当在该资产整体完工时停止借款费用的资本化。

IAS 38

Intangible assets

1. Definitions

An intangible asset is an identifiable **non-monetary asset without physical substance**. The asset must be:

a) **Controlled** by the entity as a result of events in the past

Control by the entity means:

○ **Control over** technical knowledge or know-how only exists if it is **protected by a legal right.** 只有当受法律保护的时候才是可控制的。

○ The **skill of employees**, arising out of the benefits of training costs, are most **unlikely to be recognisable** as an intangible asset, because an entity **does not control** the future actions of its staff.（员工的技能是不能控制的,不是无形资产,常考）

○ **market share and customer loyalty** cannot normally be intangible assets, since an entity **cannot control** the actions of its customers.（拥有的市场份额及客户忠诚度是不可控制的,不是无形资产,常考）

b) Something from which the entity expects **future economic benefits to flow**

c) Identifiable means:

○ If an intangible asset is acquired **separately through purchase**（可单独购买）, there may be a transfer of a legal right that would help to make an asset identifiable.

○ An intangible asset may be **identifiable if it is separable**, ie if it could be rented or sold separately.

Internally generated goodwill can not be recognized as an asset because they are subjective and cannot be measured reliably.

2. Research and development costs

1) Research——费用化

Research costs should therefore **be written off as an expense** as they are incurred. There is **too much uncertainty** about the likely success or otherwise of the project.（For example, new knowledge 只是一些简单的额认知,search and investigation 一些简单的调查研究,possible alternatives 一些可能的方案）

2) Development——满足条件的资本化,其余的费用化

Development costs may qualify for recognition as intangible assets provided that the **following strict criteria can be demonstrated**. (**PIRATE**)(同时满足下列条件就**应当"must"**资本化)

P — How the intangible asset will generate **Probable** future economic benefits.(未来经济利益很可能流入)

I — **Intention** to complete the intangible asset and use or sell it(主观上的意愿)

R — **Resources** (financial resources, technical resources, and others)(资源充足)

A — **Ability** to use or sell the intangible asset(客观上的能力)

T — **Technical** feasibility of completing the intangible asset so that it will be available for use or sale(技术上的可行性)

E — Its ability to measure the **Expenditure** attributable to the intangible asset during its development reliably(相关的成本费用能够可靠的计量)

3. Measurement

1) Initial measurement

Intangible assets should **be initially be measured at cost**, but subsequently they can be carried at cost or at a revalued amount.

The costs allocated to an internally generated intangible asset should be **only costs that can be directly attributed or allocated on a reasonable and consistent basis** to creating, producing or preparing the asset for its intended use.(其实本质上和 PPE 是一样的,详见 PPE)

2) Subsequent measurement

Applying the **cost model**, an intangible asset should be **carried at its cost, less any accumulated amortisation and less any accumulated impairment losses**.

The **revaluation model allows an intangible asset to be carried at a revalued amount**, which is its fair value at the date of revaluation, less any subsequent accumulated amortisation and any subsequent accumulated impairment losses.(其实本质上和 PPE 是一样的,详见 PPE)

3) Amortisation period and amortisation method

An intangible asset with a **finite useful** life **should be amortized** over its expected useful life.(使用年限确定的无形资产应当摊销)

Amortisation should **start when the asset is available for use**.

The amortisation charge for each period should normally be **recognized in profit or loss**.

An intangible asset with an **indefinite useful life should not be amortised**.(IAS 36 requires that such an asset is **tested for impairment at least annually**.使用年限不确定的无形资产,不应摊销,应当每年进行减值测试)

4. Goodwill

1) 宏观的商誉概念

Goodwill is created by **good relationships between a business and its customers.** 比如：

a) By building up a reputation (by word of mouth perhaps) for high quality products or high standards of service

b) By responding promptly and helpfully to queries and complaints from customers

c) Through the personality of the staff and their attitudes to customers

2) Purchased goodwill (收购过程中产生的商誉)

Purchased goodwill is **shown in the consolidated statement of financial position** because it has been paid for. It has **no tangible substance**. (商誉只会出现在合并报表中)

Goodwill acquired in a business combination is recognised as an asset and is **initially measured at cost.**

Cost is the **excess of** the cost of the combination over the acquirer's interest in the net fair value of the acquiree's identifiable assets, liabilities and contingent liabilities.

Negative goodwill arises when the acquirer's interest in the net fair value of the acquiree's identifiable assets, liabilities and contingent liabilities exceeds the cost of the business combination.

IFRS 3 refers to negative goodwill as the 'excess of acquirer's interest in the net fair value of acquiree's identifiable assets, liabilities and contingent liabilities over cost'.

Any negative goodwill remaining should be recognised immediately in profit or loss. (若出现了负商誉,直接计入当期损益!)

IAS 36

Impairment of assets

1. Scope
IAS 36 applies to all tangible, intangible and financial assets except（本准则适用范围不包括，即为下列资产准则的减值有自己的准则规定。）：
IAS 2 Inventories
IFRS 15 Assets arising from construction contracts
IAS 12 Deferred tax assets
IAS 19 Employee benefits
IAS 32 Financial instruments：presentation
IFRS 5 Non-current assets held for

2. Indications of a possible impairment of assets（减值迹象的判断）
1) **Internal sources of information**：（内部因素）
   a) Evidence of obsolescence or physical damage（过时或毁损）
   b) The asset's economic performance（经济表现，比如产量降低）
2) **External sources of information**（外部因素，企业无法控制的因素）
   a) A fall in the asset's market value that is more significant than would normally be expected from passage of time over normal use（市价的降低）
   b) A significant change in the technological, market, legal or economic environment of the business in which the assets are employed（技术、市场、法律、经济环境的改变）
   c) An increase in market interest rates or market rates of return on investments likely to affect the discount rate used in calculating value in use（折现率越高，折现价值越低）
   d) The **carrying amount of the entity's net assets** being more than its **market capitalization**.（净资产账面价值大于市价，整体减值）

Even if there are **no indications of impairment**, the following assets **must always be tested for impairment annually**.（以下资产不管有没有减值迹象都要每年进行减值测试）
   a) An intangible asset with an indefinite useful life（使用寿命不确定的无形资产）
   b) Goodwill acquired in a business combination（企业合并过程中产生的商誉）
减值分录：

DR：Impairment loss
　　CR：Goodwill/Intangible asset

3. Measurement

If the recoverable amount of an asset is lower than the carrying amount, the carrying amount should be reduced by the difference（ie the impairment loss）which should be charged as an expense in profit or loss.

CA＞recoverable amount → impaired

CA＜recoverable amount → do nothing（除非是特别明显的增值，比如用 revaluation model 产生的增值）

The recoverable amount of an asset should be measured as the higher value of：

a) The asset's fair value less costs of disposal

b) Its value in use(present value of future cash flow)

4. Cash generating units(资产组的减值)

A cash-generating unit is the smallest identifiable group of assets（最小资产组合）for which independent cash flows can be identified and measured.

An impairment loss should be recognized for a cash-generating unit if（and only if）the recoverable amount for the cash-generating unit is less than the carrying amount in the statement of financial position for all the assets in the unit.（当且仅当 carrying amount＞recoverable amount 的时候才产生减值）

减值分摊的顺序，几乎每次考试必考。

When an impairment loss is recognized for a cash-generating unit，the loss should be allocated between the assets in the unit in the following order：

a) First，to any assets that are obviously damaged or destroyed（先分摊至明显减值的资产）

b) Next，to the goodwill allocated to the cash generating unit（再分给商誉）

c) Then to all other assets in the cash-generating unit，on a pro rata basis 剩下的才是其他资产的，这儿主要指的是 NCA(包括无形资产)，通常按照账面价值的比例分配，切记，流动资产不要分配！

In allocating an impairment loss，the carrying amount of an asset should not be reduced below the highest of：（减值后的各资产的账面价值不得低于以下三者之中最高者）

a) Its fair value less costs of disposal

b) Its value in use

c) Zero

IAS 20

Government grants

1. Definitions

1) Government grants

Assistance by government in the form of transfers of resources to an entity in return for past or future compliance with certain conditions relating to the operating activities of the entity.

They exclude those forms of government assistance which cannot reasonably have a value placed upon them and transactions with government which cannot be distinguished from the normal trading transactions of the entity.

政府补助是指企业从政府无偿取得货币性资产或非货币性资产。其主要形式包括政府对企业的无偿拨款、税收返还、财政贴息，以及无偿给予非货币性资产等。

政府如以企业所有者身份向企业投入资本，享有相应的所有权权益，政府与企业之间是投资者与被投资者的关系，属于互惠交易。

企业从政府取得的经济资源，如果与企业销售商品或提供劳务等活动密切相关，且来源于政府的经济资源是企业商品或服务的对价或者是对价的组成部分，应当按照《企业会计准则第 14 号——收入》的规定进行会计处理，不适用政府补助准则。

2) Grants related to assets

Government grants whose primary condition is that an entity qualifying for them should purchase, construct or otherwise acquire non-current assets.

与资产相关的政府补助，是指企业取得的、用于购建或以其他方式形成长期资产的政府补助。

2. Accounting treatment

IAS 20 requires grants to be recognised as income over the relevant periods to match them with related costs which they have been received to compensate. This should be done on a systematic basis.

Grants should not, therefore, be credited directly to equity.

It would be against the accruals assumption to credit grants to income on a receipts basis, so a systematic basis of matching must be used. A receipts basis would only be acceptable if no other basis was available.

Where grants are received in relation to a depreciating asset, the grant will be recognised over the periods in **which the asset is depreciated and in the same proportions.**

政府补助的无偿性决定了其应当最终计入损益而非直接计入所有者权益。其会计处理有两种方法：

一是总额法，将政府补助全额确认为收益；

二是净额法，将政府补助作为相关资产账面价值或所补偿费用的扣减。

2.1 Grants related to assets 与资产相关的政府补助

There are two choices here for how government grants related to assets (including non-monetary grants at fair value) should be shown in the statement of financial position：

a) Set up the grant as deferred income. 总额法

会计处理：

取得时：

| 借：银行存款（××资产） | DR：Bank or PPE |
| 贷：递延收益 | CR：Deferred income |

摊销时：

| 借：递延收益 | DR：Deferred income |
| 贷：其他收益 | CR：Other income |

b) Deduct the grant in arriving at the carrying amount of the asset.

将补助冲减相关资产账面价值。

2.2 Grants related to income 与收益相关的政府补助

These grants are a credit in profit or loss, but there is a choice in the method of disclosure：

a) Present as a separate credit or under a general heading, e.g. 'other income'

b) Deduct from the related expense

ACCA F7 主要考察与资产相关的政府补助，收益相关的稍作了解即可。

下面是收益相关政府补助的具体处理：（了解即可）

（1） 与收益相关的政府补助，**若用于补偿企业以后期间的相关成本费用或损失：**

在收到时应当先判断企业能否满足政府补助所附条件。根据政府补助准则的规定，只有满足政府补助确认条件的才能予以确认。客观情况通常表明企业能够满足政府补助所附条件，企业应当将补助确认为递延收益，并在确认相关费用和损失的期间，计入当期损益或冲减相关成本。

（2） 与收益相关的政府补助，**若用于补偿企业已发生的相关成本费用或损失的：**

直接计入当期损益或冲减相关成本，这类补助通常与企业已经发生的行为有关，是对企业已发生的成本费用或损失的补偿，或是对企业过去行为的奖励，如果企业已经实际收到补助资金，应当按照实际收到的金额计入当期损益或冲减相关成本，如果会计期末企业尚未收到补助资金，但企业在符合了相关政策规定后就相应获得了收款权，且与之相关的经济利益很可能流入企业，企业应当在这项补助成为应收款时按照应收的金额予以确认，计入当期损益或冲减相关成本。

3. Repayment of government grants   政府补助的退回

If a grant must be repaid it should be accounted for as a revision of an accounting estimate:

作为会计估计的变更处理,但是:

对于属于前期差错的政府补助退回,应当按照前期差错更正进行追溯调整。(F7 不考这个,稍作了解)

a) Repayment of a grant related to income: apply first against any unamortised deferred income set up in respect of the grant; any excess should be recognised immediately as an expense.

b) Repayment of a grant related to an asset 净额法下: increase the carrying amount of the asset.

The cumulative additional depreciation that would have been recognised to date in the absence of the grant should be immediately recognised as an expense.

总额法下: or reduce the deferred income balance by the amount repayable.

政府补助的退回应当分别下列情况进行会计处理:

(1) 初始确认时冲减相关资产成本的,应当调整资产账面价值;

(2) 存在尚未摊销的递延收益的,冲减相关递延收益账面余额,超出部分计入当期损益;

(3) 属于其他情况的,直接计入当期损益。

IFRS 15

Revenue from contracts with customers

1. Definitions

Revenue is income arising in the ordinary course of an entity's activities and it may be called different names, such as sales, fees, interest, dividends or royalties.

收入,是指企业在日常活动中形成的、会导致所有者权益增加的、与所有者投入资本无关的经济利益的总流入。

2. IFRS 15 REVENUE FROM CONTRACTS WITH CUSTOMERS

Recognition and measurement

Step 1 Identify the contract with the customer

A contract with a customer is within the scope of IFRS 15 only when:

a) The parties have approved the contract and are committed to carrying it out.

b) Each party's rights regarding the goods and services to be transferred can be identified.

c) The payment terms for the goods and services can be identified.

d) The contract has commercial substance

e) It is probable that the entity will collect the consideration to which it will be entitled.

f) The contract can be written, verbal or implied

第一步:识别与客户订立的合同

a) 合同各方已批准该合同并承诺将履行各自义务

b) 该合同明确了合同各方与所转让商品或提供劳务相关的权利和义务

c) 该合同有明确的与所转让商品相关的支付条款

d) 该合同具有商业实质,即履行该合同将改变企业未来现金流量的风险/时间分布或金额

e) 企业因向客户转让商品而有权取得的对价很可能收回

Step 2 Identify the separate performance obligations

A company would account for a performance obligation separately only if the promised good or service is distinct.

第二步：识别合同中的单项履约义务

合同开始日,企业应当对合同进行评估,识别该合同所包含的各单项履约义务,并确定各单项履约义务是在某一时段内履行,还是在某一时点履行,然后,在履行了各单项履约义务时分别确认收入。

Step 3　Determine the transaction price

The transaction price is the amount of consideration a company expects to be entitled to from the customer in exchange for transferring goods or services.

第三步：确定交易价格

企业应当按照分摊至各单项履约义务的交易价格计量收入。

交易价格是指企业因向客户转让商品而预期有权收取的对价金额。

Step 4　Allocate the transaction price to the performance obligations

Where a contract contains more than one distinct performance obligation a company allocates the transaction price to all separate performance obligations in proportion to the stand-lone selling price of the good or service underlying each performance obligation

第四步：将交易价格分摊至各单项履约义务

当合同中包含两项或多项履约义务时,为了使企业分摊至每一单项履约义务的交易价格能够反映其因向客户转让已承诺的相关商品(或提供已承诺的相关服务)而预期有权收取的对价金额,企业应当在合同开始日,按照各单项履约义务所承诺商品的单独售价的相对比例,将交易价格分摊至各单项履约义务。

Step 5　Recognise revenue when (or as) a performance obligation is satisfied

The entity satisfies a performance obligation by transferring control of a promised good or service to the customer. A performance obligation can be satisfied at a point in time, such s when goods are delivered to the customer, or over time.

A performance obligation satisfied over time meets the criteria in Step 5 above and, if it entered into more than one accounting period, would previously have been described as a long-term contract.

第五步：履行每一单项履约义务时确认收入

企业应当在履行了合同中的履约义务,即客户取得相关商品控制权时确认收入。企业应当根据实际情况,首先判断履约义务是否满足在某一时段内履行的条件,如不满足,则该履约义务属于在某一时点履行的履约义务。对于在某一时段内履行的履约义务,企业应当选取恰当的方法来确定履约进度;对于在某一时点履行的履约义务,企业应当综合分析控制权转移的迹象,判断其转移时点。

3. Performance obligations satisfied over time

Methods of measuring the amount of performance completed to date encompass output methods and input methods.

Output methods recognise revenue on the basis of the value to the customer of the goods or services transferred. They include surveys of performance completed, appraisal of units produced or delivered etc.

Input methods recognise revenue on the basis of the entity's inputs, such as labour hours, resources consumed, costs incurred. If using a cost-based method, the costs incurred must contribute to the entity's progress in satisfying the performance obligation.

This will be the point in time at which the customer obtains control of the promised asset and the entity satisfies a performance obligation.

在某一时段内履行的履约义务的收入确认方法

企业应当考虑商品的性质,采用产出法或投入法确定恰当的履约进度,并且在确定履约进度时,应当扣除那些控制权尚未转移客户的商品和服务。

(1) 产出法

产出法主要是根据已转移给客户的商品对于客户的价值确定履约进度,主要包括按照实际测量的完工进度、评估已实现的结果、已达到的里程碑、时间进度、已完工或交付的产品等确定履约进度的方法。

(2) 投入法

投入法主要是根据企业履行履约义务的投入确定履约进度,主要包括以投入的材料数量、花费的人工工时或机器工时、发生的成本和时间进度等投入指标确定履约进度。

Performance obligations satisfied at a point in time

Some indicators of the transfer of control are:

a) The entity has a present right to payment for the asset.

b) The customer has legal title to the asset.

c) The entity has transferred physical possession of the asset.

d) The significant risks and rewards of ownership have been transferred to the customer.

e) The customer has accepted the asset.

某一时点履行的履约义务。当一项履约义务不属于在某一时段内履行的履约义务时,应当属于在某一时点履行的履约义务。对于在某一时点履行的履约义务,企业应当在客户取得相关商品控制权时点确认收入。在判断客户是否已取得商品控制权时,企业应当考虑下列迹象:

a) 企业就该商品享有现时收款权利,即客户就该商品负有现时付款义务。

b) 企业已将该商品的法定所有权转移给客户,即客户已拥有该商品的法定所有权。

c) 企业已将该商品实物转移给客户,即客户已占有该商品实物。

4. Common types of transaction 常见/特殊交易

4.1 Warranties

If a customer has the option to purchase a warranty separately from the product to which it relates, it constitutes a distinct service and is accounted for as a separate performance obligation.

If the customer does not have the option to purchase the warranty separately, for instance if the warranty is required by law, that does not give rise to a performance obligation and the warranty is accounted for in accordance with IAS 37.

附有质量保证条款的销售

对于附有质量保证条款的销售,企业应当评估该质量保证是否在向客户保证所销售商品符合既定标准之外提供了一项单独的服务。企业提供额外服务的,应当作为单项履约义务,按照本准则规定进行会计处理;否则,质量保证责任应当按照《企业会计准则第13号——或有事项》规定进行会计处理。

在评估质量保证是否在向客户保证所销售商品符合既定标准之外提供了一项单独的服务时,企业应当考虑该质量保证是否为法定要求、质量保证期限以及企业承诺履行任务的性质等因素。客户能够选择单独购买质量保证的,该质量保证构成单项履约义务。

4.2 Principal versus agent

An entity must establish in any transaction whether it is acting as principal or agent.

It is a principal if it controls the promised good or service before it is transferred to the customer. It is acting as an agent if its performance obligation is to arrange for the provision of goods or services by another party.

Satisfaction of this performance obligation will give rise to the recognition of revenue in the amount of any fee or commission to which it expects to be entitled in exchange for arranging for the other party to provide its goods or services.

Indicators that an entity is an agent rather than a principal include the following:

Another party is primarily responsible for fulfilling the contract.

The entity does not have inventory risk before or after the goods have been ordered by a customer, during shipping or on return.

The entity does not have discretion in establishing prices for the other party's goods or services and, therefore, the benefit that the entity can receive from those goods or services is limited.

The entity's consideration is in the form of a commission.

The entity is not exposed to credit risk for the amount receivable from a customer in exchange for the other party's goods or services

主要责任人和代理人

企业应当根据其在向客户转让商品前是否拥有对该商品的控制权,来判断其从事交易时的身份是主要责任人还是代理人。企业在向客户转让商品前能够控制该商品的,该企业为主要责任人,应当按照已收或应收对价总额确认收入;否则,该企业为代理人,应当按照预期有权收取的佣金或手续费的金额确认收入,该金额应当按照已收或应收对价总额扣除应支付给其他相关方的价款后的净额,或者按照既定的佣金金额或比例等确定。

企业与客户订立的包含多项可明确区分商品的合同中,企业需要分别判断其在这不同履约义务中的身份是主要责任人还是代理人。

当存在第三方参与企业向客户提供商品时,企业向客户转让特定商品之前能够控制该商品,从而应当作为主要责任人的情形包括:

(1) 企业自该第三方取得商品或其他资产控制权后,再转让给客户

(2) 企业能够主导该第三方代表本企业向客户提供服务

(3) 企业自该第三方取得商品控制权后,通过提供重大的服务将该商品与其他商品整合成合同约定的某组合产出转让给客户

4.3 Repurchase agreements

Under a repurchase agreement an entity sells an asset and promises, or has the option, to repurchase it.

Repurchase agreements generally come in three forms.
a) An entity has an obligation to repurchase the asset (a forward contract)
b) An entity has the right to repurchase the asset (a call option)
c) An entity must repurchase the asset if requested to do so by the customer (a put option)

If the entity is obliged to repurchase at the request of the customer (a put option), it must consider whether or not the customer is likely to exercise that option.

售后回购,是指企业销售商品的同时承诺或有权选择日后再将该商品(包括相同或几乎相同的商品,或以该商品作为组成部分的商品)购回的销售方式。对于不同类型的售后回购交易,企业应当区分下列两种情形分别进行会计处理:

(1) 企业因存在与客户的远期安排而负有回购义务或企业享有回购权利的,表明客户在销售时点并未取得相关商品控制权,企业应当作为租赁交易或融资交易进行相应的会计处理。其中,回购价格低于原售价的,应当视为租赁交易;回购价格不低于原售价的,应当视为融资交易,在收到客户款项时确认金融负债,并将该款项和回购价格的差额在回购期间内确认为利息费用等。企业到期未行使回购权利的,应当在该回购权利到期时终止确认金融负债,同时确认收入。

(2) 企业负有应客户要求回购商品义务的,应当在合同开始日评估客户是否具有行使该要求权的重大经济动因,客户具有行使该要求权重大经济动因的,企业应当将售后回购作为租赁交易或融资交易,按照上述第1种情形进行会计处理;否则,企业应当将其作为附有销售退回条款的销售交易进行会计处理。在判断客户是否具有行权的重大经济动因时,企业应当综合考虑各种相关因素,包括回购价格与预计回购时市场价格之间的比较,以及权利的到期日等。例如,如果回购价格明显高于该资产回购时的市场价值,则表明客户有行权的重大经济动因。

5. Presentation and disclosure

A contract liability is recognised and presented in the statement of financial position where a customer has paid an amount of consideration prior to the entity performing by transferring control of the related good or service to the customer.

When the entity has performed but the customer has not yet paid the relatedconsideration, this will give rise to either a contract asset or a receivable

A contract asset is recognised when the entity's right to consideration is conditional on something other than the passage of time, for instance future performance. A receivable is recognised when the entity's right to consideration is unconditional except for the passage of time.

"合同资产"核算企业已向客户转让商品而有权收取对价的权利。仅取决于时间流逝因素的权利不在本科目核算。"合同负债"核算企业已收或应收客户对价而应向客户转让商品的义务。

6. Performance obligations satisfied over time

Where performance obligations are satisfied over time, an entity must determine what amounts to include as revenue and costs in each accounting period.

Statement of profit or loss

Sales revenue and associated costs should be recorded as the contract activity progresses.

a) Include an appropriate proportion of total contract value as sales revenue in profit or loss.

Sales revenue is the value of work carried out to date.

b) The costs incurred in completing that amount of the performance obligation are matched with this sales revenue, resulting in the reporting of results which can be attributed to the proportion of work completed.

本期确认收入＝合同的交易价格×履约进度－以前期间已确认收入

本期确认费用＝合同预计总成本×履约进度－以前期间已确认费用

本期确认毛利＝本期确认收入－本期确认费用

IAS 32

Financial instruments: presentation

1. Definition

1) Financial instrument

Financial instrument is any contract that gives rise to a financial asset of one entity and a financial liability or equity instrument of another entity.

金融工具,是指形成一方的金融资产并形成其他方的金融负债或权益工具的合同。

2) Financial assets

Any asset that is:

a) cash

b) an equity instrument of another entity

c) a contractual right to receive cash or another financial asset from another entity; or to

d) exchange financial instruments with another entity under conditions that are potentially favourable to the entity.

金融资产,是指企业持有的现金、其他方的权益工具(比如持有上市公司股票)以及符合下列条件之一的资产:

a) 从其他方收取现金或其他金融资产的合同权利;

b) 在潜在有利条件下,与其他方交换金融资产或金融负债的合同权利;

c) 将来须用或可用企业自身权益工具(自己的股票)进行结算的非衍生工具合同,且企业根据该合同将收到可变数量的自身权益工具;

d) 将来须用或可用企业自身权益工具进行结算的衍生工具合同,但以固定数量的自身权益工具交换固定金额的现金或其他金融资产的衍生工具合同除外。

Examples

Trade receivable 应收账款;Options 期权;Investment in equity shares 权益性投资

3) Financial liabilities

A contractual obligation:

a) to deliver cash or another financial asset to another entity, or

b) to exchange financial instruments with another entity under conditions that are potentially unfavourable.

金融负债是指企业符合下列条件之一的负债：

a) 向其他方交付现金或其他金融资产的合同义务。

b) 在潜在不利条件下，与其他方交换金融资产或金融负债的合同义务。

c) 将来须用或可用企业自身权益工具进行结算的非衍生工具合同，且企业根据该合同将交付可变数量的自身权益工具。

d) 将来须用或可用企业自身权益工具进行结算的衍生工具合同（将来结算会涉及现金），但以固定数量的自身权益工具交换固定金额的现金或其他金融资产的衍生工具合同除外。

Examples

Trade payable 应付账款；Debenture loans 债券；Redeemable preference shares 可赎回优先股

4) Equity instrument

Any contract that evidences a residual interest in the assets of an entity after deducting all of its liabilities.

权益工具，是指能证明拥有某个企业在扣除所有负债后的资产中的剩余权益的合同。

5) Distinguish of debt and equity instrument

（区分金融负债和权益工具需考虑的因素）

Entities which issue financial instruments should classify them (or their component parts) as either financial liabilities, or equity

The classification depends on the following.

a) The substance of the contractual arrangement on initial recognition 合同所反映的经济实质

b) The definitions of a financial liability and an equity instrument 工具的特征

2. Compound instruments

Compound instruments may combine features of both equity instruments and financial liabilities. For example, Convertible debt, in such case, equity and liability should be accounted separately in financial statement. IAS 32 requires compound financial instruments be split into their component parts:

A financial liability Calculate the present value for the liability component.

An equity instrument (conversion right) Deduct the liability from the instrument as a whole to leave a residual value for the equity component.

Transaction cost should be deducted from the proceeds

复合金融工具企业发行的某些非衍生金融工具（如可转换公司债券等）既含有负债成分，又含有权益成分。对此，企业应当在初始确认时将负债和权益成分进行分拆，分别进行处理。在进行分拆时，应当先确定负债成分的公允价值并以此作为其初始确认金额，再按照该金融工具整体的发行价格扣除负债成分初始确认金额后的金额确定权益成分的初始确认金额。

3. Measurement 计量

1) Initial measurement 初始计量

Financial instruments are initially measured at the fair value of the consideration given or received plus (or minus in the case of financial liabilities), in case of a financial instrument not at fair value through profit or loss, transaction costs.

企业初始确认金融资产或金融负债，应当按照公允价值计量。对于以公允价值计量且其变动计入当期损益的金融资产和金融负债，相关交易费用应当直接计入当期损益；对于其他类别的金融资产或金融负债，相关交易费用应当计入初始确认金额。

Classification	Initial cost
Fair value through profit or loss (FVTPL) 以公允价值计量且其变动计入当期损益的金融资产和金融负债	Fair value of the consideration Transaction cost is debited to profit or loss immediately 公允价值，交易费用计入当期损益
Others(Amortized cost/FVTOCI) 其他类别的金融资产或金融负债（摊余成本计量的/以公允价值计量且其变动计入其他综合收益的）	Financial assets：Fair value of the consideration + Transaction cost Financial liabilities：Fair value of the consideration — Transaction cost 公允价值＋交易费用（金融资产）－交易费用（金融负债）

2) Subsequent measurement

On initial recognition, IFRS 9 requires that financial assets are classified as measured at either：

Amortised cost, or Fair value Subsequent measurement depends on whether the financial asset is a debt instrument or an equity instrument.

金融资产的后续计量与金融资产的分类密切相关。

Debt instrument

A debt instrument that meets the following conditions can be measured at amortised cost (net of any write down for impairment)：

金融资产同时符合下列条件的，应当分类为以摊余成本计量的金融资产：

a) Business model test： The objective of the entity's business model is to hold the financial asset to collect the contractual cash flows (rather than to sell the instrument prior to its contractual maturity to realize its fair value changes).

业务模式评估：企业管理该金融资产的业务模式是以收取合同现金流量为目标。

b) Cash flow characteristics test： The contractual terms of the financial asset give rise on specified dates to cash flows that are solely payments of principal and interest on the principal outstanding.

金融资产的合同现金流量特征：该金融资产的合同条款规定，在特定日期产生的现金流量，仅为对本金和以未偿付本金金额为基础的利息的支付。

3) Subsequent measurement-debt instrument

Assets held at amortised cost are measured using the effective interest method.

The effective interest method is a method of calculating the amortised cost of a financial instrument and of allocating the interest income or interest expense over the relevant period.

The effective interest rate is the rate that exactly discounts estimated future cash payments or receipts through the expected life of the financial instrument to the net carrying amount.

以摊余成本计量的金融资产的会计处理应采用实际利率法：实际利率法，是指计算金融资产或金融负债的摊余成本以及将利息收入或利息费用分摊计入各会计期间的方法。

实际利率，是指将金融资产或金融负债在预计存续期的估计未来现金流量，折现为该金融资产账面余额（不考虑减值）或该金融负债摊余成本所使用的利率。

4) Fair value option 公允价值选择权

IFRS 9 allows the option to initially measure a financial asset at fair value through profit or loss where a mismatch would otherwise arise between the asset and a related liability. In this case, the asset will also be subsequently measured at fair value through profit or loss.

在初始确认时，为了提供更相关的会计信息，企业可以将一项金融资产、一项金融负债或者一组金融工具（金融资产、金融负债或者金融资产及负债）指定为以公允价值计量且其变动计入当期损益的金融资产或金融负债，但该指定应当满足下列条件之一：

a) 该指定能够消除或显著减少会计错配。

b) 根据正式书面文件载明的企业风险管理或投资策略，以公允价值为基础对金融负债组合或金融资产和金融负债组合进行管理和业绩评价，并在企业内部以此为基础向关键管理人员报告。

5) Subsequent measurement-equity instruments

All equity investments in scope of IFRS 9 are to be measured at fair value in the statement of financial position, with value changes recognized in profit or loss.

Other comprehensive income option: If an equity investment is not held for trading, an entity can make an irrevocable election at initial recognition to measure it at fair value through other comprehensive income(FVTHOCI) with only dividend income recognized in profit or loss. Equity derivatives are excluded from adoption this designation.

企业的权益工具投资应当分类为以公允价值计量且其变动计入当期损益的金融资产。

特殊情况：非交易性权益工具投资（业务模式为长期持有/获取稳定分红/不关心价格波动），直接指定为以公允价值计量且其变动计入其他综合收益的金融资产。该指定一经做出，不得撤销。

4. Reclassification

For financial assets, reclassification is required between FVTPL and amortised cost, or vice versa, if and only if the entity's business model objective for its financial assets changes so its previous model assessment would no longer apply.

If classification is appropriate, it must be done prospectively from the reclassification date.

An entity does not restate any previously recognized gains, losses or interest.

企业改变其管理金融资产的业务模式时,应当按照规定对所有受影响的相关金融资产进行重分类。企业对所有金融负债均不得进行重分类。企业对金融资产进行重分类,应当自重分类日起采用未来适用法进行相关会计处理,不得对以前已经确认的利得、损失(包括减值损失或利得)或利息进行追溯调整。

IFRS 16

Leases

1. Definitions

1) Lease

A contract or part of a contract, that conveys the right to use an asset, the underlying asset, for a period of time in exchange for consideration.

租赁,是指在一定期间内,出租人将资产的使用权让与承租人以获取对价的合同。

2) Underlying asset

An asset that is the subject of a lease, for which the right to use an underlying asset for the lease term.

使用权资产,是指承租人可在租赁期内使用租赁资产的权利。

3) Lease payments

a) fixed payment, less any lease incentives

b) variable lease payments that depend on an index or rate

c) the exercise price of a purchase option

d) payment of lease termination penalties if applicable

租赁付款额,是指承租人向出租人支付的与在租赁期内使用租赁资产的权利相关的款项,包括:

(1) 固定付款额及实质固定付款额,存在租赁激励的,扣除租赁激励相关金额;

(2) 取决于指数或比率的可变租赁付款额,该款项在初始计量时根据租赁期开始日的指数或比率 确定;

(3) 购买选择权的行权价格,前提是承租人合理确定将行使该选择权;

(4) 行使终止租赁选择权需支付的款项,前提是租赁期反映出承租人将行使终止租赁选择权;

(5) 根据承租人提供的担保余值预计应支付的款项。(此点 F7 中不要求过多掌握)

4) Lease term

The non-cancelable period for which the lessee has contracted to lease the asset together with any further terms for which the lessee has the option to continue to lease the asset.

租赁期,是指承租人有权使用租赁资产且不可撤销的期间。

承租人有续租选择权,即有权选择续租该资产,且合理确定将行使该选择权的,租赁期还应当包含续租选择权涵盖的期间。

承租人有终止租赁选择权,即有权选择终止租赁该资产,但合理确定将不会行使该选择权的,租赁期应当包含终止租赁选择权涵盖的期间。

发生承租人可控范围内的重大事件或变化,且影响承租人是否合理确定将行使相应选择权的,承租人应当对其是否合理确定将行使续租选择权、购买选择权或不行使终止租赁选择权进行重新评估。(此点 F7 中不要求过多掌握)

5) Lease incentives

Payments made by the lessor to the lessee, or the reimbursement or assumption by the lessor of costs of the lessee.

租赁激励,是指出租人为达成租赁向承租人提供的优惠,包括出租人向承租人支付的与租赁有关的款项、出租人为承租人偿付或承担的成本等。

2. Identifying a lease

At inception of a contract, an entity shall assess whether the contract is, or contains, a lease.

A contract is, or contains, a lease if the contract conveys the right to control the use of an identified asset for a period of time in exchange for consideration.

在合同开始日,企业应当评估合同是否为租赁或者包含租赁。如果合同中一方让渡了在一定期间内控制一项或多项已识别资产使用的权利以换取对价,则该合同为租赁或者包含租赁。

除非合同条款和条件发生变化,企业无需重新评估合同是否为租赁或者包含租赁。

The right to control the use of an identified asset depends on the lessee having:

√ The right to obtain substantially all of the economic benefits from use of the identified assets; and

√ The right to direct the use of the identified asset.

为确定合同是否让渡了在一定期间内控制已识别资产使用的权利,企业应当评估合同中的客户是否有权获得在使用期间内因使用已识别资产所产生的几乎全部经济利益,并有权在该使用期间主导已识别资产的使用。

This arises if either:

The customer has the right to direct how and for what purpose the asset is used during the whole of its period of use, or The relevant decisions about use are pre-determined and the customer can operate the asset without the supplier having the right to change those operating instructions.

存在下列情况之一的,可视为客户有权主导对已识别资产在整个使用期间内的使用:

(1) 客户有权在整个使用期间主导已识别资产的使用目的和使用方式。

(2) 已识别资产的使用目的和使用方式在使用期开始前已预先确定,并且客户有权在整个使用期间自行或主导他人按照其确定的方式运营该资产,或者客户设计了已识别资产并在设计时已预先确定了该资产在整个使用期间的使用目的和使用方式。

3. Recognition

At the commencement date, a lessee shall recognise a right-of-use asset and a lease liability.

在租赁期开始日,承租人应当对租赁确认使用权资产和租赁负债

4. Initial measurement of the right-of-use asset

At the commencement date, a lessee shall measure the right-of-use asset at cost.

The cost of the right-of-use asset shall comprise:

a) the amount of the initial measurement of the lease liability;

b) any lease payments made at or before the commencement date;

c) less any lease incentives received;

d) any initial direct costs incurred by the lessee.

使用权资产应当按照成本进行初始计量。该成本包括:

(1) 租赁负债的初始计量金额;

(2) 在租赁期开始日或之前支付的租赁付款额,存在租赁激励的,扣除已享受的租赁激励相关金额;

(3) 承租人发生的初始直接费用;

(4) 承租人为拆卸及移除租赁资产、复原租赁资产所在场地或将租赁资产恢复至租赁条款约定状态预计将发生的成本。

Initial measurement of the lease liability

At the commencement date, a lessee shall measure the lease liability at the present value of the lease payments that are not paid at that date. The lease payments shall be discounted using the interest rate implicit in the lease, if that rate can be readily determined.

租赁负债应当按照租赁期开始日尚未支付的租赁付款额的现值进行初始计量。

在计算租赁付款额的现值时,承租人应当采用租赁内含利率作为折现率;

无法确定租赁内含利率的,应当采用承租人增量借款利率作为折现率。(此点 F7 中不要求过多掌握)

租赁内含利率,是指使出租人的租赁收款额的现值与未担保余值的现值之和等于租赁资产公允价值与出租人的初始直接费用之和的利率。

承租人增量借款利率,是指承租人在类似经济环境下为获得与使用权资产价值接近的资产,在类似期间以类似抵押条件借入资金须支付的利率。(此点 F7 中不要求过多掌握)

5. Subsequent measurement

5.1 Subsequent measurement of the right-of-use asset

After the commencement date, a lessee shall measure the right-of-use asset applying a cost model, unless it is an investment property or belongs to a class of assets to which the revaluation model applies.

在租赁期开始日后,承租人应当采用成本模式对使用权资产进行后续计量。

If the lease transfers ownership of the underlying asset to the lessee by the end of the lease term or if the cost of the right-of-use asset reflects that the lessee will exercise a purchase option, the lessee shall depreciate the right-of-use asset from the commencement date to the end of the useful life of the underlying asset.

Otherwise, the lessee shall depreciate the right-of-use asset from the commencement date to the earlier of the end of the useful life of the right-of-use asset or the end of the lease term.

承租人能够合理确定租赁期届满时取得租赁资产所有权的，应当在租赁资产剩余使用寿命内计提折旧。无法合理确定租赁期届满时能够取得租赁资产所有权的，应当在租赁期与租赁资产剩余使用寿命两者孰短的期间内计提折旧。

5.2 Subsequent measurement of the lease liability

After the commencement date, a lessee shall measure the lease liability by:

a) increasing the carrying amount to reflect interest on the lease liability;

b) reducing the carrying amount to reflect the lease payments made; and

c) remeasuring the carrying amount to reflect any reassessment or lease modifications or to reflect revised in-substance fixed lease payments

说了一大堆，其实就四个字："摊余成本"

6. Presentation

Right-of-use assets separately from other non-current assets.

Lease liabilities should be either presented separately from other liabilities or disclosed in the notes.

承租人应当在资产负债表中单独列示使用权资产和租赁负债。其中，租赁负债通常分别非流动负债和一年内到期的非流动负债列示。

7. Recognition exemptions

Instead of applying the recognition requirements of IFRS 16 described below, a lessee may elect to account for lease payments as an expense on a straight-line basis over the lease term or another systematic basis for the following two types of leases:

a) Short-term leases. These are leases with a lease term of twelve months or less. This election is made by class of underlying asset. A lease that contains a purchase option cannot be a short-term lease.

b) Low value leases. These are leases where the underlying asset has a low value when new, such as tablet and personal computers or small items of office furniture.

对于短期租赁和低价值资产租赁，承租人可以选择不确认使用权资产和租赁负债。

短期租赁，是指在租赁期开始日，租赁期不超过 12 个月的租赁。

包含购买选择权的租赁不属于短期租赁。（此点 F7 中不要求过多掌握）

低价值资产租赁，是指单项租赁资产为全新资产时价值较低的租赁。

低价值资产租赁的判定仅与资产的绝对价值有关，不受承租人规模、性质或其他情况影响。

承租人转租或预期转租租赁资产的,原租赁不属于低价值资产租赁。(此点 F7 中不要求过多掌握)

作出该选择的,承租人应当将短期租赁和低价值资产租赁的租赁付款额,在租赁期内各个期间按照直线法或其他系统合理的方法计入相关资产成本或当期损益。其他系统合理的方法能够更好地反映承租人的受益模式的,承租人应当采用该方法。(此点 F7 中不要求过多掌握)

8. Sale and leaseback transactions

If an entity(the seller-lessee)transfers an asset to another entity(the buyer-lessor)and leases that asset back from the buyer-lessor,both the seller-lessee and the buyer-lessor shall account for the transfer contract and the lease.

An entity shall apply the requirements for determining when a performance obligation is satisfied in IFRS 15 to determine whether the transfer of an asset is accounted for as a sale of that asset

- ✓ Transfer of the asset is a sale (sale and operating leaseback)
- ✓ Transfer of the asset is not a sale (sale and finance leaseback)

承租人和出租人应当按照《企业会计准则第 14 号——收入》的规定,评估确定售后租回交易中的资产转让是否属于销售。

If the transfer of an asset by the seller-lessee satisfies the requirements of IFRS 15 to be accounted for as a sale of the asset

The seller-lessee shall measure the right-of-use asset arising from the leaseback at the proportion of the previous carrying amount of the asset that relates to the right of use retained by the seller-lessee.

Accordingly, the seller-lessee shall recognise only the amount of any gain or loss that relates to the rights transferred to the buyer-lessor.

If the fair value of the consideration for the sale of an asset does not equal the fair value of the asset, or if the payments for the lease are not at market rates, an entity shall make the following adjustments to measure the sale proceeds at fair value:

a) any below-market terms shall be accounted for as a prepayment of lease payments;

b) and any above-market terms shall be accounted for as additional financing provided by the buyer-lessor to the seller-lessee.

售后租回交易中的资产转让属于销售的,承租人应当按原资产账面价值中与租回获得的使用权有关的部分,计量售后租回所形成的使用权资产,并仅就转让至出租人的权利确认相关利得或损失;出租人应当根据其他适用的企业会计准则对资产购买进行会计处理,并根据本准则对资产出租进行会计处理。

如果销售对价的公允价值与资产的公允价值不同,或者出租人未按市场价格收取租金,则企业应当将销售对价低于市场价格的款项作为预付租金进行会计处理,将高于市场价格的款项作为出租人向承租人提供的额外融资进行会计处理；同时，承租人按照公允价值调整相关销售利得或损失，出租人按市场价格调整租金收入。

在进行上述调整时，企业应当基于以下两者中更易于确定的项目：销售对价的公允价值与资产公允价值之间的差额、租赁合同中付款额的现值与按租赁市价计算的付款额现值之间的差额。

售后租回交易中的资产转让不属于销售的，承租人应当继续确认被转让资产，同时确认一项与转让收入等额的金融负债，并按照《企业会计准则第22号——金融工具确认和计量》对该金融负债进行会计处理；出租人不确认被转让资产，但应当确认一项与转让收入等额的金融资产，并按照《企业会计准则第22号——金融工具确认和计量》对该金融资产进行会计处理。

IAS 37

Provisions, contingent liabilities and contingent assets

1. Provisions（预计负债）

1) Definition

A provision **is a liability of uncertain timing or amount**.（强调,预计负债是一个负债,只是时间或者金额不确定而已。）

A liability is a **present obligation** of the entity arising from **past events**, the settlement of which is expected to result in an **outflow from the entity of resources** embodying economic benefits.

2) Recognition

IAS 37 states that a provision should be recognized as a liability in the financial statements when：（同时满足下列条件应当确认预计负债）

a) An entity has a **present obligation**（**legal or constructive**）as a result of a **past event**

b) It is **probable** that an **outflow of resources embodying economic benefits** will be required to settle the obligation

c) A **reliable estimate can be made** of the amount of the obligation

IAS 37 defines a **constructive obligation（推定义务的定义）** as：

a) By an established pattern of **past practice**, published policies or a sufficiently specific current statement the entity has indicated to other parties **that it will accept certain responsibilities**; and（比如质保服务）

b) As a result, the entity has created a **valid expectation** on the part of those other parties that it will discharge those responsibilities.

3) Measurement

The amount recognised as a provision should be the **best estimate(最佳估计值)** of the expenditure required to settle the present obligation at the end of the reporting period.

Allowance is made for uncertainty. Where the provision being measured involves **a large population of items**, the obligation is estimated by **weighting all possible outcomes by their associated probabilities**, ie **expected value**.（若为多个事项,用期望值法）

Where the provision involves **a single item**, such as the outcome of **a legal case**, provision is made in full for the **most likely outcome**.（若为单个事项,则用最有可能的

结果。)

4) Reimbursements(针对预计负债收到的赔偿怎么处理)

Some or all of the expenditure needed to settle a provision may be expected to be **recovered from a third party**. If so, the reimbursement should be **recognized only when it is virtually certain**（>95%的可能性）that **reimbursement will be received** if the entity settles the obligation.

a) The reimbursement **should be treated as a separate asset**（确认为一项单独的资产），and the amount recognized should not be greater than the provision itself.（并且确认的金额不能比预计负债本身的金额还大）

b) The provision and the amount recognized for reimbursement **may be netted off in profit or loss**.（可以在利润表中抵消，比如10块钱的预计负债费用，8块钱的赔偿，净损益就是2块钱。)

5) Changes in provisions（预计负债的价值要进行调整，少记就补记，多记就冲销。)

Increase in provision	Decrease in provision
DR：Expenses 　　CR：Provisions	DR：Provisions 　　CR：Expenses

6) Onerous contracts(亏损合同)

An onerous contract is a contract entered into with another party under which the **unavoidable costs of fulfilling the terms of the contract exceed any revenues expected to be received from the goods or services** supplied or purchased directly or indirectly under the contract and where the entity would have to **compensate the other party if it did not fulfil the terms of the contract**.

亏损合同是指履行合同义务不可避免会发生的成本超过预期经济利益的合同。

If an entity has a contract that is onerous, the **present obligation** under the contract should be recognized and measured as a provision.

待执行合同变为亏损合同，同时该亏损合同产生的义务满足预计负债的确认条件的，应当确认为预计负债。

7) Decommissioning or abandonment costs(弃置费用)

All the costs of decommissioning may be capitalised.（资本化，并且是按照折现后的金额资本化！）

Dr：PPE
　　Cr：Provision

8) Provision for restructuring(企业重组产生的预计负债)

IAS 37 defines a restructuring as：

A programme that is planned and is controlled by management and **materially changes one of two things.**（组织架构或者管理层的改变）

a) The scope of a business undertaken by an entity（企业的经营范围改变）

b) The manner in which that business is conducted（企业经营方式的改变）

IAS 37 Provisions, contingent liabilities and contingent assets

重组,是指企业制定和控制的,将显著改变企业组织形式、经营范围或经营方式的计划实施行为。

属于重组的事项主要包括:

(1) 出售或终止企业的部分业务;

(2) 对企业的组织结构进行较大调整;

(3) 关闭企业的部分营业场所,或将营业活动由一个国家或地区迁移到其他国家或地区。

The IAS gives the following examples of events that may fall under the definition of restructuring.

a) The sale or termination of a line of business

b) The closure of business locations in a country or region or the relocation of business activities from one country region to another

c) Changes in management structure, for example, the elimination of a layer of management

d) Fundamental reorganizations that have a material effect on the nature and focus of the entity's operations

The **question is whether or not an entity has an obligation — legal or constructive — at the end of the reporting period**. For this to be the case:(重组过程中,同时满足下列条件才能确认预计负债)

企业承担的重组义务满足或有事项确认条件的,应当确认为预计负债。企业应当按照与重组有关的直接支出确定预计负债金额。

(1) An entity must have a **detailed formal plan** for the restructuring.

有详细、正式的重组计划,包括重组涉及的业务、主要地点、需要补偿的职工人数及其岗位性质、预计重组支出、计划实施时间等;

(2) It must have raised a valid expectation in those affected that it will carry out the restructuring by starting to implement that plan or announcing its main features to those affected by it.

该重组计划已对外公告,重组计划已经开始实施,或已向受其影响的各方通告了该计划的主要内容,从而使各方形成了对该企业将实施重组的合理预期。

Costs to be included within a restructuring provision (重组中应当确认为预计负债的项目):

The IAS states that a restructuring provision should include **only the direct expenditures** arising from the restructuring, which are those that are both:(企业应当按照与重组有关的直接支出确定预计负债金额。)

(1) Necessarily entailed by the restructuring; and(重组过程中必须发生的)

(2) Not associated with the ongoing activities of the entity.(不能和之后的继续进行的业务相关)

F7 常考的不能计入重组预计负债成本的项目:

(1) Investment in new systems and distribution networks(对新分销系统的投资,该支出与继续进行的活动相关)

（2）Retraining or relocating continuing staff（重新培训与安置员工）

（3）Marketing（市场推广费用）

即为：**直接支出不包括留用职工岗前培训、市场推广、新系统和营销网络投入等支出。**

2. Contingent liabilities（或有负债）

1）Definition

IAS 37 defines a contingent liability as：

A **possible obligation** that arises from past events and whose existence will be confirmed only by the occurrence or non-occurrence of one or more **uncertain future events not wholly within the control of the entity**; or A **present obligation** that arises from past events **but is not recognized** because：

a）It is **not probable** that an **outflow of resources embodying economic benefits** will be required to settle the obligation；or

b）The **amount** of the obligation **cannot be measured with sufficient reliability**.

上述内容其实说白了就是不能满足负债的所有条件，所以就叫作或有负债。

2）Recognition

An entity should not recognise a contingent asset or liability, but they should be disclosed. （不在报表上确认，但是要披露。）

3. Contingent assets（或有资产）

1）Definition

IAS 37 defines a contingent asset as：

A **possible asset** that arises from past events and whose existence will be confirmed by the occurrence or non-occurrence of one or more **uncertain future events not wholly within control of the entity**.

2）Recognition

A contingent asset **must not be recognized**.（或有资产一定不能在报表上确认！）

Only when the realization of the related economic benefits is **virtually certain** should recognition take place. At that point, the asset is no longer a contingent asset！（只有当基本确定的时候，才能确认为资产！）

3）Disclosure

Contingent assets must **only be disclosed** in the notes if they are **probable**.（当很可能产生的时候才披露！）

	Provision	Contingent liability	Contingent asset
Probable（50%＜发生的可能性≤95%）	Recognize	Recognize	Disclose
Possible（5%＜发生的可能性≤50%）	Disclose	Disclose	Do nothing
Remote（0＜发生的可能性≤5%）	Do nothing	Do nothing	Do nothing

IAS 10

Events after reporting period

Events occurring after the reporting period are those events, **both favourable and unfavourable**, that **occur between the end of the reporting period and the date on which the financial statements are authorised for issue**. Two types of events can be identified.

资产负债表日后事项,是指资产负债表日至财务报告批准报出日之间发生的有利或不利事项。它包括资产负债表日后调整事项和资产负债表日后非调整事项。

Those that **provide evidence of conditions that existed at the end of the reporting period — adjusting**(资产负债表日后调整事项,是指对资产负债表日已经存在的情况提供了新的或进一步证据的事项。)

Those that are indicative of conditions that **arose after the reporting period — non-adjusting**(资产负债表日后非调整事项,是指表明资产负债表日后发生的情况的事项。)

Those that provide evidence of conditions that existed at the end of the reporting period — adjusting Examples	Those that are indicative of conditions that arose after the reporting period — non-adjusting Examples
evidence of a permanent diminution in property value prior to the year end 资产负债表日后取得确凿证据,表明某项资产在资产负债表日发生了减值或者需要调整该项资产原先确认的减值金额	acquisition of, or disposal of, a subsidiary after the year end 资产负债表日后发生企业合并或处置子公司
sale of inventory after the reporting period for less than its carrying value at the year end 存货发生减值	announcement of a plan to discontinue an operation 资产负债表日后声明终止经营
amounts received or paid in respect of legal or insurance claims which were in negotiation at the year end (法律诉讼案件是本期已经发生的,只是结果不确定)	major purchases and disposals of assets 资产负债表日后重大资产购买及处置
determination after the year end of the sale or purchase price of assets sold or purchased before the year end 资产负债表日后进一步确定了资产负债表日前购入资产的成本或售出资产的收入	destruction of a production plant by fire after the reporting period 资产负债表日后的火灾

(Continued)

evidence of a permanent diminution in the value of a long-term investment prior to the year end 长期资产的减值	announcement or commencing implementation of a major restructuring 资产负债表日后的重大重组
discovery of error or fraud which shows that the financial statements were incorrect 资产负债表日后发现了财务报表舞弊或差错	share transactions after the reporting period 资产负债表日后发行新的股票
	litigation commenced after the reporting period 资产负债表日后才发生的诉讼
	dividends proposed or declared after the end of the reporting period are not recognised as a liability in the accounts at the reporting date, but are disclosed in the notes to the accounts 资产负债表日后企业利润分配方案中拟分配的以及经审议批准宣告发放的现金股利和利润

IAS 2

Inventory

1. Introduction

Statement of financial position → Closing inventory
Statement of profit or loss → Cost of sales

2. Definition

Inventories are assets:
Held for sale in the ordinary course of business(在正常经营过程中持有待售的)
In the process of production for such sale(**work in progress** 在产品)
In the form of **materials**(原材料)

3. Cost of inventory

The cost of inventory should **comprise all** the followings:
a) Costs of purchase 采购过程中发生的成本
b) Costs of conversion 生产转换过程中的成本
c) Other costs incurred in bringing the inventory to their present location and condition 其他使存货达到预定可销售状态所必需的成本

Purchase cost:
Purchase price（买价）
Non-recovered duty and tax (irrecoverable)(不可抵扣的税费)
Transport，handling，carriage inwards(往里面运的运费) and others
Less any trade discount and rebates(扣除任何形式的商业折扣)

Conversion costs:
Cost directly related to unit production e.g. direct material，direct labour(直接材料 直接人工)
Fixed and variable production overhead that incurred in converting materials into finished goods，allocated on systematic basis(制造费用，比如折旧费)

* **Fixed production overhead:** Indirect costs of production that remains relatively constant **regardless of the volume of production.**(与产量无关的费用，固定费用)
E.g. Cost of factory management and administration（Salary of factory manager 车

间管理人员的工资)

Allocated to inventories **based on normal capacity**(标准水平) of the production facility

＊**Variable production overhead：**Indirect costs of production，that **vary directly with the volume of production**(随着产量会改变的，变动费用)

E.g. Indirect material and labour

Allocation of variable overhead is based on the **actual(实际水平) use** of production facility.

Excluded cost：(着重记忆：不应包含进存货成本的有哪些？)

a) **Abnormal wastage**(however，**normal wastage is included** as cost of inventory)(非正常损耗不计入成本，正常损耗计入成本)

b) Selling costs (marketing，**carriage outwards**)

c) Storage cost (**except** costs which are necessary in the production process before a further production stage 除非是为了进入下一个生产环节所必须得仓储成本才能计入成本，否则仓储成本都不计入存货成本)

d) **Administrative overheads unrelated** to production

e) **Foreign exchange difference**

f) **Interest costs on Cr purchase** of inventory

4. Counting inventory

1) Continuing counting (continuous/perpetual) 永续盘存制

A business holds **considerable** quantities of **varied** inventory

A card，or a **computerised record**，is kept for every item of inventory，showing receipts and issues from the stores，and a running total.(时时刻刻都在计算存货"收发存"数量)

2) Physical count/Periodic count 实地盘存制/定期盘存制

A business holds **easily counted** and **relatively small amounts** of inventory quantities of inventories on hand at the reporting date can be determined by physically counting them in an inventory count at that date.(在期末实地去盘点我们的存货有多少)

做账区别如下：

	Perpetual count	Periodic count
Purchase of inventory at $8	DR：Inventory　　　　　　　$8 CR：Trade payable/Cash　　$8	DR：Purchase　　　　　　　$8 CR：Trade payable/Cash　　$8
Sales of inventory at $12	DR：Trade receivable/Cash　$10 CR：Sales　　　　　　　　　$10	DR：Trade receivable/Cash　$10 CR：Sales　　　　　　　　　$10
Cost of sales	DR：Cost of sales　　　　　$8 CR：Inventory　　　　　　　$8	DR：Cost of sales　　　　　$8 CR：Inventory　　　　　　　$8

3) Physical count 实地盘存制下的存货怎么做账？(F3重点，非F7重点，F7重点在永

续盘存制及存货减值上！)

a) Opening inventory ＄8（假设期初库存有 8 美元的存货）

DR：Cost of sales	＄8
CR：Opening inventory	＄8

b) Purchase ＄10（假设本期购进 10 美元的存货）

DR：Cost of sales	＄10
CR：Purchase	＄10

c) Closing inventory ＄2（期末，实际去仓库盘点发现我们有 2 美元的存货）

DR：closing inventory	＄2
CR：cost of sales	＄2

Cost of sales ＝ 8 ＋ 10 － 2 ＝ ＄16

为什么是这样？

逻辑是在实地盘存制下，我们先假设期初(＄8)及本期增加的(＄10)存货在当期都卖出去了，到了期末的时候去仓库实地盘点，得到还有＄2 的存货，倒挤出实际卖出去的存货只有＄16．

得到公式，实地盘存制下：

Cost of sales＝Opening inventory＋Purchase — Closing inventory

5. Valuing inventory — price

1) Items not ordinarily interchangeable

Cost of inventories should be assigned by **specific identification** of their **individual costs**

针对不可互换、不可互相替代的产品，应当单独确认每个存货的成本。

2) Interchangeable items 针对同质、可相互替换的存货

a) First in，first out（FIFO）先进先出法

Components are used in the order in which they are received from suppliers

b) Last in，first out（LIFO）后进先出法（了解即可，准则不允许使用）

Components used formed part of the most recent delivery，and inventories are the oldest receipts. And LIFO is not permitted by IAS2 Inventory.

c) Average cost（AVCO）加权平均法

As purchase prices change with each new consignment，the average price of components held is **constantly changed.** Each component is valued at the average price of all components held at that moment.

（i）Moving(continuous)average cost 移动加权平均法

Cost of inventory ＝ cost of inventory currently in the store ＋ cost of new items received － cost of issued/No. Of inventory currently in the store ＋ No. Of new items received － No. Of inventory issued

（ii）Periodic average 期末一次加权平均

Cost of inventory ＝ cost of opening inventory ＋ cost of all purchase in the period/No.

Of opening inventory + No. Of all purchase in the period

3) Impairment of inventory(F7 考试重点)

Inventory should be valued at the lower of cost and net realisable value. (IAS2) （背下这句话！）

Net realizable value is the estimated selling price in the ordinary course of business less the estimated costs of completion and the estimated costs necessary to make the sale.

文字变公式：**NRV = Selling price — Cost of completion — Cost necessary to make the sale**

If cost of inventory is larger than net realisable value, then impairment loss occurs.

Dr: Impairment loss (SPL)　　　　　　　　　　　　　　　XXX
　　　Cr: Inventory (SOFP)　　　　　　　　　　　　　　　XXX

IAS 41

Agriculture

1. Definitions

Agricultural activity(农业生产行为) is the management by an entity of the **biological transformation** of biological assets for sale, into agricultural produce or into additional biological assets.(比如苹果树会长出苹果,奶牛会产出牛奶)

Agricultural produce(农产品) is the harvested product of an entity's biological assets.

Biological assets(生物资产) are living animals or plants.(生物资产,是指有生命的动物和植物。)

Biological transformation(生物转化), compromises the processes of growth(生长), degeneration(退化), production(生产) and procreation(繁衍) that cause qualitative and quantitative changes in a biological asset.(其实就是发生数量和质量上的改变)

A group of biological assets is an aggregation of similar living animals or plants.

Harvest(收获) is the detachment of produce from a biological asset or the cessation of a biological asset's life processes.

The IAS distinguishes between two broad categories of agricultural production system.

a) Consumable: animals/plants themselves are harvested.

消耗性生物资产,是指为出售而持有的、或在将来收获为农产品的生物资产,包括生长中的大田作物、蔬菜、用材林以及存栏待售的牲畜等。

b) Bearer: animals/plants bear produce for harvest, such as grape vines, rubber trees and oil palms. These plants are used solely to grow produce crops over several periods and are not in themselves consumed. When no longer productive they are usually scrapped. They are **similar to assets in a manufacturing activity. (IAS16)**

生产性生物资产,是指为产出农产品、提供劳务或出租等目的而持有的生物资产,包括经济林、薪炭林、产畜和役畜等。

2. Recognition

The recognition criteria **are very similar to those for other assets**, in that animals or plants should be recognized as assets in the following circumstances.(其实生物资产的确认条件和其他资产的确认条件是相似的)

a) The entity **controls** the asset as a result of **past events**.

b) It is **probable** that the **future economic benefits** associated with the asset will flow to the entity.

c) The **fair value or cost** of the asset to the entity can be **measured reliably**.

3. Measurement

1) Initial measurement

The IAS requires that at each year end all biological assets within the scope should be **measured at fair value less estimated point-of-sale costs.**

If a **fair value cannot be determined** because market determined prices or values are not available. Then the biological asset **can be measured at cost less accumulated depreciation and impairment losses.**（公允价值不能合理取得的话，就按照类似于PPE成本模型来计量）

This alternative basis is only allowed on initial recognition.（后续计量是不允许采用成本模型的）

2) Subsequent measurement

In the statement of financial position the biological assets **must be shown at fair value less estimated point of sale costs**, incorporating the consequences of all biological transformations.

A **gain or loss** arising on initial recognition of a biological asset at fair value less estimated point of sale costs and **from a change in fair value** less estimated point of sale costs is **included in profit or loss** in the period in which it arises.（公允价值变动计入当期损益）

4. Presentation

In the statement of financial position biological assets should **be classified as a separate class of assets** falling under neither current nor non-current classifications.（在报表上一定要单独列报生物资产）

5. Agricultural produce

Agricultural produce that is harvested for trading or processing activities within integrated agricultural/agribusiness operations **should be measured at fair value at the date of harvest and this amount is deemed cost** for application of IAS 2 to consequential inventories.（是农产品的时候就按照 FV — cost to sell 来计量，变成存货的时候存货的 cost 为转换日当天的 FV。）

Notes: 通常变为存货的时点就是"enters **trading activities** or **production processes**"

Agricultural produce should be classified as inventory in the statement of financial position and disclosed separately either in the statement of financial position or in the notes.

IAS 12

Income tax

1. 所得税核算的基本原理

资产负债表债务法

所得税会计采用资产负债表债务法核算所得税,资产负债表债务法是从资产负债表出发,通过比较资产负债表上列示的资产、负债按照企业会计准则规定确定的账面价值与按照税法规定确定的计税基础,对于两者之间的差异分别应纳税暂时性差异与可抵扣暂时性差异,确认相关的递延所得税负债与递延所得税资产,并在此基础上确定每一会计期间利润表中的所得税费用。

所得税准则规范的是资产负债表中递延所得税资产和递延所得税负债的确认和计量。减少未来期间应交所得税的暂时性差异形成递延所得税资产,即未来期间由税前会计利润计算应纳税所得额时会纳税调整减少的暂时性差异确认递延所得税资产;增加未来期间应交所得税的暂时性差异形成递延所得税负债,即未来期间由税前会计利润计算应纳税所得额时会纳税调整增加的暂时性差异应确认递延所得税负债。

2. 资产的计税基础

资产的计税基础,指企业收回资产账面价值的过程中,计算应纳税所得额时按照税法可以自应税经济利益中抵扣的金额。

The tax base of an asset is the amount that will be deductible for tax purposes against any taxable economic benefits that will flow to the entity when it recovers the carrying value of the asset. Where those economic benefits are not taxable, the tax base of the asset is the same as its carrying amount. So where the carrying amount and the tax base of the asset are different, a temporary difference exists.

资产的计税基础 = 未来可税前列支的金额
Tax base of asset = future tax deductible amount
某一资产负债表日的计税基础 = 成本 − 以前期间已税前列支的金额

针对固定资产:
账面价值 = 实际成本 − 会计累计折旧 − 固定资产减值准备
计税基础 = 实际成本 − 税法累计折旧

3. 负债的计税基础

负债的计税基础,是指负债的账面价值减去未来期间计算应纳税所得额时按照税法规定可予抵扣的金额。

The tax base of a liability will be its carrying amount, less any amount that will be deducted for tax purposes in relation to the liability in future periods. For revenue received in advance, the tax base of the resulting liability is its carrying amount, less any amount of the revenue that will not be taxable in future periods.

负债的计税基础 = 账面价值 – 未来期间按照税法规定可予税前扣除的金额

Tax base of liability = CV – future tax deductible amount

4. 暂时性差异

暂时性差异,是指资产或负债的账面价值与其计税基础之间的差额。根据暂时性差异对未来期间应纳税所得额影响的不同,分为应纳税暂时性差异和可抵扣暂时性差异。

These temporary differences give rise to deferred tax, because there is a delay between profits being reported for accounting purposes and tax levied on those profits.

A temporary difference is the difference between the carrying values of an asset or liability and its tax base.

某些不符合资产、负债的确认条件,未作为财务报告中资产、负债列示的项目,如果按照税法规定可以确定其计税基础,该计税基础与其账面价值之间的差额也构成暂时性差异。

1) 应纳税暂时性差异

应纳税暂时性差异,是指在确定未来收回资产或清偿负债期间的应纳税所得额时,将导致产生应税金额的暂时性差异。

A temporary difference that will result in taxable amounts in the future when the carrying amount of the asset is recovered or the liability is settled. (carrying value > tax base)

应纳税暂时性差异通常产生于以下情况:

(1) 资产的账面价值大于其计税基础;

(2) 负债的账面价值小于其计税基础

2) 可抵扣暂时性差异

可抵扣暂时性差异,是指在确定未来收回资产或清偿负债期间的应纳税所得额时,将导致产生可抵扣金额的暂时性差异。

A temporary difference that will result in amounts that are tax deductible in the future when the carrying amount of the asset is recovered or the liability is settled. (carrying value < tax base)

可抵扣暂时性差异一般产生于以下情况:

(1) 资产的账面价值小于其计税基础

(2) 负债的账面价值大于其计税基础

5. 递延所得税负债的确认和计量

1) 递延所得税负债的确认原则

除所得税准则中明确规定可不确认递延所得税负债的情况以外,企业对于所有的应纳税暂时性差异均应确认相关的递延所得税负债。除直接计入所有者权益的交易或事项以及企业合并中取得资产、负债相关的以外,在确认递延所得税负债的同时,应增加利润表中的所得税费用。

2) 递延所得税负债的计量

递延所得税负债应以相关应纳税暂时性差异转回期间适用的所得税税率计量。无论应纳税暂时性差异的转回期间如何,递延所得税负债的确认不要求折现。

$$\text{Deferred tax liability} = (\text{Carrying value} - \text{Tax Base}) \times \text{Tax Rate}$$

Deferred tax should not be discounted

The tax rate in force when the asset is realised or the liability is settled should be used to calculate deferred tax. This rate must be based, however, on tax rates and legislation that has been enacted or substantially enacted by the balance sheet date.

6. 递延所得税资产的确认和计量

1) 递延所得税资产的确认

资产、负债的账面价值与其计税基础不同产生可抵扣暂时性差异的,在估计未来期间能够取得足够的应纳税所得额用以利用该可抵扣暂时性差异时,应当以很可能取得用来抵扣可抵扣暂时性差异的应纳税所得额为限,确认相关的递延所得税资产。

2) 递延所得税资产的计量

适用税率的确定。确认递延所得税资产时,应估计相关可抵扣暂时性差异的转回时间,采用转回期间适用的所得税税率为基础计算确定。无论相关的可抵扣暂时性差异转回期间如何,递延所得税资产均不予折现。

Tax charged to profit or loss	
Estimated tax for the year (go to SOFP as current liability)	X
Less: over provision of last year Add: under provision of last year	(X)/X
Add: increase/decrease in deferred tax	X/(X)
Tax charge in P/L	X

Presentation of published financial statements

Statement of profit or loss and other comprehensive income of ABC Company for the year ended XX.XX.XXXX

	$
Sales revenue	X
Cost of sales	(X)
Gross profit	X

(Continued)

	$
Other income	X
Distribution cost	(X)
Administration cost	(X)
Other operation expenses	(X)
Profit from operating	X
Finance cost	(X)
Profit before tax	X
Tax	(X)
Profit for the year	X
Other comprehensive income:	
Items that will not be reclassified to profit or loss:	
Gains on property revaluation	X
Investments in equity instruments	X
Remeasurement gains (losses) on defined benefit pension plans	X
Share of gains (losses) on property revaluation of associates	X
Income tax relating to items that will not be reclassified	X
Total comprehensive income	X

Statement of financial position of ABC Company as at XX.XX.XXXX

Assets	$	$
Non-current assets		
Property, plant and equipment	X	
Intangible assets	X	
Goodwill	X	
Investments	X	
		X
Current assets		
Inventory	X	
Trade receivable	X	
Other current assets	X	
Cash and cash equivalents	X	
		X

(Continued)

Assets	$	$
Total assets		X̲
Equities and liabilities		
Equity		
Share capital	X	
Retained earnings	X	
Other components of equity	X	
		X
Non-current liabilities		
Long-term loan	X	
Long-term provisions	X	
		X
Current liabilities		
Trade and other payable	X	
Short term borrowing (Bank overdraft)	X	
Current portion of long-term borrowings	X	
Short-term provisions	X	
Current tax payable	X	
		X
Total equity and liabilities		X̲

Statement of changes in equity of ABC Company for the year ended 31 December 20×8

	Share capital $	Share premium $	Revaluation surplus $	Retained earnings $	Total $
Balance at 1.1. XXXX	X	X	X	X	X
Changes in accounting policy				(X)	(X)
Restated balance	X̲	X̲	X̲	X̲	X̲
Changes in equity for XXXX					
Dividends				(X)	(X)
Total comprehensive income for the year			X	X	X
Issue of share capital	X	X			X
Balance at 31.12.XXXX	X̲	X̲	X̲	X̲	X̲

Group introduction

1. Trade investment(通常持股比例在小于 20%)

A trade investment is a **simple investment** in the shares of another entity **that is not an associate or a subsidiary.**

A trade investment is a simple investment in the shares of another entity,that is **held for the accretion of wealth** 财富增值(为了增值买卖或是长期获利),and is **not an associate or a subsidiary.**

Dr:Investment　　　　　　　　　　　(在报表上通常列式在非流动资产部分)XX
　　Cr:Cash　　　　　　　　　　　　　　　　　　　　　　　　　　　　XX

2. Associate

Associate:An entity over which the investor **has significant influence**. 重大影响(IAS28)

The existence of significant influence is usually evidenced in the **following ways:**

a) Representation on the board of directors(董事会)(or equivalent) of the investee(董事会当中有代表)

b) **Participation** in the policy making process(可参与决策)

c) Material transactions between investor and investee(有重大交易,比如为主要供应商)

d) Interchange of management personnel(内部高管的互换)

e) Provision of essential technical information(提供核心技术信息)

Note: If an investor **holds 20% or more of the voting power**(投票权) **of the entity**, it can be presumed that the investor has **significant influence** over the entity,unless it can be clearly shown that this is not the case.(通常来说持股比例超过 20%就代表有重大影响)

1) **Equity method in consolidated financial statements — IAS28**

a) P acquire A 40% shares in cash for 1,000

Dr:Investment in associate　　　　　　　　　　　　　　　1,000
　　Cr:Cash　　　　　　　　　　　　　　　　　　　　　　　1,000

b) After acquisition,A makes a profit of $500

Dr:Investment in associate　　　　　　　　　　　(500*40%)200
　　Cr:Share of profit of associate　　　　　　　　(500*40%)200

c) At the same time,A make a dividend $200

Dr: Cash (200*40%) 80
　　Cr: Investment in associate (200*40%) 80

The F3/FFA syllabus requires you to **understand the principle** of equity accounting, **but** you will **not be expected to perform calculations** using equity accounting techniques in your exam.(理解即可,F3 中不会考到你复杂的计算)

2) Cost method in single financial statements

a) P acquire A 40% shares in cash for 1,000

Dr: Investment in associate　　　　　　　　　　　　　1,000
　　Cr: Cash　　　　　　　　　　　　　　　　　　　　1,000

b) After acquisition, A makes a profit of $500—Do nothing

c) P received dividend from A 200

Dr: Cash　　　　　　　　　　　　　　　　　　　　　　200
　　Cr: Investment income　　　　　　　　　　　　　　200

3. Group

The parent has **power over more than 50% of the voting rights** by virtue of agreement with other investors.

The parent has power to **govern(监管、控制)** the financial and operating policies of the entity by statute or under an agreement(控制财务经营决策)

The parent has the power to **appoint or remove a majority** of members of the board of directors (or equivalent governing body)(任命或罢免董事会大多数成员)

The parent has power to cast **a majority of votes** at meetings of the **board of directors**(董事会当中大多数的投票权)

Control can usually be assumed to exist when the parent owns **more than half (ie over 50%) of the voting power** of an entity unless it can be clearly shown that such ownership does not constitute control (these situations will be very rare).(通常来说持有拥有投票权的股权超过 50%即形成控制)

1) Definition

Subsidiary 子公司

An entity that is controlled by another entity (known as the parent).

Parent 母公司

An entity that has one or more subsidiaries.

Group 集团

A parent and all its subsidiaries.

Control

The power to govern the financial and operating policies of an entity so as to obtain benefits from its activities.

Consolidation means presenting the results, assets and liabilities of a group of companies **as if they were one company.**

2) Basic principle for consolidation

IFRS 10 requires a parent to present consolidated financial statements 母公司编制合并报表（also referred to as group accounts）in which the accounts of the parent and subsidiary（or subsidiaries）are combined and presented as a single entity.

This presentation means that the substance, rather than the legal form, of the relationship between parent and subsidiaries will be presented.

Consolidated financial statements ignore the legal boundaries of the separate legal entities.

They are important because the users of the parent's financial statements need to know about the financial position, results of operations and changes in financial position of the group as a whole.

IFRS 10 requires that, when a parent issues consolidated financial statements, it should consolidate all subsidiaries, both foreign and domestic

Basis principle of consolidation is：

Adding together 加总求和

Cancellation of like items internal to the group 抵销内部交易

Consolidate as if you owned everything then show the extent to which you do not own everything（先假设你拥有100%，再体现你不拥有的东西"少数股东权益"）

The consolidated statement of financial position

1. Introduction

1）日期

DOA：date of acquisition（收购日，形成控制那一天）

DOC：date of consolidation（合并日，母公司会计期末）

2）P → 100% 控股的情况

Investment in subsidiary：对子公司的投资（即为我们花了多少钱买子公司）

= Fair value of net assets of S + Goodwill

= Net assets + Fair value adjustment + Goodwill

= Total assets − Total liabilities + Fair value adjustment + Goodwill

即为：Goodwill 商誉 = investment in subsidiary − FV of net assets（考试更常用的公式是这个）

3）P → 50%～100%（非100%）控股的情况

Investment in subsidiary：对子公司的投资（即为我们花了多少钱买子公司）

= Fair value of net assets of S + Goodwill − Non-controlling interest (NCI)

= Net assets + Fair value adjustment + Goodwill-NCI

= Total assets − Total liabilities + Fair value adjustment + Goodwill − NCI

即为：Goodwill 商誉 = investment in subsidiary + NCI − FV of net assets of S（考试更常用的公式是这个）

2. Consolidation principle

Basic consolidation consists of two procedures

Cancelling out items which appear as an asset in one company and a liability in another(内部交易,比如应收应付的抵销)

Then **adding together all the uncanceled assets and liabilities** on a line by line basis.(逐行相加剩下的所有资产负债)

The asset 'investment in subsidiaries' in the parent company accounts always cancels with the share capital of the subsidiary companies. The only share capital in the consolidated accounts is that of the parent company.

(这儿简单理解为:花了"investment in subsidiaries"账户里所列示的钱把子公司的 equity 从子公司股东那儿买过来了,买过来的形式是相关的资产和负债一起打包买过来,所以如果再加一遍 equity 就会重复,所以 equity 应当抵销。)

3. Goodwill arising on consolidation

Goodwill is **the difference between consideration paid and the fair value of net assets of subsidiary at acquisition.**

Fair value adjustment:

The **land and buildings**(考试中通常这两项都是公允价值会高于账面价值) of the subsidiary may be worth more than their carrying amount at acquisition. If this is the case, it must be taken into account in the consolidated financial statements.

Goodwill calculation:

Consideration transferred	X
Non-controlling interest	X
Less fair value of identifiable net assets of subsidiary company at acquisition date:	
Share capital	X
Share premium	X
Retained earnings at acquisition	X
Fair value adjustments at acquisition	X
	(X)
Goodwill	X

The **consideration paid** by the parent for the shares in the subsidiary can take **different forms**.(收购所支付的对价有不同的形式)

The calculation of goodwill **must be based on the fair value** of the consideration transferred.

a) Cash

b) Shares of parent company — fair value of shares is their **market price** on the date of acquisition (number of shares issued * **share price of P**)

4. Non-controlling interest(NCI)(少数股东权益)

The **non-controlling interest (NCI)** shows the extent to which net assets controlled by the group are **owned by other parties**.

IFRS 10 defines non-controlling interest as the equity in a subsidiary not attributable, directly or indirectly, to a parent.

NCI is **shown in the equity section** of the consolidated statement of financial position and is included in the consolidated financial statements at its fair value plus the NCI's share of post-acquisition retained earnings and other reserves.

Fair value of NCI at date of acquisition (DOA)	X
Plus: NCI's share of S's post-acquisition retained earnings	X
NCI at reporting date/date of Consolidation(DOC)	X

> 专题介绍

合并报表中的特殊事项处理

1. 联营企业顺流交易逆流交易怎么处理?

1.1 Introduction

Often a group will be able to exercise significant influence over another company by virtue of a substantial shareholding which falls short of 50%. Such a company is called an associated undertaking of the group.

An associated undertaking is therefore defined as an entity over which the group exercises significant influence, but not control. If the group holds 20% or more of the company's equity we presume that significant influence exists however this presumption can be rebutted if there is clear evidence to the contrary.

1.2 DEFINITION

Significant influence—is the power **to participate in** the financial and operating policy decisions of an entity in which an investment is held, but is not control over these policies.

联营企业投资,是指投资方能够对被投资单位施加重大影响的股权投资。重大影响是指投资方对被投资单位的财务和生产经营决策**有参与决策的权力**,但并不能控制或与其他方一起共同控制这些政策的制定。

Equity accounting — a method of accounting whereby the investment is initially recorded at cost and **adjusted thereafter** for the post-acquisition change in the investor's share of net assets of the associate.

权益法,是指投资以初始投资成本计量后,在投资持有期间根据投资企业享有被投资单位所有者权益份额的变动对投资的账面价值进行调整的方法。

The rules on accounting for associated undertakings are contained mainly in IAS 28 Investments in associates.

IAS 28 requires the use of the equity method to account for associates in consolidated financial statement. The investing group will have to disclose its share of associate's profit after tax on the face of consolidated statement of profit or loss as 'Share of profit from associates'.

1.3 在合并报表中的处理

In the consolidated statement of financial position the investment in associates

should be shown as：
  Cost of the investment in the associate；长期股权投资——投资成本（投资时点）
  Plus：Group share of post acquisition profits；长期股权投资——损益调整（持有期间被投资单位净损益及利润分配变动）
  Less：Any amounts paid out as dividends；（支付给集团母公司的股利）
  Less：Any amount written off the investment（减值准备）

权益法核算下，长期股权投资代表的是享有被投资单位的净资产的份额，投资收益代表的是享有被投资单位净损益的份额。

投资企业与其联营企业及合营企业之间的未实现内部交易损益抵销与投资企业与子公司之间的未实现内部交易损益抵销有所不同，母子公司之间的未实现内部交易损益在合并财务报表中是全额抵销的，而**投资企业与其联营企业及合营企业之间的未实现内部交易损益抵销仅仅是投资企业或是纳入投资企业合并财务报表范围的子公司享有联营企业或合营企业的权益份额部分**。投出或出售的资产不构成业务的（**注意仅指不构成业务的**，F7 中不考察构成业务的会计处理。"构成业务"是一个专业术语）应当分别顺流交易和逆流交易进行会计处理。

  'Upstream' transactions：sales of assets from an associate to the investor. 逆流交易
  'Downstream' transactions：sales of assets from the investor to an associate. 顺流交易
  Profits and losses resulting from 'upstream' and 'downstream' transactions are **eliminated to the extent of the investor's interest in the associate.**

1.3.1 If H sold goods to A 顺流交易

F7 中记住这个调整分录就行：

Dr：Group reserve（注意一定要 * shareholding%）
   Cr：Investment in associate（注意一定要 * shareholding%）

我们来看下处理逻辑原理：

假设，ABC 公司于 2019 年 1 月取得 XYZ 公司 20%有表决权股份，能够对 XYZ 公司施加重大影响。假定 ABC 公司取得该项投资时，XYZ 公司各项可辨认资产、负债的公允价值与其账面价值相同。2019 年 1 月，ABC 公司将其成本为 600 万元的某商品以 1 000 万元的价格出售给 XYZ 公司。至 2019 年资产负债表日，XYZ 公司仍未对外出售该存货。XYZ 公司 2019 年实现净利润为 2 000 万元。假定不考虑所得税因素。

ABC 公司在该项交易中实现利润 400 万元，**其中的 80 万元（400×20％）万元是针对本企业持有的对联营企业的权益份额，在采用权益法计算确认投资损益时应予抵销**，即 ABC 公司应当进行的账务处理为：（ABC 公司单体报表中的处理）

  借：长期股权投资——损益调整[（20 000 000 − 4 000 000）×20%] 3 200 00
    贷：投资收益 3 200 000
  上述分录可分解为：
  借：长期股权投资——损益调整（20 000 000×20%） 4 000 000
    贷：投资收益 4 000 000
  借：投资收益（4 000 000×20%） 800 000
    贷：长期股权投资——损益调整 800 000

那么，假设 ABC 公司存在子公司，即 ABC 公司需要编制合并报表，那么此交易在合并报表中的调整如下：

借：营业收入（10 000 000×20%）　　　　　　　　　　　　　　　2 000 000
　　贷：营业成本（6 000 000×20%）　　　　　　　　　　　　　　1 200 000
　　　　投资收益　　　　　　　　　　　　　　　　　　　　　　　　800 000

接下来，简单理解：（收入－成本）最终会形成 Group reserve，投资收益最终会形成长期股权投资。即最终在合并报表中的分录结果为：

借：营业收入（10 000 000×20%）　　　　　　　　　　　　　　　2 000 000
　　贷：营业成本（6 000 000×20%）　　　　　　　　　　　　　　1 200 000
　　　　长期股权投资　　　　　　　　　　　　　　　　　　　　　800 000

即为 F7 中的：
Dr：Group reserve　　　　　　　　　　　　　　　　　　　　　800,000
**　　Cr：Investment in associate　　　　　　　　　　　　　　　800,000**

1.3.2　If A sold good to H 逆流交易

F7 中记住这个调整分录就行：
Dr：Group RE　　　　　　　　　　　　　　　　　　（注意 * shareholding%）
**　　Cr：Group inventory　　　　　　　　　　　　　（注意 * shareholding%）**

同样，我们来看下处理逻辑原理：

假设，ABC 公司于 2019 年 1 月取得 XYZ 公司 20%有表决权股份，能够对 XYZ 公司施加重大影响。假定 ABC 公司取得该项投资时，XYZ 公司各项可辨认资产、负债的公允价值与其账面价值相同。2019 年 1 月，XYZ 公司将其成本为 600 万元的某商品以 1 000 万元的价格出售给 ABC 公司，ABC 公司将取得的商品作为存货。至 2019 年资产负债表日，ABC 公司仍未对外出售该存货。XYZ 公司 2019 年实现净利润为 3 200 万元。假定不考虑所得税因素。

ABC 公司在按照权益法确认应享有 XYZ 公司 2019 年净损益时，应进行以下账务处理：（ABC 公司单体报表中的处理）

借：长期股权投资——损益调整[（32 000 000－4 000 000）×20%]　5 600 000
　　贷：投资收益　　　　　　　　　　　　　　　　　　　　　　5 600 000

上述分录可分解为：

借：长期股权投资——损益调整（32 000 000×20%）　　　　　　6 400 000
　　贷：投资收益　　　　　　　　　　　　　　　　　　　　　　6 400 000
借：投资收益（4 000 000×20%）　　　　　　　　　　　　　　　800 000
　　贷：长期股权投资——损益调整　　　　　　　　　　　　　　800 000

同样假设 ABC 公司存在子公司，即 ABC 公司需要编制合并报表，那么此交易在合并报表中的调整如下：

借：长期股权投资——损益调整[（10 000 000－6 000 000）×20%]　800 000
　　贷：存货　　　　　　　　　　　　　　　　　　　　　　　　800 000

简单理解，最终"长期股权投资——损益调整"在合并报表中的结果为形成集团的投资收益，**即 F7 中的"Group RE"**。所以在合并报表中的调整结果为：

借：投资收益　　　　　　　　　　　　　　　　　　　　　800 000
　　　　贷：存货　　　　　　　　　　　　　　　　　　　　　　800 000

即为 ACCA F7 中的：

Dr：Group RE　　　　　　　　　　　　　　　　　　　　800,000
　　Cr：Group inventory　　　　　　　　　　　　　　　　800,000

很多同学会有疑问，在合并报表中为什么变成了调存货？

因为在合并财务报表中，因该未实现内部交易损益体现在投资企业持有存货的账面价值当中。

记住，调整的一定是持股比例部分！（＊Shareholding％）（投资企业与其联营企业及合营企业之间的未实现内部交易损益抵销仅仅是投资企业或是纳入投资企业合并财务报表范围的子公司享有联营企业或合营企业的权益份额部分。）

2. 购买日的合并财务报表处理

2.1　使用的合并方法：购买法

All business combination must be accounted for the **Acquisition method**.

购买法是将企业合并视为购买企业以一定的价款购进被购买企业的机器设备、存货等资产项目，同时承担该企业的所有负债的行为，从而按合并时的公允价值计量被购买企业的净资产，**将投资成本（购买价格）超过净资产公允价值的差额确认为商誉的会计方法。**

体现到公式当中就是：

a）100%持股比例时：

Investment in subsidiary（支付的对价 consideration，这个数字只会出现在母公司单体报表中）

　　＝Fair value of net assets of subsidiary（子公司净资产公允价值）＋Goodwill（商誉）

　　＝Net assets（账面价值）＋Fair value adjustment（公允价值调整）＋Goodwill

　　＝Total assets－Total liabilities＋Fair value adjustment＋Goodwill

但我们常用的公式是这个（看到题通常先算商誉）：

Goodwill ＝ Investment in subsidiary － FV of net assets of subsidiary

b）非100%控股时：

Investment in subsidiary（支付的对价 consideration，这个数字只会出现在母公司单体报表中）

　　＝Fair value of net assets＋Goodwill－Non-controlling interest（NCI）（少数股东权益）

　　＝Net assets＋Fair value adjustment＋Goodwill－NCI

　　＝Total assets－Total liabilities＋Fair value adjustment＋Goodwill－NCI

但我们常用的公式是这个（看到题通常先算商誉）：

Goodwill ＝ Investment in subsidiary ＋ NCI － FV of net assets of Subsidiary

2.2　基本合并思路

a) The carrying amount of the parent's investment in each subsidiary and the parent's portion of equity of each subsidiary are eliminated or cancelled（母公司支付的对价，即为 **'Investment in S'** 与子公司的权益相抵消，但在 ACCA 考试中是不用写抵消分录的。）

感兴趣的同学可以了解下，抵消分录为：

购买日合并抵消分录：

借：股本

　　资本公积

　　其他综合收益

　　盈余公积

　　未分配利润

　　商誉(借方差额)

　　贷：长期股权投资

　　　　少数股东权益

b) Non-controlling interests in the net income of consolidated subsidiaries are adjusted against group income, to arrive at the net income attributable to the owners of the parent

c) Non-controlling interests in the net assets of consolidated subsidiaries should be presented separately in the consolidated statement of financial position（这儿其实体现了合并财务报表的合并理论，即为："母公司理论、实体理论、所有权理论。"目前国际财务报告准则及我国企业会计准则主要采用的是实体理论。)

2.3 举例：购买日合并财务报表编制(合并资产负债表)

P 公司于 2×20 年 6 月 30 日发行 1 000 万股普通股（每股面值 1 元，市场价格为 8.75 元），取得了 S 公司 70% 的股权。P 公司和 S 公司资产负债表有关数据如表所示：假定不考虑所得税影响。

2×20 年 6 月 30 日　　　　　　　　　　　　　　　　　　　　　　　　　单位：万元

项目	P 公司	S 公司	
	账面价值	账面价值	公允价值
资产：			
货币资金	4,312.50	450.00	450.00
存货	6,200.00	255.00	450.00
应收账款	3,000.00	2,000.00	2,000.00
长期股权投资	5,000.00	2,150.00	3,800.00
固定资产：			
固定资产原值	10,000.00	4,000.00	5,500.00
减：累计折旧	3,000.00	1,000.00	0.00
固定资产净值	7,000.00	3,000.00	
无形资产	4,500.00	500.00	1,500.00
商誉	0.00	0.00	0.00

(Continued)

项目	P公司	S公司	
	账面价值	账面价值	公允价值
资产总计	30,012.50	8,355.00	13,700.00
负债和所有者权益:			
短期借款	2,500.00	2,250.00	2,250.00
应付账款	3,750.00	300.00	300.00
其他负债	375.00	300.00	300.00
负债合计	6,625.00	2,850.00	2,850.00
实收资本(股本)	7,500.00	2,500.00	
资本公积	5,000.00	1,500.00	
盈余公积	5,000.00	500.00	
未分配利润	5,887.50	1,005.00	
所有者权益合计	23,387.50	5,505.00	10,850.00
负债和所有者权益总计	30,012.50	8,355.00	

(1) 计算确定长期股权投资。(发行股票方式取得股权, Acquired shares by share for share exchange)

　　借：长期股权投资　　　　　　　　　　　　　　　　　8 750
　　　　贷：股本　　　　　　　　　　　　　　　　　　　　1 000
　　　　　　资本公积——股本溢价　　　　　　　　　　　7 750
　　DR：Investment in Subsidiary　　　　　　　　　　　8,750
　　　　CR：Share capital　　　　　　　　　　　　　　　1,000
　　　　　　Share premium　　　　　　　　　　　　　　7,750

(2) 计算确定商誉。(Calculation of Goodwill)

　　合并商誉＝企业合并成本－合并中取得被购买方可辨认净资产公允价值份额
　　　　　　＝8 750－10 850×70％＝1 155(万元)

按照上面给出的英文公式：

Goodwill = Investment in subsidiary + NCI − FV of net assets of Subsidiary
　　　　 = 8,750 + 10,850 * 30%(NCI at the date of acquisition 考试的时候通常会给,实际上是算出来的) − 10,850 = 1,155(万元)

(后面会给大家讲到 Partial Goodwill and Full Goodwill 这儿大家先不用纠结。)

(3) 编制调整抵消分录。[ACCA 考试中不会考察,因为 ACCA 考的都是合并日(DOC)的财务报表,而不是收购日(DOA)的财务报表,这儿只是带着大家看下怎么把子公司的资产负债整体"加"到合并财务报表里。不过也正是因为不考察,就导致很多同学其实并不知道有这个调整过程。]

借：存货 195
　　长期股权投资 1 650
　　固定资产 2 500
　　无形资产 1 000
　　贷：资本公积 5 345
借：实收资本 2 500
　　资本公积 6 845
　　盈余公积 500
　　未分配利润 1 005
　　商誉 1 155
　　贷：长期股权投资 8 750
　　　　少数股东权益 3 255

DR：Inventory 195
　　Investment in equity shares 1,650
　　PPE 2,500
　　Intangible assets 1,000
　　CR：Capital Reserves 1,000
DR：Share capital 2,500
　　Capital reserves 6,845
　　Surplus reserves 500
　　Retained earnings 1,005
　　Goodwill 1,155
　　CR：Investment in subsidiary 8,750
　　　　NCI 3,255

(4) 编制购买日的合并资产负债表

2×20 年 6 月 30 日　　　　　　　　　　　　　　　　　　　　单位：万元

项目	P公司	S公司		抵销分录		合并金额
	账面价值	账面价值	公允价值	借方	贷方	
资产：						
货币资金	4 312.50	450.00	450.00			4 762.50
存货	6 200.00	255.00	450.00	195.00		6 650.00
应收账款	3 000.00	2 000.00	2 000.00			5 000.00
长期股权投资	5 000.00	2 150.00	3 800.00	1 650.00	8 750.00	8 800.00
固定资产：						
固定资产原值	10 000.00	4 000.00	5 500.00	2 500.00		16 500.00
减：累计折旧	3 000.00	1 000.00	0.00			4 000.00

(Continued)

项目	P公司 账面价值	S公司 账面价值	S公司 公允价值	抵销分录 借方	抵销分录 贷方	合并金额
固定资产净值	7 000.00	3 000.00				
无形资产	4 500.00	500.00	1 500.00	1 000.00		6 000.00
商誉	0.00	0.00	0.00	1 155.00		1 155.00
资产总计	30 012.50	8 355.00	13 700.00			44 867.50
负债和所有者权益:						
短期借款	2 500.00	2 250.00	2 250.00			4 750.00
应付账款	3 750.00	300.00	300.00			4 050.00
其他负债	375.00	300.00	300.00			675.00
负债合计	6 625.00	2 850.00	2 850.00			9 475.00
实收资本(股本)	7 500.00	2 500.00		2 500.00		8 500.00
资本公积	5 000.00	1 500.00		6 845.00	5 345.00	12 750.00
盈余公积	5 000.00	500.00		500.00		5 000.00
未分配利润	5 887.50	1 005.00		1 005.00		5 887.50
少数股东权益					3 225.00	3 225.00
所有者权益合计	23 387.50	5 505.00	10 850.00			35 392.50
负债和所有者权益总计	30 012.50	8 355.00				44 867.50

3. 合并过程中的特殊事项处理

3.1 Partial Goodwill and Full Goodwill 部分商誉及完全商誉会计处理

1) Partial goodwill: 部分商誉

Non-controlling interest is measured at its proportion share of subsidiary's net assets thus goodwill is relating to parent only.

部分商誉法指在非同一控制下的企业控股合并交易中将购买方的合并成本超过取得的被购买方可辨认净资产公允价值份额的差额,确认为商誉的初始计量金额的方法。

(部分商誉法下计算出来的商誉与NCI无关,都是属于Parent的,题干中会直接告诉你的,若商誉发生减值,减值损失都是母公司的。)

部分商誉法下商誉发生减值的会计处理:

Dr: Group retained earnings (Amount of impairment)
　　Cr: Goodwill (Amount of impairment)

2) Full goodwill: 完全商誉

Non-controlling interest is measured at fair value, goodwill represent that of both the parent and the NCI

完全商誉法，将母公司和少数股东的合并成本之和同被合并企业可辨认净资产公允价值相比较，将其差额确认为完全商誉的方法。

（计算出来的商誉与 Parent 和 NCI 都有关系。F7 考试常考的是这种。若发生减值，**减值损失要分给母公司也要分给 NCI**。）

完全商誉法下商誉发生减值的会计处理：

Dr：Group retained earning（Amount of impairment ∗ shareholding% of Parent）
Dr：NCI（Amount of impairment ∗ shareholding% of NCI）
　　Cr：goodwill（Amount of impairment）

3.2　Deferred consideration 关于递延对价的处理

Discounted at PV of future cash flow using cost of capital/discount factor/effective interest rate.

Including in non-current liability in P's book.

Interest on deferred consideration deducted from group retained earning

Example：

The parent acquired 75% of the subsidiary's 80 m $1 shares on 1 January 20×8. It paid $3.50 per share and agreed to pay a further $108 m on 1 January 20×9.

The parent company's cost of capital is 8%.

In the financial statements for the year to 31 December 20×6 the cost of the combination will be：

Cash paid：80 m shares ∗ 75% ∗ $3.5 per share = $210 m

Deferred consideration：$108 m/(1+8%) = $100 m

Total consideration = $210 m + $100 m = $310 m

Unwinding of the discount on the deferred consideration：$100 m ∗ 8% = $8 m，which should be charged to finance cost.

3.3　Share for share exchange 发行股票方式收购的会计处理

√ Calculate the value of consideration（use the market price）
√ Add extra share capital and share premium to group account

Dr：Cash　　　　　　　　　　　　　　　　　　　　　　　　XX
　　Cr：Share capital　　　　　　　　　　　　　　　　　　　XX
　　Cr：Share premium　　　　　　　　　　　　　　　　　　XX

Issue cost should be deducted from proceeds of issue（i.e. share premium）**not included** in the cost of the acquisition.

Professional fees and similar incremental costs incurred directly in making the acquisition—**all such costs should be expensed**

合并方在非同一控制下的企业合并中发生的中介费用应计入管理费用。（**费用化处理而非资本化**）

例子：

甲公司 20×9 年 1 月 1 日以定向增发公司普通股票的方式，购买取得 A 公司 70% 的股权。甲公司定向增发普通股股票 10 000 万股（每股面值为 1 元），甲公司普通股股票面值每股为 1 元,市场价格每股为 2.95 元。

借：长期股权投资——A 公司		29 500
贷：股本		10 000
资本公积		19 500
DR：Investment in subsidiary(10,000 * 2.95)		29,500
CR：Share capital(10,000 * 1)		10,000
Share premium (10,000 * 1.95)		19,500

3.4　Contingent consideration 或有对价的会计处理

The revised standard requires the acquirer to recognise the acquisition date fair value of all contingent consideration as part of the consideration.

IFRS 3 requires that all contingent consideration is now recognised.

In an exam question，the acquisition date fair value（or how to calculate it）of any contingent consideration would be given.

非同一控制下企业合并长期股权投资确认与计量应考虑或有对价。

合并成本中包含或有对价的公允价值。

购买方应当将合并协议约定的或有对价作为企业合并转移对价的一部分,按照其在购买日的公允价值计入企业合并成本。根据《企业会计准则——金融工具确认和计量》《企业会计准则第 22 号——金融工具列报》以及其他相关准则的规定,或有对价符合金融负债或权益工具定义的,购买方应当将拟支付的或有对价确认为一项负债或权益;符合资产定义并满足资产确认条件的,购买方应当将符合合并协议约定条件的、对已支付的合并对价中可收回部分的权利确认为一项资产。

Example：

The parent acquired 60% of the subsidiary's $100 m share capital on 1 Jan 20×8 for a cash payment of 150 m and a further payment of $50 m on 31 March 20×9 if the subsidiary's post acquisition profits have exceeded an agreed figure by that date.

In the financial statements for the year to 31 December 20×8 $50 m will be added to the cost of the combination，discounted as appropriate.

(下面的文字部分 F7 不考察,学 SBR 的同学要注意下。)

购买日 12 个月内出现对购买日已存在情况的新的或进一步证据需要调整或有对价的,应当予以确认并对原计入合并商誉的金额进行调整;其他情况下发生的或有对价变化或调整,应当区分情况进行会计处理：或有对价为权益性质的,不进行会计处理;或有对价为资产或负债性质的,如果属于会计准则规定的金融工具,应当按照以公允价值计量且其变动计入当期损益进行会计处理,不得指定为以公允价值计量且其变动计入其他综合收益的金融资产。

3.5　Assets and liabilities not previously recognised in the acquiree's financial statements

被收购方单体报表中没有确认的项目,合并报表需要确认：

a) A **tax benefit** arising from the acquiree's tax losses that was not recognised by the acquiree

b) **Contingent liabilities** are recognised if their fair value can be measured reliably

c) The acquiree may also have **internally-generated assets** such as brand names which have not been recognised as intangible assets.

As the acquiring company is giving valuable consideration for these assets, they are now recognised as assets in the consolidated financial statements.

（1）合并中取得的被购买方除无形资产以外的其他各项资产（不仅限于被购买方原已确认的资产），其所带来的未来经济利益预期很可能流入企业且公允价值能够可靠计量的，应当单独予以确认并按照公允价值计量。

（2）企业合并中取得的无形资产的确认。

非同一控制下的企业合并中，购买方在对企业合并中取得的被购买方资产进行初始确认时，应对被购买方拥有的但在其财务报表中未确认的无形资产进行充分辨认和合理判断，满足以下条件之一的，应确认为无形资产：

① 源于合同性权利或其他法定权利；

② 能够从被购买方中分离或者划分出来，并能单独或与相关合同、资产和负债一起，用于出售、转移、授予许可、租赁或交换。

（3）合并中取得的被购买方除或有负债以外的其他各项负债，履行有关的义务很可能导致经济利益流出企业且公允价值能够可靠地计量的，应当单独予以确认为负债并按照公允价值计量。

（4）合并中取得的被购买方的或有负债，在购买日其公允价值能够可靠计量的，应当单独确认为负债并按照公允价值计量。

3.6 Negative goodwill 负商誉的会计处理

Negative goodwill arises where the cost of the investment is less than the valued of net assets purchased. The negative goodwill is very rare. In this situation, IFRS 3 refers to it as a 'gain on a bargain purchase.

First reassess the cost of investment and fair value of net assets of subsidiary to identify any error.

Once it is established that negative goodwill has arisen it should **be credited directly to the profit or loss.**

购买方对合并成本小于合并中取得的被购买方可辨认净资产公允价值份额的差额（负商誉），应当按照下列规定处理：

对取得的被购买方各项可辨认资产、负债及或有负债的公允价值以及合并成本的计量**进行复核；**

经复核后合并成本仍小于合并中取得的被购买方可辨认净资产公允价值份额的，**其差额应当计入当期损益（营业外收入）**，并在会计报表附注中予以说明。

4. 内部销售存货交易的抵销处理

Intra-group transactions-inventory 内部销售存货交的抵销处理

In the buying company's accounts, inventory will be valued at acquisition cost which now includes the profit element earned by the selling company.

The problem is that from the group's point of view this profit **has not yet been realised** because no sale has been made outside the group and therefore closing inventories are overstated by the profit element.

直接看例子：

P 公司系 S 公司的母公司。P 公司本期个别利润表的营业收入中有 2 000 万元，系向 S 公司销售商品实现的收入，其商品成本为 1 400 万元，销售毛利率为 30%。S 公司本期从 P 公司购入的商品本期均未实现销售，期末存货中包含有 2 000 万元从 P 公司购进的商品，该存货中包含的未实现内部销售损益为 600 万元。编制合并报表内部交易的抵销分录（单位：万元）：

借：营业收入　　　　　　　　　　　　　　　　　　　　　　　2 000
　　贷：营业成本　　　　　　　　　　　　　　　　　　　　　1 400
　　　　存货　　　　　　　　　　　　　　　　　　　　　　　　600

DR：Sales　　　　　　　　　　　　　　　　　　　　　　　　2,000
　　CR：Cost of sales　　　　　　　　　　　　　　　　　　1,400
　　CR：Inventory　　　　　　　　　　　　　　　　　　　　　600

分录归纳整理：

借：期初未分配利润（年初存货中包含的未实现内部销售利润）（注：F7 中一般不考这个金额，记住下面的分录就行）

　　营业收入（本期内部商品销售产生的收入）

　　贷：营业成本

　　　　存货（期末存货中未实现内部销售利润）

上述抵销分录的原理为：本期发生的未实现内部销售收入与本期发生存货中未实现内部销售利润之差即为本期发生的未实现内部销售成本。抵销分录中的"期初未分配利润"和"存货"两项之差即为本期发生的存货中未实现内部销售利润。

变为 F7 中的分录即为：

1) P-S 母公司卖给子公司的情况

a) 资产负债表中（SOFP）：

DR：Retained earnings（Unrealized profit）

　　CR：Inventory（Unrealized profit）

b) 利润表中（SOP/L）：

DR：Sales（Intra-group sales）

　　CR：Cost of sale（Intra-group sales — URP）

将上述分录合并：

DR：Retained earnings b/f（URP b/f）（F7 中一般此项为 0，即为期初无未实现内部销售利润）

DR：Sales（Intra-group sales）

　　CR：Cost of sales（Intra-group sales — URP）

　　CR：Inventory（Unrealized profit）

2) S to P（子公司卖给母公司）

子公司卖给母公司存货就会产生一个问题，即"少数股东是否承担未实现内部交易损益？"

合并财务报表准则第三十六条：母公司向子公司出售资产所发生的未实现内部交易损益，应当全额抵销"归属于母公司所有者的净利润"。子公司向母公司出售资产所发生的未实现内部交易损益，应当按照母公司对该子公司的分配比例在"归属于母公司所有者的净利润"和"少数股东损益"之间分配抵销。

则分录变为：

1) 资产负债表中(SOFP)

DR：Group retained earnings（Unrealized profit * P% shareholding）
DR：Retained earnings of NCI（Unrealized profit * NCI% shareholding）
　　CR：Inventory（Unrealized profit）

2) 利润表中(SOP/L)：

DR：sales（intra-group sales）
　　CR：cost of sale（intra-group sales — URP）

合并则为：

DR：Retained earnings b/f of Parent（URP b/f * P% shareholding）（F7中一般此项为0，即为期初无未实现内部销售利润）

DR：Retained earnings b/f of NCI（URP b/f * NCI% shareholding）（F7中一般此项为0，即为期初无未实现内部销售利润）

DR：Sales（Intra-group sales）
　　CR：Cost of sales（Intra-group sales — URP）
　　CR：Inventory（Unrealized profit）

看例子：

S公司系P公司子公司，P公司拥有S公司80%的股份。2×19年3月1日，S公司向P公司出售一批存货，成本为80万元，未计提存货跌价准备，售价为100万元，至2×19年12月31日，P公司将上述存货对外出售70%。编制合并报表内部交易的抵销分录：

计算未实现损益(URP) = (100 − 80) * (1 − 70%) = 6(万元)

抵销分录：

1) 资产负债表中：

DR：Retained earnings（60 000 * 80%）	48,000
DR：NCI（60 000 * 20%）	12,000
CR：Inventory	60,000

2) 利润表中：

DR：Sales（1,000,000）	1,000,000
CR：Cost of sales（1,000,000 − 60,000）	940,000

IAS 21

Foreign currency transactions

1. Definition

Foreign currency(外币): A currency other than the functional currency of the entity.

Functional currency（记账本位币）: The currency of the primary economic environment in which the entity operates.（记账本位币,是指企业经营所处的主要经济环境中的货币。）

Presentation currency(列报的货币): The currency in which the financial statements are presented.

Exchange rate(汇率): The ratio of exchange for two currencies.

Exchange difference(汇兑损益): The difference resulting from translating a given number of units of one currency into another currency at different exchange rates.（一种货币换另外一种货币时,由于汇率不同所产生的差异。）

Closing rate(期末汇率): The spot exchange rate at the year-end date.（报表日期末汇率）

Spot exchange rate(即期汇率): The exchange rate for immediate delivery.（即期汇率,通常是指银行公布的当日本位币外汇牌价的中间价。）

Monetary items（货币性项目）: Units of currency held and assets and liabilities to be received or paid in a fixed or determinable number of units of currency.（货币性项目,是指企业持有的货币和将以固定或可确定的金额收取的资产或者偿付的负债。）

Conversion(兑换) is the process of exchanging amounts of one foreign currency for another.（货币兑换是将一种外币兑换成另一种外币的过程）

Profits (or losses) on conversion would be included in profit or loss（计入当期损益）for the year in which conversion (whether payment or receipt) takes place.

Translation(外币报表折算) is required at the end of an accounting period when a company still holds assets or liabilities in its statement of financial position which were obtained or incurred in a foreign currency.（主要指期末外币报表折算）

2. Determining an entity's functional currency

An entity considers the following factors in determining its functional currency：
企业选定记账本位币,应当考虑下列因素:

a) The currency that **mainly influences sales prices for goods and services**（this will often be the currency in which sales prices for its goods and services are denominated and settled）；（该货币主要影响商品和劳务的销售价格，通常以该货币进行商品和劳务的计价及结算）and of the country whose competitive **forces and regulations mainly determine the sales prices of its goods and services**.

b) The currency that **mainly influences labour, material and other costs** of providing goods or services（this will often be the currency in which such costs are denominated and settled）.（采购成本所主要使用的货币。）

c) The currency in which funds from financing activities are generated and the currency in which receipts from operating activities are usually retained（融资活动获得的货币以及保存从经营活动中收取款项所使用的货币。）

3. Foreign currency transactions

IAS 21 states that a foreign currency transaction should be recorded，on initial recognition the functional currency，by applying the exchange rate between the reporting currency and the foreign currency at the date of the transaction to the foreign currency amount.（外币交易应当在初始确认时，采用交易发生日的即期汇率将外币金额折算为记账本位币金额）

An average rate for a period may be used if exchange rates do not fluctuate significantly.（也可以采用按照系统合理的方法确定的、与交易发生日即期汇率近似的汇率折算。）

Monetary items：Report foreign currency monetary items using the closing rate（货币性项目，采用资产负债表日即期汇率折算，因资产负债表日即期汇率与初始确认时或者前一资产负债表日即期汇率不同而产生的汇兑差额，计入当期损益。）

Non-monetary items：

a) Report non-monetary items(e.g. non-current assets，inventories) **which are carried at historical cost** in a foreign currency using the exchange rate at the date of the transaction(historical rate)［以历史成本计量的外币非货币性项目，仍采用交易发生日的即期汇率折算，不改变其原记账本位币金额（即不产生汇兑差额）。］

b) Report non-monetary items **which are carried at fair value** in a foreign currency using the exchange rates that existed when the values were measured.［以公允价值计量的外币非货币性项目，如交易性金融资产（股票、基金等），采用公允价值确定日的即期汇率折算，折算后的记账本位币金额与原记账本位币金额的差额，作为公允价值变动处理，计入当期损益（公允价值变动损益）。］

Notes：Exchange differences are recognized as part of **profit or loss** for the period in which they arise.（正常情况，汇兑损益都计入当期损益 profit or loss）Any differences that relate to items charged to Other Comprehensive Income，such as revaluations，should also be charged to OCI（但是特殊情况也会计入 OCI 中，遵循"从哪里来，就到哪里去"的原则。属于 P/L 的就计入 P/L，属于 OCI 的就计入 OCI。）

IAS 8

Accounting policies, changes in accounting estimates and errors

Accounting policies are the specific principles, bases, conventions, rules and practices adopted by an entity in preparing and presenting financial statements. (会计政策,是指企业在会计确认、计量和报告中所采用的原则、基础和会计处理方法。)

IAS 8 allows accounting policies to be changed only if:(当且仅当出现下列情况允许会计政策发生改变)

a) Required by IFRS (法律、行政法规或者国家统一的会计制度等要求变更)

b) The change will result in a more relevant and reliable presentation of events or transactions.(会计政策变更能够提供更可靠、更相关的会计信息。)

A change in accounting policy occurs if there has been a change in(三种类型的会计政策变更):

a) Recognition, e.g. An expense is now recognized rather than an asset(一般地,对会计确认的指定或选择是会计政策,其相应的变更是会计政策变更。比如把费用确认为资产)

b) Presentation, e.g. Depreciation is now included in cost of sales rather than administrative expenses.(一般地,对列报项目的指定或选择是会计政策,其相应的变更是会计政策变更。比如列报的改变,报表上列式的位置发生了改变)

c) Measurement, e.g. Stating assets at replacement cost rather than historical cost. (一般地,对计量基础的指定或选择是会计政策,其相应的变更是会计政策变更。比如计量的标准发生了改变。)

注意特点:In the case of tangible non-current assets, if a policy of revaluation is adopted for the first time then this is treated, not as a change of accounting policy under IAS 8, but as a revaluation under IAS 16 Property, plant and equipment.(考试迷惑性的考点:第一次采用某个模型,不属于会计政策的变更!比如第一次采用 revaluation model,第一次采用租赁准则等。)

The required treatment for dealing with changes policies is that(会计政策变更的处理):

a) The change should be **applied retrospectively**(追溯调整)(追溯调整法,是指对某项交易或事项变更会计政策,视同该项交易或事项初次发生时即采用变更后的会计政策,并以此对财务报表相关项目进行调整的方法。)

b) With an adjustment to the opening balance of retained earnings in the statement of changes in equity. (所有者权益变动表的期初金额应当调整:"prior year adjustment 以前年度损益调整")

c) Comparative information should be restated unless it is impracticable to do so

Changes in accounting estimates

Estimates arise in relation to business activities because of the uncertainties inherent within them. **Judgments are made based on** the most up to date information and the use of such estimates is a necessary part of the preparation of financial statements. **It does not undermine their reliability.**

会计估计,是指企业对结果不确定的交易或事项以最近可利用的信息为基础所作的判断。

第一,会计估计的存在是由于经济活动中内在的不确定性因素的影响。

第二,进行会计估计时,往往以最近可利用的信息或资料为基础。

第三,进行会计估计并不会削弱会计确认和计量的可靠性。

Examples:

A necessary irrecoverable debt allowance 坏账准备的计提

Useful lives of depreciable assets 固定资产使用年限的估计

Residual value of non-current assets 固定资产的残值估计

Depreciation methods 折旧方法的估计

Provision for obsolescence of inventory provision 存货滞销减值准备的计提

Warranty provision 质保服务

Changes in accounting estimates result from new information or new developments and, accordingly, are not corrections of errors. **Changes in accounting estimate are not applied retrospectively.** [会计估计的变更不进行追溯调整! 通常采用"未来适用法",即为影响当期(the period of the change, if the change affects that period only)及未来期间(the period of the change and future periods, if the change affects both)。]

IFRS 5

Non-current assets held for sale and discontinued operations

1. The objective of IFRS 5

a) To set out requirements for the classification, measurement and presentation of non-current assets held for sale, in particular requiring that such assets **should be presented separately** on the face of statement of financial position（资产负债表中单独披露持有代售资产）

b) To set out updated rules for the presentation of **discontinued operational** in particular requiring that the results of discontinued operations should be **presented separately in the income statement.**（利润表也要单独列报终止经营相关业务经营成果）

2. Disposal group

A group of assets to be disposed of, by sale or otherwise, together as a group in a single transaction, and liabilities directly associated with those assets that will be transferred in the transaction. (In practice a disposal group could be a subsidiary, a cash-generating unit or a single operation within an entity.) 处置组,是指在一项交易中作为整体通过出售或其他方式一并处置的一组资产,以及在该交易中转让的与这些资产直接相关的负债。

3. Classification as held for sale

A non-current asset should be classified **as 'held for sale'** if its carrying amount **will be recovered principally through a sale transaction rather than through continuing use.** For this to be the case, the following conditions must apply（非流动资产或处置组划分为持有待售类别,应当同时满足下列条件）：

a) The asset must be available for immediate sale in its present condition（根据类似交易中出售此类资产或处置组的惯例,在当前状况下即可立即出售。）

b) The sale must be highly probable, meaning that（出售极可能发生,同时满足下列条件）：

○ Management are committed to a plan to sell the asset（企业已经就一项出售计划作

出决议）

  ○ There is an active program to locate a buyer; and（有具体的程序能找到买家，且获得确定的购买承诺）

  ○ The asset must be marketed for sale at a price that is reasonable in relation to its current fair value.（和当前市场价值很接近）

  ○ The sale is expected to be completed within 12 months of its classification as held for sale(预计出售将在一年内完成）

  ○ It is unlikely that the plan will be significantly changed or will be withdrawn（不会随意变更、撤销本计划）

4. Measurement

a) Non-current assets that qualify as held for sale should be measured **at the lower of their carrying amount and fair value less costs to sell**. Any impairment loss recognised, to write down an asset to its fair value less costs to sell, Should normally be charged to the profit or loss.

分录即为：

DR：Impairment loss
　　CR：NCA held for sale

企业初始计量持有待售的非流动资产或处置组时，其账面价值高于公允价值减去出售费用后的净额的，应当将账面价值减记至公允价值减去出售费用后的净额，减记的金额确认为资产减值损失，计入当期损益，同时计提持有待售资产减值准备。

b) It should cease to be depreciated (or amortized). Depreciation is a measure of consumption, which is no longer relevant as the asset will be sold rather than consumed（持有待售的非流动资产不应计提折旧或摊销。）

c) A non-current asset (or disposal group) that is no longer classified as held for sale (for example, because the sale has not taken place within one year) is measured at the lower of(不满足"held for sale"的条件就变回为PPE，变回PPE的计量标准如下）：

  ○ Its carrying amount before it was classified as held for sale, adjusted for any depreciation that would have been charged had the asset not been held for sale(划分为持有待售类别前的账面价值，按照假定不划分为持有待售类别情况下本应确认的折旧、摊销或减值等进行调整后的金额）

  ○ Its recoverable amount at the date of the decision not to sell(可收回金额）

5. Presentation

a) Assets and liabilities held for sale should not be offset(持有待售资产和负债不应当相互抵销）

b) The major classes of assets and liabilities held for sale should be **separately disclosed** either on the face of the statement of financial position or in the notes.

c) IFRS 5 requires non-current assets or disposal groups held for sale to be **shown as a** separate component of current assets/current liabilities.("持有待售资产"和"持有待售负债"应当分别作为流动资产和流动负债列示。)

6. Discontinued operations

A discontinued operation is a component of an enterprise that either has been disposed of, or is classified as held for sale, and（终止经营,是指企业满足下列条件之一的、能够单独区分的组成部分,且该组成部分已经处置或划分为持有待售类别）:

a) Represents, a separate major line of business or geographical area of operations（该组成部分代表一项独立的主要业务或一个单独的主要经营地区）

b) Is part of a single co-ordinated plan to dispose of a separate major line of business or geographical area of operations; or(该组成部分是拟对一项独立的主要业务或一个单独的主要经营地区进行处置的一项相关联计划的一部分)

c) Is a subsidiary acquired exclusively with a view to resale（该组成部分是专为转售而取得的子公司,取得的目的就是转售）

An enterprise must disclose a single amount on the face of the income statement, comprising the total of（企业应当在利润表中分别列示持续经营损益和终止经营损益）the post-tax profit or loss(一定是税后的利润!) of discontinued operations.

IAS 33

Earings per share

1. Definitions

1.1 Earnings per share

Earnings per share is a measure of the amount of profits earned by a company for each ordinary share

每股收益是指普通股股东每持有一股普通股所能享有的企业净利润或需承担的企业净亏损。

1.2 Potential ordinary shares 潜在普通股

a) Debt or equity instruments, including preference shares, that are convertible intoordinary shares

b) Share warrants and options

c) Employee plans that allow employees to receive ordinary shares as part of their remuneration and other share purchase plans

d) Shares that would be issued upon the satisfaction of certain conditions resulting from contractual arrangements, such as the purchase of a business or other assets

2. 基本每股收益计算

Basic EPS is calculated by dividing the net profit or loss for the period attributable to ordinary shareholders by the weighted average number of ordinary shares outstanding during the period.

Basic EPS = Net profit/(loss) attributable to ordinary shareholders/Weighted average number of ordinary shares outstanding during the period

基本每股收益 = 归属于普通股股东的当期净利润/发行在外普通股的加权平均数

*Earnings

Earnings includes all items of income and expense (including tax and non-controlling interests) less the results of discontinued operations where these are presented, less net profit attributable to preference shareholders, including preference dividends.

Preference dividends deducted from net profit consist of:

a) Preference dividends on non-cumulative preference shares declared in respect of the period

b) The full amount of the required preference dividends for cumulative preference shares for the period, whether or not they have been declared

企业存在发行在外的除普通股以外的金融工具的，在计算基本每股收益时，基本每股收益中的分子，即归属于普通股股东的净利润不应包含其他权益工具的股利或利息，其中，对于发行的不可累积优先股等其他权益工具应扣除当期宣告发放的股利，对于发行的累积优先股等其他权益工具，无论当期是否宣告发放股利，均应予以扣除。

3. Capitalisation/bonus issue and share

In both cases, ordinary shares are issued to existing shareholders for no additional consideration. The number of ordinary shares has increased without an increase in resources. This problem is solved by adjusting the number of ordinary shares outstanding before the event for the proportionate change in the number of shares outstanding as if the event had occurred at the beginning of the earliest period reported

Change the number of shares outstanding, without a corresponding change in resources:

增加或减少其发行在外普通股或潜在普通股的数量，但并不影响所有者权益总额，既不影响企业所拥有或控制的经济资源也不改变企业的盈利能力。

a) Capitalisation or bonus issue (sometimes called a stock dividend) 股票股利
b) Bonus element in any other issue, e.g. a rights issue to existing shareholders
c) Share split 拆股
d) Reverse share split (consolidation of shares) 并股

4. Rights issue

A rights issue of shares is an issue of new shares to existing shareholders at a price below the current market value.

This means that there is a bonus element included.

To arrive at figures for EPS when a rights issue is made, we need to calculate first of all the theoretical ex-rights value.

This is a weighted average value per share, and is perhaps explained most easily with a numerical example.

RIGHTS ISSUE-PROCEDURES

a) The EPS for the corresponding previous period should be multiplied by the following fraction.

Theoretical ex-rights fair value per share/Fair value per share immediately before the exercise of rights

b) To obtain the EPS for the current year you should:

i) Multiply the number of shares before the rights issue by the fraction of the year before the date of issue and by the following fraction

Fair value per share immediately before the exercise of rights/Theoretical ex-rights fair value per share

ii) Multiply the number of shares after the rights issue by the fraction of the year after the date of issue and add to the figure arrived at in (i)

○ 每股理论除权价格=(行权前发行在外普通股的公允价值总额+配股收到的款项)/行权后发行在外的普通股股数

○ 调整系数=行权前发行在外普通股的每股公允价值/每股理论除权价格

○ 因配股重新计算的上年度基本每股收益=上年度基本每股收益/调整系数

○ 本年度基本每股收益=归属于普通股股东的当期净利润/(配股前发行在外普通股股数×调整系数×配股前普通股发行在外的时间权重+配股后发行在外普通股加权平均数)

5. Diluted eps 稀释每股收益

Diluted EPS is calculated by adjusting the net profit due to continuing operations attributable to ordinary shareholders and the weighted average number of shares outstanding for the effects of all dilutive potential ordinary shares.

A company may have in issue some securities which do not (at present) have any claim to a share of equity earnings, but may give rise to such a claim in the future.

a) Convertible loan stock or convertible preferred shares which give their holders the right at some future date to exchange their securities for ordinary shares of the company, at a pre-determined conversion rate

b) Options or warrants, In other words, a future increase in the number of ordinary shares will cause a dilution or 'watering down' of equity, and it is possible to calculate a diluted earnings per share.

潜在普通股是否具有稀释性的判断标准是看其对持续经营每股收益的影响,即假定潜在普通股当期转换为普通股,若会减少持续经营每股收益或增加持续经营每股亏损,表明具有稀释性,否则,具有反稀释性。

5.1 Earnings

The earnings calculated for basic EPS should be based on continuing operations and adjusted by:

a) Any dividends on dilutive potential ordinary shares that were deducted to arrive at earnings for basic EPS

b) Interest recognised in the period for the dilutive potential ordinary shares (convertible debt)

c) Any other changes in income or expenses

分子的调整

计算稀释每股收益时,应当根据下列事项对归属于普通股股东的当期净利润进行调整:
(1) 当期已确认为费用的稀释性潜在普通股的利息(比如可转债的利息要调整);
(2) 稀释性潜在普通股转换时将产生的收益或费用。

上述调整应当考虑相关的所得税影响。

5.2 Per share

The number of ordinary shares is the weighted average number of ordinary shares calculated for basic EPS plus the weighted average number of ordinary shares that would be issued on the conversion of all the dilutive potential ordinary shares into ordinary shares.

分母的调整。计算稀释每股收益时,当期发行在外普通股的加权平均数应当为计算基本每股收益时普通股的加权平均数与假定稀释性潜在普通股转换为已发行普通股而增加的普通股股数的加权平均数之和。

计算稀释性潜在普通股转换为已发行普通股而增加的普通股股数的加权平均数时,以前期间发行的稀释性潜在普通股(比如去年就发行的认股权证),应当假设在当期期初转换为普通股;当期发行的稀释性潜在普通股,应当假设在发行日转换普通股。

INTERPRETATION OF FINANCIAL STATEMENTS

1. Profitability and return

a) Gross profit margin = Gross profit/sales * 100% 毛利率

This ratio is of fundamental importance in the analysis.(每一块钱销售收入能带来多少毛利润)

b) Operating profit margin = PBIT(Profit before interest and tax)/Sales * 100%

A high profit margin means a high profit per $1 of sales, but if this also means that sales prices are high, there is a strong possibility that sales turnover will be depressed, and so asset turnover lower.(每一块钱销售收入能带来多少息税前利润)

c) *Asset turnover* = ("Sales revenue" × 100%)/(*Capital employed*)(资产周转率,每一块钱的资本能为企业带来多少收入)

Capital employed = equity + long term liability 占用的资本(占用资金的"长期"来源)
= Total assets − Current liability

Reflect the pure business profitability, without considering the cost of capital employed.

Can be interpreted by comparing it with previous period or competitor or market borrowing rates

A high asset turnover means that the company is generating a lot of sales, but to do this it might have to keep its prices down and so accept a low profit margin per $1 of sales.

d) Return on Capital Employed = (PBIT × 100%)/(Capital employed)

ROCE = Operating profit margin × Asset turnover

ROE = (Profit after tax and preference divident)/(Equity shareholder 'funds)

ROCE measures the overall efficiency of a company in employing the resources available to it.

2. Liquidity

A simple measure of how much of the total current assets is financed by current liability.(衡量多少短期负债支撑着多少短期资产)

1) Current ratio = (Current asset)/(current liability)

If, for example the result is 2:1, this means only a limited portion of assets are funded by the current liabilities. Acceptable current ratio is 1.5

2) Quick ratio（or acid test ratio 酸性测试比率）=（Current asset − inventoryinventory)/(Current liability)

Inventory are not very liquid asset

Acceptable 0.8, but ideally be at least 1

3) Working capital

Working capital analysis can help us to interpret the liquidity ratio more in depth. Through the analysis we can assess the management's efficiency in controlling the main elements of working capital: inventory, receivable and payable.

a) Receivables days = (Trade receivables balance × 365)/(credit sales)

Estimated average receivable collection period(应收账款平均回收周期，多少天能收回应收账款)

Increased receivable days may indicate poor credit control. However, some companies must allow generous credit terms to win customers.

b) Payable days = (Trade payable balance × 365)/(credit purchase)

Estimated average period to settle the payment to suppliers

Increased payable days may indicate deteriorated liquidity.（暗示资金流动性出现了问题）

c) Inventory turnover = (inventory balance × 365)/(cost of sales)

Indicate the average number of days that inventory is held for in a business(存货持有的天数)

Increased inventory days may indicate inefficiency of inventory management.

d) Operating cycle + = inventory days + receivable days − payable days(企业一个经营循环需要多少天)

3. Debt and gearing (long-term solvency)

Debt ratios are concerned with how much the company owes in relation to its size, whether its debt burden seems heavy or light.

1) Gearing ratio = [(long − term debts) × 100%]/(capital employed)

Shows a company's long term capital structure

No absolute limit, over 50% is said to be highly geared.

If gearing is too high, company may find it difficult to borrow in future.（比如获得新借款难、借款成本更高）

2) Leverage = (Shareholder's equity)/(capital employed)

3) Debt ratio = (Total debts × 100%)/(Total assets) 资产负债率

Reflect the debt burden of a company

The safe limit varies amount companies, depending on the nature of business

General bench marking：50%

4）Interest coverage=（Profit before interest and tax）/（Interest charge）利息保障倍数

Shows whether a company earns enough profit to pay interest.

A fall on PBIT would have significant influence on profits available for ordinary shareholder.

3 times is considered to be acceptable limits.

4. Shareholders' investment ratios

a）**Earnings per share（EPS）**：Earnings per share is the amount of net profit for the period that is attributable to each ordinary share which is outstanding during all or part of the period（详见 EPS 章节）

b）**Dividend per share** = Dividends/No. of shares

c）**Dividend cover** = Earnings per share/Dividend per（ordinary）share ［It shows the proportion of profit for the year that is available for distribution to shareholders that has been paid（or proposed）and what proportion will be retained in the business to finance future growth.］

d）**P/E ratio**：The Price/Earnings（P/E）ratio is the ratio of a company's current share price to the earnings per share.

e）Dividend yiled = Dividend on the share for the year * 100%/Current market value of the share（ex-dividends）

The dividend per share is taken as the **dividend for the previous year** and ex-dividends means that the share price **does not include the right to the most recent dividend**.（用上一年的股利来计算，同时股价是不含股息的股价，题中若给到你股息你要记得扣除！）

5. Limitations of financial statements and ratio analysis

a）Problems of **historical cost information**：Financial statements are affected by the obvious shortcomings of **historical cost information** and are also subject to manipulation and becomes less relevant as time goes by.（都是历史的信息，可能被操纵，且信息可能是过时的"out of date"）

b）**Listed companies** produce their financial statements with one eye on the stock market and，where possible，they like to produce financial statements which show analysts what they are expecting to see.（上市公司可能进行财务造假，比如 reducing gearing 降低杠杆，让报表更好看）

c）Transactions with related parties，cannot be assumed to have been engaged in **'at arm's length'** or in the best interests of the entity itself.（与关联方的交易可能是不公允的,并不是为了企业利益而进行的交易。）

d）Seasonal trading(季节性交易)：May distort reported results.

e）**Major asset acquisitions（重大资产购买）** just before the end of an accounting period can also distort results. The statement of financial position will show an **increased level of assets and corresponding liabilities**（probably a loan or lease payable），but the income which will be earned from utilisation of the asset will not yet have materialised.（资产在期末买了，资产增加的同时相应的负债增加，但是资产并没有在当年投入使用，没有为公司在该期间带来收益。）

f）A company may have acquired or **disposed of a subsidiary or division** during the year and the effect of this will **need to be isolated** in order to assess the underlying performance.（考试的时候在进行 ratio analysis 的时候一定要注意剔除 one-off 一次性事项的影响来分析报表，比如重大资产处置、购买或者收购子公司等。）

IAS 22

Statement of cash flow

1. The need for statement of cash flow

a) Cash flow statement concentrates on the sources and uses of cash and are a useful indicator of a company's liquidity and solvency.（反映一个公司的流动性及偿付能力的重要指标）

b) Shareholders might believe that if a company makes a profit after tax, then this is the amount which it could afford to pay as a dividend.

c) Survival of a business entity depends not so much on profits as on its ability to pay its debts when they fall due.（债务到期，有钱还，企业才能活下去）

d) Cash is less likely to be manipulated than profit(相比利润，现金相对来说不容易被操纵）

2. Definition

IAS 7（Revised）Cash Flow Statements defines the followings：

Cash comprises **cash on hand and deposits** payable on demand；

Cash equivalents are **short-term（三个月内可变现）**, highly liquid investments that are convertible to **known amounts of cash** and which are subject to **insignificant risk** of changes in value.

An investment maturity date should **normally be three months** from its acquisition date.

The **bank overdrafts** are repayable on demand and will be included in cash and cash equivalents.（**bank overdrafts** 记着作为现金及现金等价物的减项）

Cash flows are inflows and outflows of cash and cash equivalents.

3. Presentation of statement of cash flow

IAS 7 requires statements of cash flows to report cash flows during the period classified by **operating, investing and financing activities.**

1) OPERATING ACTIVITY (CFO) 经营活动产生的现金流量

Operating activities are the **principle revenue** producing activities of enterprise and other activities **that are not investing or financing activities.**

Most of operating cash flows will be those items which determine the net profit or loss of the entity. Examples of cash flow from operating activities：

a) Cash receipts from the sale of goods and the rendering of services 销售商品及提供劳务收到的现金

b) Cash receipts from royalties，fees，commissions and other revenue

c) Cash payments to suppliers for goods and services 采购商品及接受劳务支付的现金

d) Cash payments to and on behalf of employees（e.g.工资）

INVESTING ACTIVITIES(CFI)投资活动产生的现金流量

Investing activities are the acquisition and disposal of long-term assets and other investments not included in cash equivalents.

Examples of cash flows arising from investing activities：

a) Cash payments to acquire non-current assets 购买 NCA

b) Cash receipts from sales of non-current assets 处置 NCA

c) Cash payments to acquire other investment（shares or debentures of other enterprises）购买其他公司股票或债券

d) Cash receipts from sales of other investment 处置投资

e) Cash advances 预付款 and loans made to other parties 对其他企业进行贷款

f) Cash receipts from the repayment of advances and loans made to other parties 其他企业偿还贷款

2) FINANCING ACTIVITIES(CFF)筹资活动产生的现金流量

Financing activities are activities that result in changes in the composition of the equity capital and borrowings of the enterprise.（改变企业债务和股权比例的）

Examples of cash flows which might arise under these headings：

a) Cash proceeds from issuing shares 发行股票获得的现金

b) Cash payments to owners to redeem the enterprises' shares 赎回股票支付的现金

c) Cash proceeds from borrowings 借款

d) Cash repayments of debt 偿还负债

IAS 7（Revised）allows **two methods** of reporting cash flows from operating activities：

The **DIRECT method** whereby major classes of gross cash receipts and gross cash payments are disclosed

The **INDIRECT method**. whereby net profit or loss is adjusted for the effects of：

transactions of a non-cash nature 非现金交易（非收现收入/非付现成本）

any deferrals or Accruals of past or future operating cash receipts or payments，and items of income or expense associated with investing or financing cash flows

IAS 7（Revised）**encourages** enterprises to report cash flows from operation activities doing the **direct method**. It is believed that the direct method will provide more useful information about an entity's cash flows，**but it may not be practical or cost effective** in many circumstances.

When the indirect method is adopted, the net cash flow from operating activities is determined by adjusting net profit or loss for the effects of:（间接法是通过调整"PBT"税前利润来反映现金流）

Changes during the period in inventories and operating receivables and payables 存货/应收/应付

Non-cash items such as depreciation 折旧调整

All other items for which the cash effects are investing or financing cash flows 投资/筹资相关的调整

4. Interest and dividends

Cash flows from interest and dividends received and paid should each be disclosed separately.（利息及股利需要单独披露）

Each should be classified in a **consistent manner** from period to period.

Interest paid should be classified as an operating cash flow（正常经营活动中的利息）or a financing cash flow.（为了融资支付的利息）**支付的利息，题干中未明确说明就放在经营活动中）**

Interest received and dividends received should be classified as operating cash flows or, **more usually, as investing cash flows.**（收到的利息/股利通常作为投资活动的现金流量）

Dividends paid by the enterprise should be classified as an operating cash flow, so that users can assess the enterprises' ability to pay dividends out of operating cash flows, or **more usually, as a financing cash flow**, showing the cost of obtaining financial resources.（支付的股利通常作为筹资活动的现金流量）

5. Format

1) Direct method format

Statement of Cash Flow for the year ended XXXX

Cash flow from operating activities	
Cash receipts from customers	X
Cash paid to suppliers and employees	(X)
Cash generated from operations	X
-Interest paid	(X)
-Income tax paid	(X)
Net cash flow from operation activity	X
Other parts is same as indirect format	

2) **Indirect method format**(考试通常考的都是间接法，记住格式！)

Statement of cash flows of ABC Company for the year ended XX.XX.XXXX

IAS 22 Statement of cash flow

	$
Cash flows from operation activities	
Profit before taxation	X
Adjustment for:	
Depreciation/amortization charged	X
Loss/profit on disposal on non-current assets	X/(X)
Finance costs	X
Investment income	(X)
Net cash flow before working capital changes	X
Working capital changes:	
(increase)/(decrease) in inventory	(X)/X
(increase)/(decrease) in trade receivable	(X)/X
Increase/(decrease) in trade payable	X/(X)
Cash generated from operations	X
-interest paid	(X)
-income tax paid	(X)
Net cash flows from operation activity	X
Cash flows from investing activities:	
Purchase of property, plant and equipment	(X)
Proceeds from sale of equipment	X
Interest received/investment income received	X
Dividends received	X
Net cash flows from investing activities	X
Cash flows from financing activities:	
Proceeds from issuance of share capital	X
Proceeds from long-term borrowing	X
Loan repayment	(X)
Dividends paid	(X)
Net cash flows from financing activities	X
Net increase/decrease in cash and cash equivalents	X/(X)
Cash and cash equivalents at the beginning of period	X
Cash and cash equivalents at the end of period	X

ACCOUNTING FOR INFLATION

1. Advantages and Disadvantages of historical cost accounting

Advantages of historical cost accounting	Disadvantages of historical cost accounting
Amounts used are objective and free from bias	Lead to understatement of assets in the statement of financial position
Amounts are reliable, they can always be verified, they exist on invoices and documents	Depreciation will also be understated
Amounts in the statement of financial position can be matched perfectly with amounts in the statement of cash flows	An organisation selling in an inflationary market will see its revenue and profits rise, but this is 'paper profit', distorted by the understated depreciation and cost of sales
Opportunities for creative accounting are less than under systems which allow management to apply their judgement to the valuation of assets	Understatement of assets will depress a company's share price and make it vulnerable to takeover. In practice, listed companies avoid this by revaluing land and buildings in line with market values
It has been used for centuries and is easily understood	Understated depreciation and understated cost of sales lead to overstatement of profits, compounded by price inflation
	Overstated profits can lead to too much being distributed to shareholders, leaving insufficient amounts for investment
	Overstated profits will lead shareholders to expect higher dividends and employees to demand higher wages
	Overstated profits lead to overstated tax bills

2. Current value accounting

Under CVA, the original cost of an asset would be replaced with its **discounted present value**(会用折现值来代替).

Current value accounting attempts to address the problems of historical cost accounting in an **inflationary environment**.

There are two different theoretical approaches to accounting for price changes:

1) The current purchasing power approach (CPP)

CPP accounting is a method of accounting fo**r general (not specific) inflation**（考虑的是一般的通货膨胀）. It does so by expressing asset values in a stable monetary unit, the $ of current purchasing power.

CPP measures profits as the increase in the **current purchasing power of equity**（衡量的是购买力）.

Profits are therefore stated after allowing for the **declining purchasing power**（反映购买力的下降）of money due to price inflation.

Monetary items(cash, receivables, payables) **cannot be restated as their amount is fixed**.(货币性质的科目是不会重新计量的)

Non-monetary items(not-current assets and inventories) are **restated in line with the general price** index(一般物价指数)(at ＄c) and the balancing figure is equity.

Advantages of CPP accounting	Disadvantages of CPP accounting
The restatement of asset values in terms of a stable money value provides a more meaningful basis of comparison with other companies	It is not clear what ＄c means.'Generalised purchasing power' as measured by a retail price index, or indeed any other general price index, has no obvious practical significance.(实际上这个通胀指数没有明显的实务的作用)
Profit is measured in 'real' terms and excludes 'inflationary value increments'	The use of indices inevitably involves approximations in the measurements of value.(指数本身也只是一个不精确的数字)
CPP avoids the subjective valuations of current value accounting, because a single price index is applied to all non-monetary assets.(CPP 用的都是统一的 index,避免了主观的估值)	The value of assets in a CPP statement of financial position has less meaning than a current value statement of financial position.(就算考虑了通货膨胀,和真实数据还是有差距的)
Since it is based on historical cost accounting, raw data is easily verified, and measurements of value can be readily audited	

2) The current cost accounting approach（CCA）

CCA is based on a **physical concept of capital maintenance**. Profit is recognized after the **operating capability of the business** has been maintained.(生产力提高才是盈利)

The conceptual basis of CCA is that the value of assets consumed or sold, and the value of assets in the statement of financial position, should be stated at their value to the business (also known as 'deprival value').(处置时的价值)

The deprival value of an asset is the loss which a business entity would suffer if it were deprived of the use of the asset.(不使用该资产来生产会产生的损失是多少)

Value to the business, or deprival value, can be:

a) **Replacement cost:** in the case of non-current assets, it is assumed that the replacement cost of an asset would be its net replacement cost（NRC）, its gross replacement cost minus an appropriate provision for depreciation to reflect the amount of its life already 'used up'. (In simple terms you should remember that in **CCA deprival value is nearly always replacement cost**.)

b) **Net realisable value（NRV）:** what the asset could be sold for, net of any disposal costs.

c) **Economic value（EV）**, or value in use: what the existing asset will be worth to the company over the rest of its useful life.

ACCA 知识精要

CCA preserves the operating capability of the company but does not necessarily preserve it against the declining value in the purchasing power of money (against inflation).（考虑的是生产能力而不是购买力）

As mentioned previously, CCA is a system which takes account of **specific price inflation**（考虑的是具体价格通胀）(changes in the prices of specific assets or groups of assets) but not of general price inflation.（这是与 CPP 最主要的区别）

Advantages and disadvantages of current cost accounting

Advantages of current cost accounting	Disadvantages of current cost accounting
Assets are valued after management has considered the opportunity cost of holding them, and the expected benefits from their future use	It is impossible to make valuations of EV or NRV without subjective judgements. The measurements used are therefore not objective
It can be implemented fairly easily in practice, by making simple adjustments to the historical cost accounting profits.	There are several problems to be overcome in deciding how to provide an estimate of replacement costs for non-current assets
	It is arguable that the total assets will, therefore, have an aggregate value which is not particularly meaningful because of this mixture of different concepts
	It can be argued that 'deprival value' is an unrealistic concept, because the business entity has not been deprived of the use of the asset

3. Concepts of capital and capital maintenance

1) Financial capital maintenance（财务资本保全）

Profit is the increase in **nominal money capital** over the period and this is the concept **used in CPP, and used under historical cost accounting.**（钱增加了,利润才增加。）

2) Physical capital maintenance（实物资本保全）

Profit is the increase in the physical **productive capacity** over the period. This is the concept used in **CCA**.（生产力提升了,利润才提升。）

NOT FOR PROFIT ORGANISATION

3 Es: economy, efficiency and effectiveness

4 Cs(Best Value):

a) Challenging why, how and by whom a service is provided

b) Comparing performance against other local authorities

c) Consulting service users, the local community, etc.

d) Using fair Competition to secure efficient and effective services

AUDIT AND ASSURANCE

Format of the exam

Section	Style of question type	Description	Proportion of exam
A	客观题	3 questions×10 marks Each question will contain 5 segment and each worth 2 marks	30
B	主观题	1 question×30 marks 2 questions×20 marks	70
Total			100

Part 1

Introduction

1.1 Purpose of the audit process

For auditor to express their opinion and provide assurance to shareholders that the financial **statements** are prepared, **in all material respects**, in accordance with an applicable financial reporting framework.

1.2 Materiality

Information is material if its **omission or misstatement** could **influence the economic decision** of users taken on the basis of the financial statements. 低于重要性水平,报告是可接受的

Both the amount (quantity) and nature (quality) of misstatements need to be considered.

The higher the anticipated risk, the lower the value of materiality will be. 重要性取决于审计风险的水平。预期风险越高,重要性的数值设定应该越低。

The lower the materiality level is set, the more work will need to be performed to ensure audit risk is kept at an acceptably low level. 重要性的数值设定越低,需要做的工作也越多。

During planning, the auditor establishes materiality for financial statements as a whole by exercising judgement.

- Amount (quantity) 数量重大

  ≥0.5% of sales revenue

  ≥1% of total assets

  ≥5% of profit before tax

- Nature (quality) 性质重大: 如重大的关联方交易

1.3 Reasonable assurance

合理保证:审计师给不了100%保证

The highest level of assurance given, as in the case of statutory audit, is described as reasonable assurance. 非绝对的保证 is not absolute assurance because there are 固有局限性 inherent limitations of an audit which result in the auditor forming an opinion on evidence that is 有说服力的而不是结论性的 persuasive rather than conclusive.

Reasons:

- Audit is not objective. Judgement has to be made.
- Not all items in the financial statements are tested, there is sampling risk.

Part 1 Introduction

1.4 Assurance engagement 鉴证业务

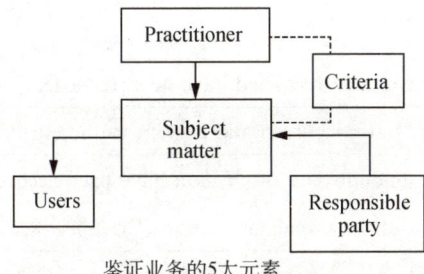

鉴证业务的5大元素

An assurance engagement is an engagement in which a **practitioner** expresses a conclusion designed to enhance the degree of confidence of the **intended users other than the responsible party** about the outcome of the evaluation or measurement of a **subject matter against criteria**.

	External audit	Non-assurance review
Level of Assurance	Reasonable assurance Highest level Positive expression	Limited assurance Moderate level Negative expression
level of opinion	In our opinion, the financial statements present fairly, in all material respects, in accordance with International Financial Reporting Standards	Based on our work described in this report, nothing has come to our attention that causes us to believe that the financial statements do not present fairly, in all material respects, in accordance with International Financial Reporting Standards

1.5 Process of external audit

- Agree the scope of work to be performed 同意工作范围
- Formalise all of the terms of the engagement in a contract (engagement letter) 签合同
- Plan the work 计划工作
- Obtain sufficient appropriate evidence on which to base the conclusion 充分恰当的证据
- Perform overall review and form opinion 总览并形成意见
- Issue report to the client 报告

1.6 Logic of audit assertion 认定

资产负债表认定	Account balances at the period-end All assets, liabilities and equity interests
Completeness 完整	should have been recorded have been recorded. 该记得都记了
Existence 存在	Exist 记了的都存在
Valuation 估值	included in the financial statements at appropriate amounts 数值正确
Rights & Obligations 权利和义务	The entity holds or controls the rights/obligation to the entity

(Continued)

利润表认定	Classes of transactions for the period All transactions and events				
Completeness 完整	should have been recorded have been recorded. 该记得都记了				
Occurrence 发生	Recorded have occurred and pertain to the entity. 记了的都发过				
Accuracy 准确性	Relative amounts and other data have been recorded appropriately. 数值正确				
Classification 分类	Recorded in the proper accounts. 记录在恰当的科目				
Cut-off 截止	Recorded in the correct accounting period. 正确的会计期间				
		Asset	Liability	Income	Expense
Completeness			低估		低估
Existence/Occurrence		高估		高估	
Valuation/Accuracy		高估		高估	

1.7 Purpose of audit planning

○ Helping the auditor to devote appropriate attention to important areas of the audit.

○ Helping the auditor to identify and resolve potential problems on a timely basis.

○ Helping the auditor to properly organize and manage the audit engagement so that it is performed in an effective and efficient manner.

○ Assisting in the selection of engagement team members with appropriate levels of capabilities and competence to respond to anticipated risks and the proper assignment of work to them

○ Facilitating the direction and supervision of engagement team members and the review of their work.

○ Assisting, where applicable, in coordination of work down by experts.

Part 2

Audit risk

The risk that the auditor expresses an inappropriate audit opinion when the financial statements are materially misstated. Auditor should obtain sufficient evidence to reduce the risk to an acceptably low level.

Audit risk model is comprised of:

Audit risk = RoMM(重大错报风险)×Detection risk(检查发现)
= inherent risk(固有风险)×control risk(控制风险)×detection risk

2.1 Inherent risk

This is the susceptibility(敏感性) of an assertion to a misstatement that could be material, either individually or when aggregated with other misstatements, assuming that there were no related internal controls. 与内控无关

E.g. Complex calculation

The heavy use of accounting estimates

The influence of external environment

2.2 Control risk

有相关内控,但没起到组织风险的作用

This is a risk that the misstatement occur in an assertion could be material and that's not be prevented by the internal control of the company, either individually or aggregated with other misstatements.

Some control risk will always exist because of the inherent limitations of internal control

2.2.1 Control risk 出现的诱因,内控的固有局限性:

a) Human error (inexperience)

b) Process being deliberately circumvented 控制流程被绕开

c) Management overriding controls 管理层凌驾于控制之上

d) Occurrence of unforeseen circumstances 意外情况

e) Inadequate information 信息不足

2.2.2 舞弊三角理论:

a) An incentive to commit fraud (Motive) 动机—under pressure

b) A perceived opportunity to commit fraud (Opportunity) 机会—High volume of complex transactions

    c）An ability to rationalize the fraudulent action（Dishonesty）自我合理化

2.3 Detection Risk 检查风险

This is the risk that the auditor's procedures will not detect a misstatement that exists in an assertion that could be material either individually or when aggregated with other misstatements.

2.3.1 Sampling risk 抽样风险

Sampling risk is the risk that auditor's conclusion，based on a sample，may be different from the conclusion that would have been reached if the entire population were subjected to the same audit procedure. Sampling risk must be reduced to an acceptably low level.

2.3.2 Indicators of Non-sampling risk

    a）Poor planning

    b）New client

    c）Financial constraints 预算不足

    d）Auditor's lack of experience

    e）Time pressure

    f）Lack of industry knowledge

2.4 Business risk

A risk resulting from significant conditions，events，circumstances，actions or inactions that could adversely affect an entity's ability to achieve its objectives and execute its strategies，or from the setting of inappropriate objectives and strategies（ISA 315）站在企业股东或者经理人角度看待企业的风险，而不是审计人员。如：经济环境下行、供应商及客户的违约、产品过时、存货积压、政治风险、环境风险、丑闻曝光等。

A business risk is a threat to cause the under-performance of business.

☐ Net current liabilities（or net liabilities overall）

☐ Borrowing facilities not agreed

☐ Default on loan agreements/ceasing dividend payment

☐ Unplanned sales of non-current assets/entrench staff

☐ Missing tax payments

☐ Delay paying staff

☐ Negative cash flow

☐ Regulated industry/license

☐ Overtrading

☐ Patent infringement

☐ Unable to obtain credit from suppliers/bank

☐ Major technology changes in the industry

☐ Breach of law and regulations

☐ Legal claims against the company

□ Loss of key management or staff without replacement
□ Over reliance on a small number of products or staff
□ Significant depends on/loss of major customer
□ Late paying suppliers
□ Low liquidity ratio or high gearing ratio
□ Business diversification

2.5 Responsibility

Risks dependent on the entity:
— business risk (risk in business)
— RoMM/inherent risk/control risk (risk in the financial statement)

Risks dependent on the auditor:
— detection risk (risk of not detecting MM)

2.6 Risk assessment

□ Understanding the entity and its environment 了解公司和它所处的行业环境

□ Assess the risk of material misstatement at the financial statement and assertion level 从报表层和认定层,来评估重大误报。

2.6.1 Methods of risk assessment-AEIOU

○ Analytical Procedures (A)

□ Ratio analysis (receivable days)

□ Trend analysis (sales)

□ Proof in total (payroll) Analytical procedures

Operating margin = operating profit/revenue

Revenue increase ratio

Return on capital employed = operating profit/(equity + non-current liabilities)

Interest cover = operating profit/finance cost ($\geqslant 1$)

Current ratio = current asset/current liability ($\geqslant 2$)

Gearing = non-current lia/(non-current liability + equity) = debt/equity ($\geqslant 0.5$)

Inventory turnover = (average inventory/cost of sales) × 365

Trade receivables days = (Trade receivables/sales revenue) × 365

Trade payables days = (Trade payables/cost of sales) × 365

Cash change\revenue change\liability change

○ Enquiry (E)

Enquiry of knowledgeable parties and document

External confirmation obtained in the form of a direct written response to the auditor from a third party

○ Inspection (I)

Inspection of records, documents

Physically inspection of assets

○ Observation (O)

Observe a process performed by others
  ○ Reperform（U）

□ Recalculation consists of checking the mathematical accuracy of documents or records.

□ Reperform involves the auditor's independent execution of procedures or controls that were originally performed by client.

2.6.2 Common audit risks

◇ Numbers are misstated

◇ Disclosure is missing or inadequate

◇ Basis of preparation is not appropriate

Situation	Audit risk
Tight audit deadline/time table	Place additional pressure on the team in obtaining sufficient and appropriate evidence, increasing detection risk
There is a new website directly linked to the finance system which records sales automatically	There is increased risk over completeness of income if the system fails to record all sales made on the website. Revenue may be understated
Change/upgrading computerized accounting system	If any errors occurred during change or set up process, the financial information may be incorrectly stated in financial statement
Change of key personnel in making financial reporting	The successor may be not familiar with client's financial reporting enough, leading increased errors in financial statement
Consignment 委托代销	There is a risk that the sale and inventory may be overstated
Good-in-transit at the year end 年底有在途，考分类错误	Inventory may not be recorded incorrect accounting period（cut-off issue）
Goods damage/obsolescence/defect/fashion or Consumer electronics/sale on deep discount	Potential indication that NRV ＜ Cost, leading overstatement of inventory
Ongoing court case 未判决诉讼	There is a risk that the either the provision, as well as the expenses, are understated or that a contingent liability is not appropriately disclosed in the financial statements
Transaction/accounting treatment involves significant accounting estimates	Management may intend to produce the favorable result, especially when their personal rewards are linked to company's financial performance
Complicated business nature/in specialized industry	Audit team may not be sufficiently qualified to assess, increasing detection risk
Change of accounting standards	Client may be lack of experience to apply new accounting standard, leading increased errors in financial statement

Part 2　Audit risk

(Continued)

Situation	Audit risk
Client is under loan	Breach of covenant may cause severe liquidity pressure, even going concern problem, management may manipulate the financial statements to meet financial requirements of covenant
Client expands into new industry/ product line	There is a risk that the results of the new products division are not separately disclosed as operating segment
New client of audit firm 首次鉴证业务	Opening balances may be misstated 期初余额 Audit team should be suitably experienced. Adequate time should be allocated for team members to obtain an understanding of the company. Review previous auditor's work to assess the opening balances
Inventory is stored at a third-party warehouse	It may be difficult to obtain sufficient appropriate evidence over the quantity and condition of inventory held. There is increased detection risk over completeness, existence and valuation of inventory
It takes up to one period to manufacture products(WIP)	here is likely to be a material work in progress (WIP) inventory balance at the year end. Determining the value and quantity of WIP is complex. There is a risk of misstatement of WIP inventory
Loss of key customer/Sales have fallen dramatically	If sales is not compensated from other source, Client may not be able to continue to operate for the foreseeable future. There is a risk that disclosures of material uncertainties relating to going concern may be inadequate
Client is planning to list on the stock exchange next year/ negotiating with bank or potential investor	There is an increased risk of 'window dress' of the financial statements. There is a risk of overstatement of assets and profits, and understatement of expenses and liabilities
Account balance has no movement	There is a risk that the prior year figure has been incorrectly presented in the current year column
closing down and workforce redundancy	according to the requirement of IAS 37 Provisions, Contingent Liabilities and Contingent Assets a redundancy provision will be required for any staff not yet paid at the year end. If dose not doing so, the provision may be understated
R&D — capitalised incorrectly	According to the requirement of IAS 38: the expenditure should be expensed when the new product is in research stage, when the product is in its final stage, satisfying more strict criteria it can be capitalised, so under some pressure, intangible assets could be overstated

Part 3

Internal control

Internal control describes the process designed, implemented and maintained by those charged with governance, management（治理层 + 管理层 = BOD）and other personnel to provide them with reasonable assurance that an entity will achieve its objectives 确保企业实现它的目标 with regard to

□ The reliability of financial reporting (internal and external)财务报告可靠
□ The effectiveness and efficiency of operations and 运营有效果,有效率
□ Compliance with applicable laws and regulations 合法

3.1 Five Components of an internal control system 内控五要素

The control environment 控制环境	Sets the tone or Tone from the top by creating a culture attitudes, awareness and actions of management 如：文化基调
The entity's risk assessment process 公司的风险评估程序	How management identifies risks and decides upon actions to manage them 如何识别和管理风险：风险识别 identity→风险评估 assessment→风险应对 response
The information system 信息系统	Consists of infrastructure, software, people, procedures and data. 硬件、软件、程序、数据
Control activities 控制活动	The policies and procedures that help ensure that management directives are carried out
Monitoring of controls 控制监督	Assess the design and operation of controls over time Ongoing monitoring is part of regular management activity

3.2 Control activities

□ Segregation of duties：assignment of roles to different people(权责分离)
□ Information processing：computer controls including general IT controls including general control and application control (电脑控制)
□ Authorisation：transactions should be approved a responsible official(授权)
□ Physical control：restrict access to physical assets like cash (物理控制)
□ Performance reviews：review the performance of the company and compare it to the budget or the prior year.（回顾企业表现）

□ Arithmetical control：check the arithmetical accuracy of the records（数字准确性）

□ Account reconciliations：compare the account with other source, often from the third party（对账）

3.3 Computer control

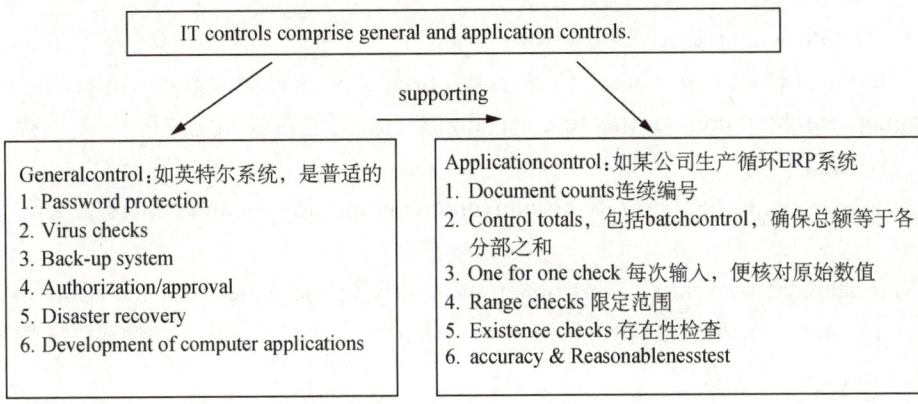

3.4 Obtaining an understanding of the entity's internal controls

The auditors must keep a record of the client's systems which must be updated each year.

There are several techniques for recording the assessment of control risk；that is, the system. One or more of the following may be used depending on the complexity of the system. 掌握各种方法的优缺点。各种方法的选择，取决于系统的复杂程度

○ Narrative notes 文字性笔记

优点：简单、易记录，员工讨论的简单笔记

缺点：当系统比较复杂的时候，需要大量文字，比较啰唆 cumbersome，替代方案是图标格式。

○ Flow charts 流程图

优点：简单，逻辑性强，整个系统图在一张表里集中表现

缺点：比较耗费时间，而且有时需要文字补充

○ Internal control questionnaires（ICQs）问卷

Comprise a series of questions on each key transaction cycle（sales，purchases etc）which seek to determine whether a control exists.

优点：

ICQs identify where internal controls exist

Quick to prepare

Can be completed by junior staff

缺点：容易让雇主的员工 Overstate the level of control，Give a distorted view 夸大事实、模棱两可。如：有些模棱两可的问题，因为回答说是，给人以做了的错觉，但实际上或许并未做。可能包含大量不相关的问题/控制。没有相关权重。

○ Internal control evaluation questionnaires（ICEQs）评估问卷 are slightly more robust in that they ask questions which enable the auditor to elicit the controls which exist. A questionnaire listing control objectives, that requires the client to explain how they meet each objective.

优点：Quick to prepare, timely method to record.

缺点：对审计师的经验有一定要求。

3.5 Limitations of internal control

□ Human error can cause failures although a well-designed internal control environment can help control this to a certain extent. 尽管内控制定的很好，但内控靠人来执行，人会出错。

□ Processes being deliberately circumvented by employees and others 人为绕开内控程序。

□ Management overriding controls, presumably in the belief that the controls put in place are inconvenient or inappropriate and should not apply to them. 管理层凌驾于内控之上。

□ The occurrence of unforeseen circumstances 发生不可预计的情况。

Control systems are designed to cope with a given range of variables and when an event happens out with that range, the system may be unable to cope.

□ Poor judgement in decision-making. Internal control failures can sometimes arise from individual decisions being made based on inadequate information provision or by inexperienced staff. 信息不足或人员素质不够导致的决策失误。

Part 4

Test of control and substantive procedures

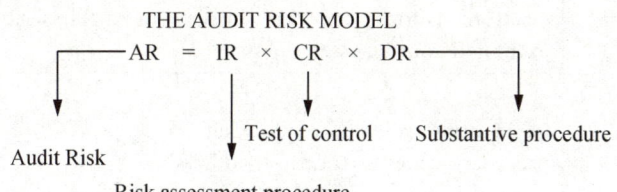

Tests of control evaluate the operating effectiveness of controls in preventing, or detecting and correcting, material misstatements at the assertion level.

Example tests of control over wages and salaries

— Inspect numerical sequence of clock cards/timesheets; if any breaks in the sequence are noted, enquire of management as to missing payroll records.

— Review a sample of timesheets/clock cards for evidence of authorisation of overtime by a responsible official.

— Observe whether there is adequate segregation of duties between human resources and payroll departments.

Substantive procedures are aimed at detecting material misstatements at the assertion level. They include **tests of details** of transactions, balances, disclosures and **substantive analytical procedures.** (细节测试与实质性分析程序)

Example substantive procedures over wages and salaries.

— Perform a proof in total of total payroll taking into account joiners and leavers and any annual pay rise, compare any trends to prior years and discuss significant fluctuations with management.

— For a sample of employees, recalculate the gross and net pay and agree to the payroll records to verify accuracy.

— Re-perform calculation of statutory deductions to confirm whether correct deductions for this year have been included within the payroll expense.

ACCA 知识精要

Seven procedures for obtaining evidence:

手段	举例	局限性
Inquiry 询问	Inquiry consists of seeking information from knowledgeable persons, both financial and non-financial, within the entity or outside the entity	依赖于回答人的正值度和知道多少
External confirmation 外部函证（仅限于实质性审查）	An external confirmation represents audit evidence obtained by the auditor as a direct written response to the auditor from a third party, in paper form, electronic form or by other medium	需要可靠的第三方出具函证
Inspection 检查	Inspection involves examining records or documents, whether internal or external, in paper form, electronic form, or other media, or a physical examination of an asset	依赖于公司内控的有效性；实物资产，只能查存在性，不能确认价值
Observation 观察	Observation consists of looking at a process or procedure being performed by others	只反映观察时履行步骤，没看到的时候就不知道了，具有时效限制
Reperformance 重新执行	Reperformance involves the auditor's independent execution of procedures or controls that were originally performed as part of the entity's internal control	适用范围比较窄，只适用于可以独立操作的。
Recalculation 重新计算	Recalculation consists of checking the mathematical accuracy of documents or records. Recalculation may be performed manually or electronically	
Analytical procedures 分析性复核（仅限于实质性审查）	Analytical procedures consist of evaluations of financial information through analysis of plausible relationships among both financial and non-financial data. Analytical procedures also encompass such investigation as is necessary of identified fluctuations or relationships that are inconsistent with other relevant information or that differ from expected values by a significant amount	依赖于数字的准确性

Part 5

Cycle and substantive procedures

5.1 Purchase cycle

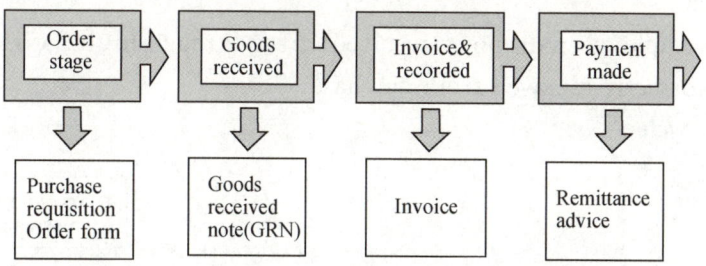

Control objective	Activities of control
1) Ensure the purchase can enjoy competitive price and satisfied quality	Authorized supplier list.
2) Ensure the goods being purchased are really required by the company	Authorized and signed by purchasing manager and accounting manager
3) Ensure the goods received are the items on orders and with correct quantity and good quality.	Compare orders before receiving to ensure the name, quantity and quality of goods received
4) Ensure all goods ordered have been received in time	After receiving the order, fill in the GRN on the order. Periodically review the order. No GRN indicates that the order is not received
5) Ensure all purchase transactions have been accounted for the transaction has been accounted for correctly	1. Make the serial number of the account, the skip number means the omission of the account. 如 001-002-003 2. Ensure that the invoice information matches GRN
6) Ensure all payments have been authorised properly and thus no error or fraud in payment such as payment twice	After the invoice is entered into the account, it shall be signed by the financial personnel

Analytical review of Purchase and sale costs:

□ Compare the overall level of purchase/cost against prior years and budget and investigate any significant fluctuations.

☐ Obtain a schedule of purchase/cost for the year broken down into the detailed categories and compare this to the prior year breakdown and for any unusual movements discuss with management.

☐ Calculate the gross profit margin and compare this to the prior year and investigate any significant fluctuations.

☐ Select a sample of purchase and agree these to the goods receive notes and invoices through to inclusion in the sales ledger to ensure completeness of purchase.

☐ Select a sample of purchase invoices for suppliers and recalculate the discounts allowed to ensure that these are accurate.

☐ Select a sample of GRN both pre and post year end; follow these through to purchase invoices in the correct accounting period to ensure that cut-off has been correctly applied.

☐ Select a sample of credit notes received, trace through to the original invoice and ensure invoice correctly removed from purchase.

5.2 Sales cycle

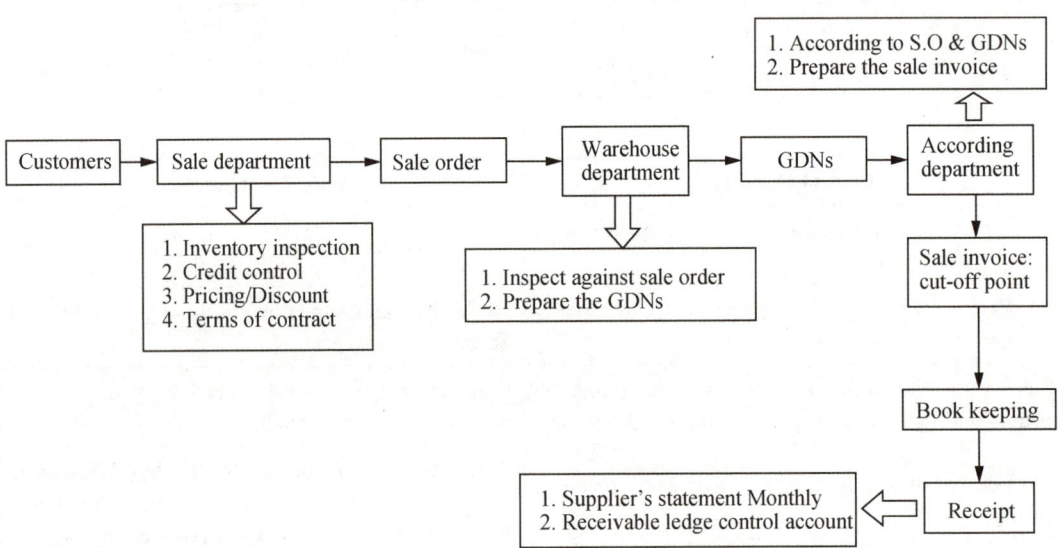

Control objective 控制目标

☐ Ensure that orders are only accepted if goods are available to be processed for customers.

☐ Ensure that sales discounts are only provided to valid customers.

☐ Ensure that goods are not supplied to poor credit risks.

☐ Ensure that goods are despatched for all orders on a timely basis.

☐ Ensure that goods are despatched correctly to customers and that they are of an adequate quality.

☐ Ensure that all goods despatched are correctly invoiced.

☐ Ensure completeness of income for goods despatched.

□ Ensure that all orders are recorded completely and accurately.

□ Order forms should be sequentially numbered and where there are gaps in the sequence, they should be investigated to identify any missing orders.

□ Customer credit limits should be reviewed more regularly by a responsible official.

□ The invoicing system should be amended to prevent sales clerks from being able to manually enter sales discounts onto invoices.

Substantive procedures of sales revenue

□ Compare the overall level of revenue against prior years and budget and investigate any significant fluctuations.

□ Obtain a schedule of sales for the year, compare this to the prior year and for any unusual movements discuss with management.

□ Calculate the gross profit margin for XX and compare this to the prior year and investigate any significant fluctuations.

□ Select a sample of trade customer orders placed online and agree these to the despatch notes and sales invoices through to inclusion in the sales ledger to ensure completeness of revenue.（反过来讲就是 occurrence）

□ Select a sample of sales invoices and agree the sales prices back to the supporting documentation to ensure the accuracy of invoices.

□ Select a sample of sales invoices for larger customers and recalculate the discounts allowed to ensure that these are accurate.

□ Select a sample of despatch notes both pre and post year end; follow these through to sales invoices in the correct accounting period to ensure that cut-off has been correctly applied.截止

□ Select a sample of sales invoice and make sure the correct client's name in sales invoice（right & obligation）. 控制权

5.3 Substantive procedures of trade receivables

□ Calculate average receivable days and compare this to prior year, investigate any significant differences.

□ Perform a positive trade receivables circularisation of a representative sample of company's year-end balances, for any non-replies, with company's permission, send a reminder letter to follow up.

□ Select a sample of year-end receivable balances and agree back to valid supporting documentation of GDN and sales order to ensure existence.（反过来就是 completeness）

□ Select a sample of goods despatched notes（GDNs）before and just after the year end and follow through to the sales invoice to ensure they are recorded in the correct accounting period.（理解性应用）

□ Review customer correspondence for any aged balances to assess whether there are any invoices in dispute.

□ Review the after date cash receipts and follow through to pre-year-end receivable balances.

☐ Review board minutes to assess whether there are any material disputed receivables.

☐ Inspect the aged receivables report to identify any slow moving balances, discuss these with the credit control manager to assess whether an allowance or write down is necessary

5.4 Substantive procedures of trade payables

☐ Calculate the trade payable days for XXX and compare to prior years, investigate any significant difference, in particular any decrease for this year.

☐ Select a sample of payable balances and perform a trade payables' circularisation, follow up any non-replies and any reconciling items between the balance confirmed and the trade payables' balance.

☐ Select a sample of year-end payable balances and agree back to valid supporting documentation of GRNs and purchase order to ensure existence.

☐ Select a sample of GRNs before the year end and after the year end and follow through to inclusion in the correct period's payables balance, to ensure they are recorded in the correct accounting period.（理解性应用）

☐ Obtain supplier statements and reconcile these to the purchase ledger balances, and investigate any reconciling items.（月结单）

☐ Review after date payments, if they relate to the current year then follow through to the purchase ledger or accrual listing to ensure completeness.

☐ Enquire of management their process for identifying goods received but not invoiced or logged in the purchase ledger and ensure that it is reasonable to ensure completeness of payables.

5.5 Inventory

5.5.1 Inventory control and test of control

Inventory controls are designed to ensure safe custody. Such controls include：

☐ Restriction of access to inventory

☐ Documentation and authorization of movements

☐ Regular independent inventory counting

☐ Review of inventory condition

Tests must be undertaken on how inventory movements are recorded and how inventory is secured.

5.5.2 Inventory count

1) Plan

☐ Review prior year working papers 查看去年工作底稿,辨识风险和熟悉存货内容

☐ Obtain last year's inventory count memo 查看去年的库存清点工作纪要

☐ Determine arrangements with management in advance 跟管理层讨论安排

☐ Ascertain whether any inventory is held by third parties 确认是否有库存在他人

仓库

- Review client's inventory count instructions 查看客户的库存清点程序
- Consider the need for an expert 考虑下是否需要专家介入
- Prepare audit programme for the count 准备库存盘点的审计方案

2) Determine procedures to cover a representative selection of inventories 确认样本量

3) Count

- Observe the counting teams to confirm whether the inventory count instructions are being followed correctly.
- Confirm the procedures for identifying and segregating damaged goods are operating correctly.
- Identify and record any inventory held for third parties (if any) and confirm that it is excluded from the count.
- Obtain a photocopy of the completed sequentially numbered inventory sheets for follow up testing on the final audit.
- Identify and make a note of the last goods received notes (GRNs) and goods despatched notes (GDNs) for the year end in order to perform cut-off procedures.

4) Final

- Trace own test count items through to final inventory summary
- Inspect replies from third parties
- Follow up cut-off details

5.5.3　Substantive procedures of inventory

- Select a sample of inventory from the inventory sheet and perform physical count. Confirm that items inspected.
- For inventory held by third parties send confirmation to verify the inventory balance at the year end.
- For the sample of inventory physically count trace them to inventory sheet.
- Perform a review of the average inventory days for the current year and compare to prior year inventory days. Discuss any significant variations with management.
- Compare the gross margin for current year with prior year. Fluctuations in gross margin could be due to inventory valuation issues. Discuss significant variations in the margin with management.
- Select a representative sample of goods in inventory at the year end, agree the cost per the records to a recent purchase invoice and ensure that the cost is correctly stated.
- Review aged inventory reports and identify any slow moving goods, discuss with management why these items have not been written down.
- For a sample of manufactured items obtain cost sheets and confirm: 自产产品成本
  — raw material costs to recent purchase invoices 原材料价格跟采购单一致
  — labour costs to time sheets or wage records 人工成本跟工资记录出勤记录一致

— overheads allocated are of a production nature.制造成本分摊合理

□ Follow up any damaged/obsolete items noted by the auditor at the inventory counts attended，to ensure that the inventory records have been updated correctly.

□ Select a sample of year end goods and review post year end sales invoices to ascertain if NRV is above cost or if an adjustment is required.

5.6 Wage system

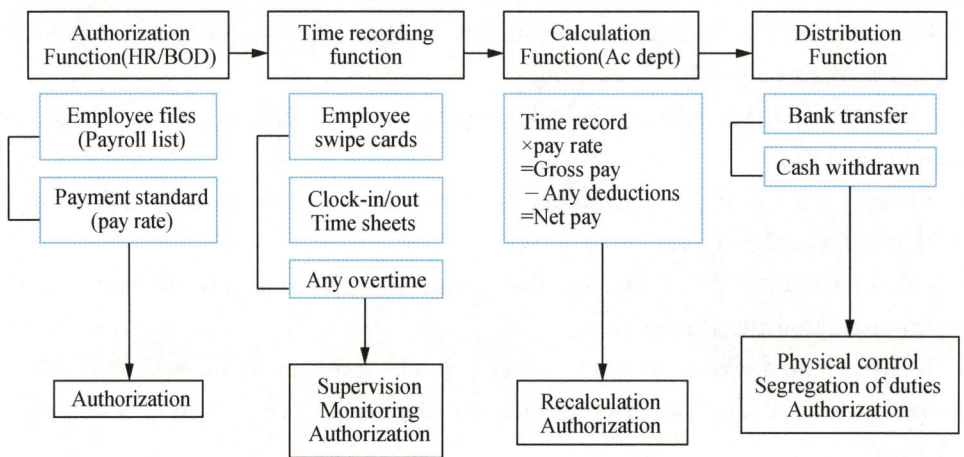

5.6.1 Control objectives 控制目标

○ Employees are only paid for work that they have done

○ Gross pay has been calculated correctly 税前工资计算正确

○ Overtime has been authorised properly 加班有合理授权

○ Net pay has been calculated correctly 税后工资计算正确

○ Gross and net pay have been recorded accurately in the general ledger 工资入账正确

○ Only genuine employees are paid 只有真正的员工是付工资的

○ Correct amounts are paid to taxation authorities. 工资所得税，支付正确

5.6.2 Substantive procedures of Wage/Payroll

○ Compare the total payroll expense to the prior year and investigate any significant differences.

○ Review monthly payroll charges，compare this to the prior year and budgets and discuss with management any significant variances.

○ Perform a proof in total of total wages and salaries，incorporating joiners and leavers and the pay increase. Compare this to the actual wages in the financial statements and investigate any significant differences.

○ Agree the total wages and salaries expense per the payroll system to the trial balance，investigate any differences.

○ Agree the individual wages and salaries per the payroll to the personnel records and records of hours worked per clocking in cards (计时卡).

○ For bank transfer, agree the total net pay per the payroll records to the bank transfer listing of payments and to the cashbook.

○ For cash payment, agree the total cash withdrawn for wage payments equates to the weekly wages paid plus any surplus cash subsequently banked to confirm completeness and accuracy.

○ Agree the year-end tax liabilities to the payroll records, and subsequent payment to the post year-end cash book to confirm completeness.

○ Recalculate statutory deductions to confirm whether correct deductions for this year have been included within the payroll expense.

5.7 Cash

5.7.1 Control of cash

Deficiencies	Controls	Test of control
A junior clerk opens the post unsupervised. This could result in cash being misappropriated.	A second staff independent of the accounts team should assist with the mail, one should open the post and the second should record cash received in the cash log.	Observe the mail opening process, to assess if the control is operating effectively.
Cash and cheques are secured in a small locked box and only banked every few days. A small locked box is not adequate for security of to considerable cash receipts, as it can easily be stolen.	Cash and cheques should be ideally banked daily, if not then it should be stored in a fire proof safe, and access to this safe should be restricted to supervised individuals.	Enquire of management where the cash receipts not banked are stored. Inspect the location to ensure cash is suitably secure.
Cash and cheques are only banked every few days and any member of the finance team performs this.	Cash and cheques should be banked every day by appointed person.	Inspect the paying-in-books to see if cash and cheques have been banked daily or less frequently. Review bank statements against the cash received log to confirm all amounts were banked promptly.
The cashier updates both the cash book and the sales ledger. This is weak segregation of duties, as the cashier could incorrectly enter a receipt and this would impact both the cash book and the sales ledger. In addition weak segregation of duties could increase the risk of a 'teeming and lading' fraud.	The cashier should update the cash book from the cash received log. A member of the sales ledger team should update the sales ledger.	Observe the process for recording cash received into the relevant ledgers and note if the segregation of duties is occurring.

(Continued)

Deficiencies	Controls	Test of control
Bank reconciliations are not performed every month and they do not appear to be reviewed by a senior member of the finance department. Errors in the cash cycle may not be promptly identified if reconciliations are performed infrequently.	Bank reconciliations should be performed monthly. A responsible individual should then review them.	Review the file of reconciliations for evidence of regular performance and review by senior finance team members.

5.7.2 Substantive procedures of bank

○ Obtain the company's bank reconciliation and check the additions to ensure arithmetical accuracy.

○ Verify the reconciliation's balance per the cash book to the year end cash book.

○ Review the cash book and bank statements for any unusual items or large transfers around the year end, as this could be evidence of window dressing.

○ Verify the balance per the bank statement to an original year end bank statement and also to the bank confirmation letter.

○ Obtain a bank confirmation letter from XX's bankers for all of its accounts.

○ Agree all balances listed on the bank confirmation letter to the company's bank reconciliations or trial balance to ensure completeness of bank balances.

○ Examine the bank confirmation letter for details of any security provided by XX as this may require disclosure.

○ Trace all of the outstanding lodgements to the pre year-end cash book, post year-end bank statement and also to paying-in-book pre year end.

○ Trace all unpresented cheques through to a pre year-end cash book and post year-end statement. For any unusual amounts or significant delays obtain explanations from management.

5.8 PPE

5.8.1 Risk assessment

确认: In order to expand their flight network, Donald Co will need to acquire more airplanes; they have placed orders for another six planes at an estimated total cost of $20 m and the company is not sure whether these planes will be received by the year end.	according to the requirement of IAS16: only assets which physically exist at the year end should be included in property, plant and equipment, if dose not follow this requirement the non current asset will be overstated.
升级改造: company has spent an estimated $15 m on refurbishing their existing planes	according to the requirement of IAS16: if the expenditure is in capital nature, it will be capitalised, otherwise, it should be expensed as repairs

(Continued)

重估：The land and buildings are to be revalued at the year end.	The revaluation needs to be carried out and recorded in accordance with IAS 16 Property, Plant and Equipment; otherwise non-current assets may be incorrectly valued
处置：During the year a small warehouse has been disposed of at a profit/loss.	the asset needs to have been correctly removed from property plant and equipment to ensure the non-current asset register is not overstated, and the profit on disposal should be included within the income statement.
租赁（控制权问题）	Only warehouses owned by the client should be included within PPE. There is a risk of overstatement of PPE and understatement of rental expenses if the client has capitalised all warehouses.
会计估计变更：The directors have reviewed the asset lives and depreciation rates of plant and machinery, resulting in the depreciation charge reducing.	Under IAS 16 Property, Plant and Equipment, asset lives should be reviewed annually, and if the asset lives have increased as a result of this review such that the depreciation decreases, then this change may be reasonable. However, there is a risk that this reduction has occurred in order to achieve profit target

5.8.2　Substantive procedures of PPE

1）完整性

○ Obtain a list of PPE register, recalculate it and agree the total to the general ledger and F/S.

○ Reconcile the PPE register with the opening position.

○ Select a sample of PPE from the register and perform physical inspection. Confirm that items inspected：

— Exist

— Are in use

— Are in good condition

○ For the sample of asset physically exist trace them to register.

2）Addition 新增（存在）& revaluation 重估

○ Obtain a breakdown of additions, cast the list and agree to the non-current asset register to confirm completeness of plant & equipment (P&E).

○ Select a sample of additions and agree cost to supplier invoice.

○ For a sample of additions recorded physically verify them on the factory floor.

○ If any assets have been revalued during the year then assess the reasonableness of the valuer. In particular consider their experience, independence, scope of work and assumptions used.

○ Agree the revalued amounts to a valuation report, for a sample recalculate the revaluation surplus and agree to the revaluation reserve.

3) Depreciation

○ Review depreciation policies for reasonableness by comparison to prior year, industry practices, the entity's replacement policy and the profits/losses arising on disposal of assets.

○ For a sample of assets recalculate the depreciation charge for the year and agree to the entity asset register.

○ Perform a proof in total calculation of depreciation, considering the timing of additions and disposals and compare this expectation to the actual charge, and investigate any significant differences.

4) Disposal

○ Obtain a breakdown of disposals, cast the list and agree all assets removed from the non-current asset register to confirm existence.

○ Select a sample of disposals and agree sale proceeds to supporting documentation such as sundry sales invoices.

○ Recalculate the profit/loss on disposal and agree to the income statement.

5) Control & Right 所有权

○ Verify ownership of property via inspection of title deeds 房产证 and land registration documents.

○ For a sample of additions agree to purchase invoices to verify invoice relates to the entity

○ Review any new lease agreements to ensure assets are correctly treated as finance or operating leases.

○ Inspect vehicle registration documents 车辆登记证 to confirm ownership of motor vehicles.

5.9　IAS37 Provisions, Contingent Liabilities and Contingent Assets

5.9.1　Provisions

A provision should be recognised where a reliable estimate can be made in relation to a probable outflow of economic resources and a present obligation has taken place.

If these criteria have been met, it would be reasonable that full amount be recognized.

Provision shall be reviewed and adjusted at each statement of financial position date.（经济利益很可能流出,概率50%＜X≤95%,全额确认在流动负债）

5.9.2　Contingent Liabilities

A contingent liability should be disclosed if there is a possible outflow of economic benefit.

If an amount is possible, rather than probable to be paid, then it is treated as a contingent liability, and a note to the accounts should be provided to describe the nature of the situation, an estimate of the possible financial effect and an indication of any uncertainties.（经济利益可能流出,概率5%＜X≤50%,全额披露）

5.9.3 Contingent Assets

Only when the realisation of income is virtually certain, then the related asset is not a contingent asset and its recognition is appropriate.（只有当经济利益基本确定流入企业时，方可在资产负债表中确认）

5.9.4 Substantive procedures of Redundancy

○ Discuss with the directors of Chuck Industries as to whether they have formally announced their intention to make the sales ledger department redundant, to confirm that a present obligation exists at the year end. 与高层讨论，是否真的有裁员。

○ If announced before the year end, review supporting documentation to verify that the decision has been formally announced. 如年底前宣布，查看相应的证据（通知、告示等）。

○ Review the board minutes to ascertain whether it is probable that the redundancy payments will be paid. 查看 BOD 会议纪要，确认裁员赔款支付的可能性。

○ Obtain a breakdown of the redundancy calculations by employee and cast it to ensure completeness. 需要计算的明细表，来计算裁员的费用，确保完整性。

○ Recalculate the redundancy provision to confirm completeness and agree components of the calculation to supporting documentation. 重新计算下裁员的费用。

○ Review the post year-end period to identify whether any redundancy payments have been made, compare actual payments to the amounts provided to assess whether the provision is reasonable. 查看年后的账，看看是否已支付，将实际支付的跟当时预期的比较，看是否合理。

○ Obtain a written representation from management to confirm the completeness of the provision. 获取管理层的保证来确认预期事项的完整性。

○ Review the disclosure of the redundancy provision to ensure compliance with IAS 37 Provisions, Contingent Liabilities and Contingent Assets. 看下裁员的披露，是否符合 IAS 37 的要求。

5.9.5 Substantive procedures of Food poisoning

○ Review the correspondence from the customers claiming food poisoning to assess whether Balotelli has a present obligation as a result of a past event. 查看客户反应，评估公司是否对过去事件有当前责任。

○ With the client's permission, send an enquiry letter to the lawyers of Balotelli to obtain their view as to the probability of the claim being successful. 询问律师观点，胜率多少。

○ Review board minutes to understand whether the directors believe that the claim will be successful or not. 查看管理层的会议纪要，确认官司的胜率（赔款可能性）。

○ Review the post year-end period to assess whether any payments have been made to any of the claimants. 查看年后付款，评估下是否私下付款给被告。

○ Discuss with management as to whether they propose to include a contingent liability disclosure or not, consider the reasonableness of this. 跟管理层讨论或有负债的合

理披露。

- Obtain a written management representation confirming management's view that the lawsuit is unlikely to be successful and hence no provision is required. 获取管理层的保证来确认索赔可能不大，不是预计负债。
- Review the adequacy of any disclosures made in the financial statements.

Part 6

Subsequent event

Subsequent events are events occurring between the period end and the date of the auditor's report and also include facts discovered after the auditor's report has been issued.

Auditors should consider the effect of such events on the financial statements and on their audit opinion.

There are two types of event defined by IAS 10.

a) Those that provide evidence of conditions that existed at the year-end date (adjusting events).

b) Those that are indicative of conditions that arose after the year-end date (non-adjusting events).

You should be familiar with adjusting and non-adjusting events from your financial reporting studies.

Adjusting events	Non-adjusting events
Settlement of a court case	Dividends declared after the year end
Sale of inventory after year end providing evidence of its net realisable value at year end	Fire causing destruction of major plant
Bankruptcy of a major customer	Announcement of a major restructuring

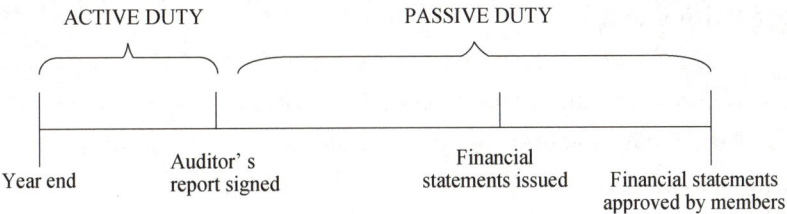

6.1 Auditor's responsibility

Auditors have a responsibility to review subsequent events before they sign the auditor's report. Period between the year-end date and the date the auditor's report is signed 财年结束后,至审计报告签署前

The auditor shall perform audit procedures designed to obtain sufficient appropriate audit evidence that all events occurring between the date of the financial statements and the date of the auditor's report that require adjustment of, or disclosure in, the financial statements have been identified. 审计师有积极的责任执行审计程序，来辨别财报是否正确，该披露的是否披露。

The auditor is not, however, expected to perform additional audit procedures on matters to which previously applied audit procedures have provided satisfactory conclusions. 如果审计师对当年的财务报告已经比较满意了，那么不会再执行额外的审计程序。

May have to take action if they become aware of subsequent events after the date they sign the auditor's report. Period between the date the auditor's report is signed and the date the financial statements are issued. 审计报告已签署，至财报公布前。

The auditor has no obligation to perform any audit procedures regarding the financial statements after the date of the auditor's report. 签署审计报告后，审计师没有责任来主动发现问题。

6.2 期后事项答题步骤与思路

S1. 描述题意

S2. 依据年底是否存在，判断调整和非调整

S3. 判断重要性：金额重大（计算）、性质重大（指明风险）

S4. 审计程序

6.2.1 Evidence of NRV of inventories

S1.

S2. This information was obtained after the year end but provides further evidence of the net realizable value of inventory at the year end and hence is an adjusting event.

IAS 2 Inventories requires that inventory is valued at the lower of cost and net realizable value. The inventory of $0.85 million must be written down to its net realizable value of $0.1 million.

S3. It represents 13.4% (0.75/5.6) of profit before tax and 1.4% (0.75/55) of revenue. Hence, the directors should amend the financial statements by writing down the inventory to $0.1 million.

S4.

○ Review the board minutes/quality control reports to assess whether this event was the only case of defective inventory as there could potentially be other inventory which requires writing down. 查看会议纪要。

○ Discuss the matter with the directors, checking whether the company has sufficient inventory to continue trading in the short term. 是否有足够存货维持公司运作。

○ Obtain a written representation confirming that the company's going concern status is not impacted. 获取管理层的保证书，来证明公司还能持续经营，万能写法。

○ Obtain a schedule showing the defective inventory and agree to supporting production documentation that it was produced prior to 30 April, as otherwise it would not require a write down at the year end. 次品存货明细。

○ Discuss with management how they have assessed the scrap value of $0.1 million and agree this amount to any supporting documentation to confirm the value.

6.2.2 Resolution of a court case

S1.

S2. Although the settlement was agreed after the year end, it provides further evidence that the company had a present obligation as at 30 September. 因为是年中官司，期后同意。

The financial statements should be adjusted with the contingent liability disclosures being removed and instead a provision of $0.6 million being recorded.

S3. The sum being claimed is $1 million but the probable payment is $0.6 million, as it represents 8% of profit and hence management should provide for this amount.

S4.

○ The auditor should contact the company's lawyers to ask their view as to whether the settlement is probable and whether $0.6 million is the likely amount. 律师意见。

○ Review the correspondence with the supplier to confirm that the amount they are willing to accept is in fact $0.6 million.

○ Discuss with management as to whether it is probable that they will pay this sum and obtain a written representation confirming this.

6.2.3 Bankruptcy of a major customer

S1.

S2. This information was received after the year end but provides further evidence of the recoverability of the receivable balance at the year end. The receivables balance is overstated and consideration should be given to adjusting this balance, if material, through the use of an allowance for receivables or by being written off. 因为客户难以支付，所以要计提坏账准备或购销坏账。

S3. It represents 7.4% (0.283/3.8 m) of profit before tax and 2.5% (0.283/11.2 m) of revenue. The directors should amend the 2014 financial statements by writing down or writing off the receivable balance.

S4. The following audit procedures should be applied:

○ The correspondence with the customer should be reviewed to assess whether there is any likelihood of payment.

○ Discuss with management as to why they feel an adjustment is not required in the 2014 financial statements.

○ Review the post year-end period to see if any payments have been received from the customer.

6.2.4 Non-adjusting events

S3. As a material non-adjusting event, the directors should consider including a disclosure note detailing the explosion and the value of assets impacted. 因为是重要调整项，需要在财报中披露。

S4.

○ Obtain a schedule showing the damaged property，plant and equipment and agree the net book value to the non-current assets register to confirm what the value of damaged assets was.

○ Obtain the latest inventory records for this storage location to ascertain the likely level of inventory at the time of the explosion.

○ Discuss with the directors whether they will disclose the effect of the explosion in the financial statements.

○ Discuss with the directors why they do not believe that they are able to claim on their insurance；if a claim was to be made，then only uninsured losses would require disclosure，and this may be an immaterial amount.

6.2.5　Event after the audit report has been signed

○ Discuss the matter with the directors to determine their course of action.

○ Where the directors decide to amend the disclosure in the financial statements，audit the amendment and then re-draft and re-date the audit report as appropriate.

○ Where the directors decide not to amend the disclosure in the financial statements, the auditor can consider other methods of contacting the members. For example, the auditor can speak in the upcoming general meeting to inform the members of the event.

Part 7

Going concern

IAS 1 Presentation of Financial Statements requires that management automatically prepare financial statements on a going concern basis unless they believe that the company will soon cease trading.

7.1 Going concern indicators

Financial

- Net liability or net current liability position.
- Negative operating cashflows.
- Substantial operating losses or significant deterioration in the value of assets used to generate cash flows.
- Indications of withdrawal of financial support by creditors
- Inability to obtain new financing

Operational

- Management intention to liquidate the entity or to cease operations
- Loss of a major market, key customer, license, or principal supplier.
- Labour difficulties or stock outs.
- Emergence of a highly successful competitor.

Other

- Non-compliance with capital or other statutory requirements.
- Changes in legislation or government policy expected to adversely affect the entity.
- Pending legal or regulatory proceedings against the entity that may, if successful, result in claims that are unlikely to be satisfied.
- Uninsured or under-insured catastrophes when they occur.

7.2 Responsibility for going concern

- To carry out appropriate audit procedures that will identify whether or not an organisation can continue as a going concern.执行适当的审计程序来判断公司是否可持续经营
- To ensure that the organisation's management have been realistic in their use of the going concern assumption when preparing the financial statements 确保企业运用了恰当的持续经营假设

○ To report to the members where they consider that the going concern assumption has been used inappropriately, for example, when the financial statements indicate that the organisation is a going concern, but audit procedures indicate this may not be the case. 如果企业不恰当运用了可持续经营假设，需通报给公司股东。

7.3 Going concern procedures

— Obtain Elounda's cash flow forecast and review the cash in and out flows. Assess the assumptions for reasonableness and discuss the findings with management to understand if the company will have sufficient cash flows to meet liabilities as they fall due.

— Discuss with management their ability to settle the next instalment due for repayment to the bank and the lump sum payment of \$800k in January 20×7 and ensure these have been included in the cash flow forecast.

— Review current agreements with the bank to determine whether any key ratios or covenants have been breached with regards to the bank loan or any overdraft.

— Review the company's post year-end sales and order book to assess the levels of trade and if the revenue figures in the cash flow forecast are reasonable.

— Review post year-end correspondence with suppliers to identify whether any restrictions in credit have arisen, and if so, ensure that the cash flow forecast reflects the current credit terms or where necessary an immediate payment for trade payables.

— Enquire of the lawyers of Co as to the existence of litigation and claims; if any exist, then consider their materiality and impact on the going concern basis.

— Perform audit tests in relation to subsequent events to identify any items which might indicate or mitigate the risk of going concern not being appropriate.

— Review the post year-end board minutes to identify any other issues which might indicate financial difficulties for the company.

— Review post year-end management accounts to assess if in line with cash flow forecast and to identify any issues which may be relevant to the going concern assessment.

— Consider whether any additional disclosures as required by IAS 1 Presentation of Financial Statements in relation to material uncertainties over going concern should be made in the financial statements.

— Obtain a written representation confirming the directors' view that Co is a going concern.

Part 8

Written representations

管理层声明,管理层的发誓书,必要不充分的证据,有它不够,没它不行

ISA 580 requires the auditor to request management to provide written representations as follows:

That it has fulfilled its responsibilities for the preparation of the financial statements

Specific issues require disclosure (such as fraud, laws & regulations, estimates, going concern, related parties and subsequent events).

The appropriate use of accounting policies as well as a number of specific disclosures (such as plans that might affect asset values and details of any contingent liabilities).

The auditor should obtain written representations from management on matters material to the financial statements when other sufficient appropriate audit evidence cannot reasonably be expected to exist.

The representations should relate to matters where they are critical to obtaining sufficient appropriate audit evidence. Representations cannot be a substitute for other audit evidence that auditors expect to be available.

If management refuse to sign written representations:

○ Auditor should write letter setting out his understanding and ask for management confirmation.

○ If management refuses to provide a representation that the auditor considers necessary, this constitutes a scope limitation and the auditor should express a qualified opinion or disclaimer of opinion.

○ Discuss the matter with management

○ Re-evaluate the integrity of management and evaluate the effect

○ Take appropriate actions, including determining the impact on the auditor's report

Part 9

Reporting

9.1 Format
- Title
- Addressee
- Opinion
- Basis for Opinion
- Material Uncertainty of Going Concern
- Emphasis of matter
- Key Audit Matters-required for listed Co
- Other Matter
- Responsibilities of Management and Those Charged with Governance
- Auditor's Responsibilities for the Audit of the Financial Statements
- Report on Other Legal and Regulatory Requirements
- Name of audit engagement partner
- Signature of audit engagement partner and/or audit firm
- Auditor's address
- Date of the auditor's report

9.2 Audit opinion

9.2.1 Unmodified opinion — 'The financial statements present fairly, in all material respects ...'
- Unmodified opinion:

Free from material misstatement as a whole

- Unmodified opinion with emphasis of matter paragraph:

Free from material misstatement as a whole, but have important matters to draw reader's attention

9.2.2 Modified opinion — If the financial statements as a whole are not free from material misstatement or the auditors are unable to obtain sufficient appropriate evidence
- Qualified opinion

Material misstatement, but not pervasive

No appropriate sufficient evidence, but not pervasive

○ Adverse opinion

Material misstatement, and pervasive

○ Disclaimer

No appropriate sufficient evidence

Nature of Matter Giving Rise to the Modification	Auditor's Judgment about the Pervasiveness of the Effects or Possible Effects on the Financial Statements	
	Material but Not Pervasive	Material and Pervasive
Financial statements are materially misstated	Qualified opinion	Adverse opinion
Inability to obtain sufficient appropriate audit evidence	Qualified opinion	Disclaimer of opinion

9.3 Responsibility for the financial statements

9.3.1 Management's responsibility for the financial statements 管理层的责任

Management is responsible for the preparation and fair presentation of these financial statements in accordance with International Financial Reporting Standards, and for such internal control as management determines is necessary to enable the preparation of financial statements that are free from material misstatement, whether due to fraud or error.

9.3.2 Auditor's responsibility

Our responsibility is to

a) express an opinion on these financial statements based on our audit. We conducted our audit in accordance with

b) International Standards on Auditing. Those standards require that we comply with

c) ethical requirements and

d) plan and perform the audit to obtain reasonable assurance about whether the financial statements are free from material misstatement.

e) An audit involves performing procedures to obtain audit evidence about the amounts and disclosures in the financial statements.

f) The procedures selected depend on the auditor's judgement, including the assessment of the risks of material misstatement of the financial statements, whether due to fraud or error.

g) In making those risk assessments, the auditor considers internal control relevant to the entity's preparation and fair presentation of the financial statements in order to design audit procedures that are appropriate in the circumstances, but not for the purpose of expressing an opinion on the effectiveness of the entity's internal control. 查看内控只是为了设计审计程序,但绝不是为了对企业内控有效性发表意见!

h) An audit also includes evaluating the appropriateness of accounting policies used and the reasonableness of accounting estimates made by management, as well as evaluating the overall presentation of the financial statements.

i) We believe that the audit evidence we have obtained is sufficient and appropriate to provide a basis for our audit opinion.

9.4 Emphasis of Matter:

A paragraph included in the auditor's report that refers to a matter appropriately presented or disclosed in the financial statements that, in the auditor's judgment, is of such importance that it is fundamental to users' understanding of the financial statements.

It should be positioned immediately after the Basis for Opinion paragraph and should be clearly identified as an "Emphasis of Matter".

○ If there is a Key Audit Matters section in the report, then it is up to the auditor's judgment whether to place the EoM before this (i.e. straight after the Basis for Opinion) or after it.

○ An EoM paragraph is not used when the issue has been covered as a key audit matter.

○ Matters need to be emphasized include:

a) Exceptional litigation & regulatory action

b) Early apply for new accounting standard

c) Major disaster

Form:

We draw attention to Note X of the financial statements, which describes the effects of a fire in the Company's production facilities. Our opinion is not modified in respect of this matter.

9.5 Other Matter paragraph

A paragraph included in the auditor's report that refers to a matter other than those presented or disclosed in the financial statements that, in the auditor's judgment, is relevant to users' understanding of the audit, the auditor's responsibilities or the auditor's report.

○ Other Matter paragraph states:

That the financial statements of the prior period were audited by the predecessor auditor.

The type of opinion expressed by the predecessor auditor and, if the opinion was modified, the reasons therefore.

The date of that report.

○ Some specific circumstances must use it:

Where prior period financial statements were audited by a predecessor auditor.

Where prior period financial statements were not audited.

When reporting on prior period financial statements in connection with the current period audit, if the auditor's opinion on such prior period financial statements differs from the opinion the auditor previously expressed.

○ The Other Matter paragraph can also be used whenever the auditor thinks it is necessary. Examples include:

The auditor is unable to withdraw from the engagement and yet is unable to obtain sufficient appropriate audit evidence.

An Other Matter paragraph must not refer to something that has been included as a key audit matter.

○ The Other Matter paragraph is included after the Basis for Opinion paragraph, after any Emphasis of Matter paragraph and after any Key Audit Matters section.

9.6 Material uncertainty related to going concern paragraph 专有名词，一个单词不可错

	Material Uncertainty Exist	Assumption is inappropriate
Adequate disclosure	Unmodified opinion with a material uncertainty related to going concern paragraph	Unmodified opinion and EoM paragraph to draw attention to alternative basis of preparation
Inadequate disclosure	Qualified or adverse opinion	Adverse opinion

Emphasis of matter paragraphs are not used in relation to going concern anymore. They used to be used where there was a 'material uncertainty' that was appropriately disclosed, but now the auditor uses a material uncertainty related to going concern paragraph instead.

9.7 Key Audit Matters (KAMs)

Those matters that, in the auditor's professional judgment, were of most significance in the audit of the financial statements of the current period.

○ Areas of higher risk of material misstatement

e.g. Sales recognition of long-term service contract or prepaid income

○ Significant management judgement

e.g. Finite useful life of intangible assets

○ Effect of significant events or transactions

e.g. Material related party transactions

□ KAMs are part of every listed company auditor's report, and can be included by other auditors if needed.

□ KAMs do not constitute a modification of the report or of the opinion.

□ KAMs are not a substitute for Emphasis of Matter and Other Matter paragraphs.

□ KAMs must always relate to matters already disclosed within the financial statements.

□ When a modified opinion is expressed, the matter that gives rise to the modified opinion must not be included as a KAM.

□ Where the auditor disclaims an opinion on the financial statements, a KAMs section must not be included in the auditor's report.

强调事项段

审计报告的强调事项段是指审计报告中含有的一个段落,该段落提及已在财务报表中恰当列报或披露的事项,根据注册会计师的职业判断,该事项对财务报表使用者理解财务报表至关重要。

需要增加强调事项段的情形举例:
(1) 异常诉讼或监管行动的未来结果存在不确定性。
(2) 提前应用(在允许的情况下)对财务报表有广泛影响的新会计准则。
(3) 存在已经或持续对被审计单位财务状况产生重大影响的特大灾难。

其他事项段

审计报告的其他事项段是指审计报告中含有的一个段落,该段落提及未在财务报表中列报或披露的事项,根据注册会计师的职业判断,该事项与财务报表使用者理解审计工作、注册会计师的责任或审计报告相关。

需要增加其他事项段的情形
(1) 与使用者理解审计工作相关的情形;
(2) 与使用者理解注册会计师的责任或审计报告相关的情形;
(3) 对两套以上财务报表出具审计报告的情形;
(4) 限制审计报告分发和使用的情形。

二者的差别主要是看其是否披露,以及是理解财务报表还是理解审计工作、注册会计师责任、审计报告。

关键事项段

关键审计事项,是指注册会计师根据职业判断认为对当期财务报表审计最为重要的事项,并且是已经得到满意解决的事项。

9.8 Impact on audit report

	Due to insufficient appropriate evidence	
↙		↘
Material but not pervasive		Material and pervasive
↓		↓
Qualified opinion 'except for'		Disclaimer of opinion 'we do not express an opinion'
	Due to material misstatement	
↙		↘
Material but not pervasive		Material and pervasive
↓		↓
Qualified opinion 'except for'		Adverse opinion do not present fairly'

1) Qualified opinion

The basis for qualified opinion paragraph should be included just after the opinion paragraph, the matter about modification in relation to XXXX (matters)

○ The opinion paragraph would be qualified 'except for' — due to material misstatement.

○ The opinion paragraph would be qualified 'except for' — due to insufficient appropriate audit evidence.

2) Adverse opinion & Disclaimer

The basis for Adverse opinion/Disclaimer paragraph should be included just after the opinion paragraph, the matter about modification in relation to XXXX (matters).

e.g. a) Auditor should modify the opinion in report when the F/S as a whole are not free from material misstatement based on evidence.

b) In this case, the auditor must exercise professional judgement and assess whether XXX is material but not pervasive or material and pervasive.

c) If the impact of XXX is material but not pervasive, he auditor will include a 'Qualified Opinion' paragraph at the start of the auditor's report which will state that the financial statements are presented fairly in all material respects 'except for' the absence of this disclosure. The qualified opinion paragraph will be followed immediately by a 'Basis for Qualified Opinion' paragraph which will give details of XXX.

d) If XXX will have a fundamental impact on the users' understanding of the financial statements. On this basis, an adverse audit opinion on the grounds of material misstatement is appropriate. The auditor will include an 'Adverse Opinion' paragraph at the start of the auditor's report which will state that the financial statements are not presented fairly in all material respects. The adverse opinion paragraph will be followed immediately by a 'Basis for Adverse Opinion' paragraph which will give details of XXX in this respect are fundamental and pervasive to the financial statements and therefore require an adverse opinion.

3) How to judge the impact ot misstatement is pervasive?

a) Those specific elements, accounts or items in the financial statements and represent or could represent a substantial portion of the financial statements

b) Those that relate to disclosures which are fundamental to users' understanding of the financial statements

c) Non-consolidation of a subsidiary (pervasive material misstatement leading to adverse opinion)

d) Inability to obtain sufficient appropriate audit evidence about multiple elements of the financial statements

e) When going concern basis to prepare financial is not appropriate

Part 10

Professional ethics

10.1 The fundamental principles

○ **Integrity** 正直 — Members should be **straightforward** and honest in all professional and business relationships (ie truth is fundamental).

○ **Objectivity** 客观 — Members should not allow **bias, conflicts of interest or undue influence of others** to override professional or business judgement (ie fairness is fundamental also).

○ **Professional competence and due care** 职业胜任能力及应有关注（勤勉尽责）— Members have a continuing duty to **maintain** professional **knowledge and skill** at a level required to ensure that a client or employer receives **competent** professional service based on current developments in practice, legislation and techniques. Members should **act diligently** and in accordance with applicable technical and professional standards when providing professional services.

○ **Confidentiality** 保密 — Members should respect the confidentiality of **information acquired** as a result of professional and business relationships and **should not disclose** any such information to third parties **without proper and specific authority or unless there is a legal or professional right or duty to disclose.** Confidential information acquired as a result of professional and business relationships should not be used for the **personal advantage** of members or third parties.

○ **Professional behaviour** 职业行为 — Members should comply with relevant laws and regulations and should avoid any action that **discredits the profession.**

10.2 Ethics Threat

Self-interest threat

○ This would arise in situations where the audit firm or a member of the engagement team has some financial or other interest in the audit client.

- ○ Providing a loan to a client.
- ○ Earning fees on a contingent basis, ie profit related.
- ○ Owning shares in a client.
- ○ Undue dependence on fees from a client.

Self-review threat
○ The self-review threat occurs when a **previous judgement** needs to be **reviewed** by members responsible for that judgement. The situation tends to arise when the auditor has provided other services to a client.

○ Key examples would be:

○ The auditor providing a **specialist valuation** (e.g. pension liabilities).

○ The audit firm providing internal audit services and subsequently relying on the work for the external audit.

○ Reporting on the operation of financial systems after being involved in their design or implementation.

Advocacy threat
○ The advocacy threat occurs when members **promote** a position or opinion to the point that subsequent objectivity may be compromised.

○ Specific examples would be:

○ Acting as an **advocate** on behalf of an assurance client in litigation or disputes with third parties.

○ Promoting shares in a listed entity when that entity is a financial statement audit client.

○ Financing

Familiarity threat
○ The familiarity threat occurs when, because of a close relationship, members become too sympathetic to the interest of others.

○ Circumstances which would create a familiarity threat would include:

○ Long association with a client.

○ Acceptance of gifts or preferential treatment unless the value is clearly insignificant. Over-familiarity with the management of the organisation such that judgement could be compromised.

Intimidation threat 威胁
○ The intimidation threat occurs when members are prevented from acting objectively by threats, actual or perceived.

○ Such a threat will occur in the following circumstances:

○ The threat of dismissal or replacement of the member, or a close or
immediate family member

○ A dominant personality attempting to influence the decision making process or controlling relations with auditors.

○ Being threatened with litigation.

○ Being pressured to reduce inappropriately the extent of work performed in order to reduce fees.

10.3 Safeguards
○ Both Client A and Client B should be notified that the audit firm would be acting

as auditors for each company and, if necessary, consent obtained.

○ The use of separate engagement teams, with different engagement partners and team members; once an employee has worked on one audit such as Goofy Co then they would be prevented from being on the audit of Mickey Co for a period of time. This separation of teams is known as building a 'Chinese wall'.

○ Procedures to prevent access to information, for example, strict physical separation of both teams, confidential and secure data filing.

○ Clear guidelines for members of each engagement team on issues of security and confidentiality. These guidelines could be included within the audit engagement letters.

○ Potentially the use of confidentiality agreements signed by employees and partners of the firm.

○ Regular monitoring of the application of the above safeguards by a senior individual in the audit firm not involved in either audit.

10.4 Application

Situation	Ethical threat	Managing risk
Long association	A familiarity threat arises where an engagement partner is associated with a client for a long period of time. XX has been involved in the audit of XX for X years and hence may not maintain her professional scepticism and objectivity	XX firm should monitor the relationship between engagement and client staff, and should consider rotating engagement partners when a long association has occurred. In addition, ACCA's Code of Ethics and Conduct recommends that engagement partners rotate off an audit after seven years for listed and public interest entities. Therefore consideration should be given to appointing an alternative audit partner
Close relationship	Personal relationships between the client and members of the audit team can create a familiarity or self-interest threat. ACCA's Code of Ethics and Conduct does not specifically prohibit friendships between the audit client and the team. However, due to the senior positions held by both parties then there is a risk that independence may be perceived to have been threatened	Consideration should be given to rotating the partner off this engagement and replacing with an alternative partner
Staff discount	This is a familiarity or self-interest threat. Only goods of an insignificant value are allowed to be accepted. A discount of XX% may not appear to be significant, but as these are luxury XX then this may still be a significant value	The audit firm should should review the discount for significance. If it is deemed to be of significant value then the offer of discount should be declined

(Continued)

Situation	Ethical threat	Managing risk
Gift/ Hospitality	The finance director has offered the team a free weekend away at a luxury hotel. This represents a self-interest threat as the acceptance of goods and services, unless insignificant in value, is not permitted	As it is unlikely that a weekend at a luxury hotel for the whole team has an insignificant value, then this offer should be politely declined
Financial interest-shares	A self-interest threat can arise when an audit firm has a financial interest in the company. In this case the partner's son will receive shares as part of his remuneration. As the son is an immediate family member of the partner then if he holds the shares it will be as if the partner holds these shares, and this is prohibited	In this case as holding shares is prohibited by ACCA's Code of Ethics and Conduct then either the son should refuse the shares or more likely the engagement partner will need to be removed from the audit
Financial interest-Loan	The XX (client) has offered a XX (audit team member) a loan at discounted interest rates. XX (client) does provide loans and hence the provision of a loan can be provided within the normal course of business. However, if the loan is on preferential rates, as this is, then it would represent a self-interest threat	This loan must not be accepted by the XX (audit team member) due to the preferential terms. However, if the terms of the loan are amended so that the interest rate charged is in line with XX (client)'s normal levels, then the provision of the loan is acceptable. And the audit firm should perform an external quality review
Fee proportion	The total fee income from XX (client) is XX% (>15%) of the total fees for the audit firm. If the fees for audit and recurring work exceed 15% then there is a self-interest threat. The fees for XX (client) include XX (tax and audit) that are assumed to be recurring, however the XX (secondment) fees would not recur each year	The firm should assess if the recurring fees will exceed 15%. If this is the case then it might need to consider whether the appearance of independence will still be met if the XX (tax and audit) work is retained. No further work should be accepted in the current year from the client, and it might be advisable to perform external quality control reviews. It may also become necessary to consider resigning from either the tax or the audit engagement
Contingent fee	Fees based on the outcome or results of work performed are known as contingent fees and are prohibited by ACCA's Code of Ethics and Conduct. Hence XX's request that XX% of the external audit fee is based on profit after tax would represent a contingent fee	XX (Firm) will not be able to accept contingent fees and should communicate to XX(client) that the external audit fee needs to be based on the time and level of work performed

(Continued)

Situation	Ethical threat	Managing risk
Contingent fee	Agreeing to accept taxation work on the percentage of the tax saved is essentially accepting a contingent fee. There will be pressure to gain the highest tax refund for the client and this could tempt the audit firm to suggest illegal tax avoidance schemes	The audit firm must confirm that assistance with taxation work is acceptable, although the fee must be based on time and experience for the job, not the contingent fee
Outstanding fee	Last year's audit fee is still outstanding. This amounts to 20% of the total fee and is likely to be a significant value. A self-interest threat can arise if the fees remain outstanding, as XX firm may feel pressure to agree to certain accounting adjustments in order to have the previous year and the current year fee paid. In addition outstanding fees could be perceived as a loan to a client, this is strictly prohibited	XX should chase the outstanding fees. If they remain outstanding, the firm should discuss with those charged with governance the reasons for the continued non-payment, and ideally agree a payment schedule which will result in the fees being settled before much more work is performed for the current year audit
Prepare account	Whilst X (firm) is able to prepare accounts for unlisted clients, this does increase the risk of self-review as the audit team could be auditing their own work	they must ensure that this work is undertaken by a team separate to the audit team
Employment relationship	The assistant finance director of X (client) has joined X (firm) as a partner and has been proposed as the review partner. This represents a self-review threat, as he was in a position to influence the financial statements whilst working at X(client); if he is the review partner there could be a risk of him reviewing his own work	This partner must not be involved in the audit of X (client) for a period of at least two years. An alternative review partner should be appointed
Financing activity	X (client) has asked the engagement partner of to attend meetings with potential investors. This represents an advocacy threat as the audit firm may be perceived as promoting investment in X (client) and this threatens objectivity	The engagement partner should politely decline this request from X (client), as it represents too great a threat to independence
Represent the client in court	Representing XX(client) in court could be seen as an advocacy threat-that is the audit firm is promoting the position of the client. Objectivity could be compromised because the audit firm is seen to take the position that the client is correct, affecting judgement on the tax issue	To remain independent, the audit firm should decline to represent the client in court

(Continued)

Situation	Ethical threat	Managing risk
Obtain assignments	X(client) has implied to X(firm) that they must complete the audit quickly and with minimal questions/issues if they wish to obtain the assurance assignments. This creates an intimidation threat on the team as they may feel pressure to cut corners and not raise issues, and this could compromise the objectivity of the audit team	The engagement partner should politely inform the finance director that the team will undertake the audit in accordance with all relevant ISA sand their own quality control procedures. This means that the audit will take as long as is necessary to obtain sufficient, appropriate evidence to form an opinion. If any residual concerns remain or the intimidation threat continues then X (firm) may need to considering resigning from the engagement

10.5 Confidentiality

a) Auditors acquiring information in the course of their professional work should not disclose any such information to third parties without first obtaining permission from their clients. 审计师在审计过程中获取的信息在未经获得客户同意的前提下，不应披露给第三方。

b) Confidentiality is an implied term of auditors' contracts with their clients. For this reason auditors should not disclose confidential information to other persons, against their client's wishes. The obligation of confidentiality continues even though a professional relationship has ended. 保密是个暗示条款，即使合同里没有写，也视作审计师应该履行保密业务。工作结束也不得泄露客户的信息。违反需承担法律责任。

c) There are, however, circumstances where auditors may disclose information to third parties without first obtaining permission. These can be categorised as obligatory and voluntary disclosures. 在某些情况下，审计师有披露的豁免权，分为法律强制义务披露（不披露犯法）和主动披露。

d) Obligatory disclosure 法律强制义务披露

○ Auditors are obliged to make disclosure where, for example, there is a statutory right or duty to disclose, such as if the auditor suspects the client is involved in money laundering, terrorism or drug trafficking in which case they must immediately notify the relevant authorities. 当审计怀疑客户涉及洗黑钱、恐怖组织、贩毒等罪，必须立刻通报相关机构。

○ In addition, auditors must make disclosure if compelled by the process of law, for example under a court order or summons, under which they are obliged to disclose information. 另外，当法律程序要求披露时，例如法庭传唤审计出庭作证。

e) Voluntary disclosure 主动披露

○ In certain circumstances auditors are free, as opposed to obliged, to disclose information without obtaining the client's permission first. These circumstances can be categorised into the four areas below：下述情况，可以不经客户批准，披露信息

○ Public interest 公众利益 — An auditor may disclose information which would otherwise be confidential if disclosure can be justified in the 'public interest'. This would be perhaps if those charged with governance are involved in fraudulent activities. 例如：牵涉舞弊交易、破产边缘骗供应商货款，向他人借款等。

○ Protect a member's interest 保护事务所利益 — Members/auditors may disclose information to defend themselves against a negligence action，disciplinary proceedings or if suing for unpaid fees. 譬如事务所起诉客户追讨费用，或者应客户疏忽的诉时，向法庭披露信息作为辩护材料。

○ Authorised by statute/laws 法律授权 — There are cases of express statutory provision where disclosure of information to a proper authority overrides the duty of confidentiality.

○ Non-governmental bodies 非政府组织 — Auditors may be approached by non-governmental bodies seeking information concerning suspected acts of misconduct not amounting to a crime or civil wrong. Disclosure should only be made to those bodies with statutory powers to compel disclosure. 譬如环保组织怀疑企业污染环境，接洽审计师想获取一些信息。事务所有严格的程序来界定审计师是否可以披露，比较复杂。

Part 11

Corporate governance

Corporate governance is the system by which companies are directed and controlled.

Good corporate governance is important because the owners of a company and the people who manage the company are not always the same.（经营权和所有权分离，代理问题）

According to the UK Corporate Governance Code the 'purpose of corporate governance is to facilitate effective, entrepreneurial and prudent management that can deliver the long-term success of the company'. 根据 UK 公司治理法，公司治理的目的就是为了有效管理，实现企业长期繁荣

Corporate governance considers the responsibilities of directors, how the board of directors should be run and structured, the need for good internal controls and the relationship with external auditors. 公司治理考虑了董事的责任，管理层的构架和运作方式，好内控的需求以及跟外部审计的关系。

BOD structure

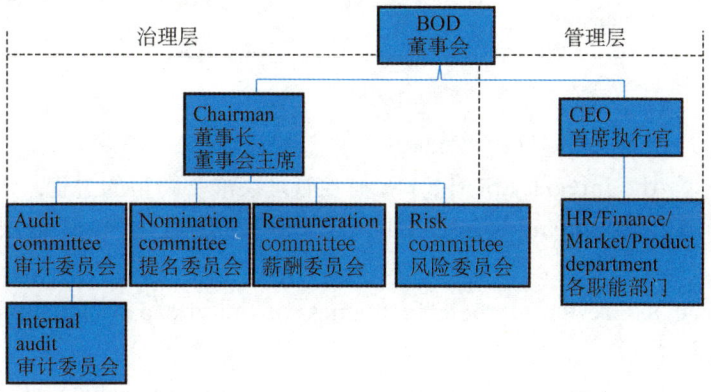

Responsibilities of CG

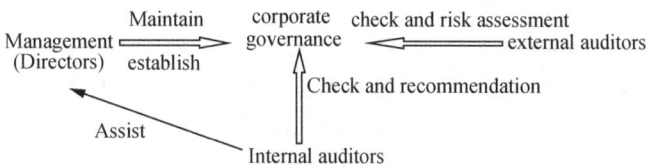

Deficiencies	Analysis	Recommendation
CEO 和 chairmen 是一个人	xxx has too much power over the key decisions of the company.	CEO and chairmen should be two different person. Another person should be appointed as the chairmen.（一般是再找一个 NED）
5个执行董事2个非执行董事	ED can dominate in the board, which may not be in the best interest of the shareholders.	There should be a balance of ED and NED. Three more NEDs should be appointed to balance the board.
Nomination of directors(special experience, skills, competence and independence)	xxx may be preferred to appoint directors will support his decisions. There is not clear and transparent process for determining appointments.	A nomination committee comprising NEDs should be established to suggest for the appropriate directors and ensure there is no basis.
performance is not reviewed	If the performance is not reviewed, there is no accountability for poor management. 没有人对差的管理负责	Performance targets should be set and reviewed. Directors should be required to explain any under performance.
xx 为自己和别人设定工资	Xxx may pay directors, who support his decisions, more, or, he may also pay himself more.	Remuneration committee comprising of NEDs should decide the salaries of board members, and the remuneration should be related their actual performance.
默认内控的复核全由外审做	External auditors only review internal controls that relating to the F/S. their purposes are to evaluate the control risk.	An internal audit function should be established to assess the effectiveness of the internal control and also provide recommendations.
没有内审部门和审计委员会	Corporate governance codes require an audit committee for listed company.	An audit committee should be established with NEDs. Audit committee's main function is about internal and external audit.

1.1 Audit committee

1.1.1 Characters of audit committee

a) **Monitoring** the integrity of the FS. 监控管理层准备财报的过程。

b) **Reviewing** the company's internal financial controls. 复核管理层内部财务控制（内控）。

c) **Monitoring and reviewing** the effectiveness of the internal audit function. 复核内审的运作效率(内审独立性)。

d) **Making recommendations** in relation to the appointment and removal of the external auditor and their remuneration. 由审计委员会提出外审的任命和解雇以及相应薪酬(外审独立性)。

e) **Reviewing and monitoring** the external auditor's independence and objectivity and the effectiveness of the audit process. 复核并监督外审的独立性、客观性以及审计程序的有效性。

f) **Developing and implementing policy** on the engagement of the external auditor to supply non-audit services. 把控外审可以提供的非审计服务。

g) **Reviewing** arrangements for confidential reporting by employees and investigation of possible improprieties (whistleblowing). 复核由职员提供的机密报告，调查不当行为。

1.1.2　Benefits of audit committee

a) It provides the internal audit department with an independent reporting mechanism compared to reporting to the directors who may wish to hide or amend unfavorable internal audit reports. 增加内审的独立性。

b) The audit committee will assist the internal auditor by ensuring that recommendations in internal audit reports are adopted and performed. 帮助内审。

c) Shareholder and public confidence in published financial information is enhanced because it has been reviewed by an independent committee. 独立部门监控财报编制，提升股东和公众的信心。

d) The committee helps the executive directors fulfill any obligations under corporate governance to implement and maintain an appropriate system of internal control within the company. 监督执行董事完善内控。

Bluebird does not currently have any non-executive directors, hence once appointed, they will bring considerable external experience to the board as well as challenging the decisions of executive directors and contributing to independent judgements.

e) The committee should assist in providing better communication between the directors, external auditors and management arranging meetings with the external auditor. 增进交流(审计委员会和外审交流)。

f) Strengthens the independence of company's external auditor by providing a clear reporting structure and separate appointment mechanism from the board. 增强外审的独立性。

g) The finance director will benefit in that he will be able to raise concerns and discuss accounting issues with the audit committee. 审计委员会让财务总监可以有人讨论，提高财务上的技术。

1.2　Internal Audit

全球约有137 000多名学生	External Audit	Internal Audit
Objective 目标	The main objective of the external auditor is to express an opinion on the truth and fairness of the financial statements. 对财报的正直公允发表意见	The main objective of internal audit is to improve a company's operations, by reviewing the efficiency and effectiveness of the company's internal controls. 通过评估公司的内控，改善公司运营的效率和有效性
Reporting 报告对象	External auditors report to the shareholders or members of the company. External audit reports are contained within the financial statements and hence are publicly available. 和财务报告一起，报告给股东，因此面对公众的	Internal auditors normally report to management or those charged with governance (such as the audit committee). Internal audit reports not publicly available and are only intended to be seen by the addressee of the report. 报告给董事会成员，理想的话报告给审计师委员会，如果没有AC，那么报告给财务总监等。非面对公众

(Continued)

全球约有 137 000 多名学生	External Audit	Internal Audit
Scope of work 工作范围	The external auditor's work is limited to verifying the truth and fairness of the financial statements of the company.确保财报的正直公允	The internal auditor can have a wide scope of work and it is determined by the requirements of management or those charged with governance. Commonly internal audit focus on the company's internal control environment, but any other area of a company's operations can be reviewed.范围很广,由管理层和治理层来定工作范围。一般来说,IC 关注于内控环境
Relationship with company 跟公司关系	External auditors are appointed by the company's shareholders. They are independent of the company.由公司股东任命,独立于公司管理层	Internal auditors are appointed by management. As internal auditors are normally employees of the company they lack independence. However, the internal audit department can be outsourced and this can increase their independence.由管理层任命,则相对来说缺乏独立性(理想是由治理层 audit committee 来定,这样独立性会提高)。如果外包内审的话,则独立性有所改善

1.2.1 The factors to consider before establishing an internal audit department

a) The costs of establishing an IA department will be significant, therefore prior to committing to these costs and management time, a cost benefit analysis should be performed. 建立 IA 部门的成本,做成本效益分析。

b) The size and complexity of Sunflower should be considered. The larger, more complex and diverse a company is, then the greater the need for an IA department. At Sunflower there are 25 supermarkets and a head office and therefore it would seem that the company is diverse enough to gain benefit from an IA department. 考虑下企业的规模、员工人数、复杂性.公司越大情况越复杂,IA 部门设立的必要性越高。

c) The role of any IA department should be considered. The finance director should consider what tasks he would envisage IA performing. He should consider whether he wishes them to undertake inventory counts at the stores, or whether he would want them to undertake such roles as internal controls reviews. 考虑 IA 部门设立的工作内容,扮演的角色。

d) If the possibility of fraud is high, then the greater the need for an IA department to act as both a deterrent and also to possibly undertake fraud investigations. As Sunflower operates 25 food supermarkets, it will have a significant risk of fraud of both inventory and cash. 考虑舞弊存在的可能性(这点比较重要)。IA 部门的存在是对舞弊的一种威慑,如果有舞弊存在,IA 将协助做进一步调查。

e) The finance director should assess the current control environment and determine whether there are departments or stores with a history of control deficiencies. If this is the case, then it increases the need for an IA department. 查看当前内控情况,如果当前系

统出现过控制缺陷,就更需要 IA 部门。

1.2.2 Functions for internal audit department

Testing cash controls	Currently the internal audit department undertakes inventory counts at each of the stores. This role could be increased to include controls testing over cash receipts and cash counts. These controls should be tested at each location as well as performance of a cash count to reduce the level of fraud and error reported.不仅清点库存,还测试现金控制,降低舞弊或出错风险
Overall review of financial/ operational controls	The department could undertake reviews of controls at head office, as well as individual stores and make recommendations to management over such areas as the purchasing process as well as the sales cycle.查看总部和分店的管理,给管理层针对这些领域的意见
Fraud investigations	It is likely that as a retailer, Greystone would have problems with theft of inventory as well as cash. Internal audit could be asked to review the main areas of fraud risk and develop controls to mitigate these risks. If fraud is suspected then internal audit could be asked to investigate these cases further.查看容易招致舞弊的点,建立控制。如果有怀疑,进行必要的深入调查
IT system reviews	Greystone is likely to have a relatively complex computer system linking all of the tills in the stores to head office. The internal audit department could be asked to perform a review over the computer environment and controls.查看 IT 系统的环境和控制
Value for money review	The internal audit department could be asked to assess whether Greystone are obtaining value for money in areas such as the just in time ordering system recently introduced.查看公司是否有金钱价值,譬如是否零库存管理
Regulatory compliance 合规检查	Greystone operates in countries throughout the world and hence will be subject to varying degrees of law and regulation. The internal audit department could help ensure compliance with those regulations.查看公司是否合规经营。跨国公司可能面临不同国家有不同政策,有相对宽泛的法规要求

1.2.3 Value for money

A value for money audit focuses on whether the best combination of services has been obtained for the lowest level of resources.是否最小的资源投入导致了最好的产出结果?

In performing a value for money audit there are three areas which an auditor will commonly focus on being economy, efficiency and effectiveness, and these are known as the "3 Es".

○ Economy — Keeping the cost of resources used to a minimum. 投入最少 ✓

○ Effectiveness — How well the organisation's objectives have been achieved. 产出结果好

○ Efficiency — The relationship between the output from goods and services and the resources used to produce them. 投入/产出关系

1.2.4 Limitations of establishing and maintaining an internal audit department

a) The internal auditors of Bush-Baby will be employees of the company and so this can impair their independence, as they may not report issues to those charged with governance for fear of losing their job. 独立性（必须写）：内审部门作为公司的员工，独立性会有问题。他们可能不会汇报问题给治理层，怕惹怒高管。

b) Although some internal auditors are professionally qualified, there is no requirement to be qualified, as there is for external auditors. Hence, there may be gaps in the experience and technical knowledge of the internal audit department. 有效性（必须写）：尽管某些内审是有专业资质的，但这不是强行要求，只有外部审计师是强行规定需要资质的。

c) The cost of establishing an internal audit department can be significant; hence prior to recruiting a team, the management of Bush-Baby should consider carefully the roles the team can perform and whether this will generate sufficient value for money. 成本效益分析

d) As Bush-Baby has not previously had any form of internal audit, there may be some resistance from employees of the company. They may be uncomfortable with the idea of their work being reviewed, especially if the first role of the department is to undertake fraud investigations. 内审部门是来查问题的，新成立 IA 部门，员工会有抵触情绪，尤其是 IA 上马就查舞弊，会弄得人心惶惶。

1.2.5 Outsourcing the internal audit department

Advantage

☐ No need to spend money in recruiting further staff

☐ As the current internal audit department is small, then outsourcing can provide the number of staff needed straight away.

☐ The audit firm is likely to have staff with specialist skills already available.

☐ Outsourcing can be an efficient means to control the costs of internal audit as any associated costs such as training will be eliminated. In addition, the costs for the internal audit service will be agreed in advance. This will ensure budget can be made accordingly.

☐ If the internal audit department is outsourced, Saxophone will have total flexibility in its internal audit service. Staff can be requested from Cello to suit the company's workloads and requirements. This will ensure that, when required, extra staff is readily available for as long or short a period as needed.

☐ The audit firm will benefit from the internal audit service being outsourced as this will generate additional fee income.

Disadvantage

☐ If there is an existing internal audit department, then they may need to be made redundant and this could be costly. Staff may oppose the outsourcing if it results in redundancies

☐ Each visit the staff members are different and hence they may not fully understand the company. This will decrease the quality of the services provided and increase the time spent in explaining the system to the auditors.

□ If the current internal audit team is not deployed elsewhere in the company, valuable internal audit knowledge and experience may be lost. If company then decided at a future date to bring the service back in-house, this might prove to be too difficult.

□ As well as the cost of potential redundancies, the internal audit fee charged may over a period of time increase, proving to be very expensive.

□ Knowledge of company systems and confidential data will be available. Although the engagement letter would provide confidentiality clauses, this may not stop breaches of confidentiality.

□ Once outsourced it will need to discuss areas of work and timings well in advance with auditor firm.

□ If auditor firm provides both external audit and internal audit services, there may be a self-review threat especially where the internal audit work is relied upon by the external auditor team. The firm would need to take steps to ensure that separate teams are put in place as well as additional safeguards.

1.3 ISA 260 Communication with Those Charged with Governance

1.3.1 Importance of reporting to those charged with governance(TCWG)

In accordance with ISA 260 Communication with Those Charged with Governance, it is important for the auditors to report to those charged with governance as it helps in the following ways:

a) It assists the auditor and those charged with governance in understanding matters related to the audit, and in developing a constructive working relationship. This relationship is developed while maintaining the auditor's independence and objectivity.

b) It helps the auditor in obtaining, from those charged with governance, information relevant to the audit. For example, those charged with governance may assist the auditor in understanding the entity and its environment, in identifying appropriate sources of audit evidence and in providing information about specific transactions or events.

c) It helps those charged with governance in fulfilling their responsibility to oversee the financial reporting process, thereby reducing the risks of material misstatement of the financial statements.

1.3.2 Matters to be communicated to those charged with governance

○ The auditor's responsibilities with regards to providing an opinion on the financial statements and that they have carried out their work in accordance with International Standards on Auditing.

○ The auditor should explain the planned approach to the audit as well as the audit timetable.

○ Any key audit risks identified during the planning stage should be communicated.

○ In addition, any significant difficulties encountered during the audit should be communicated.

- Also significant matters arising during the audit, as well as significant accounting adjustments.
- During the audit any significant deficiencies in the internal control system identified should be communicated in writing or verbally.
- Those charged with governance should be notified of any written representations required by the auditor.
- Other matters arising from the audit that are significant to the oversight of the financial reporting process.
- If any suspected frauds are identified during the audit, these must be communicated.
- If the auditors are intending to make any modifications to the audit opinion, these should be communicated to those charged with governance.
- For listed entities, a confirmation that the auditors have complied with ethical standards and appropriate safeguards have been put in place for any ethical threats identified.

Part 12

Other matters

12.1 Differences between an interim and a final audit Interim audit

The interim audit is that part of the audit which takes place before the year end. The auditor uses the interim audit to carry out procedures which would be difficult to perform at the year end because of time pressure. There is no requirement to undertake an interim audit; factors to consider when deciding upon whether to have one include the size and complexity of the company along with the effectiveness of internal controls.

Typical procedures undertaken during the interim audit include documenting and testing of internal controls, testing of profit and loss transactions for the year to date and identification of potential problems which may affect the final audit work.

Final audit The final audit will take place after the year end and concludes with the auditor forming and expressing an opinion on the financial statements for the whole year subject to audit. It is important to note that the final opinion takes account of conclusions formed at both the interim and final audit.

Typical work carried out at the final audit includes follow up of items noted at the inventory count, obtaining confirmations from third parties, analytical reviews of figures in the financial statements, substantive procedures of account balances and transactions, review of events after the reporting period and going concern review.

12.2 Test of control and substantive procedures

a) Tests of control evaluate the operating effectiveness of controls in preventing, or detecting and correcting, material misstatements at the assertion level.

Example tests of control over wages and salaries

— Inspect numerical sequence of clock cards/timesheets; if any breaks in the sequence are noted, enquire of management as to missing payroll records.

— Review a sample of timesheets/clock cards for evidence of authorisation of overtime by a responsible official.

— Observe whether there is adequate segregation of duties between human resources and payroll departments.

b) Substantive procedures are aimed at detecting material misstatements at the assertion level. They include tests of details of transactions, balances, disclosures and substantive analytical procedures.

Example substantive procedures over wages and salaries

— Perform a proof in total of total payroll taking into account joiners and leavers and any annual pay rise, compare any trends to prior years and discuss significant fluctuations with management.

— For a sample of employees, recalculate the gross and net pay and agree to the payroll records to verify accuracy.

— Re-perform calculation of statutory deductions to confirm whether correct deductions for this year have been included within the payroll expense

12.3　ISA 240 The Auditor's Responsibilities Relating to Fraud in an Audit of Financial Statements

Maple & Co must conduct an audit in accordance with ISA 240 The Auditor's Responsibilities Relating to Fraud in an Audit of Financial Statements and are responsible for obtaining reasonable assurance that the financial statements taken as a whole are free from material misstatement, whether caused by fraud or error.

In order to fulfil this responsibility, Maple & Co is required to identify and assess the risks of material misstatement of the financial statements due to fraud.

They need to obtain sufficient appropriate audit evidence regarding the assessed risks of material misstatement due to fraud, through designing and implementing appropriate responses. In addition, Maple & Co must respond appropriately to fraud or suspected fraud identified during the audit.

When obtaining reasonable assurance, Maple & Co is responsible for maintaining professional scepticism throughout the audit, considering the potential for management override of controls and recognising the fact that audit procedures which are effective in detecting error may not be effective in detecting fraud.

To ensure that the whole engagement team is aware of the risks and responsibilities for fraud and error, ISAs require that a discussion is held within the team. For members not present at the meeting, Sycamore's audit engagement partner should determine which matters are to be communicated to them.

12.4　Reliability of audit evidence

— The reliability of audit evidence is increased when it is obtained from independent sources outside the entity.

— The reliability of audit evidence which is generated internally is increased when the related controls imposed by the entity, including those over its preparation and maintenance, are effective.

— Audit evidence obtained directly by the auditor is more reliable than audit evidence obtained indirectly or by inference.

— Audit evidence in documentary form, whether paper, electronic or other medium, is more reliable than evidence obtained orally.

— Audit evidence provided by original documents is more reliable than audit evidence provided by photocopies or facsimiles, the reliability of which may depend on the controls over their preparation and maintenance.

12.5 Levels of assurance

The level of assurance provided by audit and review engagements is as follows:

External audit — A high but not absolute level of assurance is provided, this is known as reasonable assurance. This provides comfort that the financial statements present fairly in all material respects (or are true and fair) and are free of material misstatements.

Review engagements — where an opinion is being provided, the practitioner gathers sufficient evidence to be satisfied hat the subject matter is plausible; in this case negative assurance is given whereby the practitioner confirms that nothing has come to their attention which indicates that the subject matter contains material misstatements.

12.6 Matters to be included in an audit engagement letter

☐ The objective and scope of the audit;

☐ The responsibilities of the auditor;

☐ The responsibilities of management;

☐ Identification of the financial reporting framework for the preparation of the financial statements;

☐ Expected form and content of any reports to be issued;

☐ Elaboration of the scope of the audit with reference to legislation;

☐ The form of any other communication of results of the audit engagement;

☐ The fact that some material misstatements may not be detected;

☐ Arrangements regarding the planning and performance of the audit, including the composition of the audit team;

☐ The expectation that management will provide written representations;

☐ The basis on which fees are computed and any billing arrangements;

☐ A request for management to acknowledge receipt of the audit engagement letter and to agree to the terms of the engagement;

☐ Arrangements concerning the involvement of internal auditors and other staff of the entity;

☐ Any obligations to provide audit working papers to other parties;

☐ Any restriction on the auditor's liability;

☐ Arrangements to make available draft financial statements and any other information;

☐ Arrangements to inform the auditor of facts which might affect the financial statements, of which management may become aware during the period from the date of the auditor's report to the date the financial statements are issued.

12.7 Steps prior to accepting the audit

ISA 210 Agreeing the Terms of Audit Engagements provides guidance to Salt &

Pepper & Co (Salt & Pepper) on the steps they should take in accepting the new audit client, Cinnamon. It sets out a number of processes that the auditor should perform prior to accepting a new engagement, in addition to considering whether preconditions for the audit are in place.

Salt & Pepper should consider any issues which might arise which could threaten compliance with ACCA's Code of Ethics and Conduct or any local legislation, including conflict of interest with existing clients. If issues arise, then their significance must be considered.

In addition, they should consider whether they are competent to perform the work and whether they would have appropriate resources available, as well as any specialist skills or knowledge required for the audit of Cinnamon.

Salt & Pepper should consider what they already know about the directors of Cinnamon; they need to consider the reputation and integrity of the directors. If necessary, the firm may want to obtain references if they do not formally know the directors.

Additionally, Salt & Pepper should consider the level of risk attached to the audit of Cinnamon and whether this is acceptable to the firm. As part of this, they should consider whether the expected audit fee is adequate in relation to the risk of auditing Cinnamon.

Salt & Pepper should communicate with the outgoing auditor of Cinnamon to assess if there are any ethical or professional reasons why they should not accept appointment. They should obtain permission from Cinnamon's management to contact the existing auditor; if this is not given, then the engagement should be refused.

If given permission to respond, the auditors should reply to Salt & Pepper, who should carefully review the response for any issues that could affect acceptance.

12.8 Preconditions for the audit

ISA 210 Agreeing the Terms of Audit Engagements requires auditors to only accept a new audit engagement when it has been confirmed that the preconditions for an audit are present.

To assess whether the preconditions for an audit are present, Salt & Pepper must determine whether the financial reporting framework to be applied in the preparation of Cinnamon's financial statements is acceptable. In considering this, the auditor should assess the nature of the entity, the nature and purpose of the financial statements and whether law or regulations prescribes the applicable reporting framework.

In addition, they must obtain the agreement of Cinnamon's management that it acknowledges and understands its responsibility for the following:

— Preparation of the financial statements in accordance with the applicable financial reporting framework, including where relevant their fair presentation;

— For such internal control as management determines is necessary to enable the preparation of financial statements which are free from material misstatement, whether due to fraud or error; and

— To provide Salt & Pepper with access to all relevant information for the preparation of the financial statements, any additional information that the auditor may request from management and unrestricted access to persons within Cinnamon from whom the auditor determines it necessary to obtain audit evidence.

If the preconditions for an audit are not present, Salt & Pepper shall discuss the matter with Cinnamon's management. Unless required by law or regulation to do so, the auditor shall not accept the proposed audit engagement:

— If the auditor has determined that the financial reporting framework to be applied in the preparation of the financial statements is unacceptable;

— If management agreement of their responsibilities has not been obtained.

FINANCIAL MANAGEMENT

Part A

Financial management function

Chapter 1

Financial management and financial objectives

1. The nature and purpose of financial management

1.1 Explain the <u>nature</u> and <u>purpose</u> of financial management.

○ Concept of financial management: management of the finances of an organisation in order to achieve the financial objectives of the organisation(财务管理的概念：管理一个组织的财务，以实现该组织的财务目标)

○ Objective of financial management for private sector: maximise shareholders' wealth

Three decisions(财务管理体现在三个方面)

a) investment: non-current asset, working capital, financial assets 投资

b) Finance: internal vs external, debt vs equity, long term debt vs short term debt 融资

c) Dividend: profitability, cash flow, growth, legal restriction, shareholder expectation 股利分配

1.2 Explain the relationship between financial management and financial and management accounting.

	Management Accounting	Financial Accounting
Use	Internal	External & internal
Mandatory	No legal requirement	By law
Format	No strict rules	By law & accounting standards
Scope	On specific areas	On the business as a whole
Account	Non-monetary	Monetary
	Historic record and future plan	Historic record

Chapter 1 Financial management and financial objectives

2. Financial objectives and the relationship with corporate strategy

2.1 Discuss the relationship between financial objectives, corporate objectives and corporate strategy.

Corporate strategy: is concerned with the overall purpose and scope of the organisation and how value will be added to the different parts (business units) of the organisation.

Corporate objectives: are relevant for the organisation as a whole, relating to key factors for business success. (for example: Profitability, Market share, Growth, Cash flow, Customer satisfaction, Industrial relations)(公司目标有多种,但公司的主要财务目标是股东利益最大化)

For the private sector, the primary **financial objective** of the company is to maximise shareholders' wealth.

Non-financial objectives(非财务目标)
a) The welfare of employees 员工福利
b) The welfare of management 管理者的福利
c) The provision of a service 提供的服务
d) The fulfillment of responsibilities towards customers 履行对客户的责任
e) The fulfillment of responsibilities towards suppliers 履行对供应商的责任
f) The welfare of society as a whole 整个社会的财富

2.2 Identify and describe a variety of financial objectives, including:
a) shareholder wealth maximisation
b) profit maximisation
c) earnings per share growth

Maximisation of wealth VS Maximisation of profit (重点,区别体现在哪些方面)

a) Future profit vs current profit (未来利益和现在的利益): shareholder may not want managers to maximise current profits at the expense of future profits

b) Quality of earning (盈利的质量): business may increase its profit by taking a high level of risk. the profit is of poor quality to shareholders. Risk averse shareholders may sell the shares (从而导致股票价格下降)

c) Paper figure vs cash flow (利润只是纸质数字,股东财富最大化是现金流)

d) Measurement (计算的方式不同)
e.g. EPS = PAT/No of shares vs total shareholder return/TSR = $[(P_1 - P_0) + D_1]/P_0$

3. Stakeholders and impact on corporate objectives

Companies should also balance objectives of other stakeholders

Conflict of interest: Takeover, Time horizon, Risk, Reward

The danger that managers may not act in the best interest of shareholder is referred to as the agency problem

Resolved by incentive schemes and corporate governance (CG: restrict behavior of directors from regulatory level) (用激励和公司治理的方法解决利益冲突)

3.1 Performance-related pay: (和业绩相关的奖励) links part of the remuneration of directors to some aspect of corporate performance, such as levels of profit or earnings per share. One problem here is that it is difficult to choose an aspect of corporate performance which is not influenced by the actions of the directors, leading to the possibility of managers influencing corporate affairs for their own benefit rather than the benefit of shareholders, for example, focusing on short-term performance while neglecting the longer term.

3.2 Executive share options plans (ESOPs) (高管股票分享计划)

○ Share options allow directors to purchase shares at a specified price on a specified future date, encouraging them to make decisions which exert an upward pressure on share prices.

○ Unfortunately, a general increase in share prices can lead to directors being rewarded for poor performance, while a general decrease in share prices can lead to managers not being rewarded for good performance.

○ However, share option schemes can lead to a culture of performance improvement and so can bring continuing benefit to stakeholders.

3.3 Corporate governance

Codes of best practice-it seeks to reduce corporate risk and increase corporate accountability

3.4 ratio(掌握好每个 ratio 的计算方法)

3.4.1 Profitability and return

ROCE = PBIT/capital employed

= Profit margin * asset turnover

= PBIT/revenue * revenue/capital employed

ROE = earning/equity

total shareholder return TSR = $[(P_1 - P_0) + D_1]/P_0$

3.4.2 Debt and gearing(Solvency)

Gearing = Debt/equity

Interest cover = PBIT/interest

3.4.3 Liquidity

Current ratio = current asset/current liability

Acid test ratio = current asset-inventory/current liability

Chapter 1 Financial management and financial objectives

3.4.4 Shareholders' investment
Dividend yield = PAT/dividend paid
EPS = PAT/No of shares
Price earning ratio = MV of share/EPS

4. Financial and other objectives in not-for-profit organisations

4.1 not-for-profit organisations(NFP)
The primary objective of many NFP organisations will be the effective provision of a service, not the creation of profit. This has implications for reporting of results.

The organisation will need to be open and honest in showing how it has managed its budget and allocated funds raised.

4.2 Value for money（非盈利组织主要用 3 个 E 来考察业绩）:
can be defined as getting the best possible combination of services from the least resources, which means maximising the benefits for the lowest possible cost.

a) Economy — purchase of inputs of appropriate quality at minimum cost

b) Efficiency — use of these inputs to maximise output

c) Effectiveness — use of these inputs to achieves it goals (quality, speed of response)

4.3 Performance measurement(业绩评价的方法):

a) cost and benefit analysis

b) judgment: by experts

c) comparisons(with historical/benchmarking/budgeting)

考试时文字题套路：

Financial Objective

无论上市公司还是 NFP(not for profit)，都需要 keep spending within budget. 都可以运用 accounting ratios 来分析财务目标。

a) 上市公司
- 股东利益最大化
- 具体如：股价增长，EPS 增长，股息增长
- Operating profit & revenue 增长
- 现金流 NPV 健康，否则会有 going concern 问题。可以算 quick ration，gearing，interest cover 判断
- Net cash income 净收入，赚钱的，是重要财务指标

b) NFP 非营利组织
- 最大化 Net cash income，有足够收入支持公益服务
- 尽可能多的筹集资金，实现慈善目的
- Value for money，实现 3Es

题目：2011-12-Q4，2013-06-Q1(通过真题的大题来看答案，总结自己答题的思路)

Part B

Financial management environment

Chapter 2

The economic environment for business

1. The economic environment for business

1.1 Identify and explain the main macroeconomic policy targets.

Main economic objective：

a) Economic growth 经济的增长
b) Control price inflation 控制通货膨胀
c) Full employment 实现充分就业
d) Balance of payment 国际收支平衡

1.2 Define and discuss the role of fiscal, monetary, interest rate and exchange rate policies in achieving macroeconomic policy targets

Macroeconomic policy 宏观经济政策

a) Fiscal policy 财政政策
  - Taxation 税收
  - Government borrowing 政府借款
  - Government spending 政府支出

财政政策一般是由政府部分实施的政策

b) Monetary policy 货币政策
  - Interest rate 利率
  - Exchange rate 外汇率
  - Credit availability 借贷能力
  - Money supply 货币的供应量

货币政策一般是由中央银行实施的政策

c) External trade policy：Promoting economic growth by stimulating exports and Import controls 外部贸易政策（主要是控制进出口平衡 多出口少进口）

d) Exchange rate policy：

Many factors will influence the exchange rate：

○ Import and export
○ Level of interest rate
○ Inflation
○ Government influence
○ Speculation

1.3 Explain how government economic policy interacts with planning and decision-making in business

Expansionary policy 经济扩张政策
{ Increase spending 增加政府支出
Reduce borrowing interest 降低借款利
Reduce tax 减税 }

Contractionary policy 经济紧缩政策
{ Decrease spending 减低政府支出
Increase borrowing interest 增加借款利率
Increase tax 增税 }

★ **Achieving low inflation：（背诵记忆）**

Policy	Impact on a business's planning & decision marking
Fiscal policy ○ Cutting spending ○ Raising tax	Lower consumer spending, export markets attractive Higher prices(if VAT) so lower sales Lower profits from investment Dividend policy affected if taxes on dividends increased
Monetary policy High interest rate	Less likely to use debt finance, consumer demand falls
Exchange rate policy High exchange rate	Export markets become less attractive

★ **Achieving balance of payments stability(背诵记忆)**

Policy	Impact on a business's planning & decision marking
Fiscal policy ○ Cutting spending ○ Raising tax	Designed to cut spending on imports but will have a knock on effect on domestic sales
Monetary policy High interest rate	Designed to attract capital into the domestic economy from abroad, but reduces investment by local firms
Exchange rate policy High exchange rate	Design to make exports more competitive

1.4 Explain the need for, and the interaction with, planning and decision-making in business of: competition policy, government assistance for business, green policies, corporate governance regulation

1) Competition policy

e.g. the Competition Commission prevents takeovers that are against the public interest. 竞争委员会阻止违背公众利益的收购。

Competition commission will investigate an acquisition if it will result in the combined entity acquiring 25% or more of market share（竞争委员会会调查收购如果他们的收获导致了整个集团获得了25%以上的市场份额）

2) Government assistance for business

grants may be available to attract firms to invest in depressed areas. 政府可能会拨款

来吸引公司到经济萧条地区投资。

3) Green policies：

may either threaten a business（e.g. tax on petrol 汽油）or create opportunities（e.g. subsidies for loft insulation）

Advantage：① customers，② society，③ employee，④ investors(对顾客,社会,员工和投资者,考试时结合题意进行论述）

4) Corporate governance regulation

Chapter 3

Financial markets and institutions

1. **The nature and role of financial markets and institutions**

Identify the nature and role of money and capital markets, both nationally and internationally.

1) **Describe the role of the money markets（货币市场的角色）**

a）providing short-term liquidity to the private sector and the public sector 向私营部门和公营部门提供短期流动资金

b）providing short-term trade finance 提供短期的融资

c）allowing an organisation to manage its exposure to foreign currency risk and interest rate risk. 管理货币和利率风险

2) **Explain the characteristics and role of the principal money market instruments**

a）interest-bearing instruments

b）discount instruments

c）derivative product

2. **Explain the role of financial intermediaries**

Role of financial intermediary：
- Risk diversification 风险分散
- Aggregation 汇总资金
- Maturity transformation
- Hedging
- Making a market
- advice

3. **The nature and role of money markets**

3.1 Financial markets are the markets where individuals and organisations with surplus funds lend funds to other individuals and organisations that want to borrow

It can be classified as following：
- Capital market and money market（资本市场和货币市场）
- Exchange traded and over the counter market（场内和场外市场）

Chapter 3 Financial markets and institutions

Exchange traded: Buyers and sellers of securities buy and sell securities in one location, the exchange. Such as: London Stock Exchange and the New York Stock Exchange(和股票交易所交易)

over the counter market: Customers usually negotiate individual transactions with a financial intermediary such as a bank.(和银行交易)

○ Primary market and secondary market（主要市场和二级市场）

Primary market: Primary markets enable organisations to raise new finance.（主要是企业）

secondary market: Secondary markets enable investors to buy and sell existing investments to each other.（主要是投资者）

3.2 capital market: market concerned with medium (1-5 years) and long term (5-10 years) financial instruments

○ equity capital: ordinary shares, preference shares

○ loan capital: debenture from Eurobond market

3.3 Money markets are markets for short-term capital (short-term financial instruments, short-term lending and borrowing)

○ primary market

○ the inter-bank mark

○ the Eurocurrency market

○ the certificate of deposit market

○ the local authority market

○ the inter-company market

Money market instruments are traded over the counter between institutional investors. They include interest-bearing instruments, discount instruments and derivatives.

Money market instruments in the UK（以下每个了解清楚每种金融工具的内容考试时候知道如何区分了解清楚概念）

1) **Interest bearing instruments**: pay interest. The investor receives face value plus interest at maturity.

○ certificate of deposit (CD) 大额存单

○ repurchase agreement 回购协议

2) **Discount instrument**

○ Treasury bill 国债

○ Bank's acceptance(BA) 银行汇票

○ commercial paper 商业票据

3) **Derivatives 衍生品**

○ forwards and futures 期货

○ swaps 互换

○ options 期权

3.4 Securitisation and Disintermediation

Securitisation is the process of converting illiquid assets into marketable securities. These securities are backed by specific assets and are normally called asset-backed securities（ABS）（资产证券化：证券化是将流动性差的资产转换为有价证券的过程。这些证券由特定资产支持，通常被称为资产支持证券）

Disintermediation describes a decline in the traditional deposit and lending relationship between banks and their customers and an increase in direct relationships between the ultimate suppliers and users of financing.（去中介的过程：指的是银行与客户之间传统的存贷款关系减少，而融资的最终供应商和用户之间的直接关系增加。）

4. Eurobonds

In recent years a strong market has built up which allows large companies with excellent credit ratings to raise finance in a foreign currency.（近年来，一个强大的市场已经建立起来，它允许拥有优秀信用评级的大公司以外币融资。）

Advantage：
- Cheaper debt finance
- Unsecured no covenants
- Long-term debt in a foreign currency

5. Rates of interest and rates of return

Interest rates are effectively the 'prices' governing lending and borrowing. Interest rates on financial assets are influenced by：（利率实际上是控制借贷的"价格"。金融资产利率受以下因素影响：）

1）Risk

There is a trade-off between risk and return. Investors in riskier assets expect to be compensated for the risk. This means that investments carrying a higher degree of risk will demand a higher rate of return.（在风险和回报之间存在一种平衡。高风险资产的投资者希望从风险中得到补偿。这意味着高风险的投资会要求更高的回报率。）

2）Need to make a profit on re-lending

Financial intermediaries make their profits from re-lending at a higher rate of interest than the cost of their borrowing.（金融中介机构通过以高于借贷成本的利率转贷来获取利润。）

3）Duration of the lending

In general，longer-dated assets will earn a higher yield than similar short-dated assets but this is not always the case.（一般而言，较长期资产的收益率将高于类似的短期资产，但情况并非总是如此。）

4）Size of the loan or deposit

Administrative cost savings help to allow lower rates of interest to be charged by banks on larger loans and higher rates of interest to be paid on larger time deposits.（节省

管理成本有助于银行对大额贷款收取较低的利率,对大额定期存款支付较高的利率。)

5) Different types of financial asset

This is partly because different types of asset attract different sorts of lender/investor. For example, bank deposits attract individuals and companies, whereas long-dated government securities are particularly attractive to various institutional investors. (这在一定程度上是因为不同类型的资产吸引不同类型的贷款人/投资者。例如,银行存款吸引个人和公司,而长期的政府证券对各种机构投资者特别有吸引力。)

Part C

Working capital management

Chapter 4

Working capital

1. Describe the nature of working capital and identify its elements

Net working capital = current asset − current liabilities

1.1 factors influence the formulation of working capital policy

Working capital policies cover the level of investment in current asset, the way in which CA are financed and management of element of WC such as inventory trade receivable, cash and trade payable factors to influence working capital level:

a) the nature of the business

b) uncertainty in supplier deliveries

c) the overall level of activity of the business

d) the company's credit policy

e) the length of the operating cycle

f) the credit policy of suppliers

小册子上均为答题要点，考试时文字题结合题意拓展并且编辑成句子。

2. Identify the objectives of working capital management in terms of liquidity and profitability, and discuss the conflict between them

2.1 the objectives of working capital management

a) To ensure that it has sufficient liquid resources to continue in business
（确保公司有足够的流动资源来支撑它的发展）

b) To increase its profitability

2.2 Balance of profitability and liquidity

a) Profitability objective reflect the objective of maximising shareholder's wealth

b) Liquidity objective is to ensure the liability can be settled as they are due

c) However, these two objectives are in conflict, since liquid resources have no return or low levels of return and hence decrease profitability.

d) Liquidity may be more important objective when short-term finance is hard while profitability may become a more important objective when cash management become too conservative In short both objectives are important and neither can be neglected

2.3 Funding policy

Matching: Non-current asset and permanent current assets are financed by long-term finance

Fluctuating current asset are financed by short-term finance
- Aggressive approach: more short-term finance, more risky but cheaper
- Conservative approach: more long-term finance, expensive but lower risk

（还取决于管理者对于风险的态度）

3. The cash operating cycle

3.1 公式背

Operating cycle = inventory days + receivable days − payable days

Inventory days = finished goods/cost of sales * 365

Inventory days = WIP/cost of production * 365

Inventory days = raw material/cost of raw material purchase * 365

Receivable days = receivable/credit sales * 365

Payable days = payable/credit payable * 365

3.2 理解记忆要点即可

- Length of the working capital cycle depends on its elements, which are inventory days, trade receivables days and trade payable days. These elements usually depend on the nature of the business undertaken by a company and the way that business is conducted by its competitors.
- The length of the working capital cycle is usually therefore similar between companies in the same business sector, but can differ between business sectors.（这些因素通常取决于公司开展业务的性质及其竞争对手开展业务的方式。因此，在同一业务部门的公司之间，营运资金周期的长度通常是相似的，但在不同的业务部门之间可能会有所不同。）

3.3 Whether a working capital cycle should be positive or negative?

- If the working capital cycle had been negative, Co would have been receiving cash from its customers before it needed to pay its trade suppliers.

A company which does not give credit to its customers, such as a supermarket chain, can have a negative working capital cycle.

如果营运资本周期为消极的，则公司在需要向贸易供应商付款之前，就已经从客户那里收到现金。公司不会提供应收账款给这些公司（比如可能会出现负营运资本循环的连锁超市）

- Even if companies might generally prefer to be paid by customers before they have to pay their suppliers, the question of whether the working capital cycle should be positive or negative implies that companies are able to make such a choice, but this is not usually the case.

即使公司一般倾向于在必须向供应商付款之前先收到客户付款（即先收到应收账款再付应付账款），但营运资金周期是积极还是消极的问题暗示着公司能够作出这样的选择，但通常情况并非如此。

4. Liquidity ratios

The current ratio = CA/CL

The quick ratio = CA − inventory/CL

The accounts receivable payment period

The inventory turnover period

The accounts payable payment period

The sales revenue/net working capital ratio = revenue/net working capital

5. Over-capitalisation and working capital

If there are excessive inventories, accounts receivable and cash, and very few accounts payable, there will be an over investment by the company in current assets. Working capital will be excessive and the company in this respect will be over-capitalised.

如果存货、应收账款、现金过多，应付账款很少，则公司对流动资产的投资过多。营运资本将会过多，公司在这方面将会过度资本化。

Indicators of over-capitalisation	
Sales/working capital	Compare with previous years or similar company. A low of falling ratio may indicate over-capitalisation
Liquidity ratio	Compare with previous years or similar company.
Turnover period	Long turnover periods for inventory and account receivable or short credit period from supplies may be unnecessary working capital requirements can be reduced by improving these turnover times

6. Overtrading

In contrast with over-capitalisation, overtrading happens when a business tries to do too much too quickly with too little long-term capital, so that it is trying to support too large a volume of trade with the capital resources at its disposal.

Even if an overtrading business operates at a profit, it could easily run into serious trouble because it is short of cash. Such liquidity troubles stem from the fact that it does not have enough capital to provide the cash to pay its debts as they fall due.

与过度资本化形成对比的是，当一家企业试图用太少的长期资本以过快的速度做太多的事情时，就会发生过度贸易，从而导致它试图利用可支配的资本资源来支持过大的交易量。

即使一个过度贸易的企业在盈利，它也很容易陷入严重的麻烦，因为它缺乏现金。这种流动性问题的根源在于它根本不具备流动性有足够的资本在债务到期时提供现金支付。

6.1 Symptoms of overtrading are as follows.

a) There is a rapid increase in sales revenue. 销售收入过快增长

b) There is a rapid increase in the volume of current assets and possibly also non-current assets. Inventory turnover and accounts receivable turnover might slow down, in which case the rate of increase in inventories and accounts receivable would be even greater than the rate of increase in sales. 存货和应收账款增长幅度大于了销售收入增长幅度

c) There is only a small increase in equity capital (perhaps through retained profits). Most of the increase in assets is financed by credit, especially: 资产的增长都来源于负债，而不是内部利润累计的 retained profit

(i) Trade accounts payable — the payment period to accounts payable is likely to lengthen

(ii) A bank overdraft, which often reaches or even exceeds the limit of the facilities agreed by the bank

d) Some debt ratios and liquidity ratios alter dramatically. 流动性问题比较大

(i) The proportion of total assets financed by proprietors' capital falls, and the proportion financed by credit rises

(ii) The current ratio and the quick ratio fall

(iii) The business might have a liquid deficit; that is, an excess of current liabilities over current assets.

6.2 ways to reduce overtrading

a) Fundamental solution is to replace short-term finance with long-term finance such as loan or equity funds 公司支撑发展的资产换成更稳定的 equity 和风险相对较小的长期贷款(相比于应付账款和银行的 overdraft)

b) Restrict rate of expansion 限制扩张过快

c) Improve management of inventory and receivable 更好的管理我们的存货和应收账款适应公司的发展策略

考试时文字题套路：

1) Working Capital★

a) 每期 Working Capital 只记 incremental 变化量。

b) Tax & Tax on benefit of CA 取决于支付时间，当期还是滞后。

c) $(1 + \text{nominal DR}) = (1 + \text{inflation R})(1 + \text{real DR})$

d) 当不同科目有不同 inflation R 时，使用名义利率。

e) 当不同科目采用实际现金流时，使用实际利率。

f) 无论用名义，还是实际，得到的 NPV 差别不大。

原因：CA 节税不受通胀影响；working capital 的时差效应。

题目：2012-06-Q1，2012-12-Q1，2013-06-Q1，2013-12-Q1，2014-06-Q1，2014-12-Q4

2) Positive & Negative WC★

a) Positive working capital：T/R + Inventory − T/P = 正，一般企业都为正。先付供应商，再收款，期间需要垫资。

b) Negative working capital：T/R + Inventory − T/P = 负，如超市。

c) 正或负取决于商业模式行业惯例，竞争对手操作等外部因素，一般企业没有决定权。

题目：2004-06-Q2
3) Optimum level of cash★

a) Transactions need 交易需求：正常运作需要的现金
b) Precautionary need 预防需求：应对突发状况需要的现金（Cash buffer）
c) Speculative need 投机需求：如果有闲钱可以投资赚快钱的机会
d) Availability for finance 融资可行性：如果公司融资渠道有限，很难借到钱，那就需要保持较多的现金

题目：2012-12-Q
4) Over trading 特征★

贸易过度＝长期融资不足以支持企业的发展速度，过度依赖于短期融资

a) 销售收入/Turnover 相对于 Long-term debt 快速增长，对短期 debt 依赖度更高
b) T/R Day 增长，给客户更好的付款条件
c) Profitability 降低，给客户更低的价格
d) CA 快速增长，表现为更多库存来满足订单需求
e) Short-term debt 快速增长，无论是银行透支还是对供应商 T/P，都快速增长
f) Liquidity 下降：Current ratio & Quick ratio 都大大降低，流动性很差

题目：2012-06-Q2

Chapter 5

Managing working capital

1. management inventory

1.1 ABC system

Inventory management has traditionally been about minimising the total cost of inventory without running the risk of stock-outs.（保持最低的存货量但是同时也要预防缺货的风险）

A simple inventory classification system called an ABC system is often used to achieve this.：

A High value inventory items，requiring careful control using sophisticated methods such as the EOQ method discussed below with regular review and control

高价值存货项目，需要使用复杂的方法，如 EOQ 方法进行仔细控制，并定期检查和控制

B Medium value inventory items，as above but with less frequent review

中等价值的库存项目，如上所述，但不经常检查

C Low value inventory items，aim to keep a continuous availability

低价值库存项目，旨在保持持续的可用性

1.2 inventory cost

a) holding cost 持有成本：

warehousing and handling cost（仓储和搬运成本）

Deterioration and obsolescent（恶化和过时）

Insurance 保险

b) procuring cost 生产成本：

Ordering cost and delivery cost

c) shortage cost 缺货成本：

Contribution from lost sales

Extra cost of emergency inventory Cost of lost production and sales in a stock-out

销售损失的贡献（在缺货时失去生产和销售时）紧急库存的额外成本

d) Purchase cost of inventory 购买成本：

Relevant particularly when calculating discounts for bulk quantity purchases（在大量购买时注意 discount 问题）

1.3 Economic order quantity model（EOQ）经济下订单量

$$\text{Economic Order Quantity} = EOQ = \sqrt{\frac{2C_0 D}{C_h}}$$

D = Annual demand in units Co = Cost of placing an order

Ch. = Annual cost of holding one unit in inventory

P = Purchase price per unit Q = Number of units ordered.

a) Holding Cost = $Ch \times Q/2$

b) Ordering Cost = $Co \times D/Q$

c) average inventory level becomes Buffer inventory + $Q/2$.

The drawbacks of the EOQ model are that it:

a) Assumes 0 lead times, and 0 bulk purchase discounts — although these can be adjusted for as shown above

b) Ignores the possibility of supplier shortages or price rises

c) Ignores fluctuations in demand

d) Ignores the benefit of holding inventory to customers (choice, short lead times)

e) Ignores the hidden costs of holding inventory (see just-in-time below)

1.4 re-order level (再次下单的量)

Re-order level = maximum usage * maximum lead time.

Maximum inventory level = re-order level + re-order quantity − (minimum usage * minimum lead time)

Minimum inventory or buffer safety inventory = re-order level − (average usage * average lead time)

Average inventory = buffer safety inventory + re-order amount/2

1.5 Just-in-time (JIT)

Just-in-time procurement is a term which describes a policy of obtaining goods from suppliers at the latest possible time (ie when they are needed) and so avoiding the need to carry any materials or components inventory.指的是在尽可能晚的时间(如需要时)从供应商处获得货物,从而避免携带任何材料或部件存货的一种采购策略。

Introducing JIT might bring the following **potential benefits**.

a) Reduction in inventory holding costs

b) Reduced manufacturing lead times

c) Improved labour productivity

d) Reduced scrap/rework/warranty costs

Disadvantages:

Too reliable on supplier for both quality and reliability

May not appropriate in some business for example hospital a stock-out could be fatal

2. management receivable

2.1 Credit control policy

○ A credit analysis system

Before offering credit to particular customer, it is important to analyse the risk of trading with that customer by asking for bank references and trade references. A credit rating agency will also provide details on a customer's trading history, debt levels and payment performance. (For larger potential customers)

在向特定客户提供信贷之前,通过询问银行证明和交易证明来分析与该客户交易的风险是很重要的。信用评级机构还将提供客户交易历史、债务等细节水平和薪酬表现。(针对较大的潜在客户)

- A credit control system

a) Having granted credit to customers, a company needs to ensure that the agreed terms are being followed.

b) It will also advise on the frequency with which statements are sent to remind customers of outstanding amounts and when they are due to be paid.

c) It will be useful to prepare an aged receivables analysis at regular intervals (e.g. monthly), in order to focus management attention on areas where action needs to be taken to encourage payment by clients.

a) 在向客户提供信贷后,公司需要确保所商定的条款得到遵守。

b) 它还会建议用什么频率发送报表来提醒客户未付的款项和应付的时间。

c) 定期(例如每月)准备一份应收账款账龄化分析报告,以便使管理人员集中注意需要采取行动鼓励客户付款的领域。

- A debt collection system

a) Ideally, all customers will settle their outstanding accounts as and when they fall due. Any payments not received electronically should be banked quickly in order to decrease costs and increase profitability.

b) If accounts become overdue, steps should be taken to recover the outstanding amount by sending reminders, making customer visits and so on.

c) Legal action could be taken if necessary, although only as a last resort.

a) 理想情况下,所有客户都将在未偿账款到期时结清。任何没有通过电子方式收到的付款都应该迅速存入银行,以降低成本和增加盈利能力。

b) 如出现逾期,应采取催款通知、客户拜访等措施追回欠款。

c) 必要时可以采取法律行动,尽管只是作为最后的手段。

2.2 Managing foreign accounts receivable

1) Letters of credit

国外客户的银行给我看他们的信用等级

2) Exchange credit insurance

It can protect the exporting company against the risk of Non-payment of foreign customer

3) Invoice discounting

如果收不回来可以折价发现给其他金融机构

4) Export factoring(保理业务)

Factoring is an arrangement to have debts collected by a factor company, which advances a proportion of the money it is due to collect.

○ Non-recourse service — the factor provides protection against bad debts. If a customer defaults, the factor bear the loss.

○ Recourse service — our company must bear the loss of any bad debts thus must reimburse the factor for all bad debts.

保理是由提供保理业务的公司催收债务的一种安排,公司预付一定比例的应收款项。

○ 无追索权服务——该因素提供了对坏账的保护。如果一个客户违约,提供保理业务的公司承担损失。

○ 追索权服务——本公司必须承担任何坏账损失,因此必须对所有坏账进行补偿。

Advantages	Disadvantages
○ Saving in administrating costs ○ Professional service from factors ○ Reduction in the need for management control ○ The business receives early payment for most of its receivables in the form of finance from the factor. It can use this money to pay its suppliers.	○ Likely to be more costly than an efficiently run internal control department. ○ Customer may not wish to deal with a factor ○ Once you start factoring it is difficult to revert easily to an internal credit control ○ May indicate that the firm is in need of rapid cash, raising questions about its financial stability.

保理的优点	保理的缺点
节约管理成本 保理公司提供专业的服务 降低管理应收账款控制的成本 企业更早的收到应收账款可以用来支付应付账款等	可能更加费成本 应收账款的这个公司可能不愿意和保理公司合作 一旦你把应收账款给保理公司你就不能控制你的credit control 可能暗示你公司需要大量的资金,你的财务稳定性问题值得怀疑

3. Management payable

Cost of lost early payment

Discount = $[100/(100 - discount) \times 365]/T - 1$

If the cost > cost of capital, accept the early payment discount

考试时大题解题套路还有真题参考

1) Working Capital Cycle★

a) Working capital cycle/Cash operating cycle = T/R days + Inventory days — T/P days

i) 一般来说,Working capital 的投资规模跟 cash operating cycle 成正比,cycle 越长,WC 越多

ii) WC 规模也跟公司政策有关。激进政策,库存和 T/R 都少,cycle 短。保守政策,库存和 T/R 都多,cycle 长。

iii) Cash operating cycle 长,盈利性受影响,但风险少,不容易缺货,也更容易满足客户要货需求。

iv) Nature of Business 影响 COC,服务业的短,制造业的长。付款方式也会影响,现金

支付的就 COC 短。

 v) 同行业竞争对手的做法,会起影响作用

 vi) Risk appetite of company：保守的公司,会举长债来满足所有 permanent CA + 部分 fluctuating CA；激进的会举短债来满足所有 fluctuating CA + 部分 permanent CA

 b) Quick ration & Current ratio 变化分析

 c) Target sales/net working capital ratio 变化分析

题目：2011-06-Q4，2011-12-Q2，2014-06-Q2，2014-12-Q1，Pilot Q1

2) 营运资金管理目的

Working capital 主要关注：

a) Profitability

b) Liquidity

它们有时候冲突。

a) 盈利性表现在最大化股东利益

b) 流动性表现在满足偿债需求,运作需求。

不同管理层会采取不同策略,或 Conservative 保守(充足现金流),或 aggressive 激进(更在意盈利)。管理好 working capital 的重要性：

a) Cash 是公司商业活动的血液

b) CA 一般来说,差不多是企业一半的资产了,必须谨慎管理

c) 对 SME 来说,CL 是主要的融资来源。

题目：2013-12-Q3

3) Manage T/R 包括客户 Creditworthiness 商誉调查★

a) Credit analysis：Trade Reference 贸易记录,Bank reference 银行记录,Credit rating agency 信用评定中介

b) Credit control：Credit limit 授信额度,Review regularly 定期复核、Aged listing of T/R 账龄分析、定期对账催账

c) Debt collection：有效管理：现金收账及时存银行降低偷盗风险、增加收益、利用保理、有催账流程,采取必要法律手段、早期付款优惠

题目：2010-12-Q3，2012-12-Q2，2013-06-Q3，2015-06-Q3

4) T/R 规模影响因素

a) Trade credit 融资成本

b) 竞争对手的 T/R 条款

c) 公司可以承受的 risk 和资金压力

d) 公司的流动性 liquidity 需求

e) 对客户的资信调查题目：2010-12-Q3

5) EOQ

a) 当前 Ordering Policy 跟 EOQ 比较,计算经济性(节省开支多少)。

b) 比较早付折扣

c) 比较 bulk purchase discount

题目：2010-12-Q3，2011-06-Q4，2012-12-Q2，2013-12-Q3，Pilot Q1

6) T/P discount 计算

a) 原 term 的 T/P

b) 修改 term 的 T/P

c) T/P 变动量

d) T/P 变动引起的 Interest 跟 discount 好处比较，得到更优方案

题目：2012-12-Q2，2013-12-Q3

7) JIT 好处

a) Inventory holding costs 降低

b) Manufacturing lead times 降低，生产更有效率

c) Working capital 水平降低，资金压力少

d) 供应商关系提高，必须紧密合作，实现 JIT

e) Operating efficiency 提高，来实现 JIT

f) Rework cost 降低，因为没有时间重做，必须第一遍做对做好，质量意识提高

题目：2010-12-Q3

8) 管理海外应收 T/R

a) 付款方式的控制，譬如部分预付：30%deposit + 70%DP at sight

b) 交易通过银行，见单后银行付款（需要客户在银行有等值货款）

c) Forfeiting

d) 信用证

e) Counter trading：正对等贸易，也称对销贸易，以物换物，用物品代替货币。缺点：多方交易的法律风险、物品/服务价值波动、谈判过程艰难。

f) Export credit insurance：保险，在满足什么条件时，可以由保险公司赔付未收账款。缺点：针对不同情况，赔付比例不同，保额保费都不同。很难 100% 获赔。

g) Export factoring：比国内保理贵，不是所有国家都有。发展中国家可能没有。

来源：考官文章

9) Letter of Credit 信用证

a) 买卖双方约定物品，交货期，付款方式等。

b) 买方银行按照条款内容，出具信用证。

c) 买方银行把信用证给卖方银行，承诺满足合同条款，即付款。

d) 发货后，卖方通过银行将发货单据等寄给买方银行。

e) 买方银行确认付款。

f) 卖方可以即刻兑现 banker's acceptance，或者在货币市场折价出售。

缺点：手续费较高，合同条款要注意，买方银行需要有足够存款满足付款需求。

Chapter 6

Working capital finance

1. The management of cash

The reasons why organizations hold cash

○ **Transactions motive**: a business needs cash to meet its regular commitments of paying its accounts payable, its employees' wages, its taxes, its annual dividends to shareholders and so on.

交易的需求：企业需要现金来支付应付账款、员工工资、税收、股东年度股息等常规支出。

○ **Precautionary motive**: there is a need to maintain a 'buffer' of cash for unforeseen contingencies. This buffer may be provided by an overdraft facility, which has the advantage that it will cost nothing until it is actually used.

预防的需求：有必要为不可预见的突发事件保留现金缓冲。这个缓冲区可以由透支工具提供，它的优点是在实际使用之前不需要任何成本。

○ **Speculative motive**: Some businesses hold surplus cash as a speculative asset in the hope that interest rates will rise. However, many businesses would regard large long-term holdings of cash as not prudent.

投机的需求：一些企业持有过剩现金作为投机性资产，希望利率上升。然而，许多企业认为长期持有大量现金是不明智的。

The amount of cash that a business needs to keep in its bank account can be assessed in one of two ways:

a) A cash flow forecast

b) A mathematical model of a business's cash flows

2. Cash flow forecasting

This is the most important tool in short-term cash flow planning. Cash flow forecasts will be prepared continuously during the year and will allow a business to plan how to deal with expected cash flow surpluses or shortages.

这是短期现金流计划中最重要的工具。现金流量预测将会在全年持续编制，让企业计划如何处理预期的现金流量盈余或短缺。

You will need to produce forecasts in the exam that reflect:

a) The expected timing of receipts and payments of cash during the period

b) That not all items in the income statement will be in the cash budget e.g. depreciation

Cash forecast for the three months ended 31 March 20×1

	January	February	March
Cash receipts			
Sales receipts (W1)	X	X	X
Issue of shares		X	
Cash payments			
Purchase payments (W2)	X	X	X
Dividends/Taxes	X		
Purchase of non-current assets Wages	X	X	X
Cash surplus/deficit for month	X	(X)	X
Cash balance, beginning	X	X	(X)
Cash balance, ending	X	(X)	X

A cash flow forecast can show four positions. Management will need to take appropriate action depending on the potential position.

Cash position	Appropriate management action
Short-term surplus	Pay accounts payable early to obtain discount Attempt to increase sales by increasing accounts receivable and inventories Make short-term investment
Short-term deficit	Increase account payable by delaying payments to suppliers Reduce accounts receivable by improving collection of overdue payments Arrange a bank overdraft facility or increase the limit on an existing facility
Long-term surplus	Make long-term investments Expand Diversify Replace/update non-current asset Distribute the surplus to shareholders
Long-term deficit	Raise long-term fiance Consider shutdown/disinvestment opportunities

3. Mathematical models

How much to transfer can be calculated by using mathematical models, there are two mathematical models that you need to be aware of:

a) Baumol model

b) Miller-Orr model

Similarly to the EOQ, costs are minimised when:

$$Q=\sqrt{\frac{2CS}{i}}$$

S = the amount of cash to be used in each time period
C = the cost per sale of securities
i = the interest cost of holding cash or near cash equivalents
Q = the total amount to be raised to provide for S

3.1 Baumol model

The Baumol model is based on the idea that deciding on optimum cash balances is like deciding on optimum inventory levels. It assumes that cash is steadily consumed over time.

Drawbacks of the Baumol model

a) In reality, it is unlikely to be possible to predict amounts required over future periods with much certainty.

b) No buffer inventory of cash is allowed for. There may be costs associated with running out of cash.

c) There may be other normal costs of holding cash which increase with the average amount held.

a) 实际上,不大可能十分肯定地预测未来期间所需的数额。

b) 不允许备存现金。在现金快用完的时候可能会有相关的成本。

c) 持有现金的其他正常成本可能随持有的平均数额而增加。

3.2 Miller-Orr model

In an attempt to produce a more realistic approach to cash management, various models more complicated than the inventory approach have been developed. One of these, the Miller-Orr model, manages to achieve a reasonable degree of realism while not being too elaborate.

The Miller-Orr model setting the target cash balance, which incorporates uncertainty in the cash inflows and outflows.

为了产生一种更实际的现金管理方法,已经发展了各种比存货方法更复杂的模型。其中之一,米勒-奥尔模型,成功地实现了合理程度的现实主义,而不是过于复杂。

米勒-奥尔模型设定了目标现金余额,其中包含了现金流入和流出的不确定性。

$$\text{Return point} = \text{Lower limit} + \left(\frac{1}{3} \times \text{spread}\right)$$

The formula for the spread is:

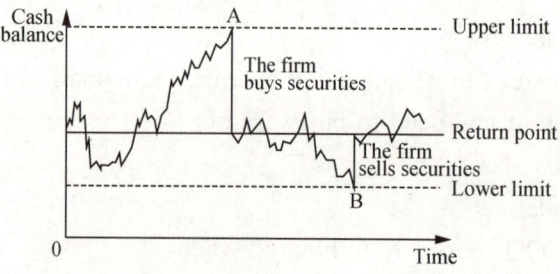

$$\text{Spread} = 3\left(\frac{3}{4} \times \frac{\text{Transaction cost} \times \text{Variance of cash flows}}{\text{Interest rate}}\right)^{\frac{1}{3}}$$

It works as follows:

a) A safety stock (lower limit) of cash is decided upon.

b) A statistical calculation is completed taking into account the variation in cash flow to agree an allowable range or spread of cash flow fluctuations.

c) Using this spread, an upper limit of cash balances is agreed.

d) The cash balance is managed to ensure that the balance at any point in time is kept between the lower and upper limits.

4. Treasury management

A large organisation will have a treasury department to manage liquidity, short-term investment, borrowings, foreign exchange risk and other, specialised areas such as forward contracts and futures. 一家大型机构将拥有一个财政部，负责管理流动性、短期投资、借款、外汇风险以及远期合约和期货等其他专业领域。

Four key functions:

a) Management of liquidity

b) Management of funding

c) Management of risk

d) Advising on corporate finance issues

5. Investing surplus cash

Temporary surpluses of cash can be invested in a variety of financial instruments.

Longer-term surpluses should be returned to shareholders if there is alack of investment opportunities.

暂时的现金盈余可以投资于各种金融工具。

如果缺乏投资机会，长期盈余应该返还给股东。

5.1 Temporary cash surpluses are likely to be:

a) Deposited with a bank or similar financial institution.

b) Invested in short-term debt instruments, such as Treasury bills or CDs. (Debt instruments are debt securities which can be traded.)

c) Invested in longer term debt instruments such as government bonds, which can be sold when the company eventually needs the cash.

d) Invested in shares of listed companies, which can be sold on the stock market when the company eventually needs the cash. Investing in equities is fairly high risk, since share prices can fall substantially, resulting in large losses on investment.

暂时的现金盈余可能是：

a) 存入银行或类似的金融机构。

b) 投资于短期债务工具，如国库券或定期存单。(债务工具是可以交易的债务证券。)

c) 投资于较长期债务工具，例如政府债券 可以在公司最终需要现金时出售。

d) 投资上市公司的股票，当公司最终需要现金时，可以在股票市场上出售。投资股票是相当高的风险，因为股票价格会大幅下跌，导致投资的巨大损失。

5.2 Long-term cash surpluses are likely to be：

a) Investments — new projects or equipment

b) Financing — repay debt, buy back shares

c) Dividends — Return to shareholders

长期现金盈余可能是：

a) 投资——新项目或设备

b) 融资——偿还债务，回购股票

c) 股息——股东的回报

6. Managing cash flow shortages

★ Working capital funding policy（重要 理解＋背）

Cash shortages can be funded by either long-term finance or short term borrowings; these will be covered in detail in later chapters.

In between these extremes is a matching policy which uses short-term finance to fund fluctuating current assets and long term finance to fund permanent current assets and non-current assets.

The likelihood of a company adopting an aggressive approach depends on：

a) Management attitude to risk

b) Strength of relationship with the bank providing an overdraft

c) Ability to raise long-term finance

公司采取激进做法的可能性取决于：

a) 管理者对风险的态度

b) 与提供透支的银行的关系强度

c) 有能力筹集长期资金

○ Working capital investment policy is concerned with the level of investment in current assets, with one company being compared with another.

○ Working capital financing policy is concerned with the relative proportions of short-term and long-term finance used by a company. While working capital investment policy is therefore assessed on an inter-company comparative basis, assessment of working capital financing policy involves analysis of financial information for one company alone.

营运资金融资政策涉及公司使用的短期和长期资金的相对比例。因此，营运资本投资政策是在公司间比较的基础上评估的，而营运资本融资政策的评估则涉及对一家公司的财务信息的分析。

○ Working capital financing policy uses an analysis of current assets into permanent current assets and fluctuating current assets. Working capital investment policy does not require this analysis.

○ 营运资本融资政策将流动资产分析为永久性流动资产和波动性流动资产。营运资本投资政策不需要这种分析。

○ Permanent current assets represent the core level of investment in current assets that supports a given level of business activity.

○ Fluctuating current assets represent the changes in the level of current assets that arise through, for example, the unpredictability of business operations, such as the level of trade receivables increasing due to some customers paying late or the level of inventory increasing due to demand being less than predicted.

○ Working capital financing policy relies on the matching principle, which is not used by working capital investment policy. The matching principle holds that long-term assets should be financed from a long-term source of finance.

○ Non-current assets and permanent current assets should therefore be financed from a long-term source, such as equity finance or bond finance, while fluctuating current assets should be financed from a short- term source, such as an overdraft or a short-term bank loan.

○ Both working capital investment policy and working capital financing policy use the terms conservative and aggressive.

○ In investment policy, the terms are used to indicate the comparative level of investment in current assets on an inter-company basis. One company has a more aggressive approach compared to another company if it has a lower level of investment in current assets, and vice verse for a conservative approach to working capital investment policy.

在投资政策中,这些术语用来表示公司间对流动资产投资的比较水平。如果一家公司在流动资产上的投资水平较低,那么它就会采取比另一家公司更激进的方法,反之,在营运资本投资政策上则采取保守的方法。

○ In working capital financing policy, the terms are used to indicate the way in which fluctuating current assets and permanent current assets are matched to short-term and long-term finance sources.

○ An aggressive financing policy means that fluctuating current assets and a portion of permanent current assets are financed from a short- term finance source.

○ A conservative financing policy means that permanent current assets and a portion of fluctuating current assets are financed from a long-term source.

○ An aggressive financing policy will be more profitable than a conservative financing policy because short-term finance is cheaper than long-term finance, as indicated for debt finance by the normal yield curve (term structure of interest rates).

○ However, an aggressive financing policy will be riskier than a conservative financing policy because short-term finance is riskier than long-term finance.

○ Overall, therefore, it can be said that while working capital investment policy and working capital financing policy use similar terminology, the two policies are very different in terms of their meaning and application.

○ It is even possible, for example, for a company to have a conservative working capital investment policy while following an aggressive working capital financing policy.

考试时大题解题套路和真题

1) Working capital Financing policy★

a) 保守的 Conservative approach：需要借长债来负担 CA 中的永久资产和部分浮动资产。

b) 激进的 Aggressive approach：需要借短债来负担 CA 中的浮动资产和部分永久资产需求。

c) 因为短期融资比长期融资便宜，所以激进的方法更盈利

d) 但短期融资利率浮动可能，信用撤回风险都比长期融资高，所以激进的方法风险更高 WC 的融资投资政策应用和意义不同，同一个公司可能有保守的投资政策和激进的融资政策

题目：2012-06-Q2

2) Working capital investment policy★

a) 保守的 Conservative approach：充足的活动现金流，宁愿举长债，有比较高的固定利息支出，现金流短缺风险较低，库存较多可能库存过期，对客户的要求比较不变通。

b) 激进的 Aggressive approach：活动现金流有限（对财务人员要求非常高了），通过降低 FC 来提高盈利能力，库存有限，因库存不足或现金不足导致营运困难的风险较高，也因此丧失声誉。比较符合高科技公司的特征。

题目：2012-06-Q2, 2014-06-Q2

3) Miller-Orr model★

Return point = lower limit + (1/3 × spread)，记住图形样子，大概知道即可。

——低于 lower limit，撤回投资，补充现金流至回归点。

——高于 upper limit，追加投资，减少现金流至回归点。

题目：2012-06-Q2

Part D

Investment appraisal

【Part D 所有的计算题一定要结合 BPP 练习册认真练习。理解公式含义,理解记忆。计算题只有多练多理解考试时候才能算出来。】

Chapter 7

Investment decision

1. Investment and the capital budgeting process

1.1 Investment

Investment can be divided into two categories: capital expenditure and revenue expenditure.

Capital expenditure is expenditure which results in the acquisition of non-current assets or an improvement in their earning capacity. It is not charged as an expense in the statement of profit or loss; the expenditure appears as a non-current asset in the statement of financial position.

资本支出是指取得非流动资产或改善其收入能力的支出。它没有作为费用记入损益表；支出在财务状况表中以非流动资产的形式出现。

Revenue expenditure is charged to the statement of profit or loss and is expenditure which is incurred:

a) For the purpose of the trade of the business — this includes expenditure classified as selling and distribution expenses, administration expenses and finance charges

b) To maintain the existing earning capacity of non-current assets

收入性支出计入利润表

Investment can be made in non-current assets or working capital.

Investment in non-current assets involves a significant amount of time.

Investment in working capital are only committed for a short period of time.

对固定资产投资需要较长的一段时间 对营运资本投资需要的时间相对较少

1.2 The capital budgeting process

A typical model for investment decision-making has a number of distinct stages.

○ Origination of proposals

Suggestion schemes, innovation group, customer research

○ Project screening

Project committee reviews for suitability & feasibility, how long the project takes to pay back the initial investment.

○ Analysis and acceptance

covered in this chapter (so you can ignore this for now)

Chapter 7　Investment decision

○ Monitoring and review

Audit by an independent team over whether the project achieves its objectives (a post audit)

2. Relevant cash flows

Only the cash flows affected by the decision to invest should be taken into account when appraising investments, these are called relevant cash flows. 只有相关现金流我们才考虑

Relevant cash flows Examples:

○ Annual incremental cash profits from the investment
○ Opportunity costs
○ Extra tax or reduction in tax (see more in Chapter 9)
○ Capital investment for the project
○ Residual value or disposal value of equipment
○ Incremental working capital requirements (working capital will be released at the end of the project)
○ Savings arose from the investment project

Non-relevant cash flows

Any costs incurred in the past, or any committed costs which will be incurred regardless of whether or not an investment is undertaken, are not relevant cash flows.

Examples:
○ Depreciation.
○ Sunk cost
○ Historic cost

3. Payback period

Payback is the time it takes the cash inflows from a capital investment project to equal the cash outflows.

A long payback period is considered risky because it relies on cash flows that are in the distant future. (payback period 越长风险越高)

Payback period = initial investment/annual cash inflow, or accumulative cash flow

Decision criteria

Accept: payback period < required payback period

Advantages:

a) it is simple to use and easy to understand
b) A simply measure of risk, rapid payback minimizes risks
c) maybe important to companies with limited cash resources for budgeting purpose
d) payback period uses cash flows rather than accounting profit less likely to be distorted

e) Emphasizes cash flow in the early years

f) the method acts as the first screening device

Disadvantages

a) it doesn't consider the time value of money

b) there is no measure of return

c) ignores cash flows after the payback period

4. Return on capital employed

ROCE is also called the accounting rate of return (ARR) or the return on investment (ROI).

Decision criteria

Accept: ROCE > target ROCE

$$ROCE = \frac{\text{Average annual profit from investment}}{\text{initial investment}} \times 100$$

$$\text{or} \quad \frac{\text{Average annual profit from investment}}{\text{average investment}} \times 100$$

$$\text{where average investment} = \frac{\text{initial outlay} + \text{scrap value}}{2}$$

Note: profit is after depreciation but before interest and tax

The ROCE method of capital investment appraisal can also be used to compare two or more projects which are mutually exclusive. The project with the highest ROCE would be selected (provided that the expected ROCE is higher than the company's target ROCE).

Advantages of ROCE

○ A quick and simple calculation

○ Consistent with methods used to evaluate the company as a whole

○ Relative score (%) is easy to understand

○ Considers the whole life of the project

Disadvantages of ROCE

○ Ignores the timing of the profits from an investment.

○ It is based on accounting profits and not cash flows.

○ A relative measure rather than an absolute measure and hence takes no account of the size of the investment

○ It takes no account of the length of the project.

○ Ignores the time value of money.

大题解题套路

ARR 计算*

(1) Total before-tax cash flow — Total depreciation = Total accounting profit

(2) Average annual profit = Total accounting profit/N 年

(3) Average investment＝(初期投资＋末期残值)/2
(4) ROCE (ARR) = Average annual profit/Average investment = %

题目：2012-12-Q1

Chapter 8

Investment appraisal using DCF methods

1. Discounted cash flow (DCF)

Discounted cash flow is an investment appraisal technique which takes into account both the timings of cash flows and also total profitability over a project's life.

$$FV = PV(1+r)^n$$

Discounting starts with the future value, and converts a future value to a present value. Discounting tells us how much an investment will be worth in today's terms.（折现就是把未来现金流折到今天的价值）

Present value is the cash equivalent now of a sum of money receivable or payable at a stated future date，discounted at a specified rate of return (discount factor).

$$PV = FV/(1+r)^n$$

2. The net present value method

Net present value or NPV is the value obtained by discounting all cash outflows and inflows of a capital investment project by a chosen target rate of return or cost of capital. The NPV is thus calculated as the PV of cash inflows minus the PV of cash outflows.（净现值方法是把一项资本投资项目所有的未来现金流出和未来现金流入按照目标的要求的资本成本折现的方法 NPV = PV of cash outflows − PV of cash inflow）

Decision Criteria

Accept：If a project has a positive NPV then it should be accepted because it increase shareholder's wealth.（NPV＞0 接受这个项目）

Reject：If a project has a negative NPV then it should be rejected. NPV = 0：Return from investment's cash inflows same as cost of capital.（NPV＜0 拒绝这个项目）

要注意记得以下公式的计算并结合计算题好好理解

Annuity

Perpetuity annuity

Delay annuity

3. The internal rate of return method

The internal rate of return (IRR) of an investment is the cost of capital at which its

NPV would be exactly $0. IRR is a discounted cash flow technique of a project that calculates the % return given by a project. This method is to accept investment projects whose IRR exceeds a target rate of return. (内含报酬率是一项投资的资本成本＝NPV时候的那个折现率,当IRR＞要求的回报率的时候我们接受这个项目)

4. NPV and IRR compared

Both NPV and IRR are superior methods for appraising investments compared to the techniques covered in the previous chapter because:

a) They account for the time value of money (unlike ROCE and payback)
b) They focus on relevant cash flows (unlike ROCE)
c) They look at the cash flows over the whole life of the project (unlike payback)
d) NPV is technically superior to IRR and simpler to calculate

Advantage of IRR

IRR gives the % return of a project; this concept is easy for non financial managers to understand and for financial managers to calculate because it does not require the calculation of a cost of capital.

Disadvantage of IRR

IRR does not indicate the size of the investment, thus the risk involve in the investment

Assume that earning throughout the period of the investment are re-invested at IRR

It can give conflicting signals with mutually exclusive project

If a project has irregular cash flows there is multiple IRRs for that project

Conclusion — NPV is a better technique

NPV does not have any of the problems of IRR. The role of IRR is to act as a tool for explaining the benefits of an investment to non-financial managers; it should not be used as the financial analysis used to justify the investment decision.

This is not to say that NPV is perfect; like any financial technique, there is the danger that the non-financial benefits of an investment are ignored.

Chapter 9

Allowing for inflation and taxation

1. Allowing for inflation

Inflation is a feature of all economies, and it must be accommodated in financial planning.

Real cash flows (cash flows in current prices) should be discounted at a real discount rate, which is a return ignoring inflation.

Nominal cash flows (the actual expected cash flows at future prices, ie including inflationary increases) should be discounted at a nominal discount rate, which is a rate relating to current market rates of return.

The relationship between real and nominal rates of interest is given by the Fisher formula.

$$(1+i) = (1+r)(1+h)$$

Where h = rate of inflation

r = real rate of interest

i = nominal (money) rate of interest

当一个 project 里 所有的 sales cost 的通货膨胀率一样的时候就用 real rate of interest；

当一个 project 里 sales cost 的通货膨胀率不一样，即有多个 inflation 时候，用 nominal rate

2. Allowing for taxation

Taxation is a major practical consideration for businesses. It is vital to take it into account in making decisions.

In investment appraisal, tax is often assumed to be payable one year in arrears.（延后一年付税）

Net operating cash flows from a project should be considered as the taxable profits.

Tax-allowable depreciation details should be checked in any question you attempt.

Tax-allowable depreciation (capital allowances)

Tax-allowable depreciation (capital allowances) is used to reduce taxable profits, and it is not the same as the depreciation charge for the purpose of reporting profit in the financial statements.（网课里的例题认真理解并记住如何计算）

3. NPV format(记住格式＋做题熟悉)

	Year 0	Year 1	Year 2	Year 3	Year 4
Sales receipts		X	X	X	
Costs	—	(X)	(X)	(X)	—
Sales less costs		X	X	X	
Taxation on profits		(X)	(X)	(X)	(X)
Capital expenditure	(X)				
Scrap value				X	
Working capital	(X)			X	
Tax benefit of tax dep'n	—	X	X	X	X
Discount factors @ post-tax cost of capital	X	X	X	X	X
Present value	(X)	X	X	X	(X)

4. Working capital

Major projects will need the injection of funds to finance the level of working capital required（normally assumed to be inventory）.

Questions will show the total amount of working capital required in each year of the project. The DCF working should only show the incremental cash flows from one year's requirement to the next.

At the end of the project，when there is no further requirement for working capital in the project，the full amount invested will be released. This is shown in the DCF calculation as an income.

在 NPV 项目里我们只需要考虑的是 incremental working capital 部分。

本章的知识点一定要结合大题进行计算后，总结。记忆。其中重要的 taxable allowance depreciation 和 tax 还有 incremental working capital 一定要记住如何计算的，还有每题的 NPV 的题的计算有部分是公式里没有的那就是题目中特有的部分考试时也要注意。

Chapter 10

Project appraisal and risk

1. Risk and uncertainty

Risk can be quantified and built into an NPV using certain techniques, e.g. expected value and risk adjusted discount factors. (风险可以被量化,用 NPV 等方法)

Uncertainty cannot be quantified, but can be described using certain techniques, e.g. sensitivity analysis, payback period, adjusted payback period and simulation. (不确定性不能被量化,但是可以用一些技术来分析,比如敏感性分析,回收期法,等)

1.1 Risk

○ Several possible outcomes 多种可能的结果

○ On basis of past relevant experience. assign probabilities to outcomes 基于过去的相关经验。为结果分配概率

○ Increases as the variability of returns increase 随着回报率的增加而增加

Techniques used for risk

a) Expected value(profitability analysis): use probabilities to create an assessment of the average expected NPV from an investment

b) Risk adjusted discount factor: using a higher cost of capital if the project is high risk this is discussed in part E 可以用期望价值和风险调整的折旧来分析风险。

1.2 Uncertainty

○ Several possible outcomes 多种可能的结果

○ Little past experience thus difficult to assign probabilities to outcomes 过去的经验很少

○ Increase as project life increase 随着项目寿命的增加而增加

Techniques used for uncertainty

Sensitivity analysis	An analysis of what% change in one variable(e.g. sales) would be needed for the NPV of a project to fall to zero
Payback period	Covered earlier the quicker the payback the less reliant a project in on the later more uncertain cash flows
Adjusted payback period	As above but uses the discounted cash flows also called discounted payback period
simulation	An analysis of how changes in more than 1 variable(e.g. market share and sales price)may affect the NPV of a project

Chapter 10 Project appraisal and risk

可以用敏感分析，回收期法，调整的回收期法来分析不确定性都可以结合题目来理解

$$\text{Sensitivity} = \frac{\text{NPV}}{\text{Present value of project variable}} \%$$

The **lower** the percentage，the **more sensitive** is NPV to that project variable

2. Sensitivity analysis(本公式会背，考试时会计算)

Some key sensitivity ratio：
○ Sensitivity of discount rate：IRR
○ Sensitivity of sale volume：PV of contribution.
○ Sensitivity of price：PV of revenue

敏感分析的分析几个主要因素对应的因子要记住

Weakness of sensitivity analysis：

a) Variable is calculated isolated. In reality，there is combination of changes.
b) No indication of probability of a change in a key factor arising.
c) Does not provide managers with clear decision rules.
d) Subjectivity：Must rely on judgment，different manager will interpret differently.
e) Critical factors may be those out of management control.

a) 在敏感分析中变量是孤立计算的。实际上，变化是多种多样的。
b) 没有显示关键因素发生变化的可能性。
c) 没有为管理者提供明确的决策规则。
d) 主观性：必须依靠判断，不同的管理者会有不同的解释。
e) 关键因素可能是那些失去管理控制的因素。

3. Probability analysis

Probability analysis of expected cash flows can often be estimated and used both to calculate an expected NPV and measure risk.

An expected value is a weighted average of all possible outcomes.

It is calculated by multiplying the value of each possible outcome，by the probability of that outcome，and summing the results.

预期现金流的概率分析经常可以用来估计和计算预期 NPV 和衡量风险。
期望值是所有可能结果的加权平均值。
计算方法是将每个可能结果的值乘以该结果的概率，然后对结果求和。

Weakness of profitability analysis：

a) Identifying the probability of each outcome can be difficult.
b) Even if the probabilities can be calculated reasonably，in practice，there may be many possible outcomes for a project and the probability distribution for a range of possible outcomes may be difficult to determine.
c) The expected NPV approach calculates an average figure which may not be capable factually occurring.

a）确定每种结果的可能性是困难的。

b）即使概率可以合理计算,在实践中,一个项目可能会有很多可能的结果,并且一系列可能结果的概率分布可能很难确定。

c）预期净现值方法计算的结果可能在现实中是无法实际发生的平均值。

考试时文字题解题套路

1) Investment appraisal

考虑 Risk 因素的 3 种方式。

a）Risk & Uncertainty：对于评价投资,很不一样

b）Risk 对于 Possible outcomes 和 Probability of each outcome

c）Uncertainty 对于 Possible outcomes 有预估,但 Probability of each outcome 不确定

2) Sensitivity analysis

分析某个变量变动,导致整个项目 NPV＝0 的时的变动率,来做投资决策。

a）可以帮助企业找出影响项目经济效益变动的最敏感性因素,分析敏感性因素变动的原因,并为进一步进行不确定性分析（如概率分析）提供依据；

b）研究不确定性因素变动如引起项目经济效益值变动的范围或极限值,分析判断项目承担风险的能力；

c）比较多方案的敏感性大小,以便在经济效益值相似的情况下,从中选出不敏感的投资方案。

3) Probability analysis

概率分析：又称风险分析,是通过研究各种不确定性因素发生不同变动幅度的概率分布及其对项目经济效益指标的影响,对项目可行性和风险性以及方案优劣作出判断的一种不确定性分析法。

a）可以用来计算 mean or average NPV（the expected NPV or ENPV）假定该可能性在未来重复发生很多次。

b）也可以用来分析最坏的结果及发生可能性,－NPV 可能性,最好的结果及可能性等等。

4) Risk-adjusted discount rate

CAPM 模型,找类似的公司 B 上杠杆下杠杆,然后得出公司引入新项目的 B 值。

5) Adjusted payback

a）根据风险调整返本期：降低项目回报周期有助于降低风险。因为回报周期越长,不确定性和风险越高。

b）根据风险调整贴现率：或者考虑风险,而修正 DF 值,给 DF 值打个折扣。结果同 1)

题目：2011-06-Q1

2) Sensitivity analysis*

a）如果概率是 quantified and measured,属于 risk,可用 Expected values 来表示预期输出。

b）Uncertainty 是不可以量化和测量的,发生有随机性,不具备重复性。一般用 Mean or Average 值来提供计算,给出输出值。

c) Risk 可以运用 Probability analysis(比 sensitivity analysis 更合适),通过计算方差来看波动区间,来看各种可能性概率。但概率分析可能基于经验之谈,可能是专家意见,含主观判断,或许不够客观。

d) 敏感性分析考虑的单个变量波动多少,对最终 NPV 的影响,可以找出 key or critical 变量。计算方法:用 NPV/变量 PV,使 NPV=0 时的变化率。但它不给出变量的可变范围,只是给管理层一个参考意见,便于他们做风险评估。

题目:2011-12-Q1,2012-06-Q1,2015-06-Q5

Chapter 11

Specific investment decisions

1. Lease or buy decisions

Leasing is a commonly used source of finance, and can be especially attractive where companies find it difficult to raise finance to fund capital expenditure.

Leasing is a contract between a lessor and a lessee for hire of a specific asset by the lessee from a manufacturer or vendor of such assets.

The lessor has ownership of the asset and so provides the initial finance for the asset.

The lessee has possession and use of the asset on payment of specified rentals over a period.

租赁是一种常用的融渠道,当公司发现难以筹集资金用于资本支出时,租赁尤其具有吸引力。

租赁是出租人和承租人之间就租赁某项资产或从某项资产的制造商或卖方处获得的合同。

出租人拥有该资产的所有权,因此为该资产提供初始融资。

承租人在一段时期内支付了规定的租金,就拥有和使用该资产。

Types of leases:

○ Operating leases (the lessor retains most of the risks and rewards of ownership)经营租赁:出租人承担风险和拥有这个资产

○ Finance leases (transfers substantially all of the risks and rewards of ownership of an asset to the lessee)融资租赁:把资产的风险和收益都转移给了承租人

○ Sale and leaseback arrangements 售后租回

The decision whether to lease or buy an asset is a financing decision which interacts with the investment decision to buy the asset.(在投资决策里我们往往要考虑是买一个资产还是租赁一个资产)

1.1 Operating leases

Operating lease is a lease where the lessor retains most of the risks and rewards of ownership.

Operating leases are rental agreements between a lessor and a lessee, for a relatively short period of time. It is useful to think of operating leases as short-term rental agreements.

Chapter 11　Specific investment decisions

经营租赁是出租人承担风险和收益,是一种在(较短时期内)承租人和出租人之间的租赁合同。如果考虑短期的投资,经营租赁是一种方法

a) The lessor supplies the equipment to the lessee.

b) The lessor is responsible for servicing and maintaining the leased equipment

c) The period of the lease is fairly short, less than the expected economic life of the asset. At the end of one lease agreement, the lessor can either lease the same equipment to someone else and obtain a good rent for it, or sell the equipment second-hand.

a) 出租人把设备出租给承租人

b) 出租人对设备的维修保养负责

c) 租赁期间是比较短的少于设备的经济寿命。租赁期结束,出租人可以把这个资产租给其他人或者转手卖给其他人

1.2　Finance leases

A finance lease is a lease that substantially transfers all the risks and rewards of ownership of an asset to the lessee. It is an agreement between the lessee and the lessor for most or all of the asset's expected useful life.

融资租赁是一种把资产的风险和收益转移给承租人的租赁方式。租赁期几乎为资产的使用寿命

a) The lessee is responsible for the upkeep, servicing and maintenance of the asset.

b) The lease has a primary period covering all or most of the useful economic life of the asset. At the end of this period, the lessor would not be able to lease the asset to someone else.

a) 承租人对资产的维修,保管负责

b) 这种租赁的时间较长,几乎为资产的使用寿命,租赁期结束,出租人不能把资产再租给或者卖给其他人

1.3　Sale and leaseback

Sale and leaseback is when a business that owns an asset agrees to sell the asset to a financial institution and lease it back on terms specified in the sale and leaseback agreement.

售后租回(相当于一种贷款 把我们的资产抵押给他们,这种情况下我们公司资金不足但是又想使用这个资产先把他们卖出去然后再每年付租金的方式租回来还可以使用然后又可以解决资金不足的问题)

1.4　Leasing may have advantages for the lessee.

a) The lessee may not have enough cash to pay for the asset, and would have difficulty obtaining a bank loan to buy it. If so, the lessee has to rent the asset to obtain use of it at all.

b) Finance leasing may be cheaper than a bank loan.

c) The lessee may find the tax relief available advantageous.

承租方可能没有足够的资金来购买资产或者获得银行贷方上有困难,如果这样租赁可以使得承租方用租这个资产的方式来获得使用权

Discounted cash flow techniques are used to evaluate the lease or buy decision so that the least-cost financing option can be chosen.

折现的现金流方式来评估租赁或者购买的抉择

2. Asset replacement decisions(本公式结合题目理解)

DCF techniques can assist asset replacement decisions, to decide how frequently an asset should be replaced. When an asset is being replaced with an identical asset, the equivalent annual cost method can be used to calculate an optimum replacement cycle.

Step 1　Calculate the present value of costs for each replacement cycle over one cycle only.

Step 2　Turn the present value of costs for each replacement cycle into an equivalent annual cost (an annuity).

The equivalent annual cost is calculated as follows.

$$\frac{\text{The PV of cost over one replacement cycle}}{\text{The cumulative present value factor for the number of years in the cycle}}$$

Equivalent annual benefit

The equivalent annual benefit is the annual annuity with the same value as the net present value of an investment project.

3. Capital rationing

Capital rationing is a situation in which a company has a limited amount of capital to invest in potential projects, such that the different possible investments need to be compared with one another in order to allocate the capital available most effectively.

资金限制是一个公司在投资潜在的项目时资金有限。这时候这些潜在的不同的项目就要比较，公司选择如何用有限的资金更有效的投资这些项目。

Capital rationing arises for two main reasons：

Soft capital rationing — a firm can get the cash but decides not to; this is typical of a larger company that wants to keep its gearing under control.（公司有资金但是想控制他们的 gearing，所以投资项目的时候会考虑资金分配问题）

Hard capital rationing — a firm cannot get cash from the capital markets; typically this means that the firm is small or does not have an established trading record.（公司没钱，然后这个时候投资项目的时候就要根据手上可利用的资金来进行决策）

3.1　Soft capital rationing may arise for one of the following reasons.

a) Management may be reluctant to issue additional share capital because of concern that this may lead to outsiders gaining control of the business.

b) Management may be unwilling to issue additional share capital if it will lead to a dilution of earnings per share.

c) Management may not want to raise additional debt capital because they do not wish to be committed to large fixed interest payments.

d) Management may wish to limit investment to a level that can be financed solely from retained earnings.

　　a）管理者不愿意多发行股本，因为考虑到这可能使得外部人获得公司的控制权

　　b）管理者不愿意多发行股本，因为这可能稀释每股收益

　　c）管理者不愿意发行债权资本，因为他们不愿意支付大额的利息支付

　　d）管理者可能想限制他们的投资水平因为投资仅仅依靠留存收益

3.2　Hard capital rationing may arise for one of the following reasons.

　　a) Raising new finance through the stock market may not be possible if share prices are depressed.

　　b) There may be restrictions on bank lending due to government control.

　　c) Lending institutions may consider an organisation to be too risky to be granted further loan facilities.

　　d) The costs associated with making small issues of capital may be too great.

　　a）如果股价不太好的情况下，从股权市场融资不太可能

　　b）由于政府控制这可能再银行贷款方面有限制

　　b）借款的机构可能考虑企业如果发行更多的债务融资风险会较大

　　d）小型的企业融资成本可能更高

3.3　Single period capital rationing

When capital rationing occurs in a single period，projects are ranked in terms of profitability index. This is the ratio of the NPV of a project to its investment cost. The projects with the highest ratios should be selected for investment.

　　Profitability index = PV/Initial Investment

Divisible projects

Assumptions：

○ The project cannot be postponed.

○ There is complete certainty about the outcome of each project

○ Projects are divisible.

Non-divisible projects

If the projects are not divisible，then the best way to deal with this situation is to use trial and error and test the NPV available from different combinations of projects.

3.4　Problems with PI

　　a) The approach can only be used if projects are divisible.

　　b) The selection criterionis fairly simplistic，taking no account of the possible strategic value of individual investments in the context of the overall objectives of the organisation.

　　c) The Profitability Index ignores the absolute size of individual projects. A project with a high index might be very small and therefore only generate a small NPV.

　　a）该方法只能在项目可分割的情况下使用。

　　b）选择标准是相当简单的，没有考虑到在组织的总体目标的背景下，个人投资可能的

战略价值。

c) 盈利能力指数忽略了单个项目的绝对规模。具有高排序的项目可能非常小，因此只生成较小的 NPV。

考试时文字题解题套路

1) Equivalent annual cost*

a) PV of cash flows

b) Cumulative present value factor：举例查表 3 年 12%的值为 2.402

c) Equivalent annual cost = PV/Equivalent annual cost

d) 比较 2 个项目，哪个净现金流出少，表示成本低，选哪个 题目：2012-06-Q1

2) Profitability Index*

a) 当有 capital limit(ration 配额)时，要以 profitability index 来 rank 项目。

b) 注意项目 divisible 可分否，mutually exclusive 相互冲突否。

c) 对于战略意义重大的项目，即使 NPV 未负，有时也会做，这个看题意。

d) Soft：企业可以融到资本，但是企业不愿意举债。

e) Hard：企业贷不到钱，政府控制了放贷量。

f) 融资顺序：内部资本 R/E——发债（固定利息成本、降低盈利）——发股（EPS 降低、控制降低）。

题目：2011-12-Q1，2014-06-Q1

3) Capital rationing*

Investment 决策的核心是最大化股东利益，只要项目有 + NPV 就投资，但这是基于 perfect capital market 的假定。现实世界，funds 受限，不可能投资所有项目。

i) Soft capital rationing — Internal factors：公司可以融资，但不愿意融资

a) Reluctance to surrender control 发股票融资，可能降低对公司控制

b) Wish only to use retain earnings 只愿意用自有资金

c) Reluctance to dilute EPS 发股票融资，会稀释 EPS

d) Reluctance to pay more interest 不愿意增加利息支付

e) Capital expenditure budgets 资本费用预算节制

ii) Hard capital rationing — External factors 公司想要融资，但融不到资

a) Depressed stock market 股票市场表现不好，投资者不愿意投资

b) Restrictions on bank lending 银行借不到款，可能信用不好，可能政府的挤出效应 crowding-out

c) Conservative lending policies 借款政策保守，企业不满足条件

d) Issue costs 发行成本太高，无法发行

题目：2011-12-Q1

4) Buy or Lease*

a) 计算 Lease 现金流：每年租赁费用 * DF

b) 计算 Borrow Buy 现金流：Maintenance 费用 * DF，再加上初期买，和末期卖的价值 * DF。这里不考虑利息。

c) 比较 1 和 2 的 NPV，然后决定

5) 经营租赁&融资租赁

i) Operating Lease 的好处：

a) 灵活，相当于短期融资；

b) 避免资产过时，尤其是资产更新换代很快时；

c) 可以以不高的成本租到技术性要求很高的设备，虽然会有额外的操作服务费。

ii) Finance leasing 的好处：

a) 融资租赁，相当于长期融资；

b) 当企业想要 NCA，但融资困难时，可以通过经营租赁和融资租赁解决。借钱是需要抵押担保的，但租赁因为物权不转移，通常更容易实现。但如果租金为暗示到账，那租赁标的会被收回。

题目：2013-12-Q

Part E

Business finance

Chapter 12

Sources of finance

1. Short-term sources of finance

A range of short-term sources of finance are available to businesses including overdrafts, short-term loans, trade credit and short-term leases. (短期的融资包含银行透支,短期贷款,短期租赁和赊销的额度)

Short-term finance is usually needed for businesses to run their day to day operations including payment of wages to employees, inventory ordering and supplies. Businesses with seasonal peaks and troughs and those engaged in international trade are likely to be heavy users of short-term finance. (短期的融资对于企业日常的经营非常的需要,日常的经验包含:给员工支付的工资,持有的存货,有季节需要的企业和参与国际贸易的都需要短期的融资)

1.1 Overdrafts

Where payments from a current account exceed income to the account for a temporary period, the bank may agree to finance a deficit balance on the account by means of an overdraft.

They can be arranged relatively quickly, and offer a level of flexibility with regard to the amount borrowed at any time, whilst interest is only paid when the account is overdrawn.

Overdrafts are normally repayable on demand.

如果经常账户的支出在一段时间内超过收入,银行可以同意通过透支的方式为账户赤字提供资金。

透支可以比较快地安排,并提供一定程度的灵活性,在任何时间的贷款金额,当透支时只需要支付透支的利息。

透支通常是按要求偿还的。

1.2 Short-term loans

A term loan is a loan for a fixed amount for a specified period, usually from a bank. It is drawn in full at the beginning of the loan period and repaid at a specified time or in defined installments. Term loans are offered with a variety of repayment schedules. Often, the interest and capital repayments are predetermined

短期贷款是在一定期间从银行借固定的金额。每期固定还款,利息和还本一般都提前在借款合同协商好。

1.3 Overdrafts and short-term loans compared

In most cases, when a customer wants finance to help with 'day to day' trading and cash flow needs, an overdraft would be the appropriate method of financing.

When a customer wants to borrow from a bank for only a short period of time, even for the purchase of a major fixed asset such as an item of plant or machinery, an overdraft facility might be more suitable than a loan.

However, a mix of overdrafts and loans might be suggested in some cases.

在大多数情况下,当客户需要融资来满足"日常"交易和现金流需求时,透支将是合适的融资方式。

当客户只想从银行借一段很短的时间,甚至是购买一项重要的固定资产,如厂房或机器时,透支安排可能比贷款更合适。

然而,在某些情况下,可能建议将透支和贷款混合使用。

1.4 Advantages of an overdraft over a loan:

a) The customer only pays interest when he is overdrawn.

b) The bank has the flexibility to review the customer's overdraft facility periodically, and perhaps agree to additional facilities, or insist on a reduction in the facility.

An overdraft can do the same job as a loan: a facility can simply be renewed every time it comes up for review

1.5 Advantages of a loan for longer term lending:

a) Both the customer and the bank know exactly what the repayments of the loan will be and how much interest is payable, and when. This makes planning (budgeting) simpler.

b) The interest rate on the loan balance is likely to be lower than the interest charged on overdrawn balances.

c) The customer does not have to worry about the bank deciding to reduce or withdraw an overdraft facility before he is in a position to repay what is owed.

d) Loans normally carry a facility letter setting out the precise terms of the agreement.

1.6 Trade credit

Trade credit represents an interest-free short-term loan.

Current assets such as raw materials may be purchased on credit with payment terms normally varying from between 30 to 90 days.

In a period of high inflation, purchasing via trade credit will be very helpful in keeping costs down. However, it is important to take into account the loss of discounts suppliers offer for early payment.

Unacceptable delays in payment will worsen a company's credit rating and additional credit may become difficult to obtain.

赊销期可能是一个无期的短期贷款

1.7 Leasing

Rather than buying an asset outright, using either available cash resources or borrowed funds, a business may lease an asset.

Operating leases are in effect a short-term source of finance for non-current assets, and finance leases are a long-term source of finance.

Many lessors are financial intermediaries such as banks and insurance companies. The range of assets leased is wide, including office equipment and computers, cars and commercial vehicles, aircraft, ships and buildings.

Leasing was covered in detail in Chapter 11.

Benefits of leasing:

operating lease:

a) Acts as source of short term-finance

b) Offers a solution to the obsolescence problem

c) Can be cancelled without penalty

d) Provide access to skilled maintenance

e) The ownership remain with the lessor

finance lease:

a) Acts as source of long term-finance

b) The ownership of the leased asset is transferred to the lessees

Both operating lease and finance lease access to non-current asset in cases where borrowing may be difficult or even not possible for a company

Summary

Types	Pros & cons(优缺点)
Overdraft A limit is agreed with a bank. interest is paid on the daily cash balance subject to instant recall	Flexible form of finance but risky because of instant recall
Short-term loan	More secure than an overdraft but less flexible
Trade credit paying suppliers later	Tempting but risks loss of supplier goods discounts
Lease finance	Operating leases covered in previous chapter

Short-term finance is usually cheaper than long-term finance so some companies adopt an "aggressive" approach and rely mainly on short-term finance. This carries risk but potentially results in higher profits.

2. Debt finance

A range of long-term sources of finance are available to businesses including debt finance, leasing, venture capital and equity finance. (长期融资包括债务融资, 租赁, 股权投资和风险投资)

Long-term finance is used for major investments and is usually more expensive and less flexible than short-term finance.（比起短期投资长期投资更加昂贵不太灵活）

The choice of debt finance that a company can make depends on：

a) The size of the company；a public issue of bonds is only available to a large company

b) The duration of the required financing

c) Whether a fixed or floating interest rate is preferred（fixed rates are more expensive，but floating rates are riskier）

d) The security（collateral）that can be offered and the security that may be demanded by a lender.

Factors to consider when choosing a source of debt finance

a) cost-issue cost，interest to be charged repayment term

b) Maturity-the period the debt is taken should be matched against the period for which the company needs the finance

c) Finance risk

d) Availability（能否借到）

2.1 type of debt finance include the following

Bank loans	Bonds(debenture/loan notes)
Available over a range of time period with flexible repayment schedules	IOUs sold to investors normally fixed interest and redeemable
Normally secured on the assets of the business by a fixed or floating charge	Secured&carry loan covenants
Must be repaid if loan covenants on gearing or asset disposal are broken	Can often be redeemed early at the company's discretion
	Carries a credit rating
Available to most companies	Often cheaper because avoid bank fees&liquid investment
Supported by the loan guarantee scheme for small business	Can be convertible
Quick to arrange	Can be zero coupon
	Can be in foreign currency(Eurobond)

2.2 Advantages of bank loans and bonds：

Bank loans	Bonds
Available to most companies	Often cheaper because avoid bank fees&liquid investment
Supported by the loan guarantee scheme for small businesses	Can be convertible
Quick to arrange	Can be zero coupon
	Can be in foreign currency（Eurobond）

Deep discount bonds are bonds or loan notes issued at a price which is at a large discount to the nominal value of the notes, and which will be redeemable at nominal value (or above nominal value) when they eventually mature. (折价发行的债券就是发行价额远远低于他们的票面价值,最终偿还的是票面价值或者高于他们的票面价值)

Zero coupon bonds are bonds that are issued at a discount to their redemption value, but no interest is paid on them. (零息债券以票面价值发行但是没有利息)

Convertible bonds can (at the holder's option) be converted into ordinary shares at some future date instead of being held to maturity. Convertibles are a hybrid of debt and equity and are a debt sweetener. This means that a lower rate of interest can be paid on the debt. (可转债可以在未来期间转换成为普通股 可转债是债和股的混合)

Conversion value = Conversion ratio × market price per share Conversion premium = Current market value − current conversion value (公式熟记,会运用)

Benefit of convertible debt: 1 self-liquidation the debt will be converted into ordinary share if the conversion value is greater than the redemption value if it is the case it will not need to be redeemed 2 lower interest rate is required 3 more attractive than bank loan for lender

3. Venture capital

Venture capital is risk capital, normally provided by a venture capital firm or individual venture capitalist, in return for an equity stake.

High growth potential, high returns, significant amounts.

The return is generated by an eventual flotation or sale of companies that they finance. Failure to hit targets set by the venture capitalist can lead to extra shares being transferred to their ownership at no additional cost. This is called an equity ratchet.

风险资本是风险资本,通常由风险投资公司或个人风险资本家提供,以换取股权。

高增长潜力,高回报,数量可观。

这些回报是由他们融资的公司最终上市或出售产生的。未能达到风险投资家设定的目标可能导致额外的股份被转移到他们的手中,而不需要额外的成本。这被称为股权棘轮。

4. Equity finance and preference shares

Equity finance is raised through the sale of ordinary shares to investors via a new issue or a rights issue.

4.1 Ordinary shares

Ordinary share owners have the right to vote on directors appointments, and to receive a share of any dividend that is agreed by the board. (普通股拥有投票权收股利)

4.2 Preference shares

Preference shares are shares which give the right to receive (fixed) dividends before any dividends can be paid to ordinary shareholders. They have no voting rights. (优先股股东比普通股股东有优先收到股利的权利但是他们没有投票权)

Advantages over debt capital

a) Dividends do not have to be paid if company performance is poor, whereas interest must be paid on debt capital regardless of profit.

b) Preference shares are not secured on company assets.

Preference shareholders usually have no voting rights so there is no dilution of control.

Disadvantage

Preference share capital is not as tax efficient as debt capital, as dividends paid are not tax deductible, whereas interest on debt is.

4.3 Stock market listing

Advantages

a) Access to a wider pool of finance

b) Improved marketability of shares

c) Enhanced public image

d) Easier to seek growth by acquisition

e) Original owners realizing holding

f) Original owners selling holding to obtain funds for other project

a) 获得更广泛的资金来源

b) 提高了股票的销售性

c) 增强公众形象

d) 更容易通过收购寻求企业增长

e) 原所有者实现持股

f) 原业主出售股权以获得其他项目的资金

Disadvantages

a) There will be significantly greater public regulation, accountability and scrutiny.

b) A wider circle of investors with more exacting requirements will hold shares.

c) There will be additional costs involved in making share issues, including brokerage commissions and underwriting fees

a) 将有更大的公共监管、问责制和审查。

b) 持有股份的投资者范围会更广,要求也会更严格。

c) 发行股票会有额外的成本,包括经纪佣金和承销费用

Methods of obtaining a listing

○ An initial public offer (IPO)

○ A placing

○ An introduction

An initial public offer (IPO) is a means of selling the shares of a company to the public at large for the first time. A large issue will probably take the form of an IPO. This is known as flotation. Subsequent issues are likely to be placings or rights issues.

A placing is an arrangement whereby, instead of offering the shares to the general public, the sponsoring investment bank arranges for most of the issue to be bought by a small number of investors, usually institutional investors such as pension funds and insurance companies.

A stock exchange introduction is a method of obtaining a quotation, no shares are made available to the market, neither existing nor newly created shares; nevertheless, the stock market grants a quotation

首次公开发行(IPO)是指公司首次向公众出售股票的一种方式。大的发行可能会采取首次公开募股的形式。这就是所谓的上市。随后的发行可能是配股。

配售是指投资银行不向公众发行股票，而是安排大部分发行股票让少数投资者购买的一种安排，这些投资者通常是养老基金和保险公司等机构投资者。

证券交易所是一种获得报价的方法，它不向市场提供股票，无论是现有的还是新创建的股票；尽管如此，股票市场还是会给出报价

Compare IPO & Placing

- Placings are much cheaper
- Placings are likely to be quicker
- Placings are likely to involve less disclosure of information
- Placing is appropriate for small issues
- IPO is appropriate for large issues

Underwriting

Underwriters are financial institutions which agree (in exchange for a fixed fee, perhaps 2.25% of the finance to be raised) to buy at the issue price any securities which are not subscribed for by the investing public.

Underwriters remove the risk of a share issue's being undersubscribed.

Ordinary offers for sale (IPOs) are likely to be underwritten.

4.4 Right issue

A rights issue is an offer to existing shareholders enabling them to buy more shares, usually at a price lower than the current market price, and in proportion to their existing shareholding.

For example, a rights issue on a one for four basis at 280c per share would mean that a company is inviting its existing shareholders to subscribe for one new share for every four shares they hold, at a price of 280c per new share.

（以低于市场的价格发行股票给现有的股东）

Advantages

a) Rights issues are cheaper than IPOs to the general public.

b) Rights issues are more beneficial to existing shareholders than issues to the general public.

c) Relative voting rights are unaffected if shareholders all take up their rights.

d) The finance raised may be used to reduce gearing in book value terms by increasing share capital and/or to pay off long-term debt which will reduce gearing in market value terms.

4.4.1 Issue price

Rights issues shares are offered at a discount to the market value. It can be difficult to judge what the amount of the discount should be.

4.4.2 Relative cost

Rights issues are cheaper than other methods of raising finance by issuing new equity, such as an initial public offer (IPO) or a placing, due to the lower transactions costs associated with rights issues.

4.4.3 Ownership and control

As the new shares are being offered to existing shareholders, there is no dilution of ownership and control, providing shareholders take up their rights.（控制权不会稀释）

4.4.4 Gearing and financial risk

Increasing the weighting of equity finance in the capital structure of XX can decrease its gearing and its financial risk. The shareholders of the company may see this as a positive move, depending on their individual risk preference positions.

4.5 Stock split

A stock split occurs where, for example, each ordinary share of $1 each is split into two shares of 50c each, thus creating cheaper shares with greater marketability. There is possibly an added psychological advantage in that investors may expect a company which splits its shares in this way to be planning for substantial earnings growth and dividend growth in the future

（股票分割,就是比如原来是每股1元的股票,分割成2股每股0.5元）

As a consequence, the market price of shares may benefit. For example, if one existing share of $1 has a market value of $6, and is then split into two shares of 50c each, the market value of the new shares might settle at, say, $3.10 instead of the expected $3, in anticipation of strong future growth in earnings and dividends.

A stock split changes the share capital but does not raise any new equity finance for the company. It also leaves the company's reserves (as shown in its statement of financial position) unaffected.

4.6 Scrip issue

A scrip issue occurs when a company issues new shares to existing shareholders in proportion to their existing holdings at no charge. The issue is made out of distributable reserves (retained profits).

The difference between a stock split and a scrip issue is that a scrip issue converts equity reserves into share capital, whereas a stock split leaves reserves unaffected.

5. Islamic finance(掌握每种的概念区别,考试考简单题)

Islamic finance operates under the principle that there should be a link between the economic activity that creates value and the financing of that activity.伊斯兰金融的原则

是，经济活动的创造价值和融资方式之间是有联系的，不能收利息，收利息犯法。

a) **Murabaha:** 类似于商业信用/贷款 Trade credit/loan,利润预先约定,无利息,借方卖了产品,借方和贷方分享收益。Pre-arranged mark up for convenience of later payment, no interest.

b) **Musharaka:** 类似于风投 Venture capital,收益共享,无分红,损失的话,按照资本投入承担。

Profit share per contract, no dividends, losses per capital contribution, both parties participate

c) **Mudaraba:** 类似于股权投资 Equity,利润预先约定,无分红,损失的话,全部由出钱的人承担。

Profit share per contract, no dividends, losses borne by capital provider, organisation runs business

d) **Ijara:** 类似于租赁 Leasing,债主拥有所有权并承担主要风险,需要负责大修和重要保险。

Whatever the other features, lessor remains asset owner and incurs risks of ownership.

e) **Sukuk:** 类似于债券 Bonds,对资产和收益享有所有权,所以既有 debt 债权性质,又有 equity 所有权性质。对于潜在的有形资产,持有股票可能是基于资产(销售/售后回租)或资产(证券化)。

Underlying tangible asset in which holder shares may be asset-based (sale/leaseback) or asset-backed (securitisation).

f) **Salam:** 类似于远期合同 Forward contract,商品约定未来某日卖,但现金可以折现到当下,预先付款。

Commodity sold for future delivery, cash received at discount from financial institution, payments received in advance.

g) **Istisna:** 类似于分期付款 Phased payments,用于项目筹措,先付首付款,然后用项目进行的钱再支付分期款。

Project funding, initial payment and then instalments from business undertaking the project.

5.1 Riba

Riba (interest) is forbidden in Islamic finance.

Making profits by lending alone and the charging of interest is forbidden under Sharia'a law. The Islamic bank arranges their business in such a way that the bank's profitability is closely tied to that of the client. The bank stands to take profit or make loss in line with the projects they are financing and as such must be more involved in the investment decision-making

5.2 Murabaha (trade credit)

Here is a pre-agreed mark-up to be paid, in recognition of the conveniencc of paying later, for an asset that is transferred immediately. There is no interest charged.

5.3 Musharaka (venture capital)

Profits are shared according to a pre-agreed contract. There are no dividends paid. Losses are shared according to capital contribution.

5.4 Mudaraba (equity)

Profits are shared according to a pre-agreed contract. There are no dividends paid. Losses are solely attributable to the provider of capital.

5.5 Ijara (leasing)

Whether an operating or finance transaction, in Ijara the lessor is still the owner of the asset and incurs the risk of ownership. This means that the lessor will be responsible for major maintenance and insurance which is different from a conventional finance lease.

5.6 Sukuk (bonds)

There is an underlying tangible asset and the Sukuk holder shares in the risk and rewards of ownership. This gives the Sukuk properties of equity finance as well as debt finance.

考试时文字答题套路

1) Long-term debt finance

a) Long-term bank loan：长期银行贷款，有固定抵押，每年固定付息。如果固定资产不足以担保，怎可能无法拿到贷款。如果付息延迟，银行可能会拿去抵押物。

b) Bonds or Loan note：企业债券，分可赎回和不可赎回。如同股票，可以在资本市场交易，也可以以外币发行。发债成本比发股成本低，是个好选择。

c) Convertible bonds or loan notes：可转债，因为有股票选择权，所以通常利率比较低。

d) Deep discount bonds and zero coupon bonds：折价债券、零息债券，因为是折价发行，往往是没有额外利息或者比较低的利息，投资者通过债券升值而收益。

e) Sale and leaseback：比较适合大宗物品售卖后回租，可以作为长期融资的一种方式。但对抵押物要求比较高

f) Venture capital：一般风投对高增长预期、高回报、金额比较大的项目感兴趣

题目：2010-12-Q2，2014-06-Q4

2) Islamic finance★

原则：伊斯兰金融是要求风险和回报由出资者和资金使用者共同承担，不允许直接收利息！

Ha：类似 Trade credit/loan，预先约定了交易的利润，必须以资产为依托，伴随资产转移，支付约定利润和本金。不收利息。举例：汽车商让银行购买一辆汽车，然后明示利润额将其出售给顾客，支付则延期进行。

Ka：类似于 Venture capital，对以一个约定的项目合同，利润共享，不支付分红。如果损失，那出资人按照股份比例分摊损失。

Ba：类似于 Equity 信托出资，对以一个约定的项目合同，利润共享，不支付分红。如果损失，那完全由出资人承担损失。

Ra：类似于 leasing，债主拥有所有权并承担主要风险，需要负责大修和重要保险。

Uk：类似于债券，对资产和收益享有所有权，所以既有 debt 债权性质，又有 equity 所有权性质。

题目：2013-12-Q4

3) Convertible loan note ★

a) 计算 average historical share price growth

b) 计算 further share price，然后计算 conversion value 并跟直接现金赎回比较，取高值。

c) DF 这算 Market value of loan note

d) 特点：

○ Self liquidating 自动清算，如果客户转股权了，即债务期满自动赎回，无需支付后续利息

○ Low interest rate 因为有了股权转换权，则利率相对于债来说，会更低

○ Increase in debt capacity on conversion 转换 = debt 降低 equity 增加，gearing 降低。举债能力更强

○ More attractive than ordinary debt 对股价乐观的投资者更喜欢，即使当前经济状况不好

题目：2012-12-Q3，2014-12-Q2

4) Right Issue 相关计算

a) 计算 Ex right price per share

b) 如果用 Right issue 资本，偿债，可以赎回多少？

c) Before-tax interest savings，然后计算税后节约的 FC

d) Earnings after 偿债，然后计算 revised EPS

e) 题目告知 P/E ratio 不变，由 revised EPS × P/E ratio 得到估价现值

f) 比较估价在偿债前和偿债后的变化，评论

题目：2015-06-Q4

5) Right Issue 考虑因素

a) Issue Price：通常是对当前估价折价发行，但折价多少？

b) Relative cost：比其他发股方式便宜，譬如 IPO（常被风投抽水 3%～5%）

c) Ownership and control：如果完全行权，不会对股权比例有稀释

d) Gearing and financial risk：增加 equity 比重，会降低杠杆和财务风险。

题目：2014-12-Q5

6) 融资方和贷款方考虑

a) 融资方考虑：

○ 成本：如利息，偿付条款

○ 到期日 Maturity：融资需要实现的目标是短期目标还是长期目标。短期借款比较灵活，长期借款一般为长约

○ Financial risk：负债会增加公司 gearing。需要考虑公司是否有能力偿付目前的利息，以及高杠杆对未来投资人投资决策的影响。

◦ Availability：是否有能力获得贷款，这与公司的规模和经营现状等有关。譬如公司想 issue traded bonds，但很少有 SMEs 可以发行

b）贷款方考虑：

◦ Risk and ability to meet financial obligation：需要查过往记录，管理层管理是否有效，未来现金流是否有能力偿付贷款

◦ Security 是否有足够抵押物。如果没有，通常会调高利息来匹配对应的高风险

◦ Legal restrictions on borrowings 公司章程对公司的负债是否有要求，不允许超过多少

题目：2012-06-Q3

7）**Traded bonds MV 影响因素**

a) Amount of interest payment 利息额高，回报高，估值高

b) Frequency of interest payments 利息支付月频繁，估值高

c) Redemption value 赎回价格越高，估值高

d) Period to redemption 赎回周期越长，折现率高，估值低

e) Cost of debt 当前市场利息水平会影响利息预期，利息预期（回报率要求）越高，折价率高，估值低

f) Convertibility 可转股权否，多了股权选择权，利息要求会低，同时还要考虑股价走势，股价好，估价高

题目：2010-12-Q2，2011-06-Q2

8）**发股 VS. Sale & Leaseback**

a）发股要评估发行量，发行价（折价多少发行），发行后的股价，EPS 等影响是多少。发股后股息政策，股东反馈。好处是可以降低杠杆，提高对外举债的能力。

b）Sale & Leaseback：是一个提高流动性的好办法，尤其将大宗固定资产 sale&leaseback，可以补充大量流动资金。取决于抵押物和贷款银行。

题目：2011-06-Q3

9）**Scrip Share 配股**

a）可以降低 gear & financial risk，提高公司举债能力。

b）公司不用派现金股息，以股份替代，缓解公司资金流动性。

c）缺点在于，如果公司需要维持当前的每股股息，则总体股息支出会提高。

题目：2011-06-Q3

Chapter 13

Dividend policy

1. Internal sources of finance

Internal sources of finance include retained earnings and increasing working capital efficiency.(增加留存收益或者营运资本)

Retained earnings

Retained earnings is surplus cash that has not been needed for operating costs, interest payments, tax liabilities, asset replacement or cash dividends.

Retained earnings belong to shareholders and are classed as equity financing.(留存收益就是本年取得的利润然后交完税后分配给股东后剩下来的留在企业的可以用的钱)

Advantages of using retained earnings

a) Retained earnings are a flexible source of finance; companies are not tied to specific amounts or specific repayment patterns.

b) Using retained earnings does not involve a change in the pattern of shareholdings and no dilution of control.

c) Retained earnings have no issue costs.

a) 留存收益是一种灵活的资金来源；公司不受特定金额或特定还款模式的限制。

b) 留存收益的使用不涉及持股模式的改变，也不涉及控制权的稀释。

c) 留存收益不存在发行成本。

Disadvantages of using retained earnings

a) Shareholders may be sensitive to the loss of dividends that will result from retention for reinvestment, rather than paying dividends.

b) Not so much a disadvantage as a misconception, that retaining profits is a cost-free method of obtaining funds. There is an opportunity cost in that if dividends were paid, the cash received could be invested by shareholders to earn a return.

a) 股东可能对股息的损失很敏感，因为保留是为了再投资，而不是支付股息。

b) 与其说是缺点不如说是一种误解，认为保留利润是一种免费获得资金的方法。如果支付股息，收到的现金可能会被股东投资以赚取回报的机会成本

2. Dividend policy

When deciding on the dividends to pay out to shareholders, one of the main considerations of the directors will be the amount of earnings they wish to retain to meet financing needs.

Dividend policy is largely a matter of common sense, and is a reflection of the investment decision and the financing decision.（我们要考虑好 是分给股东的股利多还是留存下来以便我们可以投资的钱比较多 这样的考虑下就形成了不同的股利政策）

Investment decision

If the company is going through a growth phase, it is unlikely to have sufficient liquidity to pay dividends. In this case shareholder expectations may well be for the dividend to remain low or 0. This will not be a problem as long as the share price is rising.（当公司处于高速增长的阶段我们就不分配股利,把钱都用于投资项目上来赚更多的钱）

Financing decision

If a company can borrow to finance its investments, it can still pay dividends. This is sometimes called borrowing to pay a dividend.

There are legal constraints over a company's ability to do this; it is only legal if a company has accumulated realized profits.（如果公司可以借钱,那我们就可以用借的钱来分配股利但是这一般是有法律限制,法律允许当公司有留存收益时才能分配股利）

2.1 Dividends as a signal to investors

The dividend declared can be interpreted as a signal from directors to shareholders about the strength of underlying project cash flows. Investors usually expect a consistent dividend policy from the company, with stable dividends each year or, even better, steady dividend growth.

2.2 Theories of dividend policy

Residual theory

Dividends should be the amount of after-tax profits left over (the 'residual' amount) after setting aside money to invest in all viable business opportunities.

2.3 Traditional view

The price of a share depends on both current dividends and expectations of future dividend growth, given shareholders' required rate of return.

Irrelevancy theory

Modigliani and Miller (MM) proposed that in a perfect capital market, no taxes or tax preferences so shareholders are indifferent between dividends and capital gains, and no transaction costs so the value of a company is determined solely by the 'earning power' of its assets and investments.

If a company pursues a consistent dividend policy, it will tend to attract to itself a clientele consisting of those preferring its particular payout ratio.

2.4 Scrip dividends(以股代息)

A scrip dividend is a dividend paid by the issue of additional company shares, rather than by cash. With enhanced scrip dividends, the value of the shares offered is much greater than the cash alternative, giving investors an incentive to choose the shares.（发

行股票的方式代替付股利）

Advantages of scrip dividends

a) They can preserve a company's cash position if a substantial number of shareholders take up the share option.

b) Investors may be able to obtain tax advantages if dividends are in the form of shares.

c) Investors looking to expand their holding can do so without incurring the transaction costs of buying more shares.

d) A small scrip dividend issue will not dilute the share price significantly. However, if cash is not offered as an alternative, empirical evidence suggests that the share price will tend to fall.

e) A share issue will decrease the company's gearing, and may therefore enhance its borrowing capacity.

a) 如果相当多的股东持有股票期权，他们可以保留公司的现金头寸。

b) 如果股息是股票形式的，投资者可以获得税收优惠。

c) 希望扩大持股的投资者可以在不产生购买更多股票的交易成本的情况下这样做。

d) 发行小股股利不会显著稀释股价。然而，如果不提供现金作为替代，经验证据表明，股价将倾向于下跌。

e) 股票发行将降低公司的杠杆率，并因此可能增强其借贷能力。

Disadvantages of scrip dividends

a) Assuming that dividend per share is maintained or increased, the total cash paid as a dividend will increase.

b) Scrip dividends may be seen as a negative signal by the market ie the company is experiencing cash flow issues.

a) 假设每股股息维持或增加，作为股息支付的现金总额将增加。

b) 以股派息可能被市场视为一个负面信号，即公司正在经历现金流问题。

2.5 Share repurchase

In many countries companies have the right to buy back shares from shareholders who are willing to sell them, subject to certain conditions.

Public companies with a large amount of surplus cash may offer to repurchase (and then cancel) some shares from its shareholders. A reason for this is to find a way of offering cash returns to investors without increasing dividend payments. Higher dividend payments would affect investor expectations about future dividends and dividend growth, whereas share buybacks would not affect dividend expectations at all. In addition, by reducing the number of shares in issue, the company should be able to increase the earnings per share (EPS) for the remaining shares.（拥有大量现金的公司可能想股票回购，回购回来后注销这些股票，为什么这样做的原因是这样可以不通过分配股利的方式把现金给投资者，过高的股利会影响投资者对于未来分配股利的预期，股票回顾不会影响这些预期，同时注销股票，股票数额变少，会增加我们的每股收益）

Advantages of share repurchase

a) Finding a use for surplus cash, which may be a 'dead asset'.

b) Increase in earnings per share through a reduction in the number of shares in issue. This should lead to a higher share price than would otherwise be the case, and the company should be able to increase dividend payments on the remaining shares in issue.

c) Increase in gearing. Repurchase of a company's own shares allows debt to be substituted for equity, so raising gearing. This will be of interest to a company wanting to increase its gearing without increasing its total long-term funding.

d) Readjustment of the company's equity base to more appropriate levels, for a company whose business is in decline.

e) Possibly preventing a takeover or enabling a quoted company to withdraw from the stock market.

Disadvantages of share repurchase

a) It can be hard to arrive at a price that will be fair both to the vendors and to any shareholders who are not selling shares to the company.

b) A repurchase of shares could be seen as an admission that the company cannot make better use of the funds than the shareholders.

c) Some shareholders may suffer from being taxed on a capital gain following the purchase of their shares rather than receiving dividend income.

Dividend Policy 考虑因素

a) Profitability：付分红但要保持一定的 R/E 再投资，赚更多钱

b) Liquidity：分红也是现金付款。不能影响公司现金流动性

c) Legal & other restrictions：UK 法律规定，分红不能超过累计 net realized profit

d) The need for finance：公司有融资需求，会首先考虑不分红，满足公司流动现金需求

e) The level of financial risk：如果杠杆已很高，应该用分红的钱还债，降低负债率

f) 其他影响：因为上市公司分红数据是公开的，所以会影响投资者对公司盈利能力的判断和投资偏好，是一个信号 signaling。经常分红，且分红比较高的公司，更受投资者追捧。

题目：2010-12-Q4

Chapter 14

Gearing and capital structure

1. Gearing

Gearing is the amount of debt finance a company uses relative to its equity finance.

The financial risk of a company's capital structure can be measured by a gearing ratio, a debt ratio or debt/equity ratio, or by the interest cover.

A high level of debt creates financial risk. Financial risk can be seen from different points of view.

杠杆是指公司使用的债务融资相对于其股权融资的金额。

公司资本结构的财务风险可以通过杠杆比率、债务比率或债务/权益比率或利息保障来衡量。

高水平的债务会带来金融风险。财务风险可以从不同的角度来看待。

Ordinary shareholders

Higher levels of financial gearing increase the variability of after-tax profits and earnings per share.（高的财务杠杆增加公司税后利润和每股收益的变动性）

The company as a whole

If a company builds up debts that it cannot pay when they fall due, it will be forced into liquidation.（如果公司借了太多的债务而无法偿还的时候就面临破产清算的危险）

Suppliers/lenders

If a company cannot pay its debts, the company will go into liquidation owing suppliers money that they are unlikely to recover in full. Lenders will therefore want a higher interest yield to compensate them for higher financial risk and gearing.（如果公司无法偿还他们的债务，公司会破产清 sauna，这个时候借款人可能无法全部收回他们的款项，因为他们希望更好的利率来补偿这种高的财务风险）

1.1 Financial gearing（财务杠杆）

measures the relationship between shareholders' funds（equity）and prior charge capital. It indicates the degree to which the organisation's activities are funded by borrowed funds, as opposed to shareholder funds.

$$\text{Financial gearing} = \frac{\text{Prior charge capital}}{\text{Equity capital（including reserves）}}$$

$$\text{and} = \frac{\text{Prior charge capital}}{\text{Total capital employed}^*}$$

* Either including or excluding non-controlling (minority) interests, deferred tax and deferred income

$$\text{Financial gearing} = \frac{\text{Market value of prior charge capital}}{\text{Market value of equity} + \text{Market value of prior charge capital}}$$

1.2 Operational gearing(经营杠杆)

measures the relationship between contribution and profit before interest and tax. It indicates the degree to which an organisation's profits are made up of variable (as opposed to fixed) costs. (contribution = sales-variable cost)

Financial risk, as we have seen, can be measured by financial gearing. Business risk refers to the risk of making only low profits, or even losses, due to the nature of the business that the company is involved in. One way of measuring business risk is by calculating a company's operational gearing.

$$\text{Operational gearing} = \frac{\text{Contribution}}{\text{Profit before interest and tax (PBIT)}}$$

Contribution is sales minus variable cost of sales.

The significance of operational gearing is as follows.

a) If contribution is high but PBIT is low, the company has a high proportion of fixed costs, which are only just covered by contribution. Business risk will be high.

b) If contribution is not much bigger than PBIT, the company has a low proportion of fixed costs, which are fairly easily covered by contribution. Business risk will be low

1.3 Interest coverage ratio

The interest cover ratio is a measure of financial risk which is designed to show the risks in terms of profit rather than in terms of capital values.

The reciprocal of this, the interest to profit ratio, is also sometimes used. As a general guide, an interest coverage ratio of less than three times is considered low, indicating that profitability is too low given the gearing of the company. An interest coverage ratio of more than seven is usually seen as safe. 利息覆盖率是衡量金融风险的一个指标,其目的是通过利润而不是资本价值来显示风险。它的倒数,利息与利润的比率,有时也被使用。一般情况下,低于三倍的利息覆盖率就被认为偏低,说明考虑到公司的杠杆率,公司的盈利能力太低。利息保障比率超过7通常被视为安全的。

$$\text{Interest coverage ratio} = \frac{\text{Profit before interest and tax}}{\text{Interest}}$$

1.4 The debt ratio

Another measure of financial risk is the debt ratio.

Debt ratio = Total debts : Total assets

Debt does not include long-term provisions and liabilities such as deferred taxation.

There is no firm rule on the maximum safe debt ratio but, as a general guide, you might regard 50% as a safe limit to debt.

1.5 Determinant the suitability of the gearing mix

Life cycle	A new, growing business will find it difficult to forecast cash flows with any certainty so high levels of gearing are unwise.
Operational gearing	If fixed costs are high then contribution (before fixed costs) will be high relative to profits (after fixed costs). High fixed costs mean cash flow is volatile, so high gearing is not sensible.
Stability of revenue	If operating in a highly dynamic business environment then high gearing is not sensible.
Security	If unable to offer security then debt will be difficult and expensive to obtain.

2. Effect on shareholder wealth

Debt finance may add to shareholder wealth for many reasons. (advantages)

a) Debt is a cheap source of finance And any profit left after paying the interest belongs to the shareholders.

b) The use of debt is a signal of confidence in the company's cash flows This can be true. But banks would still expect to see some equity being invested.

c) The use of debt is a discipline on management Careful cash flow management is needed.

d) The use of debt avoids dilution of earnings per share A motive in the real world but not may be valid if higher debt results in a lower P/E ratio.

Disadvantages of debt finance:

a) Debt creates higher variability in dividends (higher financial risk).

b) Debt creates higher default risks which can lead to financial distress costs such as lower sales or higher supplier costs.

债务融资可以增加股东的财富，原因有很多。

a) 债务是一种廉价的融资来源，支付利息后剩下的利润归股东所有。

b) 使用债务是对公司现金流有信心的信号。但银行仍希望看到一些股权投资。

c) 债务的使用是一种管理的纪律，谨慎的现金流管理是必要的。

d) 使用债务避免稀释每股收益但如果较高的债务导致较低的市盈率，这可能是无效的。

债务融资的弊端：

a) 债务在股息方面产生更高的可变性（更高的财务风险）。

b) 债务造成更高的违约风险，从而导致财务困境成本，如销售下降或供应商成本上升。

3. Finance for small and medium-sized entities

Small and medium-sized entities (SMEs) have the following characteristics.

a) Firms are likely to be unquoted private companies.

b) The business is owned by a few individuals, typically a family group.

c) They are not micro businesses — very small businesses that act as the owners' medium for self employment.

中小企业具有以下特点：
a）公司很可能是未上市的私营公司。
b）企业由少数个人所有，通常是一个家族集团。
c）它们不是微型企业——是作为个体经营业主中介的小型企业。

The high failure rate for small companies means that they face particular problems in raising external finance and have few shareholders which makes it difficult to raise internal finance; this is sometimes referred to as the funding gap.

Even medium-sized companies will sometimes find that they cannot obtain more debt finance, due inadequate security (in the form of assets). This is a particular problem for medium-term projects which often do not have the security offered by long-term investments in land &buildings create. The difficulty in obtaining medium-term financing is called the maturity gap.

小公司的高失败率意味着其在筹集外部资金方面面临特殊的问题，股东人数少，内部融资困难；这有时被称为资金缺口。

即使是中等规模的公司，有时也会发现由于担保不足（以资产形式），无法获得更多的债务融资。这对于中期项目来说是一个特别的问题，因为这些项目往往没有长期投资（土地或者房屋）所提供的安全性。中期融资难的现象称为期限差额。

The government has recognized these difficulties and has tried to encourage investment in SMEs.

a) Business angel financing are wealthy individuals or groups of individuals who invest directly in small businesses. They are prepared to take high risks in the hope of high returns .

b) Supply chain finance (SCF)

c) Reverse factoring is a method of financing by selling invoices at a small discount (interest rate) in order to obtain the cash in advance of the invoice due date.

d) Crowdfunding is the funding of a project by raising money from a large number of people.（internet）

政府已经认识到这些困难，并努力鼓励对中小企业的投资。（以下几种方式）

a）商业天使融资是指直接投资于小企业的富有的个人或个人团体。他们准备冒高风险，希望获得高回报。

b）供应链金融(SCF)

c）逆保理是指在发票到期日之前以低折扣（利率）出售发票以获得现金的一种融资方式。

d）众筹是指通过向大量的人募集资金来为一个项目融资。

The reason why SMEs have less agency problem than listed company

Listed company
a) there is a separation between ownership and control
b) shareholders and directors are different people the objectives of them may

be different

　　c) directors might act for their own interest rather than those of shareholders

　　d) there is asymmetry of information so it is hard for shareholders to monitor the actions and decisions of directors

　　SME

　　a) shareholders and directors usually are the same person there is no conflict due to different objective of shareholders and directors

　　b) in the case when shareholder and director are different person share of SME are often owned by a small number of shareholders who may be in regular contract with the company and its director the possibility of conflict is very much reduced

考试时文字题解题套路
1) 大公司利益冲突＞SMEs

　　a) 大公司股东和管理层之间存在 agency problem.
　　○ 股东和管理层的目标不一致
　　○ 所有权和控制权分离
　　○ 信息不对称，股东信息比较少不利于监督评判，而管理层掌握大部分信息
　　b) SMEs 上述 3 点都一致，目标一致，控制经营权集中，掌握大部分信息
　　c) 股东数来看，SMEs 股东人数少，股东跟管理层 regular contact 经常接触

题目：2012-06-Q3
2) SME 融资问题-难

SME 不容易吸引投资，投资者认为 SME 存在比较高的 uncertainty and risk：
　　a) 管理不如大公司系统，投资回报预期不明确
　　b) 内控可能不存在，或者执行不利
　　c) 外控也比较少，没有公开的监管（譬如媒体监管或上市公司财报公开要求）
　　d) 大股东凌驾于管理之上，做拍脑门的决定
　　e) 固定有形资产规模较小，不够做抵押担保
来源：考官文章

3) SME 融资渠道

SME 融资渠道：
　　a) 家人朋友
　　b) Business angel 天使投资人：指具有一定净财富的个人或者机构，对具有巨大发展潜力的初创企业进行早期的直接投资，属于一种自发而又分散的民间投资方式。
　　c) Trade credit：就是占用供应商的资金，以延长 T/P 付款期来实现
　　d) Factoring and invoice discounting 通过保理，先拿到 T/R，也可降低坏账率；提供早期折扣让客户尽快付款
　　e) Leasing：以租代买，常见的是租车、租办公室
　　f) Bank finance：中长期贷款需要足够的抵押物，中小企业资本不足，常常只能用短期借贷来满足长期资本需求，风险较高。
　　g) Venture capital：风投，追求高增长、高预期回报、高投资

h）Listing 上市

i）Supply chain financing

j）Crowdfunding

来源：考官文章

4）SME 政府扶持政策

"政府扶持中小企业（原因：支持创新、增加就业）

a）提高政府补助 grant

b）提供税收减免

c）提供专业指导和帮助——如果成立新公司及政策指导、融资指导

d）以政府信用为贷款担保，帮助中小企业贷款

e）政府背景的风投机构，投资 SME 的 equity"

来源：考官文章

5）Supplier chain finance

供应链金融：就是银行将核心企业和上下游企业联系在一起提供灵活运用的金融产品和服务的一种融资模式。即把资金作为供应链的一个溶剂，增加其流动性。

举例：A 为优质买家，信用评级高；B 为供应商。B 供给 A 货，A 签单表示 30 天付款。因为 A 信用评级高，银行见单后愿意以 A 的信用为依托，提前支付货款给 B，并以 A 的信用等级给 B 更优惠的 discount（相当于向银行短期融资的利息成本）

6）Crowdfunding 众筹

众筹：常应用于投资者对项目或想法很感兴趣，有一定信仰，所以愿意承担更高风险，更低回报。由发起人、跟投人、平台构成。具有低门槛、多样性、依靠大众力量、注重创意的特征，是指一种向群众募资，以支持发起的个人或组织的行为。一般而言是通过网络平台连结起赞助者与提案者。群众募资被用来支持各种活动，包含灾害重建、民间集资、竞选活动、创业募资、艺术创作、自由软件、设计发明、科学研究以及公共专案等。

7）Forfaiting 未偿债务买卖

卖方将单据卖给海外 Forfaiter，由 Forfaiter 承担收款风险，将货款折价提前支付给卖方。Forfaiter 可以将应收账款做成金融产品，在货币市场上出售赚取差价。Forfaiting 对卖方而言，折扣率较高，属于比较贵的方式，更适合中长期交易，且交易金额比较大时。（相当于海外保理 Factoring，只是更贵）

补充 ratio analysis

Profitability ratio

$$ROCE = \frac{PBIT}{Capital\ employed}$$

$$ROE = \frac{PAT}{Equity}$$

ROCE = net profit margin * asset turnover

$$Asset\ turnover = \frac{sales}{Capital.employed}$$

$$Net\ profit\ margin = \frac{PBIT}{sales}$$

Chapter 14 Gearing and capital structure

Gearing
Business risk

$$\text{Operational Gearing} = \frac{\text{contribution}}{\text{PBIT}}$$

Financial risk

$$\text{Financial Gearing} = \frac{\text{debt}}{\text{Equity}}$$

$$\text{Interest cover} = \frac{\text{PBIT}}{\text{interest}}$$

Liquidity ratio

$$\text{Current ratio} = \frac{\text{current.asset}}{\text{current.liability}}$$

$$\text{Quick ratio} = \frac{\text{current.asset} - \text{inventory}}{\text{current.liabilities}}$$

$$\text{Inventory days} = \frac{\text{Average.inventory} \times 365}{\text{cost.of.sales}}$$

$$\text{Receivable days} = \frac{\text{Average.receivable} \times 365}{\text{sales}}$$

$$\text{Payable days} = \frac{\text{Average.payable} \times 365}{\text{cost.of.sales}}$$

Stock market ratio (investors return)

$$\text{EPS} = \frac{\text{Profit.after.tax} - \text{perference.dividends}}{\text{No.of.ordinary.shares.in.issue}}$$

$$\text{P/E} = \frac{\text{Market.price.per.share}}{\text{EPS}} = \frac{\text{Total.market.value}}{\text{profit.after.tax}}$$

$$\text{Dividend cover} = \frac{\text{Earning.per.share}}{\text{Dividend.per.share}}$$

$$\text{Dividend yield} = \frac{\text{Dividend.per.share}}{\text{share.price}} = \frac{\text{Total.dividend}}{\text{Total.market.value}}$$

$$\text{TSR} = \frac{\text{Dividend.per.share} + \text{change.in.share.price}}{\text{share.price.at.start.of.period}}$$

Steps of ratio analysis

a) calculation of ratio

b) state the situation compare with the prior year or industry average

c) identify the possible reasons

d) Estimate the consequences or recommendation

（先计算出 ratio，然后和过去或者行业平均值比较，看题目是给的过去年份的还是行业平均值然后分析原因，最后写出结论）

Chapter 15

The cost of capital

1. Cost of capital

The cost of capital is the rate of return that the enterprise must pay to satisfy the providers of funds, and it reflects the riskiness of providing funds. (资本成本就是企业必须满足资金提供者的回报率,同时它也反映了提供资金的风险性)

1.1 Risk-return relationship

The main principle is that the higher the risk faced by the investor, the higher the return they will expect to be paid; this is the risk-return relationship. (一个主要的原则就是高的风险就要求高的回报率这就是风险和回报之间的关系)

1.2 The cost of capital can be analyzed into three elements

1) Risk-free rate of return

This is the return which would be required from an investment if it were completely free from risk. Typically, a risk-free yield is the yield on government securities.

2) Premium for business risk

This is an increase in the required rate of return due to the existence of uncertainty about the future and about a firm's business prospects.

3) Premium for financial risk

This relates to the danger of high debt levels (high gearing).

Cost of capital = Risk-free rate of return + Premium for business risk + Premium for financial risk

1.3 The creditor hierarchy

Increasing risk:
1. Creditors with a fixed charge
2. Creditors with a floating charge
3. Unsecured creditors
4. Preference shareholders
5. Ordinary shareholders

Investors will require a higher return to compensate for risk. This means that the cheapest type of finance is debt (especially if secured) and the most expensive type of finance is equity (ordinary shares). This risk-return relationship is sometimes referred to as the creditor hierarchy. (投资者对于风险可能要求更高的回报,这意味着最便宜的融资

是债务(特别是有担保的债务)最贵的融资方式是股票融资。风险回报的关系有时候也指借款人的层级,如上图所示,等级越高风险越高)

The reasons why the cost of equity is greater than the cost of debt

○ The cost of equity is the return required by ordinary shareholders (equity investors), in order to compensate them for the risk associated with their equity investment, i.e. their investment in the ordinary shares of a company.

○ If the risk of an investment increases, the return expected by the investor also increases. If the risk of a company increases, therefore, its cost of equity also increases.

○ If a company is liquidated, the order in which the claims of creditors are settled is a factor in determining their relative risk.

○ The claims of providers of debt finance (debt holders) must be paid off before any cash can be distributed to ordinary shareholders (the owners).

○ The risk faced by shareholders is therefore greater than the risk faced by debt holders, and the cost of equity is therefore greater than the cost of debt.

Interest on debt finance must be paid before dividends can be paid to ordinary shareholders, so the risk faced by ordinary shareholders is greater than the risk faced by debt holders, since the necessity of paying interest may mean that dividends have to be reduced.

权益成本高于债务成本的原因:

○ 权益成本是普通股股东(权益投资者)为补偿其权益投资(即对公司普通股的投资)所带来的风险而要求的回报。

○ 如果投资风险增加,投资者期望的回报也会增加。因此,如果一家公司的风险增加,它的权益成本也会增加。

○ 如果一家公司被清算,债权人清偿债权的顺序是决定其相对风险的一个因素。

○ 在任何现金可以分配给普通股东(所有者)之前,必须付清债务融资提供者(债权人)的债权。

○ 因此,股东所面临的风险大于债务持有人所面临的风险,股权成本也因此大于债务成本。

债务融资的利息必须在股利支付给普通股股东之前支付,因此普通股股东面临的风险要大于债权人面临的风险,因为支付利息的必要性可能意味着股利必须减少。

2. Dividend growth model(公式熟记会运用,借助题理解)

The dividend growth model can be used to estimate a cost of equity.

Assumptions:

○ The market value of share is directly related to the expected future dividends from the shares.

○ Dividends will be paid in perpetuity

○ Dividends will be constant or growing at a fixed rate

$$K_e = \frac{d_0(1+g)}{P_0} + g \text{ or } k_e = \frac{d_1}{P_0} + g$$

K_e is the cost of equity capital.

d_0 is the current net dividend, d_1 is the next year's net dividend.

g is the expected annual growth in dividend payments(算增长率的方法有2个)。

P_0 is the current market price (ex-div).

There are 2 methods of estimating g that you need to know, but the examiner may give you the rate in the exam.

○ Use historic growth;

○ Use current re-investment levels:

$$g = br$$

g is the annual growth rate in dividends.

b is the proportion of profits that are retained.

r is the rate of return on new investments.

Weaknesses of the dividend growth model:

a) The model does not explicitly incorporate risk.

b) Dividends do not grow smoothly in reality, so g is only an approximation.

c) The model fails to take capital gains into account; however, it is argued that a change of share ownership does not affect the present value of the dividend stream.

d) No allowance is made for the effects of taxation although the model can be modified to incorporate tax.

e) It assumes there are no issue costs for new shares.

f) It does not produce meaningful results where no dividend is paid (if d is zero, K_e is 0).

a) 模型没有明确地纳入风险。

b) 股息在现实中不会平稳增长，所以g只是一个近似值。

c) 模型没有考虑资本利得；然而，有人认为，股份所有权的变化并不影响股息流的现值。

d) 不考虑税收的影响，尽管该模型可以修改为考虑税的情况。

e) 假设新股不存在发行成本。

f) 如果没有红利支付，就不会产生有意义的结果(如果d为0,Ke为0)。

3. Capital asset pricing model (CAPM)

The capital asset pricing model can be used to calculate a cost of equity and incorporates risk.

The CAPM is based on a comparison of the systematic risk of individual investments with the risks of all shares in the market.

This model assumes that investors have a broad range of investments, to reduce their exposure to risk.（资本资产定价模型只考虑了系统风险,同时假设投资者拥有大量的投资

来分散风险）

Portfolio theory suggests that investors can reduce the total risk on their investments by diversifying their portfolio of investments. ［投资者可以减少他们的风险，通过投资不同的资产（不要把鸡蛋放一个篮子里）］

Unsystematic risk can be diversified away. Investors may mix a diversified market portfolio with risk-free assets to achieve a preferred mix of risk and return. (the risk specific to a share)

Market risk or systematic risk cannot be diversified away. (e.g. market crashes as a result of a global recession, war or natural catastrophe)（系统风险不能被分散化因为系统风险一般指的是战争、自然灾害、经济衰退等）

In return for accepting systematic risk, a risk-averse investor will expect to earn a return which is higher than the return on a risk-free investment. （在系统风险下，一个风险厌恶者可能希望收到的回报比无风险下的投资回报更高）

Beta factor

$\beta = 1$, system risk = market risk neutral shares

$\beta > 1$, system risk > market risk aggressive shares

$\beta < 1$, system risk < market risk defensive shares

Market risk premium or equity risk premium is the difference between the expected rate of return on a market portfolio and the risk-free rate of return over the same period.

Market risk premium = market return - risk free rate of return

$$\text{The CPAM formula}$$
$$E(r_i) = R_f + \beta_i [E(R_m) - R_f]$$

$E(r_i)$ is the cost of equity capital

$E(r_m) - R_f$ = equity risk premium

R_f is the risk-free rate of return

$E(r_m)$ is the return from the market as a whole, β_i is the beta factor of the individual security.

Compare the dividend growth model and the capital asset pricing model.

○ The dividend growth model calculates the apparent cost of equity in the capital market, provided that the current market price of the share, the current dividend and the future dividend growth rate are known.

○ While the current market price and the current dividend are readily available, it is very difficult to find an accurate value for the future dividend growth rate.

○ A common approach to finding the future dividend growth rate is to calculate the average historic dividend growth rate and then to assume that the future dividend growth rate will be similar. There is no reason why this assumption should be true.

○ The capital asset pricing model tends to be preferred to the dividend growth model as a way of calculating the cost of equity as it has a sound theoretical basis, relating the cost of equity or required return of well-diversified shareholders to the systematic risk they face through owning the shares of a company.

○ However, finding suitable values for the variables used by the capital asset pricing model (risk-free rate of return, equity beta and equity risk premium) can be difficult.

比较股利增长模型和资本资产定价模型

○ 股息增长模型计算资本市场上权益的成本,前提是股票的当前市场价格、当前股息和未来股息增长率已知。

○ 当前市场价格和当前股利是现成的,很难找到未来股利增长率的准确值。

○ 寻找未来股息增长率的一个常见方法是计算平均历史股息增长率,然后假设未来股息增长率将是相似的。没有理由证明这个假设是正确的。

○ 资本资产定价模型往往是首选的股息增长模型来计算股票的成本,因为它有一个良好的理论基础

○ 然而,为资本资产定价模型(无风险收益率、股权贝塔和股权风险溢价)所用的变量找到合适的值可能很困难。

4. Cost of debt

Lenders are only willing to lend if their initial outlay of money is fully compensated by future cash inflows. Therefore, the cost of capital is the rate at which lenders recover their initial outlay of money, and the price of debt equals the present value of cash inflows 放贷者只有在最初的资金支出能被未来的现金流入完全补偿的情况下,才愿意放贷。因此,资本成本就是贷款人收回其初始资金的比率,而债务的价格等于现金流入的现值。

4.1 Cost of irredeemable debt

For irredeemable debt, this is the (post-tax) interest as a percentage of the ex-interest market value of the bonds (or preferred shares)

Paying interest reduces taxable profits which reduces the tax charge, so the cost of debt to the company is reduced. (不可赎回的债券不能在到期日前赎回)

Without tax

$$K_d = \frac{I}{P_0}$$

I = interest paid
P_0 = market value of the debt
With tax

$$k_d = \frac{I(1-T)}{P_0}$$

T = tax

4.2 Cost of redeemable debt

For redeemable debt, the cost is given by the internal rate of return of the cash flows involved (interest and capital gain or loss at redemption).

If the debt is redeemable, the cost of raising the bond is assessed by looking at the market value, post-tax interest and redemption value cash flows.

a) Easiest to assess one unit of £100 debt

b) Tax has no effect on either the market value or the redemption value(可赎回债券假设他们的面值都是100,利用IRR来计算)

○ IRR method

Year	CF	DF@L%	PV	DF@H%	PV
0	(MV)		(X)		(X)
1-n	interest * (1-t)		X		X
n	redemption		X		X
		NPV =	N_L	NPV =	N_H

$$IRR = L\% + \frac{N_L}{N_L - N_H} \times (H\% - L\%)$$

4.3 Cost of convertible debt

Debt holders will only convert if the value of the shares is greater the redemption value of the debt.

a) If conversion is not expected, the conversion value is ignored and the bond is treated as redeemable debt, using the IRR method.

b) If conversion is expected, the IRR method for calculating the cost of redeemable debt is used, but the number of years to redemption is replaced by the number of years to conversion and the redemption value is replaced by the conversion value ie the market value of the shares into which the debt is to be converted.（可转债,未来可以转换成股票的债券,在到期日以到期价值和转换价值高的作为到期日价值）

○ IRR method

Year	CF	DF@L%	PV	DF@H%	PV
0	(MV)		(X)		(X)
1-n	interest * (1-t)		X		X
n	Higher of a) redemption b) Conversion Value		X		X
		NPV =	N_L	NPV =	N_H

$$IRR = L\% + \frac{N_L}{N_L - N_H} \times (H\% - L\%)$$

4.4 Cost of preference shares

$$K_{pref} = \frac{\text{Preference Dividend}}{\text{Market Value}_{(exdiv)}} = \frac{d}{P_0}$$

5. Weighted average cost of capital (WACC)

The weighted average cost of capital (WACC) is the average cost of capital for all the company's long term sources of finance, weighted to allow for the relative proportions of each type of capital in the overall capital structure.

The WACC is calculated by weighting the costs of the individual sources of finance according to their relative importance as sources of finance.

The WACC represents the return that the company should make on its investments to be able to provide the returns required by its finance providers.

General formula for the WACC

$$\text{WACC} = \left[\frac{V_e}{V_e + V_d}\right] k_e + \left[\frac{V_d}{V_e + V_d}\right] k_d (1 - T)$$

where k_e is the cost of equity
  k_d is the cost of debt
  V_e is the market value of equity in the firm
  V_d is the market value of debt in the firm
  T is the rate of company tax

- Market value of equity and debt
- MV of Equity = No. of ordinary share × Share price
- MV of Debt

Bond/Debenture = Book value of debenture × Debenture price/100 Loan: Market value = Book value Preference share: No. of preference share × share price

Note: 本章所有公式一定要记住,而且要结合例题好好地理解运用。考试时候是重点。

Chapter 16

Capital structure

1. Capital structure theories

1.1 The traditional view

Under the traditional theory of cost of capital, the weighted average cost of capital declines initially as gearing increases, but then rises as gearing increases further. The optimal capital structure is at the gearing level where WACC is lowest.（在传统理论下，WACC 随着 gearing 的增长刚开始先下降后面再上升,有一个最低的 WACC）

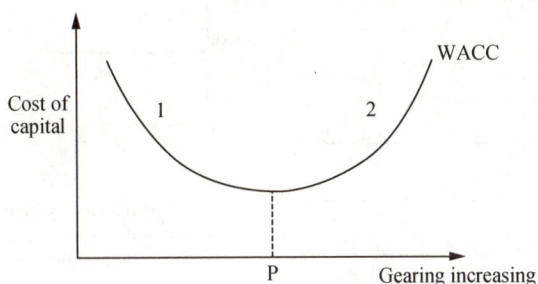

At point 1, the cost of capital falls as the level of debt finance increases. This is because debt is cheaper than equity.

Point P shows the optimum level of debt: cheap debt finance minimises the cost of capital.

At point 2, the cost of capital increases as the level of debt finance continues to increase. This is because above the optimum level of debt finance, the company is perceived to be high risk by shareholders and lenders, who start to demand a higher level of return.

1.2 Net operating income view of WACC: Modigliani-Miller (M&M)

Modigliani and Miller stated that, in the absence of tax relief on debt interest, a company's capital structure would have no impact on its WACC. WACC would be the same regardless of the company's capital structure.（不管公司的资本结构如何变化，WACC 都不会有影响）

M&M made various assumptions in arriving at this conclusion, including:

a) A perfect capital market exists, in which investors have the same information, on which they act rationally, to arrive at the same expectations about future earnings and risks.

b) There are no tax or transaction costs.

c) Debt is risk free and freely available at the same cost to investors and companies alike.

a) 完美的资本市场是存在的,在这个市场中,投资者拥有相同的信息,他们会理性地采取行动,从而对未来的收益和风险达到相同的预期。

b) 没有税收或交易成本。

c) 债务是无风险的,投资者和公司都可以以相同的成本免费获得。

If M&M's theory holds, it implies:

a) The cost of debt remains unchanged as the level of gearing increases.

b) The cost of equity rises in such a way as to keep the weighted average cost of capital constant.

a) 负债成本随着杠杆水平的提高而保持不变。

b) 权益成本的上升使加权平均资本成本保持不变。

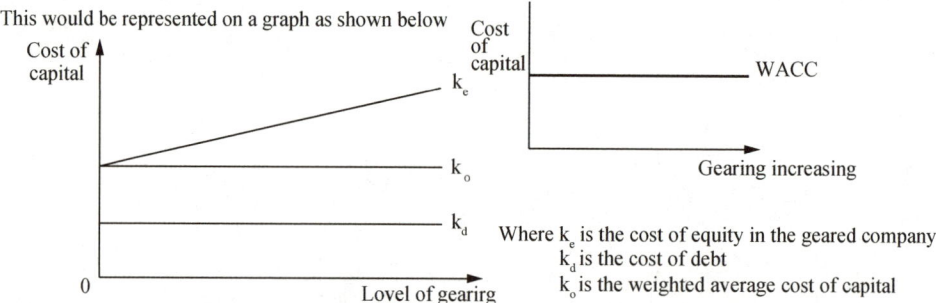

1.3 Market imperfections

Direct financial distress costs	Costs of higher debt payments, and of managing the liquidation process.
Indirect financial distress costs	Loss of sales/higher costs from suppliers. Sale of stock at below market value.
Agency costs	At high levels of gearing, restrictive covenants prevent firms investing.
Tax exhaustion	As companies increase their gearing they may reach a point where there are not enough profits from which to obtain all available tax benefits.

In 1963 Modigliani and Miller modified their theory to admit that tax relief on interest payments does lower the weighted average cost of capital. The savings arising from tax relief on debt interest are the tax shield.

However, whereas the traditional approach to gearing and WACC is that there is an optimal level of gearing where WACC is minimized, M&M took a different view. They argued that the weighted average cost of capital continues to fall, up to gearing of 100%

（M&M 理论下有税的理论下，随着 gearing 的增加，WACC 是一直下降的）

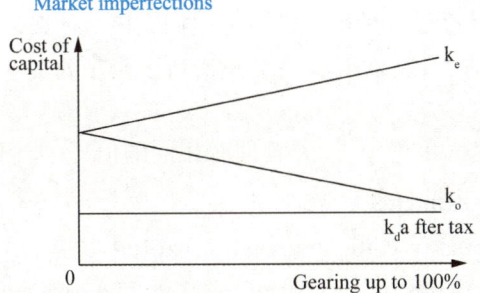

1.4 Pecking order theory

Pecking order theory has been developed as an alternative to traditional theory. This theory is based on the view that companies will not seek to minimize their WACC.

Instead they will seek additional finance in an order of preference，or 'pecking order'.

The order of preference will be：（融资的顺序是先是留存收益，然后是贷款，然后再优先股最后股票）

- Retained earnings
- Straight debt（bank loans or bonds）
- Convertible debt
- Preference shares
- Issue new equity shares

Reasons for following pecking order

a) It is easier to use retained earnings than go to the trouble of obtaining external finance and have to live up to the demands of external finance providers.

b) There are no issue costs if retained earnings are used，and the issue costs of debt are lower than those of equity.

c) Investors prefer safer securities；that is，debt with its guaranteed income and priority on liquidation.

a) 使用留存收益比获得外部融资和必须满足外部融资方的需求要容易。

b) 如果使用留存收益，不存在发行成本，而且债务的发行成本低于股本的发行成本。

c) 投资者偏好较安全的证券；即收入有保证、优先清偿的债务。

Limitations of pecking order theory

a) It fails to take into account taxation，financial distress，agency costs or how the investment opportunities that are available may influence the choice of finance.

b) Pecking order theory is an explanation of what businesses actually do，rather than what they should do.

c) This order is partly because of shares being undervalued（the stock market does not know the full benefits of the project being financed so the firm is reluctant to issue new equity).

　　a) 没有考虑税收、财务困境、代理成本或现有的投资机会如何影响金融选择。

　　b) 啄食顺序理论是对企业实际做什么的一种解释而不是他们应该做什么。

　　c) 该理论的部分原因是股票被低估了(股票市场并不知道所融资项目的全部收益,因此公司是不愿发行新股)。

2. Impact of cost of capital on investments

2.1 The relationship between company value and cost of capital

The market value of a company depends on its cost of capital. The lower a company's WACC, the higher the net present value of its future cash flows will be and therefore the higher its market value.(公司的价值取决于公司的资本成本,WACC越低,未来现金流的现值就越高,公司的价值就会越高,因为 MV = FCFF/WACC)

2.2 Using the WACC in investment appraisal

The weighted average cost of capital can be used in investment appraisal if:

a) The project being appraised is small relative to the company.

b) The existing capital structure will be maintained (same financial risk).

c) The project has the same business risk as the company.

(当投资项目的经营风险和财务风险与公司一致的时候适应)

2.3 Arguments against using the WACC(当投资项目的经营风险和财务风险发生改变时)

a) New investments undertaken by a company might have different business risk characteristics from the company's existing operations. As a consequence, the return required by investors might go up (or down) if the investments are undertaken, because their business risk is perceived to be higher (or lower).

b) The finance that is raised to fund a new investment might substantially change the capital structure and the perceived financial risk of investing in the company.

2.4 Using CAPM in investment appraisal

CAPM can be used to calculate a project-specific cost of capital.

It produces a discount rate which is based on the systematic risk of the individual investment.

It can be used to compare projects of all different risk classes.

Step 1—find a quoted company in that business

An equity beta is the beta of a share, and will be an indication of the risk of the business.

In reality an equity beta will also be affected by a company's gearing; if a company has a high equity beta this may be because it has high gearing not because it is a high risk business.

第一步先找到一个行业的类比的公司的 equity beta

Chapter 16　Capital structure

Step 2—adjust the beta to reflect differences in gearing

a) Adjust the equity beta by stripping out the impact of the other company's debt and get the ungeared beta (asset beta)

b) Convert it back to a geared beta (equity beta), which reflects the company's own gearing ratio

第二步调整 beta 使他们反映我们投资项目的风险

a) 先找到 ungeared beta(asset beta)把我们找到的行业的 beta 里他们自己企业的财务的风险去掉

$$\beta_a = \left\{\frac{V_e}{[V_e + V_d(1-T)]}\beta_e\right\} + \left\{\frac{V_d(1-T)}{[V_e + V_d(1-T)]}\beta_d\right\}$$

Where β_a is the asset beta or ungeared beta

β_e is the equity beta or geared beta

β_d is the beta factor of debt in the geared company

V_d is the market value of the debt capital in the geared company

V_e is the market value of the equity capital in the geared company

T is the rate of corporate tax

Debt is often assumed to be risk free and its beta(β_d) is then taken as zero, in which case the formula above reduces to the following form.

$$\beta_a = \beta_e \times \frac{V_e}{V_e + V_d(1-T)} \text{ or, without tax, } \beta_a = \beta_e \times \frac{V_e}{V_e + V_d}$$

beta 把我们找到的行业的 bate 里他们自己企业的财力的风险去掉

b) 然后把我们投资项目的财务风险再加上 re-geared 的过程

步骤整体如下（记住步骤然后结合例题自己多做题多理解）

先算 beta a（使用的是我们找的行业标准公司的 V_e 和 V_d）

$$\text{ungeared beta: } \beta_a = \beta_e \frac{V_e}{V_e + V_d(1-T)}$$

然后利用我们用行业标准公司求出的 beta a 再算我们自己公司的 beta e（使用的是我们自己公司的 V_e 和 V_d）

$$\text{Regeared beta: } \beta_e = \beta_a \frac{V_e + V_d(1-T)}{V_e}$$

最后用这个 Re-geared beta 的 beta e 代入到 CAPM 公式中求出 cost of equity = R_f + $\beta_e(R_m - R_f)$

Weaknesses in the formula

a) It is difficult to identify other firms with identical operating characteristics.

b) Estimates of beta values from share price information are not wholly accurate. They are based on statistical analysis of historical data and estimates using one firm's data will differ from estimates using another firm's data.

c) There may be differences in beta values between firms.

a）很难识别具有相同经营特征的其他公司。（找这个行业标准的公司比较难）

b）根据股价信息对贝塔值的估计并不完全准确。

它们基于对历史数据的统计分析，使用一家公司的数据进行的估算与使用另一家公司的数据进行的估算会有所不同。

c）公司之间可能存在 beta 值的差异。

考试时文字题解题套路

1) Cost of Capital★

a）Cost of Equity：$K_e = D_0(1+g)/P_0 + g$。应用难点：通常 g、K_e、P 的变动都是不固定的。

b）不可赎回 Preference share：$Kp = Divident/MV \text{ of shares} * 100\%$

c）可赎回 Bond，5%算现金流和10%算现金流，每年利息支出 $*(1-tax)$，IRR 法算 after-tax cost

d）Cost of Debt of bank loan = 利率 $x(1-tax\%)$

e）WACC = 各种 MV * 资本利率加总/Total value of all capital（题目会要求 Book value 算或 Market value 算，看清！）

f）CAPM(capital asset pricing model) = 先去杠杆，再上杠杆。难度：找到 β, risk-free rate of return & risk premium

g）β 反映了系统风险。β * 市场溢价 = 对承担风险的补偿需求 Asset β 反映了 business risk，同行业的 business risk 差不多 Equity β 反映了"business risk + finance risk"

题目：2010-12-Q4，2010-12-Q1，2011-12-Q3，2012-06-Q4，2012-12-Q3，2013-06-Q2，2013-12-Q2，2014-12-Q5，Pilot Q5

2) Systematic risk

a）Business risk：跟公司经营性质、运作方式有关。经营风险是指股东回报因为公司运作而波动，与 PBIT 受收入影响有关。可以通过计算 operating gearing = Contribution/PBIT 来评估。

b）Financial risk：使用 Debt 来融资，跟公司资本构架有关。财务风险是指股东回报因利息支付而波动。可以通过计算 gearing = debt/equity 或 Interest cover ratio 来评估。

c）Systematic risk：上述 2 个风险总和。尽管投资人有很多投资仍然无法避免的风险，又称市场风险。可以用 Equity beta 来评估，如果公司有 debt & equity，那么公司既有金融风险又有经营风险。如果公司没有 Debt，那么公司的 Equity beta = Asset beta。

题目：2012-06-Q4

3) Portfolios theory 投资组合

a）投资组合理论表示，多样化的投资可以降低总的风险。买 N 家公司比买 1,2 家公司安全。

b）这种可以投资组合降低的风险是非系统风险。

c）多样化投资还不能降低的风险就是金融系统风险，又可称作市场风险。

d）投资组合理论更重视总风险，即系统风险 + 非系统风险。CAPM 假设客户是多样化投资的，所以只关注系统风险。

题目：2014-06-Q3
4) MV or BV 计算 WACC

a) MV 反映在资本市场的当前状态。最明显的就是 Equity 的 MV 和 BV 就差别非常大。

b) BV 算出来的值跟 MV 比较，通常要小。WACC(BV)＜WACC(MV)

c) 有些项目，用 BV 计算是可接受的，但用 MV 计算是不可接受的。

d) 如果考虑 debt，MV 还是 BV 算出来的结果不会差别太大，因为 debt 的 MV 和 BV 在资本市场差别不大。

e) Debt 对 WACC 的贡献会因为 Equity 比重变化而变化，用 BV 还是 MV 都会造成 Debt 重要性高估或低估。

题目：2012-12-Q
5) Capital Structure 或发债为什么会影响 WACC★

公司价值可以由未来现金流的 WACC 折现后的 PV 表示。

a) 传统理论：平衡 equity and debt，存在 minimum WACC，此时资本结构 optimal。但 debt 过高有财务风险，然后 K_e 会增加，与财务风险相匹配。

b) MM（无税）：WACC 与资本结构无关，无最优资本结构。前提：perfect 资本市场，无企税。

c) MM（有税）：利息是 tax-efficient source，提高 gearing 可以降低 WACC，从而提高公司价值。

d) Market imperfection view：过高的 gearing 会增加 financial risk，从而增加破产风险。这时债务融资和股权融资成本都增加了。

e) Marginal and average cost of debt 引入一个新债，会影响 marginal cost of capital。边际成本＜WACC，则 WACC 会变小。

f) Peacking order theory 啄食理论：现实中，公司不是以最优融资结构理论来融资。一般公司融资偏好为自有资本 Retained earnings，然后是 bank loans, ordinary debt, convertible debt，优先股，普通股。

题目：2011-06-Q2，2013-12-Q2，2015-06-Q4
6) Interest Rate 增长影响★

a) 客户融资成本变高，购买大宗商品预期利息支付额变高，购买欲望下降。

b) 公司融资成本变高，K_d 变高，导致 WACC 变高。如果公司 K_d 占比较高，则对 WACC 影响更明显。另外，K_e 也会因 K_d 增长而增长，大多数公司主要以 Equity Finance 为主，所以也会推高 WACC。

c) 对 Capital investment appraisal process。利率边高后，DF 就会大，项目 NPV 就变小。为了让新项目盈利，通常会提高价格，但这会影响销售量。同时，各种成本以因为上游企业的利息支出增长而增长。总体而言，收入和净利润会下降。

题目：2012-12-Q1

Part F

Business valuations

Chapter 17

Business valuations

1. The nature and purpose of business valuations

1.1 Reasons for business valuations

For quoted companies

In making a bid for another company, it is important for the buyer to create a range of values within which a buyer would be prepared to negotiate.

When deciding to float or sell the company again the seller must create a range of values within which to negotiate.

对于上市公司：在竞购另一家公司时，对买家来说，重要的是要创造出一个可供谈判的价值范围。

在决定上市或再次出售公司时，卖方必须创造一个可在其中进行谈判的价值范围。

For unquoted companies

a) Wishes to 'go public'

b) Mergers and acquisitions

c) Shares are sold

d) Shares need to be valued for the purposes of taxation

e) Shares are pledged as collateral for a loan and the bank wants to put a value to the collateral

f) Another company is proposing to take over the unquoted company by making an offer to buy all its shares.

对于非上市公司：

a) 希望"上市"

b) 合并和收购

c) 出售股票

d) 出于税收目的，股票需要估值

e) 股票被抵押作为贷款的抵押品，银行希望对抵押品进行估价

f) 另一家公司提议通过出价购买这家未上市公司的全部股份来接管这家公司。

For subsidiary companies

when the group's holding company is negotiating the sale of the subsidiary to a management buyout team or to an external buyer

For any company

Where a shareholder wishes to dispose of their holding

1.2 Business valuation methods

Value of cash flow or earning under new ownership

Value the dividends under the existing management

Value the asset

2. Asset valuation bases

Using this method of valuation, the value of an equity share is equal to the net tangible assets divided by the number of shares.

Net tangible assets are the value in the statement of financial position of the tangible non-current assets (net of depreciation) plus current assets, minus all liabilities.

Intangible assets (including goodwill) should be excluded, unless they have a market value (for example patents and copyrights, which could be sold).

使用这种估值方法,股本的价值等于有形资产净值除以股份的数量。

有形资产净值是指有形非流动资产(折旧净值)加流动资产减去所有负债在财务状况表中的价值。

无形资产(包括商誉)应被排除在外,除非它们具有市场价值(例如可以出售的专利和版权)。

Choice of valuation bases

Key consideration: whether it is valued on a going concern or a break-up basis.

Historical cost basis (net book value) — unlikely to give a realistic value, as it is dependent on the business's depreciation and amortization policy.

Realizable basis — if the assets are to be sold, or the business as a whole broken up. This won't be relevant if a minority (non-controlling) shareholder is selling their stake, as the assets will continue in the business's use.

Replacement basis — if the assets are to be used on an ongoing basis.

关键考虑因素:它的估值是基于持续经营还是破产清算。

历史成本基础(账面净值)——不太可能给出现实的价值,因为它取决于企业的折旧和摊销政策。

可变现价值——如果资产被出售,或业务作为一个整体破产了。如果一个少数(非控股)股东出售他们的股份,这就无关紧要了,因为这些资产将继续用于企业的使用。

重置成本-如果资产将持续使用。

The net assets basis of valuation might be used in the following circumstances.

a) As a measure of the 'security' in a share value. The asset backing for shares thus provides a measure of the possible loss if the company fails to make the expected earnings or dividend payments.

b) As a measure of comparison in a scheme of merger

A merger is essentially a business combination of two or more companies, of which none obtains control over any other.

  c) As 'floor value' for a business that is up for sale

下列情况可以采用净资产计价基础。

  a) 作为衡量股票价值中"安全性"的标准。

  b) 作为合并方案中比较的衡量标准

  c) 作为待售企业的"底价"

Disadvantage

This method ignores intangible assets & future profits.

3. Income-based valuation bases

3.1 P/E ratio (earnings) method of valuation

$$P/E \text{ ratio} = \frac{Market.price}{EPS}$$

then market value per share = EPS × P/E ratio

Market valuation or capitalization = (for individual shares) P/E ratio × Earnings per share, or

(for all the company's equity) P/E ratio × Total earnings

The EPS could be a historical EPS or a prospective future EPS. For a given EPS figure, a higher P/E ratio will result in a higher price.

Significance of high P/E ratio

1) Expectations that the EPS will grow rapidly

A high price is being paid for future profit prospects. Many small but successful and fast-growing companies are valued on the stock market on a high P/E ratio.

2) Security of earnings

A well-established low-risk company would be valued on a higher P/E ratio than a similar company whose earnings are subject to greater uncertainty.

3) Status

If a quoted company (the bidder) made a share for share takeover bid for an unquoted company (the target), it would normally expect its own shares to be valued on a higher P/E ratio than the target company's shares

1）预期每股收益将迅速增长

为了未来的利润前景，人们付出了高昂的代价。许多小型但成功且快速增长的公司在股市上的市盈率都很高。

2）安全的收益

一家信誉良好的低风险公司的市盈率会高于一家盈利不确定性更大的同类公司。

3）状态

如果一家上市公司（投标人）以股份收购一家非上市公司（目标公司），其自身股票的市盈率通常会高于目标公司股票的市盈率

Problems with using P/E ratios

However, using the P/E ratios of quoted companies to value unquoted companies may be problematic. This is because a P/E ratio must be guessed at, using the P/E ratios for similar quoted companies as a guide.

3.2 Earnings yield valuation method

This method is effectively a variation on the P/E method (the EY being the reciprocal of the P/E ratio)

$$\text{Earning yield(EY)} = \frac{\text{EPS}}{\text{Market.price.per.share}}$$

$$\text{Market value} = \text{Earning}/\text{EY}$$

We can incorporate earnings growth into this method:

$$\text{Market value} = \frac{\text{Earning} \times (1+g)}{\text{EY} - g}$$

Advantage:

it gives a value from the perspective of the acquire

Disadvantage:

a) Earning yield method use profit for evaluation and profit is easy to manipulated

b) It is difficult to find an appropriate earning yield

c) Earning yield method assumes the earning yield remains constant in the future in perpetuity

4. Cash flow based valuation models

Cash flow based valuation models include the dividend valuation model, the dividend growth model and valuation on a discounted cash flow basis.

4.1 Dividend valuation model

The dividend valuation model is based on the theory that an equilibrium price for any share (or bond) on a stock market is:

○ The future expected stream of income from the security

○ Discounted at a suitable cost of capital

Equilibrium market price is thus a present value of a future expected income stream. The annual income stream for a share is the expected dividend every year in perpetuity.

○ 来自证券的未来预期收入流

○ 以合适的资本成本贴现

因此，均衡市场价格是未来预期收入流的现值。股票的年度收入流是预期股息，每年永续

The basic dividend-based formula for the market value of shares is expressed in the dividend valuation model as follows.

Dividend no growth:

$$\text{MV(ex div)} = \frac{D}{1+k_e} + \frac{D}{(1+k_e)^2} + \frac{D}{(1+k_e)^2} + \cdots = \frac{D}{k_e}$$

where MV = Ex-dividend market value of the shares

D = Constant annual dividend

k_e = Shareholders' required rate of return

The dividend growth model

$$P_0 = \frac{D_0(1+g)}{(1+k_e)} + \frac{D_0(1+g)^2}{(1+k_e)^2} + \cdots = \frac{D_0(1+g)^n}{(k_e-g)^n}$$

$$= \frac{D_1}{k_e - g}$$

where D_0 = Current year's dividend

g = Growth rate in earnings and dividends

$D_0(1+g)$ = Expected dividend in one year's time (D_1)

k_e = Shareholders' required rate of return

P_0 = Market value excluding any dividend currently payable

Disadvantages

a) It is difficult to estimating future dividend growth

b) It is inaccurate to assume that growth will be constant

c) It creates zero values for zero dividend companies

d) It creates negative values for high growth companies, if $g > K_e$

a) 未来股利增长难以估计

b) 假定增长将是恒定的是不准确的

c) 它为零股利公司创造了零价值

d) 它为高增长公司创造了负价值,(如果增长率大于股权成本)

4.2 Discounted cash flow basis of valuation

A DCF method of share valuation may be appropriate when one company intends to buy the assets of another company and to make further investments in order to improve cash flows in the future.

Step 1

Estimate the cash flows that will be obtained each year from the acquired business. The cash flows may be estimated for a maximum number of years (say, for ten years). Alternatively, there may be an assumption about annual cash flows from the business into perpetuity.

If the proposal is to buy the equity shares only, the cash flows should be cash flows after interest payments on debt of the target company and tax on the profits.

If the proposal is to buy the entire business, including liability for its debts, the cash flows should be cash flows before interest payments on debt of the target company.

估计每年从被收购企业获得的现金流。现金流量可以估计为最长年限(例如 10 年)。或者,也可以假设企业每年都要有现金流入永续经营。

如果提议只购买股权,则现金流应为目标公司支付债务利息和对利润征税后的现金流。

如果提议是收购整个企业,包括债务,现金流应该是目标公司债务利息支付前的现金流。

Step 2

Discount these cash flows at an appropriate cost of capital. This produces a value either for the equity shares or for the business as a whole. 用资本成本对现金流折现

5. Valuation of debt

Debt calculations — a few notes

a) Debt is always quoted in $100 nominal units, or blocks; always use $100 nominal values as the basis to your calculations.

b) Debt can be quoted as a percentage or as a value, e.g. 97% or $97. Both mean that $100 nominal value of debt is worth $97 market value.

c) Interest on debt is stated as a percentage of nominal value. This is known as the coupon rate. It is not the same as the redemption yield on debt or the cost of debt.

a) 通常面值就是$100 的债务

b) 债券可以折价发行,比如97%发行 就是发行价格=97% * 100 = 97

c) 利率使用面值来计算的,利率通常指的是票面利率

5.1 Irredeemable debt

For irredeemable bonds where the company will go on paying interest every year in perpetuity, without ever having to redeem the loan (ignoring taxation):

$$P_0 = \frac{i}{K_d}$$

where P_0 is the market price of the bond ex interest; that is, excluding any interest payment that might soon be due

i is the annual interest payment on the bond

K_d is the return required by the bond investors

5.2 Redeemable debt

Value of debt = (Interest earnings × annuity factor) + (Redemption value × Discounted cash flow factor)

5.3 Convertible debt

$$\text{Conversion value} = P_0(1+g)^n R$$

where P_0 is the current ex-dividend ordinary share price

g is the expected annual growth of the ordinary share price

n is the number of years to conversion

R is the number of shares received on conversion

5.4 Preference shares

Preference shares pay a fixed-rate dividend which is not tax deductible for the company.

The current ex-dividend value P_0 paying a constant annual dividend d and having a cost of capital k_{pref}.

Chapter 17 Business valuations

$$P_0 = \frac{d}{k_{pref}}$$

考试时文字题答题套路

1) Business Valuation ★

a) 最高：Cashflow or earnings (income based)；次之 Dividends (income based)；最低 Assets based (常用于清算)

○ Dividend growth model value：可以用 g，也可以用 bre = ROIx% 投资率。少数股东 (股票投资者) min value

○ P/E ratio(Earnings yield 呈倒数关系)定价：适用于非上市公司，但有投资者想买。EPS = earnings per share = MV/PE ratio。

○ 资本市场定价 Market capitalisation(equity market value)：用股价估值。这是现股东最少可以从股市拿到的钱

○ 比较可行的资产估价：Replacement basis，前提：公司持续经营。5) Net asset value，前提：公司进入清算 liquidation basis

b) 偿债顺序：固定抵押 Debt—浮动抵押 Debt—无抵押 Debt—优先股-常规股

c) Venture Capital 风投：3 高：高增长预期，高投资金额，高回报(高风险)。投资-换股权。

题目：2012-12-Q4，2013-06-Q4，Pilot Q2

2) DGM vs. Earings Yield 法 ★

a) DGM：基于现金流的估计 cashflow-base。使用的信息是本公司自己的。使用者：少数股东，即买股票投资的人。

缺陷如下：

○ g 比较难估计。DGM 模型假定 g 是 constant，这不符合现实。而且股价对 g 非常敏感，一点变动，就对股价影响很大。另外，用过去的 g 来预计未来，是不合适的。

○ K_e 比较难估计。DGM 模型假定 K_e 是 constant，这不符合现实。K_e 可以用 capital asset pricing model(CAPM)来计算。同样，基于历史数据计算所得的 K_e，未必能给给出未来预期。

○ Zero dividends 时，必须存在 dividend 增长预期，才可以使用 DGM。可以取过去几年的 Average dividend growth rate，预测未来某年股价，再然后折现成当前股价。如果没有 dividend 增长预期，不可使用该模型。

优点：

○ 上市公司的分红数据公开可查；

○ g 可以用来计算投资者卖掉股票而损失的未来收益的值，是计算最低卖价的模型。这对买卖双方都是有用信息。

b) Earning yield：基于利润的估计 profit-base。当使用行业平均值，就不具有针对性。使用者：收购方(前提是 EY 合适)但无论上述两种方式，都假设 g，K_e，EY 在未来固定，这个跟现实有悖，降低了现实意义。

题目：2011-12-Q1，2015-06-Q1，Pilot Q2

3）P/E 定价估价的问题★

a）P/E 比较适合估计非上市公司的价值。

b）用 P/E 估值的难点在于选一个合适的 P/E 值，如果用平均，或许会跟本公司实际情况不一致。

c）当公司的 business risk & financial risk 跟类似公司不一致时，P/E 值会很不一样。

d）行业领先者通常对行业平均 P/E 值有贡献作用（＞行业平均）。

e）理想的话，估算 P/E 应该用预计未来的 earnings，这个也比较难估计。

题目：2012-06-Q4，2014-12-Q2

Chapter 18

Market efficiency

1. The efficient market hypothesis

The efficient market hypothesis provides a rationale for explaining how share prices react to new information about a company, and when any such change in share price occurs. Stock market reaction to new information depends on the strength of the stock market efficiency. (有效市场假说提供了一个合理的解释(关于股票价格是如何对一个公司的信息发生变化的)。当股票价格发生变化是,市场对新信息的反映取决于市场的有效程度)

1.1 Definition of market efficiency

Different types of efficiency can be distinguished in the context of the operation of financial markets.

1) Allocative efficiency 配置效率

If financial markets allow funds to be directed towards firms which make the most productive use of them, then there is allocative efficiency in these markets. (金融市场允许资金直接流向最能有效使用资金这些资金的公司)

2) Operational efficiency 运行效率

Financial markets have operational efficiency if transaction costs are kept as low as possible. Transaction costs are kept low where there is open competition between brokers and other market participants (尽可能地把交易成本控制在较低的水平)

3) Information processing efficiency 信息处理有效性

The information processing efficiency of a stock market means the ability of a stock market to price stocks and shares fairly and quickly. An efficient market in this sense is one in which the market prices of all securities reflect all the available information.

The efficient markets hypothesis is concerned with the information processing efficiency of stock markets.

市场对股票的定价快速和公平的能力、有效的市场就是一种股票的市场定价反映了所有有效的信息

1.2 Varying degrees of efficiency

There are three degrees or 'forms' of stock market efficiency: weak form, semi-strong form and strong form.

1) Weak form efficiency

If a stock market has weak form efficiency, it is not efficient at responding to events that affect companies and should affect share prices. It does not react to much of the information that is available about a company. Instead, when stock market efficiency is weak, share prices only reflect historical information including information about past share price movements.

If stock markets exhibit weak-form efficiency, investors can't make excess profits by studying past share price movements (an approach that is sometimes called technical analysis).

弱势有效市场

当市场是弱势有效的时候,股票价格仅仅反映历史的信息。投资者不能通过观察过去的股票价格移动来获得超额收益(这种方法叫作技术分析)。

2) Semi-strong form efficiency

If a stock market displays semi-strong efficiency, current share prices reflect both:

○ All relevant information about past price movements and their implications, and

○ All knowledge which is available publicly

This means that individuals cannot 'beat the market' by reading the newspapers or annual reports, since the information contained in these will be reflected in the share price.

Stock markets are usually presumed to be semi-strong efficient.

半强势有效市场

股票价格反映过去和公开的信息。(股票价格因为反映了这些信息是所有人都能知道的所以投资者不能再利用这些信息来获得超额的收益)

3) Strong form efficiency

If a stock market displays a strong form of efficiency, share prices reflect all information whether publicly available or not:

○ From past price changes

○ From public knowledge or anticipation

○ From specialists' or experts' insider knowledge (e.g. inside knowledge of investment managers about unpublished facts)

In a strong form efficient market, share prices will respond to new developments and events before they even become public knowledge. Therefore it is not possible for investors to 'beat the market' using information not known to the market. Strong form markets are unlikely.

强势有效市场

股票价格反映过去和公开还有一些内幕信息。

1.3 Features of efficient markets

Stock markets that are efficient (or semi-efficient) are therefore markets in which:

a) The prices of securities bought and sold reflect all the relevant information available to the buyers and sellers, and share prices change quickly to reflect all new information about future prospects.

b) No individual dominates the market.

c) Transaction costs of buying and selling are not so high as to discourage trading significantly.

d) Investors are rational and so make rational buying and selling decisions, and value shares in a rational way.

e) There are low, or no, costs of acquiring information.

有效(或半有效)的股票市场是这样的市场:

a) 买卖证券的价格反映了买卖双方可以获得的所有相关信息,而股票价格变化迅速,反映了有关未来前景的所有新信息。

b) 没有一个人主导市场。

c) 买卖交易成本不高,不会严重阻碍交易。

d) 投资者是理性的,所以会做出理性的买卖决定,以理性的方式给股票估值。

e) 获取信息的成本很低,或者没有成本。

1.4 Impact of efficiency on share prices

If the stock market is efficient, share prices should vary in a rational way.

a) If a company makes an investment with a positive net present value (NPV), shareholders will get to know about it and the market price of its shares will rise in anticipation of future dividend increases.

b) If a company makes a bad investment, shareholders will find out and so the price of its shares will fall.

c) If interest rates rise, shareholders will want a higher return from their investments, so market prices will fall.

如果股票市场是有效的,股票价格应该以一种理性的方式变化。

a) 如果一家公司进行一项净现值(NPV)为正的投资,股东会了解到该投资,其股票的市场价格会因为预期未来股息增加而上升。

b) 如果一家公司做了一项糟糕的投资,股东们会发现,因此股票价格就会下跌。

c) 如果利率上升,股东将希望从他们的投资中获得更高的回报,因此市场价格将下降。

2. The valuation of shares

Fundamental analysis is based on the theory that share prices can be derived from a rational analysis of future dividends. The value of a share will be the discounted present value of all future expected dividends on the shares, discounted at the shareholders' cost of capital. The theory therefore supports the view that 'realistic' share prices can be determined by valuation models, such as the dividend growth model.

基础分析是基于股票价格可以从对未来股利的理性分析中得出的理论。股票的价值将是所有未来预期股息的现值,以股东的资本成本贴现。因此,该理论支持了这样一种观点,即"现实的"股价可以由估值模型(如股息增长模型)来决定。

Technical analysts or chartists work on the basis that past price patterns will be repeated, therefore future price movements can be predicted from historical patterns of share price movements in the past, and there are some patterns that continually reappear. Chartists do not attempt to predict every price change. They are primarily interested in trend reversals, for example when the price of a share has been rising for several months but suddenly starts to fall. One of the main problems with chartism is that it is often difficult to see a new trend until after it has happened.

技术分析师或图表分析师的工作基础是过去的价格模式将会重复,因此未来的价格运动可以从过去股价运动的历史模式中预测出来,而且有一些模式会不断重现。图表分析师不会试图预测每一个价格变化。他们主要对趋势逆转感兴趣,例如,当股价已经上涨了几个月,但突然开始下跌时。图表的一个主要问题是,在新趋势出现之前,通常很难看到它。

Random walk theory is consistent with the fundamental theory of share values. It accepts that a share should have an intrinsic price dependent on the fortunes of the company and the expectations of investors. One of its underlying assumptions is that all relevant information about a company is available to all potential investors who will act on the information in a rational manner

随机游走理论与股票价值的基本理论是一致的。它承认,股票的内在价格应取决于公司的命运和投资者的预期。它的一个基本假设是,公司的所有相关信息都可以提供给所有的潜在投资者,他们会根据这些信息以理性的方式行事

Share prices are also affected by marketability and liquidity of shares, availability and sources of information, market imperfections and pricing anomalies, market capitalisation and investor speculation.

The marketability of shares in a private company, particularly a minority shareholding, is generally very limited, a consequence being that the price can be difficult to determine.

股票价格还受到股票的市场性和流动性、信息的可获得性和来源、市场不完善和定价异常、市值和投资者投机等因素的影响。

私人公司的股票,特别是少数股权的可销售性通常非常有限,其结果是价格很难确定。

Speculation by investors and market sentiment is a major factor in the behaviour of share prices.

Behavioural finance is an alternative view to the efficient market hypothesis. It attempts to explain the market implications of the psychological factors behind investor decisions and suggests that irrational investor behaviour may significantly affect share price movements. These factors may explain why share prices appear sometimes to overreact to past price changes.

投资者的投机行为和市场情绪是影响股票价格走势的主要因素。

行为金融学是有效市场假说的另一种观点。它试图解释投资者决策背后的心理因素对市场的影响,并表明非理性的投资者行为可能会对股价走势产生重大影响。这些因素可以解释为什么股票价格有时会对过去的价格变化反应过度。

Chapter 18　Market efficiency

考试时文字题解题套路

1) Investment appraisal 方法

a) Payback period：Before depreciation but after taxation（◆提示：跟 ROCE 正好相反）优点：简单易理解、关注短期、关注低风险、倾向于快速回本

缺点：忽略 cash flow 时间价值、忽略项目总回报、项目 cut-off 要求比较任意

b) ROCE：注意 F9 用的是平均收益（accounting profit＝PV－depreciation，再除以 N 年）/平均投资（初始＋残值，除以 2），After depreciation but before interest and tax

优点：快速计算、回报率%好理解、查看了整个寿命周期

缺点：关注 accounting profit（可造假）而非 cash flow，忽略时间价值、没有考虑项目时间周期

题目：2010-12-Q1，Pilot Q4

2) Forms of efficiency★

a) Weak form efficiency：只反映 past information，可以通过基本面分析获益

b) Semi-strong form efficiency：反映 past information & public information，可以通过内幕消息获益

c) Strong form efficiency：反映所有信息，包括 past，public or private。可以通过买很多股票，取平均收益。其他：技术分析对任何 form of efficiency 都没啥作用。

题目：2010-12-Q2

3) Capital Market Efficiency★

a) 有效市场假说 efficient market hypothesis 特点：市场价格公允反映了价值和公司相关信息；没有人操控市场；交易成本是不重要的。

b) EMH 成立存在的结果：收购就以估价为参考即可，因为估价反映了公司价值；公司发行股票不需要择时，反正估价始终反映了真实情况；但实际情况是，市场不是强有效的，最多半有效，存在各种缺陷。

c) Weak-form efficiency：基本面分析可以超额利润，基于过去信息的技术分析没用。

d) Semi strong-form efficiency：公开信息/新信息，市场价格立即做出反应，有内幕消息者赚钱。

Strong-form efficiency：股票反映了内幕信息，所以即使掌握内幕信息也无法取得超额利润。

题目：2014-06-Q3

Part G

Risk management

Chapter 19

Foreign currency risk

本章节公式也要结合例题好好理解,总结解题套路。

1. Exchange rates

An exchange rate is the rate at which one country's currency can be traded in exchange for another country's currency.

The spot rate is the exchange rate currently offered on a particular currency for immediate delivery.

A forward rate is an exchange rate set now for currencies to be exchanged at a future date.

(外汇汇率就是一个国家和另外一个国家之间的货币兑换的利率,spot rate 就是现在的利率,forward rate 就是未来期间的利率)

2. Foreign currency risk

Currency risk is the risk of changes in an exchange rate or in the foreign exchange value of a currency. It is a two-way risk.

Currency risk occurs in three forms: transaction exposure (short-term), economic exposure (effect on present value of longer-term cash flows) and translation exposure (book gains or losses).

2.1 Translation risk

Translation risk is the risk that the organisation will make exchange losses when the accounting results of its foreign branches or subsidiaries are translated into the home currency. Translation losses can result, for example, from re-stating the book value of a foreign subsidiary's assets at the exchange rate on the statement of financial position date. The effect of translation risk is to create gains or losses in the reported financial results of the parent group, but they do not create cash flow gains or losses.

翻译的风险是指当外国分支机构或子公司的会计结果被翻译成本国货币时,该组织将产生汇总损失的风险。

2.2 Transaction risk

Transaction risk is the risk of adverse exchange rate movements occurring in the course of normal international trading transactions.

This arises when the prices of imports or exports are fixed in foreign currency terms and there is movement in the exchange rate between the date when the price is agreed and the date when the cash is paid or received in settlement.

For example, if an Australian company buys goods from a US supplier for an agreed price of US $1,000,000, with payment in two months' time, it is exposed to a transaction risk, that the US dollar may strengthen in value against the Australian dollar during the two-month credit period.

Transaction risk therefore affects cash flows so companies often choose to hedge or protect themselves against transaction risk.

交易风险是指在正常的国际贸易交易过程中发生的汇率不利变动的风险。

当进口或出口的价格以外币计价,并且在价格商定的日期和结算时支付或收到现金的日期之间的汇率发生变动时,就会出现这种情况。

例如,如果一家澳大利亚公司以约定的1,000,000美元的价格从美国供应商那里购买货物,两个月后付款,它就会面临交易风险,因为在两个月的信贷期内,美元可能会对澳元升值。

因此,交易风险会影响现金流,因此企业往往选择对冲或保护自己免受交易风险。

2.3 Economic risk

This refers to the effect of exchange rate movements on the international competitiveness of a company and refers to the effect on the present value of longer-term cash flows.

For example, a UK company might use raw materials which are priced in US dollars, but export its products mainly within the EU, pricing its exports in sterling. A depreciation of sterling against the dollar or an appreciation of sterling against other EU currencies will erode the competitiveness of the company.

Economic exposure can be difficult to avoid, although diversification of the supplier and customer base across different countries will reduce this kind of exposure to risk.

这是指汇率变动对公司国际竞争力的影响,是指汇率变动对长期现金流现值的影响。

例如,一家英国公司可能使用以美元计价的原材料,但其出口产品主要在欧盟内部,出口产品以英镑计价。英镑兑美元贬值或英镑兑其他欧盟货币升值,将削弱该公司的竞争力。

尽管不同国家的供应商和客户基础的多样化会减少这种风险暴露,但经济暴露是难以避免的。

3. The causes of exchange rate fluctuations

3.1 Currency supply and demand

Factors influencing the exchange rate include the comparative rates of inflation in different countries (purchasing power parity), comparative interest rates in different countries (interest rate parity), the underlying balance of payments, speculation and government policy on managing or fixing exchange rates.

Chapter 19　Foreign currency risk

影响外汇汇率的因素有不同国家的通货膨胀率,国家的货币的供需关系,政府的政策。

我们可以利用购买力平价理论(purchasing power parity)在有通货膨胀率的时候计算出未来汇率

3.2　Interest rate parity

Interest rate parity is a method of predicting foreign exchange rates based on the hypothesis that the difference between the interest rates in the two countries should offset the difference between the spot rates and the forward foreign exchange rates over the same period. High rates of inflation in a foreign country weaken its exchange rate so high interest rates are associated with weakening currencies.

利率平价理论是我们可以预计我们未来的利率基于两个国家不同的利率

$$F_0 = S_0 \times \frac{(1 + i_c)}{(1 + i_b)}$$

Where　F_0 = forward rate

　　　　S_0 = current spot rate

　　　　i_c = interest rate in country c (the overseas country) up to the future date

　　　　i_b = interest rate in country b (the base country) up to the future date

比如原来美元/欧元 那我们就是现在的利率 * (1 + 美元的 interest)/(1 + 欧元的 interest)

3.3　Purchasing power parity

Purchasing power parity theory is an alternative theory for predicting movements in a spot exchange rate over time.

Purchasing power parity theory predicts that the exchange value of foreign currency depends on the relative purchasing power of each currency in its own country and that spot exchange rates will vary over time according to relative price changes.

$$S_t = S_0 \times \frac{(1 + h_c)}{(1 + h_b)}$$

Where　S_1 = expected spot rate

　　　　S_0 = current spot rate

　　　　h_c = expected inflation rate in country c (a foreign country)

　　　　h_b = expected inflation rate in country b (the investor's country)

Note this formula is given in the exam.

比如原来美元/欧元 那我们就是现在的利率 * (1 + 美元的 inflation rate)/(1 + 欧元的 inflation rate)

3.4　The Fisher effect

Fisher effect

$$[1 + \text{nominal (money) rate}] = [1 + \text{real interest rate}][1 + \text{inflation rate}]$$
$$(1 + i) = (1 + r)(1 + h)$$

The international Fisher effect can be expressed as:

$$\frac{1+i_a}{1+i_b} = \frac{1+h_a}{1+h_b}$$

Where i_a is the nominal interest rate in country a

i_b is the nominal interest rate in country b

h_a is the inflation rate in country a

h_b is the inflation rate in country b

3.5 Four-way equivalence

The four-way equivalence model states that in equilibrium, differences between forward and spot rates, differences in interest rates, expected differences in inflation rates and expected changes in spot rates are equal to one another.

In other words the theories that we have been examining are linked. This is shown graphically below.

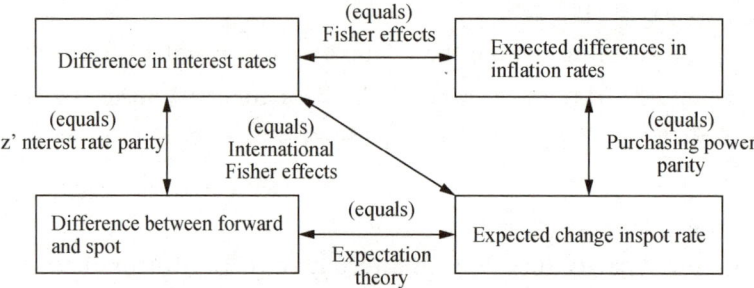

4. Foreign currency risk management

Foreign currency risk can be managed, in order to reduce or eliminate the risk. Measures to reduce currency risk are known as 'hedging'.

4.1 Currency of invoice

One easy way is to insist that all foreign customers pay in your home currency and that your company pays for all imports in your home currency.

However the exchange-rate risk has not gone away, it has just been passed onto the customer. Your customer may not be too happy with your strategy and simply look for an alternative supplier. Achievable if you are in a monopoly position.

坚持用本国货币支付

一个简单的方法是坚持所有的外国客户用你的本国货币支付,你的公司用你的本国货币支付所有的进口。

然而,汇率风险并没有消失,它只是被转嫁到客户身上。你的客户可能对你的策略不太满意,而只是寻找替代供应商。如果你处于垄断地位,你是可以做到的。

4.2 Leading and lagging

A company may decide to obtain payment early or pay late if it believes that exchange movement will be significant between now and the due date.

提前支付或者延后支付

一个公司可以支付更早或者更晚（如果他们预测到这个汇率在到期那天的变动）

4.3 Matching receipts and payments

A company can reduce or eliminate its foreign exchange transaction exposure by matching receipts and payments. Wherever possible, a company that expects to make payments and have receipts in the same foreign currency should plan to offset its payments against its receipts in the currency.

收支相符

公司可以通过收支匹配来减少或消除其外汇交易风险。如果一家公司希望用同一种外币进行付款和收款，那么它应该计划用这种货币来抵消它的付款和收款。（比如一个公司有应收美元 100 万，应付美元 60 元，那么最终就是应收美元 100 − 60 = 40 万）

4.4 Matching assets and liabilities

A company which expects to receive a substantial amount of income in a foreign currency will be concerned that this currency may weaken. It can hedge against this possibility by borrowing in the foreign currency and using the foreign receipts to repay the loan.

For example, US dollar receivables can be hedged by taking out a US dollar overdraft.

A company which has a long-term foreign investment, for example an overseas subsidiary, may also try to match its foreign assets (property, plant, etc) by a long-term loan in the foreign currency. This would reduce its risk from translation exposure.

资产负债匹配

希望获得大量外币收入的公司会担心这种货币会贬值。它可以通过借入外币并使用外汇收入偿还贷款来对冲这种可能性。

例如，美元应收账款可以通过提取美元透支来对冲。

拥有长期外国投资的公司，例如海外子公司，也可以通过长期外币贷款来匹配其外国资产（财产、厂房等）。这将降低其转换风险。

4.5 Netting

Netting is a process in which credit balances are netted off against debit balances so that only the reduced net amounts remain due to be paid by actual currency flows.

Where related companies located in different countries trade with one another, there is likely to be inter-company indebtedness denominated in different currencies.

净额是指将贷方余额与借方余额进行净额减记，以便只有减少的净额仍需由实际货币流动支付。

当位于不同国家的相关公司相互进行贸易时，公司间很可能存在以不同货币计价的债务。

4.6 Forward exchange contracts

Forward exchange rates

A forward exchange rate may be higher or lower than the spot rate. When a currency is more expensive forward than spot, it is quoted forward 'at a premium' to the spot rate. When a currency is cheaper forward than spot, it is quoted forward 'at a discount' to the spot rate.

For example, suppose that:

○ The spot rate for Swiss francs against sterling is SFr1.4460-SFr1.4560 per £1, and

○ The three-month forward rate is SFr1.4680-SFr1.4800 per £1.

a) A bank would sell 20,000 Swiss francs:

I. At the spot rate, now, for (20,000/1.4460) £13,831.26

II. Under a forward contract for settlement in three months' time, for (20,000/1.4680) £13,623.98

b) A bank would buy 20,000 Swiss francs:

I. At the spot rate, for (20,000/1.4560) £13,736.26

II. Under a forward contract for settlement in three months' time, for (20,000/1.4800) £13,513.51

In both cases, the quoted currency (Swiss franc) would be quoted forward at a discount to the spot rate.

小技巧：

首先确定我们是用乘法或者除法来乘除我们的汇率

比如我们国家货币是欧元 现在的汇率是 美元/欧元 = 10,我们未来3个月要收到100 000美元,那我们换成欧元就是 100 000 美元,除 美元/欧元 10,得到 10 000 欧元

然后我们要确定的是如果我们是付钱(借钱)我们要付的多。如果是除法我们就要选择利率较小的。乘法选择利率较大的收钱我们要收的少。如果是除法我们就要选择利率较大的。乘法选择利率较小的

A forward exchange contract is defined as:

a) An immediately firm and binding contract, e.g. between a bank and its customer

b) For the purchase or sale of a specified quantity of a stated foreign currency

c) At a rate of exchange fixed at the time the contract is made

d) For performance (delivery of the currency and payment for it) at a future time which is agreed when making the contract. (This future time will be either a specified date, or any time between two specified dates.)

a) 立即生效的有约束力的合同(如银行与客户之间的)

b) 购买或出售一定数量的规定外币

c) 按照订立合同时确定的汇率

d) 在订立合同时约定的未来时间履行(货币交付和支付)。(这个未来时间将是一个指定的日期,或者两个指定日期之间的任何时间。)

Advantages of forward contracts	Disadvantages of forward contracts
Simple	Fixed date agreements
Low or zero up-front costs	Rate quoted may be unattractive
Available for many currencies	
Normally available for more than a year ahead	

4.7 Money market hedging

Money market hedging (synthetic forward) involves borrowing in one currency, converting the money borrowed into another currency and putting the money on deposit until the time the transaction is completed, hoping to take advantage of favourable exchange rate movements.

Because of the close relationship between forward exchange rates and the interest rates in two currencies, it is possible to 'manufacture' a forward rate by using the spot exchange rate and money market lending or borrowing. This technique is known as a money market hedge or synthetic forward.

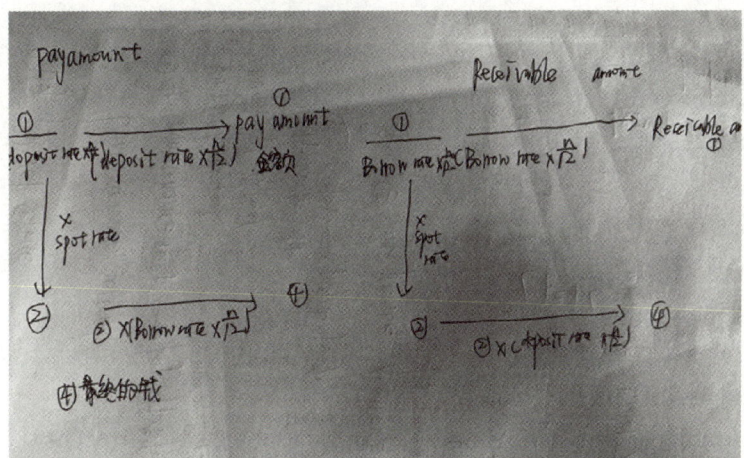

小技巧：

如果我们未来是付钱,那我们就要用 pay amount 除以 deposit rate * n/12 得到的数然后乘以 spot rate 得到②然后乘以(borrow rate * n/12)得到④就是我们最终要求的数

如果我们未来是收钱。那我们就要用 receivable amount 除以 borrow rate * n/12 得到的数然后乘以 spot rate 得到②然后乘以(deposit rate * n/12)得到④就是我们最终要求的数

Advantages of money market hedging: May be cheaper if an exporter with a cash flow deficit or an importer with a cash flow surplus

Disadvantages: More time consuming than a forward contract and normally no cheaper

5. Foreign currency derivatives

Currency future	Forward contract
Standard contracts	Bespoke contracts
Exchange traded	Traded over the counter
Flexible close out dates	Fixed date of settlement
Underlying transactions take place at the spot rate; the difference between the spot rate and futures rate is settled between two parties	Underlying transactions take place at the forward rate
Cheaper than forwards	Relatively high premium required

5.1 Currency futures

Advantages of futures

a) Transaction costs should be lower than other hedging methods.

b) Futures are tradable and can be bought and sold on a secondary market so there is pricing transparency, unlike forward contracts where prices are set by financial institutions.

c) The exact date of receipt or payment of the currency does not have to be known, because the futures contract does not have to be closed out until the actual cash receipt or payment is made.

期货的优点

a) 交易成本应低于其他套期保值方法。

b) 期货是可交易的,可以在二级市场买卖,因此有定价透明度,不像远期合约,价格是由金融机构设定的。

c) 不必知道货币的确切收付日期,因为期货合同不必在实际现金收付之前平仓。

Disadvantages of futures

a) The contracts cannot be tailored to the user's exact requirements.

b) Hedge inefficiencies are caused by having to deal in a whole number of contracts and by basis risk (the risk that the futures contract price may move by a different amount from the price of the underlying currency or commodity).

c) Only a limited number of currencies are the subject of futures contracts (although the number of currencies is growing, especially with the rapid development of Asian economies).

d) Unlike options (see below), they do not allow a company to take advantage of favourable currency movements.

期货的缺点

a) 合同不能根据用户的具体要求进行调整。

b) 套期保值的低效率是由于必须交易大量的合约和基础风险(期货合约价格变动与标的货币或商品价格变动幅度不同的风险)造成的。

c) 只有有限的几种货币是期货合约的标的(尽管货币的数量在不断增加,特别是随着亚洲经济的快速发展)。

d) 不同于期权,它们不允许公司利用有利的汇率波动。

5.2 Currency options

A currency option is a right of an option holder to buy (call) or sell (put) a quantity of one currency in exchange for another, at a specific exchange rate (the exercise rate, exercise price or strike price) on or before a future expiry date. If a buyer exercises the option, the option seller must sell or buy at this rate. If an option is not exercised, it lapses at the expiry date.

Advantages of options

a) Flexible dates (like a future)

b) Allow a company to take advantage of favourable movements in exchange rates. Options are the only form of hedging that does this.

c) Useful for uncertain transactions, can be sold if not needed

Disadvantages of options

a) Only available in large contract sizes

b) Expensive

期权的优点

a) 灵活的日期

b) 允许公司利用汇率的有利变动。期权是唯一能做到这一点的对冲形式。

c) 用于不确定的交易,如果不需要,可以出售

期权的缺点

a) 只对比较大的合同适用

b) 比较贵

5.3 Currency swaps

A swap is a formal agreement whereby two organisations contractually agree to exchange payments on different terms, e.g. in different currencies, or one at a fixed rate and the other at a floating rate.

考试时文字题解题套路

1) Foreign currency risk

a) Transaction risk:短期影响,T/R,T/P 因为汇率波动,导致收益低于预期。可以使用货币/远期 hedge 对冲。

b) Translation risk:海外资产和负债是以外币计量,因外币贬值导致资产缩水或负债提升,影响盈利表现。

c) Economic risk:长期影响,因为外汇走势影响了公司的长期现金流的 NPV,影响公司竞争力或业务发展。

题目:2013-06-Q3

2) Transaction risk 控制方式★

a) Currency of invoice:要求客户本币支付,将汇率风险转嫁给客户,一般很难执行。

尤其当竞争对手实行外币支付,就会丢客户。

b) Matching:经营支出都用外币,等于外币资产和负债互相匹配。从远期来看,是个比较好的方法。

c) Leading or lagging:提前或滞后支付,取决于对外币的预期升值或贬值。注意:晚支付可能超过供应商允许的账期,存在不良商誉的风险。

题目:2014-06-Q2,2014-12-Q3

Chapter 20

Interest rate risk

1. Interest rate risk

Interest rate risk relates to the sensitivity of profit and cash flows to changes in interest rates.

Interest rate risk is faced by companies with floating (variable) and fixed rate debt. It can arise from gap exposure and basis risk.

利率风险就是利润和现金流对利率变化的敏感程度。公司面对的利率风险有固定的利率和浮动的利率风险。他们可能是由于利率敏感性缺口和基差风险导致的

1.1 Gap exposure（利率敏感性缺口）

Gap analysis is based on the principle of grouping together assets and liabilities which are sensitive to interest rate changes according to their maturity dates.

1) A negative gap

A negative gap occurs when a firm has a larger amount of interest-sensitive liabilities maturing at a certain time or in a certain period than it has interest sensitive assets maturing at the same time. The difference between the two amounts indicates the net exposure.

With a negative gap, the company faces exposure if interest rates rise by the time of maturity.

消极的敏感性缺口

消极的敏感性缺口是指企业在某一时期或某一时期到期的对利息敏感的负债数量多于同时到期的对利息敏感的资产数量。两者之差表示净缺口。

在消极的敏感性缺口下，该公司将面临到期时利率上升的风险。

2) A positive gap

There is a positive gap if the amount of interest-sensitive assets maturing at a particular time exceeds the amount of interest-sensitive liabilities maturing at the same time. With a negative gap, the company faces exposure if interest rates rise by the time of maturity.

With a positive gap, the company will lose out if interest rates fall by maturity

积极的敏感性缺口

如果在某一特定时间到期的对利息敏感的资产数额超过同时到期的对利息敏感的负债

数额,则存在正的缺口。如果缺口为负,该公司将面临到期时利率上升的风险。

如果缺口为正,如果到期利率下降,该公司将蒙受损失

1.2 Basis risk

It may appear that a company which has size-matched assets and liabilities, and is both receiving and paying interest, may not have any interest rate exposure. However, the two floating rates may not be determined using the same basis or benchmark. For example, one loan may be linked to one-month LIBOR and the other to six-month LIBOR.

LIBOR or the London Interbank Offered Rate is the rate of interest applying to wholesale money market lending between London banks. There are different LIBOR rates for loans and deposits with different maturities.

Interest rates on interest bearing liabilities & interest bearing assets may be revised at different time periods. As one rate increases, the other rate may change by a different amount or may change later.

看起来,一个拥有规模匹配的资产和负债、同时收取和支付利息的公司可能没有任何利率风险。但是,这两个浮动利率不能使用相同的基础或基准来确定。例如,一笔贷款可能与1个月的LIBOR挂钩,而另一笔与6个月的LIBOR挂钩。

伦敦银行同业拆息是伦敦银行间批发货币市场贷款的利率。不同期限的贷款和存款有不同的LIBOR利率。

计息负债和计息资产的利率可按不同时期调整。当一种利率上升时,另一种利率可能会有不同程度的变化,或者以后会发生变化。

2. The causes of interest rate fluctuations

The causes of interest rate fluctuations include the structure of interest rates and yield curves and changing economic factors.

2.1 The structure of interest rates

There are several reasons why interest rates differ in different markets and market segments.

1) Risk

Higher risk borrowers must pay higher rates on their borrowing, to compensate lenders for the greater risk involved.

2) The need to make a profit on re-lending

Financial intermediaries make their profits from re-lending at a higher rate of interest than the cost of their borrowing.

3) The size of the loan

Deposits above a certain amount with a bank or building society may attract higher rates of interest than smaller deposits.

4) Different types of financial asset

Different types of financial asset attract different rates of interest. This is largely because of the competition for deposits between different types of financial institution.

5) The duration of the lending

利率在不同的市场和细分市场有不同的原因。

1）风险

风险较高的借款人必须为他们的借款支付更高的利率,以补偿贷款机构所涉及的更大风险。

2）需要从再贷款中获利

金融中介机构通过以高于借贷成本的利率转贷来获取利润。

3）贷款的规模

在银行或建筑协会超过一定数额的存款可能比小额存款吸引更高的利率。

4）不同类型的金融资产

不同类型的金融资产吸引不同的利率。这主要是因为不同类型的金融机构之间对存款的竞争。

5）贷款期限

2.2 The term structure of interest rates

The yield curve shows the relationship between interest rates or yield for a debt to the length of time for the debt to reach maturity.

a) Normally, the longer the term to maturity, the higher the rate of interest. This is shown by the normal yield curve in the diagram below.

b) Occasionally, interest rates may be higher for short-term maturities than longer-term maturities. When this happens, there is a negative yield curve, which is also illustrated in the diagram below.

收益率曲线反映了贷款的利率和他时间长短的关系

a）通常,到期日时间越长,利率越高

b）比起长期的贷款到期日合同,短期的贷款到期日的利润更高

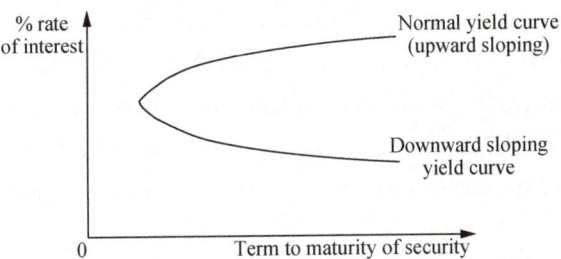

2.2 The term structure of interest rates

There are several different reasons why interest rates on a debt security or loan may differ for different maturities.

a) Liquidity preference theory provides a reason why, in theory, the yield curve is normally upward sloping, so that long-term financial assets offer a higher yield than short-term assets.

Liquidity preference means that investors prefer having cash now to deferring the use of the cash by lending or investing it. Investors also prefer having cash sooner to having cash later. They therefore want compensation in the form of a higher return for being unable to use their cash now. The required return increases with the length of time for which the cash is unavailable. Because of this, long-term interest rates, such as bond yields, tend to be higher than short-term yields, and the yield curve slopes upward.

流动性偏好理论解释了在理论上，收益率曲线通常是向上倾斜的，因此长期金融资产的收益率高于短期资产。

流动性偏好意味着投资者更喜欢现在持有现金，而不是通过放贷或投资来推迟使用现金。投资者也更愿意尽早持有现金，而不是晚些持有。因此，由于现在无法使用自己的现金，他们希望获得更高回报的补偿。所需的回报随着无法获得现金的时间长短而增加。正因为如此，长期利率，如债券收益率，往往高于短期收益率，收益率曲线向上倾斜。

b) Expectations theory states that interest rates reflect expectations of future changes in interest rates. If interest rates are expected to rise in the future, the yield curve will slope upwards. When interest rates are expected to fall, short-term rates may be higher than long-term rates, and the yield curve downward sloping. Thus, the shape of the yield curve gives an indication about how interest rates are expected to move in the future.

预期理论认为，利率反映了对利率未来变化的预期。如果预期利率在未来会上升，收益率曲线会向上倾斜。当利率预期会下降时，短期利率可能会高于长期利率，收益率曲线会向下倾斜。因此，收益率曲线的形状提供了未来利率预期走势的指标。

c) The market segmentation theory of interest rates suggests that the slope of the yield curve will reflect conditions in different segments of the market. This theory holds that the major investors are confined to a particular segment of the market and will not switch segment even if the forecast of likely future interest rates changes.

利率市场分割理论认为，收益率曲线的斜率将反映不同细分市场的情况。该理论认为，主要投资者都局限于市场的某一特定部分，即使对未来可能利率的预测发生变化，也不会转换市场的某个部分。

d) Government policy on interest rates may be significant too. A government policy of keeping interest rates relatively high may have the effect of forcing short term interest rates higher than long-term rates. Similarly, a government may have a policy of very low short-term interest rates. In the US, the eurozone and the UK, the central banks are responsible for managing short-term interest rates, through the rates at which the central bank lends to banks.

政府的利率政策可能也很重要。政府维持较高利率的政策可能会迫使短期利率高于长期利率。同样，政府可能会采取短期利率非常低的政策。在美国、欧元区和英国，央行负责通过向银行贷款的利率管理短期利率。

The significance of yield curves to financial managers

Financial managers can inspect the shape of the yield curve when deciding the term of borrowing or deposits. The curve is influenced by the market's expectations of future interest rate movements.

For instance a yield curve sloping steeply upwards suggests a rise in interest rates in the future; in this case a company will be more concerned about managing interest rate risk.

收益率曲线对财务经理的重要性

理财经理在决定存贷款期限时，可以查看收益率曲线的形状。这条曲线受到市场对未来利率走势预期的影响。

例如，一条陡峭向上的收益率曲线表明未来利率将上升；在这种情况下，公司会更加关注利率风险的管理。

2.3 The general level of interest rates

Interest rates on any one type of financial asset will vary over time. The general level of interest rates is affected by several factors.

a) Need for a real return
b) Inflation
c) Uncertainty about future rates of inflation
d) Liquidity preference of investors and the demand for borrowing
e) Balance of payments
f) Monetary policy

3. Interest rate risk management

3.1 Matching and smoothing

Matching is where liabilities and assets with a common interest rate are matched.

For example, subsidiary A of a company might be investing in the money markets at LIBOR and subsidiary B is borrowing through the same market at LIBOR. If LIBOR increases, subsidiary B's borrowing cost increases and subsidiary A's returns increase. The interest rates on the assets and liabilities are therefore matched.

This method is most widely used by financial institutions, such as banks, who find it easier to match the magnitudes and characteristics of their assets and liabilities than commercial or industrial companies.

Smoothing is where a company keeps a balance between its fixed rate and floating rate borrowing.

Using a balance of fixed and floating rate borrowing; this smoothes the impact of interest increases or decrease. Use more fixed rate finance if rate rises are expected.

匹配是指负债和资产在相同利率下的匹配。

例如，一家公司的子公司 A 可能以伦敦银行同业拆放利率投资于货币市场子公司 B 通过同一市场以伦敦银行同业拆放利率借款。如果 LIBOR 上升，子公司 B 的借款成本增加，子公司 A 的收益增加。因此，资产和负债的利率是匹配的。

这种方法在银行等金融机构中使用最为广泛，因为与商业或工业公司相比，银行更容易匹配其资产和负债的规模和特征。

平滑化是指公司在固定利率和浮动利率借款之间保持平衡。

使用固定利率和浮动利率的差额借款；这可以缓和利率上升或下降的影响。如果预期利率会上升，则使用更多的固定利率融资。

3.2 Forward rate agreements (FRAs) 注意例题，理解题，掌握计算方法和套路

Forward rate agreements hedge risk by fixing the interest rate on future short-term borrowing.

A company can enter into a FRA with a bank that fixes the rate of interest for short term borrowing from a certain time in the future. If the actual interest rate at that date proves to be higher than the rate in the FRA, the bank pays the company the difference. If the actual interest rate is lower than the FRA rate, the company pays the bank the difference.

远期利率协议通过确定未来短期借款的利率来对冲风险。

公司可以与银行建立一个远期利率协议，协商好在未来某个时间短期借款的利率（提前订好）。如果该日期的实际利率被证明高于 FRA 的利率，银行将支付该公司差额。如果实际利率低于 FRA 利率，公司将向银行支付差额。

An FRA is separate from the bank loan and allows a company to borrow in say 3 months1 time at the best rate available.

A company can enter into a FRA with a bank that fixes the rate of interest for short-term borrowing from a certain time in the future.

An FRA is not an agreement to lend or borrow. It is an agreement that fixes an interest rate on a notional amount of principal.

If the actual interest rate at that date proves to be higher than the rate in the FRA, the bank pays the company the difference. If the actual interest rate is lower than the FRA rate, the company pays the bank the difference.

FRA 与银行贷款是分开的，它允许公司以最好的利率借款 3 个月。

一家公司可以与一家银行建立 FRA，后者为未来某一特定时间的短期借款设定利率。

FRA 不是借贷协议。它是确定名义本金金额利率的协议。

如果该日期的实际利率被证明高于 FRA 的利率，银行将支付该公司差额。如果实际利率低于 FRA 利率，公司将向银行支付差额。

4. Interest rate derivatives

4.1 Interest rate futures

Interest rate futures offer a means of hedging against the risk of interest rate movements. Such contracts are effectively a gamble on whether interest rates will rise or fall. Futures contracts are frequently used by banks and other financial institutions as a means of hedging their portfolios: such institutions are often not concerned with achieving an exact match with their underlying exposure.

4.2 Interest rate option

An interest rate option grants the buyer of it the right, but not the obligation, to deal at an agreed interest rate (strike rate) at a future maturity date (the expiry date for the option). On the date of expiry of the option, the buyer must decide whether or not to exercise the right.

4.3 Interest rate caps, collars and floors

Caps set a ceiling to the interest rate; a floor sets a lower limit. A collar is the simultaneous purchase of a cap and sale of floor.

4.4 Interest rate swaps

Interest rate swaps are where two parties agree to exchange interest rate payments.

Interest rate swaps can act as a means of switching from paying one type of interest to another.

考试时文字题解题套路

1) Interest Rate 风险管理★

i) 预期短期利率增长, 则更多使用长期, 利率锁定的债, 比如 bank load 和 traded bonds.

ii) 风险管理手段 Internal Method：Matching & Smoothing

a) Matching：资金需求跟债务结构匹配。短期流动资金要求, 借短债；购买厂房设备等, 借长债

b) Smoothing：长债短债比例保持均衡

iii) External Method：Forward rate agreement 远期合同锁定利率, 差额银行赔付。

题目：2012-12-Q3

2) Forward exchange rate★

1) 类似题型：远期合同跟 money market hedge, 计算那个合算。思路：收入的币种用贷款利率, 另一个用存款利率。

2) FRA 的好处：一段时间内锁定利率, 可以控制风险, 便于确认收益或做预算。如果约定利率高于未来利率, 公司补偿银行差价。反之同理。Net effect 是锁定的。

锁定利率银行和实际交易银行可以是两家银行。

题目：2012-06-Q3, 2014-12-Q3, 2015-06-Q1, Pilot Q3

3) 利率平价 VS. 采购力平价

1) 利率平价(Interest rate parity)指所有可自由兑换货币的预期回报率相等时外汇市场所达到的均衡条件。当前国家的利息率(Interest rate)越高, 则汇率越疲软。

Forward rate = current spot rate × (1 + interest rate 外)/(1 + interest rate 本) 仅从公式看, 汇率走高的, 利率会相对低

2) 购买力平价(Purchasing Power Parity)是国家间综合价格之比, 即两种或多种货币在不同国家购买相同数量和质量的商品和服务时的价格比率, 用来衡量对比国之间价格水平的差异。当前国家的通胀(Inflation)越高, 则汇率越疲软。

题目：2011-06-Q4, 2012-06-Q3, 2014-12-Q3, Pilot Q3